W9-AHB-442

Subject & Strategy

A WRITER'S READER

Paul Eschholz

Alfred Rosa

University of Vermont

Bedford / St. Martin's
Boston • New York

For Bedford/St. Martin's

Executive Editor For Developmental Studies: Alexis Walker
Associate Production Editor: Kellan Cummings
Senior Production Supervisor: Jennifer Peterson
Marketing Manager: Molly Parke
Editorial Assistant: Karrin Varucene
Copy Editor: Mary Lou Wilshaw-Watts
Indexer: Leoni McVey
Photo Researcher: Naomi Kornhauser
Permissions Manager: Kalina Ingham Hintz
Art Director: Lucy Krikorian
Text Design: Nesbitt Graphics
Cover Design: Marine Bouvier Miller
Cover Art: AXO, Victor Vasarely, image courtesy of Masterworks Fine Art
Composition: Glyph International
Printing and Binding: Haddon Craftsmen, Inc., an RR Donnelley & Sons Company

President: Joan E. Feinberg
Editorial Director: Denise B. Wydra
Editor in Chief: Karen S. Henry
Director of Development: Erica T. Appel
Director of Marketing: Karen R. Soeltz
Director of Production: Susan W. Brown
Associate Director, Editorial Production: Elise S. Kaiser
Managing Editor: Shuli Traub

Library of Congress Control Number: 2010937894

Manufactured in the United States of America.

5 4 3 2 1 0
f e d c b a

For information, write: Bedford/St. Martin's, 75 Arlington Street, Boston, MA 02116   (617-399-4000)

ISBN: 978-0-312-61273-3

Acknowledgments

Preface for Instructors

***Subject & Strategy* is a reader for college writers. The** eighty-two essays in this edition were selected to entertain students, to inform them, and to contribute to their self-awareness and their understanding of the world around them. Above all, however, the readings were chosen to help students become better writers.

As its title suggests, *Subject & Strategy* places equal emphasis on the content and form of an essay. While all readers pay attention to content, far fewer notice the strategies — narration, description, illustration, process analysis, comparison and contrast, division and classification, definition, cause and effect analysis, and argumentation — that writers use to organize their writing and to make their subjects understandable and effective for a given audience. Because these strategies are such an essential element of the writer's craft, we have designed *Subject & Strategy* to help students understand what they are and how they work, by means of essays that skillfully model their use, and questions, writing prompts, and other pedagogy that support students in using the strategies to write well-constructed essays of their own.

Favorite Features of *Subject & Strategy*

We continue to include the key features — developed and refined over eleven previous editions — that have made *Subject & Strategy* a classic introductory text.

Timely, Teachable, and Diverse Readings

Eighty-two readings — sixty-nine selections by professional writers and thirteen student essays — offer a broad spectrum of subjects, styles, and cultural points of view. The work of well-known writers including Stephen

King, Malcolm X, Annie Dillard, Deborah Tannen, Mike Rose, Alice Walker, Michael Pollan, Bharati Mukherjee, Martin Luther King Jr., Andrew Sullivan, Steven Pinker, Barbara Ehrenreich, and Doris Lessing demonstrates for students the versatility and strengths of the different rhetorical strategies.

Thorough Coverage of the Processes of Reading and Writing

- Chapter 1, "Reading," discusses effective reading habits and provides an illustration of attentive, analytical reading using Thomas L. Friedman's essay "My Favorite Teacher."
- Chapter 2, "Writing," offers writing advice and provides a case study of a student paper in progress, which illustrates one student's writing process and shows what can be accomplished with careful, thoughtful revision.
- In Chapter 3, "Six Writers on Writing," professional writers Russell Baker, Anne Lamott, Linda Flower, William Zinsser, Donald Murray, and Stephen King offer students inspiration, insight, and advice on writing well.

Detailed Introductions to Each Rhetorical Strategy

The introduction to each rhetorical chapter opens with an example of the strategy at work in everyday life and then examines its use in written texts, discusses the various purposes for which writers use the strategy, and offers advice on how to use it in various college disciplines. This discussion is followed by detailed advice on how to write an essay using the strategy, including guidelines on selecting topics, developing thesis statements, considering audiences, gathering evidence, and using other rhetorical strategies in support of the dominant strategy.

Annotated Student Essays

An annotated student essay appears in each rhetorical chapter, offering students realistic models for successfully incorporating a particular strategy into their own writing. Discussion questions follow each essay, encouraging students to analyze and evaluate the overall effectiveness of the rhetorical strategies employed in the example.

Extensive Rhetorical Apparatus

Numerous questions and prompts for thought, discussion, in-class activities, and writing accompany each professional essay:

- **Preparing to Read** prompts ask students to write about their own knowledge and/or experiences with the subject of each selection before they read.
- **Thinking Critically about the Text** prompts ask students to analyze, elaborate on, or take issue with a key aspect of each selection. From time to time, discussion questions and writing assignments ask students to revisit their responses to these prompts and reflect on them before moving ahead with more formal writing tasks.

- **Questions on Subject** focus students' attention on the content of each selection as well as on the author's purpose. These questions help students check their comprehension and provide a basis for classroom discussion.

- **Questions on Strategy** direct students to the various rhetorical strategies and writing techniques the writer has used. These questions encourage students to put themselves in the writer's place and to consider how they might employ the strategies in their own writing. In addition, questions in this section ask students to identify and analyze places where the author has used one or more rhetorical strategies to enhance or develop the essay's dominant strategy.

- **Questions on Diction and Vocabulary** emphasize the importance of diction, word choice, and verbal context.

- **Classroom Activities** accompanying each essay — usually requiring no more than ten to fifteen minutes of class time and designed for students to complete individually, in small groups, or as a class — allow students to apply their understanding of the subject and/or the strategies at work in a given selection.

- **Writing Suggestions** focus on the particular rhetorical strategy under discussion and/or explore the subject of the essay or a related topic.

End-of-Chapter Writing Suggestions

Writing suggestions at the ends of the rhetorical chapters (Chapters 4 through 14) provide additional topics suitable to the strategy covered in each chapter. Many of the suggestions refer back to particular selections or to multiple selections in the chapter. Instructors can use these writing suggestions as complements to or substitutes for the more focused writing topics that accompany individual selections.

Advice for Writing Researched Essays

Chapter 15, "A Brief Guide to Researching and Documenting Essays," provides an overview of the research process, with a focus on finding, evaluating, and analyzing sources; taking notes; and documenting sources. Up-to-date model MLA citations are provided for the most widely used sources, along with a sample documented student essay.

Editing Advice

Chapter 16, "Editing for Grammar, Punctuation, and Sentence Style," provides a concise guide to twelve of the most common writing challenges, from run-ons and fragments to wordiness and lack of sentence variety. The introductions to the rhetorical modes chapters provide cross-references to this chapter for help with grammar, punctuation, and style problems specific to a given mode — for example, keeping verb tense consistent in narration. (The marginal icons that provide these cross-references — **1**, **2**, etc. — are a feature new to this edition.)

Thematic Contents

Immediately after the main table of contents, a second table of contents groups the reading selections into general thematic categories, providing further opportunities for discussion and writing based on the content of individual selections.

Glossary of Rhetorical Terms

The glossary at the end of *Subject & Strategy* provides concise definitions of terms italicized in the text and called out in the questions that follow each reading selection.

New to This Edition of *Subject & Strategy*

Substantially updated for its twelfth edition, *Subject & Strategy* combines the currency of a brand-new text with the effectiveness of a thoroughly class-tested one. Guided by comments and advice from instructors and students across the country who have used previous editions, we have made a number of significant changes to the text.

Engaging New Readings, Compelling Perspectives

Thirty-six readings — more than 40 percent of this edition's selections — are new, including the following:

- Stephen King's "Reading to Write," in which King explains that reading is essential for writers at all levels because it helps them tell the difference between "what works and what just lies dying (or dead) on the page";
- Vernon E. Jordan Jr.'s "Vernon Can Read!," a vivid account of Jordan's experience working as a chauffeur in the segregated South of the 1950s;
- Mike Rose's "Blue-Collar Brilliance," in which Rose makes a case for the unheralded capabilities of ordinary shift workers;
- Michael Pollan's "Eating Industrial Meat," in which Pollan reflects on the process of bringing beef to market by following the fate of one steer, Number 534, from feedlot to table;
- Bharati Mukherjee's "Two Ways of Belonging in America," in which Mukherjee contrasts her immigrant experience with her sister's; and
- Barbara Ehrenreich's "This Land Is Their Land," in which Ehrenreich argues that America's wealthy are illegitimately appropriating our common heritage — the natural landscapes that surround us.

Expanded Coverage of Writing with Sources

Students need more help than ever in managing the information available to them as they write source-based papers. The twelfth edition of *Subject & Strategy* provides this help in the following ways:

- **A brand-new Chapter 14, "Writing with Sources,"** helps students master this essential academic skill by offering sound, detailed advice on effectively integrating sources through quotation, summary, and paraphrase, and on avoiding plagiarism. The chapter also features four new essays — two student and two professional — that integrate outside sources, and it provides questions and prompts that direct students' attention to the ways in which they do so.

- **A fully revised, updated, and streamlined Chapter 15, "A Brief Guide to Researching and Documenting Essays,"** offers advice on finding sources and on the mechanics of documentation. This coverage has been designed for courses that require students to do independent research, and it dovetails smoothly with the extensive advice on integrating sources in the new Chapter 14.

- **New Writing with Sources assignments among** the end-of-chapter Writing Suggestions in every modes chapter round out this increased attention to integrating outside perspectives ethically and effectively.

A Fresh Take on Argument

To more realistically reflect the multiplicity of possible perspectives on any complex topic and to discourage students from thinking of argument as winner-take-all conflict, we have replaced the Argument Pairs of the previous edition with the following:

- new Argument Trio, in which Andrew Sullivan, Andrew Keen, and Matt Welch debate the merits of blogging; and

- new Argument Roundtable, in which seven experts from a range of fields discuss the state of marriage in the contemporary United States.

More (on) Visuals

In acknowledgment both of the increasing prominence of visuals in our culture and of the many predominantly visual learners among us, we have made every attempt to add visuals to this edition where they could serve a clear pedagogical purpose:

- **New chapter-opening images** in each rhetorical modes chapter underline the importance and ubiquity of the strategies by providing real-world examples taken from ads, cartoons, graphic novels, and other image-based texts. A brief discussion of the image opens the chapter, and a writing prompt related to the image appears among the end-of-chapter writing assignments.

- **Numerous new images** throughout the chapters serve as the basis for Classroom Activities; we reproduce images that originally appeared in selections new to this edition.

- **A new section on reading visuals** has been added to Chapter 1, in order to help students read visuals actively and critically.

A New Design

The new design of the twelfth edition of *Subject and Strategy* offers a fresh, contemporary look to the text while also adding a pedagogical advantage: Subtle visual cues now reflect essays' original publication medium (book, magazine, newspaper, or online), reinforcing the importance of context in analysis and interpretation.

The Instructor's Edition of *Subject & Strategy*

We have designed *Subject & Strategy* to be as accessible as possible to all of the kinds of people teaching composition, including new graduate students and very busy adjuncts. Toward that end, we provide an Instructor's Manual (ISBN: 978-0-312-60178-2), bound together with the student text in a special Instructor's Edition and available separately online to authorized instructors, which suggests responses to the questions and prompts that accompany each selection in *Subject & Strategy*.

You Get More Digital Choices with *Subject & Strategy*

Subject & Strategy doesn't stop with a book. Online, you'll find both free and affordable premium resources to help students get even more out of the book and your course. You'll also find convenient instructor resources, such as downloadable sample syllabi, classroom activities, and even a nationwide community of teachers. To learn more about or to order any of the products below, contact your Bedford/St. Martin's sales representative, e-mail sales support (sales_support@bfwpub.com), or visit the Web site at **bedfordstmartins.com/subjectandstrategy**.

Student Resources

Send students to free and open resources, upgrade to an expanding collection of innovative digital content, or package a standalone CD-ROM for free with *Subject & Strategy*.

- *Re:Writing*, the best *free* collection of online resources for the writing class, offers clear advice on citing sources in *Research and Documentation Online by Diana Hacker*, 30 sample papers and designed documents, and over 9,000 writing and grammar exercises with immediate feedback and reporting in *Exercise Central*. Updated and redesigned, *Re:Writing* also features five free videos from *VideoCentral* and three new visual tutorials from our popular *ix: visual exercises* by Cheryl Ball and Kristin Arola. *Re:Writing* is completely free and open (no codes required) to ensure access to all students. Visit **bedfordstmartins.com/rewriting**.

- *VideoCentral* is a growing collection of videos for the writing class that captures real-world, academic, and student writers talking about how and why they write. Writer and teacher Peter Berkow interviewed hundreds of people — from Michael Moore to Cynthia Selfe — to produce 50 brief videos about topics such as revising and getting feedback. *VideoCentral* can be packaged with *Subject & Strategy* at a significant discount. An activation code is required. To learn more, visit **bedfordstmartins.com/videocentral**.

- *Re:Writing Plus* gathers all of Bedford/St. Martin's premium digital content for composition into one online collection. It includes hundreds of model documents, the first ever peer review game, and *VideoCentral. Re:Writing Plus* can be purchased separately or packaged with the print book at a significant discount. An activation code is required. To learn more, visit **bedfordstmartins.com/rewriting**.

Instructor Resources

Bedford/St. Martin's wants to make it easy for you to find the support you need — and to get it quickly. To find everything available with *Subject & Strategy*, visit **bedfordstmartins.com/subjectandstrategy**.

- The Instructor's Manual, which suggests answers to questions and prompts for each reading, is available in PDF format and can be downloaded from the Bedford/St. Martin's online catalog.

- *TeachingCentral* offers the entire list of Bedford/St. Martin's print and online professional resources in one place. You'll find landmark reference works, sourcebooks on pedagogical issues, award-winning collections, and practical classroom advice — all free for instructors.

- *Bits* collects creative ideas for teaching a range of composition topics in an easily searchable blog. A community of teachers — leading scholars, authors, and editors — discuss revision, research, grammar and style, technology, peer review, and much more.

- Content cartridges for course management systems — Blackboard, WebCT, Angel, and Desire2Learn — allow you to easily download digital materials from Bedford/St. Martin's for your course.

Acknowledgments

We are gratified by the reception and use of the eleven previous editions of *Subject & Strategy*. Composition teachers in hundreds of community colleges, liberal arts colleges, and universities have used the book. Many teachers responded to our detailed review questionnaire, thus helping tremendously in conceptualizing the improvements to this edition. We thank Chris Allen, Piedmont Technical College; Christopher Baker, Armstrong Atlantic State University; James Boswell, Harrisburg Area Community College; Risa Botyinick, Meredith College; Arnold Bradford, Northern Virginia Community College; Maureen Connolly, Elmhurst College; Donneva Crowell, Harrisburg Area Community College, Gettysburg Campus; William Donohue, Lincoln University; Donna Eisenstat, West Virginia University Institute of

Technology; Crystal S. Gibbins, University of Nebraska–Lincoln; Valerie T. Goodwin, South Carolina State University; Betty L. Hart, University of Southern Indiana; Barbara J. Hunt, Columbus State University; Theresa James, South Florida Community College; Florence Johnson, North Dakota State College of Science; Susan Lago, William Paterson University; Jim Landers, Community College of Philadelphia; Mary Lang, Wharton County Junior College; Ellen Leonard, Springfield Technical Community College; Kathryn R. Moore, SUNY Fredonia; Peter Pellegrin, Cloud County Community College, Geary County Campus; Patrick Quinn, College of Southern Nevada; Jacqueline Shehorn, West Hills College Lemorre; Michael Sollars, Texas Southern University; Anne Taylor, North Dakota State College of Science; Patricia Jo Teel, Victor Valley College; Traci Thomas-Card, University of Wisconsin, Eau Claire; Lynn Watson, Santa Rosa Junior College; William Wend, Burlington County College; Marian Wernicke, Pensacola Junior College; and Diana L. Yeager, Hillsborough Community College.

At Bedford/St. Martin's, we thank our longtime friend and editor, Nancy Perry, and our talented and enthusiastic developmental editor, Alexis Walker, for her commitment to *Subject & Strategy*. Together we have charted some new territories for this enduring text, and the process has been truly exciting. Thanks go also to the rest of the Bedford/St. Martin's team: Joan Feinberg, Denise Wydra, Karen Henry, Erica Appel, Shuli Traub, Kellan Cummings, Molly Parke, Donna Dennison, Karrin Varucene, Naomi Kornhauser, and Warren Drabek. Special thanks go to Lisa Moore for preparing the Instructor's Manual. We are also happy to recognize those students whose work appears in *Subject & Strategy* for their willingness to contribute their time and effort in writing and rewriting their essays: Barbara Bowman, Gerald Cleary, Kevin Cunningham, Keith Eldred, Mark Jackson, Jake Jamieson, Paula Kersch, Tara E. Ketch, Laura LaPierre, Shoshanna Lew, Christine Olson, Howard Solomon Jr., and Jim Tassé. We are grateful to all of our writing students at the University of Vermont for their enthusiasm for writing and for their invaluable responses to materials included in this book. And we also thank our families for sharing in our commitment to quality teaching and textbook writing.

Finally, we thank each other. Beginning in 1971 we have collaborated on many textbooks on language and writing, all of which have gone into multiple editions. With this twelfth edition of *Subject & Strategy*, we enter the fortieth year of working together. Ours must be one of the longest-running and most mutually satisfying writing partnerships in college textbook publishing. The journey has been invigorating and challenging as we have come to understand the complexities and joys of good writing and have sought new ways to help students become better writers.

Paul Eschholz

Alfred Rosa

Contents

Preface for Instructors   iii
Thematic Contents   xxv

1   Reading   1

Developing an Effective Reading Process   1

    Step 1   Prepare Yourself to Read the Selection   1

    Step 2   Read the Selection   4

    Step 3   Reread the Selection   4

    Step 4   Annotate the Selection   4

        ➤ *What to Annotate in a Text*   5

    An Example: Annotating Rita Dove's "Loose Ends"   5

    Step 5   Analyze and Evaluate the Selection   7

        ➤ *Questions for Analysis and Evaluation*   7

The Reading Process in Action: Thomas L. Friedman's "My Favorite Teacher"   7

About the Photographs and Visual Texts in This Book   11

The Reading-Writing Connection   14

    Reading As a Writer   14

2   Writing   16

Developing an Effective Writing Process   16

    Step 1   Understand Your Assignment   17

        ➤ *Direction Words*   17

        ➤ *Formal versus Informal Writing*   20

➤ *Questions about Audience*   21

Step 2   Gather Ideas and Formulate a Thesis   21

➤ *Will Your Thesis Hold Water?*   24

Step 3   Organize and Write Your First Draft   24

➤ *Organizational Strategies*   24

➤ *Determining What Strategies to Use with a Specific Assignment*   25

➤ *Determining What Strategies to Use with an Open Assignment*   26

Step 4   Revise Your Essay   28

➤ *Tips for Revising Your Draft*   28

➤ *A Brief Guide to Peer Critiquing*   29

➤ *Questions for Revising the Larger Elements of Your Essay*   30

➤ *Questions for Revising Sentences*   30

➤ *Questions for Writing Beginnings and Endings*   31

Step 5   Edit and Proofread Your Essay   32

➤ *Questions to Ask during Editing and Proofreading*   32

A Student Essay in Progress   32

Step 1   Keith's Assignment   33

Step 2   Keith's Ideas   33

Step 3   Keith's First Draft   33

Step 4   Keith's Revised Essay   35

Step 5   Keith's Edited Essay   37

Keith Eldred, *Secular Mantras* (student essay)   38

3   Six Writers on Writing   41

Russell Baker, *Discovering the Power of My Words*   42
"And he started to read. My words! He was reading *my words* out loud to the entire class. What's more, the entire class was listening."

Anne Lamott, *Shitty First Drafts*   47
"All good writers write them. This is how they end up with good second drafts and terrific third drafts."

Linda S. Flower, *Writing for an Audience*   52
"A good piece of writing closes the gap between you and the reader."

William Zinsser, *Simplicity*   56
"Clutter is the disease of American writing. We are a society strangling in unnecessary words, circular constructions, pompous frills, and meaningless jargon."

Donald M. Murray, *The Maker's Eye: Revising Your Own Manuscripts* 60

"A piece of writing is never finished. It is delivered to a deadline, torn out of the typewriter on demand, sent off with a sense of accomplishment and shame and pride and frustration."

Stephen King, *Reading to Write* 66

"If you want to be a writer, you must do two things above all others: read a lot and write a lot."

4 Narration 73

What Is Narration? 73

Narration in Written Texts 73

Using Narration As a Writing Strategy 74

Using Narration across the Disciplines 75

Sample Student Essay Using Narration As a Writing Strategy 76

Laura LaPierre, *Why Are You Here?* (student essay) 76

Suggestions for Using Narration As a Writing Strategy 79

Planning Your Narration Essay 79

Organizing Your Narration Essay 81

Writing Your Narration Essay 82

Revising and Editing Your Narration Essay 83

➤ *Questions for Revising and Editing: Narration* 84

Malcolm X, *Coming to an Awareness of Language* 85

"I saw that the best thing I could do was get hold of a dictionary — to study, to learn some words."

Annie Dillard, From *An American Childhood* 90

"A black Buick was moving toward us down the street. We all spread out, banged together some regular snowballs, took aim, and, when the Buick drew nigh, fired."

Barry Winston, *Stranger Than True* 96

"Some kid is in trouble and would I be interested in helping him out? He's charged with manslaughter, a felony, and driving under the influence. I tell him sure, have the kid call me."

David P. Bardeen, *Not Close Enough for Comfort* 102

"I had wanted to tell Will I was gay since I was 12. As twins, we shared everything back then: clothes, gadgets, thoughts, secrets. Everything except this."

Vernon E. Jordan Jr., *Vernon Can Read!* 108

"I sat there day after day, drinking in the atmosphere of the place — the smell of the books, the feel of them, the easy chairs. The way of life that the library symbolized — the commitment to knowledge and the leisure to pursue it — struck a chord in me that still resonates."

Writing Suggestions for Narration 117

5 Description 121

What Is Description? 121

Description in Written Texts 121

Using Description As a Writing Strategy 122

Using Description across the Disciplines 124

Sample Student Essay Using Description As a Writing Strategy 125

   James C. Tassé, *Trailcheck* (student essay) 125

Suggestions for Using Description As a Writing Strategy 128

   Planning Your Description Essay 128

   Organizing Your Description Essay 129

   Revising and Editing Your Description Essay 131

      ➤ *Questions for Revising and Editing: Description* 132

Cherokee Paul McDonald, *A View from the Bridge* 133
"I was coming up on the little bridge in the Rio Vista neighborhood of Fort Lauderdale, deepening my stride and my breathing to negotiate the slight incline without altering my pace. And then, as I neared the crest, I saw the kid."

Stan Badgett, *Rock Dust* 139
"Mark stood opposite me on the other side of the stack, smiling. The next day a section of roof collapsed and killed him."

Pat Mora, *Remembering Lobo* 144
"We called her *Lobo.* The word means 'wolf' in Spanish, an odd name for a generous and loving aunt."

Robert Ramírez, *The Barrio* 150
"Members of the barrio describe their entire area as their home. It is a home, but it is more than this. The barrio is a refuge from the harshness and the coldness of the Anglo world."

Maya Angelou, *Sister Flowers* 156
"She acted just as refined as whitefolks in the movies and books and she was more beautiful, for none of them could have come near that warm color without looking gray by comparison."

Writing Suggestions for Description 163

6 Illustration 167

What Is Illustration? 167

Illustration in Written Texts 167

Using Illustration As a Writing Strategy 169

Using Illustration across the Disciplines 169

Sample Student Essay Using Illustration as a Writing Strategy 170

Paula Kersch, *Weight Management: More than a Matter of Good Looks* (student essay)   171

Suggestions for Using Illustration As a Writing Strategy   177

Planning Your Illustration Essay   177

Organizing Your Illustration Essay   179

Revising and Editing Your Illustration Essay   180

➤ *Questions for Revising and Editing: Illustration*   181

Natalie Goldberg, *Be Specific*   182
"Don't say 'fruit.' Tell what kind of fruit — 'It is a pomegranate.' Give things the dignity of their names."

Mitch Albom, *If You Had One Day with Someone Who's Gone*   186
"Have you ever lost someone you love and wanted one more conversation, one more day to make up for the time when you thought they would be here forever?"

Deborah Tannen, *How to Give Orders Like a Man*   192
"I challenge the assumption that talking in an indirect way necessarily reveals powerlessness, lack of self-confidence or anything else about the character of the speaker."

Mike Rose, *Blue-Collar Brilliance*   202
"Gripping the outer edge of the table with one hand, she'd watch the room and note, in the flow of our conversation, who needed a refill, whose order was taking longer to prepare than it should, who was finishing up."

Alice Walker, *In Full Bloom*   213
"There is always a moment in any kind of struggle when one feels in full bloom. Vivid. Alive. One might be blown to bits in such a moment and still be at peace."

Writing Suggestions for Illustration   220

7 Process Analysis   223

What Is Process Analysis?   223

Process Analysis in Written Texts   223

Using Process Analysis As a Writing Strategy   224

Directional Process Analysis   225

Informational Process Analysis   225

Evaluative Process Analysis   226

Using Process Analysis across the Disciplines   226

Sample Student Essay Using Process Analysis As a Writing Strategy   227

Shoshanna Lew, *How (Not) to Be Selected for Jury Duty* (student essay)   227

Suggestions for Using Process Analysis As a Writing Strategy   231

Planning Your Process Analysis Essay   231

Organizing and Writing Your Process Analysis Essay   232

Revising and Editing Your Process Analysis Essay   233

> ➤ *Questions for Revising and Editing: Process Analysis*   234

Mortimer Adler, *How to Mark a Book*   236
"Marking up a book is not an act of mutilation but of love."

Paul Roberts, *How to Say Nothing in 500 Words*   243
"You still have four hundred and sixty-eight [words] to go, and you've pretty well exhausted the subject. It comes to you that you do your best thinking in the morning, so you put away the typewriter and go to the movies."

Michael Pollan, *Eating Industrial Meat*   256
"'You are what you eat' is a truism hard to argue with, and yet it is, as a visit to a feedlot suggests, incomplete, for you are what what you eat eats, too."

Tiffany Sharples, *Young Love*   263
"Along with language, romance may be one of the hardest skills we'll ever be called on to acquire."

Nikki Giovanni, *Campus Racism 101*   270
"There are discomforts attached to attending predominantly white colleges, though no more so than living in a racist world."

Writing Suggestions for Process Analysis   277

8   Comparison and Contrast — 281

What Are Comparison and Contrast?   281

Comparison and Contrast in Written Texts   282

Using Comparison and Contrast As a Writing Strategy   284

Using Comparison and Contrast across the Disciplines   285

Sample Student Essay Using Comparison and Contrast As a Writing Strategy   286

Barbara Bowman, *Guns and Cameras* (student essay)   287

Suggestions for Using Comparison and Contrast As a Writing Strategy   289

Planning Your Comparison and Contrast Essay   289

Organizing and Writing Your Comparison and Contrast Essay   291

Revising and Editing Your Comparison and Contrast Essay   293

> ➤ *Questions for Revising and Editing: Comparison and Contrast*   294

Kim Hoang, *Chinese in New York, American in Beijing*   295
"I am American, but there are things about my life that are distinctly Chinese."

Bharati Mukherjee, *Two Ways to Belong in America*   301
"America spoke to me — I married it — I embraced the demotion from expatriate aristocrat to immigrant nobody, surrendering those thousands of years of 'pure culture,' the saris, the delightfully accented English."

Malcolm Jones, *Who Was More Important: Lincoln or Darwin?* 307

"It is a measure of their accomplishments, of how much they changed the world, that the era into which Lincoln and Darwin were born seems so strange to us now."

Suzanne Britt, *Neat People vs. Sloppy People* 318

"I've finally figured out the difference between neat people and sloppy people. The distinction is, as always, moral."

Bruce Catton, *Grant and Lee: A Study in Contrasts* 323

"They were two strong men, these oddly different generals, and they represented the strengths of two conflicting currents that, through them, had come into final collision."

Writing Suggestions for Comparison and Contrast 330

9 Division and Classification 333

What Are Division and Classification? 333

Division and Classification in Written Texts 333

Using Division and Classification As a Writing Strategy 336

Using Division and Classification across the Disciplines 336

Sample Student Essay Using Division and Classification As a Writing Strategy 337

Gerald Cleary, *How Loud? How Good? How Much? How Pretty?* (student essay) 338

Suggestions for Using Division and Classification As a Writing Strategy 340

Planning Your Division and Classification Essay 340

Organizing and Writing Your Division and Classification Essay 342

Revising and Editing Your Division and Classification Essay 343

➤ *Questions for Revising and Editing: Division and Classification* 344

Rosalind Wiseman, *The Queen Bee and Her Court* 345

"Our best politicians and diplomats couldn't do better than a teen girl does in understanding the social intrigue and political landscape that lead to power."

Jim Kitchens, *The Psychology of Persuasive Messaging* 359

"Fear, narcissism, consumerism, and religiosity shape our perception and understanding of public communication."

Judith Viorst, *The Truth about Lying* 366

"I'm willing to lie. But just as a last resort — the truth's always better."

Amy Rashap, *The American Dream for Sale: Ethnic Images in Magazines* 373

"Advertisers devised images that tapped into deeply held beliefs and myths of an 'all-American' lifestyle — one that didn't just sell a product, but a way of life that people could buy."

Martin Luther King Jr., *The Ways of Meeting Oppression*   384
"The problem is not a purely racial one, with Negroes set against whites. In the end, it's not a struggle between people at all, but a tension between justice and injustice."

Writing Suggestions for Division and Classification   389

10 Definition   393

What Is Definition?   393

Definition in Written Texts   393

Using Definition As a Writing Strategy   396

Using Definition across the Disciplines   397

Sample Student Essay Using Definition As a Writing Strategy   398

   Howard Solomon Jr., *Best Friends* (student essay)   398

Suggestions for Using Definition As a Writing Strategy   402

   Planning Your Definition Essay   402

   Organizing and Writing Your Definition Essay   405

   Revising and Editing Your Definition Essay   406

      ➤ *Questions for Revising and Editing: Definition*   408

Jo Goodwin Parker, *What Is Poverty?*   410
"Poverty is getting up every morning from a dirt- and illness-stained mattress. The sheets have long since been used for diapers. Poverty is living in a smell that never leaves."

G. Anthony Gorry, *Steal This MP3 File: What Is Theft?*   416
"But in the case of digital music, where the material is disconnected from the physical moorings of conventional stores and copying is so easy, many of my students see matters differently."

Deborah M. Roffman, *What Does "Boys Will Be Boys" Really Mean?*   422
"It's not so much that the boy is always *being* bad — sometimes that sort of thing can seem so outrageous it's funny. It's the underlying assumption . . . that boys, by nature, are bad."

Sojourner Truth, *Ain't I a Woman?*   429
"That man over there says that women need to be helped into carriages, and lifted over ditches, and to have the best place everywhere. Nobody ever helps me into carriages, or over mud-puddles, or gives me any best place!"

David Brooks, *The Odyssey Years*   433
"There used to be four common life phases: childhood, adolescence, adulthood, and old age. Now, there are at least six: childhood, adolescence, odyssey, adulthood, active retirement, and old age."

Writing Suggestions for Definition   438

11 Cause and Effect Analysis 441

What Is Cause and Effect Analysis? 441

Cause and Effect Analysis in Written Texts 441

Using Cause and Effect Analysis As a Writing Strategy 444

Using Cause and Effect Analysis across the Disciplines 445

Sample Student Essay Using Cause and Effect Analysis As a Writing Strategy 446

Kevin Cunningham, *Gentrification* (student essay) 446

Suggestions for Using Cause and Effect Analysis As a Writing Strategy 450

Planning Your Cause and Effect Analysis 450

Organizing and Writing Your Cause and Effect Analysis 451

Revising and Editing Your Cause and Effect Analysis 453

➤ *Questions for Revising and Editing: Cause and Effect Analysis* 454

Jon Katz, *How Boys Become Men* 455
"Men remember receiving little mercy as boys; maybe that's why it's sometimes difficult for them to show any."

Jennie Yabroff, *Here's Looking at You, Kids* 460
"'They've all seen reality TV. They make movies with their cell phones,' she says. 'Being under the microscope is just part of their lives.'"

Andrew Sullivan, *iPod World: The End of Society?* 466
"Each was in his or her own little musical world, walking to their own soundtrack, stars in their own music video, almost oblivious to the world around them. These are the iPod people."

Carl M. Cannon, *The Real Computer Virus* 471
"One of the things that makes the Internet so appealing is that anyone can pull anything off it. The other side of the coin is that anyone can put anything on it."

Michael Jonas, *The Downside of Diversity* 480
"What emerged in more diverse communities was a bleak picture of civic desolation, affecting everything from political engagement to the state of social ties."

Writing Suggestions for Cause and Effect Analysis 489

12 Argumentation 493

What Is Argumentation? 493

Argument in Written Texts 493

Persuasive and Logical Argument 494

Informational, or Exploratory, Argument 495

Focused Argument 495

Action-Oriented Argument   495

Quiet, or Subtle, Argument   496

Reconciliation Argument   496

Using Argumentation As a Writing Strategy   496

The Classical Appeals   497

Considering Audience   498

Argumentation and Other Rhetorical Strategies   498

Inductive and Deductive Reasoning   498

Using Argumentation across the Disciplines   501

Sample Student Essay Using Argumentation As a Writing Strategy   502

Mark Jackson, *The Liberal Arts: A Practical View* (student essay)   502

Suggestions for Using Argumentation As a Writing Strategy   507

Planning Your Argumentation Essay   507

Organizing and Writing Your Argumentation Essay   509

Revising and Editing Your Argumentation Essay   511

➤ *Questions for Revising and Editing: Argumentation   512*

Thomas Jefferson, *The Declaration of Independence*   513
"We hold these truths to be self-evident, that all men are created equal, that they are endowed by their Creator with certain unalienable Rights, that among these are Life, Liberty, and the pursuit of Happiness."

Richard Lederer, *The Case for Short Words*   519
"A lot of small words, more than you might think, can meet your needs with a strength, grace, and charm that large words do not have."

Martin Luther King Jr., *I Have a Dream*   525
"I have a dream that my four little children will one day live in a nation where they will not be judged by the color of their skin but by the content of their character."

Steven Pinker, *In Defense of Dangerous Ideas*   531
"Dangerous ideas are likely to confront us at an increasing rate, and we are ill-equipped to deal with them."

Barbara Ehrenreich, *This Land Is Their Land: How the Rich Confiscate Natural Beauty from the Public*   541
"And if your heart doesn't bleed for the dishwasher or landscaper who commutes two to four hours a day, at least shed a tear for the wealthy vacationer who gets stuck in the ensuing traffic."

ARGUMENT TRIO: ON BLOGGING   547

Andrew Sullivan, *Why I Blog*   548
"Blogging is to writing what extreme sports are to athletics: more free-form, more accident-prone, less formal, more alive. It is, in many ways, writing out loud."

Andrew Keen, *Web 2.0*   560

"This Web 2.0 dream is Socrates' nightmare: technology that arms every citizen with the means to be an opinionated artist or writer."

Matt Welch, *Blogworld and Its Gravity:*
            The New Amateur Journalists Weigh In   565

"So what have these people contributed to journalism? Four things: personality, eyewitness testimony, editorial filtering, and uncounted gigabytes of new knowledge."

ARGUMENT ROUNDTABLE: ALPHA WIVES: THE TREND AND THE TRUTH   572

Stephanie Coontz, *Women Finally Start to Catch Up*   574

"Women today are far less likely than their forerunners in the Great Depression to consider it 'unmanly' if their husband can't support his family."

Claudia Goldin, *The Benefits of the Breadwinning Wife*   575

"More educated women are healthier, live longer, have healthier children, more stable marriages, and higher incomes."

Ralph Richard Banks, *The Marriage Decline*   577

"Middle class black women are more unmarried than at any time since slavery and, as a result, have fewer children than any other group of women in our society."

Andrew J. Cherlin, *The Housewife Anomaly*   578

"We are returning to the more typical kind of family in which women's work of all sorts — which now includes earning money — is crucial."

Janet Reibstein, *It's about Respect*   580

"As the powerful woman becomes more common, she may be alluring to some men, but to other men this is a problem if it leads to an inequality of respect."

Kathleen Gerson, *No Role Reversals*   581

"If we fail to help women and men create shared lives that integrate family and work in a flexible, egalitarian way, our worst fears may be realized."

Barbara Dafoe Whitehead, *Separate and Unequal Mating*
            Markets   582

"For noncollege-educated women, marriage is becoming the exception rather than the rule."

Writing Suggestions for Argumentation   585

13 Combining Strategies   589

What Does It Mean to Combine Strategies?   589

Combining Strategies in Written Texts   590

Sample Student Essay Using a Combination of Strategies   591

Tara E. Ketch, *Kids, You Can't Read That Book!*
            (student essay)   592

**Suggestions for Using a Combination of Strategies
in an Essay**   598

Planning Your Combined Strategies Essay   598

Organizing Your Combined Strategies Essay   600

Revising and Editing Your Combined Strategies Essay   601

➤ *Questions for Revising and Editing: Combining Strategies*   601

Lars Eighner, *On Dumpster Diving*   602
"I like the frankness of the word *scavenging*. I live from the refuse of others. I am a scavenger."

Doris Lessing, *On Not Winning the Nobel Prize*   608
"We are a jaded lot, we in our threatened world. We are good for irony and even cynicism. Some words and ideas we hardly use, so worn out have they become. But we may want to restore some words that have lost their potency."

George Orwell, *Shooting an Elephant*   615
"The wretched prisoners huddling in the stinking cages of the lockups, the grey, cowed faces of the long-term convicts, the scarred buttocks of the men who had been flogged with bamboos — all these oppressed me with an intolerable sense of guilt."

Jonathan Swift, *A Modest Proposal*   624
"I have been assured by a very knowing American of my acquaintance in London, that a young healthy child well nursed is at a year old a most delicious, nourishing, and wholesome food, whether stewed, roasted, baked, or broiled; and I make no doubt that it will equally serve in a fricassee or a ragout."

Writing Suggestions for Combining Strategies   634

14 Writing with Sources   635

What Does It Mean to Write with Sources?   635

Writing with Sources   635

Learning to Summarize, Paraphrase, and Quote From Your Sources   637

Summarizing   637

Paraphrasing   638

Using Direct Quotation   639

Integrating Borrowed Material into Your Text   640

Avoiding Plagiarism   642

Using Quotation Marks for Language Borrowed Directly   643

Using Your Own Words and Word Order When Summarizing and Paraphrasing   644

➤ *Preventing Plagiarism*   645

Sample Student Essay Using Library and Internet Sources   646

Christine Olson, *Distortions in the Media* (student essay)   646

Lily Huang, *The Case of the Disappearing Rabbit* 653
"For the first time in geological history, you can watch glacial ice move, and by the current projection, 20 years from now there will be nothing to see."

Ed Yong, *East Meets West: How the Brain Unites Us All* 661
"Nowhere is our love affair with otherness more romanticized than in our attitudes toward the cultures of East and West."

Jake Jamieson, *The English-Only Movement: Can America Proscribe Language with a Clear Conscience?* (student essay) 672

15 A Brief Guide to Researching and Documenting Essays 682

Establishing a Realistic Schedule 682

Finding and Using Sources 683

Conducting Keyword Searches 685

Using Subject Directories to Define and Develop Your Research Topic 686

Evaluating Your Sources 687

Analyzing Your Sources 689

Developing a Working Bibliography 690

Taking Notes 692

Documenting Sources 693

In-Text Citations 694

List of Works Cited 695

16 Editing for Grammar, Punctuation, and Sentence Style 706

1 Run-Ons: Fused Sentences and Comma Splices 706

2 Sentence Fragments 708

3 Comma Faults 709

4 Subject-Verb Agreement 710

5 Unclear Pronoun References 711

6 Pronoun-Antecedent Agreement 713

7 Dangling and Misplaced Modifiers 714

8 Faulty Parallelism   715

9 Weak Nouns and Verbs   716

10 Shifts in Verb Tense, Mood, and Voice   717

11 Wordiness   718

12 Sentence Variety   720

Glossary of Rhetorical Terms   724
Acknowledgments   733
Index   741

Thematic Contents

Consumerism

    Michael Pollan, *Eating Industrial Meat*   256

    Gerald Cleary, *How Loud? How Good? How Much?*
    How Pretty? (student essay)   338

    Barbara Ehrenreich, *This Land Is Their Land: How the Rich*
    Confiscate Natural Beauty from the Public   541

    Lars Eighner, *On Dumpster Diving*   602

Contemporary Social Issues

    Michael Pollan, *Eating Industrial Meat*   256

    Jo Goodwin Parker, *What Is Poverty?*   410

    Kevin Cunningham, *Gentrification* (student essay)   446

    Michael Jonas, *The Downside of Diversity*   480

    Steven Pinker, *In Defense of Dangerous Ideas*   531

    Barbara Ehrenreich, *This Land Is Their Land: How the Rich*
    Confiscate Natural Beauty from the Public   541

    ARGUMENT ROUNDTABLE: Alpha Wives: The Trend and the Truth   572

    Tara E. Ketch, *Kids, You Can't Read That Book!* (student essay)   592

    Doris Lessing, *On Not Winning the Nobel Prize*   608

Discoveries/Epiphanies

    Barry Winston, *Stranger Than True*   96

    Cherokee Paul Mcdonald, *A View from the Bridge*   133

    Kim Hoang, *Chinese in New York, American in Beijing*   295

    Lily Huang, *The Case of the Disappearing Rabbit*   653

Education

Thomas L. Friedman, *My Favorite Teacher*   7

Russell Baker, *Discovering the Power of My Words*   42

Stephen King, *Reading to Write*   66

Mortimer Adler, *How to Mark a Book*   236

Nikki Giovanni, *Campus Racism 101*   270

Mark Jackson, *The Liberal Arts: A Practical View*
(student essay)   502

Steven Pinker, *In Defense of Dangerous Ideas*   531

Tara E. Ketch, *Kids, You Can't Read That Book!* (student essay)   592

Doris Lessing, *On Not Winning the Nobel Prize*   608

Family and Friends

David P. Bardeen, *Not Close Enough for Comfort*   102

Pat Mora, *Remembering Lobo*   144

Maya Angelou, *Sister Flowers*   156

Mitch Albom, *If You Had One Day with Someone
Who's Gone*   186

Howard Solomon Jr., *Best Friends* (student essay)   398

ARGUMENT ROUNDTABLE: Alpha Wives: The Trend and the Truth   572

Historical Perspectives

Malcolm Jones, *Who Was More Important: Lincoln
or Darwin?*   307

Bruce Catton, *Grant and Lee: A Study in Contrasts*   323

Jim Kitchens, *The Psychology of Persuasive Messaging*   359

Amy Rashap, *The American Dream for Sale: Ethnic Images
in Magazines*   373

Thomas Jefferson, *The Declaration of Independence*   513

Jonathan Swift, *A Modest Proposal*   624

The Immigrant Experience

Robert Ramírez, *The Barrio*   150

Bharati Mukherjee, *Two Ways to Belong in America*   301

Jim Kitchens, *The Psychology of Persuasive Messaging*   359

Michael Jonas, *The Downside of Diversity*   480

Life's Decisions

Barry Winston, *Stranger Than True*   96

David P. Bardeen, *Not Close Enough for Comfort*   102

Mitch Albom, *If You Had One Day with Someone Who's Gone*   186

Shoshanna Lew, *How (Not) to Be Selected for Jury Duty* (student essay)   227

Tiffany Sharples, *Young Love*   263

George Orwell, *Shooting an Elephant*   615

Jonathan Swift, *A Modest Proposal*   624

Media in America

Amy Rashap, *The American Dream for Sale: Ethnic Images in Magazines*   373

Andrew Sullivan, *iPod World: The End of Society?*   466

Andrew Sullivan, *Why I Blog*   548

Andrew Keen, *Web 2.0*   560

Matt Welch, *Blogworld and Its Gravity: The New Amateur Journalists Weigh In*   565

Christine Olson, *Distortions in the Media* (student essay)   646

Moral Values

Alice Walker, *In Full Bloom*   213

Barbara Bowman, *Guns and Cameras* (student essay)   287

Judith Viorst, *The Truth about Lying*   366

G. Anthony Gorry, *Steal This MP3 File: What Is Theft?*   416

Thomas Jefferson, *The Declaration of Independence*   513

Martin Luther King Jr., *I Have a Dream*   525

Steven Pinker, *In Defense of Dangerous Ideas*   531

Doris Lessing, *On Not Winning the Nobel Prize*   608

The Natural World

James C. Tassé, *Trailcheck* (student essay)   125

Cherokee Paul McDonald, *A View from the Bridge*   133

Stan Badgett, *Rock Dust*   139

Michael Pollan, *Eating Industrial Meat*   256

Barbara Bowman, *Guns and Cameras* (student essay)   287

Barbara Ehrenreich, *This Land Is Their Land: How the Rich Confiscate Natural Beauty from the Public*   541

Lily Huang, *The Case of the Disappearing Rabbit*   653

Parenting

Rita Dove, *Loose Ends*   3

Rosalind Wiseman, *The Queen Bee and Her Court*   345

Deborah M. Roffman, *What Does "Boys Will Be Boys" Really Mean?*   422

Tara E. Ketch, *Kids, You Can't Read That Book!*
(student essay)   592

Peer Pressure

Annie Dillard, *From* An American Childhood   90

Paula Kersch, *Weight Management: More Than a Matter of Good Looks* (student essay)   171

Rosalind Wiseman, *The Queen Bee and Her Court*   345

Deborah M. Roffman, *What Does "Boys Will Be Boys" Really Mean?*   422

People and Personalities

Suzanne Britt, *Neat People vs. Sloppy People*   318

Rosalind Wiseman, *The Queen Bee and Her Court*   345

Ed Yong, *East Meets West: How the Brain Unites Us All*   661

The Power of Language

Russell Baker, *Discovering the Power of My Words*   42

Malcolm X, *Coming to an Awareness of Language*   85

Vernon E. Jordan Jr., *Vernon Can Read!*   108

Jim Kitchens, *The Psychology of Persuasive Messaging*   359

Thomas Jefferson, *The Declaration of Independence*   513

Tara E. Ketch, *Kids, You Can't Read That Book!*
(student essay)   592

Doris Lessing, *On Not Winning the Nobel Prize*   608

Jake Jamieson, *The English-Only Movement: Can America Proscribe Language with a Clear Conscience?*
(student essay)   672

Race in America

Malcolm X, *Coming to an Awareness of Language*   85

Vernon E. Jordan Jr., *Vernon Can Read!*   108

Alice Walker, *In Full Bloom*   213

Nikki Giovanni, *Campus Racism 101*   270

Kim Hoang, *Chinese in New York, American in Beijing*   295

Martin Luther King Jr., *The Ways of Meeting Oppression*   384

Martin Luther King Jr., *I Have a Dream*   525

Sense of Place

Stan Badgett, *Rock Dust*   139

Robert Ramírez, *The Barrio*   150

Kim Hoang, *Chinese in New York, American in Beijing*   295

Barbara Ehrenreich, *This Land Is Their Land: How the Rich Confiscate Natural Beauty from the Public*   541

Lily Huang, *The Case of the Disappearing Rabbit*   653

Ed Yong, *East Meets West: How the Brain Unites Us All*   661

Sense of Self

Keith Eldred, *Secular Mantras* (student essay)   38

Laura LaPierre, *Why Are You Here?* (student essay)   76

Paula Kersch, *Weight Management: More Than a Matter of Good Looks* (student essay)   171

Tiffany Sharples, *Young Love*   263

Kim Hoang, *Chinese in New York, American in Beijing*   295

David Brooks, *The Odyssey Years*   433

Jennie Yabroff, *Here's Looking at You, Kids*   460

Andrew Sullivan, *Why I Blog*   548

Technology and the Internet

Jennie Yabroff, *Here's Looking at You, Kids*   460

Andrew Sullivan, *iPod World: The End of Society?*   466

Carl M. Cannon, *The Real Computer Virus*   471

Andrew Sullivan, *Why I Blog*   548

Andrew Keen, *Web 2.0*   560

Matt Welch, *Blogworld and Its Gravity: The New Amateur Journalists Weigh In*   565

Women and Men

Deborah Tannen, *How to Give Orders Like a Man*   192

Tiffany Sharples, *Young Love*   263

Deborah M. Roffman, *What Does "Boys Will Be Boys" Really Mean?*   422

Sojourner Truth, *Ain't I a Woman?*   429

Jon Katz, *How Boys Become Men*   455

ARGUMENT ROUNDTABLE: Alpha Wives: The Trend and the Truth   572

The World of Work

Vernon E. Jordan Jr., *Vernon Can Read!*   108

James C. Tassé, *Trailcheck* (student essay)   125

Stan Badgett, *Rock Dust*   139

Deborah Tannen, *How to Give Orders Like a Man*   192

Mike Rose, *Blue-Collar Brilliance*   202

Writing about Writing

Russell Baker, *Discovering the Power of My Words*   42

Anne Lamott, *Shitty First Drafts*   47

Linda Flower, *Writing for an Audience*   52

William Zinsser, *Simplicity*   56

Donald M. Murray, *The Maker's Eye: Revising Your Own Manuscripts*   60

Stephen King, *Reading to Write*   66

Natalie Goldberg, *Be Specific*   182

Paul Roberts, *How to Say Nothing in 500 Words*   243

Richard Lederer, *The Case for Short Words*   519

Andrew Sullivan, *Why I Blog*   548

Matt Welch, *Blogworld and Its Gravity: The New Amateur Journalists Weigh In*   565

CHAPTER 1

Reading

Subject & Strategy **places equal emphasis on content and** form — that is, on the *subject* of an essay and on the *strategies* an author uses to write it. All readers pay attention to content. Far fewer, however, notice form — the strategies authors use to organize their writing and the means they use to make it clear, logical, and effective.

When you learn to read actively and analytically, you come to appreciate the craftsmanship involved in writing — a writer's choice of an appropriate organizational strategy or strategies and his or her use of descriptive details, representative and persuasive examples, sentence variety, and clear, appropriate, vivid diction.

Developing an Effective Reading Process

Active, analytical reading requires, first of all, that you commit time and effort to it. Second, it requires that you try to take a positive interest in what you are reading, even if the subject matter is not immediately appealing. To help you get the most out of your reading, this chapter provides guidelines for an effective reading process.

Step 1: Prepare Yourself to Read the Selection

Instead of diving right into any given selection in *Subject & Strategy*, you need first to establish a context for what you will be reading. What's the essay about? What do you know about the author's background and reputation? Where was the essay first published? Who was the intended audience? And, finally, how much do you already know about the subject of the selection?

The materials that precede each selection in this book — the *title, headnote,* and *Preparing to Read* prompt — are intended to help you establish this context. From the *title* you often discover the writer's position on an

1

Organizational* Strategies

Narration	Telling a story or giving an account of an event
Description	Presenting a picture in words
Illustration	Using examples to explain a point or an idea
Process Analysis	Explaining how something is done or happens
Comparison and Contrast	Demonstrating likenesses and differences
Division and Classification	Breaking down a subject into its parts and placing them in appropriate categories
Definition	Explaining what something is
Cause and Effect Analysis	Explaining the causes of an event or the effects of an action
Argumentation	Using reason and logic to persuade

* Also known as *rhetorical* or *writing* strategies.

issue or attitude toward the topic. The title can also give clues about the writer's intended audience and reasons for composing the piece.

Each *headnote* contains four essential elements:

1. A *photo* of the author lets you put a face to a name.

2. The *biographical note* provides information about the writer's life and work, as well as his or her reputation and authority to write on the subject.

3. The *publication information* for the selection that appears in the book tells you when the essay was published and where it first appeared. This information can also give you insight into the intended audience.

4. The *content and rhetorical highlights* of the selection preview the subject and outline key aspects of the writing strategies used by the author.

Finally, the *Preparing to Read* journal prompt encourages you to reflect and record your thoughts and opinions on the topic before you begin reading.

Carefully review the following context-building materials that accompany Rita Dove's essay "Loose Ends" to see how they can help you establish a context for the reading. The essay itself appears on pages 5–6.

TITLE

Loose Ends

AUTHOR

RITA DOVE

HEADNOTE

Pulitzer Prize–winning poet Rita Dove was born in Akron, Ohio, in 1952 and received her bachelor's degree from Miami University of Ohio in 1973. After two semesters as a Fulbright scholar at Tübingen Universität in Germany, Dove enrolled in the University of Iowa's Writers' Workshop, where she earned her master's degree in 1977. From 1981 to 1989, she taught at Arizona State University; currently, she is Commonwealth Professor of English at the University of Virginia. Dove served as poet laureate of the United States from 1993 to 1995.

Biographical note

Dove has published nine poetry collections, including *The Yellow House on the Corner* (1980), *Museum* (1983), *Mother Love* (1995), *On the Bus with Rosa Parks* (1999), *American Smooth* (2004), and *Sonata Mulattica* (2009); a book of short stories, *Fifth Sunday* (1985); and a novel, *Through the Ivory Gate* (1992). Her most famous work is *Thomas and Beulah* (1986), a collection of poems loosely based on the lives of her maternal grandparents.

This much-sought-after speaker and performer enjoys classical voice training, ballroom dancing, and playing her viola da gamba, a seventeenth-century stringed instrument. When asked in a recent interview what a person needs to succeed, Dove replied, "I think that without imagination we can go nowhere. And imagination is not something that's just restricted to the arts. Every scientist that I have met who has been a success has had to imagine. You have to imagine it possible before you can see something, sometimes."

Publication information

"Loose Ends" was first published in 1995 in *The Poet's World*, a collection of lectures and essays. Starting with a simple anecdote about her daughter's behavior, Dove prepares readers for what she has to say about Americans, reality, and television. Notice how she uses comparison and contrast to highlight what she sees as our culture's seeming preference for television over reality.

Content and rhetorical highlights

■ Preparing to Read

Journal prompt

What are your thoughts about the new "reality" television programs? In what ways, if at all, do these programs reflect "real" life? How do these shows differ from regular television fare?

From reading these preliminary materials, what expectations do you have for "Loose Ends"? While Dove's *title* does not give any specific indication of her topic, it does suggest that she will be writing about something that is not neatly organized or prepackaged. The *biographical note* reveals that Dove is an acclaimed poet and teacher and includes the titles of her various books, which suggest her African American heritage and her interest in the minority experience. From the *publication information* for the selection, you learn that the essay first appeared in *The Poet's World*, a collection of essays published during Dove's last year as poet laureate. This suggests that the subject of the essay is likely to be reflective. The *content and rhetorical highlights* advise you to look at Dove's use of comparison and contrast to spotlight differences between real life and life depicted on television. Finally, the *journal prompt* asks for your thoughts and opinions about "reality" televison. After reading Dove's essay, you can compare your thoughts about "reality" television and real life with her reflections.

Step 2: Read the Selection

Always read the selection at least twice, no matter how long it is. The first reading lets you get acquainted with the essay and get an overall sense of what the writer is saying, and why. As you read, you may find yourself modifying the sense of the writer's message and purpose that you derived from the title, headnote, and your response to the writing prompt. Circle words you do not recognize so that you can look them up in a dictionary. Put a question mark alongside any passages that are not immediately clear. However, you will probably want to delay most of your annotating until a second reading so that your first reading can be fast, enabling you to concentrate on the larger issues of message and purpose.

Step 3: Reread the Selection

Your second reading should be quite different from your first. You will know what the essay is about, where it is going, and how it gets there; now you can relate the individual parts of the essay more accurately to the whole. Use your second reading to test your first impressions, developing and deepening your sense of how (and how well) the essay is written. Because you now have a general understanding of the essay, you can pay special attention to the author's purpose and means of achieving it. You can look for strategies of organization and style and adapt them to your own work.

Step 4: Annotate the Selection

When you annotate a selection you should do more than simply underline what you think are important points. It is easy to underline so much that the notations become almost meaningless, and it's common to forget why you underlined passages in the first place, if that's all you do. Instead, as you read, write down your thoughts in the margins or on a separate piece of paper. Mark the selection's main point when you find it stated directly. Look for the strategy or strategies the author uses to explore and support that point, and jot this information down. If you disagree with a statement or conclusion, object in the margin: "No!" If you feel skeptical, write "Why?" or "Explain." If you are impressed by an argument or turn of phrase, write "Good point!" Place vertical lines or a star in the margin to indicate especially important points.

What to Annotate in a Text

Here are some examples of what you may want to mark in a selection as you read:

▸ Memorable statements or important points

▸ Key terms or concepts

▸ Central issues or themes

▸ Examples that support a major point

▸ Unfamiliar words

▸ Questions you have about a point or passage

▸ Your responses to a specific point or passage

Remember that there are no hard-and-fast rules for annotating elements. Choose a method of annotation that will make sense to you when you go back to recollect your thoughts and responses to the essay. Jot down whatever marginal notes come naturally to you. Most readers combine brief written responses with underlining, circling, highlighting, stars, or question marks.

Above all, don't let annotating become burdensome. A word or phrase is usually as good as a sentence. One helpful way to focus your annotations is to ask yourself questions such as those on page 7 while reading the selection a second time.

▪ An Example: Annotating Rita Dove's "Loose Ends"

Begins w/ anecdote—why?

For years the following scene would play daily at our house: 1
Home from school, my daughter would (heave) her backpack off her shoulder and let it (thud) to the hall floor, and then (dump) her jacket on top of the pile. My husband would

Nice description— comes alive!

tell her to pick it up — as he did every day — and hang it in the closet. Begrudgingly with a (snort) and a (hrrumph), she would comply. The ritual interrogation began:

"Hi, Aviva. How was school?"   2

Daughter Aviva: bored (?) by school

"Fine."   3

"What did you do today?"   4

"Nothing."   5

Don't get it—kids like veg. casseroles??

And so it went, every day. We cajoled, we pleaded, we   6
threatened with rationed ice-cream sandwiches and <u>new
healthy vegetable casseroles</u>, we attempted subterfuges such
as: "What was Ms. Boyers wearing today?" or: "Any new
pets in science class?" but her answer remained the same:
I dunno.

Daughter loves TV, bored by school—main problem of essay?

Asked, however, about that week's episodes of "MathNet,"   7
her favorite series on Public Television's *Square One*, or asked
for a quick gloss of a segment of *Lois and Clark* that we happened to miss, and she'd spew out the details of a complicated
story, complete with character development, gestures, every
twist and back-flip of the plot.

Not sure how she means "greater" here

Is TV (greater) than reality? Are we to take as damning   8
evidence the soap opera stars attacked in public by viewers
who obstinately believe in the on-screen villainy of Erica
or Jeannie's evil twin? Is an estrangement from real life
the catalyst behind the escalating violence in our schools,
where children imitate the gun-'em-down pyrotechnics of
cop-and-robber shows? Such a conclusion is too easy. Yes,
the influence of public media on our perceptions is enormous, but the relationship of <u>projected reality</u>—i.e., TV—to
<u>imagined reality</u>—i.e., an existential moment—is much
more complex. <u>It is not that we confuse TV with reality, but
that we prefer it to reality</u>—the manageable struggle resolved
in twenty-six minutes, the witty repartee within the family
circle instead of the grunts and silence common to most real
families; the sharpened conflict and defined despair instead
of vague anxiety and invisible enemies. "<u>Life, my friends,
is boring.</u> We must not say so," wrote (John Berryman) and
many years and "Dream Songs" later he leapt from a bridge
in Minneapolis. <u>But there is a devastating corollary to that
statement: Life, friends, is ragged.</u> (Loose ends) are the rule.

"projected reality" = TV; "imagined reality" = real life??

Thesis?

"instead ofs" mark point-by-pt contrast btw TV and real life

Poet? look him up

Part of thesis? Title!

Sums it up for us

<u>What happens when my daughter tells the television's story</u>   9
<u>better than her own is simply this:</u> The TV offers an easier tale
to tell. The salient points are there for the plucking—indeed,
they're the only points presented—and all she has to do is
to recall them. Instant Nostalgia! Life, on the other hand,
(slithers) about and (runs down blind alleys) and sometimes
just (fizzles) at the climax. "The world is ugly, / And the people are sad," sings the country bumpkin in (Wallace Stevens's)
"Gubinnal." Who isn't tempted to ignore the (inexorable) fact
of our insignificance on a dying planet? We all yearn for our
own private patch of blue.

Describes life as—a rat? (but: "fizzles"?)

Look up Stevens and "inexorable"

Now that you have learned what you should do to prepare yourself to
read a selection, what you should look for during a first reading and during

a second reading, and what you should annotate, it is time to move on to the next step: analyzing a text by asking yourself questions as you reread it.

Step 5: Analyze and Evaluate the Selection

As you continue to study the selection, analyze it for a deeper understanding and appreciation of the author's craft and try to evaluate its overall effectiveness as a piece of writing. Here are some questions you may find helpful as you start the process:

Questions for Analysis and Evaluation

1. What is the writer's topic?

2. What is the writer's main point or thesis?

3. What is the writer's purpose in writing?

4. What strategy or strategies does the writer use? *Where* and *how* does the writer use them?

5. Do the writer's strategies suit his or her subject and purpose? Why or why not?

6. How effective is the essay? Does the writer make his or her points clear and persuade the reader to accept them?

Each essay in *Subject & Strategy* is followed by study questions similar to these but specific to the essay. Some of the questions help you analyze the content of an essay, while others help you analyze the writer's use of the rhetorical strategies. In addition, there are questions about the writer's diction and style. As you read the essay a second time, look for details related to these questions, and then answer the questions as fully as you can.

The Reading Process in Action:
Thomas L. Friedman's "My Favorite Teacher"

To give you practice using the five-step reading process that we have just explored, we present an essay by Thomas L. Friedman, including the headnote material and the Preparing to Read prompt. Before you read Friedman's essay, think about the title, the biographical and rhetorical information in the headnote, and the Preparing to Read prompt. Make some notes of your expectations about the essay and write out a response to the prompt. Next, continue following the five-step process outlined in this chapter. As you read the essay for the first time, try not to stop; take it all in as if in one breath. The second time through, pause to annotate the text. Finally, using the questions listed above, analyze and evaluate the essay.

My Favorite Teacher

THOMAS L. FRIEDMAN

New York Times foreign affairs columnist Thomas L. Friedman was born in Minneapolis, Minnesota, in 1953. He graduated from Brandeis University in 1975 and received a Marshall Scholarship to pursue modern Middle East studies at St. Anthony's College, Oxford University, where he earned a master's degree. He has worked for the *New York Times* since 1981 — first in Lebanon, then in Israel, and since 1989 in Washington, D.C. He was awarded the Pulitzer Prize in 1983 and 1988 for his reporting and again in 2002 for his commentary. Friedman's 1989 best-seller, *From Beirut to Jerusalem*, received the National Book Award for nonfiction. His most recent books are *The Lexus and the Olive Tree: Understanding Globalization* (2000), *Longitudes and Attitudes: Exploring the World after September 11* (2002), *The World Is Flat: A Brief History of the Twenty-First Century* (2005), and *Hot, Flat, and Crowded: Why We Need a Green Revolution — And How It Can Renew America* (2008).

In the following essay, which first appeared in the *New York Times* on January 9, 2001, Friedman pays tribute to his tenth-grade journalism teacher. As you read Friedman's profile of Steinberg, note the descriptive detail he selects to create the dominant impression of "a woman of clarity in an age of uncertainty."

▪ Preparing to Read

If you had to name your three favorite teachers of all time, who would they be? Why do you consider each one a favorite? Which one, if any, are you likely to remember twenty-five years from now? Why?

Last Sunday's *New York Times Magazine* published its annual review of people who died last year who left a particular mark on the world. I am sure all readers have their own such list. I certainly do. Indeed, someone who made the most important difference in my life died last year — my high school journalism teacher, Hattie M. Steinberg.   1

I grew up in a small suburb of Minneapolis, and Hattie was the legendary journalism teacher at St. Louis Park High School, Room 313. I took her intro to journalism course in 10th grade, back in 1969, and have never needed, or taken, another course in journalism since. She was that good.   2

Hattie was a woman who believed that the secret for success in life was   3
getting the fundamentals right. And boy, she pounded the fundamentals of
journalism into her students — not simply how to write a lead or accurately
transcribe a quote, but, more important, how to comport yourself in a professional way and to always do quality work. To this day, when I forget to
wear a tie on assignment, I think of Hattie scolding me. I once interviewed an
ad exec for our high school paper who used a four-letter word. We debated
whether to run it. Hattie ruled yes. That ad man almost lost his job when it
appeared. She wanted to teach us about consequences.

Hattie was the toughest teacher I ever had. After you took her journal-   4
ism course in 10th grade, you tried out for the paper, *The Echo*, which she
supervised. Competition was fierce. In 11th grade, I didn't quite come up to
her writing standards, so she made me business manager, selling ads to the
local pizza parlors. That year, though, she let me write one story. It was about
an Israeli general who had been a hero in the Six-Day War, who was giving a
lecture at the University of Minnesota. I covered his lecture and interviewed
him briefly. His name was Ariel Sharon. First story I ever got published.

Those of us on the paper, and the yearbook that she also supervised, lived in   5
Hattie's classroom. We hung out there before and after school. Now, you have to
understand, Hattie was a single woman, nearing 60 at the time, and this was the
1960s. She was the polar opposite of "cool," but we hung around her classroom
like it was a malt shop and she was Wolfman Jack. None of us could have articu-
lated it then, but it was because we enjoyed being harangued by her, disciplined
by her and taught by her. She was a woman of clarity in an age of uncertainty.

We remained friends for 30 years, and she followed, bragged about and   6
critiqued every twist in my career. After she died, her friends sent me a pile of
my stories that she had saved over the years. Indeed, her students were her family — only closer. Judy Harrington, one of Hattie's former students, remarked
about other friends who were on Hattie's newspapers and yearbooks: "We all
graduated 41 years ago; and yet nearly each day in our lives something comes
up — some mental image, some admonition that makes us think of Hattie."

Judy also told the story of one of Hattie's last birthday parties, when one   7
man said he had to leave early to take his daughter somewhere. "Sit down,"
said Hattie. "You're not leaving yet. She can just be a little late."

That was my teacher! I sit up straight just thinkin' about her.   8

Among the fundamentals Hattie introduced me to was the *New York*   9
Times. Every morning it was delivered to Room 313. I had never seen it before
then. Real journalists, she taught us, start their day by reading the *Times* and
columnists like Anthony Lewis and James Reston.

I have been thinking about Hattie a lot this year, not just because she died   10
on July 31, but because the lessons she imparted seem so relevant now. We've
just gone through this huge dot-com-Internet-globalization bubble — during
which a lot of smart people got carried away and forgot the fundamentals of
how you build a profitable company, a lasting portfolio, a nation state or a

thriving student. It turns out that the real secret of success in the information age is what it always was: fundamentals — reading, writing and arithmetic, church, synagogue and mosque, the rule of law and good governance.

The Internet can make you smarter, but it can't make you smart. It can   11 extend your reach, but it will never tell you what to say at a P.T.A. meeting. These fundamentals cannot be downloaded. You can only upload them, the old-fashioned way, one by one, in places like Room 313 at St. Louis Park High. I only regret that I didn't write this column when the woman who taught me all that was still alive.

Once you have read and reread Friedman's essay, write your own answers to the six basic questions listed on page 7. Then compare your answers with those that follow.

1. **What is the writer's *topic*?**

   Friedman's topic is his high school journalism teacher, Hattie M. Steinberg; more broadly, his topic is the "secret for success in life," as taught to him by Steinberg.

2. **What is the writer's *main point* or *thesis*?**

   Friedman writes about Steinberg because she was "someone who made the most important difference in my life" (paragraph 1). His main point seems to be that "Hattie was a woman who believed that the secret for success in life was getting the fundamentals right" (3). Friedman learned this from Hattie and applied it to his own life. He firmly believes that "the real secret of success in the information age is what it always was: fundamentals" (10).

3. **What is the writer's *purpose* in writing?**

   Friedman's purpose is to memorialize Steinberg and to explain the importance of the fundamentals that she taught him more than forty years ago. He wants his readers to realize that there are no shortcuts or quick fixes on the road to success. Without the fundamentals, success often eludes people.

4. **What *strategy* or *strategies* does the writer use? *Where* and *how* does the writer use them?**

   Overall, Friedman uses the strategy of illustration, fleshing out his profile of Steinberg with specific examples of the fundamentals she instilled in her students (paragraphs 3 and 9). Friedman uses description as well to develop his profile of Steinberg. We learn that she was Friedman's "toughest teacher" (4), that she was "a single woman, nearing 60 at the time," that she was "the polar opposite of 'cool,'" and that she was "a woman of clarity in an age of uncertainty" (5). Finally, Friedman's brief narratives about an advertising executive, Ariel Sharon, Steinberg's classroom hangout, and one of the teacher's last birthday parties give readers insight into her personality by showing us what she was like instead of simply telling us.

5. **Do the writer's *strategies* suit his *subject* and *purpose*? Why or why not?**

Friedman uses exemplification as a strategy to show why Steinberg had such a great impact on his life. Friedman knew that he was not telling Steinberg's story, or writing narration, so much as he was showing what a great teacher she was. Using examples of how Steinberg affected his life and molded his journalistic skills allows Friedman to introduce his teacher as well as to demonstrate her importance.

In developing his portrait of Steinberg in this way, Friedman relies on the fundamentals of good journalism. When taken collectively, his examples create a poignant picture of this teacher. Steinberg would likely have been proud to see her former student demonstrating his journalistic skills in paying tribute to her.

6. **How effective is the essay? Does the writer make his points clear and persuade the reader to accept them?**

Friedman's essay serves his purpose extremely well. He helps his readers visualize Steinberg and understand what she gave to each of her journalism students. In his concluding two paragraphs, Friedman shows us that Steinberg's message is as relevant today as it was more than forty years ago in St. Louis Park High School, Room 313.

About the Photographs and Visual Texts in This Book

With this edition we have given *Subject & Strategy* a new visual dimension. Each chapter now opens with a photograph or visual text that provides insight into the chapter's modal strategy. In addition, we have illustrated at least one essay in each chapter with a photograph that captures one or more themes in the essay. Finally, we have included an assortment of visual texts in the Classroom Activities that accompany each essay in *Subject & Strategy.* It is our hope that, by adding a new, visual medium to the mix of written essays and text-based analytical activities and assignments, we can demonstrate not only another approach to themes and strategies but also how a different medium portrays these themes and strategies.

There's nothing unnatural or wrong about looking at a photograph and naming its subject or giving it a label. For example, summarizing the content of the photograph on page 13 of a village scene in Gujarat, India, is easy enough. We'd simply say, *"Here's a photograph of a woman in traditional dress."*

The problem comes when we mistake *looking* for *seeing*. If we think we are seeing and truly perceiving but are only looking, we miss a lot. Our visual sense can become uncritical and nonchalant, perhaps even numbed to what's going on in a photograph.

To reap the larger rewards, we need to move in more closely on an image. If we take a closer look, we will see all kinds of important details that we perhaps missed the first time around. We see elements in harmony as well as conflict. We see comparisons and contrasts. We see storytelling. We see process and change. We see highlights and shadows, foreground and background, light and dark, and a myriad of shades in between. There is movement — even in still photographs. There is tension and energy, peace and harmony, and line and texture. We see all this because we are seeing and not merely looking.

If we examine the photograph of the woman again and truly *see* it, we might observe the following:

1. The woman is holding a child. It looks as if the child, who appears to be well fed, is wearing a necklace but is otherwise naked. The woman is barefoot, but she's also wearing jewelry — a necklace and a bracelet. She is in traditional dress — the skirt goes down to her ankles, and there is some kind of scarf that goes over the back of her hair.

2. The woman is focusing on something to the photographer's right (her left). She is looking into the sun, which is low on the horizon. We know this because there is a long shadow behind her.

3. There is a satellite dish on the roof of the building in the photo. It is neither a huge dish indicating early technology nor a relatively small one indicating recent digital satellite technology. On the peak of the roof of the building is a small cross.

4. There is non-Western writing on the wall of the building. Some of the writing is smudged. The writing doesn't appear to be graffiti because it is very neatly rendered.

5. The building appears to be simply constructed out of rough, concrete-like material, while the roof is covered with tiles.

6. At what looks like the entrance to the building are two large sacks, still tied at their tops.

7. The road is not paved; all we see is dirt and stone. The fact that the woman is standing barefoot on this surface makes us wonder if she's uncomfortable.

© Sean Sprague/Stock Boston

8. There are trees poking out from behind the building. They are not palm trees; they might even be evergreens.

9. The most unusual thing about the photograph is the juxtaposition of the satellite dish with the rudimentary building in what appears to be an underdeveloped rural setting.

Based on these detailed observations, we can begin to identify a number of themes at work in the photo: cultural diversity, cultural contradictions, culture clashes (East versus West; first world versus third), technology, and imperialism. Likewise, we can see that several rhetorical strategies are at work: comparison and contrast predominantly, but also description and exemplification.

A similar close analysis of the other photographs in this book will enhance your understanding of how themes and strategies work in these visual texts. Practice in visual analysis will, in turn, add to your understanding of the reading selections. In reading, too, we need to train ourselves to pay close attention to catch all nuances and to be attuned to what is *not* expressed as well as to what is. By sharpening our observational skills, we penetrate to another level of meaning — a level not apparent to a casual reader. Finally, strengthening your ability to see and read deeply will also strengthen your ability to write. We need to see first, clearly and in detail, before we attempt, as writers, to find the appropriate words to make others see.

The Reading-Writing Connection

Reading and writing are two sides of the same coin. Active reading is one of the best ways to learn to write and to improve writing skills. By reading we can see how others have communicated their experiences, ideas, thoughts, and feelings in their writing. We can study how they have effectively used the various elements of the essay — thesis, organizational strategies, beginnings and endings, paragraphs, transitions, effective sentences, word choice, tone, and figurative language — to say what they wanted to say. By studying the style, technique, and rhetorical strategies of other writers — by reading, in effect, *as* writers — we learn how to write more effectively ourselves.

Reading As a Writer

What does it mean to read as a writer? Most of us have not been taught to read with a writer's eye, to ask why we like one piece of writing and not another. Likewise, most of us do not ask ourselves why one piece of writing is more believable or convincing than another. When you learn to read with a writer's eye, you begin to answer these important questions and, in the process, come to appreciate what is involved in selecting a subject.

At one level, reading stimulates your imagination by providing you with ideas on what to write about. After reading Thomas L. Friedman's "My Favorite Teacher," Malcolm X's "Coming to an Awareness of Language," David P. Bardeen's "Not Close Enough for Comfort," or the selection from Annie Dillard's *An American Childhood,* you might decide to write about a turning point in your life. Or, after reading Pat Mora's "Remembering Lobo," Maya Angelou's "Sister Flowers," or Robert Ramírez's "The Barrio," you might be inspired to write about a person or place of similar personal significance to you.

Reading also provides you with information, ideas, and perspectives that can serve as jumping-off points for your own essays. For example, after reading Rosalind Wiseman's "The Queen Bee and Her Court," you might want to elaborate on what she has written, agreeing with her examples or generating better ones; qualify her argument or take issue with it; or use a variation of her classification scheme to discuss male relationships (i.e., "The King and His Court"). Similarly, if you wanted to write an essay in which you take a stand on an issue, you would find the essays on various controversies in the "Argumentation" chapter an invaluable resource.

Reading actively and analytically will also help you recognize effective writing and learn to emulate it. When you see, for example, how Deborah Tannen uses a strong thesis statement about the value of directness and indirectness in human communication to control the parts of her essay, you can better appreciate the importance of having a clear thesis statement in your writing. When you see the way Andrew Sullivan ("iPod World: The End of Society?") uses transitions to link key phrases and important ideas so that readers can recognize how the parts of his essay are meant to flow together, you have a better idea of how to achieve such coherence in your writing. And when you see how Suzanne Britt ("Neat People vs. Sloppy People") uses a point-by-point organizational pattern to show the differences between neat and sloppy people, you see a powerful way in which you can organize an essay using the strategy of comparison and contrast.

Perhaps the most important reason to master the skill of reading like a writer is that, for everything you write, you will be your own first reader. How well you scrutinize your own drafts will affect how well you revise them, and revising well is crucial to writing well.

CHAPTER 2

Writing

Nothing is more important to your success in school and in the workplace than learning to write well. You've heard it so often you've probably become numb to the advice. Let's ask the big question, however. Why is writing well so important? The simple answer is that no activity develops your ability to think better than writing does. Writing allows you to develop your thoughts and to "see" and reflect critically on what you think: In that sense, writing also involves its twin sister, reading. Small wonder, then, that employers in all fields are constantly looking for people who can read and write well. Simply put, employers want to hire and retain the best minds they can to further their business objectives, and the ability to read and write well is a strong indication of a good mind.

In today's technology-driven economy, there is virtually no field of work that doesn't require clear, accurate, and direct expression in writing, whether it be writing internal memos, self-appraisals, laboratory reports, bids for contracts, proposals for new products or procedures, loan or grant applications, sales reports, market analyses, or some other type of document. Starting with the ability to write an effective job-application letter and résumé and continuing on to advancement through the ranks of an organization—and perhaps more than any other factor — your ability to organize your thoughts and clearly present them will affect your overall success on the job and in life.

College is a practical training ground for learning to write. In college, with the help of instructors, you will write essays, analyses, term papers, reports, reviews of research, critiques, and summaries. Take advantage of the opportunity college provides to develop your skills as a writer: What you learn now will be fundamental, not only to your education, but also to your later success.

Developing an Effective Writing Process

Writers cannot rely on inspiration alone to produce effective writing. Good writers follow a writing *process*: They analyze their assignment, gather ideas, draft, revise, edit, and proofread. It is worth remembering, however, that the writing process is rarely as simple and straightforward as this. Often the process is recursive, moving back and forth among different stages. Moreover, writing is personal — no two people go about it exactly the same way. Still, it is possible to describe basic guidelines for developing a writing process, thereby allowing you to devise your own reliable method for undertaking a writing task.

Step 1: Understand Your Assignment

A great deal of the writing you do in college will be in response to very specific assignments. Your American history professor, for example, may ask you to write a paper in which you explain the causes of the Spanish-American War; your environmental studies professor may ask you to report both the pro and con arguments for regulating industrial carbon emissions; or your English professor may ask you to compare and contrast the text and film versions of H. G. Wells's *The War of the Worlds*. It is important, therefore, that you understand exactly what your instructor is asking you to do. The best way to understand assignments such as these (or exam questions, for that matter) is to identify *subject* words (words that indicate the content of the assignment) and *direction* words (words that indicate your purpose or the writing strategy you should use). In the first example given above, the subject words are *Spanish-American War* and the direction word is *explain*. In the second example, the subject words are *industrial carbon emissions* and the direction word is *report*. Finally, the subject words in the third example are *text and film versions of H. G. Wells's* The War of the Worlds, while the direction words are *compare and contrast.*

Most direction words are familiar to us, but we are not always sure how they differ from one another or exactly what they are asking us to do. The following list of direction words, along with explanations of what they call for, will help you analyze paper and exam assignments.

Direction Words

Analyze: take apart and examine closely

Argue: make a case for a particular position

Categorize: place into meaningful groups

Compare: look for differences; stress similarities

Contrast: look for similarities; stress differences

Critique: point out positive and negative features

Define: provide the meaning for a term or concept

Evaluate: judge according to some standard

Explain: make plain or comprehensible

Illustrate: show through examples

Interpret: explain the meaning of something

(*continued on next page*)

(continued from previous page)

List: catalog or enumerate steps in a process

Outline: provide abbreviated structure for key elements

Prove: demonstrate truth through logic, fact, or example

Review: summarize key points

Synthesize: bring together or make connections among elements

Trace: delineate a sequence of events

Finding a Subject Area and Focusing on a Topic. Although you will often be given specific assignments in your writing course, you may sometimes be given the freedom to choose your subject matter and topic. In this case, begin by determining a broad subject that you like to think about and might enjoy writing about — a general subject like the Internet, popular culture, or foreign travel. Something you've recently read — one of the essays in *Subject & Strategy,* for example — may help bring particular subjects to mind. You might consider a subject related to your career ambitions — perhaps business, journalism, teaching, law, medicine, architecture, or computer programming. Another option is to list some subjects you enjoy discussing with friends: food, sports, television programs, or politics. Select several likely subjects, and explore their potential. Your goal is to arrive at an appropriately narrowed topic.

Suppose, for example, you select as possible subject areas "farming" and "advertising." You could develop each according to the following chart.

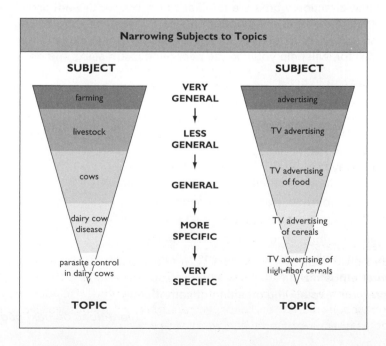

Narrowing Subjects to Topics		
SUBJECT		**SUBJECT**
farming	**VERY GENERAL**	advertising
livestock	**LESS GENERAL**	TV advertising
cows	**GENERAL**	TV advertising of food
dairy cow disease	**MORE SPECIFIC**	TV advertising of cereals
parasite control in dairy cows	**VERY SPECIFIC**	TV advertising of high-fiber cereals
TOPIC		**TOPIC**

Determine Your Purpose

All effective writing springs from a clear purpose. Most good writing seeks specifically to accomplish any one of the following three purposes:

- To express thoughts and feelings about life experiences
- To inform readers by explaining something about the world around them
- To persuade readers to adopt some belief or take some action

In *expressive writing*, or writing from experience, you put your thoughts and feelings before all other concerns. When Annie Dillard reacts to being caught throwing a snowball at a car (Chapter 4), when Malcolm X shows his frustration at not having appropriate language to express himself (Chapter 4), and when Stan Badgett describes the rock dust covering every surface in the coal mine where he worked (Chapter 5), each one is writing from experience. In each case, the writer has clarified an important life experience and has conveyed what he or she learned from it.

Informative writing focuses on telling the reader something about the outside world. In informative writing, you report, explain, analyze, define, classify, compare, describe a process, or examine causes and effects. When Michael Pollan explains how the beef we eat travels from factory farms to our tables (Chapter 7) and when Deborah Tannen discusses examples of orders given and received in the workplace (Chapter 6), each one is writing to inform.

Argumentative writing seeks to influence readers' thinking and attitudes toward a subject and, in some cases, to move them to a particular course of action. Such persuasive writing uses logical reasoning, authoritative evidence, and testimony, and it sometimes includes emotionally charged language and examples. In writing their arguments, Richard Lederer uses numerous examples to show us the power of short words (Chapter 12) and Thomas Jefferson uses evidence and clearly expressed logic to argue that the fledgling American colonies are within their rights to break away from Britain (Chapter 12).

Know Your Audience

The best writers always keep their audience in mind. Once they have decided on a topic and a purpose, writers present their material in a way that empathizes with their readers, addresses their difficulties and concerns, and appeals to their rational and emotional faculties. Based on knowledge of their audience, writers make conscious decisions on content, sentence structure, and word choice.

Writing for an Academic Audience. Academic writing most often employs the conventions of formal standard English, or the language of educated professionals. Rather than being heavy or stuffy, good academic writing is lively and engaging and holds the reader's attention by presenting interesting ideas supported with relevant facts, statistics, and detailed information. Informal writing, usually freer and simpler in form, is typically used in notes, journal entries, e-mail, text messages, instant messaging, and the like.

In order not to lessen the importance of your ideas and your credibility, be sure that informal writing does not carry over into your academic writing. Always keeping your audience and purpose in mind will help you achieve an appropriate style.

When you write, your audience might be an individual (your instructor), a group (the students in your class), a specialized group (art history majors), or a general readership (readers of your student newspaper). To help identify your audience, ask yourself the questions posed at the top of page 21.

Formal versus Informal Writing

Formal Writing	Informal Writing
Uses standard English, the language of public discourse typical of newspapers, magazines, books, and speeches	Uses nonstandard English, slang, colloquial expressions (*anyways, dude, freaked out*), and shorthand (*OMG, IMHO, GR8*)
Uses mostly third person	Uses first and second person most often
Avoids most abbreviations (*Professor, brothers, miles per gallon, Internet, digital video recorder*)	Uses abbreviations and acronyms (*Prof., bros., mpg, Net, DVR*)
Uses an impersonal tone (*The speaker took questions from the audience at the end of her lecture.*)	Uses an informal tone (*It was great the way she answered questions at the end of her talk.*)
Uses longer, more complex sentences	Uses shorter, simpler sentences
Adheres to the rules and conventions of proper grammar	Takes a casual approach to the rules and conventions of proper grammar

Questions about Audience

▸ Who are my readers? Are they a specialized or a general group?

▸ What do I know about my audience's age, gender, education, religious affiliation, economic status, and political views?

▸ What does my audience know about my subject? Are they experts or novices?

▸ What does my audience need to know about my topic in order to understand my discussion of it?

▸ Will my audience be interested, open-minded, resistant, or hostile to what I have to say?

▸ Do I need to explain any specialized language so that my audience can understand my subject? Is there any language that I should avoid?

▸ What do I want my audience to do as a result of reading my essay?

Step 2: Gather Ideas and Formulate a Thesis

Ideas and information (facts and details) lie at the heart of good prose. Ideas grow out of information; information supports ideas. Before you begin to draft, gather as many ideas as possible and as much information as you can about your topic in order to inform and stimulate your readers intellectually.

Brainstorming.   A good way to generate ideas and information about your topic is to *brainstorm*: Simply list everything you know about your topic, freely associating one idea with another. At this point, order is not important. Write quickly, but if you get stalled, reread what you have written; doing so will jog your mind in new directions. Keep your list handy so that you can add to it over the course of several days.

Here, for example, is a student's brainstorming list on why Martin Luther King Jr.'s "I Have a Dream" speech (page 525) is enduring:

WHY "I HAVE A DREAM" IS MEMORABLE

• Delivered on steps of Lincoln Memorial during civil rights demonstration in Washington, D.C.; crowd of more than 200,000 people

• Repetition of "I have a dream"

• Allusions to the Bible, spirituals

• "Bad check" metaphor and other memorable figures of speech

- Echoes other great American writings—Declaration of Independence and Gettysburg Address
- Refers to various parts of the country and embraces all races and religions
- Sermon format
- Displays energy and passion

Clustering.   Clustering allows you to generate material and to sort it into meaningful groupings. Put your topic, or a key word or phrase about your topic, in the center of a sheet of paper and draw a circle around it. Draw four or five (or more) lines radiating out from this circle, and jot down main ideas about your topic; draw circles around them as well. Repeat the process by drawing lines from the secondary circles and adding examples, details, and any questions you have.

Here is a student's cluster on television news programs:

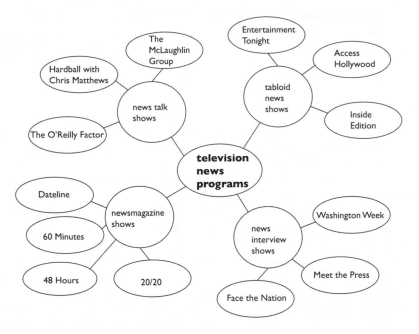

Researching.   You may want to supplement what you know about your topic with research. This does not necessarily mean formal library work or even online research. Firsthand observations and interviews with people knowledgeable about your topic are also forms of research. Whatever your form of research, take careful notes, so you can accurately paraphrase an author or quote an interviewee.

Rehearsing Ideas.   Consider rehearsing what you are going to write by taking ten or fifteen minutes to talk your way through your paper with a roommate, friend, or family member. Rehearsing in this way may suit your personality and the way you think. Moreover, rehearsing may help you generate new ideas.

Formulating a Thesis.   The thesis of an essay is its main idea, the major point the writer is trying to make.

A thesis should be

- The most important point you make about your topic

- More general than the ideas and facts used to support it

- Focused enough to be covered in the space allotted for the essay

The thesis is often expressed in one or two sentences called a *thesis statement.* Here's an example of a thesis statement about television news programs:

> The so-called serious news programs are becoming too like tabloid
> news shows in both their content and their presentation.

A thesis statement should not be a question but rather an assertion. If you find yourself writing a question for a thesis statement, answer the question first — this answer will be your thesis statement.

An effective strategy for developing a thesis statement is to begin by writing, "What I want to say is that . . ."

> *What I want to say is that* unless language barriers between patients
> and health care providers are bridged, many patients' lives in our most
> culturally diverse cities will be endangered.

Later you can delete the formulaic opening, and you will be left with a thesis statement.

To determine whether your thesis is too general or too specific, think hard about how easy it will be to present data — that is, facts, statistics, names, examples or illustrations, and opinions of authorities — to support it. If you stray too far in either direction, your task will become much more difficult. A thesis statement that is too general will leave you overwhelmed by the number of issues you must address. For example, the statement "Malls have ruined the fabric of American life" would lead to the question "How?" To answer it, you would probably have to include information about traffic patterns, urban decay, environmental damage, economic studies, and so on. To cover all of this in the time and space you have for a typical college paper would mean taking shortcuts, and your paper would be ineffective. On the other hand, too specific a thesis statement will leave you with too little information to present. "The Big City Mall should not have been built because it reduced retail sales at existing Big City stores by 21.4 percent" does not leave you with any opportunity to develop an argument.

The thesis statement is usually presented near the beginning of the essay. One common practice in shorter college papers is to position the thesis statement as the final sentence of the first paragraph.

Will Your Thesis Hold Water?

Once you have a possible thesis statement in mind for an essay, ask yourself the following questions:

▶ Does my thesis statement take a clear position on an issue? If so, what is that position?

▶ Is my thesis the most important point I make about my topic?

▶ Is my thesis neither too general nor too specific? Will I be able to argue it in the time and space allotted?

Step 3: Organize and Write Your First Draft

There is nothing mysterious or difficult about the nine organizational strategies discussed in this book. In fact, you're familiar with most of them already. Whenever you tell a story, for example, you use the strategy of *narration*. When you need to make a decision, you *compare and contrast* the things you must choose between. When you want to describe how to make a pizza, you use the strategy of *process analysis* to figure out how to explain it. What might make these strategies seem unfamiliar, especially in writing, is that most people use them more or less intuitively. Sophisticated thinking and writing, however, do not come from simply using these structures, but rather from using them consciously and purposefully.

Writing strategies are not like blueprints or plaster molds that determine in advance exactly how the final product will be shaped. Rather, these strategies are flexible and versatile, with only a few fundamental rules or directions to define their shape — like the rules for basketball, chess, or other strategic games. Such directions leave plenty of room for imagination and variety. In addition, because these strategies are fundamental ways of thinking, they will help you in all stages of the writing process — from prewriting and writing a first draft through revising and editing your piece.

Organizational* Strategies

Narration	Telling a story or giving an account of an event
Description	Presenting a picture in words
Illustration	Using examples to explain a point or an idea
Process Analysis	Explaining how something is done or happens
Comparison and Contrast	Demonstrating likenesses and differences

Division and Classification	Breaking down a subject into its parts and placing them in appropriate categories
Definition	Explaining what something is
Cause and Effect Analysis	Explaining the causes of an event or the effects of an action
Argumentation	Using reason and logic to persuade

*Also known as *rhetorical* or *writing* strategies.

Determining a Strategy for Developing Your Essay.   Good essays often employ components of more than one strategy. In determining which strategies to use, the language of the writing assignment is very important. If a description is called for, or you need to examine causes and effects, or, as is often the case, you are asked to argue for a position on an important issue, the language of the assignment will include key direction words and phrases that will indicate the primary strategy or strategies you should use in developing your essay.

The first column in the following chart lists some key direction words and phrases you may encounter in your writing assignments. The second column lists the strategy that is most likely called for by the use of those words.

Determining What Strategies to Use with a Specific Assignment

Key Direction Words and Phrases	Suggested Writing Strategy
Give an account of; tell the story of; relate the events of	*Narration*
Describe; present a picture; discuss the details of	*Description*
Show; demonstrate; enumerate; discuss; give examples of	*Illustration*
Explain how something is done; explain how something works; explain what happens; analyze the steps	*Process Analysis*
Compare; contrast; explain differences; explain similarities; evaluate	*Comparison and Contrast*
Divide and classify; explain what the components are; analyze the parts of	*Division and Classification*

(*continued on next page*)

(*continued from previous page*)

Explain; define a person, place, or thing; give the meaning of   *Definition*

Explain causes; explain effects; give the reasons for; explain the consequences of   *Cause and Effect Analysis*

Argue for or against; make a case for or against; state your views on; persuade; convince; justify   *Argumentation*

Often in academic writing your instructor may not give you a specific assignment; instead, he or she may ask only that you write a paper of a specific length. In such cases you are left to determine for yourself what strategy or strategies might best accomplish your purpose. If you are not given a specific assignment and are uncertain as to what strategy or strategies you should use in developing your essay, you might try the following four-step method:

Determining What Strategies to Use with an Open Assignment

1. State the main idea of your essay in a single phrase or sentence.

2. Restate the main idea as a question — in effect, the question your essay will answer.

3. Look closely at both the main idea and the question for key words or concepts that go with a particular strategy, just as you would when working with an assignment that specifies a topic.

4. Consider other strategies that would support your primary strategy.

Choosing Strategies across the Disciplines. The examples below show how a student writing in different disciplines might decide what strategies to use.

American Literature

1. MAIN IDEA: John Updike relies on religion as a major theme in his fiction.
2. QUESTION: In what instances does John Updike use religion as a major theme?
3. STRATEGY: Illustration. The phrase "in what instances" suggests that it is necessary to show examples of where Updike uses the theme of religion to further his narrative purposes.
4. SUPPORTING STRATEGIES: Definition. What is meant by *religion* needs to be clear.

Biology

1. MAIN IDEA: Mitosis is the process by which cells divide.
2. QUESTION: How does the process of mitosis work?
3. STRATEGY: Process analysis. The words *how*, *process*, and *work* suggest a process analysis essay.
4. SUPPORTING STRATEGIES: Illustration. A good process analysis includes examples of each step in the process.

Political Science

1. MAIN IDEA: The threat of terrorism has changed the way people think about air travel.
2. QUESTION: What effects does terrorism have on air travel?
3. STRATEGY: Cause and effect. The phrase "what effects" asks for a listing of the effects.
4. SUPPORTING STRATEGIES: Illustration. The best presentation of effects is through vivid examples.

These are just a few examples of how to decide on a writing strategy and supporting strategies that are suitable for your topic. In every case, your reading can guide you in recognizing the best plan to follow. In Chapter 13, you will learn more about combining strategies.

Writing Your First Draft.   First drafts are exploratory and sometimes unpredictable. While writing your first draft, you may find yourself getting away from your original plan. What started as a definition essay may develop into a process analysis or an effort at argumentation. For example, a definition of *school spirit* could turn into a process analysis of how a pep rally is organized or an argument about why school spirit is important (or detrimental). A definition of *manners* could become an instructive process analysis on how to be a good host, or it could turn into an argument that respect is based on the ways people treat one another. A definition of *democracy* could evolve into a process analysis of how democracy works in the United States or into an argument for democratic forms of government.

If your draft is leaning toward a different strategy from the one you first envisioned, don't force yourself to revert to your original plan. Allow your inspiration to take you where it will. When you finish your draft, you can see whether the new strategy works better than the old one or whether it would be best to go back to your initial strategy. Use your first draft to explore your ideas; you will always have a chance to revise later.

It may also happen that, while writing your first draft, you run into a difficulty that prevents you from moving forward. For example, suppose you want to tell about something that happened to you, but you aren't certain whether you should be using the pronoun *I* so often. If you turn to the essays in Chapter 4 to see how authors of narrative essays handle this problem, you will find that it isn't necessarily a problem at all. For an account of a personal experience, it's perfectly acceptable to write *I* as often as you need to. Or suppose that after writing several pages describing someone you think is quite a character, you find that your draft seems flat and doesn't express how lively and funny the person really is. If you read the introduction to Chapter 5, you will learn that descriptions need lots of factual, concrete detail; the chapter selections give further proof of this. You suddenly realize that just such detail is what's missing from your draft.

If you do run into difficulties writing your first draft, don't worry or get upset. Even experienced writers run into problems at the beginning. Just try to keep going. Think about your topic, and consider your details and what you want to say. You might even want to go back and look over your original invention work or information you've gathered.

Step 4: Revise Your Essay

Once you have completed your first draft, set it aside awhile and do something else. When you are refreshed and again ready to give it your full attention, you are ready to revise.

Revision is a vital part of the writing process. It is not to be confused with editing or "cleaning up" a draft but should be regarded as a set of activities wherein a rough draft may be transformed into a polished essay that powerfully expresses your ideas. In fact, many writers believe that all writing is essentially *re*writing. When you revise, you give yourself a chance to re-see how well you have captured your subject, to see what has worked and what still needs to be done.

In revising, you might need to reorganize your paragraphs or the sentences within some paragraphs, generate more information because you have too few examples, revise your thesis statement so that it better fits your argument, or find better transitions to bind your sentences and thoughts together. Rather than an arduous task, many writers find revision a very satisfying process because they are able to bring their work into sharper focus and give themselves a better chance of connecting with their audience.

The following sections offer proven techniques for initiating and carrying out one or more revisions of your developing essays.

Tips for Revising Your Draft

☐ Triple-space your draft so that you can make changes more easily.

☐ Make revisions on a hard copy of your paper.

☐ Read your paper aloud, listening for parts that do not make sense.

☐ Have a fellow student read your essay and critique it.

Taking Advantage of Peer Critiques.   When you critique work with other students — yours or theirs — it is important to maximize the effectiveness and efficiency of the exercise. The tips outlined in the following box will help you get the most out of peer critiques.

A Brief Guide to Peer Critiquing

When critiquing someone else's work:

- ▸ Read the essay carefully. Read it to yourself first and, if possible, have the writer read it to you at the beginning of the session. Some flaws only become obvious when read aloud.

- ▸ Ask the writer to state his or her purpose for writing and to identify the thesis statement within the paper itself.

- ▸ Be positive, but be honest. Never denigrate the paper's content or the writer's effort, but do your best to identify how the writer can improve the paper through revision.

- ▸ Try to address the most important issues first. Think about the thesis and the organization of the paper before moving on to more specific topics like word choice.

- ▸ Do not be dismissive, and do not dictate changes. Ask questions that encourage the writer to reconsider parts of the paper that you find confusing or ineffective.

When someone critiques your work:

- ▸ Give your reviewer a copy of your essay before your meeting.

- ▸ Listen carefully to your reviewer, and try not to argue each issue. Record comments, and evaluate them later.

- ▸ Do not get defensive or explain what you wanted to say if the reviewer misunderstands what you meant. Try to understand the reviewer's point of view, and learn what you need to revise to clear up the misunderstanding.

- ▸ Consider every suggestion, but only use the ones that make sense to you in your revision.

- ▸ Be sure to thank your reviewer for his or her effort on your behalf.

Revising the Larger Elements of Your Essay.   During revision, you should focus first on the larger issues of thesis, purpose, content, organization, and paragraph structure to make sure that your writing says what you want it to say. One way to begin is to make an informal outline of your first draft — not as you planned it, but as it actually came out. What does your outline tell you about the strategy you used? Does this strategy suit your purpose? Perhaps you meant to compare your two grandmothers, but you have not clearly shown their similarities and differences.

Consequently, your draft is not one unified comparison and contrast essay but two descriptive essays spliced together.

Even if you are satisfied with the overall strategy of your draft, an outline can still help you make improvements. Perhaps your classification essay on types of college students is confusing because you create overlapping categories: computer science majors, athletes, and foreign students (a computer science major could, of course, also be an athlete, a foreign student, or both). You may uncover a flaw in your organization, such as a lack of logic in an argument or faulty parallelism in a comparison and contrast. Now is the time to discover these problems and to fix them.

The following list of questions addresses the larger elements of your essay: thesis, purpose, organization, paragraphs, and evidence.

Questions for Revising the Larger Elements of Your Essay

▶ Have I focused my **topic**?

▶ Does my **thesis statement** clearly identify my topic and make an assertion about it?

▶ Is the **writing strategy** I have chosen the best one for my purpose?

▶ Are my **paragraphs** adequately developed, and does each support my thesis?

▶ Is my **beginning** effective in capturing my reader's interest and introducing my topic?

▶ Is my **conclusion** effective? Does it grow naturally from what I've said in the rest of my essay?

▶ Have I accomplished my **purpose**?

Writing Beginnings and Endings. Beginnings and endings are very important to the effectiveness of an essay, but they can be daunting to write. Inexperienced writers often feel they must write their essays sequentially when, in fact, it is usually better to write both the beginning and the ending after you have completed most or all of the rest of your essay. Once you see how your essay develops, you will know better how to capture your reader's attention and introduce the rest of the essay. As you work through the revision process, ask yourself the questions in the box below.

Questions for Revising Sentences

▶ Do my sentences convey my thoughts clearly, and do they emphasize the most important parts of my thinking?

▶ Are all my sentences complete sentences?

> ▸ Are my sentences stylistically varied? Do I alter their pattern and rhythm for emphasis? Do I use some short sentences for dramatic effect?
>
> ▸ Are all my sentences written in the active voice?
>
> ▸ Do I use strong action verbs and concrete nouns?
>
> ▸ Is my diction fresh and forceful? Do I avoid wordiness?
>
> ▸ Have I achieved an appropriate degree of formality in my writing?
>
> ▸ Have I committed any errors in usage?

Revising the Smaller Elements of Your Essay. Once you have addressed the larger elements of your essay, you should turn your attention to the finer elements of sentence structure, word choice, and usage. The following questions focus on these concerns.

If, after serious efforts at revision, you still find yourself dissatisfied with specific elements of your draft, look at some of the essays in *Subject & Strategy* to see how other writers have dealt with similar situations. For example, if you don't like the way the essay starts, find some beginnings you think are particularly effective. If your paragraphs don't seem to flow into one another, examine how various writers use transitions. If you have lapsed into informal language, take a look at how other writers express themselves. If an example seems unconvincing, examine the way other writers include details, anecdotes, facts, and statistics to strengthen their illustrations.

Remember that the readings in this text are a resource for you as you write, as are the strategy chapter introductions, which outline the basic features of each strategy. In addition, the six readings in Chapter 3, "Six Writers on Writing," will provide you with inspiration and advice to help you through the writing process.

Questions for Writing Beginnings and Endings

▸ Does my introduction grab the reader's attention?

▸ Is my introduction confusing in any way? How well does it relate to the rest of the essay?

▸ If I state my thesis in the introduction, how effectively is it presented?

▸ Does my essay come to a logical conclusion or does it seem to just stop?

▸ Does the conclusion relate well to the rest of the essay? Am I careful not to introduce topics or issues that I did not address in the essay?

(continued on next page)

(*continued from previous page*)

> ▶ Does my conclusion underscore important aspects of the essay, or is it merely a mechanical rehashing of what I wrote earlier?

Step 5: Edit and Proofread Your Essay

During the *editing* stage, you check your writing for errors in grammar, punctuation, capitalization, spelling, and manuscript format. Chapter 16 of this book provides help for common problems with grammar, punctuation, and sentence style. A dictionary and a grammar handbook may be necessary for less common or more specific editing questions.

After editing, proofread your work carefully before turning it in. Though you may have used your computer's spell-checker, you might find that you have typed *their* instead of *there* or *form* instead of *from*. (A computer won't know the difference, as long as you've spelled *some* word correctly.)

Questions to Ask during Editing and Proofreading

▶ Do I have any sentence fragments, comma splices, or run-on sentences?   ⟍ E1–2

▶ Have I used commas properly in all instances?   ⟍ E3

▶ Do my verbs agree in number with their antecedents?   ⟍ E4

▶ Do my pronouns clearly and correctly refer to their antecedents?   ⟍ E5–6

▶ Do any dangling or misplaced modifiers make my meaning unclear?   ⟍ E7

▶ Are my sentences parallel in structure?   ⟍ E8

▶ Have I used specific nouns and strong verbs wherever possible?   ⟍ E9

▶ Have I made any unnecessary shifts in person, tense, or number?   ⟍ E10

▶ Have I eliminated unnecessary words?   ⟍ E11

▶ Are my sentences appropriately varied and interesting?   ⟍ E12

▶ Have I checked for misspellings, mistakes in capitalization, commonly confused words like *its* and *it's*, and typos?

▶ Have I followed the prescribed guidelines for formatting my manuscript?

A Student Essay in Progress

When he was a first-year student at the University of Vermont, Keith Eldred enrolled in Written Expression, an introductory writing course.

Step 1: Keith's Assignment

Near the middle of the semester, Keith's assignment was to write a three-to-five-page definition essay. After reading the introduction to Chapter 10 in *Subject & Strategy* (pages 393–96) and the essays his instructor assigned from that chapter, Keith was ready to get to work.

Step 2: Keith's Ideas

Keith had already been introduced to the Hindu concept of the *mantra*, and he decided that he would like to explore this concept, narrowing his focus to the topic of mantras as they operate in the secular world. To get started, he decided to brainstorm. His brainstorming provided him with several examples of what he intended to call *secular mantras*; a dictionary definition of the word *mantra*; and the idea that a good starting point for his rough draft might be the story of "The Little Engine That Could." Here are the notes he jotted down.

> Mantra: "a mystical formula of invocation or incantation" (Webster's)
>
> Counting to ten when angry
>
> "Little Engine That Could" (possible beginning)
>
> "Let's Go Bulls" → action because crowd wants players to say it to themselves
>
> Swearing (not always a mantra)
>
> Tennis star—"Get serious!"
>
> "Come on, come on" (at traffic light)
>
> "Geronimo" "Ouch!"
>
> Hindu mythology

Step 3: Keith's First Draft

After mulling over his list, Keith began to organize his ideas with the following scratch outline:

> 1. Begin with story of "Little Engine That Could"
> 2. Talk about the magic of secular mantras
> 3. Dictionary definition and Hindu connections
> 4. Examples of individuals using mantras
> 5. Crowd chants as mantras—Bulls
> 6. Conclusion—talk about how you can't get through the day without using mantras

Based on this outline as well as what he learned from *Subject & Strategy* about definition as a writing strategy, Keith came up with the following first draft of his essay.

Secular Mantras: Magic Words
Keith Eldred

Do you remember "The Little Engine That Could"? If you recall, 1
it's the story about the tiny locomotive that hauled the train over
the mountain when the big, rugged locomotives wouldn't. Do you
remember how the Little Engine strained and heaved and chugged
"I think I can—I think I can—I think I can" until she reached the
top of the mountain? That's a perfect example of a secular mantra
in action.

A secular mantra (pronounced man-truh) is any word or group 2
of words that helps a person use his or her energy. The key word
here is "helps"—repeating a secular mantra doesn't *create* energy; it
just makes it easier to channel a given amount. The Little Engine, for
instance, obviously had the strength to pull the train up the mountain; apparently, she could have done it without saying a word. But we
all know she wouldn't have been able to, any more than any one of
us would be able to skydive the first time without yelling "Geronimo"
or not exclaim "Ouch" if we touched a hot stove. Some words and
phrases simply have a certain magic that makes a job easier or
that makes us feel better when we repeat them. These are secular
mantras.

It is because of their magical quality that these expressions are 3
called "secular mantras" in the first place. A mantra (Sanskrit for
"sacred counsel") is "a mystical formula of invocation or incantation"
used in Hinduism (*Webster's*). According to Hindu mythology, Manu,
lawgiver and progenitor of humankind, created the first language
by teaching people the thought-forms of objects and substances.
"VAM," for example, is the thought-form of what we call "water."
Mantras, groups of these ancient words, can summon any object or
deity if they are miraculously revealed to a seer and properly repeated
silently or vocally. Hindus use divine mantras to communicate with
gods, acquire superhuman powers, cure diseases, and for many
other purposes. Hence, everyday words that people concentrate on to
help themselves accomplish tasks or cope with stress act as secular
mantras.

All sorts of people use all sorts of secular mantras for all sorts of 4
reasons. A father counts to 10 before saying anything when his son
brings the car home dented. A tennis player faults and chides himself,
"Get serious!" A frustrated mother pacing with her wailing baby mutters, "You'll have your own kids someday." A college student writhing

before an exam instructs himself not to panic. A freshly spanked child glares at his mother's back and repeatedly promises never to speak to her again. Secular mantras are everywhere.

Usually, we use secular mantras to make ourselves walk faster or keep silent or do some other act. But we can also use them to influence the actions of other persons. Say, for instance, the Chicago Bulls are behind in the final minutes of a game. Ten thousand fans who want them to win scream, "Let's go, Bulls!" The Bulls are roused and win by 20 points. Chalk up the victory to the fans' secular mantra, which transferred their energy to the players on the court.

5

If you're not convinced of the power of secular mantras, try to complete a day without using any. Don't mutter anything to force yourself out of bed. Don't utter a sound when the water in the shower is cold. Don't grumble when the traffic lights are long. Don't speak to the computer when it's slow to boot up. And don't be surprised if you have an unusually long, painful, frustrating day.

6

Step 4: Keith's Revised Essay

Keith read his paper aloud in class, and other students had an opportunity to ask him questions about secular mantras. As a result of this experience, Keith had a good idea of what he needed to do in subsequent drafts, and he made the following notes so that he wouldn't forget what he needed to do.

- Do a better job of defining *secular mantra*—expand it and be more specific—maybe tell what secular mantras are not
- Get more example, especially from everyday experiences and TV
- Don't eliminate background information about mantras
- Class thought Bulls example didn't work—keep or delete?
- Keep "The Little Engine That Could" example at beginning of paper
- Write new conclusion—present conclusion doesn't follow from paper

In subsequent drafts, Keith worked on each of the areas he had listed. While revising, he found it helpful to reread portions of the selections in Chapter 10. His reading led him to new insights about how to strengthen his essay. As he revised further, he found that he needed to make yet other unanticipated changes.

Keith revised his definitions of *mantra* and *secular mantra* to include the following meanings for the related *terms*.

Historical definition of *mantra* revised

Mantra means "sacred counsel" in Sanskrit and refers to a "mystical formula of invocation or incantation" used in Hinduism (*Webster's*). According to Hindu mythology, the god Manu created the first language by teaching humans the thought-form of every object and substance. "VAM," for example, was what he told them to call the stuff we call "water." But people altered or forgot most of Manu's thought-forms. Followers of Hinduism believe mantras, groups of these ancient words revealed anew by gods to seers, can summon specific objects or deities if they are properly repeated, silently or vocally. Hindus repeat mantras to gain superhuman powers, cure diseases, and for many other purposes. Sideshow fakirs chant "AUM" ("I agree" or "I accept") to become immune to pain when lying on beds of nails.

Definition of secular *mantra* expanded

Our "mantras" are "secular" because, unlike Hindus, we do not attribute them to gods. Instead, we borrow them from tradition or invent them to fit a situation, as the Little Engine did. They work not by divine power but because they help us, in a way, to govern transmissions along our central nervous systems.

Explanation of how secular mantras work added

Secular mantras give our brains a sort of dual signal-boosting and signal-damping capacity. The act of repeating them pushes messages, or impulses, with extra force along our nerves or interferes with incoming messages we would rather ignore. We can then perform actions more easily or cope with stress that might keep us from functioning the way we want to. We may even accomplish both tasks at once. A skydiver might yell "Geronimo," for example, both to amplify the signals telling his legs to jump and to drown out the ones warning him he's dizzy or scared.

He also rewrote the conclusion, adding yet more examples of secular mantras, this time drawn largely from television advertising. Finally, he made his conclusion more of a natural outgrowth of his thesis and purpose and thus a more fitting conclusion for his essay.

Sentence of examples moved from paragraph 4	You probably have favorite secular mantras already. Think about it. How many of us haven't uttered the following at least once: "Just do it"; "I'm lovin' it"; "Got milk?"; "Can you hear me now?"; or "Have it your way"? How about the phrases you mumble to yourself from your warm bed on chilly mornings? And those words you chant to ease your impatience when the traffic lights are endless? And the reminders you mutter
Final sentence, which links to thesis and purpose, added	so that you'll remember to buy bread at the store? If you're like most people, you'll agree that your life is much less painful and frustrating because of those magic words and phrases.

Step 5: Keith's Edited Essay

After expanding his definitions and strengthening his conclusion, as well as making other necessary revisions, Keith was now ready to edit his essay. His instructor told him to avoid the use of first- or second-person address in his essay, and to correct sentences starting with coordinating conjunctions like *and* or *but*. In addition, he had to correct smaller but equally important errors in word choice, spelling, punctuation, and mechanics. He had put aside these errors to make sure his essay had the appropriate content. Now he needed to make sure it was grammatically correct. For example, here is how he edited the first paragraph of his essay:

> ~~Do you~~ ^Rremember "The Little Engine That Could"? ~~If you recall,~~
> ^{That's} ~~it's~~ the story about the tiny loc^oamotive that hauled the train over the
> mountain when the big, rugged loc^oamotives wouldn't. ~~Do you~~ ^Rremem-
> ber how the Little Engine strained and heaved and chugged, "I think
> I can—I think I can—I think I can" until she reached the top of the
> mountain? That's a perfect example of a secular mantra in action.

By the deadline, Keith had written his essay, revised and edited it, printed it, proofread it one last time, and turned it in. Here is the final draft of his essay:

Secular Mantras
Keith Eldred

"The Little Engine That Could" is a story about a tiny locomotive   1
that hauls a train over a mountain when the big, rugged locomotives
refuse: The Little Engine strains and heaves and chugs, repeating
"I think I can—I think I can—I think I can" until she reaches the top of
the mountain. This refrain—"I think I can—I think I can"—is a perfect
example of a secular mantra in action.

A secular mantra (pronounced "man-truh") is any word or group   2
of words that focus energy when consciously repeated. Most readers of this essay have already used a secular mantra today without
realizing it. Some additional explanation is necessary, however, in order
to understand what distinguishes a secular mantra from any other
kind of phrase.

To be a secular mantra, a phrase must help the speaker focus and   3
use energy. Thus, "I wish I were at home" is not a secular mantra if
it's simply a passing thought. The same sentence becomes a secular
mantra if, walking home on a cold day, a person repeats the sentence
each time she takes a step, willing her feet to move in a steady,
accelerated rhythm, and take her quickly someplace warm. By the
same token, every curse word a person mutters in order to bear down
on a job is a secular mantra, while every curse word that same person
unthinkingly repeats is simple profanity.

It is important to understand, however, that secular mantras   4
only help people use energy: They don't create it. The Little Engine,
for instance, obviously had enough power to pull the train up the
mountainside—she could have done it without a peep. Still, puffing
"I think I can" clearly made her job easier, just as, say, chanting
"left-right-left" makes marching in step easier for soldiers. Any such
word or phrase that, purposefully uttered, helps a person perform
something difficult qualifies as a secular mantra.

Why, though, use the term *secular mantra* to describe these phrases,   5
rather than something else? *Mantra* means "sacred counsel" in Sanskrit
and refers to a "mystical formula of invocation or incantation" used
in Hinduism (*Webster's*). According to Hindu mythology, the god Manu
created the first language by teaching humans the thought-form of
every object and substance. VAM, for example, was what Manu taught
humans to call "water." People unfortunately forgot or altered most of
Manu's thought-forms, however. Followers of Hinduism believe that
mantras, groups of these ancient words revealed anew by gods to seers,
can summon specific objects or deities if they are properly repeated,

silently or aloud. Hindus repeat mantras to gain superhuman powers, cure diseases, and for many other purposes. Sideshow fakirs chant *AUM* ("I agree" or "I accept") to become immune to pain when lying on a bed of nails.

The mantras that are the topic of this paper are called *secular* because Western culture does not claim that they are divine in origin; instead, they derive from tradition or are invented to fit a situation, as in the case of the Little Engine. In addition, most Westerners assume that they work not by divine power but through the mind-body connection, by helping govern transmissions along the central nervous system. 6

The Western, scientific explanation for the power of secular mantras runs something like this: Secular mantras give people's brains a sort of dual signal-boosting and signal-damping capacity. The act of repeating them pushes messages, or impulses, with extra force along the nerves or blocks incoming messages that would interfere with the task at hand. People repeating mantras are thus enabled to perform actions more easily or cope with stress that might keep them from functioning optimally. Mantras may even convey both benefits at once: A skydiver might yell "Geronimo!," for example, both to amplify the signals telling his legs to jump and to drown out the signals warning him he's dizzy or afraid. 7

Anyone can use words in this way to help accomplish a task. A father might count to ten to keep from bellowing when Junior returns the family car with a huge dent. A tennis player who tends to fault may shout "Get serious!" as he serves, to concentrate harder on controlling the ball. An exhausted new mother with her wailing baby can make her chore less painful by muttering, "Someday you'll do chores for me." Chanting "Grease cartridge" always cools this writer's temper because doing so once headed off a major confrontation with a friend while working on a cantankerous old Buick. 8

Most readers of this essay probably have favorite secular mantras already. Most people—at least those exposed in any way to contemporary popular culture—have at one point uttered one of the following: "Just do it"; "No worries"; "It's all good"; "I'm king of the world!!"; "We are the champions!"; or something similar. Many people have ritual phrases they mutter to get themselves to leave their warm beds on chilly mornings; others blurt out habitual phrases to help them get over impatience when traffic lights don't change or to help them endure a courtesy call to a neighbor they've never really liked. Most people, if they really think about it, will admit that the seeming magic of secular mantras has made their lives much less painful, less frustrating, and perhaps even a little more fun. 9

While it's not perfect, "Secular Mantras" is a fine essay of definition. Keith provides a clear explanation of the concept, offers numerous examples to illustrate it, and suggests how mantras work and how we use them. Keith's notes, rough draft, samples of revised and edited paragraphs, and final draft demonstrate how such effective writing is accomplished. By reading analytically — both his own writing and that of experienced writers — Keith came to understand the requirements of the strategy of definition. An honest and thorough appraisal of his rough draft led to thoughtful revisions, resulting in a strong and effective piece of writing.

CHAPTER 3

Six Writers on Writing

Like any other craft, writing involves learning basic skills as well as more sophisticated techniques that can be refined and then shared among practitioners. Some of the most important lessons a student writer encounters may come from the experiences of other writers: suggestions, advice, cautions, corrections, encouragement. This chapter contains essays in which writers discuss their habits, difficulties, and judgments while they express both the joy of writing and the hard work it can entail. These writers deal with the full range of the writing process — from freeing the imagination in journal entries to correcting punctuation errors for the final draft. The advice they offer is pertinent and sound.

Discovering the Power of My Words

RUSSELL BAKER

Russell Baker has had a long and distinguished career as a newspaper reporter and columnist. He was born in Morrisonville, Virginia, in 1925 and enlisted in the navy in 1943 after graduating from Johns Hopkins University. In 1947, he secured his first newspaper job, as a reporter for the *Baltimore Sun*, then moved to the *New York Times* in 1954, where he wrote the "Observer" column from 1962 to 1998. His incisive wit, by turns melancholic and sharp-edged, is well represented in such quips as these: "Children rarely want to know who their parents were before they were parents, and when age finally stirs their curiosity, there is no parent left to tell them" and "Is fuel efficiency really what we need most desperately? I say that what we really need is a car that can be shot when it breaks down."

Baker's columns have been collected in numerous books over the years. In 1979, he was awarded the Pulitzer Prize, journalism's highest award, as well as the George Polk Award for Commentary. Baker's memoir, *Growing Up* (1983), also received a Pulitzer. His autobiographical follow-up, *The Good Times*, was published in 1989. His other works include *Russell Baker's Book of American Humor* (1993); *Inventing the Truth: The Art and Craft of Memoir*, with William Zinsser and Jill Ker Conway (revised 1998); and *Looking Back* (2002), a collection of Baker's essays for the *New York Review of Books*. From 1993 to 2004 he hosted the distinguished PBS series *Exxon Mobil Masterpiece Theatre*.

The following selection is from *Growing Up*. As you read Baker's account of how he discovered the power of his own words, note particularly the joy he felt hearing his writing read aloud.

■ Preparing to Read

What has been your experience with writing teachers in school? Have any of them helped you become a better writer? What kind of writer do you consider yourself now — excellent, above average, good, below average? Why?

The notion of becoming a writer had flickered off and on in my head . . . but it wasn't until my third year in high school that the possibility took hold. Until then I'd been bored by everything associated with English courses. I found English grammar dull and baffling. I hated the assignments to turn out "compositions," and went at them like heavy labor, turning out   1 leaden, lackluster paragraphs that were agonies for teachers to read and for me to write. The classics thrust on me to read seemed as deadening as chloroform.

When our class was assigned to Mr. Fleagle for third-year English I anticipated another grim year in that dreariest of subjects. Mr. Fleagle was notorious among City students for dullness and inability to inspire. He was said to be stuffy, dull, and hopelessly out of date. To me he looked to be sixty or seventy and prim to a fault. He wore primly severe eyeglasses, his wavy hair was primly cut and primly combed. He wore prim vested suits with neckties blocked primly against the collar buttons of his primly starched white shirts. He had a primly pointed jaw, a primly straight nose, and a prim manner of speaking that was so correct, so gentlemanly, that he seemed a comic antique.

I anticipated a listless, unfruitful year with Mr. Fleagle and for a long time was not disappointed. We read *Macbeth*. Mr. Fleagle loved *Macbeth* and wanted us to love it, too, but he lacked the gift of infecting others with his own passion. He tried to convey the murderous ferocity of Lady Macbeth one day by reading aloud the passage that concludes

> . . . I have given suck, and know
> How tender 'tis to love the babe that milks me.
> I would, while it was smiling in my face,
> Have plucked my nipple from his boneless gums . . .

The idea of prim Mr. Fleagle plucking his nipple from boneless gums was too much for the class. We burst into gasps of irrepressible snickering. Mr. Fleagle stopped.

"There is nothing funny, boys, about giving suck to a babe. It is the — the very essence of motherhood, don't you see."

He constantly sprinkled his sentences with "don't you see." It wasn't a question but an exclamation of mild surprise at our ignorance. "Your pronoun needs an antecedent, don't you see," he would say, very primly. "The purpose of the Porter's scene, boys, is to provide comic relief from the horror, don't you see."

Late in the year we tackled the informal essay. "The essay, don't you see, is the . . ." My mind went numb. Of all forms of writing, none seemed so boring as the essay. Naturally we would have to write informal essays. Mr. Fleagle distributed a homework sheet offering us a choice of topics. None was quite so simpleminded as "What I Did on My Summer Vacation," but most seemed to be almost as dull. I took the list home and dawdled until the night before the essay was due. Sprawled on the sofa, I finally faced up to the grim task, took the list out of my notebook, and scanned it. The topic on which my eye stopped was "The Art of Eating Spaghetti."

This title produced an extraordinary sequence of mental images. Surging up from the depths of memory came a vivid recollection of a night in

Belleville when all of us were seated around the supper table — Uncle Allen, my mother, Uncle Charlie, Doris, Uncle Hal — and Aunt Pat served spaghetti for supper. Spaghetti was an exotic treat in those days. Neither Doris nor I had ever eaten spaghetti, and none of the adults had enough experience to be good at it. All the good humor of Uncle Allen's house reawoke in my mind as I recalled the laughing arguments we had that night about the socially respectable method for moving spaghetti from plate to mouth.

8   Suddenly I wanted to write about that, about the warmth and good feeling of it, but I wanted to put it down simply for my own joy, not for Mr. Fleagle. It was a moment I wanted to recapture and hold for myself. I wanted to relive the pleasure of an evening at New Street. To write it as I wanted, however, would violate all the rules of formal composition I'd learned in school, and Mr. Fleagle would surely give it a failing grade. Never mind. I would write something else for Mr. Fleagle after I had written this thing for myself.

9   When I finished it the night was half gone and there was no time left to compose a proper, respectable essay for Mr. Fleagle. There was no choice next morning but to turn in my private reminiscence of Belleville. Two days passed before Mr. Fleagle returned the graded papers, and he returned everyone's but mine. I was bracing myself for a command to report to Mr. Fleagle immediately after school for discipline when I saw him lift my paper from his desk and rap for the class's attention.

> And he started to read. My words! He was reading *my words* out loud to the entire class. What's more, the entire class was listening.

10   "Now, boys," he said, "I want to read you an essay. This is titled 'The Art of Eating Spaghetti.'"

11   And he started to read. My words! He was reading *my words* out loud to the entire class. What's more, the entire class was listening. Listening attentively. Then somebody laughed, then the entire class was laughing, and not in contempt and ridicule, but with open-hearted enjoyment. Even Mr. Fleagle stopped two or three times to repress a small prim smile.

12   I did my best to avoid showing pleasure, but what I was feeling was pure ecstasy at this startling demonstration that my words had the power to make people laugh. In the eleventh grade, at the eleventh hour as it were, I had discovered a calling. It was the happiest moment of my entire school career. When Mr. Fleagle finished he put the final seal on my happiness by saying, "Now that, boys, is an essay, don't you see. It's — don't you see — it's of the very essence of the essay, don't you see. Congratulations, Mr. Baker."

13   For the first time, light shone on a possibility. It wasn't a very heartening possibility, to be sure. Writing couldn't lead to a job after high school, and it was hardly honest work, but Mr. Fleagle had opened a door for me. After that I ranked Mr. Fleagle among the finest teachers in the school.

■ Thinking Critically about the Text

In his opening paragraph Baker states, "I hated the assignments to turn out 'compositions,' and went at them like heavy labor, turning out leaden, lackluster paragraphs that were agonies for teachers to read and for me to write." Have you ever had any assignments like these? How are such assignments different from Mr. Fleagle's assignment to write an informal essay about "The Art of Eating Spaghetti"? How do you think Baker would respond to the following cartoon about writing assignments?

"When writing your essays, I encourage you to think for yourselves while you express what I'd most agree with."

■ Discussing the Craft of Writing

1. How does Baker describe his teacher, Mr. Fleagle, in the second para-graph? What dominant impression does Baker create of this man? (Glossary: *Dominant Impression*)
2. Mr. Fleagle's homework assignment offered Baker and his classmates "a choice of topics." Is it important to have a "choice" of what you write about? Explain.
3. Once Baker's eye hits the topic of "The Art of Eating Spaghetti" on Mr. Fleagle's list, what happens? What triggers Baker's urge to write about the night his Aunt Pat served spaghetti for supper?

4. Why is Baker reluctant to submit his finished essay?
5. In paragraph 11 Baker states, "And he started to read. My words! He was reading *my words* out loud to the entire class. What's more, the entire class was listening. Listening attentively." Why do you suppose this episode was so memorable to Baker? What surprised him most about it?
6. What insights into the nature of writing does Baker's narrative offer? Explain.

Shitty First Drafts

ANNE LAMOTT

Born in San Francisco in 1954, Anne Lamott graduated from Goucher College in Baltimore and is the author of six novels, including *Rose* (1983), *All the New People* (1989), *Crooked Little Heart* (1997), and *Blue Shoes* (2002). She has also been a food reviewer for *California* magazine, a book reviewer for *Mademoiselle*, and a columnist for *Salon.* Her nonfiction books include *Operating Instructions: A Journal of My Son's First Year* (1993), in which she describes life as a single parent; *Traveling Mercies: Some Thoughts on Faith* (1999), in which she charts her journey toward faith in God; *Plan B: Further Thoughts on Faith* (2005); and *Grace (Eventually): Thoughts on Faith* (2007). Lamott has taught at the University of California–Davis, as well as at writing conferences around the country. Reflecting on the importance of writing and reading, Lamott has written, "Writing and reading decrease our sense of isolation. They deepen and widen and expand our sense of life: They feed the soul."

In the following selection, taken from Lamott's popular book about writing, *Bird by Bird: Some Instructions on Writing and Life* (1994), she argues for the need to let go and write those "shitty first drafts" that lead to clarity and sometimes brilliance in subsequent drafts.

■ Preparing to Read

Many professional writers view first drafts as something they have to do before they can begin the real work of writing — revision. How do you view the writing of your first drafts? What patterns, if any, do you see in your writing behavior when working on them? Is the work liberating or restricting? Pleasant or unpleasant?

Now, practically even better news than that of short assignments is the idea of shitty first drafts. All good writers write them. This is how they end up with good second drafts and terrific third drafts. People tend to look at successful writers, writers who are getting their books published and maybe even doing well financially, and think that they sit down at their desks every morning feeling like a million dollars, feeling great about who they are and how much talent they have and what a great story they have to tell; that they take in a few deep breaths, push back their sleeves, roll their necks a few times to get all the cricks out, and dive in, typing fully formed passages as fast as a court reporter. But this is just the fantasy of the uninitiated. I know some very great writers, writers you love who write beautifully and have made a great deal of money, and not *one* of them sits down routinely feeling wildly enthusiastic and confident. Not one of them writes elegant first drafts. All right, one of them does, but we do not like her very much. We do not think that she has a rich inner life or that God likes her or can even stand her. (Although when I mentioned this to my priest friend Tom, he said you can safely assume you've created God in your own image when it turns out that God hates all the same people you do.)

> All good writers write them. This is how they end up with good second drafts and terrific third drafts.

Very few writers really know what they are doing until they've done it. Nor do they go about their business feeling dewy and thrilled. They do not type a few stiff warm-up sentences and then find themselves bounding along like huskies across the snow. One writer I know tells me that he sits down every morning and says to himself nicely, "It's not like you don't have a choice, because you do — you can either type or kill yourself." We all often feel like we are pulling teeth, even those writers whose prose ends up being the most natural and fluid. The right words and sentences just do not come pouring out like ticker tape most of the time. Now, Muriel Spark is said to have felt that she was taking dictation from God every morning — sitting there, one supposes, plugged into a Dictaphone, typing away, humming. But this is a very hostile and aggressive position. One might hope for bad things to rain down on a person like this.

For me and most of the other writers I know, writing is not rapturous. In fact, the only way I can get anything written at all is to write really, really shitty first drafts.

The first draft is the child's draft, where you let it all pour out and then let it romp all over the place, knowing that no one is going to see it and that you can shape it later. You just let this childlike part of you channel whatever voices and visions come through and onto the page. If one of the characters wants to say, "Well, so what, Mr. Poopy Pants?," you let her. No one is going to see it. If the kid wants to get into really sentimental, weepy, emotional territory, you let him. Just get it all down on paper, because there may be something great in those six crazy pages that you would never have gotten to by more rational, grown-up means. There may be something in the very last line of the very last paragraph on page six that you just love, that is so beautiful or wild that you now know what you're supposed to be writing about, more or less, or in what direction you might go — but there was no way to get to this without first getting through the first five and a half pages.

I used to write food reviews for *California* magazine before it folded. (My ⁵ writing food reviews had nothing to do with the magazine folding, although every single review did cause a couple of canceled subscriptions. Some readers took umbrage at my comparing mounds of vegetable puree with various ex-presidents' brains.) These reviews always took two days to write. First I'd go to a restaurant several times with a few opinionated, articulate friends in tow. I'd sit there writing down everything anyone said that was at all interesting or funny. Then on the following Monday I'd sit down at my desk with my notes, and try to write the review. Even after I'd been doing this for years, panic would set in. I'd try to write a lead, but instead I'd write a couple of dreadful sentences, xx them out, try again, xx everything out, and then feel despair and worry settle on my chest like an X-ray apron. It's over, I'd think, calmly. I'm not going to be able to get the magic to work this time. I'm ruined. I'm through. I'm toast. Maybe, I'd think, I can get my old job back as a clerk-typist. But probably not. I'd get up and study my teeth in the mirror for a while. Then I'd stop, remember to breathe, make a few phone calls, hit the kitchen and chow down. Eventually I'd go back and sit down at my desk, and sigh for the next ten minutes. Finally I would pick up my one-inch picture frame, stare into it as if for the answer, and every time the answer would come: All I had to do was to write a really shitty first draft of, say, the opening paragraph. And no one was going to see it.

So I'd start writing without reining myself in. It was almost just typing, ⁶ just making my fingers move. And the writing would be *terrible*. I'd write a lead paragraph that was a whole page, even though the entire review could only be three pages long, and then I'd start writing up descriptions of the food, one dish at a time, bird by bird, and the critics would be sitting on my shoulders, commenting like cartoon characters. They'd be pretending to snore, or rolling their eyes at my overwrought descriptions, no matter how hard I tried to tone those descriptions down, no matter how conscious I was of what a friend said to me gently in my early days of restaurant reviewing. "Annie," she said, "it is just a piece of *chicken*. It is just a bit of *cake*."

But because by then I had been writing for so long, I would eventually ⁷ let myself trust the process — sort of, more or less. I'd write a first draft that was maybe twice as long as it should be, with a self-indulgent and boring beginning, stupefying descriptions of the meal, lots of quotes from my black-humored friends that made them sound more like the Manson girls than food lovers, and no ending to speak of. The whole thing would be so long and incoherent and hideous that for the rest of the day I'd obsess about getting creamed by a car before I could write a decent second draft. I'd worry that people would read what I'd written and believe that the accident had really been a suicide, that I had panicked because my talent was waning and my mind was shot.

The next day, though, I'd sit down, go through it all with a colored pen, ⁸ take out everything I possibly could, find a new lead somewhere on the second page, figure out a kicky place to end it, and then write a second draft. It always turned out fine, sometimes even funny and weird and helpful. I'd go over it one more time and mail it in.

Then, a month later, when it was time for another review, the whole 9 process would start again, complete with the fears that people would find my first draft before I could rewrite it.

Almost all good writing begins with terrible first efforts. You need to 10 start somewhere. Start by getting something — anything — down on paper. A friend of mine says that the first draft is the down draft — you just get it down. The second draft is the up draft — you fix it up. You try to say what you have to say more accurately. And the third draft is the dental draft, where you check every tooth, to see if it's loose or cramped or decayed, or even, God help us, healthy.

What I've learned to do when I sit down to work on a shitty first draft is 11 to quiet the voices in my head. First there's the vinegar-lipped Reader Lady, who says primly, "Well, *that's* not very interesting, is it?" And there's the emaciated German male who writes these Orwellian memos detailing your thought crimes. And there are your parents, agonizing over your lack of loyalty and discretion; and there's William Burroughs, dozing off or shooting up because he finds you as bold and articulate as a houseplant; and so on. And there are also the dogs: let's not forget the dogs, the dogs in their pen who will surely hurtle and snarl their way out if you ever *stop* writing, because writing is, for some of us, the latch that keeps the door of the pen closed, keeps those crazy ravenous dogs contained.

Quieting these voices is at least half the battle I fight daily. But this is 12 better than it used to be. It used to be 87 percent. Left to its own devices, my mind spends much of its time having conversations with people who aren't there. I walk along defending myself to people, or exchanging repartee with them, or rationalizing my behavior, or seducing them with gossip, or pretending I'm on their TV talk show or whatever. I speed or run an aging yellow light or don't come to a full stop, and one nanosecond later am explaining to imaginary cops exactly why I had to do what I did, or insisting that I did not in fact do it.

I happened to mention this to a hypnotist I saw many years ago, and he 13 looked at me very nicely. At first I thought he was feeling around on the floor for the silent alarm button, but then he gave me the following exercise, which I still use to this day.

Close your eyes and get quiet for a minute, until the chatter starts up. 14 Then isolate one of the voices and imagine the person speaking as a mouse. Pick it up by the tail and drop it into a mason jar. Then isolate another voice, pick it up by the tail, drop it in the jar. And so on. Drop in any high-maintenance parental units, drop in any contractors, lawyers, colleagues, children, anyone who is whining in your head. Then put the lid on, and watch all these mouse people clawing at the glass, jabbering away, trying to make you feel like shit because you won't do what they want — won't give them more money, won't be more successful, won't see them more often. Then imagine that there is a volume-control button on the bottle. Turn it all the way up for a minute, and listen to the stream of angry, neglected, guilt-mongering voices. Then turn it all the way down and watch the frantic mice lunge at the glass, trying to get to you. Leave it down, and get back to your shitty first draft.

A writer friend of mine suggests opening the jar and shooting them all in   15
the head. But I think he's a little angry, and I'm sure nothing like this would ever occur to you.

■ Thinking Critically about the Text

What do you think of Lamott's use of the word *shitty* in her title and in the essay itself? Is it in keeping with her tone? (Glossary: *Tone*) Are you offended by the word? Explain. What would be lost or gained if she used a different word?

■ Discussing the Craft of Writing

1. Lamott says that the perception most people have of how writers work is different from the reality. She refers to this in paragraph 1 as the "fantasy of the uninitiated." What does she mean?
2. In paragraph 7 Lamott refers to a time when, through experience, she "eventually let [herself] trust the process — sort of, more or less." She is referring to the writing process, of course, but why "more or less"? Do you think her wariness is personal, or is she speaking for all writers? Explain.
3. From what Lamott has to say, is writing a first draft more about content or psychology? Do you agree when it comes to your own first drafts? Explain.
4. What is Lamott's thesis? (Glossary: *Thesis*)
5. Lamott adds humor to her argument for "shitty first drafts." Give some examples. Does her humor add to or detract from the points she makes? Explain.
6. In paragraph 5, Lamott narrates her experiences in writing a food review, during which she refers to an almost ritualistic set of behaviors. What is her purpose in telling her readers this story about her difficulties? (Glossary: *Purpose*) Is this information helpful? Explain.

Writing for an Audience

LINDA S. FLOWER

 Linda S. Flower is a professor of English at Carnegie Mellon University, where she directed the Business Communication program for a number of years and is currently the director of the Center for the Study of Writing and Literacy. She has been a leading researcher on the composing process, and the results of her investigations shaped and informed her influential writing text *Problem-Solving Strategies for Writing in College and Community* (1997). She has also written *The Construction of Negotiated Meaning: A Social Cognitive Theory of Writing* (1994).

In this selection, which is taken from *Problem-Solving Strategies,* Flower's focus is on audience — the people for whom we write. She believes that writers must establish a "common ground" between themselves and their readers that lessens their differences in knowledge, attitudes, and needs. Although we can never be certain who might read what we write, it is nevertheless important for us to have a target audience in mind. Many of the decisions that we make as writers are influenced by that real or imagined reader.

▪ Preparing to Read

Imagine for a moment that you just received a speeding ticket for going sixty-five miles per hour in a thirty-mile-per-hour zone. How would you describe the episode to your best friend? To your parents? To the judge in court? Sketch out the three versions. What differences, if any, do you find in the three versions? Explain.

The goal of the writer is to create a momentary common ground between   1
the reader and the writer. You want the reader to share your knowledge and your attitude toward that knowledge. Even if the reader eventually disagrees, you want him or her to be able for the moment to *see things as you see them.* A good piece of writing closes the gap between you and the reader.

Analyze Your Audience

The first step in closing that gap is to gauge the distance between the two of   2
you. Imagine, for example, that you are a student writing your parents, who

have always lived in New York City, about a wilderness survival expedition you want to go on over spring break. Sometimes obvious differences such as age or background will be important, but the critical differences for writers usually fall into three areas: the reader's *knowledge* about the topic; his or her *attitude* toward it; and his or her personal or professional *needs*. Because these differences often exist, good writers do more than simply express their meaning; they pinpoint the critical differences between themselves and their reader and design their writing to reduce those differences. Let us look at these areas in more detail.

> A good piece of writing closes the gap between you and the reader.

Knowledge

This is usually the easiest difference to handle. What does your reader need to know? What are the main ideas you hope to teach? Does your reader have enough background knowledge to really understand you? If not, what would he or she have to learn? 3

Attitudes

When we say a person has knowledge, we usually refer to his conscious awareness of explicit facts and clearly defined concepts. This kind of knowledge can be easily written down or told to someone else. However, much of what we "know" is not held in this formal, explicit way. Instead it is held as an attitude or image — as a loose cluster of associations. For instance, my image of lakes includes associations many people would have, including fishing, water skiing, stalled outboards, and lots of kids catching night crawlers with flashlights. However, the most salient or powerful parts of my image, which strongly color my whole attitude toward lakes, are thoughts of cloudy skies, long rainy days, and feeling generally cold and damp. By contrast, one of my best friends has a very different cluster of associations: to him a lake means sun, swimming, sailing, and happily sitting on the end of a dock. Needless to say, our differing images cause us to react quite differently to a proposal that we visit a lake. Likewise, one reason people often find it difficult to discuss religion and politics is that terms such as "capitalism" conjure up radically different images. 4

As you can see, a reader's image of a subject is often the source of attitudes and feelings that are unexpected and, at times, impervious to mere facts. A simple statement that seems quite persuasive to you, such as "Lake Wampago would be a great place to locate the new music camp," could have little impact on your reader if he or she simply doesn't visualize a lake as a "great place." In fact, many people accept uncritically any statement that fits in with their own attitudes — and reject, just as uncritically, anything that does not. 5

Whether your purpose is to persuade or simply to present your perspective, it helps to know the image and attitudes that your reader already holds. The more these differ from your own, the more you will have to do to make him or her *see* what you mean.

Needs

When writers discover a large gap between their own knowledge and attitudes and those of the reader, they usually try to change the reader in some way. Needs, however, are different. When you analyze a reader's needs, it is so that you, the writer, can adapt to him. If you ask a friend majoring in biology how to keep your fish tank from clouding, you don't want to hear a textbook recitation on the life processes of algae. You expect a friend to adapt his or her knowledge and tell you exactly how to solve your problem.

The ability to adapt your knowledge to the needs of the reader is often crucial to your success as a writer. This is especially true in writing done on a job. For example, as producer of a public affairs program for a television station, 80 percent of your time may be taken up planning the details of new shows, contacting guests, and scheduling the taping sessions. But when you write a program proposal to the station director, your job is to show how the program will fit into the cost guidelines, the FCC requirements for relevance, and the overall programming plan for the station. When you write that report, your role in the organization changes from producer to proposal writer. Why? Because your reader needs that information in order to make a decision. He may be *interested* in your scheduling problems and the specific content of the shows, but he *reads* your report because of his own needs as station director of the organization. He has to act.

In college, where the reader is also a teacher, the reader's needs are a little less concrete but just as important. Most papers are assigned as a way to teach something. So the real purpose of a paper may be for you to make connections between two historical periods, to discover for yourself the principle behind a laboratory experiment, or to develop and support your own interpretation of a novel. A good college paper doesn't just rehash the facts; it demonstrates what your reader, as a teacher, needs to know — that you are learning the thinking skills his or her course is trying to teach.

Effective writers are not simply expressing what they know, like a student madly filling up an examination bluebook. Instead they are *using* their knowledge: reorganizing, maybe even rethinking their ideas to meet the demands of an assignment or the needs of their reader.

■ Thinking Critically about the Text

What does Flower believe constitutes a "good college paper" (paragraph 9)? Do you agree? Why or why not?

■ Discussing the Craft of Writing

1. How, according to Flower, does a competent writer achieve the goal of closing the gap between himself or herself and the reader? How does a writer determine what a reader's "personal or professional needs" (paragraph 2) are?
2. What, for Flower, is the difference between knowledge and attitude? Why is it important for writers to understand this difference?
3. In paragraph 4, Flower discusses the fact that many words have both positive and negative associations. How do you think words come to have associations? (Glossary: *Connotation/Denotation*) Consider, for example, such words as *home, anger, royalty, welfare, politician*, and *strawberry shortcake*.
4. Flower wrote this selection for college students. How well did she assess your needs as a member of this audience? Does Flower's use of language and examples show a sensitivity to her audience? Provide specific examples to support your view.
5. When using technical language in a paper on a subject you are familiar with, why is it important for you to know your audience? Explain. How could your classmates, friends, or parents help you?

Simplicity

WILLIAM ZINSSER

 Born in New York City in 1922, William Zinsser was educated at Princeton University. After serving in the army in World War II, he worked at the *New York Herald Tribune* as an editor, writer, and critic. During the 1970s he taught a popular course in nonfiction at Yale University, and from 1979 to 1987 he was general editor of the Book-of-the-Month Club. Zinsser has written more than a dozen books, including *The City Dwellers* (1962), *Pop Goes America* (1966), *Spring Training* (1989), and three widely used books on writing: *On Writing Well, 30th Anniversary Edition: The Classic Guide to Writing Nonfiction* (2006); *Writing with a Word Processor* (1983); and *Writing to Learn* (1988). Currently, he teaches journalism at Columbia University, and his freelance writing regularly appears in leading magazines.

The following selection is taken from *On Writing Well*. This book grew out of Zinsser's many years of experience as a professional writer and teacher. In this essay, Zinsser exposes what he believes is the writer's number one problem — "clutter." He sees Americans "strangling in unnecessary words, circular constructions, pompous frills, and meaningless jargon." His solution is simple: Writers must know what they want to say and must be thinking clearly as they start to compose. Then self-discipline and hard work are necessary to achieve clear, simple prose. No matter what your experience as a writer has been, you will find Zinsser's observations sound and his advice practical.

■ Preparing to Read

Some people view writing as "thinking on paper." They believe that by seeing something written on a page they are better able to "see what they think." Write about the relationship, for you, between writing and thinking. Are you one of those people who likes to see ideas on paper while trying to work things out? Or do you like to think through ideas before writing about them?

Clutter is the disease of American writing. We are a society strangling in unnecessary words, circular constructions, pompous frills, and meaningless jargon.   1

Who can understand the clotted language of everyday American commerce: the memo, the corporation report, the business letter, the notice from the bank explaining its latest "simplified" statement? What member of an   2

> We are a society strangling in unnecessary words, circular constructions, pompous frills, and meaningless jargon.

insurance or medical plan can decipher the brochure explaining his costs and benefits? What father or mother can put together a child's toy from the instructions on the box? Our national tendency is to inflate and thereby sound important. The airline pilot who announces that he is presently anticipating experiencing considerable precipitation wouldn't think of saying it may rain. The sentence is too simple — there must be something wrong with it.

But the secret of good writing is to strip every 3 sentence to its cleanest components. Every word that serves no function, every long word that could be a short word, every adverb that carries the same meaning that's already in the verb, every passive construction that leaves the reader unsure of who is doing what — these are the thousand and one adulterants that weaken the strength of a sentence. And they usually occur in proportion to education and rank.

During the 1960s the president of my university wrote a letter to mol- 4 lify the alumni after a spell of campus unrest. "You are probably aware," he began, "that we have been experiencing very considerable potentially explosive expressions of dissatisfaction on issues only partially related." He meant that the students had been hassling them about different things. I was far more upset by the president's English than by the students' potentially explosive expressions of dissatisfaction. I would have preferred the presidential approach taken by Franklin D. Roosevelt when he tried to convert into English his own government's memos, such as this blackout order of 1942:

> Such preparations shall be made as will completely obscure all Federal buildings and non-Federal buildings occupied by the Federal government during an air raid for any period of time from visibility by reason of internal or external illumination.

"Tell them," Roosevelt said, "that in buildings where they have to keep 5 the work going to put something across the windows."

Simplify, simplify. Thoreau said it, as we are so often reminded, and 6 no American writer more consistently practiced what he preached. Open *Walden* to any page and you will find a man saying in a plain and orderly way what is on his mind:

> I went to the woods because I wished to live deliberately, to front only the essential facts of life, and see if I could not learn what it had to teach, and not, when I came to die, discover that I had not lived.

How can the rest of us achieve such enviable freedom from clutter? The 7 answer is to clear our heads of clutter. Clear thinking becomes clear writing; one can't exist without the other. It's impossible for a muddy thinker to write good

English. He may get away with it for a paragraph or two, but soon the reader will be lost, and there's no sin so grave, for the reader will not easily be lured back.

Who is this elusive creature, the reader? The reader is someone with an | 8 attention span of about 30 seconds—a person assailed by many forces competing for attention. At one time these forces were relatively few: newspapers, magazines, radio, spouse, children, pets. Today they also include a galaxy of electronic devices for receiving entertainment and information—television, VCRs, DVDs, CDs, video games, the Internet, e-mail, cell phones, BlackBerries, iPods—as well as a fitness program, a pool, a lawn, and that most potent of competitors, sleep. The man or woman snoozing in a chair with a magazine or a book is a person who was being given too much unnecessary trouble by the writer.

It won't do to say that the reader is too dumb or too lazy to keep pace with | 9 the train of thought. If the reader is lost, it's usually because the writer hasn't been careful enough. The carelessness can take any number of forms. Perhaps a sentence is so excessively cluttered that the reader, hacking through the verbiage, simply doesn't know what it means. Perhaps a sentence has been so shoddily constructed that the reader could read it in several ways. Perhaps the writer has switched pronouns in mid-sentence, or has switched tenses, so the reader loses track of who is talking or when the action took place. Perhaps Sentence B is not a logical sequel to Sentence A; the writer, in whose head the connection is clear, hasn't bothered to provide the missing link. Perhaps the writer has used a word incorrectly by not taking the trouble to look it up.

Faced with such obstacles, readers are at first tenacious. They blame them- | 10 selves—they obviously missed something, and they go back over the mystifying sentence, or over the whole paragraph, piecing it out like an ancient rune, making guesses and moving on. But they won't do that for long. The writer is making them work too hard, and they will look for one who is better at the craft.

Writers must therefore constantly ask: What am I trying to say? Surprisingly | 11 often they don't know. Then they must look at what they have written and ask: Have I said it? Is it clear to someone encountering the subject for the first time? If it's not, some fuzz has worked its way into the machinery. The clear writer is someone clearheaded enough to see this stuff for what it is: fuzz.

I don't mean that some people are born clearheaded and are therefore | 12 natural writers, whereas others are naturally fuzzy and will never write well. Thinking clearly is a conscious act that writers must force on themselves, as if they were working on any other project that requires logic: making a shopping list or doing an algebra problem. Good writing doesn't come naturally, though most people seem to think it does. Professional writers are constantly bearded by people who say they'd like to "try a little writing sometime"—meaning when they retire from their real profession, like insurance or real estate, which is hard. Or they say, "I could write a book about that." I doubt it.

Writing is hard work. A clear sentence is no accident. Very few sen- | 13 tences come out right the first time, or even the third time. Remember this in moments of despair. If you find that writing is hard, it's because it *is* hard.

■ Thinking Critically about the Text

What assumptions does Zinsser make about readers? According to Zinsser, what responsibilities do writers have to readers? How do these responsibilities manifest themselves in Zinsser's writing?

■ Discussing the Craft of Writing

1. What exactly is clutter? When do words qualify as clutter, and when do they not?
2. In paragraph 2, Zinsser states that "Our national tendency is to inflate and thereby sound important." What do you think he means by *inflate*? Provide several examples to illustrate how people use language to inflate.
3. One would hope that education would help in the battle against clutter, but, as Zinsser notes, wordiness "usually occur[s] in proportion to education and rank" (paragraph 3). Do your own experiences or observations support Zinsser's claim? Explain.
4. Zinsser believes that writers need to ask themselves two questions — "What am I trying to say?" and "Have I said it?" — constantly as they write. How would these questions help you eliminate clutter from your own writing? Give some examples from one of your essays.
5. In order "to strip every sentence to its cleanest components," we need to be sensitive to the words we use and know how they function within our sentences. For each of the "adulterants that weaken the strength of a sentence," which Zinsser identifies in paragraph 3, provide an example from your own writing.
6. Zinsser knows that sentence variety is an important feature of good writing. Locate several examples of the short sentences (seven or fewer words) he uses in this essay, and explain how each relates in length, meaning, and impact to the sentences around it.   \E12

The Maker's Eye: Revising Your Own Manuscripts

Donald M. Murray

 Donald M. Murray (1924–2006) was born in Boston, Massachusetts. He taught writing for many years at the University of New Hampshire, his alma mater. He served as an editor at *Time* magazine, and he won the Pulitzer Prize in 1954 for editorials that appeared in the *Boston Globe*. Murray's published works include novels, short stories, poetry, and sourcebooks for teachers of writing, like *A Writer Teaches Writing* (revised 2003), *The Craft of Revision* (5th ed., 2003), and *Learning by Teaching* (1982), in which he explores aspects of the writing process. *Write to Learn* (6th ed., 1998), a textbook for college composition courses, is based on Murray's belief that writers learn to write, simply put, by writing. In 2001 he published *My Twice-Lived Life: A Memoir*. Until his death in December 2006, he wrote the weekly column "Now and Then" for the *Boston Globe*.

In the following essay, first published in the *Writer* in October 1973 and later revised, Murray discusses the importance of revision to the work of the writer. Most professional writers live by the maxim that "writing is *re*writing." And to rewrite or revise effectively, we need to become better readers of our own work, open to discovering new meanings and sensitive to our use of language. Murray draws on the experiences of many writers to make a compelling argument for careful revising and editing.

■ **Preparing to Read**

Thinking back on your education to date, what did you think you had to do when teachers told you to revise a piece of your writing? How did the request to revise make you feel? Write about your earliest memories of revising some of your writing. What kinds of changes do you remember making?

When students complete a first draft, they consider the job of writing done — and their teachers too often agree. When professional writers complete a first draft, they usually feel that they are at the start of the writing process. When a draft is completed, the job of writing can begin.

That difference in attitude is the difference between amateur and professional, inexperience and experience, journeyman and craftsman. Peter F. Drucker, the prolific business writer, calls his first draft "the zero draft" — after that he can start counting. Most writers share the feeling that the first draft, and all of those which follow, are opportunities to discover what they have to say and how best they can say it.

> A piece of writing is never finished. It is delivered to a deadline, torn out of the typewriter on demand, sent off with a sense of accomplishment and shame and pride and frustration.

To produce a progression of drafts, each of which says more and says it more clearly, the writer has to develop a special kind of reading skill. In school we are taught to decode what appears on the page as finished writing. Writers, however, face a different category of possibility and responsibility when they read their own drafts. To them the words on the page are never finished. Each can be changed and rearranged, can set off a chain reaction of confusion or clarified meaning. This is a different kind of reading which is possibly more difficult and certainly more exciting.

Writers must learn to be their own best enemy. They must accept the criticism of others and be suspicious of it; they must accept the praise of others and be even more suspicious of it. Writers cannot depend on others. They must detach themselves from their own pages so that they can apply both their caring and their craft to their own work.

Such detachment is not easy. Science-fiction writer Ray Bradbury supposedly puts each manuscript away for a year to the day and then rereads it as a stranger. Not many writers have the discipline or the time to do this. We must read when our judgment may be at its worst, when we are close to the euphoric moment of creation.

Then the writer, counsels novelist Nancy Hale, "should be critical of everything that seems to him most delightful in his style. He should excise what he most admires, because he wouldn't thus admire it if he weren't . . . in a sense protecting it from criticism." John Ciardi, the poet, adds, "The last act of the writing must be to become one's own reader. It is, I suppose, a schizophrenic process, to begin passionately and to end critically, to begin hot and to end cold; and, more important, to be passion-hot and critic-cold at the same time."

Most people think that the principal problem is that writers are too proud of what they have written. Actually, a greater problem for most professional writers is one shared by the majority of students. They are overly critical, think everything is dreadful, tear up page after page, never complete a draft, see the task as hopeless.

The writer must learn to read critically but constructively, to cut what is bad, to reveal what is good. Eleanor Estes, the children's book author, explains: "The writer must survey his work critically, coolly, as though he were a stranger to it. He must be willing to prune, expertly and hard-heartedly. At the end of each revision, a manuscript may look . . . worked over, torn apart, pinned together, added to, deleted from, words changed and words changed back. Yet the book must maintain its original freshness and spontaneity."

Most readers underestimate the amount of rewriting it usually takes to   9
produce spontaneous reading. This is a great disadvantage to the student writer, who sees only a finished product and never watches the craftsman who takes the necessary step back, studies the work carefully, returns to the task, steps back, returns, steps back, again and again. Anthony Burgess, one of the most prolific writers in the English-speaking world, admits, "I might revise a page twenty times." Roald Dahl, the popular children's writer, states, "By the time I'm nearing the end of a story, the first part will have been reread and altered and corrected at least 150 times. . . . Good writing is essentially rewriting. I am positive of this."

Rewriting isn't virtuous. It isn't something that ought to be done. It is   10
simply something that most writers find they have to do to discover what they have to say and how to say it. It is a condition of the writer's life.

There are, however, a few writers who do little formal rewriting, pri-   11
marily because they have the capacity and experience to create and review a large number of invisible drafts in their minds before they approach the page. And some writers slowly produce finished pages, performing all the tasks of revision simultaneously, page by page, rather than draft by draft. But it is still possible to see the sequence followed by most writers most of the time in rereading their own work.

Most writers scan their drafts first, reading as quickly as possible to catch   12
the larger problems of subject and form, and then move in closer and closer as they read and write, reread and rewrite.

The first thing writers look for in their drafts is *information*. They know   13
that a good piece of writing is built from specific, accurate, and interesting information. The writer must have an abundance of information from which to construct a readable piece of writing.

Next, writers look for *meaning* in the information. The specifics must   14
build to a pattern of significance. Each piece of specific information must carry the reader toward meaning.

Writers reading their own drafts are aware of *audience*. They put them-   15
selves in the reader's situation and make sure that they deliver information which a reader wants to know or needs to know in a manner which is easily digested. Writers try to be sure that they anticipate and answer the questions a critical reader will ask when reading the piece of writing.

Writers make sure that the *form* is appropriate to the subject and the   16
audience. Form, or genre, is the vehicle which carries meaning to the reader, but form cannot be selected until the writer has adequate information to discover its significance and an audience which needs or wants that meaning.

Once writers are sure the form is appropriate, they must then look at the *structure*, the order of what they have written. Good writing is built on a solid framework of logic, argument, narrative, or motivation which runs through the entire piece of writing and holds it together. This is the time when many writers find it most effective to outline as a way of visualizing the hidden spine by which the piece of writing is supported.   17

The element on which writers may spend a majority of their time is *development*. Each section of a piece of writing must be adequately developed. It must give readers enough information so that they are satisfied. How much information is enough? That's as difficult as asking how much garlic belongs in a salad. It must be done to taste, but most beginning writers underdevelop, underestimating the reader's hunger for information.   18

As writers solve development problems, they often have to consider questions of *dimension*. There must be a pleasing and effective proportion among all the parts of the piece of writing. There is a continual process of subtracting and adding to keep the piece of writing in balance.   19

Finally, writers have to listen to their own voices. *Voice* is the force which drives a piece of writing forward. It is an expression of the writer's authority and concern. It is what is between the words on the page, what glues the piece of writing together. A good piece of writing is always marked by a consistent, individual voice.   20

As writers read and reread, write and rewrite, they move closer and closer to the page until they are doing line-by-line editing. Writers read their own pages with infinite care. Each sentence, each line, each clause, each phrase, each word, each mark of punctuation, each section of white space between the type has to contribute to the clarification of meaning.   21

Slowly the writer moves from word to word, looking through language to see the subject. As a word is changed, cut, or added, as a construction is rearranged, all the words used before that moment and all those that follow that moment must be considered and reconsidered.   22

Writers often read aloud at this stage of the editing process, muttering or whispering to themselves, calling on the ear's experience with language. Does this sound right — or that? Writers edit, shifting back and forth from eye to page to ear to page. I find I must do this careful editing in short runs, no more than fifteen or twenty minutes at a stretch, or I become too kind with myself. I begin to see what I hope is on the page, not what actually is on the page.   23

This sounds tedious if you haven't done it, but actually it is fun. Making something right is immensely satisfying, for writers begin to learn what they are writing about by writing. Language leads them to meaning, and there is the joy of discovery, of understanding, of making meaning clear as the writer employs the technical skills of language.   24

Words have double meanings, even triple and quadruple meanings. Each word has its own potential of connotation and denotation. And when   25 writers rub one word against the other, they are often rewarded with a sudden insight, an unexpected clarification.

The maker's eye moves back and forth from word to phrase to sentence to paragraph to sentence to phrase to word. The maker's eye sees the need for variety and balance, for a firmer structure, for a more appropriate form. It peers into the interior of the paragraph, looking for coherence, unity, and emphasis, which make meaning clear. 26

I learned something about this process when my first bifocals were prescribed. I had ordered a larger section of the reading portion of the glass because of my work, but even so, I could not contain my eyes within this new limit of vision. And I still find myself taking off my glasses and bending my nose toward the page, for my eyes unconsciously flick back and forth across the page, back to another page, forward to still another, as I try to see each evolving line in relation to every other line. 27

When does this process end? Most writers agree with the great Russian writer Tolstoy, who said, "I scarcely ever reread my published writings; if by chance I come across a page, it always strikes me: all this must be rewritten; this is how I should have written it." 28

The maker's eye is never satisfied, for each word has the potential to ignite new meaning. This article has been twice written all the way through the writing process [. . .]. Now it is to be republished in a book. The editors made a few small suggestions, and then I read it with my maker's eye. Now it has been re-edited, re-revised, re-read, and re-re-edited, for each piece of writing to the writer is full of potential and alternatives. 29

A piece of writing is never finished. It is delivered to a deadline, torn out of the typewriter on demand, sent off with a sense of accomplishment and shame and pride and frustration. If only there were a couple more days, time for just another run at it, perhaps then . . . 30

■ Thinking Critically about the Text

Murray notes that writers often reach a stage in their editing where they read aloud, "muttering or whispering to themselves, calling on the ear's experience with language" (paragraph 23). What do you think writers are listening for? Try reading several paragraphs of Murray's essay aloud. Discuss what you heard.

■ Discussing the Craft of Writing

1. How does Murray define *information* and *meaning* (paragraphs 13–14)? Why is the distinction between the two terms important?
2. What are the essential differences between revising and editing? What types of language concerns are dealt with at each stage? Why is it important to revise before editing?

3. According to Murray, when in the writing process do writers become concerned about the individual words they are using? What do you think Murray means when he says in paragraph 24 that "language leads [writers] to meaning"?

4. The phrase "the maker's eye" appears in Murray's title and in several places throughout the essay. What do you suppose he means by this? Consider how the maker's eye could be different from the reader's eye.

5. What does Murray see as the connection between reading and writing? How does reading help the writer? What should writers be looking for in their reading?

6. What kinds of writing techniques or strategies does Murray use in his essay? Why should we read a novel or magazine article differently than we would a draft of one of our own essays?

7. According to Murray, writers look for information, meaning, audience, form, structure, development, dimension, and voice in their drafts. What rationale or logic do you see, if any, in the way Murray has ordered these items? Are these the kinds of concerns you have when reading your drafts? Explain.

8. How do you react to the following cartoon? Do you find it humorous? Why or why not? How do you think Murray would react? Explain.

© Mark Parisi, Permission required for use.

Reading to Write

STEPHEN KING

 Born in 1947, Stephen King is a 1970 graduate of the University of Maine. He worked as a janitor in a knitting mill, a laundry worker, and a high school English teacher before he struck it big with his writing. Today, many people consider King's name synonymous with the macabre; he is, beyond dispute, the most successful writer of horror fiction today. He has written dozens of novels and hundreds of short stories, novellas, and screenplays, among other works. His books have sold well over 300 million copies worldwide, and many of his novels have been made into popular motion pictures, including *Stand by Me*, *Misery*, *The Green Mile*, and *Dreamcatcher*. His fiction, starting with *Carrie* in 1974, includes *Salem's Lot* (1975), *The Shining* (1977), *The Dead Zone* (1979), *Christine* (1983), *Pet Sematary* (1983), *The Dark Half* (1989), *The Girl Who Loved Tom Gordon* (1999), *From a Buick 8* (2002), *Everything's Eventual: Five Dark Tales* (2002), *The Colorado Kid* (2005), *Cell* (2006), *Lisey's Story* (2006), *Duma Key* (2008), and *Under the Dome* (2009). Other works include *Danse Macabre* (1980), a nonfiction look at horror in the media, and *On Writing: A Memoir of the Craft* (2000).

In the following passage taken from *On Writing*, King discusses the importance of reading in learning to write. Reading, in his words, "offers you a constantly growing knowledge of what has been done and what hasn't, what is trite and what is fresh, what works and what just lies there dying (or dead) on the page."

■ Preparing to Read

In your opinion, are reading and writing connected in some way? If the two activities are related, what is the nature of that relationship? Do you have to be a reader to be a good writer, or is writing an activity that can be learned quite apart from reading?

If you want to be a writer, you must do two things above all others: Read a   1
lot and write a lot. There's no way around these two things that I'm aware of, no shortcut.

I'm a slow reader, but I usually get through seventy or eighty books a   2
year, mostly fiction. I don't read in order to study the craft; I read because I like to read. It's what I do at night, kicked back in my blue chair. Similarly, I don't read fiction to study the art of fiction, but simply because I like stories. Yet there is a learning process going on. Every book you pick up has its own

lesson or lessons, and quite often the bad books have more to teach than the good ones.

When I was in the eighth grade, I happened upon a paperback novel by Murray Leinster, a science fiction pulp writer who did most of his work during the forties and fifties, when magazines like *Amazing Stories* paid a penny a word. I had read other books by Mr. Leinster, enough to know that the quality of his writing was uneven. This particular tale, which was about mining in the asteroid belt, was one of his less successful efforts. Only that's too kind. It was terrible, actually, a story populated by paper-thin characters and driven by outlandish plot developments. Worst of all (or so it seemed to me at the time), Leinster had fallen in love with the word *zestful*. Characters watched the approach of ore-bearing asteroids with *zestful smiles*. Characters sat down to supper aboard their mining ship with *zestful anticipation*. Near the end of the book, the hero swept the large-breasted, blonde heroine into a *zestful embrace*. For me, it was the literary equivalent of a smallpox vaccination: I have never, so far as I know, used the word *zestful* in a novel or a story. God willing, I never will.

Asteroid Miners (which wasn't the title, but that's close enough) was an important book in my life as a reader. Almost everyone can remember losing his or her virginity, and most writers can remember the first book he/she put down thinking: *I can do better than this, Hell, I am doing better than this!* What could be more encouraging to the struggling writer than to realize his/her work is unquestionably better than that of someone who actually got paid for his/her stuff?

> If you want to be a writer, you must do two things above all others: Read a lot and write a lot.

One learns most clearly what not to do by reading bad prose — one novel like *Asteroid Miners* (or *Valley of the Dolls*, *Flowers in the Attic*, and *The Bridges of Madison County*, to name just a few) is worth a semester at a good writing school, even with the superstar guest lecturers thrown in.

Good writing, on the other hand, teaches the learning writer about style, graceful narration, plot development, the creation of believable characters, and truth-telling. A novel like *The Grapes of Wrath* may fill a new writer with feelings of despair and good old-fashioned jealousy — "I'll never be able to write anything that good, not if I live to be a thousand" — but such feelings can also serve as a spur, goading the writer to work harder and aim higher. Being swept away by a combination of great story and great writing — of being flattened, in fact — is part of every writer's necessary formation. You cannot hope to sweep someone else away by the force of your writing until it has been done to you.

So we read to experience the mediocre and the outright rotten; such experience helps us to recognize those things when they begin to creep into our own work, and to steer clear of them. We also read in order to measure ourselves against the good and the great, to get a sense of all that can be done. And we read in order to experience different styles.

You may find yourself adopting a style you find particularly exciting, and there's nothing wrong with that. When I read Ray Bradbury as a kid, I wrote like Ray Bradbury — everything green and wondrous and seen through a lens smeared with the grease of nostalgia. When I read James M. Cain, everything I wrote came out clipped and stripped and hard-boiled. When I read Lovecraft, my prose became luxurious and Byzantine. I wrote stories in my teenage years where all these styles merged, creating a kind of hilarious stew. This sort of stylistic blending is a necessary part of developing one's own style, but it doesn't occur in a vacuum. You have to read widely, constantly refining (and redefining) your own work as you do so. It's hard for me to believe that people who read very little (or not at all in some cases) should presume to write and expect people to like what they have written, but I know it's true. If I had a nickel for every person who ever told me he/she wanted to become a writer but "didn't have time to read," I could buy myself a pretty good steak dinner. Can I be blunt on this subject? If you don't have time to read, you don't have the time (or the tools) to write. Simple as that. |8

Reading is the creative center of a writer's life. I take a book with me everywhere I go, and find there are all sorts of opportunities to dip in. The trick is to teach yourself to read in small sips as well as in long swallows. Waiting rooms were made for books — of course! But so are theater lobbies before the show, long and boring checkout lines, and everyone's favorite, the john. You can even read while you're driving, thanks to the audiobook revolution. Of the books I read each year, anywhere from six to a dozen are on tape. As for all the wonderful radio you will be missing, come on — how many times can you listen to Deep Purple sing "Highway Star"? |9

Reading at meals is considered rude in polite society, but if you expect to succeed as a writer, rudeness should be the second-to-least of your concerns. The least of all should be polite society and what it expects. If you intend to write as truthfully as you can, your days as a member of polite society are numbered, anyway. |10

Where else can you read? There's always the treadmill, or whatever you use down at the local health club to get aerobic. I try to spend an hour doing that every day, and I think I'd go mad without a good novel to keep me company. Most exercise facilities (at home as well as outside it) are now equipped with TVs, but TV — while working out or anywhere else — really is about the last thing an aspiring writer needs. If you feel you must have the news analyst blowhards on CNN while you exercise, or the stock market blowhards on MSNBC, or the sports blowhards on ESPN, it's time for you to question how serious you really are about becoming a writer. You must be prepared to do some serious turning inward toward the life of the imagination, and that means, I'm afraid, that Geraldo, Keith Olbermann, and Jay Leno must go. Reading takes time, and the glass teat takes too much of it. |11

Once weaned from the ephemeral craving for TV, most people will find 12 they enjoy the time they spend reading. I'd like to suggest that turning off that endlessly quacking box is apt to improve the quality of your life as well as the quality of your writing. And how much of a sacrifice are we talking about here? How many *Frasier* and *ER* reruns does it take to make one American life complete? How many Richard Simmons infomercials? How many whiteboy/fatboy Beltway insiders on CNN? Oh man, don't get me started. Jerry-Springer-Dr.-Dre-Judge-Judy-Jerry-Falwell-Donny-and-Marie, I rest my case.

When my son Owen was seven or so, he fell in love with Bruce 13 Springsteen's E Street Band, particularly with Clarence Clemons, the band's burly sax player. Owen decided he wanted to learn to play like Clarence. My wife and I were amused and delighted by this ambition. We were also hopeful, as any parent would be, that our kid would turn out to be talented, perhaps even some sort of prodigy. We got Owen a tenor saxophone for Christmas and lessons with Gordon Bowie, one of the local music men. Then we crossed our fingers and hoped for the best.

Seven months later I suggested to my wife that it was time to discontinue 14 the sax lessons, if Owen concurred. Owen did, and with palpable relief — he hadn't wanted to say it himself, especially not after asking for the sax in the first place, but seven months had been long enough for him to realize that, while he might love Clarence Clemons's big sound, the saxophone was simply not for him — God had not given him that particular talent.

I knew, not because Owen stopped practicing, but because he was prac- 15 ticing only during the periods Mr. Bowie had set for him: half an hour after school four days a week, plus an hour on the weekends. Owen mastered the scales and the notes — nothing wrong with his memory, his lungs, or his eye-hand coordination — but we never heard him taking off, surprising himself with something new, blissing himself out. And as soon as his practice time was over, it was back into the case with the horn, and there it stayed until the next lesson or practice time. What this suggested to me was that when it came to the sax and my son, there was never going to be any real playtime; it was all going to be rehearsal. That's no good. If there's no joy in it, it's just no good. It's best to go on to some other area, where the deposits of talent may be richer and the fun quotient higher.

Talent renders the whole idea of rehearsal meaningless; when you find 16 something at which you are talented, you do it (whatever *it* is) until your fingers bleed or your eyes are ready to fall out of your head. Even when no one is listening (or reading, or watching), every outing is a bravura performance, because you as the creator are happy. Perhaps even ecstatic. That goes for reading and writing as well as for playing a musical instrument, hitting a baseball, or running the four-forty. The sort of strenuous reading and writing program I advocate — four to six hours a day, every day — will not seem strenuous if you really enjoy doing these things and have an aptitude for them; in fact, you may be following such a program already. If you feel you need permission to do all the reading and writing your little heart desires, however, consider it hereby granted by yours truly.

The real importance of reading is that it creates an ease and intimacy   17
with the process of writing; one comes to the country of the writer with one's papers and identification pretty much in order. Constant reading will pull you into a place (a mind-set, if you like the phrase) where you can write eagerly and without self-consciousness. It also offers you a constantly growing knowledge of what has been done and what hasn't, what is trite and what is fresh, what works and what just lies there dying (or dead) on the page. The more you read, the less apt you are to make a fool of yourself with your pen or word processor.

■ Thinking Critically about the Text

What does King mean when he writes that reading a bad novel is "worth a semester at a good writing school, even with the superstar guest lecturers thrown in" (paragraph 5)? Do you take his observation seriously? In your own words, what can one learn about writing by reading a bad novel? What can one learn by reading a good novel?

■ Discussing the Craft of Writing

1. In paragraph 3, King berates the author Murray Leinster for his repeated use of the word *zestful*. He says he himself has, as far as he knows, never used the word. Why do you suppose he doesn't like the word? Have you ever used it in your own writing? Explain. (Glossary: *Diction*)
2. In paragraph 7 King says that "we read in order to experience different styles." What examples does he use to support this statement? If you have learned from someone else's style, what exactly was it that you learned? (Glossary: *Evidence*)
3. Authors, especially those as famous as King, are very much sought after as guests on television shows, at writing conferences, and at celebrity and charity events. Why does King believe that it is incompatible for one to be both a member of polite society and an author? Do you agree with him? Why or why not?
4. King does not like TV. What does he find wrong with it, especially for writers?
5. Admittedly, not everyone who wants to write well also aspires to be a great novelist. What value, if any, does King's advice about reading and writing have for you as a college student? Explain.

CHAPTER 4

Narration

What Is Narration?

Whenever you recount an event or tell a story or an anecdote to illustrate an idea, you are using narration. In its broadest sense, narration includes any account of an event, or a series of events, presented in a logical sequence. As the tremendous popularity in our culture of narrative forms like action movies, television dramas, celebrity gossip, graphic novels, and even the Facebook status update attests, nearly everyone loves a good story. Given a decent character and a good beginning, we all want to find out what happens next.

For one example of narration in popular culture, take a look at the page from Gene Luen Yang's *American-Born Chinese* reproduced on the opposite page. Yang constructs his narrative with a series of pictures that provide snapshots of key moments in the evolution of young love. As we "read" the images, we mentally fill in the gaps between frames to form a continuous progression of events, or narrative, of his hero's sudden infatuation.

Narration in Written Texts

In the area of written texts, most of us associate narration with novels and short fiction. Narration is also useful and effective, however, in nonfiction writing, such as biography, autobiography, history, and news reporting. A good narrative essay provides a meaningful account of some significant event — anything from an account of recent U.S. involvement in the Middle East to a personal experience that gave you new insight about yourself or others. A narrative may present a straightforward message or moral, or it may make a more subtle point about us and the world we live in.

Consider, for example, the following narrative by E. J. Kahn Jr. about the invention of Coca-Cola, as both a medicine and a soft drink, from his book *The Big Drink: The Story of Coca-Cola.*

Writer establishes a context for his narrative.	In 1886 — a year in which, as contemporary Coca-Cola officials like to point out, Conan Doyle unveiled Sherlock Holmes and France unveiled the Statue of Liberty — [John Styth] Pemberton unveiled a syrup that
Writer uses third-person point of view.	he called Coca-Cola. He had taken out the wine and added a pinch of caffeine, and, when the end product tasted awful, had thrown in some extract of cola (or kola) nut and a few other oils, blending the mixture in a three-legged iron pot in his back yard and swishing it around
Writer organizes the narrative chronologically, using time markers.	with an oar. He distributed it to soda fountains in used beer bottles, and [his bookkeeper Frank M.] Robinson, with his flowing bookkeeper's script, presently devised a label on which "Coca-Cola" was written in the fashion that is still employed. Pemberton looked upon his concoction less as a refreshment than as a headache cure, especially for people whose throbbing temples could be traced to overindulgence. On a morning late in 1886, one such victim of the night before dragged himself into an Atlanta drugstore and asked for a dollop of Coca-Cola.
Writer focuses on the discovery that led to Coca-Cola's becoming a popular soft drink.	Druggists customarily stirred a teaspoonful of syrup into a glass of water, but in this instance the factotum on duty was too lazy to walk to the fresh-water tap, a couple of feet off. Instead, he mixed the syrup with some charged water, which was closer at hand. The suffering customer perked up almost at once, and word quickly spread that the best Coca-Cola was a fizzy one.

A good narrative essay, like the paragraph above, has four essential features. The first is *context*: The writer makes clear when the action happened, where it happened, and to whom. The second is *point of view*: The writer establishes and maintains a consistent relationship to the action, either as a participant or as a reporter looking on. The third is *selection of detail*: The writer carefully chooses what to include, focusing on those actions and details that are most important to the story while playing down or even eliminating others. The fourth is *organization*: The writer arranges the events of the narrative in an appropriate sequence, often a strict chronology with a clear beginning, middle, and end.

As you read the selections in this chapter, watch for these features and for how each writer uses them to tell his or her story. Think about how each writer's choices affect the way you react to the selections.

Using Narration As a Writing Strategy

The most basic and most important purpose of narration is to share a meaningful experience with readers. Another important purpose of narration is to report and instruct — to give the facts, to tell what happened. Journalists and historians, in reporting events of the near and more distant past, provide us with information that we can use to form opinions about a current issue or to better understand the world around us. A biographer gives us another person's life as a document of an individual's past but also, perhaps, as a portrait of more general human potential. And naturalists recount the drama of encounters between predators and prey in the wild. We expect writers to make these narratives as objective as possible and to distinguish between facts and opinions.

Narration is often used in combination with one or more of the other rhetorical strategies. In an essay that is written primarily to explain a process — reading a book, for example — a writer might find it useful to tell a brief story or anecdote demonstrating an instance when the process worked especially well (Mortimer Adler, "How to Mark a Book," Chapter 7). In the same way, a writer attempting to define the term *poverty* might tell several stories to illustrate clearly the many facets of poverty (Jo Goodwin Parker, "What Is Poverty?," Chapter 10). Finally, a writer could use narrative examples to persuade — for example, to argue for a reconsideration of the intelligence demanded in the blue-collar workplace (Mike Rose, "Blue-Collar Brilliance," Chapter 6) or to demonstrate for readers the power and clarity of monosyllabic words (Richard Lederer, "The Case for Short Words," Chapter 12).

Using Narration across the Disciplines

When writing essays in the academic disciplines, you will have many opportunities to use the strategy of narration to both organize and strengthen the presentation of your ideas. To determine whether or not narration is the right strategy for you in a particular paper, use the four-step method described in Chapter 2 (Determining a Strategy for Developing Your Essay, pages 25–26). Consider the following examples, which illustrate how this four-step method works for typical college papers.

American History

1. MAIN IDEA: Although Abraham Lincoln was not the chief speaker at Gettysburg on November 19, 1863, the few remarks he made that day shaped the thinking of our nation as perhaps few other speeches have.
2. QUESTION: What happened at Gettysburg on November 19, 1863, that made Abraham Lincoln's speech so memorable and influential?
3. STRATEGY: Narration. The thrust of the main idea as well as the direction words *what happened* say "tell me the story," and what better way to tell what happened than to narrate the day's events?
4. SUPPORTING STRATEGY: Cause and Effect Analysis. The story and how it is narrated can be used to explain the impact of this speech on our nation's thinking.

Anthropology

1. MAIN IDEA: Food-gathering and religious activities account for a large portion of the daily lives of native peoples in rural Thailand.
2. QUESTION: What happens during a typical day or week in rural Thailand?
3. STRATEGY: Narration. The direction words in both the statement of the main idea (*account* and *daily*) and the question (*what happens*) cry out for a narration of what does happen during any given day.
4. SUPPORTING STRATEGY: Illustration. The paper might benefit from specific examples of the various chores related to food gathering as well as examples of typical religious activities.

Life Science

1. MAIN IDEA: British bacteriologist Sir Alexander Fleming discovered penicillin quite by accident in 1928, and that discovery changed the world.
2. QUESTION: How did Fleming happen to discover penicillin, and why was this discovery so important?
3. STRATEGY: Narration. The direction words *how* and *did happen* call for the story of Fleming's accidental discovery of penicillin.
4. SUPPORTING STRATEGY: Argument. The claims that Fleming's discovery was *important* and *changed the world* suggest that the story needs to be both compelling and persuasive.

Sample Student Essay Using Narration As a Writing Strategy

After reading several personal narratives — the selection from Annie Dillard's *An American Childhood* and Malcolm X's "Coming to an Awareness of Language" in particular — Laura LaPierre decided to write a narrative of her own. Only weeks prior to writing this essay Laura had received some very bad news. It was the experience of living with this news that she decided to write about. The writing was painful, and not everyone would feel comfortable with a similar task. Laura, however, welcomed the opportunity because she came to a more intimate understanding of her own fears and feelings as she moved from one draft to the next. What follows is the final draft of Laura's essay.

Title: Asks central question that paper will answer.	**Why Are You Here?** Laura LaPierre
Beginning: Engages the reader and establishes context — when, where, who.	Balancing between a crutch on one side and an IV pole with wheels on the other, I dragged my stiff leg along the smooth, sterile floor of the hospital hall.

1

Details: Creates image of harsh, unfriendly environment.

Point of View: First person.

Organization: Straightforward chronological organization.

Descriptive details create dominant impression of a dull, uninviting room.

Organization: Time reference maintains flow.

Details show that people in group are obviously ill, but specifics are not revealed.

All around me nurses, orderlies, and doctors bustled about, dodging well-meaning visitors laden with flowers and candy. The fluorescent lights glared down with a brightness so sharp that I squinted and thought that sunglasses might be in order. Sticking close to the wall, I rounded the corner and paused to rest for a moment. I breathed in the hot, antiseptic-smelling air which I had grown accustomed to and sighed angrily.

Tears of hurt and frustration pricked at the corner of my eyes as the now familiar pain seared my leg. I tugged my bathrobe closer around my shoulder and, hauling my IV pole with me, I continued down the hall. One, two—second door on the left, she had said. I opened the heavy metal door, entered, and realized that I must be a little early because no one else was there yet. After glancing at my watch, I sat down and looked around the room, noting with disgust the prevalence of beige: beige walls, beige ceiling, shiny beige floor tiles. A small cot stood in one corner with a beige bedspread, and in the opposite corner there was a sink, mirror, and beige waste basket. The only relief from the monotony was the circle of six or seven chairs where I sat. They were a vivid rust color and helped to brighten the dull room. The shades were drawn, and the lights were much dimmer than they had been in the hall. My eyes gradually relaxed as I waited.

People began to drift in until five of the seats were filled. A nurse was the head of the odd-looking group. Three of us were attached by long tubes to IV poles, and then there was a social worker. The man to my left wore a slightly faded, royal blue robe. He had a shock of unruly gray hair above an angular face with deeply sunken cheeks. His eyes were sunken, too, and glassy with pain. Yet he smiled and appeared untroubled by his IV pole.

Wearing a crisp white uniform and a pretty sweater, the nurse, a pleasant-looking woman in her late twenties, appeared friendly and sympathetic, though not to the point of being sappy.

2

3

4

My impressions were confirmed as she began to speak.

Dialogue adds life to narrative.

"Okay. I guess we can begin. Welcome to our group, we meet every Monday at . . . ." She went on, but I wasn't paying attention anymore. I looked around the group and my eyes came to rest on the man sitting next to the nurse. In contrast to the other man's shriveled appearance, this man was robust. He was tall, with a protruding belly and a ruddy complexion. Unlike the other man, he seemed at war with his IV pole. He constantly fiddled with the tube and with the tape that held the needle in his arm. Eyes darting around the room, he nervously watched everyone.   5

Details reveal writer's restlessness, perhaps uneasiness.

Comparison and contrast: Describes other patients in the room.

I heard the nurse continue, "So, let's all introduce ourselves and tell why we are here." We went around the circle clockwise, starting with the nurse, and when we got to the social worker, I looked up and surveyed her while she talked. Aside from contributing to the beige monotony with her pants, she was agreeable both in appearance and disposition.   6

Dialogue continues. Central question of title introduced.

When it was my turn, I took a deep breath and with my voice quavering began, "My name is Laura and —"   7

Description shows writer's fear.

"Hi, Laura!" interrupted the cheerful man on my left. I turned and smiled weakly at him.   8

Cheerful man momentarily relieves tension.

Fighting back the tears, I continued, "And I have bone cancer."   9

Laura faces her fear—her moment of truth.

Analyzing Laura LaPierre's Narration Essay: Questions for Discussion

1. What context does Laura provide for her narrative? What else, if anything, would you have liked to know about the situation? What would have been lost had she told you more?

2. Laura tells her story in the first person. How would the narrative have changed had she used a third-person point of view?

3. For you, what details conveyed Laura's fear at being in the hospital? Are there places where she could have done more "showing" and less "telling"? Explain.

4. Laura uses a straightforward chronological organization for her narrative. Can you see any places where she might have used a flashback? What would have been the effect?

5. What meaning or importance do you think this experience holds for Laura?

Suggestions for Using Narration As a Writing Strategy

As you plan, write, and revise your narrative essay, be mindful of the writing process guidelines described in Chapter 2. Also, pay particular attention to the basic requirements and essential ingredients for this writing strategy.

■ Planning Your Narration Essay

Planning is an essential part of writing a good narrative essay. You can save yourself a great deal of inconvenience by taking the time to think about the key components of your essay before you actually begin to write.

Select a Topic That Has Meaning for You. In your writing course, you may have the freedom to choose the story you want to narrate, or your instructor may give you a list of topics from which to choose. Instead of jumping at the first topic that looks good, however, brainstorm a list of events that have had an impact on your life and that you could write about. Such a list might include your first blind date, catching frogs as a child, making a team or a club, the death of a loved one, a graduation celebration, a trip to the Grand Canyon, the loss of a pet, learning to drive a car, or the breakup of a relationship.

As you narrow your options, look for an event or an incident that is particularly memorable. Memorable experiences are memorable for a reason; they offer us important insights into our lives. Such experiences are worth narrating because people want to read about them.

Determine Your Point and Purpose. Before you begin writing, ask yourself why the experience you have chosen is meaningful. What did you learn from it? How are you different as a result of the experience? What has changed? Your narrative point (the meaning of your narrative) and purpose in writing will influence which events and details you include and which you leave out. Suppose, for example, you choose to write about how you learned to ride a bicycle. If you mean mainly to entertain, you will probably include a number of unusual incidents unique to your experience. If your purpose is mainly to report or inform, it will make more sense to concentrate on the kinds of details that are common to most people's experience. However, if your purpose is to tell your readers step-by-step how to ride a bicycle, you should use process analysis, a strategy used by writers whose purpose is to give directions for how something is done or to explain how something works (see Chapter 7).

The most successful narrative essays, however, do more than entertain or inform. While narratives do not ordinarily have a formal thesis statement, readers will more than likely expect your story to make a statement or to arrive at some meaningful conclusion — implied or explicit — about your experience. The student essay by Laura LaPierre, for example, shows how important it was for her to confront the reality of her bone cancer. In addressing her fears, she gains a measure of control over her life.

As you prepare to write, then, look for the significance in the story you want to tell — some broader, more instructive points it could make about the ways of the world. Learning to ride a bicycle may not suggest such points to you, and it may therefore not be a very good subject for your narrative essay. However, the subject does have possibilities. Here's one: Learning to master a difficult, even dangerous, but definitely useful skill like riding a bicycle is an important experience to have in life. Here's another: Learning to ride a bicycle is an opportunity for you to acquire and use some basic physics, such as the laws of gravity and the behavior of a gyroscope. Perhaps you can think of others. If, however, you do not know why you are telling the story and it seems pointless even to you, your readers will pick up on the ambivalence in your writing, and you should probably find another, more meaningful story to tell.

Establish a Context.   Early in your essay, perhaps in the opening paragraphs, establish the context, or setting, of your story — the world within which the action took place:

> *When it happened* — morning; afternoon; 11:37 on the dot; 1997; winter
> *Where it happened* — in the street; at Wendy's; in Pocatello, Idaho
> *To whom it happened* — to me; to my father; to the assistant; to
>   Teri Hopper

Without a clear context, your readers can easily get confused or even completely lost. And remember, readers respond well to specific contextual information because such details make them feel as if they are present, ready to witness the narrative.

Choose the Most Appropriate Point of View.   Consider what point of view to take in your narrative. Did you take part in the action? If so, it will seem most natural for you to use the first-person (*I, we*) point of view. On the other hand, if you weren't there at all and must rely on other sources for your information, you will probably choose the third-person (*he, she, it, they*) point of view, as did the author writing about the invention of Coca-Cola earlier in this chapter. However, if you were a witness to part or all of what happened but not a participant, then you will need to choose between the more immediate and subjective quality of the first person and the more distanced, objective effect of the third person. Whichever you choose, you should maintain the same point of view throughout your narrative.

Gather Details That "Show, Don't Tell."   When writing your essay, you will need enough detail about the action, the people involved, and the context to let your readers understand what is going on. Start collecting details by asking yourself the traditional reporter's questions:

- Who was involved?

- What happened?

- Where did it happen?

- When did it happen?

- Why did it happen?

- How did it happen?

Generate as many details as you can because you never know which ones will ensure that your essay *shows* and doesn't *tell* too much. For example, instead of telling readers that she dislikes being in the hospital, Laura LaPierre shows us what she sees, feels, hears, and smells and lets us draw our own conclusion about her state of mind.

As you write, you will want to select and emphasize details that support your point, serve your purpose, and show the reader what is happening. You should not, however, get so carried away with details that your readers become confused or bored by excess information: In good storytelling, deciding what to leave out can be as important as deciding what to include.

■ Organizing Your Narration Essay

Identify the Sequence of Events in Your Narrative.   Storytellers tend to follow an old rule: Begin at the beginning, and go on till you come to the end; then stop. Chronological organization is natural in narration because it is a retelling of the original order of events; it is also easiest for the writer to manage and the reader to understand.

Some narratives, however, are organized using a technique called *flashback*: The writer may begin midway through the story, or even at the end, with an important or exciting event, then use flashbacks to fill in what happened earlier to lead up to that event. Some authors begin in the present and then use flashbacks to shift to the past to tell the story. Whatever organizational pattern you choose, words and phrases like "for a month," "afterward," and "three days earlier" will help you and your reader keep the sequence of events straight.

It may help you in organizing to jot down a quick outline before tackling the first draft of your narrative. Here's the outline that Laura LaPierre used to order the events in her narrative chronologically.

Narration about my first group meeting at the hospital

Point: At some point I had to confront the reality of my illness.

Context: Hospital setting

1. Start slow walk down hospital hall attached to IV pole.
2. Sights, sounds, and smells of hospital hallway set scene.
3. Locate destination—first one to arrive for group meeting.
4. Describe "beige" meeting room.
5. Other patients arrive.
6. Young nurse leads our group meeting.
7. We start by introducing ourselves.
8. My turn—my moment of truth.

Such an outline can remind you of your point, your organization, and the emphasis you want when you write your first draft.

■ Writing Your Narration Essay

Keep Your Verb Tense Consistent. Most narratives are in the past tense, and this is logical: They recount events that have already happened, even if very recently. But writers sometimes use the present tense to create an effect of immediacy, as if the events were happening as you read about them. The important thing to remember is to be consistent. If you are recounting an event that has already occurred, use the past tense throughout. For an event in the present, use the present tense consistently. If you find yourself jumping from a present event to a past event, as in the case of a flashback, you will need to switch verb tenses to signal the change in time.

E10

Use Narrative Time for Emphasis. The number of words or pages you devote to an event does not usually correspond to the number of minutes or hours the event took to happen. You may require several pages to recount an important or complex quarter of an hour, but then pass over several hours or days in a sentence or two. Length has less to do with chronological time than with the amount of detail you include, and that's a function of the amount of emphasis you want to give to a particular incident.

Use Transitional Words to Clarify Narrative Sequence. Transitional words like *after, next, then, earlier, immediately,* and *finally* are useful, as they help your readers smoothly connect and understand the sequence of events that makes up your narrative. Likewise, a specific time mark like "on April 20," "two weeks earlier," and "in 2004" can indicate time shifts and can signal to readers how much time has elapsed between events.

Inexperienced writers sometimes overuse these words; this makes their writing style wordy and tiresome. Use these conventional transitions when you really need them, but when you don't — when your readers can follow your story without them — leave them out.

Use Dialogue to Bring Your Narrative to Life.   Having people in a narrative speak is a very effective way of showing rather than telling or summarizing what happened. Snippets of actual dialogue make a story come alive and feel immediate to the reader.

Consider this passage from an early draft of a student narrative:

> I hated having to call a garage, but I knew I couldn't do the work myself and I knew they'd rip me off. Besides, I had to get the car off the street before the police had it towed. I felt trapped without any choices.

Now compare this early draft with the revised draft below, in which the situation is revealed through dialogue.

> "University Gulf, Glen speaking. What can I do for ya?"
>
> "Yeah, my car broke down. I think it's the timing belt, and I was wondering if you could give me an estimate."
>
> "What kind of car is it?" asked Glen.
>
> "A Nissan Sentra."
>
> "What year?"
>
> "1995," I said, emphasizing the 95.
>
> "Oh, those are a bitch to work on. Can ya hold on for a second?"
>
> I knew what was coming before Glen came back on the line.

With dialogue, readers can hear the direct exchange between the car owner and the mechanic. You can use dialogue in your own writing to deliver a sense of immediacy to the reader.

■ Revising and Editing Your Narration Essay

Share Your Draft with Others.   Try sharing the draft of your essay with other students in your writing class to make sure that your narrative makes sense. Ask them if there are any parts that they do not understand. Have them tell you what they think is the point of your narrative. If their answers differ from what you intended, have them indicate the passages that led them to their interpretations so that you can change your text accordingly. To maximize the effectiveness of conferences with your peers, utilize the guidelines presented on page 29. Feedback from these conferences often provides one or more places where you can start revising.

Question Your Own Work While Revising and Editing. Revision is best done by asking yourself key questions about what you have written. Begin by reading, preferably aloud, what you have written. Reading aloud forces you to pay attention to every single word, and you are more likely to catch lapses in the logical flow of thought.

For help with twelve common writing problems, see Chapter 16, "Editing for Grammar, Punctuation, and Sentence Style." After you have read your paper through, answer the following questions for revising and editing, and make the necessary changes.

Questions for Revising and Editing: Narration

1. Is my narrative well focused, or do I try to cover too long a period of time?

2. What is my reason for telling this story? Is that reason clearly stated or implied for readers?

3. Have I established a clear context for my readers? Is it clear when the action happened, where it happened, and to whom?

4. Have I used the most effective point of view to tell my story? How would my story be different had I used a different one?

5. Have I selected details that help readers understand what is going on in my narrative, or have I included unnecessary details that get in the way of what I'm trying to say? Do I give enough examples of the important events in my narrative?

6. Is the chronology of events in my narrative clear? Have I taken advantage of opportunities to add emphasis, drama, or suspense with flashbacks or other complications of the chronological organization?

7. Have I used transitional expressions or time markers to help readers follow the sequence of events in my narrative?

8. Have I employed dialogue in my narrative to reveal a situation, or have I told about or summarized the situation too much?

9. Have I avoided run-on sentences and comma splices? Have I used sentence fragments only deliberately to convey mood or tone?

E1–2

10. Have I avoided other errors in grammar, punctuation, and mechanics? Is my sentence style as clear, smooth, and persuasive as possibe?

E3–12

11. Is the meaning of my narrative clear, or have I left my readers thinking, "So what?"

Coming to an Awareness of Language

MALCOLM X

Born Malcolm Little in Omaha, Nebraska, in 1925, Malcolm X rose from a world of street crime to become one of the most powerful and articulate African American leaders in the United States during the 1960s. On February 21, 1965, his life was cut short at age thirty-nine; he was shot and killed as he addressed an afternoon rally in Harlem. Malcolm X told his life story in *The Autobiography of Malcolm X* (1964), written with the assistance of *Roots* author Alex Haley. The book, a moving account of his life and his struggle for fulfillment, is still read by hundreds of thousands each year. In 1992, the life of this influential African American leader was reexamined in Spike Lee's film *Malcolm X*.

The following selection from *The Autobiography* refers to a period Malcolm X spent in federal prison. In the selection, Malcolm X explains how he was frustrated by his inability to express his ideas and how this frustration led him to a goal: acquiring the skills of reading and writing. Later he would say, "As I see it, the ability to read awoke inside me some long dormant craving to be mentally alive."

■ Preparing to Read

Our educational system places a great emphasis on our having a large and varied working vocabulary. Has anyone ever stressed to you the importance of developing a good vocabulary? What did you think when you heard this advice? In what ways can words be used as powerful tools? How would you judge your own vocabulary?

I've never been one for inaction. Everything I've ever felt strongly about, 1
I've done something about. I guess that's why, unable to do anything else, I soon began writing to people I had known in the hustling world, such as Sammy the Pimp, John Hughes, the gambling house owner, the thief Jumpsteady, and several dope peddlers. I wrote them all about Allah and Islam and Mr. Elijah Muhammad. I had no idea where most of them lived. I addressed their letters in care of the Harlem or Roxbury bars and clubs where I'd known them.

I never got a single reply. The average hustler and criminal was too 2
uneducated to write a letter. I have known many slick, sharp-looking hustlers, who would have you think they had an interest in Wall Street; privately, they would get someone else to read a letter if they received one.

Besides, neither would I have replied to anyone writing me something as wild as "the white man is the devil."

What certainly went on the Harlem and Roxbury wires was that Detroit 3 Red was going crazy in stir, or else he was trying some hype to shake up the warden's office.

During the years that I stayed in the Norfolk Prison Colony, never did any 4 official directly say anything to me about those letters, although, of course, they all passed through the prison censorship. I'm sure, however, they monitored what I wrote to add to the files which every state and federal prison keeps on the conversion of Negro inmates by the teachings of Mr. Elijah Muhammad.

> I saw that the best thing I could do was get hold of a dictionary— to study, to learn some words.

But at that time, I felt that the real reason was 5 that the white man knew that he was the devil.

Later on, I even wrote to the Mayor of Boston, 6 to the Governor of Massachusetts, and to Harry S. Truman. They never answered; they probably never even saw my letters. I handscratched to them how the white man's society was responsible for the black man's condition in this wilderness of North America.

It was because of my letters that I happened to stumble upon starting to 7 acquire some kind of a homemade education.

I became increasingly frustrated at not being able to express what I wanted 8 to convey in letters that I wrote, especially those to Mr. Elijah Muhammad. In the street, I had been the most articulate hustler out there — I had commanded attention when I said something. But now, trying to write simple English, I not only wasn't articulate, I wasn't even functional. How would I sound writing in slang, the way I would *say* it, something such as, "Look, daddy, let me pull your coat about a cat. Elijah Muhammad —"

Many who today hear me somewhere in person, or on television, or 9 those who read something I've said, will think I went to school far beyond the eighth grade. This impression is due entirely to my prison studies.

It had really begun back in the Charlestown Prison, when Bimbi first 10 made me feel envy of his stock of knowledge. Bimbi had always taken charge of any conversation he was in, and I had tried to emulate him. But every book I picked up had few sentences which didn't contain anywhere from one to nearly all of the words that might as well have been in Chinese. When I just skipped those words, of course, I really ended up with little idea of what the book said. So I had come to the Norfolk Prison Colony still going through only book-reading motions. Pretty soon, I would have quit even these motions, unless I had received the motivation that I did.

I saw that the best thing I could do was get hold of a dictionary — to 11 study, to learn some words. I was lucky enough to reason also that I should try to improve my penmanship. It was sad. I couldn't even write in a straight line. It was both ideas together that moved me to request a dictionary along with some tablets and pencils from the Norfolk Prison Colony school.

I spent two days just riffling uncertainly through the dictionary's pages. 12 I'd never realized so many words existed! I didn't know *which* words I needed to learn. Finally, just to start some kind of action, I began copying.

In my slow, painstaking, ragged handwriting, I copied into my tablet 13 everything printed on that first page, down to the punctuation marks.

I believe it took me a day. Then, aloud, I read back, to myself, everything I'd 14 written on the tablet. Over and over, aloud, to myself, I read my own handwriting.

I woke up the next morning, thinking about those words — immensely 15 proud to realize that not only had I written so much at one time, but I'd written words that I never knew were in the world. Moreover, with a little effort, I also could remember what many of these words meant. I reviewed the words whose meanings I didn't remember. Funny thing, from the dictionary first page right now, that "aardvark" springs to my mind. The dictionary had a picture of it, a long-tailed, long-eared, burrowing African mammal, which lives off termites caught by sticking out its tongue as an anteater does for ants.

I was so fascinated that I went on — I copied the dictionary's next page. 16 And the same experience came when I studied that. With every succeeding page, I also learned of people and places and events from history. Actually the dictionary is like a miniature encyclopedia. Finally the dictionary's A section had filled a whole tablet — and I went on into the B's. That was the way I started copying what eventually became the entire dictionary. It went a lot faster after so much practice helped me to pick up handwriting speed. Between what I wrote in my tablet, and writing letters, during the rest of my time in prison I would guess I wrote a million words.

I suppose it was inevitable that as my word-base broadened, I could for 17 the first time pick up a book and read and now begin to understand what the book was saying. Anyone who has read a great deal can imagine the new world that opened. Let me tell you something: from then until I left that prison, in every free moment I had, if I was not reading in the library, I was reading on my bunk. You couldn't have gotten me out of books with a wedge. Between Mr. Muhammad's teachings, my correspondence, my visitors . . . and my reading of books, months passed without my even thinking about being imprisoned. In fact, up to then, I never had been so truly free in my life.

■ Thinking Critically about the Text

We are all to one degree or another prisoners of our own language. Sometimes we lack the ability to communicate as effectively as we would like.

Why do you think this happens, and what do you think can be done to remedy it? How can improved language skills also improve a person's life?

▪ Questions on Subject

1. In paragraph 8, Malcolm X refers to the difference between being "articulate" and being "functional" in his speaking and writing. What is the distinction he makes? In your opinion, is it a valid one?
2. Malcolm X offers two possible reasons for the warden's keeping track of African American inmates' conversion to the teachings of Elijah Muhammad. What are those two assertions, and what is their effect on the reader?
3. What is the nature of the freedom that Malcolm X refers to in the final sentence? In what sense can language be said to be liberating?

▪ Questions on Strategy

1. Malcolm X narrates his experiences as a prisoner using the first-person *I*. Why is the first person particularly appropriate? What would be lost or gained had he narrated his story using the third-person pronoun *he*?
2. In the opening paragraph, Malcolm X refers to himself as a man of action and conviction. What details does he include to support this assertion?
3. Many people think of "vocabulary building" as learning strange, multisyllabic, difficult-to-spell words. But acquiring an effective vocabulary does not have to be so intimidating. How would you characterize Malcolm X's vocabulary in this narrative? Did you find his word choice suited to what he was trying to accomplish in this selection?
4. What is Malcolm X's narrative point in this passage? How do you know? What does he learn about himself as a result of this experience?
5. In reflecting on his years in prison, Malcolm X comes to an understanding of the events that caused him to reassess his life and take charge of his own education. Identify those events, and discuss the changes that resulted from Malcolm X's actions. How does his inclusion of these causal links enhance the overall narrative? (Glossary: *Cause and Effect Analysis*)

▪ Questions on Diction and Vocabulary

1. Although Malcolm X taught himself to be articulate in writing, we can still hear a street-savvy voice in his writing. Cite examples of his diction that convey a streetwise sound. (Glossary: *Diction*)
2. What do you do when you encounter new words in your reading? Do you skip those words as Malcolm X once did, do you take the time to look them up, or do you try to figure out their meanings from the context? Explain the strategies you use to determine the meaning of a word from its context. Can you think of other strategies?

3. Refer to your desk dictionary to determine the meanings of the following words as Malcolm X uses them in this selection: *hustler* (paragraph 2), *slick* (2), *hype* (3), *frustrated* (8), *emulate* (10), *riffling* (12),
inevitable (17).

■ Classroom Activity Using Narration

Good narrative depends on a sense of continuity or flow, a logical ordering of events and ideas. The following sentences, which make up the first
paragraph of E. B. White's essay "Once More to the Lake," have been
rearranged. Place the sentences in what seems to be a coherent sequence
based on such language signals as transitions, repeated words, pronouns,
and temporal references. Be prepared to explain your reason for the placement of each sentence.

1. I have since become a salt-water man, but sometimes in summer there
are days when the restlessness of the tides and the fearful cold of the
sea water and the incessant wind that blows across the afternoon and
into the evening make me wish for the placidity of a lake in the woods.
2. We all got ringworm from some kittens and had to rub Pond's Extract
on our arms and legs night and morning, and my father rolled over
in a canoe with all his clothes on; but outside of that the vacation was
a success and from then on none of us ever thought there was any
place in the world like that lake in Maine.
3. A few weeks ago this feeling got so strong I bought myself a couple
of bass hooks and a spinner and returned to the lake where we used
to go, for a week's fishing and to revisit old haunts.
4. One summer, along about 1904, my father rented a camp on a lake in
Maine and took us all there for the month of August.
5. We returned summer after summer — always on August 1st for one month.

■ Writing Suggestions

1. Using Malcolm X's essay as a model, write a narrative about some
goal you have set and achieved in which you were motivated by a
strong inner conflict. What was the nature of your conflict? What feeling did it arouse in you, and how did the conflict help you to accomplish your goal?
2. **Writing with Sources.** Malcolm X solved the problems of his own near-
illiteracy by carefully studying the dictionary. Would this be a practical
solution to the national problem of illiteracy? In your experience, what
does it mean to be literate? After investigating contemporary illiteracy
in your college library or on the Internet, write a proposal on what can
be done to promote literacy in this country. You might also consider
what is being done now in your community. For models of and advice
on integrating sources, see Chapters 14 and 15.

From An American Childhood

ANNIE DILLARD

 Born in Pittsburgh, Pennsylvania, in 1945, Annie Dillard has written in many genres. After graduating from Hollins College, where she wrote a thesis on Thoreau's *Walden*, she launched her writing career. Her first two books were both published in 1974, before she was thirty years old; the first was a collection of poems entitled *Tickets for a Prayer Wheel* and the second was *Pilgrim at Tinker Creek*, a Pulitzer Prize–winning book of essays based on her observations of and reflections about nature. She has explored the world of fiction, writing books of criticism — *Living by Fiction* (1982) and *Encounters with Chinese Writers* (1984) — and a novel, *The Living* (1992). In 2000, she published a collection of essays, *For the Time Being*. Her most recent book is *The Maytrees: A Novel* (2007). For a number of years she was a writer-in-residence at Wesleyan University.

In one of her early essays, Dillard expressed a mistrust of memoirs, saying, "I don't recommend, or even approve, writing personally. It can lead to dreadful writing." By 1987, however, she had put this warning aside to publish an autobiography, *An American Childhood*, from which this selection is taken. The book details Dillard's memories of her years growing up in Pittsburgh and is filled with the wonder and joy of living. This selection reflects the tone of the book as a whole.

■ Preparing to Read

What activity are you passionate about — an activity that makes you give your all? A sport is a good example of a pursuit that demands and rewards total involvement, but you might also want to consider other types of activities like making music, dancing, painting, playing computer games, or reading. What satisfactions result from wholehearted participation in the activity of your choice?

Some boys taught me to play football. This was fine sport. You thought   1
up a new strategy for every play and whispered it to the others. You went out for a pass, fooling everyone. Best, you got to throw yourself mightily at someone's running legs. Either you brought him down or you hit the ground flat out on your chin, with your arms empty before you. It was all or nothing. If you hesitated in fear, you would miss and get hurt: You would take a hard fall while the kid got away, or you would get kicked in the face while

the kid got away. But if you flung yourself wholeheartedly at the back of his knees — if you gathered and joined body and soul and pointed them diving fearlessly — then you likely wouldn't get hurt, and you'd stop the ball. Your fate, and your team's score, depended on your concentration and courage. Nothing girls did could compare with it.

Boys welcomed me at baseball, too, for I had, through enthusiastic practice, what was weirdly known as a boy's arm. In winter, in the snow, there was neither baseball nor football, so the boys and I threw snowballs at passing cars. I got in trouble throwing snowballs, and have seldom been happier since. 2

On one weekday morning after Christmas, six inches of new snow had just fallen. We were standing up to our boot tops in snow on a front yard on trafficked Reynolds Street, waiting for cars. The cars traveled Reynolds Street slowly and evenly; they were targets all but wrapped in red ribbons, cream puffs. We couldn't miss. 3

We all spread out, banged together some regular snowballs, took aim, and, when the Buick drew nigh, fired.

I was seven; the boys were eight, nine, and ten. The oldest two Fahey boys were there — Mikey and Peter — polite blond boys who lived near me on Lloyd Street, and who already had four brothers and sisters. My parents approved Mikey and Peter Fahey. Chickie McBride was there, a tough kid, and Billy Paul and Mackie Kean too, from across Reynolds, where the boys grew up dark and furious, grew up skinny, knowing, and skilled. We had all drifted from our houses that morning looking for action, and had found it here on Reynolds Street. 4

It was cloudy but cold. The cars' tires laid behind them on the snowy street a complex trail of beige chunks like crenellated castle walls. I had stepped on some earlier; they squeaked. We could have wished for more traffic. When a car came, we all popped it one. In the intervals between cars we reverted to the natural solitude of children. 5

I started making an iceball — a perfect iceball, from perfectly white snow, perfectly spherical, and squeezed perfectly translucent so no snow remained all the way through. (The Fahey boys and I considered it unfair actually to throw an iceball at somebody, but it had been known to happen.) 6

I had just embarked on the iceball project when we heard tire chains come clanking from afar. A black Buick was moving toward us down the street. We all spread out, banged together some regular snowballs, took aim, and, when the Buick drew nigh, fired. 7

A soft snowball hit the driver's windshield right before the driver's face. It made a smashed star with a hump in the middle. 8

Often, of course, we hit our target, but this time, the only time in all of 9
life, the car pulled over and stopped. Its wide black door opened; a man got
out of it, running. He didn't even close the car door.

He ran after us, and we ran away from him, up the snowy Reynolds side- 10
walk. At the corner, I looked back; incredibly, he was still after us. He was in
city clothes: a suit and tie, street shoes. Any normal adult would have quit,
having sprung us into flight and made his point. This man was gaining on us.
He was a thin man, all action. All of a sudden, we were running for our lives.

Wordless, we split up. We were on our turf; we could lose ourselves in 11
the neighborhood backyards, everyone for himself. I paused and considered.
Everyone had vanished except Mikey Fahey, who was just rounding the corner of a yellow brick house. Poor Mikey, I trailed him. The driver of the Buick
sensibly picked the two of us to follow. The man apparently had all day.

He chased Mikey and me around the yellow house and up a backyard 12
path we knew by heart: under a low tree, up a bank, through a hedge, down
some snowy steps, and across the grocery store's delivery driveway. We
smashed through a gap in another hedge, entered a scruffy backyard and ran
around its back porch and tight between houses to Edgerton Avenue; we ran
across Edgerton to an alley and up our own sliding woodpile to the Halls'
front yard; he kept coming. We ran up Lloyd Street and wound through mazy
backyards toward the steep hilltop at Willard and Lang.

He chased us silently, block after block. He chased us silently over picket 13
fences, through thorny hedges, between houses, around garbage cans, and
across streets. Every time I glanced back, choking for breath, I expected he
would have quit. He must have been as breathless as we were. His jacket
strained over his body. It was an immense discovery, pounding into my hot
head with every sliding, joyous step, that this ordinary adult evidently knew
what I thought only children who trained at football knew: that you have to
fling yourself at what you're doing, you have to point yourself, forget yourself,
aim, dive.

Mikey and I had nowhere to go, in our own neighborhood or out of it, 14
but away from this man who was chasing us. He impelled us forward; we
compelled him to follow our route. The air was cold; every breath tore my
throat. We kept running, block after block; we kept improvising, backyard
after backyard, running a frantic course and choosing it simultaneously, failing always to find small places or hard places to slow him down, and discovering always, exhilarated, dismayed, that only bare speed could save us — for
he would never give up, this man — and we were losing speed.

He chased us through the backyard labyrinths of ten blocks before he 15
caught us by our jackets. He caught us and we all stopped.

We three stood staggering, half blinded, coughing, in an obscure hilltop 16
backyard: a man in his twenties, a boy, a girl. He had released our jackets, our

pursuer, our captor, our hero: He knew we weren't going anywhere. We all played by the rules. Mikey and I unzipped our jackets. I pulled off my sopping mittens. Our tracks multiplied in the backyard's new snow. We had been breaking new snow all morning. We didn't look at each other. I was cherishing my excitement. The man's lower pants legs were wet; his cuffs were full of snow, and there was a prow of snow beneath them on his shoes and socks. Some trees bordered the little flat backyard, some messy winter trees. There was no one around: a clearing in a grove, and we the only players.

It was a long time before he could speak. I had some difficulty at first   17
recalling why we were there. My lips felt swollen; I couldn't see out of the sides of my eyes; I kept coughing.

"You stupid kids," he began perfunctorily.   18

We listened perfunctorily indeed, if we listened at all, for the chewing   19
out was redundant, a mere formality, and beside the point. The point was that he had chased us passionately without giving up, and so he had caught us. Now he came down to earth. I wanted the glory to last forever.

But how could the glory have lasted forever? We could have run through   20
every backyard in North America until we got to Panama. But when he trapped us at the lip of the Panama Canal, what precisely could he have done to prolong the drama of the chase and cap its glory? I brooded about this for the next few years. He could only have fried Mikey Fahey and me in boiling oil, say, or dismembered us piecemeal, or staked us to anthills. None of which I really wanted, and none of which any adult was likely to do, even in the spirit of fun. He could only chew us out there in the Panamanian jungle, after months or years of exalting pursuit. He could only begin, "You stupid kids," and continue in his ordinary Pittsburgh accent with his normal righteous anger and the usual common sense.

If in that snowy backyard the driver of the black Buick had cut off our   21
heads, Mikey's and mine, I would have died happy, for nothing has required so much of me since as being chased all over Pittsburgh in the middle of winter — running terrified, exhausted — by this sainted, skinny, furious redheaded man who wished to have a word with us. I don't know how he found his way back to his car.

■ Thinking Critically about the Text

As a child, did you ever do something exhilarating, satisfying, or fun even though you knew that it was "wrong"? Compare your experience to Dillard's. To what extent should children be held responsible for their deliberate misbehavior? What would have been an appropriate consequence for Dillard and her companions? If you had chased them down, what would you have done?

■ Questions on Subject

1. In this essay, Dillard separates the behavior of boys from that of both girls and adults. What characteristics does she identify that distinguish the actions of boys? Why is she able to play with them?
2. What is Dillard's main point? Where does she state it explicitly?
3. Why was the driver "sensible" to choose Mikey and the author as the targets of his chase?
4. What made the chase so unusual and exciting? Why was the end of the chase disappointing? Was there any way it could have ended that would have been more satisfying to the author? Why or why not?

■ Questions on Strategy

1. In an unusual rhetorical strategy, Dillard opens her essay in the first person but immediately switches to second person. (Glossary: *Point of View*) What is her purpose for using two points of view and especially for shifting from one to the other? In what ways does Dillard's use of the second-person point of view evoke childhood?
2. This narrative essay begins with two nonnarrative introductory paragraphs whose connection to the rest of the story may not be immediately clear. Note especially the apparently paradoxical sentence that closes the introduction: "I got in trouble throwing snowballs, and have seldom been happier since." (Glossary: *Paradox*) How do these paragraphs, and particularly this sentence, help the reader understand the story that follows?
3. The event that prompted this narrative was in itself small and seemingly insignificant, but Dillard describes it with such intensity that the reader is left in no doubt as to its tremendous significance for her. Show how she uses carefully crafted description to lift her story from the ordinary to the remarkable. (Glossary: *Description*)

■ Questions on Diction and Vocabulary

1. In paragraph 14, Dillard describes the chase using parallel word structures: "He impelled us forward; we compelled him to follow our route." In paragraph 16, find the parallel noun phrases that Dillard uses to characterize the young man who chased them. What is the impact on the reader of these parallel word structures? (Glossary: *Parallelism*) This essay contains numerous examples of parallelism; find several others that add to the impact you have identified.
2. Notice the use of strong verbs (*flung, popped, smashed*) throughout the narrative. How do strong verbs work to enhance a narrative?
3. Dillard uses a great deal of description in her narrative essay. Look up and define these words, vital to her descriptions, as she uses them: *crenellated* (paragraph 5), *reverted* (5), *turf* (11), *impelled* (14), *compelled* (14), *labyrinths* (15), *obscure* (16), *perfunctorily* (18, 19),

exalting (20). How do these words contribute to the impact of the finished piece?

■ Classroom Activity Using Narration

The number of words or paragraphs a writer devotes to the retelling of an event does not usually correspond to the number of minutes or hours the event took to happen. A writer may require multiple paragraphs to recount an important or complex ten- or twenty-minute encounter but then pass over several hours, days, or even years in several sentences. In narration, length has less to do with chronological real time than with the amount of emphasis the writer wants to give to a particular incident. Identify several passages in Dillard's essay where she uses multiple paragraphs to retell a relatively brief encounter and where she uses a paragraph or two to cover a long period of time. Why do you suppose Dillard chose to tell her story in this manner?

■ Writing Suggestions

1. Children know what it means to plunge headlong, fearlessly and eagerly, into a challenging situation. One of the most wonderful encounters a child can have is with an adult who is still able to summon up that child-like enthusiasm — one who can put aside grown-up ideas of respectability and caution in order to accomplish something. In this narrative, Dillard reveres a man who is willing to pursue his young tormentors until he catches them. Recall and write about an enthusiastic adult — a parent, a relative, a teacher, a chance acquaintance — who abandoned grown-up behavior to inspire you as a child. In what way did he or she do so? As Annie Dillard does, make your story lively and detailed.

2. **Writing with Sources.** After reading the selection from *An American Childhood*, how accountable do you think children should be for their misconduct or poor performance? Using Dillard's essay and your own experience, write an essay in which you look at the question of holding people responsible for their actions. Your essay could take the form of an argument, in which you take a definite position, or of a narrative, in which you tell the story of a childhood punishment that you received or witnessed. If you choose to narrate a childhood experience, be sure to be clear about your response to the punishment: Was it justified? Appropriate? Effective? Why or why not? You might find it helpful to talk with your parents or another adult about the incident and to review what you wrote in response to Thinking Critically about the Text. In addition, it might be useful to exchange "punishment" stories with classmates and discuss the issues that arise before you start writing.

For models of and advice on integrating sources, see Chapters 14–15.

Stranger Than True

BARRY WINSTON

Barry Winston is a practicing attorney in Chapel Hill, North Carolina. He was born in New York City in 1934 and served in the Marine Corps from 1953 to 1955. He later graduated from the University of North Carolina, from which he also received his law degree. His specialty is criminal law. He was admitted to the North Carolina Bar in 1961 and for almost fifty years has been an active defense lawyer. He is listed in the *Bar Register of Preeminent Lawyers*.

"Stranger Than True" was published in *Harper's* magazine in December 1986. In the story, Winston recounts his experience defending a young college graduate accused of driving while under the influence of alcohol and causing his sister's death. The story is characterized by Winston's energetic and strong voice. In commenting on his use of narrative detail, Winston says, "I could have made it twice as long, but it wouldn't have been as good a story." What do you think he meant by this comment?

■ Preparing to Read

The American judicial system works on the basis of the presumption of innocence. In short, you are innocent until proven guilty. But what about a situation in which all the evidence seems to point to a person's guilt? What's the purpose of a trial in such a case?

L et me tell you a story. A true story. The court records are all there if anyone   1
wants to check. It's three years ago. I'm sitting in my office, staring out the window, when I get a call from a lawyer I hardly know. Tax lawyer. Some kid is in trouble and would I be interested in helping him out? He's charged with manslaughter, a felony, and driving under the influence. I tell him sure, have the kid call me.

So the kid calls and makes an appointment to see me. He's a nice kid, fresh   2
out of college, and he's come down here to spend some time with his older sister, who's in med school. One day she tells him they're invited to a cookout with some friends of hers. She's going directly from class, and he's going to take her car and meet her there. It's way out in the country, but he gets there before she does, introduces himself around, and pops a beer. She shows up after a while and he pops another beer. Then he eats a hamburger and drinks a third beer. At some point his sister says, "Well, it's about time to go," and they head for the car.

> The next thing he remembers, he's waking up in a hospital room, hurting like hell, bandages and casts all over him, and somebody is telling him he's charged with manslaughter and DUI . . .

And, the kid tells me, sitting there in my office, the next thing he remembers, he's waking up in a hospital room, hurting like hell, bandages and casts all over him, and somebody is telling him he's charged with manslaughter and DUI because he wrecked his sister's car, killed her in the process, and blew fourteen on the Breathalyzer. I ask him what the hell he means by "the next thing he remembers," and he looks me straight in the eye and says he can't remember anything from the time they leave the cookout until he wakes up in the hospital. He tells me the doctors say he has post-retrograde amnesia. I say of course I believe him, but I'm worried about finding a judge who'll believe him.

I agree to represent him and send somebody for a copy of the wreck report. It says there are four witnesses: a couple in a car going the other way who passed the kid and his sister just before their car ran off the road, the guy whose front yard they landed in, and the trooper who investigated. I call the guy whose yard they ended up in. He isn't home. I leave word. Then I call the couple. The wife agrees to come in the next day with her husband. While I'm talking to her, the first guy calls. I call him back, introduce myself, tell him I'm representing the kid and need to talk to him about the accident. He hems and haws and I figure he's one of those people who think it's against the law to talk to defense lawyers. I say the D.A. will tell him it's O.K. to talk to me, but he doesn't have to. I give him the name and number of the D.A. and he says he'll call me back.

Then I go out and hunt up the trooper. He tells me the whole story. The kid and his sister are coming into town on Smith Level Road, after it turns from fifty-five to forty-five. The Thornes — the couple — are heading out of town. They say this sports car passes them, going the other way, right after that bad turn just south of the new subdivision. They say it's going like a striped-ass ape, at least sixty-five or seventy. Mrs. Thorne turns around to look and Mr. Thorne watches in the rearview mirror. They both see the same thing: halfway into the curve, the car runs off the road on the right, whips back onto the road, spins, runs off on the left, and disappears. They turn around in the first driveway they come to and start back, both terrified of what they're going to find. By this time, Trooper Johnson says, the guy whose front yard the car has ended up in has pulled the kid and his sister out of the wreck and started CPR on the girl. Turns out he's an emergency medical technician. Holloway, that's his name. Johnson tells me that Holloway says he's sitting in his front room, watching television, when he hears a hell of a crash in his yard. He runs outside and finds the car flipped over, and so he pulls the kid out from the driver's side, the girl from the other side. She dies in his arms.

And that, says Trooper Johnson, is that. The kid's blood/alcohol content   6
was fourteen, he was going way too fast, *and* the girl is dead. He had to charge
him. It's a shame, he seems a nice kid, it was his own sister and all, but what the
hell can he do, right?

The next day the Thornes come in, and they confirm everything Johnson   7
said. By now things are looking not so hot for my client, and I'm thinking it's
about time to have a little chat with the D.A. But Holloway still hasn't called me
back, so I call him. Not home. Leave word. No call. I wait a couple of days and
call again. Finally I get him on the phone. He's very agitated, and won't talk to
me except to say that he doesn't have to talk to me.

I know I better look for a deal, so I go to the D.A. He's very sympathetic.   8
But. There's only so far you can get on sympathy. A young woman is dead,
promising career cut short, all because somebody has too much to drink and
drives. The kid has to pay. Not, the D.A. says, with jail time. But he's got to plead
guilty to two misdemeanors: death by vehicle and driving under the influence.
That means probation, a big fine. Several thousand dollars. Still, it's hard for me
to criticize the D.A. After all, he's probably going to have the MADD mothers
all over him because of reducing the felony to a misdemeanor.

On the day of the trial, I get to court a few minutes early. There are the   9
Thornes and Trooper Johnson, and someone I assume is Holloway. Sure enough,
when this guy sees me, he comes over and introduces himself and starts right
in: "I just want you to know how serious all this drinking and driving really is,"
he says. "If those young people hadn't been drinking and driving that night,
that poor young girl would be alive today." Now, I'm trying to hold my temper
when I spot the D.A. I bolt across the room, grab him by the arm, and say, "We
gotta talk. Why the hell have you got all those people here? That jerk Holloway.
Surely to God you're not going to call him as a witness. This is a guilty plea!
My client's parents are sitting out there. You don't need to put them through a
dog-and-pony show."

The D.A. looks at me and says, "Man, I'm sorry, but in a case like this, I   10
gotta put on witnesses. Weird Wally is on the bench. If I try to go without witnesses, he might throw me out."

The D.A. calls his first witness. Trooper Johnson identifies himself,   11
tells about being called to the scene of the accident, and describes what he
found when he got there and what everybody told him. After he finishes,
the judge looks at me. "No questions," I say. Then the D.A. calls Holloway.
He describes the noise, running out of the house, the upside-down car in
his yard, pulling my client out of the window on the left side of the car and
then going around to the other side for the girl. When he gets to this part,
he really hits his stride. He describes, in minute detail, the injuries he saw
and what he did to try and save her life. And then he tells, breath by breath,
how she died in his arms.

The D.A. says, "No further questions, your Honor." The judge looks at me. 12
I shake my head, and he says to Holloway, "You may step down."

One of those awful silences hangs there, and nothing happens for a minute. 13
Holloway doesn't move. Then he looks at me, and at the D.A., and then at the
judge. He says, "Can I say something else, your Honor?"

All my bells are ringing at once, and my gut is screaming at me, Object! 14
Object! I'm trying to decide in three quarters of a second whether it'll be worse
to listen to a lecture on the evils of drink from this jerk Holloway or piss off
the judge by objecting. But all I say is, "No objections, your Honor." The judge
smiles at me, then at Holloway, and says, "Very well, Mr. Holloway. What did
you wish to say?"

It all comes out in a rush. "Well, you see, your Honor," Holloway says, 15
"it was just like I told Trooper Johnson. It all happened so fast. I heard the
noise, and I came running out, and it was night, and I was excited, and the
next morning, when I had a chance to think about it, I figured out what had
happened, but by then I'd already told Trooper Johnson and I didn't know what
to do, but you see, the car, it was upside down, and I did pull that boy out of
the left-hand window, but don't you see, the car was upside down, and if you
turned it over on its wheels like it's supposed to be, the left-hand side is really
on the right-hand side, and your Honor, that boy wasn't driving that car at all.
It was the girl that was driving, and when I had a chance to think about it the
next morning, I realized that I'd told Trooper Johnson wrong, and I was scared
and I didn't know what to do, and that's why" — and now he's looking right at
me — "why I wouldn't talk to you."

Naturally, the defendant is allowed to withdraw his guilty plea. The charges 16
are dismissed and the kid and his parents and I go into one of the back rooms
in the courthouse and sit there looking at one another for a while. Finally, we
recover enough to mumble some Oh my Gods and Thank yous and You're
welcomes. And that's why I can stand to represent somebody when I know
he's guilty. ∎

∎ Thinking Critically about the Text

Much abuse is heaped on lawyers who defend clients whose guilt seems
obvious. How does Winston's story help explain why lawyers need to
defend "guilty" clients?

∎ Questions on Subject

1. Why does the D.A. bring in witnesses for a case that has been
   plea-bargained? What is ironic about that decision? (Glossary: *Irony*)

2. Why was Holloway reluctant to be interviewed by Winston about what he saw and did in the aftermath of the accident? What might he have been afraid of?
3. Why did Holloway finally ask to speak to the court? Why do you suppose Winston chose not to object to Holloway's request?
4. What do you think is the point of Winston's narrative?

■ Questions on Strategy

1. Winston establishes the context for his story in the first three paragraphs. What basic information does he give readers?
2. What details does Winston choose to include in the story? Why does he include them? Is there other information that you would like to have had? Why do you suppose Winston chose to omit that information?
3. Explain how Winston uses sentence variety to pace his narrative. What effect do his short sentences and sentence fragments have on you?
4. What does Winston gain as a writer by telling us that this is "a true story," one that we can check out in the court records?
5. During the courtroom scene (paragraphs 9–15), Winston relies heavily on dialogue. (Glossary: *Dialogue*) What does he gain by using dialogue? Why do you suppose he uses dialogue sparingly in the other parts of his narrative?
6. How does Winston use description to differentiate the four witnesses to the accident? (Glossary: *Description*) Why is it important for him to give his readers some idea of their differing characters?

■ Questions on Diction and Vocabulary

1. How would you characterize Winston's voice in this story? How is that voice established? (Glossary: *Voice*)
2. What, if anything, does Winston's diction tell you about Winston himself? (Glossary: *Diction*) What effect does his diction have on the tone of his narrative? (Glossary: *Tone*)
3. Refer to your desk dictionary to determine the meanings of the following words as Winston uses them in this selection: *felony* (paragraph 1), *agitated* (7), *misdemeanor* (8), *probation* (8), *bolt* (9).

■ Classroom Activity Using Narration

Effective narration uses strong verbs and clear, vivid description. Newspaper writers, because they must concisely and vividly evoke everyday events, are acutely aware of the need for effective narration. It is not enough for them to say that the city council discussed the resolution, the tornado happened, or the team won; they must choose language that efficiently brings the discussion, the weather, and the game to life. For this reason, verbs such as *argued, tore, destroyed, buried, trounced,* and the like are common in the headlines of our local papers, and great care is taken to ensure that meaning is conveyed efficiently but accurately.

Sometimes these efforts go astray. As an exercise in both editing for and using strong verbs, consider the following real newspaper headlines— headlines that should have been reconsidered before the paper went to press. First, identify the source of the unintended humor in each head-line. Then—as illustrated in the sample below—rewrite the headline using effective narration techniques.

Sample headline: **Red Tape Holds Up New Bridges**

Bureaucratic   Delays
Edited headline: ₐ**Red Tape** ₐ~~Holds Up~~ **New Bridges**

New Study of Obesity Looks for Larger Test Group

Kids Make Nutritious Snacks

Local High School Dropouts Cut in Half

Hospitals Sued by 7 Foot Doctors

Police Begin Campaign to Run Down Jaywalkers

Typhoon Rips Through Cemetery: Hundreds Dead

Man Kills Self Before Shooting Wife and Daughter

Juvenile Court to Try Shooting Defendant

If Strike Isn't Settled Quickly, It May Last Awhile

■ **Writing Suggestions**

1. "Stranger Than True" is a first-person narrative told from the defense lawyer's point of view. Imagine that you are a newspaper reporter covering this case. What changes would you have to make in Winston's narrative to make it a news story? Make a list of the changes you would have to make, and then rewrite the story.

2. Holloway's revelation in the courtroom catches everyone by surprise. Analyze the chain of events in the accident and the assumptions that people made based on the accounts of those events. After reading the introduction to Chapter 11 (Cause and Effect Analysis), write a cause and effect essay in which you explain some of the possible reasons why Holloway's confession is so unexpected. (Glossary: *Cause and Effect Analysis*)

Not Close Enough for Comfort

DAVID P. BARDEEN

 David P. Bardeen was born in 1974 in New Haven, Connecticut, and grew up in Seattle, Washington. He graduated cum laude from Harvard University in 1996 and then worked for J. P. Morgan & Co. as an investment banking analyst. In 2002, he received his J.D. from the New York University School of Law, where he was the managing editor of the *Law Review*. After graduation, he joined the law firm of Cleary, Gottlieb, Steen & Hamilton and became a member of the New York Bar. Bardeen is proficient in Spanish, and his practice focuses on international business transactions involving clients in Latin America. A freelance writer on a variety of topics, he is also active with Immigration Equality, a national organization fighting for equality for lesbian, gay, bisexual, transgender, and HIV-positive immigrants.

In the following article, which appeared in the *New York Times Magazine* on February 29, 2004, Bardeen tells the story of a lunch meeting at which he reveals a secret to his twin brother, a secret that had derailed their relationship for almost fifteen years.

■ Preparing to Read

Recall a time when a parent, sibling, friend, teacher, or some other person close to you kept a secret from you. How did the secret affect your relationship? How did you feel once the secret was revealed? How has the relationship fared since?

I had wanted to tell Will I was gay since I was twelve. As twins, we shared 1 everything back then: clothes, gadgets, thoughts, secrets. Everything except this. So when we met for lunch more than a year ago, I thought that finally coming out to him would close the distance that had grown between us. When we were kids, we created our own language, whispering to each other as our bewildered parents looked on. Now, at twenty-eight, we had never been further apart.

I asked him about his recent trip. He asked me about work. Short ques- 2 tions. One-word answers. Then an awkward pause.

Will was one of the last to know. Partly it was his fault. He is hard to pin down 3 for brunch or a drink, and this was not the sort of conversation I wanted to have over the phone. I had actually been trying to tell him for more than a month, but he kept canceling at the last minute — a friend was in town, he'd met a girl.

But part of me was relieved. This was the talk I had feared the most. Coming out is, in an unforgiving sense, an admission of fraud. Fraud against yourself primarily, but also fraud against your family and friends. So, once I resolved to tell my secret, I confessed to my most recent "victims" first. I told my friends from law school — those I had met just a few years earlier and deceived the least — then I worked back through college to the handful of high-school friends I still keep in touch with. **4**

> I had wanted to tell Will I was gay since I was 12. As twins, we shared every-thing back then: clothes, gadgets, thoughts, secrets. Everything except this.

Keeping my sexuality from my parents had always seemed permissible, so our sit-down chat did not stress me out as much as it might have. We all mislead our parents. "I'm too sick for school today." "No, I wasn't drinking." "Yes, Mom, I'm fine. Don't worry about me." That deception is understood and, in some sense, expected. But twins expect complete transparency, however romantic the notion. **5**

Although our lives unfolded along parallel tracks — we went to college together, both moved to New York and had many of the same friends — Will and I quietly drifted apart. When he moved abroad for a year, we lost touch almost entirely. Our mother and father didn't think this was strange, because like many parents of twins, they wanted us to follow divergent paths. But friends were baffled when we began to rely on third parties for updates on each other's lives. "How's Will?" someone would ask. "You tell me," I would respond. One mutual friend, sick of playing the intermediary, once sent me an e-mail message with a carbon copy to Will. "Dave, meet Will, your twin," it said. "Will, let me introduce you to Dave." **6**

Now, here we were, at lunch, just the two of us. "There's something I've been meaning to tell you," I said. "I'm gay." I looked at him closely, at the edges of his mouth, the wrinkles around his eyes, for some hint of what he was thinking. **7**

"O.K.," he said evenly. **8**

"I've been meaning to tell you for a while," I said. **9**

"Uh-huh." He asked me a few questions but seemed slightly uneasy, as if he wasn't sure he wanted to hear the answers. Do Mom and Dad know? Are you seeing anyone? How long have you known you were gay? I hesitated. **10**

I've known since I was young, and to some degree, I thought Will had always known. How else to explain my adolescent melancholy, my withdrawal, the silence when the subject changed to girls, sex, and who was hot. As a teen-ager I watched, as if from a distance, as my demeanor went from outspoken to sullen. I had assumed, in the self-centered way kids often do, that everyone noticed this change — and that my brother had guessed the reason. To be fair, he asked me once in our twenties, after I had ended yet another brief relationship with a woman. "Of course I'm not gay," I told him, as if the notion were absurd. **11**

"How long have you known?" he asked again.   12

"About fifteen years," I said. Will looked away.   13

Food arrived. We ate and talked about other things. Mom, Dad, the mayor,   14
and the weather. We asked for the check and agreed to get together again soon.
No big questions, no heart to heart. Just disclosure, explanation, follow-up,
conclusion. But what could I expect? I had shut him out for so long that I suppose ultimately he gave up. Telling my brother I was gay hadn't made us close,
as I had naively hoped it would; instead it underscored just how much we had
strayed apart.

As we left the restaurant, I felt the urge to apologize, not for being gay, of   15
course, but for the years I'd kept him in the dark, for his being among the last to
know. He hailed a cab. It stopped. He stepped inside, the door still open.

"I'm sorry," I said.   16

He smiled. "No, I think it's great."   17

A nice gesture. Supportive. But I think he misunderstood.   18

A year later, we are still only creeping toward the intimacy everyone   19
expects us to have. Although we live three blocks away from each other, I can't
say we see each other every week or even every two weeks. But with any luck,
next year, I'll be the one updating our mutual friends on Will's life. ■

■ Thinking Critically about the Text

How do you think Will felt when David announced that he was gay? Do
you think Will had any clue about David's sexual orientation? What in
Will's response to David's announcement led you to this conclusion? Why
do you think it has been so difficult for them to recapture the "intimacy
everyone expects [them] to have" (paragraph 19) in the year following
David's coming out to Will?

■ Questions on Subject

1. Why do you suppose Bardeen chose to keep his sexual orientation
   a secret from his brother? Why was this particular "coming-out"
   so difficult? Was Bardeen realistic in thinking that "Will had always
   known" (paragraph 11) that he was gay?
2. What does Bardeen mean when he says, "But twins expect complete transparency, however romantic the notion" (paragraph 5)?
3. Why does Bardeen feel the need to apologize to his brother as they
   part? Do you think his brother understood the meaning of the apology? Why or why not?

4. What do you think Bardeen had hoped would happen after he confided his secret to his brother? Was this hope unrealistic?

5. What harm had Bardeen's secret done to his relationship with his brother? What is necessary to heal the relationship?

■ Questions on Strategy

1. Bardeen narrates his coming-out using the first-person pronoun *I*. (Glossary: *Point of View*) Why is the first person particularly appropriate for telling a story such as this one? Explain.

2. How has Bardeen organized his narrative? (Glossary: *Organization*) In paragraphs 3 through 6, Bardeen uses flashbacks to give readers a context for his relationship with his twin. What would have been lost or gained had he begun his essay with paragraphs 3 through 6?

3. During the lunch meeting part of the narrative (paragraphs 7–17), Bardeen uses dialogue. (Glossary: *Dialogue*) What does he gain by doing this? Why do you suppose he uses dialogue sparingly elsewhere?

4. Bardeen uses a number of short sentences and deliberate sentence fragments. What effect do these have on you? Why do you suppose he uses some sentence fragments instead of complete sentences?

5. Bardeen's title plays on the old saying "too close for comfort." What does his title suggest to you? (Glossary: *Title*) How effectively does it capture the essence of his relationship with his brother? Explain.

6. In paragraphs 6 and 11 Bardeen uses comparison and contrast to highlight the similarities and differences between himself and Will. (Glossary: *Comparison and Contrast*) Which did you find more interesting and revealing, the similarities or differences? Why?

■ Questions on Diction and Vocabulary

1. How would you describe Bardeen's voice in this narrative? How is that voice established? What, if anything, does Bardeen's diction tell you about him as a person? (Glossary: *Diction*) Explain.

2. Bardeen says that "[c]oming out is, in an unforgiving sense, an admission of fraud" (paragraph 4). Why do you suppose he uses the word *fraud* to describe how he felt about his coming-out? What does he mean when he says "in an unforgiving sense"? What other words might he have used instead of *fraud*?

3. Refer to your desk dictionary to determine the meanings of the following words as Bardeen uses them in this selection: *baffled* (paragraph 6), *melancholy* (11), *demeanor* (11), *sullen* (11), *intimacy* (19).

■ Classroom Activity Using Narration

Beginning at the beginning and ending at the end is not the only way to tell a story. Think of the individual incidents or events in a story that you would like to tell or perhaps one that you are already working on. Don't write the story itself; simply make a list of the events that you need to include. Be sure to identify at least six to ten key events in your story. Start by listing the events in chronological order. Now play with the arrangement of those events; try to develop one or two alternative sequences that include the use of flashback. Using your list of events, discuss with other class members how flashback can improve the dramatic impact of your narrative.

■ Writing Suggestions

1. Using your Preparing to Read response for this selection, write an essay about a secret you once had and how it affected relationships with those close to you. What exactly was your secret? Why did you decide to keep this information secret? How did you feel while you kept your secret? What happened when you revealed your secret? What insights into secrets do you have as a result of this experience?

2. In paragraph 4 Bardeen states, "So, once I resolved to tell my secret, I confessed to my most recent 'victims' first. I told my friends from law school — those I had met just a few years earlier and deceived the least — then I worked back through college to the handful of high-school friends I still keep in touch with." Write an essay in which you compare and contrast your level of honesty among your friends or a larger community and your level of honesty among your family or people with whom you are very close. (Glossary: *Comparison and Contrast*) Are there secrets you would be more likely to share with one group than another? If so, how would you classify those secrets? (Glossary: *Classification; Division*) Do you think it is easier to be honest with people who do or do not know you very well? Why?

3. In paragraph 4 Bardeen states, "Coming out is, in an unforgiving sense, an admission of fraud. Fraud against yourself primarily, but also fraud against your family and friends." Do you agree with Bardeen, or do you think he is being too hard on himself? Explain.

4. The "coming out" photograph on the next page of college students at a gay rights rally was taken on October 11, 2003 — National Coming Out Day — in Austin, Texas. How do you "read" this photograph? (For a discussion of how to analyze photographs and other visual texts, see pages 11–14.) Why do you suppose viewers' eyes are drawn to the young man's T-shirt? How do you interpret the message on his T-shirt? What significance, if any, do you attach to his being the only one wearing sunglasses? In your mind, is the young man being forthright, or is he holding back? Using Bardeen's essay, this photograph, and your own observations and experiences, write an essay about the mixed feelings and emotions as well as the potential misunderstandings attendant on "coming out."

National Coming Out Day rally, October 11, 2003

Vernon Can Read!

VERNON E. JORDAN JR.

Prominent civil rights lawyer, business executive, and Washington power broker Vernon E. Jordan Jr. was born in Atlanta, Georgia, in 1935. Jordan attended DePauw University, where he was the only African American student in his class; he majored in political science and graduated in 1957. Next he enrolled at Howard University School of Law, and upon graduation in 1960 he joined the nationwide effort to desegregate the U.S. educational system. In a landmark event in 1961, Jordan helped escort Charlayne Hunter past angry white protesters on her way to the admissions office at the University of Georgia. Later, Jordan served as the Georgia field director for the NAACP and as director of the Voter Education Project for the Southern Regional Council. In 1970 he became the executive director of the United Negro College Fund, and a year later he was appointed president and CEO of the National Urban League. He survived a white supremacist's assassination attempt in 1980 and later resigned from the National Urban League to return to private law practice. A close friend of former president Bill Clinton, Jordan served on the transition team shortly after Clinton was elected president in 1992. He is the author of two books, *Vernon Can Read! A Memoir* (2001) and *Make It Plain: Standing Up and Speaking Out* (2008). For his dedication to volunteerism, Jordan received the Alexis de Tocqueville Award from the United Way in 1977, and in 2001 he was singled out by the NAACP for its highest award — the Spingarn Medal, an honor given to "the man or woman of African descent and American citizenship who shall have made the highest achievement during the preceding year or years in any honorable field of human endeavor."

In the following selection from *Vernon Can Read!*, Jordan recounts how he earned money for college working as the chauffeur for former Atlanta mayor Robert Maddox. His story starts in the year 1955. As you read Jordan's narrative, notice how he uses dialogue to bring the important scenes to life.

■ **Preparing to Read**

Describe what race relations are like where you live. Is there clear evidence of racism in daily life, or are such attitudes subtle and kept under wraps? Have you noticed any changes in race relations since Barack Obama was elected president in 2008?

In the summer of 1955, at the end of my sophomore year in college, I worked as a chauffeur in my hometown of Atlanta, Georgia. It had not been my first choice of jobs. I was originally supposed to work as a salesman for the Continental Insurance Company, which had made me an offer during a campus interview at my school, DePauw University. When the interviewer said there was an opening for me in the company's Atlanta office, I jumped at the chance. It was the perfect arrangement for me. I would have a job in the place where I most wanted to be — at home in Atlanta. At the end of the term, brimming with the confidence of a young man with two years of college behind me, I packed my bags and headed south thinking everything was in place. 1

> **I sat there day after day, drinking in the atmosphere of the place—the smell of the books, the feel of them, the easy chairs.**

After a few days settling in with my family, I put on my best suit and headed downtown to the Fulton National Bank Building, where Continental had its offices. I went up to the receptionist's desk to present myself. 2

"My name is Vernon Jordan," I said. "I'm a student at DePauw University, and I'm here to begin my summer internship." 3

The receptionist seemed in need of a translator to help clarify what I had just said. She was, at that moment, like a machine whose gears had ground to a halt and was struggling to get restarted. When she finally realized she'd heard what she thought she'd heard, she called for the man in charge of summer workers. "You won't believe this," she told him, "but there's a colored boy out here who says he's a summer intern." 4

The supervisor, a tall fellow who looked to be in his mid-thirties, came out. I introduced myself. 5

"I'm Vernon Jordan. I was hired to be a summer intern in your office." 6

His reaction was not unlike the receptionist's. But he quickly composed himself and took me inside his office. An awkward moment passed before he said, "They didn't tell us." 7

"They didn't tell you what?" I asked, even though I suspected where he was heading. 8

"They didn't tell us you were colored," he replied. At that time in history, we had not yet become "black." 9

He went on. "You know, you can't work here. It's just impossible. You just can't." 10

Of course, segregation was still very much a fact of life in Georgia in the summer of 1955. I was well aware of that, and of the rules that were still propping up the system. But I had thought — hoped — during those months after my interview that I had somehow made my way around them. It was my policy then, and it remains the same today, never to expect defeat before making 11 an honest effort. Also, by then I'd come to think of Jim Crow as a lame horse that was about to be put down. The feeling was in the air. And I wanted to do whatever I could to help speed the process along. But it wouldn't happen on that day at the Continental Insurance Company.

Although I was disappointed, I knew there was nothing to be done about 12 the situation at that particular moment. As I got up to go, my never-to-be-supervisor, not wanting to leave things as they stood, said, "I'll tell you what I'll do. I'm going to call J. L. Wolfe Realty. We do business with them sometimes, and we can see if they can give you an office."

While Continental was willing to honor its commitment to hire me, under 13 no circumstances could I sit in its offices as an employee. J. L. Wolfe Realty, a black-owned real estate and insurance business on Auburn Avenue — "Sweet Auburn," the heart of Atlanta's black business district — was the proposed solution.

The Continental representative called Wolfe Realty and explained the 14 situation. The head of the company agreed to give me an office out of which I sold Continental's income-protection insurance policies to black businesses employing five or more people. On occasion, my white supervisor came down to my office to make calls.

It was absurd. As a black person, I could not sell the policies of a white 15 company to black businesses while sitting in the white company's office. Yet my white supervisor could come in to the black business office and sell the white company's policies to black firms. This was a prime example of the craziness, the backwardness, the inefficiency of Southern life.

The job was also very boring. . . . When I could stand it no longer, my 16 mother, who knew I was deeply unhappy, suggested an alternative. The summer was passing, and the opportunities for other office jobs had dwindled. I wanted to work. So why not, she asked, work the balance of the time using other skills I had? I was a good driver and, like many young men in the 1950s, I was in love with cars. My mother ran a catering business, which meant she had contacts within most, if not all, the prominent white households in Atlanta.

That is how I became a chauffeur for Robert F. Maddox. 17

Robert Maddox was one of the leading figures in Atlanta's white elite 18 for most of the early part of the twentieth century. He was mayor of the city in 1910, and before that he had been active in the civic and social affairs of the town. A man of finance, he was the president of the First National Bank of Atlanta and president of the American Banking Association. Maddox's interests and influence were wide-ranging. He had a fabulous garden on his grounds and was, for a time, the president of the Garden Clubs of America.

In many ways Maddox was a symbol of the New South — open to busi- 19 ness and economic development and devoted to progress, as long as it was within certain boundaries. When Booker T. Washington gave his famous

Atlanta Exposition address (sometimes called the Atlanta Compromise), Maddox had been among the dignitaries on the platform, listening while the "wizard of Tuskegee" assured whites that blacks would make no immediate press for social equality.

Maddox was very proud of having built the first very large home in Buckhead, one of Atlanta's most exclusive neighborhoods. When I encountered him, he was well into his eighties, a widower living alone in that spectacular house, attended by a small group of servants: Joe, the chauffeur and butler, whose place I took for the month of August, when he was away; Lizzie, the cook, a middle-aged woman who played the piano at the Mount Zion Baptist Church; and Troy, the yardman. `20`

Every morning I picked up Lizzie and brought her to work. If needed, I would then press one of Maddox's Palm Beach suits as Lizzie fixed his breakfast. When she finished doing that, she would take the meal up to Maddox and then return to prepare my breakfast, which I ate in the butler's pantry. Lizzie also made breakfast for Troy. But Troy worked in the yard and, according to age-old protocol, was not allowed to eat inside the house. His meal was handed out to him by Lizzie, and he sat on the back porch of that huge southern house and had his breakfast. `21`

My routine varied little. Maddox, in his old age, was a creature of habit. He would come downstairs, get his hat, and select one of his many walking canes. We'd go out to the car, a four-door blue Cadillac. In a bid for independence, Maddox usually insisted upon opening the passenger door himself, although he could have used my help. I would drive him from the back of the house around to the front and stop near the rose garden. At that moment, Troy, cued by the idling of the car's engine, would appear from the garden with a single rose — sometimes red, sometimes white or yellow — for Maddox's lapel. Then our day's journey began. `22`

At Maddox's insistence, we took the same route each day: down West Paces Ferry Road, right on Habersham, down to Peachtree Battle, left on Peachtree Street, and down to the First National Bank Building, where Maddox kept an office. He would go up and stay sometimes ten minutes, sometimes two hours — I never knew what to expect. But I knew that whenever he finished, our next destination would be the Capital City Club, where Maddox, and sometimes a companion we might pick up along the way, went to have a drink and lunch. Then it was back home for Maddox's afternoon nap. So, by 1:30 at the latest, my duties as chauffeur were over. I had nothing to do until six o'clock, when I took on the mantle of butler and served dinner. `23`

Maddox had a wonderful library that soon became a place of refuge for me during the dead hours of the afternoon. Shakespeare, Thoreau, Emerson — it had everything. What I read most eagerly, however, were the various books of speeches in his collection. There are few things I enjoy more `24` than a good speech and good preaching. I've tried my hand at doing both. The experience of saying aloud what needs to be said in front of a group of willing listeners is intoxicating. The good speaker or preacher is apart from the audience but always with them in some fundamental way — rising when they rise, falling when they fall, directing them but being directed as well. When a speaker has a talent for doing this, there is nothing more exciting to watch. This is all better as live theater, but the power of a truly well-written speech can come through even when read silently.

One book in Maddox's library contained Booker T. Washington's Atlanta   25
Exposition address. Maddox was deeply impressed with Washington, as the well-thumbed pages of that part of the book showed. Maddox had vigorously underlined one particular passage, to the point of damaging the page, where Washington had said of the races, "In all things purely social we can be as separate as the fingers yet one as the hand in all things essential to mutual progress." This was Maddox's credo, but, obviously, not mine. I was, after all, sitting in his private library.

I sat there day after day, drinking in the atmosphere of the place — the   26
smell of the books, the feel of them, the easy chairs. The way of life that the library symbolized — the commitment to knowledge and the leisure to pursue it — struck a chord in me that still resonates. I wanted all this for myself and my family. This was what going to college was for, to become a part of a community that appreciated and had access to a place like this. I knew I belonged there. . . .

One afternoon, as I sat reading, Maddox walked in on me. He had awak-   27
ened early from his afternoon nap and had come down in his underwear, with a bottle of Southern Comfort in one hand and a glass in the other. He was clearly startled to see me there.

"What are you doing in the library, Vernon?"   28
"I'm reading, Mr. Maddox."   29
"Reading? I've never had a nigger work for me who could read," he said.   30
"Mr. Maddox, I can read. I go to college."   31
"You do what?" he asked.   32
"I go to college."   33
"You go to college over there at those colored schools?"   34
"No, sir. I go to DePauw University in Greencastle, Indiana."   35
He pondered this for a moment.   36
"White children go to that school."   37
"Yes, sir."   38
Then the inevitable.   39
"White *girls* go to that school."   40
"Yes, sir."   41
"What are you studying to be, a preacher or a teacher?"   42

"Actually, I'm going to be a lawyer, Mr. Maddox." 43

"Niggers aren't supposed to be lawyers." 44

"I'm going to be a lawyer, Mr. Maddox." 45

"Hmmm. Well, don't you know I have some place downstairs for you all 46
to sit and do what you want to do?"

"I know. But I didn't think you'd want me to take these books down there. 47
They should stay in the library."

He looked around and finally said, "Just read then — just go ahead." He 48
turned and walked out. I thought the matter was closed. I soon found out it
was not.

His children and their spouses came for dinner that evening, which was 49
not uncommon. Ed Smith, married to Maddox's daughter, Laura, was the
chairman of the First National Bank, and Maddox's son, Baxter, was its executive vice president. Maddox was at his customary place at the head of the
table. As I moved among them serving soup in my white jacket and bow tie
with a napkin draped over my arm, Maddox said, "I have an announcement
to make."

"Yes, Papa?" one of his children said. 50

Silence. 51

"Vernon can read." 52

More silence. Maddox went on. 53

"And he's going to school with white children." 54

No one made a sound. Finally, and with a great deal of emotion, Maddox 55
said, "I knew all this was coming. But I'm glad I won't be here when it does."

The truth is that his guests were all quite embarrassed by this display 56
because they knew I could read. They knew I was a college student. Maddox's
children had hired me, through my mother. My ability to read was not a
detail they had thought to mention to him. Why should they have?

For my part, the whole business seemed so absurd that there was noth- 57
ing to say. I served dinner, poured the water and wine, and left them to themselves. This was not the last of it. . . .

When I have told this story to younger people, they often ask why I was 58
not more angry at Maddox. How could I have continued working for him
under those circumstances? While I was certainly annoyed by what was
going on, I did not think then — and I do not think now — that it would have
done any good to lash out at this elderly man for his aggressive backwardness. Each of us has to decide for ourselves how much nonsense we can take
in life, and from whom we are willing to take it. It all depends, of course, on
the situation and people involved.

I knew Maddox, or more precisely, I knew his type. I was aware of and 59
had borne the brunt of the forces that helped shape him. He had lived his
life as though Booker T. Washington's program for black-white relations in

the South had been enacted. To me, Robert Maddox was not an evil man. He was just an anachronism. And with the brashness of youth I mentally noted (and counted on) the fact that his time was up. I do not mean just his physical time on earth — but I believed that the "time" that helped shape him was on its way out. His half-mocking, half-serious comments about my education were the death rattle of his culture. When he saw that I was in the process of crafting a life for myself that would make me a man in some of the same ways he thought of being a man, he was deeply unnerved. That I was doing it with money gained from working in his household was probably even more unnerving. These things, however, were his problem. As far as I was concerned, I was executing a plan for my life and had no time to pause and reeducate him.

I kept reading in Maddox's library, but he never again announced to any- 60
one that I could read. This story does not have a happy ending, with the old man coming to see the error of his ways and taking on the role of mentor to the young man; I would find mentors in other places. The character of our relationship, however, did change slightly, but perceptibly, after he was forced to focus on who I really was. He became much more inclined to speak to me at times other than when he wanted me to do something for him. As we drove around, he sometimes tossed out a comment about a current issue with the expectation that I might know something about it. At the very least we could have a conversation. That held true over the course of the next few years when I worked for him during the summers and on vacations from school.

The story is told, and I am not sure it is true, that in 1961, when I escorted 61
Charlayne Hunter through the mobs at the University of Georgia to desegregate that institution, Maddox was watching the well-publicized event on television. By that time he was no longer living in the house (in 1963 he would sell the property to the state of Georgia, where the governor's mansion now stands), and he was living in a smaller place in Atlanta attended by a nurse.

The nurse recognized me and said, "Mr. Maddox, do you know who that 62
colored lawyer is?"

"I don't believe I do."   63

"It's your chauffeur, Vernon."   64

Maddox looked hard at the screen and said, "I always knew that nigger 65
was up to no good."

■ **Thinking Critically about the Text**

How did Jordan answer people who asked why he was not more angry at Maddox or how he could have continued working for him? How else might he have answered? What, if anything, do you think Jordan learned from working for Maddox?

▪ Questions on Subject

1. Why was Jordan excited about the prospect of the summer internship at Continental Insurance Company in Atlanta? What happened
   when he showed up for his first day on the job? What does this incident reveal about race relations in 1955?
2. In paragraph 11, Jordan says, "It was my policy then, and it remains
   the same today, never to expect defeat before making an honest effort." What do you think of his policy? What does it say about Jordan's
   character?
3. True to its commitment to Jordan, Continental Insurance Company
   struck a deal with Wolfe Realty, "a black-owned real estate and insurance business," to provide Jordan with work for the summer. Why did
   Jordan ultimately tire of this arrangement? How did Jordan come to
   be Robert F. Maddox's chauffeur?
4. What do you think Jordan means when he says, "Maddox was a symbol of the New South" (paragraph 19)?
5. What did Maddox's library come to represent or symbolize for Jordan?
   Have you ever had similar feelings sitting in such a room? Explain.
6. What does Jordan mean when he says Maddox's "half-mocking,
   half-serious comments about my education were the death rattle
   of his culture" (paragraph 59)? How did Jordan's relationship with
   Maddox change during the time Jordan was in Maddox's employ?

▪ Questions on Strategy

1. How does Jordan establish a context for his narrative in the selection's opening paragraph?
2. Throughout the scene with the receptionist and supervisor at Continental Insurance Company, Jordan relies heavily on dialogue. (Glossary:
   Dialogue) What would have been lost if Jordan had simply described
   this scene without dialogue? Explain. Where else does he use dialogue?
   To what effect?
3. In narration, length has less to do with chronological real time than
   with the amount of emphasis the writer wants to give a particular
   incident. Identify several passages in Jordan's essay where he uses
   multiple paragraphs to recount a relatively brief encounter or incident, and where he uses only a paragraph or two to cover a long
   period of time. What does this tell you about the relative importance
   of the material being narrated? Explain.
4. How effective did you find Jordan's conclusion (paragraphs 60–65)?
   How else might he have concluded the narrative? (Glossary: *Beginnings/
   Endings*)

▪ Questions on Diction and Vocabulary

1. How would you describe Jordan's diction in this narrative? (Glossary:
   Diction) What does his use of language tell you about him?

2. In paragraph 11, Jordan says, "I'd come to think of Jim Crow as a lame horse that was about to be put down." Who or what is *Jim Crow*? And do you think the lame horse simile is appropriate and effective for 1955? (Glossary: *Figures of Speech*)

3. Refer to a dictionary to determine the meanings of the following words as Jordan uses them in this selection: *segregation* (paragraph 11), *protocol* (21), *cued* (22), *mantle* (23), *resonates* (26), *brunt* (59), and *anachronism* (59).

■ Classroom Activity Using Narration

Dialogue is an effective way to bring life to your narrative, to let the people in your story speak for themselves. It is important, however, that you create dialogue that flows logically from one speaker to another. The following sentences, which include dialogue, have been scrambled. Using language cues in each of the sentences, rearrange them in chronological order.

1. The sky was gray and gloomy for as far as she could see, and sleet hissed off the glass.

2. "Oh, hi, Sarah, I'm glad you called," she said happily, but her smile dimmed when she looked outside.

3. As Betsy crossed the room, the phone rang, startling her.

4. "No, the weather's awful, so I don't think I want to leave the house today — I'm still nursing that cold, you know," she sighed.

5. "Hello?" she said, and she wandered over to the window, dragging the phone cord behind her.

6. "Thought you'd like to get a coffee on a day like today," Sarah urged.

■ Writing Suggestions

1. In the opening paragraph, Jordan tells us that during the summer of 1955 he worked as a chauffeur but then confesses that "[i]t had not been my first choice of jobs." As it turned out, Jordan's experiences working in the Maddox household were important, perhaps even life-changing. Have you ever had to settle for something that wasn't your first choice? Perhaps, like Jordan, you didn't get the summer job you wanted, or you didn't get accepted at the college you had your heart set on. Write a narrative essay about such an experience. What did you learn from it?

2. When Maddox asks Vernon, "What are you studying to be, a preacher or a teacher?" (paragraph 42) Vernon promptly and confidently replies, "Actually, I'm going to be a lawyer, Mr. Maddox" (43). What are you studying to be? What do you see yourself doing five or ten years from now? What is your "dream" job? Does it involve something that you are passionate about? Have you shared this idea with your parents and friends? If so, are they supportive? Write an essay in which you identify your dream job, explain why you believe it is right for you, and tell how you are going to get there.

WRITING SUGGESTIONS FOR NARRATION

1. Using Malcolm X's, David P. Bardeen's, or Vernon E. Jordan Jr.'s essay as a model, narrate an experience that gave you a new awareness of yourself. Use enough telling detail in your narrative to help your reader visualize your experience and understand its significance for you. You may find the following suggestions helpful in choosing an experience to narrate in the first person:

   a. my greatest success

   b. my biggest failure

   c. my most embarrassing moment

   d. my happiest moment

   e. a truly frightening experience

   f. an experience that, in my eyes, turned a hero or an idol into an ordinary person

   g. an experience that turned an ordinary person I know into one of my heroes

   h. the experience that was the most important turning point in my life

2. Each of us can tell of an experience that has been unusually significant in teaching us about our relationship to society or to life's institutions — schools, social or service organizations, religious groups, government. Think about your past, and identify one experience that has been especially important for you in this way. After you have considered this event's significance, write an essay recounting it. In preparing to write your narrative, you might benefit from reading George Orwell's account of acting against his better judgment in "Shooting an Elephant" (pages 615–21). To bring your experience into focus and to help you decide what to include in your essay, ask yourself: Why is this experience important to me? What details are necessary for me to re-create the experience in an interesting and engaging way? How can my narrative be most effectively organized? What point of view will work best?

3. Like Annie Dillard in the selection from *An American Childhood*, we have all done something we know we should not have done. Sometimes we have gotten away with our transgressions, sometimes not. Sometimes our actions have no repercussions; sometimes they have very serious ones. Tell the story of one of your escapades, and explain why you have remembered it so well.

4. Many people love to tell stories (that is, they use narration!) to illustrate an abstract point, to bring an idea down to a personal level, or to render an idea memorable. Often, the telling of such stories can

be entertaining as well as instructive. Think about a belief or position that you hold dear (e.g., every individual deserves respect, recycling matters, voluntarism creates community, people need artistic outlets, nature renews the individual), and try to capture that belief in a sentence or two. Then, narrate a story that illustrates your belief or position.

5. **Writing with Sources.** As a way of gaining experience with third-person narration, write an article intended for your school or community newspaper in which you report on what happened at one of the following:

   a. the visit of a state or national figure to your campus or community

   b. a dormitory meeting

   c. a current event of local, state, or national significance

   d. an important sports event

   e. a current research project of one of your professors

   f. a campus gathering or performance

   g. an important development at a local business or at your place of employment

   You may find it helpful to read the third-person narrative about the invention of Coca-Cola on page 74 before starting to write your own narrative. In order to provide context for your article, consider interviewing one or more people involved and/or doing some background research on the object of your narrative. For models of and advice on integrating sources, see Chapters 14 and 15.

6. **Writing with Sources.** Imagine that you are a member of a campus organization seeking volunteers for a community project. Your job is to write a piece for the school newspaper to solicit help for your organization. To build support for the project, narrate one or more stories about the rewards of lending a hand to others within the community. In order to provide context for your article, consider interviewing one or more people who already volunteer or do some background research on the need for the community project. For models of and advice on integrating sources, see Chapters 14 and 15.

7. Take some time to study the excerpt from Gene Luen Yang's *American-Born Chinese* reproduced at the beginning of this chapter (page 72).

   a. First, take a few minutes to describe what's going on in this excerpt. Who are the characters? Where are they? What happens? Next, consider how you know this. What aspects of the narrative are conveyed by written elements? What parts are conveyed by visual elements only?

b. Write a short paper in which you discuss what you discovered about the differences between visual and written narratives.

c. **Writing with Sources.** Consider broadening and deepening your exploration of the differences between visual and written narratives by reading what others have to say about using visuals to convey meaning. (One good source for such discussion is Scott McCloud's *Understanding Comics.*) Alternatively, consider writing a paper in which you compare and contrast two genres (graphic novels and films, perhaps) or two examples of a given genre (for instance, Gene Luen Yang's *American-Born Chinese* and Marjane Satrapi's *Persepolis*).

CHAPTER 5

Description

What Is Description?

Describing something with words is often compared to painting a verbal picture. Both verbal description (like a magazine article profiling a celebrity) and visual description (like a photograph, painting, or drawing accompanying the article) seek to transform fleeting perceptions into lasting images — through words in the case of an article and pixels, paints, or pencils in the case of a photograph, painting, or drawing. Both verbal and visual descriptions enable us to imaginatively experience the subject using some or all of our five senses. Both kinds of description convey information about a subject, telling us something we didn't know before. Both can convey a dominant impression of the subject. And, finally, both verbal and visual descriptions can be classed as primarily objective or subjective, depending on how much they reveal the perspective of the person doing the describing.

The photograph opposite — one of a series of portraits of Ella Watson, a custodial worker in a federal government building, taken by Gordon Parks in August 1942 — is a good example of description conveyed through strictly visual cues, principally lighting and composition (the arrangement of the flag, mop, and broom, with an unsmiling Watson at the center).

Description in Written Texts

Description is a key element in many kinds of written texts. Consider, for example, the following description by Bernd Heinrich from his book *One Man's Owl* (1987). In this selection, Heinrich describes trekking through the woods in search of owls. First, try to see, hear, smell, and feel the scene he describes: Form the jigsaw puzzle of words and details into a complete experience. Once you've accomplished this, define the dominant impression Heinrich creates.

Writer sets the scene with description of the landscape.

By mid-March in Vermont, the snow from the winter storms has already become crusty as the first midday thaws refreeze during the cold nights. A solid white cap compacts the snow, and you can walk on it without breaking through to your waist. The maple sap is starting to run on warm days, and one's blood quickens.

Writer describes the sights and sounds of the birds in early spring.

Spring is just around the corner, and the birds act as if they know. The hairy and downy woodpeckers drum on dry branches and on the loose flakes of maple bark, and purple finches sing merrily from the spruces. This year the reedy voices of the pine siskins can be heard everywhere on the ridge where the hemlocks grow, as can the chickadees' two-note, plaintive song. Down in the bog, the first red-winged blackbirds have just returned, and they can be heard yodeling from the tops of dry cattails. Flocks of rusty blackbirds fly over in long skeins, heading north.

Writer reveals his position and relies on auditory details as night approaches.

From where I stand at the edge of the woods overlooking Shelburne Bog, I feel a slight breeze and hear a moaning gust sweeping through the forest behind me. It is getting dark. There are eery creaking and scraping noises. Inside the pine forest it is becoming black, pitch black. The songbirds are silent. Only the sound of the wind can be heard above the distant honks of Canada geese flying below the now starry skies. Suddenly I hear a booming hollow "hoo-hoo-*hoo*-hoo — ." The deep resonating hoot can send a chill down any spine, as indeed it has done to peoples of many cultures. But I know what the sound is, and it gives me great pleasure.

Heinrich could have described the scene with far fewer words, but that description would likely not have conveyed his dominant impression — one of comfort with the natural surroundings. Heinrich reads the landscape with subtle insight; he knows all the different birds and understands their springtime habits. The reader can imagine the smile on Heinrich's face when he hears the call of the owl.

Using Description As a Writing Strategy

Writers often use the strategy of description to inform — to provide readers with specific data. You may need to describe the results of a chemical reaction for a lab report; the style of a Renaissance painting for an art history term paper; the physical capabilities and limitations of a stroke patient for a case study; or the acting of Meryl Streep in a movie you want your friends to see. Such descriptions will sometimes be scientifically objective, sometimes intensely impressionistic. The approach you use will depend on the subject itself, the information you want to communicate about it, and the format in which the description appears.

Another important use of description is to create a mood or atmosphere or even to convey your own views — to develop a *dominant impression*. Pat Mora uses the strategy of description to capture the fierce determination and joy that Lobo, her spinster aunt, found in leading "[a] life of giving."

> Lobo was a woman of fierce feelings, of strong opinions. She was a woman who literally whistled while she worked. The best way to cheer her when she'd visit my young children was to ask for her help. Ask her to make a bed, fold laundry, set the table or dry dishes, and the whistling would begin as she moved about her task. Like all of us, she loved being needed. Understandable, then, that she muttered in annoyance when her body began to fail her. She was a woman who found self-definition and joy in visibly showing her family her love for us by bringing us hot *té de canela* (cinnamon tea) in the middle of the night to ease a cough, by bringing us comics and candy whenever she returned home. A life of giving.

Each of the descriptions in this chapter, is distinguished by the strong dominant impression the writer creates.

There are essentially two types of description: objective and subjective. *Objective description* is as factual as possible, emphasizing the actual qualities of the subject being described while subordinating the writer's personal responses. For example, a witness to a mugging would try to give authorities a precise, objective description of the assailant, unaffected by emotional responses, so that a positive identification could be made. In the excerpt from his book, Bernd Heinrich objectively describes what he sees: "The hairy and downy woodpeckers drum on dry branches and on the loose flakes of maple bark, and purple finches sing merrily from the spruces."

Subjective or *impressionistic description*, on the other hand, conveys the writer's personal opinion or impression of the object, often in language rich in modifiers and figures of speech. A food critic describing a memorable meal would inevitably write about it impressionistically, using colorful or highly subjective language. (In fact, relatively few words in English can describe the subtleties of smell and taste in neutral terms.) In "Rock Dust," Stan Badgett uses subjective description to capture his experience of fatigue, fear, and fellowship working in the mines, all of which is pervaded by the sight, smell, and feel of rock dust.

Notice that with objective description, it is usually the person, place, or thing being described that stands out, whereas with subjective description the response of the person doing the describing is the most prominent feature. Most topics, however, lend themselves to both objective and subjective description, depending on the writer's purpose. You could write, for example, that you had "exactly four weeks" to finish a history term paper (objective) or that you had "all the time in the world" or "an outrageously short amount of time" (subjective). Each type of description can be accurate and useful in its own way.

Although descriptive writing can stand alone, and often does, it is also used with other types of writing. In a narrative, for example, descriptions provide the context for the story — and make the characters, settings, and events come alive. Description may also help to define an unusual object or thing, such as a giraffe, or to clarify the steps of a process, such as diagnosing an illness. Wherever it is used, good description creates vivid and specific pictures that clarify, create a mood, and build a dominant impression.

Using Description across the Disciplines

When writing essays in the academic disciplines, you will have many opportunities to use the strategy of description to both organize and strengthen the presentation of your ideas. To determine whether or not description is the right strategy for you in a particular paper, use the four-step method described in Chapter 2 (Determining a Strategy for Developing Your Essay, pages 25–26). Consider the following examples:

History

1. MAIN IDEA: Roman medicine, while primitive in some ways, was in general very advanced.
2. QUESTION: What primitive beliefs and advanced thinking characterize Roman medicine?
3. STRATEGY: Description. The direction word *characterize* signals the need to describe Roman medical practices and beliefs.
4. SUPPORTING STRATEGY: Comparison and contrast might be used to set off Roman practices and beliefs from those in later periods of history.

Chemistry

1. MAIN IDEA: The chemical ingredients in acid rain are harmful to humans and the environment.
2. QUESTION: What are the components of acid rain?
3. STRATEGY: Description. The direction word *components* suggests the need for a description of acid rain, including as it does sulfuric acid, carbon monoxide, carbon dioxide, chlorofluorocarbons, and nitric acid.
4. SUPPORTING STRATEGY: Cause and effect might be used to show the harm caused by acid rain. Process analysis might be used to explain how acid rain develops.

Psychology

1. MAIN IDEA: Law enforcement officers who are under abnormal stress manifest certain symptoms.
2. QUESTION: What comprises the symptoms?

3. STRATEGY: Description. The direction word *comprises* suggests the need for a picture or description of the *symptoms*.
4. SUPPORTING STRATEGY: Comparison and contrast might be used to differentiate those officers suffering from stress. Process analysis might be used to explain how to carry out an examination to identify the symptoms of stress. Argumentation might be used to indicate the need for programs to test for excessive stress on the job.

Sample Student Essay Using Description As a Writing Strategy

Jim Tassé wrote the following essay while he was a student at the University of Vermont, where he majored in English and religion. Tassé hopes to teach eventually, perhaps at the college level, but his most immediate interests include biking and singing with a rock band. As his essay "Trailcheck" reveals, Tassé is an enthusiastic skier. His experience working on ski patrol during winter breaks provided him with the subject for a striking description.

Trailcheck

Jim Tassé

Context presented—early morning in January and preparations for trailcheck

At a quarter to eight in the morning, the sharp cold of the midwinter night still hangs in the air of Smuggler's Notch. At the base of Madonna Mountain, we stamp our feet and turn up our collars while waiting for Dan to get the chairlift running. Trailcheck always begins with this cold, sleepy wait—but it can continue in many different ways. The ski patrol has to make this first run every morning to assess the trail conditions before the mountain opens—and you never know what to expect on top of the Mad Dog, Madonna Mountain. Sometimes we take our first run down the sweet, light powder that fell the night before; sometimes we have to ski the rock-hard boilerplate ice that formed when yesterday's mush froze. But there's always the cold—the dank, bleary cold of 8 a.m. in January.

Description of trailcheck begins with explanation of what it is.

Use of present tense gives immediacy to the description.

I adjust my first-aid belt and heft my backpack up a little higher, cinching it tight. I shiver, and

1

2

pull my hat down a bit lower. I am sleepy, cold, and impatient. Dan's finally got the lift running, and the first two patrollers, Chuck and Ken, get on. Three more chairs get filled, and then there's me. Looks like I'm riding up alone. The chairlift jars me a little more awake as it hits the back of my boots. I sit down and am scooped into the air.

3

Description of the total experience is enhanced by appealing to the reader's senses — especially touch, hearing, and sight.

It's a cold ride up, and I snuggle my chin deep into my parka. The bumps of the chair going over the lift-tower rollers help keep me awake. Trees piled high and heavy with snow move silently past. Every so often, in sudden randomness, a branch lets go a slide and the air fills with snow dust as the avalanche crashes from branch to branch, finally landing with a soft thud on the ground. Snow dances in the air with kaleidoscopic colors, shining in the early daylight.

4

Well-selected details contribute to the description of the wintry mountain and the magic of the day.

I imagine what it would have been like on the mountain on a similar day three hundred years ago. A day like this would have been just as beautiful, or maybe even more so — the silent mountain, all trees and cold and sunshine, with no men and no lifts. I think of the days when the fog rolls out of the notch, and the wind blows cold and damp, and the trees are close and dark in the mist, and I try to imagine how terrifyingly wild the mountain would have been centuries ago, before the white man came and installed the chairlift that takes me to the top so easily. I think how difficult it would have been to climb through the thick untamed forest that bristles out of the mountain's flanks, and I am glad I don't have to walk up Madonna this sleepy-eyed morning.

5

I watch the woods pass, looking for the trails of small animals scrolled around the trees. Skiing should be nice with all the new snow. Arriving at the top, I throw up the safety bar, tip my skis up, make contact, stand, and ski clear of the lift. The view from the mountaintop is incredible. I can see over the slopes of Stowe, where another patrol is running trailcheck just as we are. Across the state, Mt. Washington hangs above the horizon like a mirage,

Back toward Burlington, I can see the frozen lake sprawling like a white desert.

I toss my backpack full of lunch and books to Marty, who's going into the patrol shack to get the stove fired up. I stretch my legs a little as we share small talk, waiting for the mountain captain to say we can go down. I tighten my boots. Finally, Ken's radio crackles out the word, and I pull down my goggles and pole forward.

6

Opening sentence and two fragments following signal the end of the ride up the mountain and the beginning of the trailcheck.

Wake up! The first run of the day. Trailcheck. Today the run is heaven—eight inches of light dry powder. My turns are relaxed giant slaloms that leave neat S's in the snow behind me. No need to worry about ice or rocks—the snow covers every-thing with an airy cushion that we float on, fly on, our skis barely on the ground. We split up at the first intersection, and I bear to the left, down the Glades. My skis gently hiss as they break the powder, splitting the snow like a boat on calm water. I blast through deep drifts of snow, sending gouts and geysers of snow up around me. The air sparkles with snow, breaking the light into flecks of color.

7

Strong action verbs bring the description alive.

What a day! Some mornings I ride up in fif-teen-below-zero cold, only to ski down icy hardpack on which no new snow has fallen for days. There are rocks and other hazards to be noted and later marked with bamboo poles so skiers don't hit them. Fallen branches must be cleared from the trail. On days like that, when the snow is lousy and I have to worry about rocks gouging the bottoms of the skis, trailcheck is work—cold, necessary work done too early in the morning. But when the run is like today, the suffering is worthwhile.

8

Contrast enhances description of the trailcheck.

I yelp with pleasure as I launch myself off a knoll and gently land in the soft whiteness, blast-ing down a chute of untracked powder that empties out into a flatter run. I can hear the other patroller whooping and yelling with me in the distance. Turns are effortless; a tiny shift of weight and the skis respond like wings. I come over the next pitch, moving fast, and my skis hit an unseen patch of ice; my tails slide, too late to get the edge in, and POOF!

9

Dominant impression of ecstatic playfulness emerges.

I tumble into the snow in an explosion of snow dust. For a second I lie panting. Then I wallow in ecstasy, scooping the handfuls of powder over myself, the sweet light snow tingling in the air. After a moment I hop up and continue down, sluicing the S-turns on the whipped-cream powder.

Reaching the patrol room, I click off my skis   10
and stamp the snow from myself. No longer do I feel the night's cold breath in the air—just the sting of

Concluding comment sums up the writer's experience in one word.

the melting snow on my face. Ken looks at me as I drip and glisten over my trail report, and asks: "Good run, Jim?"

I grin at him and say, "Beau-ti-ful!"   11

Analyzing Jim Tassé's Description Essay: Questions for Discussion

1. How does Tassé support his dominant impression in this essay?

2. How does Tassé *show* that the mountain is beautiful rather than simply *say* that it is?

3. How and where does Tassé indicate the importance of a trailcheck?

Suggestions for Using Description As a Writing Strategy

As you plan, write, and revise your essay of description, be mindful of the writing process guidelines described in Chapter 2. Pay particular attention to the basic requirements and essential ingredients of this writing strategy.

■ Planning Your Description Essay

Planning is an essential part of writing a good description essay. You can save yourself a great deal of work by taking the time to think about key building blocks of your essay before you actually begin to write.

Determine a Purpose.   Begin by determining your purpose: Are you trying to inform, express your emotions, persuade, or entertain? While it is not necessary, or even desirable, to state your purpose explicitly, it is necessary that you have one that your readers recognize. If your readers do not see a purpose in your writing they may be tempted to respond by asking, "So what?" Making your reason for writing clear in the first place will help you avoid this pitfall.

Use Description in the Service of an Idea.   Your readers will want to know why you chose to describe what you did. You should always write description with a thesis in mind, an idea you want to convey to your readers. For example, you might describe a canoe trip as one of both serenity and exhilarating danger, which for you symbolize the contrasting aspects of nature. In his essay "A View from the Bridge," Cherokee Paul McDonald uses description in the service of an idea, and that idea is description itself: McDonald needs to describe a fish so that a blind boy can "see" it. In the process of describing, the author comes to an epiphany: The act of describing the fish brings him closer to the essence of it. He realizes then that he has received from the boy more than he has given.

Show, Don't Tell: Use Specific Nouns and Action Verbs.   Inexperienced writers often believe that adjectives and adverbs are the basis for effective descriptions. They're right in one sense, but not wholly so. Although strong adjectives and adverbs are crucial, description also depends on well-chosen nouns and verbs. *Vehicle* is not nearly as descriptive as something more specific — *Jeep*, *snowmobile*, or *Honda Civic*. Similarly, the verb *talk* does far less to describe the *way* something is said than do any of a host of possible substitutes (see page 130). The more specific and strong you make your nouns and verbs, the more lively and interesting your descriptions will be.

When you have difficulty thinking of specific action nouns and verbs to use, reach for a thesaurus — but only if you are sure you can discern the best word for your purpose. Inexpensive paperback editions are available at any bookstore, and most word-processing programs have a thesaurus utility. A thesaurus will help you keep your descriptions from getting repetitive and will be invaluable when you need to find a specific word with just the right meaning.

\ **E9**

■ Organizing Your Description Essay

Create a Dominant Impression.   After generating as many details as possible describing your subject, reread them and select those that will be most helpful in developing a dominant impression. Suppose that you wish to depict the hospital emergency room as a place of great tension. You will then naturally choose details to reinforce that sense of tension: the worried looks on the faces of a couple sitting in the corner, the quick movements of the medical staff as they tend to a patient on a wheeled stretcher, the urgent whisperings of two interns out in the hallway, the

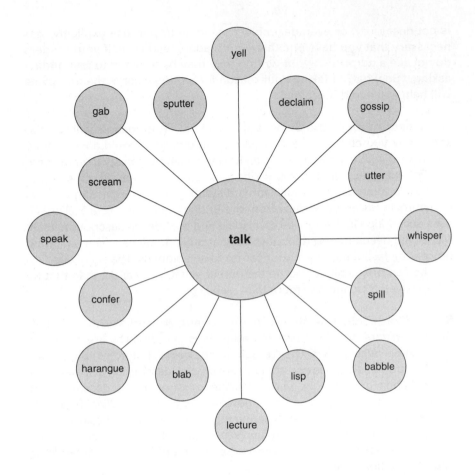

incessant paging of Dr. Thomas. If the dominant impression you want to create is of the emergency room's sterility, however, you will choose different details: the smell of disinfectant, the spotless white uniforms of the staff members, the stainless steel tables and chairs, the gleaming instruments the nurse hands to the physician.

Organize Your Details to Create a Vivid Picture.   Once you have decided which details to include and which to leave out, you need to arrange your details in an order that serves your purpose and is easy for the reader to follow.

In describing some subjects, it might make sense to imagine what the reader would experience first. A description of an emergency room, for example, could begin at the entrance, move through the waiting area, pass the registration desk, and proceed into the treatment cubicles. A description of a restaurant kitchen might conjure up the smells and sounds that escape through the swinging doors even before moving on to the first glimpse inside the kitchen.

Other patterns of organization include moving from general to specific, from smallest to largest, from least to most important, or from the usual to the unusual. Keep in mind that the last details you present will probably stay in the reader's mind the longest and that the first details will also have special force.

Before you begin your first draft, you may find it useful to sketch out an outline of your description. Here's a sample outline for Bernd Heinrich's description earlier in this introduction:

Description of Shelburne Bog

Dominant impression: Comfort with the natural surroundings

Paragraph 1: Snow-crusted landscape in mid-March

Paragraph 2: Activity and sounds of the birds (e.g., woodpeckers, finches, chickadees, and red-winged blackbirds) described from the edge of the woods

Paragraph 3: Activity and sounds inside the pine forest behind the speaker, culminating with the familiar call of the owl

Such an outline can remind you of the dominant impression you want to create and can suggest which specific details may be most useful to you.

■ Revising and Editing Your Description Essay

Share Your Work with Others.   Try sharing your draft with other students in your writing class to make sure that your description makes sense. Ask them if there are any parts that they do not understand. Have them tell you what they think is the point of your description. If their answers differ from what you intended, have them indicate which passages led them to their interpretation so that you can change your text accordingly. To maximize the effectiveness of conferences with your peers, use the guidelines presented on page 29. Feedback from these conferences often provides one or more places where you can start revising.

Question Your Own Work While Revising and Editing.   Revision is best done by asking yourself key questions about what you have written. Begin by reading, preferably aloud, what you have written. Reading aloud forces you to pay attention to every single word, and you are more likely to catch lapses in the logical flow of thought. After you have read your paper through, answer the following questions for revising and editing, and make the necessary changes. For help with twelve common writing problems, see Chapter 16, "Editing for Grammar, Punctuation, and Sentence Style."

Questions for Revising and Editing: Description

1. Do I have a clear purpose for my description? Have I answered the "so what" question?

2. Is the subject of my description interesting and relevant to my audience?

3. What senses have I chosen to use to describe it? For example, what does it look like, sound like, or smell like? Does it have a texture or taste that is important to mention?

4. Which details must I include in my essay? Which are irrelevant or distracting to my purpose and should be discarded?

5. Have I achieved the dominant impression I wish to leave with my audience?

6. Does the organization I have chosen for my essay make it easy for the reader to follow my description?

E9
7. How carefully have I chosen my descriptive words? Are my nouns and verbs strong and specific?

8. Have I used figurative language, if appropriate, to further strengthen my description?

E1–12
9. Does my paper contain any errors in grammar, punctuation, or mechanics? Is my sentence style as clear, smooth, and persuasive as possible?

A View from the Bridge

CHEROKEE PAUL MCDONALD

A fiction writer and journalist, Cherokee Paul McDonald was raised and schooled in Fort Lauderdale, Florida. In 1970, he returned home from a tour of duty in Vietnam and joined the Fort Lauderdale Police Department, where he remained until 1980, resigning with the rank of sergeant. During this time, McDonald received a degree in criminal science from Broward Community College. He left the police department to become a writer and worked a number of odd jobs before publishing his first book, *The Patch*, in 1986. McDonald has said that almost all of his writing comes from his police work, and his common themes of justice, balance, and fairness reflect his life as part of the "thin blue line" (the police department). In 1991, he published *Blue Truth*, a memoir. His first novel, *Summer's Reason*, was released in 1994. His most recent book, *Into the Green: A Reconnaissance by Fire* (2001), is a memoir of his three years as an artillery forward observer in Vietnam.

"A View from the Bridge" was originally published in *Sunshine* magazine in 1990. The essay shows McDonald's usual expert handling of fish and fishermen, both in and out of water, and reminds us that things are not always as they seem.

■ Preparing to Read

The great American philosopher and naturalist Henry David Thoreau has written: "The question is not what you look at, but what you see." We've all had the experience of becoming numb to sights or experiences that once struck us with wonderment; but sometimes, with luck, something happens to renew our appreciation. Think of an example from your own experience. What are some ways we can retain or recover our appreciation of the remarkable things we have come to take for granted?

I was coming up on the little bridge in the Rio Vista neighborhood of Fort Lauderdale, deepening my stride and my breathing to negotiate the slight incline without altering my pace. And then, as I neared the crest, I saw the kid. 1

He was a lumpy little guy with baggy shorts, a faded T-shirt and heavy sweat socks falling down over old sneakers. 2

Partially covering his shaggy blond hair was one of those blue baseball caps with gold braid on the bill and a sailfish patch sewn onto the peak. 3

Covering his eyes and part of his face was a pair of those stupid-looking '50s-style wrap-around sunglasses.

He was fumbling with a beat-up rod and reel, and he had a little bait bucket by his feet. I puffed on by, glancing down into the empty bucket as I passed. 4

"Hey, mister! Would you help me, please?" 5

The shrill voice penetrated my jogger's concentration, and I was determined to ignore it. But for some reason, I stopped. 6

> The shrill voice penetrated my jogger's concentration, and I was determined to ignore it. But for some reason, I stopped.

With my hands on my hips and the sweat dripping from my nose I asked, "What do you want, kid?" 7

"Would you please help me find my shrimp? It's my last one and I've been getting bites and I know I can catch a fish if I can just find that shrimp. He jumped outta my hand as I was getting him from the bucket." 8

Exasperated, I walked slowly back to the kid, and pointed. 9

"There's the damn shrimp by your left foot. You stopped me for *that*?" 10

As I said it, the kid reached down and trapped the shrimp. 11

"Thanks a lot, mister," he said. 12

I watched as the kid dropped the baited hook down into the canal. Then I turned to start back down the bridge. 13

That's when the kid let out a "Hey! Hey!" and the prettiest tarpon I'd ever seen came almost six feet out of the water, twisting and turning as he fell through the air. 14

"I got one!" the kid yelled as the fish hit the water with a loud splash and took off down the canal. 15

I watched the line being burned off the reel at an alarming rate. The kid's left hand held the crank while the extended fingers felt for the drag setting. 16

"No, kid!" I shouted. "Leave the drag alone . . . just keep that damn rod tip up!" 17

Then I glanced at the reel and saw there were just a few loops of line left on the spool. 18

"Why don't you get yourself some decent equipment?" I said, but before the kid could answer I saw the line go slack. 19

"Ohhh, I lost him," the kid said. I saw the flash of silver as the fish turned. 20

"Crank, kid, crank! You didn't lose him. He's coming back toward you. Bring in the slack!" 21

The kid cranked like mad, and a beautiful grin spread across his face. 22

"He's heading in for the pilings," I said. "Keep him out of those pilings!" 23

The kid played it perfectly. When the fish made its play for the pilings, he kept just enough pressure on to force the fish out. When the water exploded and the silver missile hurled into the air, the kid kept the rod tip up and the line tight. 24

As the fish came to the surface and began a slow circle in the middle of the canal, I said, "Whooee, is that a nice fish or what?" 25

The kid didn't say anything, so I said, "Okay, move to the edge of the bridge and I'll climb down to the seawall and pull him out." 26

When I reached the seawall I pulled in the leader, leaving the fish lying on its side in the water. 27

"How's that?" I said. 28

"Hey, mister, tell me what it looks like." 29

"Look down here and check him out," I said, "He's beautiful." 30

But then I looked up into those stupid-looking sunglasses and it hit me. The kid was blind. 31

"Could you tell me what he looks like, mister?" he said again. 32

"Well, he's just under three, uh, he's about as long as one of your arms," I said. "I'd guess he goes about 15, 20 pounds. He's mostly silver, but the silver is somehow made up of *all* the colors, if you know what I mean." I stopped. "Do you know what I mean by colors?" 33

The kid nodded. 34

"Okay. He has all these big scales, like armor all over his body. They're silver too, and when he moves they sparkle. He has a strong body and a large powerful tail. He has big round eyes, bigger than a quarter, and a lower jaw that sticks out past the upper one and is very tough. His belly is almost white and his back is a gunmetal gray. When he jumped he came out of the water about six feet, and his scales caught the sun and flashed it all over the place." 35

By now the fish had righted itself, and I could see the bright-red gills as the gill plates opened and closed. I explained this to the kid, and then said, more to myself, "He's a beauty." 36

"Can you get him off the hook?" the kid asked. "I don't want to kill him." 37

I watched as the tarpon began to slowly swim away, tired but still alive. 38

By the time I got back up to the top of the bridge the kid had his line secured and his bait bucket in one hand. 39

He grinned and said, "Just in time. My mom drops me off here, and she'll be back to pick me up any minute." 40

He used the back of one hand to wipe his nose. 41

"Thanks for helping me catch that tarpon," he said, "and for helping me to see it." 42

I looked at him, shook my head, and said, "No, my friend, thank you for letting *me* see that fish." 43

I took off, but before I got far the kid yelled again. 44

"Hey, mister!" 45

I stopped. 46

"Someday I'm gonna catch a sailfish and a blue marlin and a giant tuna and *all* those big sportfish!" 47

As I looked into those sunglasses I knew he probably would. I wished I could be there when it happened. ■ 48

■ Thinking Critically about the Text

The jogger and the kid are very different from each other, but they share an interest in fishing. What role does the tarpon play in this story? What can a shared interest do for a relationship between two people?

■ Questions on Subject

1. Why is the narrator angry with the kid at the beginning of the story?
2. What clues lead up to the revelation that the kid is blind? Why does it take the narrator so long to realize it?
3. "Why don't you get yourself some decent equipment?" the narrator asks the kid (paragraph 19). Why does McDonald include this question? Speculate about the answer.
4. Near the end of the story, why does the narrator say to the kid, "No, my friend, thank you for letting *me* see that fish" (paragraph 43)?
5. The boy boasts that one day he will catch big sport fish, too. Why does the narrator say he "wished [he] could be there when it happened" (paragraph 48)?

■ Questions on Strategy

1. Notice the way the narrator chooses and actually adjusts some of the words he uses to describe the fish to the kid. Why does he do this? What is McDonald's desired effect?
2. By the end of the essay, we know much more about the kid than the fact that he is blind, but, after the initial description, McDonald characterizes him only indirectly. As the essay unfolds, what do we learn about the kid, and by what techniques does the author convey this knowledge?
3. Reread the description of the kid (paragraphs 2 and 3). Which details gain significance as events unfold over the course of the essay?
4. McDonald is able to move his story along rather quickly by being selective about what he tells the reader. For example, examine paragraphs 9–13 and explain how the author moves the action forward.
5. This essay, descriptive in theme and intent, is structured as a narrative. (Glossary: *Narration*) What makes the combination of story and description effective? Suppose McDonald had started his essay with a statement like this: "If you really want to see something clearly, try describing it to a blind child." How would such an opening change the impact of the essay? Which other rhetorical strategies might McDonald have used along with the new opening?

■ Questions on Diction and Vocabulary

1. What is the metaphor in paragraph 24? Why is it apt? How does this metaphor enhance McDonald's description? (Glossary: *Figures of Speech*)
2. What is the connotation of the word *view* in the title? Of the word *bridge*? (Glossary: *Connotation/Denotation*)
3. You may be unfamiliar with some of the fishing-related vocabulary in this essay. What sort of fish is a tarpon? In the context of fishing, define *drag* (paragraph 16), *pilings* (23), *seawall* (26), *leader* (27).

■ Classroom Activity Using Description

Think about your topic — the person, place, thing, or concept that lies at the center of your descriptive essay. Make a list of all the details that you can gather through your five senses as well as those that simply come to mind when you consider your topic. Determine a dominant impression that you would like to create, and then choose those details from your list that will best help you form it. Your instructor may wish to have you and your classmates go over the items on your lists in class and discuss how effective the items will be in building the dominant impressions.

■ Writing Suggestions

1. In a group of three or four students, take turns describing some specific beautiful or remarkable thing as if your classmates were blind. You may actually want to bring an object to observe while your classmates cover their eyes. Help each other find the best words to create a vivid verbal picture. Write your description in a couple of brief paragraphs, retaining the informal style of your speaking voice.
2. McDonald's "A View from the Bridge" and the *Calvin and Hobbes* cartoon on page 138 are just two "fish stories" in the long and rich tradition of that genre. In their own ways, both the essay and the cartoon play on the ironic notion that fishing is a quiet sport but one in which the unexpected frequently occurs. (Glossary: *Irony*). For the narrator in McDonald's story, there is the revelation of the difference between merely looking and truly seeing. For Calvin, there is that sudden splash in the water (this time, alas, not the sign of a great catch). Write an essay in which you tell a "fish story" of your own, one that reveals a larger, significant truth or life lesson. Pay particular attention to the pattern of organization you choose, and be sure to revise your essay to tighten up your use of the pattern. If possible, incorporate some elements of surprise as well.

Rock Dust

STAN BADGETT

Stan Badgett was born in Topeka, Kansas, in 1947. After attending public school for a few years in Kansas he moved to Colorado, where he currently lives. Badgett spent most of his working life at manual labor — in brickyards, in construction sites, and in coal mines — before, as he writes, "becoming serious about education" in his later years. He eventually earned his B.A. in fine arts in 1993 and his M.A. in liberal studies in language and communication from Regis University in 2001. Badgett has written a number of short stories, articles, and poems. When asked to comment about writing, and "Rock Dust" in particular, Badgett replied, "I wanted to capture the physical and psychological sensation of being continuously inundated with dust — so swirlingly ambiguous, so alienating. I couldn't shake the sensation even years after leaving the coal mine, so it had to be written down. The mine is such a foreign environment. I also wanted to memorialize the death of Mark Edwards, whom I barely got to know, and to capture Big Bird, a white-faced clown figure. He was a hero to me, a mischief maker, an icon of resistance."

"Rock Dust" first appeared in the *Minnetonka Review* in 2008. Badgett reports that he struggled to get the piece right: "I sent an early version to my good friend Rodney who was supportive, but not highly enthusiastic. The piece needed lots of work. I labor at this stuff, twisting words and phrases inside out. But — boy, oh, boy — it's lots of fun, watching meaning mutate before your eyes. The real joy comes when it begins to approximate the truth."

■ Preparing to Read

Many people — armed forces personnel, fire fighters, police officers, chemical plant workers, construction employees, rescue workers, factory workers — willingly engage in dangerous occupations. What factors encourage such employment, diminishing the risks and making the advantages seem more attractive? Have you ever done dangerous work? If so, what motivated you?

Cold, white dust collects on mine timbers like rime frost, lies a foot deep on   1
the floor. You glide through it, surf through it — the dust is soft like talcum powder. You kick it up with your feet as you walk. Plop, plop.

Federal law requires everything in the coal mine to be covered with pulverized limestone — it's supposed to dampen an explosion. There are rock dust "stations" underground — yellow holding tanks buried under years of accumulated dust. You have to dig through layers of it just to find the hatch door. 2

Rock dusters (men on graveyard who spray the mine with dust) wrap up in burlap to stay warm while they're minding the tanks. You get chilled down if you're not wrapped up. You push a lever to pump white dust through the lines, then settle back for a twenty-minute snooze. 3

Four-inch aluminum pipes transport rock dust to all parts of the mine. The pipes run along the roof at skewed angles, suspended from J-hooks and baling wire. Every so often, flexible hoses hang down from shut-off valves. Here and there, little plumes of dust emanate from quaint pots and drums resembling old-fashioned stills. These are called "trickle dusters." 4

You wake from your nap and walk the dust lines, opening valves along the way, blasting the passageway with thick, choking clouds of white. You get dizzy, can't tell right or left, up or down. A man approaching from a few feet away — his caplight beaming right into your eyes — seems to be drifting in from another planet. The stuff frosts the insides of your nose, cakes your eyebrows and eyelashes, grits your teeth. It sifts into your boots and fills up your gloves. Sometimes you wonder how, after so many years of this, there is any room left in the tunnels at all — you'd think they'd be totally plugged up with dust. You go out the hole at 6:45 in the morning, leaving the mine pristine white. When you come in at 11:00 that night, the tunnels are coated with a fine layer of sooty black, and it's time to start over again. 5

> **Mark stood opposite me on the other side of the stack, smiling. The next day a section of roof collapsed and killed him.**

Rock dust comes in ninety-pound sacks. It's ground-up limestone, calcium carbonate quarried from the walls of Glenwood Canyon. Tons of the stuff come into the mine every night on little railcars called the "trip." You off-load the sacks by hand, stacking them like sandbags around a combat trench. You work up a sweat. The dust-covered paper slips through your hands and sends a gritty chill down your backbone. 6

I remember bringing in a load of dust one evening and stacking the sacks. A fellow named Mark Edwards helped me. We made swift work of it, then chatted awhile. Mark stood opposite me on the other side of the stack, smiling. The next day a section of roof collapsed and killed him. 7

I have an indelible image of another man, Big Bird, whose real name was Mike. When I think of rock dust, I think of him. There had been a terrible gas explosion at the mine. Fifteen men died. There were union meetings and safety demands, and the men voted to go on strike. The last shift before going 8 on strike felt unreal. Gloom hung heavily in the tunnels. I could imagine the white flash, the concussion, the melting heat, bodies strewn across the floor. At the end of the shift we rode silently out to the track, crammed into the back of a diesel-powered Scout. We didn't know when we'd return.

At the tracks we climbed onto mine cars, which were nothing more than   9 sheets of flat steel mounted on wheels. A low guardrail of heavy pipe surrounded each car. Bags of dust were stacked on the cars four deep. As the trip lurched forward, and we began our ascent, one of the men grabbed a bag, ripped it open, scooped up several handfuls of dust, and flung them all directions.

The tension broke as one man after another grabbed a fistful of dust and   10 pitched it at the nearest smiling face. We were eating it, wiping it out of our eyes, laughing our heads off, and Big Bird planted both feet firmly on the floor of the railcar, tore a sack in two, and heaved a good forty pounds of dust at one of the slaphappy miners, plastering him against a guardrail. It was no-holds-barred the rest of the way up the tunnel. Big Bird took some hefty shots but never went down. He just stood there unbudged, coated with white from head to foot. I can still see the wet curl of his lip, the smirk of triumph in his eyes. ■

■ Thinking Critically about the Text

Badgett describes his experience spreading rock dust in mine tunnels because it is memorable and meaningful for him and it's a topic he wishes to share with his readers. In your opinion, what does the act of going down into the tunnels and the "cold, white dust" symbolize for him? Danger? Death? Camaraderie? Life? Something else? Explain.

■ Questions on Subject

1. Why do the miners spread rock dust in the tunnels every night? Why is it a frustrating job?
2. Badgett writes in paragraph 5 that after so many years of blowing limestone into the mine tunnels "you'd think they'd be totally plugged up with dust." Why do you suppose that does not happen?
3. Explosions are not the only danger encountered in coal mining. What is another ever-present danger for miners, according to Badgett?
4. What happens to lungs under the conditions that Badgett describes? Can a worker get "white lung" as well as "black lung" disease? Explain.
5. Why does Badgett have an indelible image of "Big Bird"? Who was he and what did he do that made him unforgettable?
6. What were the miners celebrating as they made their ascent from the mine?

▪ Questions on Strategy

1. Much of this essay is composed of objective, factual description, but Badgett also shares with the reader some subjective thoughts inspired by his mining experience. (Glossary: *Objective/Subjective*) Note the places where he expresses his own opinions. As a writer, what effect does he achieve through the contrast created by the use of objective and subjective details?
2. This primarily descriptive essay makes clear the author's opinion about the risks of mining. What is his argument? Does it take the form of a thesis statement? Explain.
3. What dominant impression has Badgett created in describing the tunnels covered with rock dust? (Glossary: *Dominant Impression*)
4. Comment on Badgett's use of the present tense. Where does he use it and how effective is it? When and why does he shift to the past tense?
5. How does Badgett show us, rather than tell us, that the mine is a dangerous place?

▪ Questions on Diction and Vocabulary

1. What images convey that the coal mine is a cold place to work? Badgett says in paragraph 1 that the dust looks like "rime frost." What is rime frost? How does it differ from other kinds of frost?
2. What technical mining terms does Badgett use in his description? (Glossary: *Technical Language*) Cite several examples. In your estimation, do they enhance the essay or work against the reader's comprehension and enjoyment of it? Explain.
3. Cite several examples of Badgett's use of figures of speech and explain how they help enliven his description. (Glossary: *Figures of Speech*)

▪ Classroom Activity Using Description

Think about your topic — the person, place, thing, or concept that lies at the center of your descriptive essay. Make a list of all the details that you could gather about it using your five senses, as well as those that simply come to mind when you consider your topic. Determine a dominant impression that you would like to create, and then choose those details from your list that will best help you form it. Your instructor may wish to have you and your classmates go over your lists in class and discuss how effective the item will be in building dominant impressions.

▪ Writing Suggestions

1. Write about a dangerous job you or someone you know has had. Describe the potentially harmful or life-threatening aspects of the job, conveying the danger vividly. Think about how you might use objective description

to form the basis of your representation and subjective description to convey how you and your readers might react to the danger in a more personal way. (Glossary: *Objective/Subjective*) For example, you might be a lifeguard at a local beach or community swimming pool, so think about the objective aspects of the job (work hours, responsibilities, pay, number of swimmers, life-threatening situations) as well as the subjective responses you have to the experience (boredom, fatigue, fear, worry because of low pay, annoyance with troublesome swimmers).

2. In commenting about "Rock Dust," Badgett wrote that the dangers of coal mining gave impetus to his description of the situation. Notice how he accounts for the blasphemous language the miners used, tying it to the dust in the mines; justifies the dark humor of the miners' lot; and deepens his realization of what he went through in the mines with literary allusions.

> For me, a lot of coal mining had to do with coping with vile and blasphemous language. It raged in my bowels and scoured my brain like a relentless fire. I've written extensively about it since "Rock Dust," but this semi-whimsical essay pushed me through the man-door (a little square doorway that lets you in and out of different parts of the mine). I've come to realize that dust is really the essence of all the swearing and oath-taking. As T. S. Eliot said, "I will show you fear in a handful of dust." We are destined for the dirt, our bodies at least. Ashes to ashes, dust to dust. So "Rock Dust" is really a way of laughing at my terror.
>
> In later versions of the essay, I sparingly included some details about the calamitous explosion that occurred at our coal mine in 1981. I had files full of newspaper clippings from the explosion, yet was reticent to say anything at all, out of respect for the men who died. But I needed to take this serious turn, if only momentarily. Much of swearing is about hell and damnation. On the day Dutch Creek #1 exploded, a fireball roared up and down the entries, ripping coal out of walls, pulverizing it to combustible powder. I've seen molten glass in a furnace, glowing white-hot at 2,000 degrees. The coal mine explosion exceeded that hellacious temperature.

Write an analysis of "Rock Dust" in which you explain the essay by using what Badgett has written about it. You might also consider discussing Badgett's essay by comparing and contrasting his descriptions with those in other literary works that similarly deal with work, dust, or death. If you have read John Steinbeck's *The Grapes of Wrath*, for example, what connections do you see between Steinbeck's and Badgett's use of dust as reality, metaphor, and symbol?

Remembering Lobo

PAT MORA

 Pat Mora was born in El Paso, Texas, in 1942. She grew up in a mostly Spanish-speaking household greatly influenced by her four grandparents, who had fled to El Paso during the Mexican Revolution in the early part of the twentieth century. Speaking Spanish at home and English in public school, Mora received her B.A. from Texas Western College in 1963 and her M.A. from the University of Texas at El Paso in 1967. As a writer, lecturer, teacher, university administrator, and literacy advocate, Mora has spent her career speaking and writing about the value of family, Mexican American culture, and the desert. She is the author of twenty works of fiction and nonfiction for children and adults, among them collections of poetry such as *Chants* (1984), *Borders* (1986), and *Communion* (1991) that explore bicultural and bilingual themes. *House of Houses* (1997), perhaps her most important work, is a family memoir that uses the metaphor of a house to tell the generational story of her family in the span of a single year.

In "Remembering Lobo," taken from *Nepantla: Essays from the Middle* (1993), Mora offers us a poignant portrait of her Aunt Ignacia, better known to family members as *Lobo*. With telling details and touching devotion, Mora describes her aunt and shows how Lobo "taught [her] much about one of our greatest challenges as human beings: loving well."

▪ Preparing to Read

Think about one of your favorite aunts or uncles or a dear family friend. What makes that person special to you? Is it that the person has a special affection for you? Is it because the person has special character traits that you'd like to emulate or think are in some way strange but appealing? Or is it that the person shares some family traits with your parents? Explain.

We called her *Lobo*. The word means "wolf" in Spanish, an odd name for a generous and loving aunt. Like all names it became synonymous with her, and to this day returns me to my childself. Although the name seemed perfectly natural to us and to our friends, it did cause frowns from strangers throughout the years. I particularly remember one hot afternoon when on a crowded streetcar between the border cities of El Paso and Juarez, I momentarily lost sight of her. "Lobo! Lobo!" I cried in panic. Annoyed faces peered at me, disappointed at such disrespect to a white-haired woman.

Actually the fault was hers. She lived with us for years, and when she arrived home from work in the evening, she'd knock on our front door and ask, "*¿Dónde están mis lobitos?*" "Where are my little wolves?" 2

Gradually she became our *lobo*, a spinster aunt who gathered the four of us around her, tying us to her for life by giving us all she had. Sometimes to tease her we would call her by her real name. "*¿Dónde está Ignacia?*" we would ask. Lobo would laugh and say, "She is a ghost." 3

> We called her *Lobo*. The word means "wolf" in Spanish, an odd name for a generous and loving aunt.

To all of us in nuclear families today, the notion of an extended family under one roof seems archaic, complicated. We treasure our private space. I will always marvel at the generosity of my parents, who opened their door to both my grandmother and Lobo. No doubt I am drawn to the elderly because I grew up with two entirely different white-haired women who worried about me, tucked me in at night, made me tomato soup or hot *hierbabuena* (mint tea) when I was ill. 4

Lobo grew up in Mexico, the daughter of a circuit judge, my grandfather. She was a wonderful storyteller and over and over told us about the night her father, a widower, brought his grown daughters on a flatbed truck across the Rio Grande at the time of the Mexican Revolution. All their possessions were left in Mexico. Lobo had not been wealthy, but she had probably never expected to have to find a job and learn English. 5

When she lived with us, she worked in the linens section of a local department store. Her area was called "piece goods and bedding." Lobo never sewed, but she would talk about materials she sold, using words I never completely understood, such as *piqué* and *broadcloth*. Sometimes I still whisper such words just to remind myself of her. I'll always savor the way she would order "sweet milk" at restaurants. The precision of a speaker new to the language. 6

Lobo saved her money to take us out to dinner and a movie, to take us to Los Angeles in the summer, to buy us shiny black shoes for Christmas. Though she never married and never bore children, Lobo taught me much about one of our greatest challenges as human beings: loving well. I don't think she ever discussed the subject with me, but through the years she lived her love, and I was privileged to watch. 7

She died at ninety-four. She was no sweet, docile Mexican woman dying with perfect resignation. Some of her last words before drifting into semiconsciousness were loud words of annoyance at the incompetence of nurses and doctors. 8

"*No sirven.*" "They're worthless," she'd say to me in Spanish. 9

"They don't know what they're doing. My throat is hurting and they're taking X-rays. Tell them to take care of my throat first." 10

I was busy striving for my cherished middle-class politeness. "Shh, shh," I'd say. "They're doing the best they can." 11

"Well, it's not good enough," she'd say, sitting up in anger. 12

Lobo was a woman of fierce feelings, of strong opinions. She was a woman who literally whistled while she worked. The best way to cheer her when she'd visit my young children was to ask for her help. Ask her to make a bed, fold laundry, set the table, or dry dishes, and the whistling would begin as she moved about her task. Like all of us, she loved being needed. Understandable, then, that she muttered in annoyance when her body began to fail her. She was a woman who found self-definition and joy in visibly showing her family her love for us by bringing us hot *té de canela* (cinnamon tea) in the middle of the night to ease a cough, by bringing us comics and candy whenever she returned home. A life of giving. 13

One of my last memories of her is a visit I made to her on November 2, *El Día de los Muertos*, or All Souls' Day. She was sitting in her rocking chair, smiling wistfully. The source of the smile may seem a bit bizarre to a U.S. audience. She was fondly remembering past visits to the local cemetery on this religious feast day. 14

"What a silly old woman I have become," she said. "Here I sit in my rocking chair all day on All Souls' Day, sitting when I should be out there. At the cemetery. Taking good care of *mis muertos*, my dead ones. 15

"What a time I used to have. I'd wake while it was still dark outside. I'd hear the first morning birds, and my fingers would almost itch to begin. By six I'd be having a hot bath, dressing carefully in black, wanting *mis muertos* to be proud of me, proud to have me looking respectable and proud to have their graves taken care of. I'd have my black coffee and plenty of toast. You know the way I like it. Well browned and well buttered. I wanted to be ready to work hard. 16

"The bus ride to the other side of town was a long one, but I'd say a rosary and plan my day. I'd hope that my perfume wasn't too strong and yet would remind others that I was a lady. 17

"The air at the cemetery gates was full of chrysanthemums: that strong, sharp, fall smell. I'd buy tin cans full of the gold and wine flowers. How I liked seeing aunts and uncles who were also there to care for the graves of their loved ones. We'd hug. Happy together. 18

"Then it was time to begin. The smell of chrysanthemums was like a whiff of pure energy. I'd pull the heavy hose and wash the gravestones over and over, listening to the water pelting away the desert sand. I always brought newspaper. I'd kneel on the few patches of grass, and I'd scrub and scrub, shining the gray stones, leaning back on my knees to rest for a bit and then scrubbing again. Finally a relative from nearby would say, '*Ya, ya, Nacha,*' and laugh. Enough. I'd stop, blink my eyes to return from my trance. Slightly dazed, I'd stand slowly, place a can of chrysanthemums before each grave. 19

"Sometimes I would just stand there in the desert sun and listen. I'd hear the quiet crying of people visiting new graves; I'd hear families exchanging gossip while they worked.　20

"One time I heard my aunt scolding her dead husband. She'd sweep his gravestone and say, '*¿Porqué?* Why did you do this, you thoughtless man? Why did you go and leave me like this? You know I don't like to be alone. Why did you stop living?' Such a sight to see my aunt with her proper black hat and her fine dress and her carefully polished shoes muttering away for all to hear.　21

"To stifle my laughter, I had to cover my mouth with my hands."　22

■ Thinking Critically about the Text

Mora grew up living with an extended family that included her grand-mother and aunt. Why does she "marvel at the generosity of [her] parents" in this regard (paragraph 4)? What concessions might her parents have made to help make their living arrangement work? What were the benefits of the arrangement for Mora in particular?

■ Questions on Subject

1. Why do you think Mora's aunt Ignacia wanted to be called "Lobo"?
2. What does Mora mean when she writes in paragraph 1 about the name Lobo: "Like all names it became synonymous with her, and to this day returns me to my childself" (paragraph 1)?
3. Mora writes in paragraph 13 that Lobo "found self-definition and joy in visibly showing her family her love." In what acts did Lobo specifically, according to Mora, exhibit her love?
4. Why was All Souls' Day so important to Lobo? Why was it important for her to go to the cemetery on this day?
5. When she was dying, Lobo became annoyed at her nurses. What was her problem? How does Mora inform us of Lobo's problem with her nurses? (Glossary: *Dialogue*)

■ Questions on Strategy

1. How does Mora show us Lobo's playful side?
2. How does the image of the "wolf" work in furthering Mora's purpose? (Glossary: *Figures of Speech*)
3. What advantage does Mora gain by using food, particularly drink, to help her describe Lobo? (Glossary: *Figures of Speech*)

4. Mora writes in paragraph 8 that Lobo was "no sweet, docile Mexican woman dying with perfect resignation." How does Mora show us this side of Lobo?

5. How does Mora show us Lobo's respect for All Souls' Day? (Glossary: *Dialogue; Illustration*)

■ Questions on Diction and Vocabulary

1. Why do you suppose Mora invents the term "childself" instead of using the word *childhood* (paragraph 1)? How does the new term help Mora accomplish her purpose?

2. What does Mora accomplish by adding some Spanish words and phrases to her description of Lobo?

3. Mora says in paragraph 6 that Lobo used words in referring to her job that she [Mora] "never completely understood." What were those words and why did she not bother to find out their meanings? What magic qualities might they have had for Mora?

■ Classroom Activity Using Description

Organizational possibilities are many and varied, reflecting your purpose and the subject or object you are attempting to describe. Depending on your purpose you could present the same set of details and order them in several different ways. Suppose, for example, you wanted to describe a favorite teacher you had in high school. You could present your teacher's qualities according to a logical plan ranging from the least important to the most important, or you could describe her qualities in a chronological manner from the time you first met her to the time you had to leave her class. You could also organize your description according to her obvious physical attributes and then move on to describe the more complex parts of her personality, in effect moving from the outer to the inner person.

In order to see how this works, first make a list of descriptive features for an object of your choice and then organize them according to any two of the following principles:

Smallest to largest

Least to most important

Outside to inside

Far to near

Left to right

Easiest to most difficult to understand

Specific to general

■ Writing Suggestions

1. Using Mora's essay as a model and the questions in the Preparing to Read prompt for this essay, write a description of one of your favorite

aunts or uncles or a special family friend. Keep in mind that effective description requires examples drawn from sense perceptions, telling details, thoughtful organization, showing and not telling, and the use of concrete nouns and strong action verbs, as well as figurative language. Above all, think about the dominant impression you wish to create and your larger purpose in describing the person you choose as your subject.

2. Mora returned the gift of love that her aunt bestowed on her by writing about Lobo and, in a sense, immortalized her. In similar fashion, describe a relative, friend, or even a stranger who has given you a character-building gift, whether it be perseverance, courage, dedication, honesty, or some other intangible trait — and how that gift was passed on to you by your subject. Describe how your subject was able to influence you so importantly and how you have put that gift to good use in your own life.

The Barrio

ROBERT RAMÍREZ

Robert Ramírez was born in 1949 and was raised in Edinburg, Texas, near the Mexican border. He graduated from the University of Texas–Pan American and then worked in several communications-related jobs before joining KGBT-TV in Harlingen, Texas, where he was an anchor. He then moved to finance and worked for a time in banking and as a development officer responsible for alumni fund-raising for his alma mater.

Ramírez's knowledge of the barrio allows him to paint an affectionate portrait of barrio life that nevertheless has a hard edge. His barrio is colorful but not romantic, and his description raises important societal issues as it describes the vibrant community. "The Barrio" was originally published in *Pain and Promise: The Chicano Today* (1972), edited by Edward Simmen.

■ Preparing to Read

Describe the neighborhood in which you grew up or the most memorable neighborhood you ever encountered. Did you like it? Why or why not? How strong was the sense of community between neighbors? How did it contrast with other neighborhoods nearby?

The train, its metal wheels squealing as they spin along the silvery tracks, 1
rolls slower now. Through the gaps between the cars blinks a streetlamp, and this pulsing light on a barrio streetcorner beats slower, like a weary heartbeat, until the train shudders to a halt, the light goes out, and the barrio is deep asleep.

Throughout Aztlán (the Nahuatl term meaning "land to the north"), 2
trains grumble along the edges of a sleeping people. From Lower California, through the blistering Southwest, down the Rio Grande to the muddy Gulf, the darkness and mystery of dreams engulf communities fenced off by railroads, canals, and expressways. Paradoxical communities, isolated from the rest of the town by concrete columned monuments of progress, yet stranded in the past. They are surrounded by change. It eludes their reach, in their own backyards, and the people, unable and unwilling to see the future, or even touch the present, perpetuate the past.

Leaning from the expressway or jolting across the tracks, one enters 3
a different physical world permeated by a different attitude. The physical

dimensions are impressive. It is a large section of town which extends for fifteen blocks north and south along the tracks, and then advances eastward, thinning into nothingness beyond the city limits. Within the invisible (yet sensible) walls of the barrio, are many, many people living in too few houses. The homes, however, are much more numerous than on the outside.

The barrio is a refuge from the harshness and the coldness of the Anglo world.

Members of the barrio describe the entire area 4 as their home. It is a home, but it is more than this. The barrio is a refuge from the harshness and the coldness of the Anglo world. It is a forced refuge. The leprous people are isolated from the rest of the community and contained in their section of town. The stoical pariahs of the barrio accept their fate, and from the angry seeds of rejection grow the flowers of closeness between outcasts, not the thorns of bitterness and the mad desire to flee. There is no want to escape, for the feeling of the barrio is known only to its inhabitants, and the material needs of life can also be found here.

The *tortillería* fires up its machinery three times a day, producing steaming, round, flat slices of barrio bread. In the winter, the warmth of the tortilla factory is a wool *sarape* in the chilly morning hours, but in the summer, it unbearably toasts every noontime customer.

The *panadería* sends its sweet messenger aroma down the dimly lit street, 6 announcing the arrival of fresh, hot sugary *pan dulce*.

The small corner grocery serves the meal-to-meal needs of customers, 7 and the owner, a part of the neighborhood, willingly gives credit to people unable to pay cash for foodstuffs.

The barbershop is a living room with hydraulic chairs, radio, and television, where old friends meet and speak of life as their salted hair falls aimlessly about them.

The pool hall is a junior level country club where *'chucos*, strangers in 9 their own land, get together to shoot pool and rap, while veterans, unaware of the cracking, popping balls on the green felt, complacently play dominoes beneath rudely hung *Playboy* foldouts.

The *cantina* is the night spot of the barrio. It is the country club and 10 the den where the rites of puberty are enacted. Here the young become men. It is in the taverns that the young dude shows his *machismo* through the quantity of beer he can hold, the stories of *rucas* he has had, and his willingness and ability to defend his image against hardened and scarred old lions.

No, there is no frantic wish to flee. It would be absurd to leave the familiar and nervously step into the strange and cold Anglo community when the needs of the Chicano can be met in the barrio.

The barrio is closeness. From the family living unit, familial relationships 12
stretch out to immediate neighbors, down the block, around the corner, and
to all parts of the barrio. The feeling of family, a rare and treasurable senti-
ment, pervades and accounts for the inability of the people to leave. The barrio is this attitude manifested on the countenances of the people, on the faces
of their homes, and in the gaiety of their gardens.

The color-splashed homes arrest your eyes, arouse your curiosity, and 13
make you wonder what life scenes are being played out in them. The flimsy,
brightly colored, wood-frame houses ignore no neon-brilliant color. Houses
trimmed in orange, chartreuse, lime-green, yellow, and mixtures of these and
other hues beckon the beholder to reflect on the peculiarity of each home.
Passing through this land is refreshing like Brubeck, not narcotizing like
revolting rows of similar houses, which neither offend nor please.

In the evenings, the porches and front yards are occupied with men 14
calmly talking over the noise of children playing baseball in the unpaved
extension of the living room, while the women cook supper or gossip with
female neighbors as they water their *jardines*. The gardens mutely echo the
expressive verses of the colorful houses. The denseness of multicolored plants
and trees gives the house the appearance of an oasis or a tropical island hide-
away, sheltered from the rest of the world.

Fences are common in the barrio, but they are fences and not the walls of 15
the Anglo community. On the western side of town, the high wooden fences
between houses are thick, impenetrable walls, built to keep the neighbors at
bay. In the barrio, the fences may be rusty, wire contraptions or thick green
shrubs. In either case you can see through them and feel no sense of intru-
sion when you cross them.

Many lower-income families of the barrio manage to maintain a com- 16
fortable standard of living through the communal action of family members
who contribute their wages to the head of the family. Economic need creates
interdependence and closeness. Small barefooted boys sell papers on cool,
dark Sunday mornings, deny themselves pleasantries, and give their earnings
to *mamá*. The older the child, the greater the responsibility to help the head
of the household provide for the rest of the family.

There are those, too, who for a number of reasons have not achieved 17
a relative sense of financial security. Perhaps it results from too many children too soon, but it is the homes of these people and their situation that
numbs rather than charms. Their houses, aged and bent, oozing children, are
fissures in the horn of plenty. Their wooden homes may have brick-pattern
asbestos tile on the outer walls, but the tile is not convincing.

Unable to pay city taxes or incapable of influencing the city to live up to 18
its duty to serve all the citizens, the poorer barrio families remain trapped
in the nineteenth century and survive as best they can. The backyards have
well-worn paths to the outhouses, which sit near the alley. Running water

is considered a luxury in some parts of the barrio. Decent drainage is usually unknown, and when it rains, the water stands for days, an incubator of health hazards and an avoidable nuisance. Streets, costly to pave, remain rough, rocky trails. Tires do not last long, and the constant rattling and shaking grind away a car's life and spread dust through screen windows.

The houses and their *jardines*, the jollity of the people in an adverse   19
world, the brightly feathered alarm clock pecking away at supper and cautiously eyeing the children playing nearby, produce a mystifying sensation at finding the noble savage alive in the twentieth century. It is easy to look at the positive qualities of life in the barrio, and look at them with a distantly envious feeling. One wishes to experience the feelings of the barrio and not the hardships. Remembering the illness, the hunger, the feeling of time running out on you, the walls, both real and imagined, reflecting on living in the past, one finds his envy becoming more elusive, until it has vanished altogether.

Back now beyond the tracks, the train creaks and groans, the cars jostle   20
each other down the track, and as the light begins its pulsing, the barrio, with all its meanings, greets a new dawn with yawns and restless stretchings.

■ Thinking Critically about the Text

Does Ramírez's essay leave you with a positive or negative image of the barrio? Is it a place you would like to live, visit, or avoid? Explain your answer.

■ Questions on Subject

1. Based on Ramírez's essay, what is the barrio? Why do you think that Ramírez uses the image of the train to introduce and close his essay about the barrio?
2. Why does Ramírez refer to the barrios of the Southwest as "paradoxical communities" (paragraph 2)?
3. In paragraph 4, Ramírez states that residents consider the barrio something more than a home. What does he mean? In what ways is it more than just a place where they live?
4. Why are the color schemes of the houses in the barrio striking? How do they contrast with houses in other areas of town? (Glossary: *Comparison and Contrast*)
5. Many of the barrio residents are able to achieve financial security. How are they able to do this? What is life like for those who cannot?

■ Questions on Strategy

1. Explain Ramírez's use of the imagery of walls and fences to describe a sense of cultural isolation. What might this imagery symbolize?

2. Ramírez uses several metaphors throughout his essay. (Glossary: *Figures of Speech*) Identify them, and discuss how they contribute to the essay.
3. Ramírez begins his essay with a relatively positive picture of the barrio but ends on a more disheartening note. (Glossary: *Beginnings/Endings*) Why has he organized his essay this way? What might the effect have been if he had reversed the images?
4. Ramírez goes into detail about the many groups living in the barrio. How does his subtle use of division and classification add to his description of the barrio? (Glossary: *Classification; Division*) In what ways do the groups he identifies contribute to the unity of life in the barrio?
5. Ramírez invokes such warm images of the barrio that his statement that its inhabitants do not wish to leave seems benign. In the end, however, it has a somewhat ominous ring. How does the description of the barrio have two components, one good and one bad? What are the two sides of the barrio's embrace for the residents?

■ Questions on Diction and Vocabulary

1. Ramírez uses Spanish phrases throughout his essay. Why do you suppose he uses them? What is their effect on the reader? He also uses the words *home, refuge, family,* and *closeness.* In what ways, if any, are they essential to his purpose? (Glossary: *Purpose*)
2. Ramírez calls barrio residents "the leprous people" (paragraph 4). What does the word *leprous* connote in the context of this essay? (Glossary: *Connotation/Denotation*) Why do you think Ramírez chose to use such a strong word to communicate the segregation of the community?
3. In paragraph 6, Ramírez uses personification when he calls the aroma of freshly baked sweet rolls a "messenger" who announces the arrival of the baked goods. Cite other words or phrases that Ramírez uses to give human characteristics to the barrio.

■ Classroom Activities Using Description

1. Using action verbs can make a major difference in the quality of your writing. Review a draft of a descriptive essay that you have written and look for at least three weak verbs — verbs that do not add very much descriptive punch — and make a list of at least three alternatives you could replace them with. Be sure that the meaning of each of your alternative action verbs supports your meaning and fits the context in which you use it.

2. Examine the first photo on the next page carefully. Based on the visual details in the photograph, what can you say about the community? Which details suggest the area's ethnicity and socioeconomic status? What can you say about the pace of life as depicted in the photograph? From what you see, is this an appealing neighborhood, in your judgment? How does this scene differ from the portrait of a barrio that Ramírez paints in his essay?

The photograph below shows a woman carrying her groceries past a mural honoring Hispanic heroes and revolutionaries. Prominently featured are César Chávez, an American who led migrant farmworkers in protest against poor working conditions in California in the 1950s–1970s, and Che Guevara, a revolutionary who helped Fidel Castro come to power in Cuba in the late 1950s. How does the scene contrast with the one depicted in Ramírez's essay and the one in the photo above?

© Peter Menzel/Stock Boston.

■ Writing Suggestions

1. Ramírez frames his essay with the image of a train rumbling past the sleeping residents. Using Ramírez's essay as a model, write a descriptive essay about the place you currently live and use a metaphorical image to frame your essay. (Glossary: *Figures of Speech*) What image is both a part of life where you live and an effective metaphor for it?

2. Write a comparison and contrast essay in which you compare where you live now with another residence. (Glossary: *Comparison and Contrast*) Where are you the most comfortable? What about your current surroundings do you like? What do you dislike? How does it compare with your hometown, your first apartment, or another place you have lived? If and when you move on, where do you hope to go?

Sister Flowers

MAYA ANGELOU

Best-selling author and poet Maya Angelou was born in 1928. She is an educator, historian, actress, playwright, civil rights activist, producer, and director. She is best known as the author of *I Know Why the Caged Bird Sings* (1970), the first book in a series that constitutes her recently completed autobiography, and for "On the Pulse of the Morning," a characteristically optimistic poem on the need for personal and national renewal that she read at President Clinton's inauguration in 1993. Starting with her beginnings in St. Louis in 1928, Angelou's autobiography presents a joyful triumph over hardships that test her courage and threaten her spirit. It includes the titles *All God's Children Need Traveling Shoes* (1986), *Wouldn't Take Anything for My Journey Now* (1993), and *Heart of a Woman* (1997). The sixth and final book in the series, *A Song Flung Up to Heaven*, was published in 2002. Several volumes of her poetry were collected in *Complete Collected Poems of Maya Angelou* in 1994.

In the following excerpt from *I Know Why the Caged Bird Sings*, Angelou describes a family friend who had a major impact on her early life. As you read, notice the way Angelou describes Sister Flowers's physical presence, her stately manners, and the guidance she offered her as a youngster.

■ Preparing to Read

Think about a major crisis you had to face. Was there someone who came to your aid, offering solid advice and comforting support? How would you describe that person? What physical and personality traits characterize that person?

For nearly a year [after I was raped], I sopped around the house, the Store, 1
the school, and the church, like an old biscuit, dirty and inedible. Then I met, or rather got to know, the lady who threw me my first life line.

Mrs. Bertha Flowers was the aristocrat of Black Stamps. She had the 2
grace of control to appear warm in the coldest weather, and on the Arkansas summer days it seemed she had a private breeze which swirled around, cooling her. She was thin without the taut look of wiry people, and her printed voile dresses and flowered hats were as right for her as denim overalls for a farmer. She was our side's answer to the richest white woman in town.

Her skin was a rich black that would have peeled like a plum if snagged, 3
but then no one would have thought of getting close enough to Mrs. Flowers
to ruffle her dress, let alone snag her skin. She didn't encourage familiarity.
She wore gloves too.

I don't think I ever saw Mrs. Flowers laugh, but she smiled often. A slow 4
widening of her thin black lips to show even, small white teeth, then the slow
effortless closing. When she chose to smile on me, I always wanted to thank
her. The action was so graceful and inclusively benign.

She was one of the few gentlewomen I have ever known, and has 5
remained throughout my life the measure of what a human being can be.

Momma had a strange relationship with her. Most often when she passed 6
on the road in front of the Store, she spoke to Momma in that soft yet carrying voice, "Good day, Mrs. Henderson." Momma responded with "How you,
Sister Flowers?"

Mrs. Flowers didn't belong to our church, nor was she Momma's familiar. 7
Why on earth did she insist on calling her Sister Flowers? Shame made me
want to hide my face. Mrs. Flowers deserved better than to be called Sister.
Then, Momma left out the verb. Why not ask, "How *are* you, *Mrs.* Flowers?"
With the unbalanced passion of the young, I hated her for showing her ignorance to Mrs. Flowers. It didn't occur to me for many years that they were as
alike as sisters, separated only by formal education.

Although I was upset, neither of the women was in the least shaken by 8
what I thought an unceremonious greeting. Mrs. Flowers would continue her
easy gait up the hill to her little bungalow, and Momma kept on shelling peas
or doing whatever had brought her to the front porch.

Occasionally, though, Mrs. Flowers would drift off the road and down to 9
the Store and Momma would say to me, "Sister, you go on and play." As she
left I would hear the beginning of an intimate conversation. Momma persist-
ently using the wrong verb, or none at all.

"Brother and Sister Wilcox is sho'ly the meanest — " "Is," Momma? "Is"? 10
Oh, please, not "is," Momma, for two or more. But they talked, and from the
side of the building where I waited for the ground to open up and swallow
me, I heard the soft-voiced Mrs. Flowers and the textured voice of my grand-
mother merging and melting. They were interrupted from time to time by
giggles that must have come from Mrs. Flowers (Momma never giggled in
her life). Then she was gone.

She appealed to me because she was like people I had never met person- 11
ally. Like women in English novels who walked the moors (whatever they were)
with their loyal dogs racing at a respectful distance. Like the women who sat
in front of roaring fireplaces, drinking tea incessantly from silver trays full of
scones and crumpets. Women who walked over the "heath" and read morocco-
bound books and had two last names divided by a hyphen. It would be safe to
say that she made me proud to be Negro, just by being herself.

She acted just as refined as whitefolks in the movies and books and she   12
was more beautiful, for none of them could have come near that warm color
without looking gray by comparison.

> She acted just as refined as white- folks in the movies and books and she was more beauti- ful, for none of them could have come near that warm color with- out looking gray by comparison.

It was fortunate that I never saw her in the com-   13
pany of powhitefolks. For since they tend to think
of their whiteness as an evenizer, I'm certain that I
would have had to hear her spoken to commonly
as Bertha, and my image of her would have been
shattered like the unmendable Humpty-Dumpty.

One summer afternoon, sweet-milk fresh in   14
my memory, she stopped at the Store to buy provisions. Another Negro woman of her health and
age would have been expected to carry the paper
sacks home in one hand, but Momma said, "Sister
Flowers, I'll send Bailey up to your house with
these things."

She smiled that slow dragging smile, "Thank   15
you, Mrs. Henderson. I'd prefer Marguerite, though."
My name was beautiful when she said it. "I've been
meaning to talk to her, anyway." They gave each other
age-group looks.

Momma said, "Well, that's all right then. Sister, go and change your dress.   16
You going to Sister Flowers's."

The chifforobe was a maze. What on earth did one put on to go to Mrs.   17
Flowers's house? I knew I shouldn't put on a Sunday dress. It might be sacri-
legious. Certainly not a house dress, since I was already wearing a fresh one.
I chose a school dress, naturally. It was formal without suggesting that going
to Mrs. Flowers's house was equivalent to attending church.

I trusted myself back into the Store.   18

"Now, don't you look nice." I had chosen the right thing, for once. . . .   19

There was a little path beside the rocky road, and Mrs. Flowers walked in   20
front swinging her arms and picking her way over the stones.

She said, without turning her head, to me, "I hear you're doing very good   21
school work, Marguerite, but that it's all written. The teachers report that
they have trouble getting you to talk in class." We passed the triangular farm
on our left and the path widened to allow us to walk together. I hung back in
the separate unasked and unanswerable questions.

"Come and walk along with me, Marguerite." I couldn't have refused   22
even if I wanted to. She pronounced my name so nicely. Or more correctly,
she spoke each word with such clarity that I was certain a foreigner who
didn't understand English could have understood her.

"Now no one is going to make you talk — possibly no one can. But bear   23
in mind, language is man's way of communicating with his fellow man and

it is language alone which separates him from the lower animals." That was a totally new idea to me, and I would need time to think about it.

"Your grandmother says you read a lot. Every chance you get. That's   24
good, but not good enough. Words mean more than what is set down on paper. It takes the human voice to infuse them with the shades of deeper meaning."

I memorized the part about the human voice infusing words. It seemed   25
so valid and poetic.

She said she was going to give me some books and that I not only must   26
read them, I must read them aloud. She suggested that I try to make a sentence sound in as many different ways as possible.

"I'll accept no excuse if you return a book to me that has been badly   27
handled." My imagination boggled at the punishment I would deserve if in fact I did abuse a book of Mrs. Flowers's. Death would be too kind and brief.

The odors in the house surprised me. Somehow I had never connected   28
Mrs. Flowers with food or eating or any other common experience of common people. There must have been an outhouse, too, but my mind never recorded it.

The sweet scent of vanilla had met us as she opened the door.   29

"I made tea cookies this morning. You see, I had planned to invite you   30
for cookies and lemonade so we could have this little chat. The lemonade is in the icebox."

It followed that Mrs. Flowers would have ice on an ordinary day, when   31
most families in our town bought ice late on Saturdays only a few times during the summer to be used in the wooden ice-cream freezers.

She took the bags from me and disappeared through the kitchen door. I   32
looked around the room that I had never in my wildest fantasies imagined I would see. Browned photographs leered or threatened from the walls and the white, freshly done curtains pushed against themselves and against the wind. I wanted to gobble up the room entire and take it to Bailey, who would help me analyze and enjoy it.

"Have a seat, Marguerite. Over there by the table." She carried a platter   33
covered with a tea towel. Although she warned that she hadn't tried her hand at baking sweets for some time, I was certain that like everything else about her the cookies would be perfect.

They were flat round wafers, slightly browned on the edges and butter-   34
yellow in the center. With the cold lemonade they were sufficient for childhood's lifelong diet. Remembering my manners, I took nice little lady-like bites off the edges. She said she had made them expressly for me and that she had a few in the kitchen that I could take home to my brother. So I jammed one whole cake in my mouth and the rough crumbs scratched the insides of my jaws, and if I hadn't had to swallow, it would have been a dream come true.

As I ate she began the first of what we later called "my lessons in living." 35
She said that I must always be intolerant of ignorance but understanding of
illiteracy. That some people, unable to go to school, were more educated and
even more intelligent than college professors. She encouraged me to listen
carefully to what country people called mother wit. That in those homely
sayings was couched the collective wisdom of generations.

When I finished the cookies she brushed off the table and brought a 36
thick, small book from the bookcase. I had read *A Tale of Two Cities* and
found it up to my standards as a romantic novel. She opened the first page
and I heard poetry for the first time in my life.

"It was the best of times and the worst of times . . ." Her voice slid 37
in and curved down through and over the words. She was nearly singing.
I wanted to look at the pages. Were they the same that I had read? Or were
there notes, music, lined on the pages, as in a hymn book? Her sounds began
cascading gently. I knew from listening to a thousand preachers that she was
nearing the end of her reading, and I hadn't really heard, heard to understand, a single word.

"How do you like that?" 38

It occurred to me that she expected a response. The sweet vanilla flavor 39
was still on my tongue and her reading was a wonder in my ears. I had to
speak.

I said, "Yes, ma'am." It was the least I could do, but it was the most also. 40

"There's one more thing. Take this book of poems and memorize one for 41
me. Next time you pay me a visit, I want you to recite."

I have tried often to search behind the sophistication of years for the 42
enchantment I so easily found in those gifts. The essence escapes but its aura
remains. To be allowed, no, invited, into the private lives of strangers, and
to share their joys and fears, was a chance to exchange the Southern bitter
wormwood for a cup of mead with Beowulf or a hot cup of tea and milk with
Oliver Twist. When I said aloud, "It is a far, far better thing that I do, than I
have ever done . . ." tears of love filled my eyes at my selflessness.

On that first day, I ran down the hill and into the road (few cars ever 43
came along it) and had the good sense to stop running before I reached the
Store.

I was liked, and what a difference it made. I was respected not as Mrs. 44
Henderson's grandchild or Bailey's sister but for just being Marguerite
Johnson.

Childhood's logic never asks to be proved (all conclusions are abso- 45
lute). I didn't question why Mrs. Flowers had singled me out for attention,
nor did it occur to me that Momma might have asked her to give me a
little talking to. All I cared about was that she had made tea cookies for
me and read to *me* from her favorite book. It was enough to prove that
she liked me.

■ Thinking Critically about the Text

In paragraph 44 Marguerite indicates how important it was for her to be respected and liked for "just being Marguerite Johnson." Why do you suppose she, in particular, feels that way? Why is it important for anyone to feel that way?

■ Questions on Subject

1. What is Angelou's main point in describing Sister Flowers? Why was Sister Flowers so important to her?
2. What does Angelou mean when she writes that Sister Flowers did not "encourage familiarity" (paragraph 3)?
3. Why does Sister Flowers think that reading is "good, but not good enough" for Marguerite (paragraph 24)?
4. What revelations about race relations in her community growing up does Angelou impart in this selection? What do those revelations add to the point Angelou is trying to make?
5. Why is being liked by Sister Flowers important to Marguerite?

■ Questions on Strategy

1. What dominant impression of Sister Flowers does Angelou create in this selection? (Glossary: *Dominant Impression*)
2. To which of the reader's senses does Angelou appeal in describing Sister Flowers? To which senses does she appeal in describing Sister Flowers's house?
3. At the end of her description of Sister Flowers, Angelou implies that at the time it did not occur to her that Sister Flowers might have been asked to give her "a little talking to" (paragraph 45). What clues in the description suggest that Momma asked Sister Flowers to befriend and draw out Marguerite? Why didn't Momma take on that task herself?
4. Why does Angelou have Marguerite imagine the conversations that Momma and Sister Flowers have on several occasions instead of reporting them directly (paragraph 10)?
5. Comment on Angelou's reference to the issue of subject-verb agreement in paragraph 10. Does Momma need to use standard grammar to be understood? Why is Marguerite — who rarely speaks — so embarrassed?

■ Questions on Diction and Vocabulary

1. Angelou uses figures of speech in paragraphs 1 and 3. Explain how they work and what they add to her description of herself and Sister Flowers. (Glossary: *Figures of Speech*)
2. How do Momma and Sister Flowers differ in their manner of speaking? What annoys Marguerite about the way Momma speaks? Does Momma's speech annoy Sister Flowers? Why, or why not?

3. What do you think Sister Flowers means when she tells Marguerite that "words mean more than what is set down on paper" (paragraph 24)? Why is it important for Sister Flowers to tell Marguerite about this difference between reading and speaking?

■ Classroom Activity Using Description

One of the best ways to make a description memorable is to use figurative language such as a simile (making a comparison using *like* or *as*) or a metaphor (making a comparison without the use of *like* or *as*). Create a simile or metaphor that would be helpful in describing each item in the following list. To illustrate the assignment, the first one has been completed for you.

1. a skyscraper: The skyscraper sparkled like a huge glass needle.

2. a huge explosion

3. an intelligent student

4. a crowded bus

5. a slow-moving car

6. a pillow

7. a narrow alley

8. a thick milkshake

9. hot sun

10. a dull knife

■ Writing Suggestions

1. Sister Flowers is an excellent example of a person with grace, charm, spirit, intelligence, generosity, and high-mindedness — personality traits we ourselves might possess or are capable of possessing. Describe someone you know who has similar personality traits and try to imagine what might account for such traits. Can such qualities be learned from a role model? Can they be taught in the abstract?

2. Review your response to the Preparing to Read prompt for this selection. How would you describe the person who came along at just the right time to help you when you were having a personal crisis? Write a description of that person's physical and character traits. Be sure to select the details of your description carefully so that you create a dominant impression rather than simply offering a series of loosely related descriptive details.

WRITING SUGGESTIONS FOR DESCRIPTION

1. Most description is predominantly visual; that is, it appeals to our sense of sight. Good description, however, often goes beyond the visual; it appeals as well to one or more of the other senses — hearing, smell, taste, and touch. One way to heighten your awareness of these other senses is to purposefully deemphasize the visual impressions you receive. For example, while standing on a busy street corner, sitting in a classroom, or shopping in a supermarket, carefully note what you hear, smell, taste, or feel. (It may help if you close your eyes to eliminate visual distractions as you carry out this experiment.) Use these sense impressions to write a brief description of the street corner, the classroom, the supermarket, or another spot of your choosing.

2. Select one of the following topics, and write an objective description of it. Remember that your task in writing an objective description is to inform the reader about the object, not to convey to the reader the mood or feeling that the object evokes in you.

   a. a pine tree
   b. a personal computer
   c. a café
   d. a dictionary
   e. a fast-food restaurant
   f. a basketball
   g. the layout of your campus
   h. a movie theater
   i. a houseplant
   j. your room

3. Select one of the following places, and write a multiparagraph description that captures your subjective sense impressions of that particular place.

   a. a busy intersection
   b. a bakery
   c. a dorm room
   d. a factory
   e. a service station
   f. a zoo
   g. a cafeteria
   h. a farmers' market
   i. a concert hall
   j. a locker room
   k. a bank
   l. a library

4. At college you have the opportunity to meet many new people, students as well as teachers. In a letter to someone back home, describe one of your new acquaintances. Try to capture the essence of the person you choose and to explain why this person stands out from all the other people you have met at school.

5. This chapter on description focuses on people (Sister Flowers and Lobo) as well as places (a rock-dust-covered coal mine and a barrio). Write an essay in which you compare and contrast either pair of readings. Here are some questions to get you started:

   a. If you choose to write on the selections by Mora and Angelou, ask yourself what features of Lobo and Sister Flowers the authors concentrate on. What features do they leave out or downplay? Do they give equal attention to internal and external characteristics, or do they emphasize one over the other? Which person do you get to know better, and why?

b. If you choose to write on the selections by Badgett and Ramírez, ask yourself whether you feel you come to know the coal mine or the barrio better. What techniques do the writers employ that contribute to a better understanding and appreciation? Which author makes better use of dominant impression?

6. **Writing with Sources.** Writers of description often rely on factual information to make their writing more substantial and interesting. Using facts, statistics, or other information found online or in your college library, write an essay describing one of the people, places, or things in the following list. Be sure that you focus your description, that you have a purpose for your description, and that you present your facts in an interesting manner.

a. the Statue of Liberty
b. the iPad
c. Lady Gaga
d. the Grand Canyon
e. the Great Wall of China
f. Hillary Clinton
g. Aretha Franklin
h. the Tower of London
i. the sun
j. Disney World
k. the Hubble Space Telescope
l. Maya Angelou
m. Jon Stewart
n. a local landmark

For models of and advice on integrating sources, see Chapters 14–15.

7. **Writing with Sources.** As a way of getting to know your campus, select a building, statue, sculpture, or other familiar landmark and research it. What is its significance or meaning to your college or university? Are there any ceremonies or rituals associated with the object? What are its distinctive or unusual features? When was it erected? Who sponsored it? Is it currently being used as originally intended? Once you have completed your research, write a description of your subject in which you create a dominant impression of your landmark's importance to the campus community.

You and your classmates may wish to turn this particular assignment into a collaborative class project: the compilation of a booklet of essays that introduces readers to the unique physical and historic features of your campus. To avoid duplication, the class should make a list of campus landmarks, and students should sign up for the one that they would like to write about.

For models of and advice on integrating sources, see Chapters 14–15.

8. **Writing with Sources.** Study the photograph by Gordon Parks that appears at the beginning of this chapter (page 120). First, respond to

the photograph, answering the following questions: What does the image convey to you? How would you characterize the figure of the woman, the presence of the American flag and the broom and mop? Do you see any significance in how the woman and the inanimate objects are positioned in the photograph?

Next, do some research on Parks's work. (You might start by searching for the Library of Congress's online exhibit entitled "Ella Watson, U.S. Government Charwoman.") Be sure to find out why the photo is commonly called *American Gothic*. What is its connection to American painter Grant Wood's iconic painting of the same name? In what ways is Parks's photograph a parody of or commentary on Wood's painting?

Finally, write an essay describing the photograph and discussing its history and the message you think Parks means to convey.

For models and advice on integrating sources, see Chapters 14 and 15.

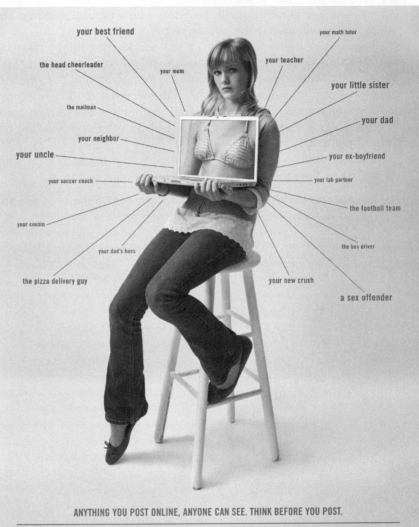

your best friend · your math tutor · the head cheerleader · your mom · your teacher · your little sister · the mailman · your neighbor · your dad · your uncle · your ex-boyfriend · your soccer coach · your lab partner · the football team · your cousin · your dad's boss · the bus driver · the pizza delivery guy · your new crush · a sex offender

ANYTHING YOU POST ONLINE, ANYONE CAN SEE. THINK BEFORE YOU POST.

www.cybertipline.com

Photo by Christian Witkin

CHAPTER 6

Illustration

What Is Illustration?

The strategy of illustration uses examples — facts, opinions, samples, and anecdotes or stories — to make a general observation, assertion, or claim more vivid, understandable, and persuasive. We use examples all the time in everyday life to make our points clearer. How often have we asked for or given an example or two when something was not evident or clear? And many of the advertisements that bombard us daily use illustration — literally and as a strategy to support a claim.

The public service announcement about online predators on the opposite page uses the strategy of illustration (as well as an effective *visual* illustration) to support its assertion that people (and especially teenagers) need to "think before [they] post": The ad presents a picture of a young woman with her computer screen displaying a somewhat revealing image of her, surrounded by twenty — yes, twenty! — examples of people (including potential predators) who can see what she posts online.

Illustration in Written Texts

In the following paragraph from "Wandering through Winter," notice how naturalist Edwin Way Teale uses examples to illustrate his generalization that "country people" have many superstitions about how harsh the coming winter will be.

Topic sentence about weather superstitions frames the entire paragraph.

In the folklore of the country, numerous superstitions relate to winter weather. Back-country farmers examine their husks — the thicker the husk, the colder the winter. They watch the acorn crop — the more acorns, the more severe the season. They observe where white-faced hornets place their paper nests — the higher they are, the deeper will be the snow. They examine the size and shape and color

Series of examples amplify and clarify the topic sentence.

of the spleens of butchered hogs for clues to the severity of the season. They keep track of the blooming of the dogwood in the spring — the more abundant the blooms, the more bitter the cold in January. When chipmunks carry their tails high and squirrels have heavier fur, the superstitious gird themselves for a long, hard winter. Without any specific basis, a wider-than-usual black band on a woolly-bear caterpillar is accepted as a sign that winter will arrive early and stay late. Even the way a cat sits beside the stove carries its message to the credulous. According to the belief once widely held in the Ozarks, a cat sitting with its tail to the fire indicates very cold weather is on the way.

Teale uses nine separate examples to illustrate and explain his topic sentence about weather-related superstitions. These examples both demonstrate his knowledge of folk traditions and entertain us. As readers, we come away from Teale's paragraph thinking that he is an authority on his subject.

Teale's examples are a series of related but varied illustrations of his main point. Sometimes, however, just one sustained example can be equally effective if the example is representative and the writer develops it well. Here is one such example by basketball legend Bill Russell from his autobiographical *Second Wind*:

Topic sentence focuses on athletes slipping into a new gear.

Extended example of Bob Beamon's record-shattering day exemplifies Russell's topic sentence.

Example illustrates that even Beamon did not anticipate his own performance.

Every champion athlete has a moment when everything goes so perfectly for him he slips into a gear that he didn't know was there. It's easy to spot that perfect moment in a sport like track. I remember watching the 1968 Olympics in Mexico City, where the world record in the long jump was just under 27 feet. Then Bob Beamon flew down the chute and leaped out over the pit in a majestic jump that I have seen replayed many times. There was an awed silence when the announcer said that Beamon's jump measured 29 feet 2¼ inches. Generally world records are broken by fractions of inches, but Beamon had exceeded the existing record by more than two feet. On learning what he had done, Beamon slumped down on the ground and cried. Most viewers' image of Beamon ends with the picture of him weeping on the ground, but in fact he got up and took some more jumps that day. I like to think that he did so because he had jumped for so long at his best that *even then* he didn't know what might come out of him. At the end of the day he wanted to be absolutely sure that he'd had his perfect day.

Few readers have experienced that "extra gear" that Russell describes, so he illustrates what he means with a single, extended example — in this case, an anecdote that gives substance to the idea he wants his readers to understand. Russell's example of Bob Beamon's record-breaking jump is not only concrete and specific, it is also memorable because it so aptly captures the essence of his topic sentence about athletic perfection. Without this extended example, Russell's claim that every great athlete "slips into a gear that he didn't know was there" would simply be a hollow statement.

Using Illustration As a Writing Strategy

Illustrating a point with examples serves several purposes for writers. First, examples make writing more vivid and interesting. Writing that consists of loosely strung together generalizations is lifeless and difficult to read, regardless of the believability of the generalizations or our willingness to accept them. Good writers try to provide just the right kind and number of examples to make their ideas clear and convincing. For example, an essay about television bloopers will be dull and pointless without some examples of on-screen blunders — accidents, pratfalls, and "tips of the slongue," as one writer calls them. Likewise, a more serious essay on the dangers of drunk driving will have more impact if it is illustrated with descriptive examples of the victims' suffering and the grief of their family and friends.

Writers also use illustration to explain or clarify their ideas. All readers want specific information and feel that it is the writer's responsibility to provide it. Even if readers can provide examples themselves, they want to see what kind of evidence the writer can present. In an essay on political leadership for a history or political science class, for instance, the assertion "Successful leaders are often a product of their times" will certainly require further explanation. Such explanation could be provided effectively through examples: Franklin D. Roosevelt, Winston Churchill, Corazon Aquino, and Nelson Mandela all rose to power because their people were looking for leadership in a time of national crisis. Keep in mind, however, that the use of these specific examples paints a different picture of the term "successful leaders" than a different set of examples would; unlike leaders like Joseph Stalin, Adolf Hitler, and Benito Mussolini, who rose to power under similar circumstances, the first group of leaders exercised their power in the interest of the people.

Illustration is so useful and versatile a strategy that it is found in many different kinds of writing, such as reports, cover letters, editorials, applications, proposals, law briefs, and reviews. In fact, there is hardly an essay in this book that does not use illustration in one way or another.

Using Illustration across the Disciplines

When writing essays in the academic disciplines, you will have many opportunities to use the strategy of illustration to both organize and strengthen the presentation of your ideas. To determine whether or not illustration is the right strategy for you in a particular paper, use the four-step method described in Chapter 2 (Determining a Strategy for Developing Your Essay, pages 25–26).

Consider the following examples, which illustrate how this four-step method works for typical college papers.

American Literature

1. MAIN IDEA: Mark Twain uses irony to speak out against racism in *The Adventures of Huckleberry Finn*.
2. QUESTION: Where does Mark Twain use irony to combat racism in *The Adventures of Huckleberry Finn*?
3. STRATEGY: Illustration. The direction words *uses* and *where* say "show me," and what better way to show than with solid, representative examples from the novel of Twain's use of irony to speak out against racism?
4. SUPPORTING STRATEGY: Argument. The examples can be used to argue in favor of a particular interpretation of Twain's work.

Criminal Justice

1. MAIN IDEA: America's criminal justice system neglects the families of capital offenders.
2. QUESTION: How has America's criminal justice system neglected the families of capital offenders?
3. STRATEGY: Illustration. Both the statement of the main idea and the question cry out for proof or evidence, and the best evidence would be a series of examples of the claimed neglect.
4. SUPPORTING STRATEGY: Process analysis. The paper might conclude with a possible remedy or solution—a step-by-step process for eliminating the current neglect.

Biology

1. MAIN IDEA: Cloning and other biotechnical discoveries give rise to serious moral and ethical issues that need our attention.
2. QUESTION: What are some of the moral and ethical issues raised by recent biotechnical discoveries that we need to address?
3. STRATEGY: Illustration. The direction words *what* and *some* call for examples of the moral and ethical issues raised by biotechnical discoveries.
4. SUPPORTING STRATEGY: Argument. The direction word *need* suggests that the examples should be both compelling and persuasive so that readers will want to address these issues.

Sample Student Essay Using Illustration As a Writing Strategy

Diets and dieting fascinated Paula Kersch, especially because she and her friends were constantly trying out the popular plans. Eventually, however, Paula began wondering: If these diets really worked, why were people always looking for new ones to try? She also wondered if these diets posed any real risks, especially when she started thinking about the more extreme ones. She made a list of the various diets she and her friends had tried and then did some research on the Internet to see what she could learn about them. On the basis of what she discovered, she developed the following thesis: "If Americans knew more about the risks that accompany these trendy diets and the seriousness of our obesity problem, perhaps they would not look for a quick fix but instead would adopt a weight-management plan that would help them achieve the desired results without compromising their health and their pocketbooks."

Before drafting her essay, Paula familiarized herself with the materials found in Chapter 14, "Writing with Sources," and Chapter 15, "A Brief Guide to Researching and Documenting Essays." What follows is the final draft of her essay. Notice how she uses examples of specific diet plans to explain her key points.

Title: Introduces the topic of the paper.

Weight Management: More than
a Matter of Good Looks
Paula Kersch

Beginning: Engages the reader by referring to common experience and observation.

Americans are obsessed with their weight. Most Americans consider themselves in need of some type of diet, and, whether they're looking to lose those extra holiday pounds or the accumulation of a lifetime, there's plenty of help out there. Bookstore owners often stock an entire section with the latest diet books, and a quick search of the Internet reveals over 250 trendy diets that are currently in vogue. This help is there because dieting is big business in America. In fact, the U.S. Centers for Disease Control and Prevention reported in 2008 that "the dieting industry earned 55 billion dollars in 2006" (*Latest*). At the same time, most experts agree that fad diets don't work (Katz, "Pandemic"). Some estimate that a full 95% of fad diets fail (Hulse).

1

Thesis: Announces the focus of the essay—trendy diets can be dangerous.

In the face of the staggering failure rate for most fad diets, why do these quick-loss plans remain so popular? If Americans knew more about the risks that accompany these trendy diets and the seriousness of our obesity problem, perhaps they would not be so quick to look for a quick fix but instead would adopt a weight-management plan that would help them achieve the desired results without compromising their health and their pocketbooks.

2

Most of the currently popular quick-weight-loss schemes appeal to Americans' desire for instant gratification. Who wants to look forward to a year of losing a pound or less a week? Most of these diets fall into one of several categories: (1) fasts and detox cleanses, (2) plans that emphasize one food group while eliminating or minimizing others, and (3) diet pills and supplements. All of these crash-dieting methods produce results. People who try them lose pounds quickly just as the ads promise—the South Beach Diet boasts seven pounds in seven days and Dr. Simeons' HCG Weight Loss Protocol, thirty-four pounds in forty-three days. Sadly, however, virtually all dieters compromise their health and gain back the weight they lose—and then some.

3

People have been using water and juice fasts and cleanses since biblical times for both spiritual and physical reasons. Most regimens last only a few days, resulting in the rapid loss of five to seven pounds in some cases. The popular Master Cleanse—also known as the Lemonade Diet—developed by Stanley Burroughs in 1941 recommends a slightly longer fourteen-day program to achieve the desired detoxification and diet results (Ogunnaike). Because humans can go without food for longer periods of time if they have water, this regimen is not necessarily dangerous. However, some people push fasts and cleanses to unhealthy extremes. Even apart from the health risks, these extremes often fail to produce the desired long-term weight-loss results.

4

Although there is a technical difference between fasting and starving, metabolically the human body does not differentiate between the two. When a person fasts, the body has to rely on burning its own reserves for energy. Because the body does not know when its next meal might be coming, the body lowers its metabolism in order to conserve fuel, thus slowing weight loss. Also, while fasting may produce lost pounds on the scale, usually it is not the fat loss most dieters aim for. Short-term fasts result in large water losses, which are almost immediately regained once the fast is broken.

5

Organization: Signals the order in which "quick-weight-loss schemes" will be discussed.

Examples of first category of trendy diets—fasts and cleanses—illustrate dangers and problems.

Parenthetical in-text citation documents information about Master Cleanse.

Writer explains in detail what happens during a fast.

The longer a fast or cleanse continues, the greater the serious risk for muscle damage in the body because the body is not getting the nutrients it needs. Additionally, people are at risk of gaining even more weight than they lost after coming off a fast because their bodies will still be functioning at a slower metabolic rate, allowing more rapid weight gain on fewer calories. Repeated fasting can permanently alter the body's base metabolic rate.

6

Writer introduces second category of trendy diets—plans that emphasize one food group while eliminating or minimizing others.

One does not have to be a nutritionist to understand that if people eat only foods from one food group and do not eat any from others, their bodies will not be able to function correctly. Over the years there have been a number of high-protein low-carb diets that promise quick weight loss by emphasizing foods high in protein, while excluding most carbohydrates. The infamous Last-Chance Diet of the 1970s, with its emphasis on a liquid-protein drink and the exclusion of all other food, led to numerous heart attacks and over sixty deaths among users. The Atkins Diet, an enormously popular diet first developed in the 1970s and later updated in *Dr. Atkins's New Diet Revolution*, is another prime example of a diet that excludes large groups of foods. Meat and fat are emphasized to the exclusion of other foods, making the diet high in cholesterol. Neither medically sound nor nutritionally safe, this diet results in a rapid and dangerous drop in weight.

7

Relevant and representative examples illustrate the range of "one food group" diets.

In spite of the fact that this and other low-carb diets—like the currently popular Dr. Arthur Agatston's South Beach Diet and Dr. Gott's No Flour, No Sugar Diet—can compromise a person's health, many people continue to follow these diets to shed their excess pounds. These and other trendy diets that emphasize single foods or food groups, like the Cabbage Soup Diet, the Grapefruit Diet, and the Apple Cider Vinegar Diet, have all been debunked as unhealthy and unrealistic solutions to a very real problem.

8

Writer introduces third category of trendy diets—pills and supplements— and provides some historical perspective.

America's search for a quick, easy solution to the weight problem is perhaps epitomized best in the popularity of diet pills and supplements. In years gone by dieters have used thyroid hormone injections, amphetamines, and fen-phen—a combination of

9

fenfluramine or dextenfluramine and phentermine—
among other things. In September 1997, however,
manufacturers took the "fen" drugs off the market at
the request of the Food and Drug Administration (FDA)
because fen-phen was linked to heart valve damage
and death (Kolata). In May of 2009, the FDA recalled
Hydroxycut, a popular dietary supplement containing
ephedra, which caused liver damage.

Nevertheless, the search for a magic bullet to   10
combat excess weight continues, motivated by the
public's desire for more attractive and healthy bodies
and corporate America's pursuit of unimaginable
profits if they are able to hit on the right formula.
In June of 2008, GlaxoSmithKline first marketed Alli
(pronounced "ally," as in supporter or friend), an
over-the-counter version of the prescription-strength
Xenical, an FDA-approved fat blocker. When used as
recommended, Alli promises to increase weight loss
by up to 50% over what might normally be lost by most
people following a healthy diet and a regular exercise
program. (Alli is not intended as a stand-alone
solution for someone with a nutritionally unhealthy
diet and no exercise regimen.)

While the future currently looks bright for   11
Alli, it remains to be seen whether it will fulfill its
promise. The FDA recommends that Alli not be used
by children or for longer than two consecutive years—
considerable restrictions. Alli also has some annoying
side effects, among them "excessive flatulence, oily
bowel movements, which can be difficult to control,
and anal leakage" (Baldwin). Some may find these side
effects minor deterrents, but others may not be willing to endure the embarrassment and inconvenience
associated with them. Some critics allege that while
Alli blocks the absorption of some fats, it may also block
some important vitamins and minerals. Dr. Sidney
Wolfe, director of Public Citizen's Health Research
Group in Washington, DC, sees no reason to take Alli
because "there are demonstrable short-term risks and
no possibility of long-term benefit" (qtd. in Mann).

It is obvious from even this cursory examination   12
of trendy dieting practices that "get-thin-quick"

Example explores the promise of diet pill Alli in detail.

Writer discusses the drawbacks of using Alli.

Quotation from medical authority used to support reservations about using Alli.

Weight
management
introduced
as healthy
alternative to
"get-thin-quick"
schemes.

schemes typically offer little more than empty
promises. According to experts, the key to real weight
loss is not dieting: The best results come from long-term
changes in lifestyle habits. Weight control is best
achieved with commonsense eating, consisting of
foods high in nutrition and low in fat and sugar, in
conjunction with regular exercise. While this kind
of weight control cannot offer fast results, it usually
proves successful where diets ultimately fail. Here's why.

Emphasis
given to eating
well-balanced
diet and
exercising
regularly.

Losing weight in a healthy manner is a slow   13
process. Most nutritionists suggest that a sensible goal
is 2-4 pounds per month. When a person follows a
sustainable eating and exercise program, that person's
body will naturally start to slim down over time. Eating
a well-balanced diet with foods from the four food
groups gives the body all the essentials it needs. The
high amounts of fiber in fruits, vegetables, and whole
grains make the stomach feel full and satisfied. When
the body receives the nutrients it needs, it functions
better as well. It is common knowledge that depression,
migraine headaches, and lethargy are often triggered
by overindulgence or nutritional deficiencies. Once
moderation is achieved and any deficiencies eliminated,
ailments tend to disappear (United States, *Nutrition*).

Many trendy diets do not advocate exercise;   14
some even claim that exercise is unnecessary. But
working out is an essential ingredient in any good
weight-management program. Exercise tones up the
body and gives people more energy and a sense of
well-being. Moderate exercise such as rapid walking
can rev up the metabolism and help the body burn
calories more efficiently. Regular exercise has the
additional benefit of increasing over time the body's
base metabolic rate so that more food may be eaten
with no weight gain (United States, *Physical*).

Benefits of
exercise
explained.

Conclusion
explains that
trendy diets
will not solve
America's
problem with
obesity.

Trendy dieting as practiced during the past two   15
decades just has not worked. Fasting, one-food-group
dieting, and diet pills and supplements often do more
harm than good in terms of nutrition and general
well-being. As a society, Americans must face the obesity
problem head-on. If we do not, the consequences will
be dire. Dr. David L. Katz, nutrition and weight-control

Quotation emphasizes the gravity of the problem, lending support to the writer's position.

expert and director of the Yale Prevention Research Center, warns that "by 2018 more than 100 million Americans will be obese, and we will be spending roughly $340 billion annually on obesity, a tripling of current levels that are already breaking the bank" ("Compelling" 3B). Long-term weight-management programs that incorporate healthy lifestyle habits offer a real solution where trendy diets fail. When overweight Americans forsake the lure of quick weight loss and understand all the negative aspects associated with these trendy diets, they will begin to get a handle on what they must do to tackle their weight problems.

Writer uses MLA style for her list of works cited.

Models of correct MLA entries for various types of publications are given on pages 695–705.

Works Cited

Baldwin, Donovan. "Pros and Cons of the New Alli Diet Pill." *SearchWarp.com*. SearchWarp.com, 20 June 2007. Web. 20 Jan. 2010.

Hulse, Dean. "Fad Diets Popular but Have Major-League Failure Rate." *News for North Dakotans*. Agriculture Communication, North Dakota State U, 8 July 1999. Web. 10 Feb. 2010.

Katz, David L. "The Compelling Case for Obesity Control." *Naples Daily News*. 3 Jan. 2010: B1+. Print.

---. "Pandemic Obesity and the Contagion of Nutritional Nonsense." *Public Health Review* 31.1 (2003): 33-44. Web. 10 Feb. 2010.

Kolata, Gina. "Companies Recall 2 Top Diet Drugs at F.D.A.'s Urging." *New York Times*. New York Times, 16 Sept. 1997. Web. 8 Feb. 2010.

Mann, Denise. "All about Alli, the Weight Loss Pill." *WebMD*. WebMD, 2007. Web. 2 Feb. 2010.

Ogunnaike, Lola. "I Heard It through the Diet Grapevine." *New York Times*. New York Times, 10 Dec. 2006. Web. 9 Feb. 2010.

United States. Dept. of Health and Human Services. Centers for Disease Control and Prevention. *Latest CDC Data Show More Americans Report Being Obese*. 17 July 2008. *CDC Online Newsroom*. Web. 20 Jan. 2010.

---.---.---. *Nutrition for Everyone*. 14 Sept. 2009. CDC. Web. 9 Feb. 2010.

---.---.---. *Physical Activity for Everyone*. 14 Sept. 2009. CDC. Web. 9 Feb. 2010.

Suggestions for Using Illustration As a Writing Strategy

As you plan, write, and revise your illustration essay, be mindful of the writing process guidelines described in Chapter 2 (see pages 16–40). Also, pay particular attention to the basic requirements and essential ingredients for this writing strategy.

■ Planning Your Illustration Essay

Planning is an essential part of writing a good illustration essay. You can save yourself a great deal of effort by taking the time to think about the key building blocks of your essay before you actually begin to write.

Focus on Your Thesis or Main Idea. Begin by thinking of how you can make your ideas clearer and more persuasive by illustrating them with examples — facts, anecdotes, and specific details. Once you have established your thesis — the main point that you will develop in your essay — you should find examples that add clarity, color, and authority.
    Consider the following thesis:

> Americans are a pain-conscious people who would rather get rid of
> pain than seek and cure its root causes.

This assertion is broad; it cries out for evidence or support. You could make it stronger and more meaningful through illustration. You might, for example, point to the sheer number of over-the-counter painkillers available and the different types of pain they address, or cite specific situations in which people you know have gone to the drugstore instead of to a doctor. In addition, you might cite sales figures for painkillers in the United States and compare them with sales figures in other countries.

Gather More Examples Than You Can Use.   Before you begin to write, bring together as many examples as you can that are related to your subject — more than you can possibly use. An example may be anything from a fact or a statistic to an anecdote or a story; it may be stated in a few words — "India's population is now approaching 1.2 billion people" — or it may go on for several pages of elaborate description or explanation.

The kinds of examples you look for and where you look for them will depend, of course, on your subject and the point you want to make about it. If you plan to write about all the quirky, fascinating people who make up your family, you can gather your examples without leaving your room: descriptions of their habits and clothing, stories about their strange adventures, facts about their backgrounds, quotations from their conversations. If, however, you are writing an essay on book censorship in American public schools, you will need to do research in the library or on the Internet and read many sources to supply yourself with examples. Your essay might well include accounts drawn from newspapers; statistics published by librarians' or teachers' professional organizations; court transcripts and judicial opinions on censorship; and interviews with school board members, parents, book publishers, and even the authors whose work has been pulled off library shelves or kept out of the classroom. The range of sources and the variety of examples are limited only by your imagination and the time you can spend on research. (For models and advice on integrating sources, see Chapters 14 and 15.)

Collecting an abundance of examples will allow you to choose the strongest and most representative ones for your essay, not merely the first ones that come to mind. Having enough material will also make it less likely that you will have to stop in mid-draft and hunt for additional examples, losing the rhythm of your work or the thread of your ideas. Moreover, the more examples you gather, the more you will learn about your subject and the easier it will be to write about it with authority.

Choose Relevant Examples.   You must make sure that your examples are relevant. Do they clarify and support the points you want to make? Suppose the main point of your planned essay is that censorship currently runs rampant in American public education. A newspaper story about the banning of *Catcher in the Rye* and *The Merchant of Venice* from the local high school's English curriculum would clearly be relevant because it concerns book censorship at a public school. The fact that James Joyce's novel *Ulysses* was once banned as obscene and then vindicated in a famous trial, although a landmark case of censorship in American history, has nothing to do with book censorship in contemporary public schools. While the case of *Ulysses* might be a useful example for other discussions of censorship, it would not be relevant to your essay.

Sometimes more than one of your examples will be relevant. In such cases, choose the examples that are most closely related to your thesis. If you were working on an essay on how Americans cope with pain, a statistic indicating the sales of a particular drug in a given year might be useful; however, a statistic showing that over the past ten years painkiller sales in America have increased more rapidly than the population has would be directly relevant to the idea that Americans are a pain-conscious people and therefore more effective as an example. Examples may be interesting in and of themselves, but they only come alive when they illustrate and link important ideas that you are trying to promote.

Be Sure Your Examples Are Representative.   Besides being relevant, your examples should also be representative — that is, they should be typical of the main point or concept, indicative of a larger pattern rather than an uncommon or isolated occurrence. In an essay on pain referred to earlier, figures showing how many people use aspirin, and for what purposes, would be representative because aspirin is the most widely used painkiller in America. Statistics about a newly developed barbiturate (a highly specialized kind of painkiller) might show a tremendous increase in its use, but the example would not be representative because not many people use barbiturates. Giving the barbiturate example might even cause readers to wonder why aspirin, which is better known, was not used as an example.

If, while working on the censorship paper, you found reports on a dozen quiet administrative hearings and orderly court cases, but only one report of a sensational incident in which books were actually burned in a school parking lot, the latter incident, however dramatic, is clearly not a representative example. You might want to mention the book burning in your essay as an extreme example, but you should not present it as typical.

What if your examples do not support your point? Perhaps you have missed some important information and need to look further. It may be, though, that the problem is with the point itself. For example, suppose you intend your censorship paper to illustrate the following thesis: "Book censorship has seriously influenced American public education." However, you have not found very many examples in which specific books were actually censored or banned outright — most attempts at censorship were ultimately prevented or overturned in the courts. You might then have to revise your original thesis: "Although there have been many well-publicized attempts to censor books in public schools, actual censorship is relatively rare and less of a problem than is commonly thought."

■ Organizing Your Illustration Essay

Sequence Your Examples Logically.   It is important to arrange your examples in an order that serves your purpose, is easy for readers to follow, and will have maximum effect. Some possible patterns of organization include chronological order and spatial order. Others include moving from the least to the most controversial, as in Martin Luther King Jr.'s "The Ways of Meeting Oppression" (pages 384–80); or from the least to the most important, as in Jo Goodwin Parker's "What Is Poverty?" (pages 410–13). Or you may hit on an order that "feels right" to you, as Edwin Way Teale did in his paragraph about winter superstitions (pages 167–68).

How many examples you include depends, of course, on the length and nature of the assignment. Before starting the first draft, you may find it helpful to work out your organization in a rough outline, using only enough words so that you can tell which example each entry refers to.

Use Transitions.   While it is important to give the presentation of your examples an inherent logic, it is also important to link your examples to the topic sentences in your paragraphs and, indeed, to the thesis of your entire essay by using transitional words and expressions such as *for example, for instance, therefore, afterward, in other words, next*, and *finally*. Such structural devices will make the sequencing of the examples easy to follow.

▪ Revising and Editing Your Illustration Essay

Share Your Work with Others.   You may find it particularly helpful to share the drafts of your essays with other students in your writing class. One of our students commented "In total, I probably wrote five or six different versions of this essay. I shared them with members of the class, and their comments were extremely insightful. I remember one student's question in particular because she really got me to focus on the problems with fad diets. The students also helped me to see where I needed examples to explain what I was talking about. The very first draft that I wrote is completely different from the one I submitted in class." To maximize the effectiveness of peer conferences, utilize the suggestions on page 29. Feedback from these conferences often provides one or more places where you can start writing.

Question Your Own Work While Revising and Editing.   Revision is best done by asking yourself key questions about what you have written. Begin by reading your paper, preferably aloud. Reading aloud forces you to pay attention to every single word. You are more likely to catch lapses in the logical flow of thought. (For help with twelve common writing problems, see Chapter 16, "Editing for Grammar, Punctuation, and Sentence Style.")

After you have read your paper through, answer the following questions for revising and editing, and make the necessary changes.

Questions for Revising and Editing: Illustration

1. Is my topic well focused?

2. Does my thesis statement clearly identify my topic and make an assertion about it?

3. Are my examples well chosen to support my thesis? Are there other examples that might work better?

4. Are my examples representative? That is, are they typical of the main point or concept, rather than bizarre or atypical?

5. Do I have enough examples to be convincing? Do I have too many examples?

6. Have I developed my examples in enough detail so as to be clear to readers?

7. Have I organized my examples in some logical pattern, and is that pattern clear to readers?

8. Does the essay accomplish my purpose?

9. Are my topic sentences strong? Are my paragraphs unified?

10. Does my paper contain any errors in grammar, punctuation, or mechanics? Is my sentence style as clear, smooth, and persuasive as possible?

E1–12

Be Specific

Natalie Goldberg

Author Natalie Goldberg has made a specialty of writing about writing. Her first and best-known work, *Writing Down the Bones: Freeing the Writer Within*, was published in 1986. Goldberg's advice to would-be writers is, on the one hand, practical and pithy; on the other, it is almost mystical in its call to know and appreciate the world. In a 2007 interview with Shara Stewart for *Ascent* magazine, Goldberg remarked that "[w]riting and Zen for me are completely interconnected. The relationship is seamless for me. . . . Writing is a practice for me, like someone else would do sitting or walking. Writing is a true spiritual practice." "Be Specific," the excerpt that appears below, is representative of the book as a whole. Amid widespread acclaim for the book, one critic commented, "Goldberg teaches us not only how to write better, but how to live better." *Writing Down the Bones* was followed by three more books about writing: *Wild Mind: Living the Writer's Life* (1990), *Living Color: A Writer Paints Her World* (1996), and *Thunder and Lightning: Cracking Open the Writer's Craft* (2000). Altogether, more than three-quarters of a million copies of these books are now in print. Goldberg has also written fiction; her first novel, *Banana Rose*, was published in 1994. Her most recent books are *Top of My Lungs* (2002), a collection of poetry and paintings; *The Great Failure: My Unexpected Path to Truth* (2004), a memoir; and *Old Friend from Far Away: The Practice of Writing Memoir* (2008).

Notice the way in which Goldberg demonstrates her advice to be specific in the following selection.

■ Preparing to Read

Suppose someone says to you, "I walked in the woods." What do you envision? Write down what you see in your mind's eye. Now suppose someone says, "I walked in the redwood forest." Again, write what you see. What's different about your two descriptions, and why?

B e specific. Don't say "fruit." Tell what kind of fruit — "It is a pomegranate." Give things the dignity of their names. Just as with human beings, it is rude to say, "Hey, girl, get in line." That "girl" has a name. (As a matter of fact, if she's at least twenty years old, she's a woman, not a "girl" at all.) Things, too, have names. It is much better to say "the geranium in the window" than "the flower in the window." "Geranium" — that one word gives us a much more   1 specific picture. It penetrates more deeply into the beingness of that flower. It immediately gives us the scene by the window — red petals, green circular leaves, all straining toward sunlight.

About ten years ago I decided I had to learn the names of plants and flowers in my environment. I bought a book on them and walked down the tree-lined streets of Boulder, examining leaf, bark, and seed, trying to match them up with their descriptions and names in the book. Maple, elm, oak, locust. I usually tried to cheat by asking people working in their yards the names of the flowers and trees growing there. I was amazed how few people had any idea of the names of the live beings inhabiting their little plot of land.

> **Don't say "fruit." Tell what kind of fruit—"It is a pomegranate." Give things the dignity of their names.**

When we know the name of something, it brings us closer to the ground. It takes the blur out of our mind; it connects us to the earth. If I walk down the street and see "dogwood," "forsythia," I feel more friendly toward the environment. I am noticing what is around me and can name it. It makes me more awake.

If you read the poems of William Carlos Williams, you will see how specific he is about plants, trees, flowers — chicory, daisy, locust, poplar, quince, primrose, black-eyed Susan, lilacs — each has its own integrity. Williams says, "Write what's in front of your nose." It's good for us to know what is in front of our noses. Not just "daisy," but how the flower is in the season we are looking at it — "The dayseye hugging the earth / in August . . . brownedged, / green and pointed scales / armor his yellow."[1] Continue to hone your awareness: to the name, to the month, to the day, and finally to the moment.

Williams also says: "No idea, but in things." Study what is "in front of your nose." By saying "geranium" instead of "flower," you are penetrating more deeply into the present and being there. The closer we can get to what's in front of our nose, the more it can teach us everything. "To see the World in a Grain of Sand, and a heaven in a Wild Flower . . ."[2]

In writing groups and classes, too, it is good to quickly learn the names of all the other group members. It helps to ground you in the group and make you more attentive to each other's work.

Learn the names of everything: birds, cheese, tractors, cars, buildings. A writer is all at once everything — an architect, French cook, farmer — and at the same time, a writer is none of these things.

---

[1] William Carlos Williams, "Daisy," in *The Collected Earlier Poems* (New York: New Directions, 1938).

[2] William Blake, "The Auguries of Innocence."

■ Thinking Critically about the Text

Natalie Goldberg found that she wasn't the only one in her neighborhood who didn't know the names of local trees and flowers. Would you be able to name many? How might you go about learning them? (Consider why Goldberg says it was "cheating" to ask people the names of their flowers and trees.) What would you gain by knowing them?

■ Questions on Subject

1. In paragraphs 3, 5, and 6, Goldberg cites a number of advantages to be gained by knowing the names of things. Review these advantages. What are they? Do they ring true?
2. Throughout the essay, Goldberg instructs readers to be specific and to be aware of the world around them. Of what besides names are the readers advised to be aware? Why?

■ Questions on Strategy

1. How does Goldberg "specifically" follow the advice she gives writers in this essay?
2. Goldberg makes several lists of the names of things. What purpose do these lists serve? How does she use these specifics to illustrate her point?
3. What specific audience is Goldberg addressing in this essay? (Glossary: *Audience*) How do you know?
4. The strategies of definition and illustration are closely intertwined in this essay; to name a thing precisely, after all, is to take the first step in defining it. (Glossary: *Definition*) What central concept is defined by Goldberg's many illustrations of naming? How might a writer use illustration to make definitions richer and more meaningful?

■ Questions on Diction and Vocabulary

1. Goldberg says that to name an object gives it dignity (paragraph 1) and integrity (4). What does she mean in each case?
2. In paragraph 1, Goldberg writes, "It [the word *geranium*] penetrates more deeply into the beingness of that flower." The word *beingness* does not appear in the dictionary. Where does it come from? Why does Goldberg use it, and what does she mean by her statement?
3. In his poem "Daisy," quoted in paragraph 4, William Carlos Williams calls the flower "dayseye." How does this spelling reinforce the central idea of the paragraph? Of the essay as a whole?
4. Refer to your desk dictionary to determine the meanings of the following words as Goldberg uses them in this selection: *pomegranate* (paragraph 1), *integrity* (4).

■ Classroom Activity Using Illustration

Specific examples are always more effective and convincing than general ones. A useful exercise in learning to be specific is to see the words we use for people, places, objects, and ideas as being positioned somewhere on a continuum of specificity. In the following chart, notice how the words become more specific as you move from left to right:

More General	General	Specific	More Specific
Organism	Reptile	Snake	Coral Snake
Food	Sandwich	Corned beef sandwich	Reuben

Fill in the missing part for each of the following lists:

More General	General	Specific	More Specific
Writing instrument		Fountain pen	Waterman fountain pen
Vehicle	Car		1958 Chevrolet Impala
Book	Reference book	Dictionary	
American		Navaho	Laguna Pueblo
	Oral medicine	Gel capsule	Tylenol Gel Caps
School	High school	Technical high school	
Celebrity	Male celebrity		Brad Pitt

■ Writing Suggestions

1. Write a brief essay advising your readers of something they should do. Title your essay, as Goldberg does, with a directive ("Be Specific"). Tell your readers how they can improve their lives by taking your advice, and give strong examples of the behavior you are recommending.
2. Goldberg likes William Carlos Williams's statement, "No idea, but in things" (paragraph 5). Using this line as both a title and a thesis, write your own argument for the use of the specific over the general in a certain field — journalism, history, political science, biology, or literature, for example. (Glossary: *Argument*) Be sure to support your argument with relevant, representative examples.

If You Had One Day with Someone Who's Gone

MITCH ALBOM

Journalist and author Mitch Albom was born in Passaic, New Jersey, in 1958. He earned a degree in sociology from Brandeis University in 1979 and master's degrees in journalism and business administration from Columbia University in 1981 and 1982. Starting in 1985, after working for newspapers in New York and Florida, Albom landed a staff position at the *Detroit Free Press*, where he writes a regular sports column. Over the years he has earned a loyal following of Detroit sports fans both as a columnist and as a host of radio and television sports talk shows. His reputation as a sportswriter blossomed with the publication of *The Live Albom: The Best of* Detroit Free Press *Sports* (1988–1995), four volumes of his sports column. With the University of Michigan's legendary football coach Bo Schembechler, he wrote *Bo: The Bo Schembechler Story* (1989) and, when Michigan won the national championship in basketball, he authored *Fab Five: Basketball, Trash Talk, and the American Dream* (1993). But it was the publication of *Tuesdays with Morrie: An Old Man, a Young Man, and Life's Greatest Lesson* (1997), the story of Albom's weekly visits with his former sociology professor Morrie Schwartz, that catapulted Albom onto the national stage. Albom followed this work of nonfiction with the two novels *The Five People You Meet in Heaven* (2003) and *For One More Day* (2006), both of which have been national best-sellers. His most recent book is *Have a Little Faith: A True Story* (2009). Albom's books have sold more than 26 million copies worldwide. In addition to numerous sportswriting awards, Albom has received humanitarian awards for his work with Dream Team, A Time to Help, Caring Athletes Team for Children's and Henry Ford Hospitals, Forgotten Harvest, and National Hospice.

In "If You Had One Day with Someone Who's Gone," an essay first published in *Parade* magazine on September 17, 2006, Albom uses the illustrative stories of five people to find out what they would do if they were granted one more day with a loved one. His examples led him to a surprising life lesson.

■ Preparing to Read

Have you ever lost or become disconnected from someone you loved or were close to — a family member or childhood friend? What were the circumstances that separated you? What would you most like to do with this person if you could be reconnected for a whole day?

Her world shattered in a telephone call. My mother was 15 years old. "Your father is dead," her aunt told her. 1

Dead? How could he be dead? Hadn't she seen him the night before, when she kissed him goodnight? Hadn't he given her two new words to look up in the dictionary? Dead? 2

"You're a liar," my mother said. 3

> **Have you ever lost someone you love and wanted one more conversation, one more day to make up for the time when you thought they would be here forever?**

But it wasn't a lie. Her father, my grandfather, had collapsed that morning from a massive heart attack. No final hugs. No goodbye. Just a phone call. And he was gone. 4

Have you ever lost someone you love and wanted one more conversation, one more day to make up for the time when you thought they would be here forever? I wrote that sentence as part of a new novel. Only after I finished did I realize that, my whole life, I had wondered this question of my mother. 5

So, finally, I asked her. 6

"One more day with my father?" she said. Her voice seemed to tumble back into some strange, misty place. It had been six decades since their last day together. Murray had wanted his little girl, Rhoda, to be a doctor. He had wanted her to stay single and go to medical school. But after his death, my mother had to survive. She had to look after a younger brother and a depressed mother. She finished high school and married the first boy she ever dated. She never finished college. 7

"I guess, if I saw my father again, I would first apologize for not becoming a doctor," she answered. "But I would say that I became a different kind of doctor, someone who helped the family whenever they had problems. 8

"My father was my pal, and I would tell him I missed having a pal around the house after he was gone. I would tell him that my mother lived a long life and was comfortable at the end. And I would show him my family — his grandchildren and his great-grandchildren — of which I am the proudest. I hope he'd be proud of me, too." 9

My mother admitted that she cried when she first saw the movie *Ghost*, where Patrick Swayze "comes back to life" for a few minutes to be with his girlfriend. She couldn't help but wish for time like that with her father. I began to pose this scenario to other people — friends, colleagues, readers. How would they spend a day with a departed loved one? Their responses said a lot about what we long for. 10

Almost everyone wanted to once again "tell them how much I loved   11
them" — even though these were people they had loved their whole lives on Earth.

Others wanted to relive little things. Michael Carroll, from San Antonio,   12
Texas, wrote that he and his departed father "would head for the racetrack,
then off to Dad's favorite hamburger place to eat and chat about old times."

Cathy Koncurat of Bel Air, Maryland, imagined a reunion with her best   13
friend, who died after mysteriously falling into an icy river. People had always
wondered what happened. "But if I had one more day with her, those questions wouldn't be important. Instead, I'd like to spend it the way we did when
we were girls — shopping, seeing a movie, getting our hair done."

Some might say, "That's such an ordinary day."   14

Maybe that's the point.   15

Rabbi Gerald Wolpe has spent nearly 50 years on the pulpit and is a   16
senior fellow at the University of Pennsylvania's Center for Bioethics. Yet, at
some moment every day, he is an 11-year-old boy who lost his dad to a sudden heart attack in 1938.

"My father is a prisoner of my memory," he said. "Would he even recog-   17
nize me today?" Rabbi Wolpe can still picture the man, a former vaudevillian,
taking him to Boston Braves baseball games or singing him a bedtime prayer.

Help me always do the right
Bless me every day and night.

If granted one more day, Rabbi Wolpe said, he "would share the good   18
and the bad. My father needed to know things. For example, as a boy, he
threw a snowball at his brother and hit him between the eyes. His brother
went blind. My father went to his death feeling guilty for that.

"But we now know his brother suffered an illness that made him suscep-   19
tible to losing his vision. I would want to say, 'Dad, look. It wasn't your fault.'"

At funerals, Rabbi Wolpe often hears mourners lament missed moments: 20
"I never apologized. My last words were in anger. *If only I could have one
more chance.*"

Maury De Young, a pastor in Kentwood, Michigan, hears similar things   21
in his church. But De Young can sadly relate. His own son, Derrick, was killed
in a car accident a few years ago, at age 16, the night before his big football
game. There was no advance notice. No chance for goodbye.

"If I had one more day with him?" De Young said, wistfully. "I'd start it   22
off with a long, long hug. Then we'd go for a walk, maybe to our cottage in
the woods."

De Young had gone to those woods after Derrick's death. He'd sat under   23
a tree and wept. His faith had carried him through. And it eases his pain now,
he said, "because I know Derrick is in heaven."

Still, there are questions. Derrick's football number was 42. The day after his   24
accident, his team, with heavy hearts, won a playoff game by scoring 42 points.
And the next week, the team won the state title by scoring — yes — 42 points.

"I'd like to ask my son," De Young whispered, "if he had something to do with that."   25

We often fantasize about a perfect day — something exotic and far away.   26
But when it comes to those we miss, we desperately want one more familiar meal, even one more argument. What does this teach us? That the ordinary is precious. That the normal day is a treasure.

Think about it. When you haven't seen a loved one in a long time, the first few   27
hours of catching up feel like a giddy gift, don't they? That's the gift we wish for when we can't catch up anymore. That feeling of connection. It could be a bedside chat, a walk in the woods, even a few words from the dictionary.

I asked my mother if she still recalled those two words her father had   28
assigned her on the last night of his life.

"Oh, yes," she said quickly. "They were 'detrimental' and 'inculcate.' I'll   29
never forget them."

Then she sighed, yearning for a day she didn't have and words she never   30
used. And it made me want to savor every day with her even more.

■ **Thinking Critically about the Text**

Albom shares with us the stories of five people who lost a loved one. In each case, the loss was sudden and unexpected. How did the suddenness of the loss affect each of the survivors? In what ways do you think sudden loss is different from losing someone to a terminal illness or old age? Explain.

■ **Questions on Subject**

1. Why did Albom's mother cry when she first viewed the movie *Ghost*?
2. When asked how they would spend a day with a departed loved one — if that were possible — how did people respond? What life lesson does Albom draw from these responses in his conclusion?
3. What do you think Rabbi Wolpe meant when he said, "My father is a prisoner of my memory" (paragraph 17)?
4. What does it say about Albom's mother and the relationship she had with her father when it's revealed that she still remembers the two vocabulary words her father gave her the night before he died six decades ago? Explain.

■ **Questions on Strategy**

1. Albom opens his essay with the story of his mother losing her father when she was fifteen years old. How effective did you find this beginning? How is Albom's conclusion connected to this beginning? (Glossary: *Beginnings/Endings*)

2. Paragraph 5 starts with the rhetorical question "Have you ever lost someone you love and wanted one more conversation, one more day to make up for the time when you thought they would be here forever?" (Glossary: *Rhetorical Question*) How does this question function in the context of Albom's essay?
3. How did Albom find the examples he uses in this essay? In what ways are Albom's examples both relevant and representative?
4. Albom often repeats key words or ideas to make the transition from one paragraph to the next. Identify several places where he has done this particularly well. What other transitional devices or expressions does he use? (Glossary: *Transitions*)
5. Why do you suppose Albom uses several one-sentence paragraphs? What would be lost had he tacked the sentence "So, finally, I asked her" (paragraph 6) on the end of the previous paragraph?

■ Questions on Diction and Vocabulary

1. Albom lets most of the people in his examples speak for themselves. What does he gain by letting people tell their own stories instead of telling us what they said? Explain.
2. What, if anything, does Albom's diction tell you about Albom himself? (Glossary: *Diction*) Do you think Albom's diction and tone are appropriate for his subject? (Glossary: *Tone*) Explain.
3. Refer to your desk dictionary to determine the meanings of the following words as Albom uses them in this selection: *scenario* (paragraph 10), *vaudevillian* (17), *lament* (20), *wistfully* (22), *giddy* (27), *detrimental* (29), *inculcate* (29).

■ Classroom Activity Using Illustration

Suppose you are writing an essay about the career choices that members of your extended family have made to see what trends or influences you could discover. Using your own extended family (great-grandparents, grandparents, parents, aunts and uncles, siblings) as potential material, make several lists of examples — for instance, one for family members who worked in agriculture or one of the trades, a second for those who worked in education, a third for those who worked in one of the professions, and a fourth for those who worked in the service sector.

■ Writing Suggestions

1. Has someone close to you — a parent, grandparent, relative, or friend — died, or has someone moved away whom you would like to see again if only for a day? Write an essay in which you first tell us something about your relationship with the person you are missing and then describe what you would do with that person for one whole day.

2. What do you value most about your relationships with family members? Do you have a special relationship with one particular parent, sibling, aunt or uncle, or grandparent? How would you describe the relationship you have with this person? What specifically do you get from him or her? Write an essay about your relationship with this family member, using relevant and representative examples to illustrate why you value having the person in your life.

How to Give Orders Like a Man

DEBORAH TANNEN

Deborah Tannen, professor of linguistics at Georgetown University, was born in 1945 in Brooklyn, New York. Tannen received her B.A. in English from the State University of New York at Binghamton in 1966 and taught English in Greece until 1968. She then earned an M.A. in English literature from Wayne State University in 1970. While pursuing her Ph.D. in linguistics at the University of California–Berkeley, she received several prizes for her poetry and short fiction. Her work has appeared in *New York*, *Vogue*, and the *New York Times Magazine*. In addition, she has authored three best-selling books on how people communicate: *You Just Don't Understand* (1990), *That's Not What I Meant* (1991), and *Talking from Nine to Five* (1994). The success of these books attests to the public's interest in language, especially when it pertains to gender differences. Tannen's other books include *The Argument Culture: Stopping America's War of Words* (1998), *I Only Say This Because I Love You: Talking to Your Parents, Partners, Sibs, and Kids When You're All Adults* (2002), *You're Wearing That? Mothers and Daughters in Conversation* (2006), and most recently *You Were Always Mom's Favorite: Sisters in Conversation Throughout Their Lives* (2009). Her research led Tannen to conclude that "in some ways, siblings and especially sisters are more influential in your childhood than your parents."

In this essay, first published in the *New York Times Magazine* in August 1994, Tannen looks at the variety of ways in which orders are given and received. Interestingly, she concludes that, contrary to popular belief, directness is not necessarily logical or effective and indirectness is not necessarily manipulative or insecure.

■ Preparing to Read

Write about a time in your life when you were ordered to do something. Who gave you the order — a friend, a parent, maybe a teacher? Did the person's relationship to you affect how you carried out the order? Did it make a difference to you whether the order giver was male or female? Why?

A university president was expecting a visit from a member of the board of trustees. When her secretary buzzed to tell her that the board member had arrived, she left her office and entered the reception area to greet him. Before ushering him into her office, she handed her secretary a sheet of paper and said: "I've just finished drafting this letter. Do you think you could type it right away? I'd like to get it out before lunch. And would you please do me a favor and hold all calls while I'm meeting with Mr. Smith?"

When they sat down behind the closed door of her office, Mr. Smith began by telling her that he thought she had spoken inappropriately to her secretary. "Don't forget," he said. "*You're* the president!"

> I challenge the assumption that talking in an indirect way necessarily reveals powerlessness, lack of self-confidence, or anything else about the character of the speaker.

Putting aside the question of the appropriateness of his admonishing the president on her way of speaking, it is revealing — and representative of many Americans' assumptions — that the indirect way in which the university president told her secretary what to do struck him as self-deprecating. He took it as evidence that she didn't think she had the right to make demands of her secretary. He probably thought he was giving her a needed pep talk, bolstering her self-confidence.

I challenge the assumption that talking in an indirect way necessarily reveals powerlessness, lack of self-confidence, or anything else about the character of the speaker. Indirectness is a fundamental element in human communication. It is also one of the elements that varies most from one culture to another, and one that can cause confusion and misunderstanding when speakers have different habits with regard to using it. I also want to dispel the assumption that American women tend to be more indirect than American men. Women and men are both indirect, but in addition to differences associated with their backgrounds — regional, ethnic, and class — they tend to be indirect in different situations and in different ways.

At work, we need to get others to do things, and we all have different ways of accomplishing this. Any individual's ways will vary depending on who is being addressed — a boss, a peer, or a subordinate. At one extreme are bald commands. At the other are requests so indirect that they don't sound like requests at all, but are just a statement of need or a description of a situation. People with direct styles of asking others to do things perceive indirect requests — if they perceive them as requests at all — as manipulative. But this is often just a way of blaming others for our discomfort with their styles.

The indirect style is no more manipulative than making a telephone call, asking "Is Rachel there?" and expecting whoever answers the phone to put Rachel on. Only a child is likely to answer "Yes" and continue holding the phone — not out of orneriness but because of inexperience with the conventional meaning of the question. (A mischievous adult might do it to tease.) Those who feel that indirect orders are illogical or manipulative do not recognize the conventional nature of indirect requests.

Issuing orders indirectly can be the prerogative of those in power. Imagine, for example, a master who says "It's cold in here" and expects a servant to make a move to close a window, while a servant who says the same thing is not likely to see his employer rise to correct the situation and make him more comfortable. Indeed, a Frenchman raised in Brittany tells me that his family never gave bald commands to their servants but always communicated orders in indirect and highly polite ways. This pattern renders less surprising the finding of David Bellinger and Jean Berko Gleason that fathers' speech to their young children had a higher incidence than mothers' of both direct imperatives like "Turn the bolt with the wrench" *and* indirect orders like "The wheel is going to fall off." 7

The use of indirectness can hardly be understood without the cross-cultural perspective. Many Americans find it self-evident that directness is logical and aligned with power while indirectness is akin to dishonesty and reflects subservience. But for speakers raised in most of the world's cultures, varieties of indirectness are the norm in communication. This is the pattern found by a Japanese sociolinguist, Kunihiko Harada, in his analysis of a conversation he recorded between a Japanese boss and a subordinate. 8

The markers of superior status were clear. One speaker was a Japanese man in his late 40s who managed the local branch of a Japanese private school in the United States. His conversational partner was a Japanese American woman in her early 20s who worked at the school. By virtue of his job, his age, and his native fluency in the language being taught, the man was in the superior position. Yet when he addressed the woman, he frequently used polite language and almost always used indirectness. For example, he had tried and failed to find a photography store that would make a black-and-white print from a color negative for a brochure they were producing. He let her know that he wanted her to take over the task by stating the situation and allowed her to volunteer to do it: (This is a translation of the Japanese conversation.) 9

> On this matter, that, that, on the leaflet? This photo, I'm thinking of changing it to black-and-white and making it clearer. . . . I went to a photo shop and asked them. They said they didn't do black-and-white. I asked if they knew any place that did. They said they didn't know. They weren't very helpful, but anyway, a place must be found, the negative brought to it, the picture developed.

Harada observes, "Given the fact that there are some duties to be performed and that there are two parties present, the subordinate is supposed to assume that those are his or her obligation." It was precisely because of his higher status that the boss was free to choose whether to speak formally or informally, to assert his power or to play it down and build rapport — an option not available to the subordinate, who would have seemed cheeky if she had chosen a style that enhanced friendliness and closeness. 10

The same pattern was found by a Chinese sociolinguist, Yuling Pan, in a meeting of officials involved in a neighborhood youth program. All spoke in ways 11 that reflected their place in the hierarchy. A subordinate addressing a superior always spoke in a deferential way, but a superior addressing a subordinate could either be authoritarian, demonstrating his power, or friendly, establishing rapport. The ones in power had the option of choosing which style to use. In this spirit, I have been told by people who prefer their bosses to give orders indirectly that those who issue bald commands must be pretty insecure; otherwise why would they have to bolster their egos by throwing their weight around?

I am not inclined to accept that those who give orders directly are really   12
insecure and powerless, any more than I want to accept that judgment of those who give indirect orders. The conclusion to be drawn is that ways of talking should not be taken as obvious evidence of inner psychological states like insecurity or lack of confidence. Considering the many influences on conversational style, individuals have a wide range of ways of getting things done and expressing their emotional states. Personality characteristics like insecurity cannot be linked to ways of speaking in an automatic, self-evident way.

Those who expect orders to be given indirectly are offended when they   13
come unadorned. One woman said that when her boss gives her instructions, she feels she should click her heels, salute, and say "Yes, boss!" His directions strike her as so imperious as to border on the militaristic. Yet I received a letter from a man telling me that indirect orders were a fundamental part of his military training. He wrote:

> Many years ago, when I was in the Navy, I was training to be a radio technician. One class I was in was taught by a chief radioman, a regular Navy man who had been to sea, and who was then in his third hitch. The students, about twenty of us, were fresh out of boot camp, with no sea duty and little knowledge of real Navy life. One day in class the chief said it was hot in the room. The students didn't react, except perhaps to nod in agreement. The chief repeated himself: "It's hot in this room." Again there was no reaction from the students.
>
> Then the chief explained. He wasn't looking for agreement or discussion from us. When he said that the room was hot, he expected us to do something about it — like opening the window. He tried it one more time, and this time all of us left our workbenches and headed for the windows. We had learned. And we had many opportunities to apply what we had learned.

This letter especially intrigued me because "It's cold in here" is the stan-   14
dard sentence used by linguists to illustrate an indirect way of getting someone to do something — as I used it earlier. In this example, it is the very obviousness and rigidity of the military hierarchy that makes the statement of a problem sufficient to trigger corrective action on the part of subordinates.

A man who had worked at the Pentagon reinforced the view that the   15
burden of interpretation is on subordinates in the military — and he noticed

the difference when he moved to a position in the private sector. He was frustrated when he'd say to his new secretary, for example, "Do we have a list of invitees?" and be told, "I don't know; we probably do" rather than "I'll get it for you." Indeed, he explained, at the Pentagon, such a question would likely be heard as a reproach that the list was not already on his desk.

The suggestion that indirectness is associated with the military must come as a surprise to many. But everyone is indirect, meaning more than is put into words and deriving meaning from words that are never actually said. It's a matter of where, when, and how we each tend to be indirect and look for hidden meanings. But indirectness has a built-in liability. There is a risk that the other will either miss or choose to ignore your meaning.   16

On January 13, 1982, a freezing cold, snowy day in Washington, Air Florida Flight 90 took off from National Airport, but could not get the lift it needed to keep climbing. It crashed into a bridge linking Washington to the state of Virginia and plunged into the Potomac. Of the seventy-nine people on board, all but five perished, many floundering and drowning in the icy water while horror-stricken bystanders watched helplessly from the river's edge and millions more watched, aghast, on their television screens. Experts later concluded that the plane had waited too long after deicing to take off. Fresh buildup of ice on the wings and engine brought the plane down. How could the pilot and co-pilot have made such a blunder? Didn't at least one of them realize it was dangerous to take off under these conditions?   17

Charlotte Linde, a linguist at the Institute for Research on Learning in Palo Alto, Califorina, has studied the "black box" recordings of cockpit conversations that preceded crashes as well as tape recordings of conversations that took place among crews during flight simulations in which problems were presented. Among the black box conversations she studied was the one between the pilot and co-pilot just before the Air Florida crash. The pilot, it turned out, had little experience flying in icy weather. The co-pilot had a bit more, and it became heartbreakingly clear on analysis that he had tried to warn the pilot, but he did so indirectly.   18

The co-pilot repeatedly called attention to the bad weather and to ice building up on other planes: 19

> Co-pilot: Look how the ice is just hanging on his, ah, back, back there, see that?
>
> . . .
>
> Co-pilot: See all those icicles on the back there and everything?
> Captain: Yeah.

He expressed concern early on about the long waiting time between deicing: 20

> Co-pilot: Boy, this is a, this is a losing battle here on trying to deice those things, it [gives] you a false feeling of security, that's all that does.

Shortly after they were given clearance to take off, he again expressed   21
concern:

> Co-pilot: Let's check these tops again since we been setting
> here awhile.
> Captain: I think we get to go here in a minute.

When they were about to take off, the co-pilot called attention to the   22
engine instrument readings, which were not normal:

> Co-pilot: That don't seem right, does it? [three-second pause]
> Ah, that's not right. . . .
> Captain: Yes, it is, there's eighty.
> Co-pilot: Naw, I don't think that's right. [seven-second pause]
> Ah, maybe it is.
> Captain: Hundred and twenty.
> Co-pilot: I don't know.

The takeoff proceeded, and thirty-seven seconds later the pilot and co-   23
pilot exchanged their last words.

The co-pilot had repeatedly called the pilot's attention to dangerous con-   24
ditions but did not directly suggest they abort the takeoff. In Linde's judgment, he was expressing his concern indirectly, and the captain didn't pick
up on it — with tragic results.

That the co-pilot was trying to warn the captain indirectly is supported   25
by evidence from another airline accident — a relatively minor one — investigated by Linde that also involved the unsuccessful use of indirectness.

On July 9, 1978, Allegheny Airlines Flight 453 was landing at Monroe   26
County Airport in Rochester, when it overran the runway by 728 feet.
Everyone survived. This meant that the captain and co-pilot could be
interviewed. It turned out that the plane had been flying too fast for a safe
landing. The captain should have realized this and flown around a second
time, decreasing his speed before trying to land. The captain said he simply
had not been aware that he was going too fast. But the co-pilot told inter-
viewers that he "tried to warn the captain in subtle ways, like mentioning
the possibility of a tail wind and the slowness of flap extension." His exact
words were recorded in the black box. The crosshatches indicate words
deleted by the National Transportation Safety Board and were probably
expletives:

> Co-pilot: Yeah, it looks like you got a tail wind here.
> Captain: Yeah.
> [?]: Yeah [it] moves awfully # slow.
> Co-pilot: Yeah the # flaps are slower than a #.
> Captain: We'll make it, gonna have to add power.
> Co-pilot: I know.

The co-pilot thought the captain would understand that if there was a   27
tail wind, it would result in the plane going too fast, and if the flaps were slow,
they would be inadequate to break the speed sufficiently for a safe landing.
He thought the captain would then correct for the error by not trying to land.
But the captain said he didn't interpret the co-pilot's remarks to mean they
were going too fast.

Linde believes it is not a coincidence that the people being indirect in   28
these conversations were the co-pilots. In her analyses of flight-crew conversations she found it was typical for the speech of subordinates to be more
mitigated — polite, tentative, or indirect. She also found that topics broached
in a mitigated way were more likely to fail, and that captains were more likely
to ignore hints from their crew members than the other way around. These
findings are evidence that not only can indirectness and other forms of mitigation be misunderstood, but they are also easier to ignore.

In the Air Florida case, it is doubtful that the captain did not realize what   29
the co-pilot was suggesting when he said, "Let's check these tops again since
we been setting here awhile" (though it seems safe to assume he did not realize the gravity of the co-pilot's concern). But the indirectness of the co-pilot's
phrasing certainly made it easier for the pilot to ignore it. In this sense, the
captain's response, "I think we get to go here in a minute," was an indirect way
of saying, "I'd rather not." In view of these patterns, the flight crews of some
airlines are now given training to express their concerns, even to superiors,
in more direct ways.

The conclusion that people should learn to express themselves more   30
directly has a ring of truth to it — especially for Americans. But direct communication is not necessarily always preferable. If more direct expression is
better communication, then the most direct-speaking crews should be the best
ones. Linde was surprised to find in her research that crews that used the most
mitigated speech were often judged the best crews. As part of the study of talk
among cockpit crews in flight simulations, the trainers observed and rated the
performances of the simulation crews. The crews they rated top in performance had a higher rate of mitigation than crews they judged to be poor.

This finding seems at odds with the role played by indirectness in the   31
examples of crashes that we just saw. Linde concluded that since every utter-
ance functions on two levels — the referential (what it says) and the relational
(what it implies about the speaker's relationships), crews that attend to the
relational level will be better crews. A similar explanation was suggested by
Kunihiko Harada. He believes that the secret of successful communication
lies not in teaching subordinates to be more direct, but in teaching higher-
ups to be more sensitive to indirect meaning. In other words, the crashes
resulted not only because the co pilots tried to alert the captains to danger
indirectly but also because the captains were not attuned to the co-pilots'
hints. What made for successful performance among the best crews might
have been the ability — or willingness — of listeners to pick up on hints, just

as members of families or longstanding couples come to understand each other's meaning without anyone being particularly explicit.

It is not surprising that a Japanese sociolinguist came up with this expla- 32
nation; what he described is the Japanese system, by which good communication is believed to take place when meaning is gleaned without being stated directly — or at all.

While Americans believe that "the squeaky wheel gets the grease" (so it's 33
best to speak up), the Japanese say, "The nail that sticks out gets hammered back in" (so it's best to remain silent if you don't want to be hit on the head). Many Japanese scholars writing in English have tried to explain to bewildered Americans the ethics of a culture in which silence is often given greater value than speech, and ideas are believed to be best communicated without being explicitly stated. Key concepts in Japanese give a flavor of the attitudes toward language that they reveal — and set in relief the strategies that Americans encounter at work when talking to other Americans.

Takie Sugiyama Lebra, a Japanese-born anthropologist, explains that one 34
of the most basic values in Japanese culture is *omoiyari*, which she translates as "empathy." Because of *omoiyari*, it should not be necessary to state one's meaning explicitly; people should be able to sense each other's meaning intuitively. Lebra explains that it is typical for a Japanese speaker to let sentences trail off rather than complete them because expressing ideas before knowing how they will be received seems intrusive. "Only an insensitive, uncouth person needs a direct, verbal, complete message," Lebra says.

Sasshi, the anticipation of another's message through insightful guess- 35
work, is considered an indication of maturity.

Considering the value placed on direct communication by Americans in 36
general, and especially by American businesspeople, it is easy to imagine that many American readers may scoff at such conversational habits. But the success of Japanese businesses makes it impossible to continue to maintain that there is anything inherently inefficient about such conversational conventions. With indirectness, as with all aspects of conversational style, our own habitual style seems to make sense — seems polite, right, and good. The light cast by the habits and assumptions of another culture can help us see our way to the flexibility and respect for other styles that is the only best way of speaking.

■ Thinking Critically about the Text

In her essay, Tannen states that "indirectness is a fundamental element in human communication" (paragraph 4). Do you agree with Tannen on this point? What does she mean when she says that it is just as important to notice what we do not say as what we actually say?

■ Questions on Subject

1. How does Tannen define indirect speech? What does she see as the built-in liability of indirect speech? Do you see comparable liability inherent in direct speech?
2. Tannen doesn't contest a finding that fathers had a higher incidence of both direct imperatives and indirect orders than mothers did. How does she interpret these results?
3. Why do you think Tannen doesn't tell her audience how to deal with an insecure boss?
4. Why is it typical for Japanese speakers to let their sentences trail off?

■ Questions on Strategy

1. What is Tannen's thesis, and where does she present it? (Glossary: *Thesis*)
2. Tannen mostly uses examples in which men give direct orders. In what ways do these examples support her thesis?
3. For what audience has Tannen written this essay? Does this help to explain why she focuses primarily on indirect communication? Why or why not? (Glossary: *Audience*)
4. Tannen gives two examples of flight accidents that resulted from indirect speech, yet she then explains that top-performing flight teams used indirect speech more often than poorly performing teams. How do these seemingly contradictory examples support the author's argument?
5. Explain how Tannen uses comparison and contrast to document the assertion that "indirectness is a fundamental element in human communication. It is also one of the elements that varies most from one culture to another, and one that can cause confusion and misunderstanding when speakers have different habits with regard to using it" (paragraph 4). (Glossary: *Comparison and Contrast*) How does this strategy enhance or support the dominant strategy of illustration in the essay?

■ Questions on Diction and Vocabulary

1. In paragraph 13, what irony does Tannen point out in the popular understanding of the word *militaristic*? (Glossary: *Irony*)
2. How would you describe Tannen's diction in this essay? (Glossary: *Diction*) Does she ever get too scientific for the general reader? If so, where do you think her language gets too technical? Why do you think she uses such language?
3. Refer to your desk dictionary to determine the meanings of the following words as Tannen uses them in this selection: *admonishing* (paragraph 3), *self-deprecating* (3), *manipulative* (5), *prerogative* (7), *subservience* (8), *cheeky* (10), *deferential* (11), *imperious* (13), *liability* (16), *mitigated* (28), *broached* (28), *gleaned* (32), *relief* (33), *empathy* (34).

■ Classroom Activity Using Illustration

Once you have established what examples you will use in a paper, you need to decide how you will organize them. Here are some major patterns of organization you may want to use:

- Chronological (oldest to newest, or the reverse)
- Spatial (top to bottom, left to right, inside to outside, and so forth)
- Most familiar to least familiar, or the reverse
- Easiest to most difficult to comprehend
- Easiest to most difficult to accept or carry out
- According to similarities or differences

Use one or more of these patterns to organize the examples in the paper you are currently working on, or to organize the lists of examples of career choice in your extended family that you generated for the classroom activity accompanying the Albom essay on page 190.

■ Writing Suggestions

1. Tannen concludes that "the light cast by the habits and assumptions of another culture can help us see our way to the flexibility and respect for other styles that is the only best way of speaking" (paragraph 36). Write an essay in which you use concrete examples from your own experience, observation, or readings to agree or disagree with her conclusion.

2. Write an essay comparing the command styles of two people — either people you know or fictional characters. You might consider your parents, professors, coaches, television characters, or characters from movies or novels. What conclusions can you draw from your analysis? (Glossary: *Comparison and Contrast*) Illustrate your essay with clear examples of the two command styles.

Blue-Collar Brilliance

MIKE ROSE

Born in Altoona, Pennsylvania, in 1944 to Italian American parents, Mike Rose moved with his family to California in the early 1950s. A graduate of Loyola University in Los Angeles, Rose is now a professor at the UCLA Graduate School of Education and Information Studies. He has written a number of books and articles on language and literacy. His best-known book, *Lives on the Boundary: A Moving Account of the Struggles and Achievements of America's Educationally Underprepared,* was recognized by the National Council of Teachers of English with its highest award in 1989. More recently, he has published *Possible Lives: The Promise of Public Education* (1995), *The Mind at Work: Valuing the Intelligence of the American Worker* (2004), *An Open Language: Selected Writings on Literacy, Learning, and Opportunity* (2006), and *Why School? Reclaiming Education for All of Us* (2009). On his blog, Rose describes his educational philosophy — based on four decades of firsthand experience — as anchored in "a deep belief in the ability of the common person, a commitment to educational, occupational, and cultural opportunity to develop that ability, and an affirmation of public institutions and the public sphere as vehicles for nurturing and expressing that ability."

In the following selection from the summer 2009 issue of *American Scholar*, Rose uses the examples of his mother, Rosie, and his uncle Joe — a waitress and an autoworker, respectively — to question society's assumptions about intelligence, work, and social class and to explain and appreciate the cognitive abilities of our nation's blue-collar workers. Notice also how he uses examples to illustrate the range of intellectual demands that he identifies in the workplace.

■ Preparing to Read

When you hear the term *blue-collar* as in "blue-collar job," what comes to mind? What has been your experience with blue-collar jobs or blue-collar workers? From your own observations, what demands do such jobs place on people? Explain.

My mother, Rose Meraglio Rose (Rosie), shaped her adult identity as   1
a waitress in coffee shops and family restaurants. When I was growing up in Los Angeles during the 1950s, my father and I would occasionally

hang out at the restaurant until her shift ended, and then we'd ride the bus home with her. Sometimes she worked the register and the counter, and we sat there; when she waited booths and tables, we found a booth in the back where the waitresses took their breaks.

> Gripping the outer edge of the table with one hand, she'd watch the room and note, in the flow of our conversation, who needed a refill, whose order was taking longer to prepare than it should, who was finishing up.

There wasn't much for a child to do at the restaurants, and so as the hours stretched out, I watched the cooks and waitresses and listened to what they said. At mealtimes, the pace of the kitchen staff and the din from customers picked up. Weaving in and out around the room, waitresses warned behind you in impassive but urgent voices. Standing at the service window facing the kitchen, they called out abbreviated orders. "Fry four on two," my mother would say as she clipped a check onto the metal wheel. Her tables were *deuces*, *four-tops*, or *six-tops* according to their size; seating areas also were nicknamed. The *racetrack*, for instance, was the fast-turnover front section. Lingo conferred authority and signaled know-how. 2

Rosie took customers' orders, pencil poised over pad, while fielding questions about the food. She walked full tilt through the room with plates stretching up her left arm and two cups of coffee somehow cradled in her right hand. She stood at a table or booth and removed a plate for this person, another for that person, then another, remembering who had the hamburger, who had the fried shrimp, almost always getting it right. She would haggle with the cook about a returned order and rush by us, saying, "He gave me lip, but I got him." She'd take a minute to flop down in the booth next to my father. "I'm all in," she'd say, and whisper something about a customer. Gripping the outer edge of the table with one hand, she'd watch the room and note, in the flow of our conversation, who needed a refill, whose order was taking longer to prepare than it should, who was finishing up. 3

I couldn't have put it in words when I was growing up, but what I observed in my mother's restaurant defined the world of adults, a place where competence was synonymous with physical work. I've since studied the working habits of blue-collar workers and have come to understand how much my mother's kind of work demands of both body and brain. A waitress acquires knowledge and intuition about the ways and the rhythms of the restaurant business. Waiting on seven to nine tables, each with two to six customers, Rosie devised memory strategies so that she could remember who ordered what. And because she knew the average time it took to prepare different dishes, she could monitor an order that was taking too long at the service station. 4

Like anyone who is effective at physical work, my mother learned to 5
work smart, as she put it, to make every move count. She'd sequence and
group tasks: What could she do first, then second, then third as she circled
through her station? What tasks could be clustered? She did everything on
the fly, and when problems arose — technical or human — she solved them
within the flow of work, while taking into account the emotional state of her
coworkers. Was the manager in a good mood? Did the cook wake up on the
wrong side of the bed? If so, how could she make an extra request or effectively return an order?

And then, of course, there were the customers who entered the restau- 6
rant with all sorts of needs, from physiological ones, including the emotions
that accompany hunger, to a sometimes complicated desire for human contact. Her tip depended on how well she responded to these needs, and so she
became adept at reading social cues and managing feelings, both the customers' and her own. No wonder, then, that Rosie was intrigued by psychology. The restaurant became the place where she studied human behavior,
puzzling over the problems of her regular customers and refining her ability
to deal with people in a difficult world. She took pride in being among the
public, she'd say. There isn't a day that goes by in the restaurant that you don't
learn something.

My mother quit school in the seventh grade to help raise her brothers and 7
sisters. Some of those siblings made it through high school, and some dropped
out to find work in railroad yards, factories, or restaurants. My father finished
a grade or two in primary school in Italy and never darkened the schoolhouse
door again. I didn't do well in school either. By high school I had accumulated a spotty academic record and many hours of hazy disaffection. I spent a
few years on the vocational track, but in my senior year I was inspired by my
English teacher and managed to squeak into a small college on probation.

My freshman year was academically bumpy, but gradually I began to see 8
formal education as a means of fulfillment and as a road toward making a living. I studied the humanities and later the social and psychological sciences
and taught for ten years in a range of situations — elementary school, adult
education courses, tutoring centers, a program for Vietnam veterans who
wanted to go to college. Those students had socioeconomic and educational
backgrounds similar to mine. Then I went back to graduate school to study
education and cognitive psychology and eventually became a faculty member in a School of Education.

Intelligence is closely associated with formal education — the type of 9
schooling a person has, how much and how long — and most people seem
to move comfortably from that notion to a belief that work requiring less
schooling requires less intelligence. These assumptions run through our
cultural history, from the post–Revolutionary War period, when mechanics
were characterized by political rivals as illiterate and therefore incapable of

participating in government, until today. More than once I've heard a manager label his workers as "a bunch of dummies." Generalizations about intelligence, work, and social class deeply affect our assumptions about ourselves and each other, guiding the ways we use our minds to learn, build knowledge, solve problems, and make our way through the world.

Although writers and scholars have often looked at the working class,   10
they have generally focused on the values such workers exhibit rather than on the thought their work requires — a subtle but pervasive omission. Our cultural iconography promotes the muscled arm, sleeve rolled tight against biceps, but no brightness behind the eye, no image that links hand and brain.

One of my mother's brothers, Joe Meraglio, left school in the ninth   11
grade to work for the Pennsylvania Railroad. From there he joined the navy, returned to the railroad, which was already in decline, and eventually joined his older brother at General Motors where, over a thirty-three-year career, he moved from working on the assembly line to supervising the paint-and-body department. When I was a young man, Joe took me on a tour of the factory. The floor was loud — in some places deafening — and when I turned a corner or opened a door, the smell of chemicals knocked my head back. The work was repetitive and taxing, and the pace was inhumane.

Still, for Joe the shop floor provided what school did not; it was like   12
schooling, he said, a place where you're constantly learning. Joe learned the most efficient way to use his body by acquiring a set of routines that were quick and preserved energy. Otherwise he would never have survived on the line.

As a foreman, Joe constantly faced new problems and became a con-   13
summate multitasker, evaluating a flurry of demands quickly, parceling out physical and mental resources, keeping a number of ongoing events in his mind, returning to whatever task had been interrupted, and maintaining a cool head under the pressure of grueling production schedules. In the midst of all this, Joe learned more and more about the auto industry, the technological and social dynamics of the shop floor, the machinery and production processes, and the basics of paint chemistry and of plating and baking. With further promotions, he not only solved problems but also began to find problems to solve: Joe initiated the redesign of the nozzle on a paint sprayer, thereby eliminating costly and unhealthy overspray. And he found a way to reduce energy costs on the baking ovens without affecting the quality of the paint. He lacked formal knowledge of how the machines under his supervision worked, but he had direct experience with them, hands-on knowledge, and was savvy about their quirks and operational capabilities. He could experiment with them.

In addition, Joe learned about budgets and management. Coming off   14
the line as he did, he had a perspective of workers' needs and management's

demands, and this led him to think of ways to improve efficiency on the line while relieving some of the stress on the assemblers. He had each worker in a unit learn his or her coworkers' jobs so they could rotate across stations to relieve some of the monotony. He believed that rotation would allow assemblers to get longer and more frequent breaks. It was an easy sell to the people on the line. The union, however, had to approve any modification in job duties, and the managers were wary of the change. Joe had to argue his case on a number of fronts, providing him a kind of rhetorical education.

Eight years ago I began a study of the thought processes involved in work like that of my mother and uncle. I cataloged the cognitive demands of a range of blue-collar and service jobs, from waitressing and hair styling to plumbing and welding. To gain a sense of how knowledge and skill develop, I observed experts as well as novices. From the details of this close examination, I tried to fashion what I called "cognitive biographies" of blue-collar workers. Biographical accounts of the lives of scientists, lawyers, entrepreneurs, and other professionals are rich with detail about the intellectual dimension of their work. But the life stories of working-class people are few and are typically accounts of hardship and courage or the achievements wrought by hard work.   15

Our culture — in Cartesian fashion — separates the body from the mind, so that, for example, we assume that the use of a tool does not involve abstraction. We reinforce this notion by defining intelligence solely on grades in school and numbers on IQ tests. And we employ social biases pertaining to a person's place on the occupational ladder. The distinctions among blue, pink, and white collars carry with them attributions of character, motivation, and intelligence. Although we rightly acknowledge and amply compensate the play of mind in white-collar and professional work, we diminish or erase it in considerations about other endeavors — physical and service work particularly. We also often ignore the experience of everyday work in administrative deliberations and policymaking.   16

But here's what we find when we get in close. The plumber seeking leverage in order to work in tight quarters and the hair stylist adroitly handling scissors and comb manage their bodies strategically. Though work-related actions become routine with experience, they were learned at some point through observation, trial and error, and, often, physical or verbal assistance from a coworker or trainer. I've frequently observed novices talking to themselves as they take on a task, or shaking their head or hand as if to erase an attempt before trying again. In fact, our traditional notions of routine performance could keep us from appreciating the many instances within routine where quick decisions and adjustments are made. I'm struck by the thinking-in-motion that some work requires, by all the mental activity that can be involved in simply getting from one place to another: the waitress rushing back through her station to the kitchen or the foreman walking the line.   17

The use of tools requires the studied refinement of stance, grip, balance, and fine-motor skills. But manipulating tools is intimately tied to knowledge of what a particular instrument can do in a particular situation and do better than other similar tools. A worker must also know the characteristics of the material one is engaging — how it reacts to various cutting or compressing devices, to degrees of heat, or to lines of force. Some of these things demand judgment, the weighing of options, the consideration of multiple variables, and, occasionally, the creative use of a tool in an unexpected way.   18

In manipulating material, the worker becomes attuned to aspects of the environment, a training or disciplining of perception that both enhances knowledge and informs perception. Carpenters have an eye for length, line, and angle; mechanics troubleshoot by listening; hair stylists are attuned to shape, texture, and motion. Sensory data merge with concept, as when an auto mechanic relies on sound, vibration, and even smell to understand what cannot be observed.   19

Planning and problem solving have been studied since the earliest days of modern cognitive psychology and are considered core elements in Western definitions of intelligence. To work is to solve problems. The big difference between the psychologist's laboratory and the workplace is that in the former the problems are isolated and in the latter they are embedded in the real-time flow of work with all its messiness and social complexity.   20

Much of physical work is social and interactive. Movers determining how to get an electric range down a flight of stairs require coordination, negotiation, planning, and the establishing of incremental goals. Words, gestures, and sometimes a quick pencil sketch are involved, if only to get the rhythm right. How important it is, then, to consider the social and communicative dimension of physical work, for it provides the medium for so much of work's intelligence.   21

Given the ridicule heaped on blue-collar speech, it might seem odd to value its cognitive content. Yet, the flow of talk at work provides the channel for organizing and distributing tasks, for troubleshooting and problem solving, for learning new information and revising old. A significant amount of teaching, often informal and indirect, takes place at work. Joe Meraglio saw that much of his job as a supervisor involved instruction. In some service occupations, language and communication are central: observing and interpreting behavior and expression, inferring mood and motive, taking on the perspective of others, responding appropriately to social cues, and knowing when you're understood. A good hair stylist, for instance, has the ability to convert vague requests (I want something light and summery) into an appropriate cut through questions, pictures, and hand gestures.   22

Verbal and mathematical skills drive measures of intelligence in the Western Hemisphere, and many of the kinds of work I studied are thought   23 to require relatively little proficiency in either. Compared to certain kinds of white-collar occupations, that's true. But written symbols flow through physical work.

Numbers are rife in most workplaces: on tools and gauges, as measure-   24
ments, as indicators of pressure or concentration or temperature, as guides to sequence, on ingredient labels, on lists and spreadsheets, as markers of quantity and price. Certain jobs require workers to make, check, and verify calculations and to collect and interpret data. Basic math can be involved, and some workers develop a good sense of numbers and patterns. Consider, as well, what might be called material mathematics: mathematical functions embodied in materials and actions, as when a carpenter builds a cabinet or a flight of stairs. A simple mathematical act can extend quickly beyond itself. Measuring, for example, can involve more than recording the dimensions of an object. As I watched a cabinetmaker measure a long strip of wood, he read a number off the tape out loud, looked back over his shoulder to the kitchen wall, turned back to his task, took another measurement, and paused for a moment in thought. He was solving a problem involving the molding, and the measurement was important to his deliberation about structure and appearance.

In the blue-collar workplace, directions, plans, and reference books   25
rely on illustrations, some representational and others, like blueprints, that require training to interpret. Esoteric symbols — visual jargon — depict switches and receptacles, pipe fittings, or types of welds. Workers them-selves often make sketches on the job. I frequently observed them grab a pencil to sketch something on a scrap of paper or on a piece of the material they were installing.

Though many kinds of physical work don't require a high literacy level,   26
more reading occurs in the blue-collar workplace than is generally thought, from manuals and catalogs to work orders and invoices, to lists, labels, and forms. With routine tasks, for example, reading is integral to understanding production quotas, learning how to use an instrument, or applying a prod-uct. Written notes can initiate action, as in restaurant orders or reports of machine malfunction, or they can serve as memory aids.

True, many uses of writing are abbreviated, routine, and repetitive, and   27
they infrequently require interpretation or analysis. But analytic moments can be part of routine activities, and seemingly basic reading and writing can be cognitively rich. Because workplace language is used in the flow of other activities, we can overlook the remarkable coordination of words, numbers, and drawings required to initiate and direct action.

If we believe everyday work to be mindless, then that will affect the work   28
we create in the future. When we devalue the full range of everyday cogni-tion, we offer limited educational opportunities and fail to make fresh and meaningful instructional connections among disparate kinds of skill and knowledge. If we think that whole categories of people — identified by class

or occupation — are not that bright, then we reinforce social separations and cripple our ability to talk across cultural divides.

Affirmation of diverse intelligence is not a retreat to a softhearted definition of the mind. To acknowledge a broader range of intellectual capacity is to take seriously the concept of cognitive variability, to appreciate in all the Rosies and Joes the thought that drives their accomplishments and defines who they are. This is a model of the mind that is worthy of a democratic society.   29

■ Thinking Critically about the Text

What, if anything, did you learn about blue-collar work as a result of reading Rose's analysis? Do you have a greater appreciation for or more insight into the intelligence required to successfully undertake most blue-collar employment? Why do you think this diversity of intelligence has not been more fully acknowledged in the past?

■ Questions on Subject

1. As a child, what did Rose learn about blue-collar work while watching his mother waitress?
2. Rose admits that he had a checkered past in elementary and high school. What prompted him to pursue a college education?
3. What does Rose see as wrong with the assumptions that "[i]ntelligence is closely associated with formal education" and that "work requiring less schooling requires less intelligence" (paragraph 9)?
4. What did Rose discover when he began to study the "thought processes involved in work like that of my mother and uncle" (paragraph 15)? What kinds of cognitive demands associated with blue-collar jobs does Rose catalog?
5. According to Rose, what happens when "we believe everyday work to be mindless" and "devalue the full range of everyday cognition" (paragraph 28)?

■ Questions on Strategy

1. What credentials does Rose have that enable him to write about intelligence and blue-collar workers and their jobs? Where in the essay does he reveal his authority?
2. How do the examples of Rose's mother, Rosie, and his uncle Joe function in the context of this essay? What exactly do these two examples illustrate?

3. How has Rose organized his essay? (Glossary: *Organization*) You may find it helpful to make an outline, identifying major points.
4. What examples does Rose use to illustrate that numbers are an important part of the blue-collar workplace? What examples can you add?

■ Questions on Diction and Vocabulary

1. How would you describe Rose's diction in this essay — formal, colloquial, informal, technical? (Glossary: *Diction*) Point to several specific examples in the text to support your choice. Did you find this diction appropriate given Rose's subject and purpose? (Glossary: *Purpose; Subject*)
2. In paragraph 5, Rose tells us that his "mother learned to work smart." What does the phrase *work smart* mean to you?
3. Refer to a dictionary to determine the meanings of the following words as Rose uses them in this selection: *impassive* (paragraph 2), *haggle* (3), *synonymous* (4), *disaffection* (7), *entrepreneurs* (15), *cognitive* (22), *rife* (24), *esoteric* (25), *disparate* (28).

■ Classroom Activity Using Illustration

The Web site thingsarefine.org, sponsored by the Portland-based advertising agency Borders Perrin Norrander (BPN), features the following text on its home page:

After considering this text, take a look at one of the downloadable posters on the site, reproduced on page 211.

After considering the Web site's message and the poster, answer the following questions: What does BPN want to persuade viewers to do? In the poster, what example does BPN use to suggest what's "fine" (or not) in the United States right now? Is the example persuasive? In small groups, discuss your answers. What conclusions about BPN's use of illustration did you come to?

■ Writing Suggestions

1. Rose confesses that after a "bumpy" first year in college he "began to see formal education as a means of fulfillment and as a road toward making a living" (paragraph 8). Write an essay in which you discuss your career aspirations and what role college plays in fulfilling them. Why are you in college? How is a formal education related to what you would like your life's work to be? What are your expectations of such work? What satisfaction and rewards do you hope to get from your work? Does your career choice have a downside?

2. Using Rose's study as a model, select a blue-collar worker you know — a grocery-store clerk, short-order cook, carpenter, landscape worker, service-station attendant, waiter, barber or hairstylist, maintenance worker, or assembly-line worker. First, observe that person working, paying special attention to the details of his or her work. Next, interview that person about his or her job. Write an essay recounting what you learned about the person you chose and the nature of his or her work. Be sure to use examples to illustrate your main points.

In Full Bloom

ALICE WALKER

 Best known for her Pulitzer Prize–winning novel *The Color Purple*, Alice Walker is a prolific writer of poetry, essays, and fiction. Walker was born in Eatonton, Georgia, in 1944, the youngest of eight children in a sharecropping family that fortunately believed in the value of education: According to Walker's biographer Evelyn White, Walker's mother once defiantly told a white plantation owner, "Don't you ever come around here again talking about how *my children* don't need to learn how to read and write." A self-described "daughter of the rural peasantry," Walker early on learned to value and appreciate the beauty and peacefulness of nature. She started first grade at age four and took advantage of educational opportunities to escape a life of poverty and servitude. With only a typewriter, a sewing machine, and a suitcase in hand, she enrolled at Spelman College in Atlanta, Georgia, where she first met Martin Luther King Jr. In 1964 she transferred to the prestigious Sarah Lawrence College in New York, and she graduated a year later and moved back to the South to join in the civil rights movement.

An African American activist and feminist, Walker often deals with controversial subjects in her writing: *The Color Purple* (1982), the novel *Possessing the Secret of Joy* (1992), and the nonfiction *Warrior Marks* (1993) are known for their unflinching portrayal of difficult subjects. Other widely acclaimed works by Walker include her collected poems, *Her Blue Body Everything We Know: Earthling Poems, 1965–1990* (1991); a memoir entitled *The Same River Twice: Honoring the Difficult* (1996); two collections of essays, *In Search of Our Mothers' Gardens* (1983) and *Anything We Love Can Be Saved: A Writer's Activism* (1997); and two collections of stories, *You Can't Keep a Good Woman Down* (1981) and *The Way Forward Is with a Broken Heart* (2000). Walker's most recent work includes *Now Is the Time to Open Your Heart: A Novel* (2004) and *We Are the Ones We Have Been Waiting For: Light in a Time of Darkness* (2006), a collection of essays. Although much of her writing deals with pain and life's hardships, her work is not pessimistic; in the words of an Amazon.com editorial review, Walker's writing represents a "quest for peace and joy in a difficult world."

The following essay, an adaptation of the introduction to *Anything We Love Can Be Saved*, appeared in the *Nation* in 2004. Here Walker reflects on her life of activism and explains its many facets, using a rich assortment of examples.

- **Preparing to Read**

When you hear the word *activist*, what do you think of? Who, for you, are today's activists? On a scale of 1–10, with 10 being most active, how would you rate yourself as an activist? Explain.

My activism — cultural, political, spiritual — is rooted in my love of nature and my delight in human beings. It is when people are at peace, content, *full*, that they are most likely to meet my expectation, selfish, no doubt, that they be a generous, joyous, even entertaining experience for me. I believe people exist to be enjoyed, much as a restful or engaging view might be. As the ocean or drifting clouds might be. Or as if they were the human equivalent of melons, mangoes, or any other kind of attractive, seductive fruit. When I am in the presence of other human beings I want to revel in their creative and intellectual fullness, their uninhibited social warmth. I want their precious human radiance to wrap me in light. I do not want fear of war or starvation or bodily mutilation to steal both my pleasure in them and their own birthright. Everything I would like other people to be for me, I want to be for them.

I have been an activist all my adult life, though I have sometimes felt embarrassed to call myself one. In the sixties, many of us were plagued by the notion that, given the magnitude of the task before us — the dismantling of American apartheid — our individual acts were puny. There was also the apparent reality that the most committed, most directly confrontational people suffered more. The most "revolutionary" often ended up severely beaten, in prison, or dead. Shot down in front of their children, blown up in cars or in church, run over by racist drunks, raped, and thrown in the river.

In Mississippi, where I lived from 1967 to 1974, people who challenged the system anticipated menace, battery, even murder, every day. In this context, I sometimes felt ashamed that my contributions at the time were not more radical. I taught in two local black colleges, I wrote about the Movement, and I created tiny history booklets which were used to teach the teachers of children enrolled in Head Start. And, of course, I was interracially married, which was illegal. It was perhaps in Mississippi during those years that I understood how the daily news of disaster can become, for the spirit, a numbing assault, and that one's own activism, however modest, fighting against this tide of death, provides at least the possibility of generating a different kind of "news." A "news" that empowers rather than defeats.

There is always a moment in any kind of struggle when one feels in full bloom. Vivid. Alive. One might be blown to bits in such a moment and still be at peace. Martin Luther King Jr. at the mountaintop. Gandhi dying with the name of God on his lips. Sojourner Truth baring her breasts at a women's rights convention in 1851. Harriet Tubman exposing her revolver to some of the slaves she had freed, who, fearing an unknown freedom, looked longingly backward to their captivity, thereby endangering the freedom of all. To be such a person or to witness anyone at this moment of transcendent presence is to know that what is human is linked, by a daring compassion, to what is divine. During my years of being close to people engaged in changing the world I have seen fear turn into courage. Sorrow into joy. Funerals into celebrations. Because whatever the consequences, people, standing side by side, have expressed who they really are, and that ultimately they believe in the love of the world and each other enough *to be that* — which is the foundation of activism.

> There is always a moment in any kind of struggle when one feels in full bloom. Vivid. Alive. One might be blown to bits in such a moment and still be at peace.

It has become a common feeling, I believe, as we have watched our heroes falling over the years, that our own small stone of activism, which might not seem to measure up to the rugged boulders of heroism we have so admired, is a paltry offering toward the building of an edifice of hope. Many who believe this choose to withhold their offerings out of shame.   5

This is the tragedy of our world.   6

For we can do nothing substantial toward changing our course on the planet, a destructive one, without rousing ourselves, individual by individual, and bringing our small, imperfect stones to the pile.   7

In this regard, I have a story to tell.   8

In the midsixties during a voter-registration campaign in south Georgia, my canvassing partner, Beverly, a local black teenager, was arrested on a bogus moving-violation charge. This was meant to intimidate her, "show her her place," and terrify her family. Those of us who feared for her safety during the night held a vigil outside the jail. I remember the raw vulnerability I felt as the swaggering state troopers — each of them three times Beverly's size, and mine — stomped in and out of the building, scowling at us. The feeling of solidarity with Beverly and our friends was strong, but also the feeling of being alone, as it occurred to me that not even my parents knew where I was. We were black and very young: We knew no one in White America paid the slightest attention to the deaths of such as us. It was partly because of this that we sometimes resented the presence of the white people who came to stand, and take their chances, with us. I was one of those to whom such resentment came easily.   9

I especially resented blond Paul from Minnesota, whose Aryan appearance meant, when he was not with us, freedom and almost worship in the race-obsessed South. I had treated him with coolness since the day we met. We certainly did not invite him to our vigil. And yet, at just the moment I felt most downhearted, I heard someone coming along the street in our direction, whistling. A moment later Paul appeared. Still whistling a movement   10 spiritual that sounded strange, even comical, on his lips, he calmly took his place beside us. Knowing his Nordic presence meant a measure of safety for us, and without being asked, he offered it. This remains a moment as bright as any I recall from that time. . . .

All we own, at least for the short time we have it, is our life. With it we   11
write what we come to know of the world. I believe the Earth is good. That people, untortured by circumstance or fate, are also good. I do not believe the people of the world are naturally my enemies, or that animals, including snakes, are, or that Nature is. Whenever I experience evil, and it is not, unfortunately, uncommon to experience it in these times, my deepest feeling is disappointment. I have learned to accept the fact that we risk disappointment, disillusionment, even despair, every time we act. Every time we decide to believe the world can be better. Every time we decide to trust others to be as noble as we think they are. And that there might be *years* during which our grief is equal to, or even greater than, our hope. The alternative, however, not to act, and therefore to miss experiencing other people at their best, reaching toward their fullness, has never appealed to me. . . .

Only justice can stop a curse.   12

■ Thinking Critically about the Text

What do you think Walker means when she writes of "the dismantling of American apartheid" in the 1960s (paragraph 2)? What was America like in the opening years of that decade? What changes did activists like Martin Luther King Jr. bring about? According to Walker, what happened to many of the activists committed to changing America?

■ Questions on Subject

1. In what is Walker's activism rooted? What expectations does Walker have for other people? Do you share her thoughts and feelings about other people? Why or why not?
2. What fears are capable of robbing people of their pleasure in each other and of their own birthright? What fears can you add to Walker's list of examples?
3. According to Walker, what is it like to witness or to be in the company of "people engaged in changing the world" (paragraph 4)?
4. Why does Walker at first resent "Paul from Minnesota"? How does she come to view him differently?
5. Why has Walker chosen to act, to "risk disappointment, disillusion ment, even despair" (paragraph 11) in her life? Why is the alternative unacceptable?

6. What has Walker learned from her activism? What advice does she offer others?

▪ Questions on Strategy

1. How does Walker illustrate her claim that "[she] sometimes felt ashamed that [her] contributions at the time [while living in Mississippi from 1967 to 1974] were not more radical" (paragraph 3)? Do you consider any of her contributions "radical"? Explain why or why not.
2. What idea does Walker illustrate with her examples of Martin Luther King Jr., Gandhi, Sojourner Truth, and Harriet Tubman (paragraph 4)? Do you find these examples convincing? What examples can you add to Walker's list?
3. In paragraph 8, Walker announces that she has a story to tell. (Glossary: *Narration*) Explain how her story of the voter registration campaign serves to illustrate her point that "we can do nothing substantial toward changing our course on the planet, a destructive one, without rousing ourselves, individual by individual, and bringing our small, imperfect stones to the pile" (paragraph 7).
4. Identify the sentence fragments in paragraphs 2 and 3. Why do you suppose Walker chose to use a sentence fragment in each case? Using one or more of the methods outlined on page 708, rewrite each of these fragments to make it a complete sentence.

▪ Questions on Diction and Vocabulary

1. In paragraph 4, Walker states, "There is always a moment in any kind of struggle when one feels in full bloom." What do you think Walker means by the phrase "in full bloom"? In what ways is this phrase an appropriate title for Walker's essay?
2. In paragraph 10, Walker refers to Paul as "Aryan" and "Nordic." What connotations do these words have? Why does Walker use them?
3. Refer to your desk dictionary to determine the meanings of the following words as Walker uses them in this selection: *revel* (paragraph 1), *puny* (2), *battery* (3), *transcendent* (4), *paltry* (5), *vulnerability* (9).

▪ Classroom Activity Using Illustration

Consider the "Back Story" feature on page 218 that ran in the November 30, 2009, issue of *Newsweek*. The graphic is based on analysis of the final statements of the 446 men and women executed in Texas since the death penalty was reinstated in 1976.

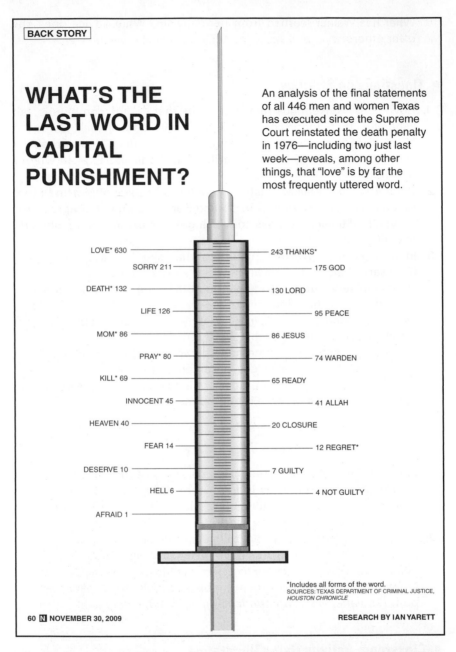

WHAT'S THE LAST WORD IN CAPITAL PUNISHMENT?

An analysis of the final statements of all 446 men and women Texas has executed since the Supreme Court reinstated the death penalty in 1976—including two just last week—reveals, among other things, that "love" is by far the most frequently uttered word.

LOVE* 630

SORRY 211

DEATH* 132

LIFE 126

MOM* 86

PRAY* 80

KILL* 69

INNOCENT 45

HEAVEN 40

FEAR 14

DESERVE 10

HELL 6

AFRAID 1

243 THANKS*

175 GOD

130 LORD

95 PEACE

86 JESUS

74 WARDEN

65 READY

41 ALLAH

20 CLOSURE

12 REGRET*

7 GUILTY

4 NOT GUILTY

*Includes all forms of the word.
SOURCES: TEXAS DEPARTMENT OF CRIMINAL JUSTICE, *HOUSTON CHRONICLE*

60 N NOVEMBER 30, 2009

RESEARCH BY IAN YARETT

What were your first thoughts after reading though the examples of the last words of men and women who were executed? Did any of the words surprise you? Did you find yourself organizing the words into groups or categories? If so, what groups? Did you draw any conclusions about the death penalty from these "last word" examples? Compare your conclusions with those of your classmates. Do these words help you answer the question at the head of the story, "What's the last word in capital punishment?"

■ Writing Suggestions

1. Write an essay in which you attempt to reconcile individual conscience with majority rule. Use well-chosen examples to illustrate each of your major points.

2. **Writing with Sources.** In his essay "Civil Disobedience," Henry David Thoreau wrote, "Under a government which imprisons any unjustly, the true place for a just man is also a prison." Using examples from recent history that you have researched in your college library or on the Web, argue for or against the validity of Thoreau's statement. Where do you think Walker would stand on this issue? Explain.

   For models of and advice on integrating sources, see Chapters 14–15.

3. **Writing with Sources.** The civil rights movement in America during the 1960s helped influence and shape the young Alice Walker, who marched in demonstrations like the one pictured in the photograph below. Research the civil rights movement in your library or on the Web, and then write about a person, a pivotal event, or some aspect of the movement that interests you. What about that person or event impresses you the most? What role did the person or event play in the national drama leading up to the signing of civil rights legislation in 1965?

   For models of and advice on integrating sources, see Chapters 14–15.

WRITING SUGGESTIONS FOR ILLUSTRATION

1. Write an essay on one of the following statements, using examples to illustrate your ideas. You should be able to draw some of your examples from personal experience and firsthand observations.

   a. Fads never go out of style.

   b. Television has produced a number of "classic" programs.

   c. Every college campus has its own unique slang terms.

   d. Making excuses sometimes seems like a national pastime.

   e. A liberal arts education can have many practical applications.

   f. All good teachers (or doctors, secretaries, auto mechanics, sales representatives) have certain traits in common.

   g. Television talk shows are an accurate (or inaccurate) reflection of our society.

   h. Good literature always teaches us something about our humanity.

   i. Grades are not always a good indication of what has been learned.

   j. Recycling starts with the individual.

2. College students are not often given credit for the community volunteer work they do. Write a letter to the editor of your local newspaper in which you demonstrate, with several extended examples, the beneficial impact that you and your fellow students have had on the community.

3. How do advertisers portray older people in their advertisements? Based on your analysis of some real ads, how fair are advertisers to senior citizens? What tactics do advertisers use to sell their products to senior citizens? Write an essay in which you use actual ads to illustrate two or three such tactics.

4. Most students would agree that in order to be happy and "well adjusted," people need to learn how to relieve stress and to relax. What strategies do you and your friends use to relax? What have been the benefits of these relaxation techniques for you? Write an article for the school newspaper in which you give examples of several of these techniques and encourage your fellow students to try them.

5. The Internet has profoundly altered the way people around the world communicate and share information. One area in which significant change is especially evident is education. While having so much information at your fingertips can be exciting, such technology is not without its problems. What are the advantages and disadvantages of the Internet for teachers and students? Write an essay in which you analyze the Internet's educational value. Document your assessment with specific examples.

6. Some people think it's important to look their best and, therefore, give careful attention to the clothing they wear. Others do not seem to care. How much stock do you put in the old saying, "Clothes make the person"? Use examples of the people on your own campus or in your community to argue your position.

7. **Writing with Sources.** Write an essay on one of the following statements, using examples to illustrate your ideas. Draw your examples from a variety of sources: your library's print and Internet resources, interviews, and information gathered from lectures and the media. As you plan your essay, consider whether you will want to use a series of short examples or one or more extended examples.

   a. Much has been (*or* should still be) done to eliminate barriers for the physically handicapped.

   b. Nature's oddities are numerous.

   c. Throughout history, dire predictions have been made about the end of the world.

   d. The past predictions of science fiction are today's realities.

   e. The world has not seen an absence of warfare since World War II.

   f. Young executives have developed many innovative management strategies.

   g. A great work of art may come out of an artist's most difficult period.

   h. The misjudgments of our presidents can be useful lessons in leadership.

   i. Genius is 10 percent talent and 90 percent hard work.

   j. Drugs have taken an economic toll on American business.

   k. Democracy has attracted renewed interest in countries outside of the United States.

   For models of and advice on integrating sources, see Chapters 14–15.

8. **Writing with Sources.** Take some time to study the public service advertisement reproduced at the beginning of this chapter (page 166). What's going on in the ad? How much of what's going on is conveyed by the written text, and how much by the visual text? How effective do you find the ad? After doing some research in your library as well as on the Internet, write an essay about online predators and what is currently being done to reduce or eliminate this problem.

   Before starting your research and drafting your essay, you will find it helpful to become familiar with Chapter 14, "Writing with Sources," and Chapter 15, "A Brief Guide to Researching and Documenting Essays."

Stop the spread of germs that make you and others sick!

Cover your Cough

Cover your mouth and nose with a tissue when you cough or sneeze

or

cough or sneeze into your upper sleeve, not your hands.

Put your used tissue in the waste basket.

Clean your Hands after coughing or sneezing.

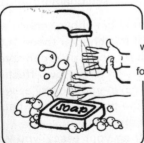

Wash hands with soap and warm water for 20 seconds

or

clean with alcohol-based hand cleaner.

CHAPTER 7

Process Analysis

What Is Process Analysis?

The strategy of process analysis involves separating an event, an operation, or a cycle of development into distinct steps, describing each step precisely, and arranging the steps in their proper order.

Whenever you explain how something occurs or how it can (and should) be done — how plants create oxygen, how to make ice cream, or merely how to get to your house — you are using process analysis. Recipes are a form of process analysis; so are the instruction and assembly manuals for the many technological devices we use around the house; and so are posters telling us what to do in case of fire, choking, or other emergency. The poster reproduced opposite is similar to the latter kind of document; sponsored by the Minnesota Department of Health, the poster was designed to help stem the tide of the H1N1 virus. In order to reach the widest possible audience, the poster uses friendly illustrations and simple instructions written in the briefest possible form.

Process Analysis in Written Texts

Each year, thousands of books and magazine articles tell us how to make home repairs, how to lose weight and get physically fit, how to improve our memories, how to play better tennis, how to manage our money. They try to satisfy our curiosity about how television shows are made, how jet airplanes work, and how monkeys, bees, or whales mate. People simply want to know how things work and how to do things for themselves, so it's not surprising that process analysis is one of the most widespread and popular forms of writing today.

Here is a process analysis written by Bernard Gladstone to explain how to light a fire in a fireplace.

First sentence establishes purpose: how to build a fire in a fireplace.

Though "experts" differ as to the best technique to follow when building a fire, one generally accepted method consists of first laying a generous amount of crumpled newspaper on the hearth between the andirons. Kindling wood is then spread generously over this layer of newspaper and one of the thickest logs is placed across the back of the andirons. This should be as close to the back of the fireplace as possible, but not quite touching it. A second log is then placed an inch or so in front of this, and a few additional sticks of kindling are laid across these two. A third log is then placed on top to form a sort of pyramid with air space between all logs so that flames can lick freely up between them.

First paragraph takes us through six steps: the result is a wood-and-paper structure.

A mistake frequently made is in building the fire too far forward so that the rear wall of the fireplace does not get properly heated. A heated back wall helps increase the draft and tends to suck smoke and flames rearward with less chance of sparks or smoke spurting out into the room.

The next three paragraphs present three common mistakes.

Another common mistake often made by the inexperienced fire-tender is to try to build a fire with only one or two logs, instead of using at least three. A single log is difficult to ignite properly, and even two logs do not provide an efficient bed with adequate fuel burning capacity.

Use of too many logs, on the other hand, is also a common fault and can prove hazardous. Building too big a fire can create more smoke and draft than the chimney can safely handle, increasing the possibility of sparks or smoke being thrown out into the room. For best results, the homeowner should start with three medium-sized logs as described above, then add additional logs as needed if the fire is to be kept burning.

Conclusion reinforces his directions for building a fire.

Using Process Analysis As a Writing Strategy

Process analysis resembles narration because both strategies present a series of events occurring over time. But a narration is the story of how things happened in a particular way, during one particular period of time; process analysis relates how things always happen — or always should happen — in essentially the same way time after time.

There are essentially two major reasons for writing a process analysis: to give directions, known as *directional process analysis*, and to inform, known as *informational process analysis*. Writers often combine one of these reasons with other rhetorical strategies to evaluate the process in question; this is known as *evaluative process analysis*. Let's take a look at each of these forms more closely.

■ Directional Process Analysis

Writers use directional process analysis to provide readers with the necessary steps to achieve a desired result. The directions may be as simple as the instructions on a frozen-food package ("Heat in microwave on high for six to eight minutes. Rotate one-quarter turn halfway through cooking time, stir, and serve") or as complex as the operator's manual for a personal computer. Mortimer Adler proposes a method for getting the most out of reading in his essay "How to Mark a Book." First he compares what he sees as the "two ways in which one can own a book" and classifies book lovers into three categories. Then he presents his directions for how one should make marginal comments to get the most out of a book. In his "How to Say Nothing in 500 Words," Paul Roberts lays out the steps by which a writer can turn a dull subject into a lively, interesting one. No matter their length or complexity, however, all directions have the same purpose: to guide the reader through a clear and logically ordered series of steps toward a particular goal.

■ Informational Process Analysis

This strategy deals not with processes that readers are able to perform for themselves, but with processes that readers are curious about or would like to understand better: how presidents are elected, how plants reproduce, how an elevator works, how the brain processes and generates language. In the following selection from his *Lives Around Us*, Alan Devoe explains what happens to an animal when it goes into hibernation.

> When the temperature of the September days falls below 50 degrees or so, the woodchuck becomes too drowsy to come forth from his burrow in the chilly dusk to forage. He remains in the deep nest-chamber, lethargic, hardly moving. Gradually, with the passing of hours or days, his coarse-furred body curls into a semicircle, like a fetus, nose-tip touching tail. The small legs are tucked in, the hand-like clawed forefeet folded. The woodchuck has become a compact ball. Presently the temperature of his body begins to fall.
>
> In normal life the woodchuck's temperature, though fluctuant, averages about 97 degrees. Now, as he lies tight-curled in a ball with the winter sleep stealing over him, this body heat drops ten degrees, twenty degrees, thirty. Finally, by the time the snow is on the ground and the woodchuck's winter dormancy has become complete, his temperature is only 38 or 40. With the falling of the body heat there is a slowing of his heartbeat and his respiration. In normal life he breathes thirty or forty times each minute; when he is excited, as many as a hundred times. Now he breathes slower and slower: ten times a minute, five times a minute, once a minute, and at last only ten or twelve times in an hour. His heartbeat is a twentieth of normal. He has entered fully into the oblivion of hibernation.

The process Devoe describes is natural to woodchucks but not to humans, so obviously he cannot be giving instructions. Rather, he has created an informational process analysis to help us understand what happens during the remarkable process of hibernation. Using transitional expressions and time markers, Devoe shows us that the process lasts for weeks, even months. He connects the progress of hibernation with changes in the weather because the woodchuck's body responds to the dropping temperature as autumn sets in rather than to the passage of specific periods of time.

■ Evaluative Process Analysis

People often want to understand processes in order to evaluate and improve them by making them simpler, quicker, safer, or more efficient. They may also wish to analyze processes to understand them more deeply or accurately. Paul Roberts's "How to Say Nothing in 500 Words," for example, describes an ineffective writing process used by some students and then compares and contrasts it with a more effective process.

Using Process Analysis across the Disciplines

When writing essays in the academic disciplines, you will have many opportunities to use the strategy of process analysis to both organize and strengthen the presentation of your ideas. To determine whether or not process analysis is the right strategy for you in a particular paper, use the four-step method described in Chapter 2 (Determining a Strategy for Developing Your Essay, pages 25–26). Consider the following examples, which illustrate how this four-step method works for typical college papers:

Psychology

1. MAIN IDEA: Most people go through a predictable grief process when a friend or loved one dies.
2. QUESTION: What are the steps in the grieving process?
3. STRATEGY: Process Analysis. The word *steps* signals the need to list the stages of the grieving process.
4. SUPPORTING STRATEGY: Description. Each step might be described and be accompanied by descriptions of the subject's behavior throughout the process.

Biology

1. MAIN IDEA: Human blood samples can be tested to determine their blood groups.
2. QUESTION: What steps are followed in typing human blood?
3. STRATEGY: Process Analysis. The word *steps* suggests a sequence of activities that is to be followed in testing blood.

4. SUPPORTING STRATEGY: Comparison and Contrast; Classification. Comparison and contrast might be used to differentiate blood characteristics and chemistry. Classification might be used to place samples in various categories.

Folklore

1. MAIN IDEA: Folklorists use several main methods for gathering their data.
2. QUESTION: How do folklorists go about collecting data?
3. STRATEGY: Process Analysis. The words *how do* and *go about* suggest process analysis.
4. SUPPORTING STRATEGY: Illustration and Argumentation. Illustration can give examples of particular data and how it is collected. Argumentation might support one method over others.

Sample Student Essay Using Process Analysis As a Writing Strategy

Shoshanna Lew was born in Pinetop, Arizona, and was a double major in English and music at the University of Vermont. After graduation, she continued her studies in musicology at graduate school. In this informative essay, Lew explains the process for selecting people to serve on juries in New York City. Notice, as you read, how she manages to explain clearly the steps in the process, as well as accommodate two audiences, those who would welcome jury duty and those who would rather be doing just about anything else.

Title: Introduces mixed feelings about the prospect of jury duty

First sentence: Effective one-word sentence

How (Not) to Be Selected
for Jury Duty
Shoshanna Lew

"SUMMONS." The red-lettered envelope slipped out from behind the junk mail and magazines. At first, I thought it must be for one of my parents, but, when I looked closer, I realized that it was *my* name on the jury duty notice. I didn't even know eighteen-year-old college students were *eligible* for jury duty, but a quick Google search told me otherwise. Great, for my summer vacation, I'd be trapped inside a jury box listening to dull testimony,

1

or worse, examining grotesque photos of bullet wounds à la a *CSI* episode. On the upside, the $44 a day for serving was more than what I was making at my summer internship.

Jury selection in New York City is a multistep process. It starts bright and early with a video extolling the virtues of the justice system in which each potential juror is participating by simply showing up on the appointed day and time. After the video finishes, the bailiff in charge of the jury pool collects everyone's cards and fields the requests of people to postpone or be exempt from their civic duty. Doctors' letters appear out of handbags and suited businesspeople wave their Blackberries to show that they are far too busy to be on a jury. As the bailiff—who determines the fate of each potential juror—dismisses people, the crowd thins down to those who will be eligible to be called to juries in the next three days. Since it is summer, my full-time student status doesn't let me off the hook. Once this process is complete, the remaining people begin doing what they will do for most of their time: They wait.

From the jury room, the courthouse looks nothing like the ones on television. Presumably—according to our introductory video—somewhere in the building lawyers are making arguments before judges, settling cases out of court, or succeeding in getting charges dropped. But in the jury room, folks read, watch television (CNN only), or nap. Suddenly, an announcement comes over the intercom. A case has been called; jury members will be empaneled—meaning a select group from the jury pool will be questioned, and some selected to sit on the jury—in fifteen minutes.

Once the bailiff is informed that a jury is being called, he brings out a bin containing cards, one for each potential juror. Just like the bins used in raffles at county fairs, the bailiff turns the crank several times and begins to pull out names. The bailiff assigns each person a number, and the lucky raffle winners are escorted into the jury room

2

3

4

where they sit in the order they were called and fill out questionnaires. Beyond the basics of name and address, jurists provide level of education, place of birth, and employment information, and disclose whether or not they have relatives working in medical, legal, or insurance professions. (Bring a family tree with you on jury duty day. You'll be asked to explain jobs of any relation!)

Organization: Paragraph addresses general questions asked of all jurors.

Unlike John Grisham's legal thrillers, in which a dramatic jury questioning occurs in a courtroom with a judge and court reporter (and some rhetorical fireworks), a real jury selection may or may not happen in front of a judge. After the lawyers acquaint themselves with the potential jurists' questionnaires, they ask all the jurors if they have any philosophical objections to the American legal system and the role of a jury in it. These questions focus on beliefs about the justice system, but are phrased to weed out only those people with the strongest opinions *against* the American justice system. (This is a good time to find your inner anarchist.) The lawyers also want to make sure that no panelist has any connection to a party to the case—be it the plaintiff, the defendant, the lawyers in the case, or others affiliated with the attorneys' firms.

Unity: Paragraph stays on topic of questions asked of all jurors.

5

Organization: Plaintiff's lawyer's questions

Once these preliminaries have been dealt with, the actual questioning begins. First, the lawyer for the plaintiff—the person with the legal complaint—presents the basis for the lawsuit. Then, the plaintiff's lawyer questions the jurors. He asks questions of the entire group, and he also addresses jurors about specific information on their questionnaires. Much of the questioning is meant to illuminate potential biases that jury members might harbor. For instance, doctors can expect to face intense scrutiny if they are being considered for a malpractice case. Jurors will also be questioned about their ability to put aside connections they have to the participants in the case—such as a shared profession or common alma mater—and be objective in weighing evidence.

6

Organization: Defense attorney's questions

When the plaintiff's lawyer has finished posing questions, the defense attorney—who represents the person being sued—takes her turn. Again, the potential jurors hear a short summary of the case but from the defense's perspective. Once more, the lawyer asks specific jurors about their backgrounds and directs inquiries to the entire group. During this part of the process people begin to be dismissed from the case. At this point, you'll probably wish for some courtroom drama to break up the monotony of the day, but you're not likely to see a war of words. Despite the numerous jokes intimating otherwise, lawyers tend to remain polite, if not cordial, during jury selection. If you are lucky enough to be one of the later jurors to be questioned, you'll have plenty of time to figure out what answers will give you the best chance of being dismissed from or accepted to—if that's your goal—the jury.

7

Organization: Final jury selection is made.

Finally, the lawyers pick their jury. Even though they dismiss some people based on their answers to questions as the inquiries are made, they make their final "picks" only after the defense finishes its part. After conferring privately, the lawyers provide a bailiff with their list of jurors and the bailiff announces the final outcome to the panel. In the reverse of a playground kickball game, the bailiff first names the people who will not be on the jury. Those who are left at the end make up Team Jury.

8

Conclusion: Why attorneys may have chosen as they did

It's difficult to know why the lawyers choose the people they do. My guess is that they look for people who seem the least likely to let their emotions play a part in weighing evidence and for those with the stamina to spend more than a week listening to dense testimony. Jury selection doesn't have the theatricality of *Law and Order*, but it is clear that the lawyers are invested in assembling the fairest jury possible—not simply the one most likely to rule in their favor—out of the candidates pulled from that raffle bin.

9

Analyzing Shoshanna Lew's Process Analysis Essay: Questions for Discussion

1. Lew shifts from the past tense (paragraph 1) to the present tense (2–9) in her essay. Why is it important for her to put the actual jury selection process in the present tense?

2. Try explaining Lew's analysis of the jury selection process to a friend. Is it more or less complex than you first thought? Did you leave any parts of the process out? Did you get the activities out of order? Explain.

3. Lew's title indicates that some people may want to serve on a jury while others may not. Serving on a jury is an important civic responsibility, so why do you think there are mixed feelings about it? How do you feel about the prospect of serving on a jury?

Suggestions for Using Process Analysis As a Writing Strategy

As you plan and revise your process analysis essay, be mindful of the writing guidelines described in Chapter 2. Pay particular attention to the basic requirements and essential ingredients of this strategy.

■ Planning Your Process Analysis Essay

Know the Process You Are Writing About. Be sure that you have more than a vague or general grasp of the process you are writing about: Make sure you can analyze it fully, from beginning to end. You can sometimes convince yourself that you understand an entire process when, in fact, your understanding is somewhat superficial. If you do outside research, it's a good idea to read explanations by several authorities on the subject. If you were analyzing the process by which children learn language, for example, you wouldn't want to rely on only one expert's account. Turning to more than one account not only reinforces your understanding of key points in the process, but it also points out various ways the process is performed; you may want to consider these alternatives in your writing.

Have a Clear Purpose. Giving directions for administering cardiopulmonary resuscitation and explaining how the El Niño phenomenon unfolds are worthy purposes for writing a process analysis paper. Many process analysis papers go beyond these fundamental purposes, however. They lay out processes to evaluate them, to suggest alternative steps, to point out shortcomings in generally accepted practices, and to suggest improvements. In short, process analysis papers are frequently persuasive or argumentative. Be sure to decide what you want your writing to do before you begin.

■ Organizing and Writing Your Process Analysis Essay

Organize the Process into Steps.   As much as possible, make each step a simple and well-defined action, preferably a single action. To guide yourself in doing so, write a scratch outline listing the steps. Here, for example, is an outline of Bernard Gladstone's directions for building a fire.

Process Analysis of Building a Fire in a Fireplace

1. Put down crumpled newspaper.

2. Lay kindling.

3. Place back log near rear wall but not touching.

4. Place next log an inch forward from the first one.

5. Bridge logs with kindling.

6. Place third log on top of kindling bridge.

Next, check your outline to make sure that the steps are in the right order and that none has been omitted. Then analyze your outline more carefully. Are any steps so complex that they need to be described in some detail — or perhaps divided into more steps? Will you need to explain the purpose of a certain step because the reason for it is not obvious? Especially in an informational process analysis, two steps may take place at the same time; perhaps they are performed by different people or different parts of the body. Does your outline make this clear? (One solution is to assign both steps the same number but divide them into substeps by labeling one of them "A" and the other "B.") When you feel certain that the steps of the process are complete and correct, ask yourself two more questions. Will the reader need any other information to understand the process — definitions of unusual terms, for example, or descriptions of special equipment? Should you anticipate common mistakes or misunderstandings and discuss them, as Gladstone does? If so, be sure to add an appropriate note or two to your scratch outline as a reminder.

Use Transitions to Link the Steps.   Transitional words and phrases like *then*, *next*, *after doing this*, and *during the summer months* can both emphasize and clarify the sequence of steps in your process analysis. The same is true of sequence markers like *first*, *second*, *third*, and so on. Devoe uses such words to make clear which stages in the hibernation process are simultaneous and which are not; Gladstone includes an occasional *first* or *then* to alert us to shifts from one step to the next.

■ Revising and Editing Your Process Analysis Essay

Energize Your Writing: Use the Active Voice and Strong Action Verbs.   Writers prefer the active voice because it stresses the doer of an action, is lively and emphatic, and uses strong descriptive verbs. The passive voice, on the other hand, stresses what was done rather than who did it and uses forms of the weak verb *to be*.   `E9`

> **active**   The coaches analyzed the game film, and the fullback decided to rededicate herself to playing defense.

> **passive**   A game film analysis was performed by the coaches, and a rededication to playing defense was decided on by the fullback.

Sometimes, however, the doer of an action is unknown or less important than the recipient of an action. In this case, it is acceptable to use the passive voice.

> The Earth's moon was formed more than 4 billion years ago.

When you revise your drafts, scan your sentences for passive constructions and weak verbs. Put your sentences into the active voice and find strong action verbs to replace weak verbs. Instead of the weak verb *run*, use *fly, gallop, hustle, jog, race, rush, scamper, scoot, scramble, tear,* or *trot,* for example. Instead of the weak verb *say, use declare, express, muse, mutter, pronounce, report, respond, recite, reply, snarl,* or *utter,* for example. Forms of the verb *to be* (*is, are, was, were, will be, should be*) are weak and nondescriptive and, therefore, should be avoided whenever possible. Here are some other common weak verbs you should replace with strong action verbs in your writing:

have, had, has	get
make	involve
concern	determine
reflect	become
provide	go
do	appear
use	

Use Consistent Verb Tense.   A verb's tense indicates when an action is taking place: some time in the past, right now, or in the future. Using verb tense consistently helps your readers understand time changes in your writing. Inconsistent verb tenses — or *shifts* — within a sentence confuse readers and are especially noticeable in narration and process analysis writing, which are sequence — and time — oriented. Generally, you should write in the past or present tense and maintain that tense throughout your sentence.   `E10`

> **inconsistent**   I mixed the eggs and sugar and then add the flour.

Mixed is past tense; *add* is present tense.

corrected   I mix the eggs and sugar and then add the flour.

The sentence is now consistently in the present tense. The sentence can also be revised to be consistently in the past tense.

corrected   I mixed the eggs and sugar and then added the flour.

Here's another example:

inconsistent   The painter studied the scene and pulls a fan brush decisively from her cup.

Studied is past tense, indicating an action that has already taken place; *pulls* is present tense, indicating an action taking place now.

corrected   The painter studies the scene and pulls a fan brush decisively from her cup.

corrected   The painter studied the scene and pulled a fan brush decisively from her cup.

Share Your Drafts with Others.   Try sharing the drafts of your essays with other students in your writing class to make sure that your process analysis works. Ask them if there are any steps in the process that they do not understand. Have them tell you what they think is the point of your essay. If their answers differ from what you intended, have them indicate the passages that led them to their interpretations so that you can change your text accordingly. To maximize the effectiveness of conferences with your peers, utilize the guidelines presented on page 29. Feedback from these conferences often provides places where you can start revising.

Question Your Own Work While Revising and Editing.   Revision is best done by asking yourself key questions about what you have written. Begin by reading, preferably aloud, what you have written. Reading aloud forces you to pay attention to every single word, and you are more likely to catch lapses in the logical flow of thought. After you have read your paper through, answer the following questions for revising and editing and make the necessary changes.

Questions for Revising and Editing: Process Analysis

1. Do I have a thorough knowledge of the process I chose to write about?

2. Have I clearly informed readers about how to perform the process (directional process analysis), or have I explained how a process occurs (informational process analysis)? Does my choice reflect the overall purpose of my process analysis paper?

3. Have I divided the process into clear, readily understandable steps?

4. Did I pay particular attention to transitional words to take readers from one step to the next?

5. Are all my sentences in the active voice? Have I used strong action verbs?   E9

6. Is my tense consistent?   E10

7. Have I succeeded in tailoring my diction to my audience's familiarity with the subject?

8. Are my pronoun antecedents clear?   E5

9. How did readers of my draft respond to my essay? Did they find any confusing passages or any missing steps?

10. Have I avoided errors in grammar, punctuation, and mechanics? Is my sentence style as clear, smooth, and persuasive as possible?   E1–12

How to Mark a Book

MORTIMER ADLER

Writer, editor, and educator Mortimer Adler (1902–2001) was born in New York City. A high school dropout, Adler completed the undergraduate program at Columbia University in three years, but he did not graduate because he refused to take the mandatory swimming test. Adler is recognized for his editorial work on the *Encyclopaedia Britannica* and for his leadership of the Great Books Program at the University of Chicago, where adults from all walks of life gathered twice a month to read and discuss the classics.

In the following essay, which first appeared in the *Saturday Review of Literature* in 1940, Adler offers a timeless lesson: He explains how to take full ownership of a book by marking it up, by making it "a part of yourself."

■ Preparing to Read

When you read a book that you must understand thoroughly and remember for a class or for your own purposes, what techniques do you use to help you understand what you are reading? What helps you remember important parts of the book and improve your understanding of what the author is saying?

You know you have to read "between the lines" to get the most out of any- 1
thing. I want to persuade you to do something equally important in the course of your reading. I want to persuade you to "write between the lines." Unless you do, you are not likely to do the most efficient kind of reading.

I contend, quite bluntly, that marking up a book is not an act of mutila- 2
tion but of love.

You shouldn't mark up a book which isn't yours. Librarians (or your 3
friends) who lend you books expect you to keep them clean, and you should. If you decide that I am right about the usefulness of marking books, you will have to buy them. Most of the world's great books are available today in reprint editions.

There are two ways in which one can own a book. The first is the property 4
right you establish by paying for it, just as you pay for clothes and furniture. But this act of purchase is only the prelude to possession. Full ownership comes only when you have made it a part of yourself, and the best way to make yourself a part

Marking up a book is not an act of mutilation but of love.

of it is by writing in it. An illustration may make the point clear. You buy a beefsteak and transfer it from the butcher's icebox to your own. But you do not own the beefsteak in the most important sense until you consume it and get it into your bloodstream. I am arguing that books, too, must be absorbed in your bloodstream to do you any good.

Confusion about what it means to *own* a book leads people to a false reverence for paper, binding, and type — a respect for the physical thing — the craft of the printer rather than the genius of the author. They forget that it is possible for a man to acquire the idea, to possess the beauty, which a great book contains, without staking his claim by pasting his bookplate inside the cover. Having a fine library doesn't prove that its owner has a mind enriched by books; it proves nothing more than that he, his father, or his wife, was rich enough to buy them.

There are three kinds of book owners. The first has all the standard sets and best-sellers — unread, untouched. (This deluded individual owns wood-pulp and ink, not books.) The second has a great many books — a few of them read through, most of them dipped into, but all of them as clean and shiny as the day they were bought. (This person would probably like to make books his own, but is restrained by a false respect for their physical appearance.) The third has a few books or many — every one of them dog-eared and dilapidated, shaken and loosened by continual use, marked and scribbled in from front to back. (This man owns books.)

Is it false respect, you may ask, to preserve intact and unblemished a beautifully printed book, an elegantly bound edition? Of course not. I'd no more scribble all over a first edition of *Paradise Lost* than I'd give my baby a set of crayons and an original Rembrandt! I wouldn't mark up a painting or a statue. Its soul, so to speak, is inseparable from its body. And the beauty of a rare edition or of a richly manufactured volume is like that of a painting or a statue.

But the soul of a book *can* be separated from its body. A book is more like the score of a piece of music than it is like a painting. No great musician confuses a symphony with the printed sheets of music. Arturo Toscanini reveres Brahms, but Toscanini's score of the C-minor Symphony is so thoroughly marked up that no one but the maestro himself can read it. The reason why a great conductor makes notations on his musical scores — marks them up again and again each time he returns to study them — is the reason why you should mark your books. If your respect for magnificent binding or typography gets in the way, buy yourself a cheap edition and pay your respects to the author.

Why is marking up a book indispensable to reading? First, it keeps you awake. (And I don't mean merely conscious; I mean wide awake.) In the second place, reading, if it is active, is thinking, and thinking tends to express itself in words, spoken or written. The marked book is usually the thought-through book. Finally, writing helps you remember the thoughts you had, or the thoughts the author expressed. Let me develop these three points.

If reading is to accomplish anything more than passing time, it must be 10 active. You can't let your eyes glide across the lines of a book and come up with an understanding of what you have read. Now an ordinary piece of light fiction, like say, *Gone with the Wind*, doesn't require the most active kind of reading. The books you read for pleasure can be read in a state of relaxation, and nothing is lost. But a great book, rich in ideas and beauty, a book that raises and tries to answer great fundamental questions, demands the most active reading of which you are capable. You don't absorb the ideas of John Dewey[1] the way you absorb the crooning of Mr. Vallee.[2] You have to reach for them. That you cannot do while you're asleep.

If, when you've finished reading a book, the pages are filled with your 11 notes, you know that you read actively. The most famous active reader of great books I know is President Hutchins, of the University of Chicago. He also has the hardest schedule of business activities of any man I know. He invariably reads with a pencil, and sometimes, when he picks up a book and pencil in the evening, he finds himself, instead of making intelligent notes, drawing what he calls "caviar factories" on the margins. When that happens, he puts the book down. He knows he's too tired to read, and he's just wasting time.

But, you may ask, why is writing necessary? Well, the physical act of writ- 12 ing, with your own hand, brings words and sentences more sharply before your mind and preserves them better in your memory. To set down your reaction to important words and sentences you have read, and the questions they have raised in your mind, is to preserve those reactions and sharpen those questions.

Even if you wrote on a scratch pad, and threw the paper away when you 13 had finished writing, your grasp of the book would be surer. But you don't have to throw the paper away. The margins (top and bottom, as well as side), the end-papers, the very space between the lines, are all available. They aren't sacred. And, best of all, your marks and notes become an integral part of the book and stay there forever. You can pick up the book the following week or year, and there are all your points of agreement, disagreement, doubt, and inquiry. It's like resuming an interrupted conversation with the advantage of being able to pick up where you left off.

---

[1]John Dewey (1859–1952) was an educational philosopher who had a profound influence on learning through experimentation.—Ed.

[2]Rudy Vallee (1901–1986) was a popular singer of the 1920s and '30s, famous for his crooning high notes.—Ed.

And that is exactly what reading a book should be: a conversation 14 between you and the author. Presumably he knows more about the subject than you do; naturally, you'll have the proper humility as you approach him. But don't let anybody tell you that a reader is supposed to be solely on the receiving end. Understanding is a two-way operation; learning doesn't consist in being an empty receptacle. The learner has to question himself and question the teacher. He even has to argue with the teacher, once he understands what the teacher is saying. And marking a book is literally an expression of your differences, or agreements of opinion, with the author.

There are all kinds of devices for marking a book intelligently and fruit- 15 fully. Here's the way I do it:

1. *Underlining:* of major points, of important or forceful statements. 16

2. *Vertical lines at the margin:* to emphasize a statement already underlined. 17

3. *Star, asterisk, or other doo-dad at the margin:* to be used sparingly, to 18 emphasize the ten or twenty most important statements in the book. (You may want to fold the bottom corner of each page on which you use such marks. It won't hurt the sturdy paper on which most modern books are printed, and you will be able to take the book off the shelf at any time and, by opening it at the folded-corner page, refresh your recollection of the book.)

4. *Numbers in the margin:* to indicate the sequence of points the author 19 makes in developing a single argument.

5. *Numbers of other pages in the margin:* to indicate where else in the book 20 the author made points relevant to the point marked; to tie up the ideas in a book, which, though they may be separated by many pages, belong together.

6. *Circling:* of key words or phrases. 21

7. *Writing in the margin, or at the top or bottom of the page, for the sake* 22 *of:* recording questions (and perhaps answers) which a passage raised in your mind; reducing a complicated discussion to a simple statement; recording the sequence of major points right through the book. I use the end-papers at the back of the book to make a personal index of the author's points in the order of their appearance.

The front end-papers are, to me, the most important. Some people 23 reserve them for a fancy bookplate. I reserve them for fancy thinking. After I have finished reading the book and making my personal index on the back end-papers, I turn to the front and try to outline the book, not page by page, or point by point (I've already done that at the back), but as an integrated structure, with a basic unity and an order of parts. This outline is, to me, the measure of my understanding of the work.

If you're a die-hard anti-book-marker, you may object that the margins, 24 the space between the lines, and the end-papers don't give you room enough. All right. How about using a scratch pad slightly smaller than the page-size of the book — so that the edges of the sheets won't protrude? Make your index, outlines, and even your notes on the pad, and then insert these sheets permanently inside the front and back covers of the book.

Or, you may say that this business of marking books is going to slow up your reading. It probably will. That's one of the reasons for doing it. Most of us have been taken in by the notion that speed of reading is a measure of our intelligence. There is no such thing as the right speed for intelligent reading. Some things should be read quickly and effortlessly, and some should be read slowly and even laboriously. The sign of intelligence in reading is the ability to read different things differently according to their worth. In the case of good books, the point is not to see how many of them you can get through, but rather how many can get through you — how many you can make your own. A few friends are better than a thousand acquaintances. If this be your aim, as it should be, you will not be impatient if it takes more time and effort to read a great book than it does a newspaper. 25

You may have one final objection to marking books. You can't lend them to your friends because nobody else can read them without being distracted by your notes. Furthermore, you won't want to lend them because a marked copy is a kind of intellectual diary, and lending it is almost like giving your mind away. 26

If your friend wishes to read your *Plutarch's Lives, Shakespeare,* or *The Federalist Papers,* tell him gently but firmly to buy a copy. You will lend him your car or your coat — but your books are as much a part of you as your head or your heart. 27

■ Thinking Critically about the Text

After you have read Adler's essay, compare your answer to the Preparing to Read prompt with Adler's guidelines for reading. What are the most significant differences between Adler's guidelines and your own? How can you better make the books you read part of yourself?

■ Questions on Subject

1. What are the three kinds of book owners Adler identifies? What are their differences?
2. According to Adler, why is marking up a book indispensable to reading? Do you agree with his three arguments? (Glossary: *Argument*) Why or why not?
3. What does Adler mean when he writes "the soul of a book *can* be separated from its body" (paragraph 8)? Is the separation a good thing? Explain.

4. Adler says that reading a book should be a conversation between the reader and the author. What characteristics does he say the conversation should have? How does marking a book help in carrying on and preserving the conversation?
5. What kinds of devices do you use for "marking a book intelligently and fruitfully" (paragraph 15)? How useful do you find these devices?

■ Questions on Strategy

1. In the first paragraph, Adler writes, "I want to persuade you to do something equally important in the course of your reading. I want to persuade you to 'write between the lines.'" What assumptions does Adler make about his audience when he chooses to use the parallel structure of "I want to persuade you . . ."? (Glossary: *Audience; Parallelism*) Is stating his intention so blatantly an effective way of presenting his argument? (Glossary: *Argument*) Why, or why not?
2. Adler expresses himself very clearly throughout the essay, and his topic sentences are carefully crafted. (Glossary: *Topic Sentence*) Reread the topic sentences for paragraphs 3–6, and identify how each introduces the main idea for the paragraph and unifies it.
3. Throughout the essay, Adler provides the reader with a number of verbal cues ("There are two ways," "Let me develop these three points"). What do these verbal cues indicate about the organizational connections of the essay? (Glossary: *Organization*) Explain how Adler's organization creates an essay that logically follows from sentence to sentence and from paragraph to paragraph.
4. Summarize in your own words Adler's process analysis about how one should mark a book. Explain how Adler's process analysis is also an argument for the correct way to read. (Glossary: *Argument*)
5. Adler's process analysis is also a description of an event or a sequence of events (how to read). Does he claim that his recommended reading process will aid the reader's understanding, increase the reader's interest, or both?

■ Questions on Diction and Vocabulary

1. Adler makes an analogy that links reading books with the statement "A few friends are better than a thousand acquaintances" (paragraph 25). (Glossary: *Analogy*) Explain how this analogy works. Why is this analogy important to Adler's overall argument?
2. Throughout the essay, Adler uses the personal pronoun *I* to describe his reading experience. (Glossary: *Point of View*) How does this personalized voice help or hinder the explanation of the process of reading?
3. What does Adler mean by the phrase "active reading"?

■ Classroom Activity Using Process Analysis

This exercise requires that you work in pairs. Draw a simple geometric design, such as the one below, without letting your partner see your drawing.

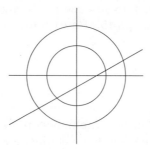

  With the finished design in front of you, write a set of directions that will allow your partner to reproduce it accurately. Before writing your directions, ask yourself how you will convey the context for your instructions, where you will begin, and how what you write may help your partner or lead your partner astray. As your partner attempts to draw the design from your instructions, do not offer any verbal advice. Let your directions speak for themselves. Once you have finished, compare your drawing to the one your partner has produced. Discuss the results with your partner and, if time allows, with the entire class.

■ Writing Suggestions

1. Write a directional process analysis in which you present your techniques for getting the most enjoyment out of a common activity. For example, perhaps you have a set routine you follow for spending an evening watching television — preparing popcorn, checking what's on, clearing off the coffee table, finding the remote control, settling into your favorite chair, and so on. Choose from the following topics:

   How to listen to music

   How to eat an ice-cream cone

   How to reduce stress

   How to wash a dog

   How to play a sport or game

2. Adler devotes a large portion of his essay to persuading his audience that marking books is a worthwhile task. (Glossary: *Persuasion*) Write an essay in which you instruct your audience about how to do something they do not necessarily wish to do or they do not think they need to do. For instance, before explaining how to buy the best MP3 player, you may need to convince readers that they *should* buy an MP3 player. Write your directional process analysis after making a convincing argument for the validity of the process you wish to present. (Glossary: *Argument*)

How to Say Nothing in 500 Words

PAUL ROBERTS

Paul Roberts (1917–1967) was a linguist, a teacher, and a writer at San Jose State College from 1946 to 1960 and at Cornell University from 1962 to 1964. His books on writing, including *English Syntax* (1954) and *Patterns of English* (1956), have helped generations of high school and college students become better writers.

"How to Say Nothing in 500 Words" is taken from his best-known book, *Understanding English* (1958). Although written over fifty years ago, the essay is still relevant for student writers today. Good writing, Roberts tells us, is not simply a matter of filling up a page; rather, the words have to hold the reader's interest, and they must say something. In this essay, Roberts uses lively prose and a step-by-step process to guide the student from the blank page to the finished essay. His bag of writing strategies holds good advice for anyone who wants to write well.

■ Preparing to Read

How do you feel about writing? Do you find writing difficult? What are some of your most memorable experiences with writing in school or during your free time? How have these experiences affected your current attitude toward writing? Explain.

Nothing about Something

It's Friday afternoon, and you have almost survived another week of classes. You are just looking forward dreamily to the weekend when the English instructor says: "For Monday you will turn in a five-hundred-word composition on college football." 1

Well, that puts a good big hole in the weekend. You don't have any strong views on college football one way or the other. You get rather excited during the season and go to all the home games and find it rather more fun than not. On the other hand, the class has been reading Robert Hutchins in the anthology and perhaps Shaw's "Eighty-Yard Run," and from the class discussion you have got the idea that the instructor thinks college football is for the birds. You are no fool, you. You can figure out what side to take. 2

After dinner you get out the portable typewriter that you got for high school graduation. You might as well get it over with and enjoy Saturday and Sunday. Five hundred words is about two double-spaced pages with normal margins. You put in a sheet of paper, think up a title, and you're off: 3

WHY COLLEGE FOOTBALL SHOULD
BE ABOLISHED

College football should be abolished because it's bad for the school and also bad for the players. The players are so busy practicing that they don't have any time for their studies.

> You still have four hundred and sixty-eight [words] to go, and you've pretty well exhausted the subject.

This, you feel, is a mighty good start. The only trouble is that it's only thirty-two words. You still have four hundred and sixty-eight to go, and you've pretty well exhausted the subject. It comes to you that you do your best thinking in the morning, so you put away the typewriter and go to the movies. But the next morning you have to do your washing and some math problems, and in the afternoon you go to the game. The English instructor turns up too, and you wonder if you've taken the right side after all. Saturday night you have a date, and Sunday morning you have to go to church. (You shouldn't let English assignments interfere with your religion.) What with one thing and another, it's ten o'clock Sunday night before you get out the typewriter again. You make a pot of coffee and start to fill out your views on college football. Put a little meat on the bones.

WHY COLLEGE FOOTBALL SHOULD
BE ABOLISHED

In my opinion, it seems to me that college football should be abolished. The reason why I think this to be true is because I feel that football is bad for the colleges in nearly every respect. As Robert Hutchins says in his article in our anthology in which he discusses college football, it would be better if the colleges had race horses and had races with one another, because then the horses would not have to attend classes. I firmly agree with Mr. Hutchins on this point, and I am sure that many other students would agree too.

One reason why it seems to me that college football is bad is that it has become too commercial. In the olden times when people played football just for the fun of it, maybe college football was all right, but they do not play football just for the fun of it now as they used to in the old days. Nowadays college football is what you might call a big business. Maybe this is not true at all schools, and I don't think it is especially true here at State, but certainly this is the case at most colleges and universities in America nowadays, as Mr. Hutchins points out in his very interesting article. Actually the coaches and alumni go around to the high schools and offer the high school stars large salaries to come to their colleges and play football for them. There was one case where a high school star was offered a convertible if he would play football for a certain college.

Another reason for abolishing college football is that it is bad for the players. They do not have time to get a college education, because they are so busy playing football. A football player has to practice every afternoon from three to six, and then he is so tired that he can't concentrate on his studies. He just feels like dropping off to sleep after dinner, and then the next day he goes to his classes without having studied and maybe he fails the test.

(Good ripe stuff so far, but you're still a hundred and fifty-one words from home. One more push.)

Also I think college football is bad for the colleges and the universities because not very many students get to participate in it. Out of a college of ten thousand students only seventy-five or a hundred play football, if that many. Football is what you might call a spectator sport. That means that most people go to watch it but do not play it themselves.

(Four hundred and fifteen. Well, you still have the conclusion, and when you retype it, you can make the margins a little wider.)

These are the reasons why I agree with Mr. Hutchins that college football should be abolished in American colleges and universities.

On Monday you turn it in, moderately hopeful, and on Friday it comes 5 back marked "weak in content" and sporting a big D.

This essay is exaggerated a little, not much. The English instructor will 6 recognize it as reasonably typical of what an assignment on college football will bring in. He knows that nearly half of the class will contrive in five hundred words to say that college football is too commercial and bad for the players. Most of the other half will inform him that college football builds character and prepares one for life and brings prestige to the school. As he reads paper after paper all saying the same thing in almost the same words, all bloodless, five hundred words dripping out of nothing, he wonders how he allowed himself to get trapped into teaching English when he might have had a happy and interesting life as an electrician or a confidence man.

Well, you may ask, what can you do about it? The subject is one on which 7 you have few convictions and little information. Can you be expected to make a dull subject interesting? As a matter of fact, this is precisely what you are expected to do. This is the writer's essential task. All subjects, except sex, are dull until somebody makes them interesting. The writer's job is to find the argument, the approach, the angle, the wording that will take the reader with him. This is seldom easy, and it is particularly hard in subjects that have been much discussed: College Football, Fraternities, Popular Music, Is Chivalry Dead?, and the like. You will feel that there is nothing you can do with such subjects except repeat the old bromides. But there are some things you can do which will make your papers, if not throbbingly alive, at least less insufferably tedious than they might otherwise be.

Avoid the Obvious Content

Say the assignment is college football. Say that you've decided to be against it. 8 Begin by putting down the arguments that come to your mind: it is too commercial, it takes the students' minds off their studies, it is hard on the players, it makes the university a kind of circus instead of an intellectual center, for most schools it is financially ruinous. Can you think of any more arguments just off hand? All right. Now when you write your paper, *make sure that you don't use any of the material on this list*. If these are the points that leap to your mind, they will leap to everyone else's too, and whether you get a C or a D may depend on whether the instructor reads your paper early when he is fresh and tolerant or late, when the sentence "In my opinion, college football has become too commercial," inexorably repeated, has brought him to the brink of lunacy.

Be against college football for some reason or reasons of your own. If 9 they are keen and perceptive ones, that's splendid. But even if they are trivial or foolish or indefensible, you are still ahead so long as they are not everybody else's reasons too. Be against it because the colleges don't spend enough money on it to make it worthwhile, because it is bad for the characters of spectators, because the players are forced to attend classes, because the football stars hog all the beautiful women, because it competes with baseball and is therefore un-American and possibly Communist inspired. There are lots of more or less unused reasons for being against college football.

Sometimes it is a good idea to sum up and dispose of the trite and con- 10 ventional points before going on to your own. This has the advantage of indicating to the reader that you are going to be neither trite nor conventional. Something like this:

> We are often told that college football should be abolished because it has become too commercial or because it is bad for the players. These arguments are no doubt very cogent, but they don't really go to the heart of the matter.

Then you go to the heart of the matter.

Take the Less Usual Side

One rather simple way of getting interest into your paper is to take the side 11 of the argument that most of the citizens will want to avoid. If the assignment is an essay on dogs, you can, if you choose, explain that dogs are faithful and lovable companions, intelligent, useful as guardians of the house and protectors of children, indispensable in police work — in short, when all is said and done, man's best friends. Or you can suggest that those big brown eyes conceal, more often than not, a vacuity of mind and an inconstancy of purpose; that the dogs you have known most intimately have been mangy, ill-tempered brutes, incapable of instruction; and that only your nobility of mind and fear of arrest prevent you from kicking the flea-ridden animals when you pass them on the street.

Naturally, personal convictions will sometimes dictate your approach. 12 If the assigned subject is "Is Methodism Rewarding to the Individual?" and you are a pious Methodist, you have really no choice. But few assigned subjects, if any, will fall in this category. Most of them will lie in broad areas of discussion with much to be said on both sides. They are intellectual exercises and it is legitimate to argue now one way and now another, as debaters do in similar circumstances. Always take the side that looks to you hardest, least defensible. It will almost always turn out to be easier to write interestingly on that side.

This general advice applies where you have a choice of subjects. If you are 13 to choose among "The Value of Fraternities" and "My Favorite High School Teacher" and "What I Think about Beetles," by all means plump for the beetles. By the time the instructor gets to your paper, he will be up to his ears in tedious tales about the French teacher at Bloombury High and assertions about how fraternities build character and prepare one for life. Your views on beetles, whatever they are, are bound to be a refreshing change.

Don't worry too much about figuring out what the instructor thinks 14 about the subject so that you can cuddle up with him. Chances are his views are no stronger than yours. If he does have convictions and you oppose them, his problem is to keep from grading you higher than you deserve in order to show he is not biased. This doesn't mean that you should always cantankerously dissent from what the instructor says; that gets tiresome too. And if the subject assigned is "My Pet Peeve," do not begin, "My pet peeve is the English instructor who assigns papers on 'my pet peeve.'" This was still funny during the War of 1812, but it has sort of lost its edge since then. It is in general good manners to avoid personalities.

Slip Out of Abstraction

If you will study the essay on college football . . . you will perceive that one 15 reason for its appalling dullness is that it never gets down to particulars. It is just a series of not very glittering generalities: "football is bad for the colleges," "it has become too commercial," "football is a big business," "it is bad for the players," and so on. Such round phrases thudding against the reader's brain are unlikely to convince him, though they may well render him unconscious.

If you want the reader to believe that college football is bad for the play-   16
ers, you have to do more than say so. You have to display the evil. Take your
roommate, Alfred Simkins, the second-string center. Picture poor old Alfy
coming home from football practice every evening, bruised and aching, ago-
nizingly tired, scarcely able to shovel the mashed potatoes into his mouth. Let
us see him staggering up to the room, getting out his econ textbook, peering
desperately at it with his good eye, falling asleep and failing the test in the
morning. Let us share his unbearable tension as Saturday draws near. Will he
fail, be demoted, lose his monthly allowance, be forced to return to the coal
mines? And if he succeeds, what will be his reward? Perhaps a slight ripple of
applause when the third-string center replaces him, a moment of elation in
the locker room if the team wins, of despair if it loses. What will he look back
on when he graduates from college? Toil and torn ligaments. And what will
be his future? He is not good enough for pro football, and he is too obscure
and weak in econ to succeed in stocks and bonds. College football is tearing
the heart from Alfy Simkins and, when it finishes with him, will callously toss
aside the shattered hulk.

This is no doubt a weak enough argument for the abolition of college   17
football, but it is a sight better than saying, in three or four variations, that
college football (in your opinion) is bad for the players.

Look at the work of any professional writer and notice how constantly   18
he is moving from the generality, the abstract statement, to the concrete
example, the facts and figures, the illustration. If he is writing on juvenile
delinquency, he does not just tell you that juveniles are (it seems to him)
delinquent and that (in his opinion) something should be done about it. He
shows you juveniles being delinquent, tearing up movie theatres in Buffalo,
stabbing high school principals in Dallas, smoking marijuana in Palo Alto.
And more than likely he is moving toward some specific remedy, not just a
general wringing of the hands.

It is no doubt possible to be *too* concrete, too illustrative or anecdotal,   19
but few inexperienced writers err this way. For most the soundest advice is
to be seeking always for the picture, to be always turning general remarks
into seeable examples. Don't say, "Sororities teach girls the social graces." Say,
"Sorority life teaches a girl how to carry on a conversation while pouring
tea, without sloshing the tea into the saucer." Don't say, "I like certain kinds
of popular music very much." Say, "Whenever I hear Gerber Spinklittle play
'Mississippi Man' on the trombone, my socks creep up my ankles."

Get Rid of Obvious Padding

The student toiling away at his weekly English theme is too often tormented   20
by a figure: five hundred words. How, he asks himself, is he to achieve this
staggering total? Obviously by never using one word when he can somehow
work in ten.

He is therefore seldom content with a plain statement like "Fast driving is dan-   21
gerous." This has only four words in it. He takes thought, and the sentence becomes:

> In my opinion, fast driving is dangerous.

Better, but he can do better still:

> In my opinion, fast driving would seem to be rather dangerous.

If he is really adept, it may come out:

> In my humble opinion, though I do not claim to be an expert on
> this complicated subject, fast driving, in most circumstances, would
> seem to be rather dangerous in many respects, or at least so it would
> seem to me.

Thus four words have been turned into forty, and not an iota of content has
been added.

Now this is a way to go about reaching five hundred words, and if you are   22
content with a D grade, it is as good a way as any. But if you aim higher, you
must work differently. Instead of stuffing your sentences with straw, you must
try steadily to get rid of the padding, to make your sentences lean and tough.
If you are really working at it, your first draft will greatly exceed the required
total, and then you will work it down, thus:

> It is thought in some quarters that fraternities do not contribute
> as much as might be expected to campus life.
> Some people think that fraternities contribute little to campus life.

> The average doctor who practices in small towns or in the
> country must toil night and day to heal the sick.
> Most country doctors work long hours.

> When I was a little girl, I suffered from shyness and embarrass-
> ment in the presence of others.
> I was a shy little girl.

> It is absolutely necessary for the person employed as a marine
> fireman to give the matter of steam pressure his undivided attention
> at all times.
> The fireman has to keep his eye on the steam gauge.

You may ask how you can arrive at five hundred words at this rate. Simply.   23
You dig up more real content. Instead of taking a couple of obvious points
off the surface of the topic and then circling warily around them for six paragraphs, you work in and explore, figure out the details. You illustrate. You say
that fast driving is dangerous, and then you prove it. How long does it take to
stop a car at forty and at eighty? How far can you see at night? What happens
when a tire blows? What happens in a head-on collision at fifty miles an hour?

Pretty soon your paper will be full of broken glass and blood and headless tor-
sos, and reaching five hundred words will not really be a problem.

Call a Fool a Fool

Some of the padding in freshman themes is to be blamed not on anxiety   24
about the word minimum but on excessive timidity. The student writes, "In
my opinion, the principal of my high school acted in ways that I believe every
unbiased person would have to call foolish." This isn't exactly what he means.
What he means is, "My high school principal was a fool." If he was a fool, call
him a fool. Hedging the thing about with "in-my-opinion's" and "it-seems-
to-me's" and "as-I-see-it's" and "at-least-from-my-point-of-view's" gains you
nothing. Delete these phrases whenever they creep into your paper.

The student's tendency to hedge stems from a modesty that in other cir-   25
cumstances would be commendable. He is, he realizes, young and inexperienced, and he half suspects that he is dopey and fuzzy-minded beyond the
average. Probably only too true. But it doesn't help to announce your incompetence six times in every paragraph. Decide what you want to say and say it as
vigorously as possible, without apology and in plain words.

Linguistic diffidence can take various forms. One is what we call *euphe-*   26
mism. This is the tendency to call a spade "a certain garden implement" or
women's underwear "unmentionables." It is stronger in some eras than others and in some people than others but it always operates more or less in
subjects that are touchy or taboo: death, sex, madness, and so on. Thus we
shrink from saying, "He died last night" but say instead, "passed away," "left
us," "joined his Maker," "went to his reward." Or we try to take off the tension
with a lighter cliché: "kicked the bucket," "cashed in his chips," "handed in
his dinner pail." We have found all sorts of ways to avoid saying *mad*: "mentally ill," "touched," "not quite right upstairs," "feeble-minded," "innocent,"
"simple," "off his trolley," "not in his right mind." Even such a now plain word
as *insane* began as a euphemism with the meaning "not healthy."

Modern science, particularly psychology, contributes many polysyllables   27
in which we can wrap our thoughts and blunt their force. To many writers
there is no such thing as a bad schoolboy. Schoolboys are maladjusted or unori-
ented or misunderstood or in need of guidance or lacking in continued success
toward satisfactory integration of the personality as a social unit, but they are
never bad. Psychology no doubt makes us better men or women, more sympathetic and tolerant, but it doesn't make writing any easier. Had Shakespeare
been confronted with psychology, "To be or not to be" might have come out,
"To continue as a social unit or not to do so. That is the personality problem.
Whether 'tis a better sign of integration at the conscious level to display a psy-
chic tolerance toward the maladjustments and repressions induced by one's
lack of orientation in one's environment or —" But Hamlet would never have
finished the soliloquy.

Writing in the modern world, you cannot altogether avoid modern jar-   28
gon. Nor, in an effort to get away from euphemism, should you salt your
paper with four-letter words. But you can do much if you will mount guard
against those roundabout phrases, those echoing polysyllables that tend to
slip into your writing to rob it of its crispness and force.

Beware of the Pat Expression

Other things being equal, avoid phrases like "other things being equal." Those   29
sentences that come to you whole, or in two or three doughy lumps, are sure
to be bad sentences. They are no creation of yours but pieces of common
thought floating in the community soup.

Pat expressions are hard, often impossible, to avoid, because they come too   30
easily to be noticed and seem too necessary to be dispensed with. No writer avoids
them altogether, but good writers avoid them more often than poor writers.

By "pat expressions" we mean such tags as "to all practical intents and pur-   31
poses," "the pure and simple truth," "from where I sit," "the time of his life," "to
the ends of the earth," "in the twinkling of an eye," "as sure as you're born," "over
my dead body," "under cover of darkness," "took the easy way out," "when all
is said and done," "told him time and time again," "parted the best of friends,"
"stand up and be counted," "gave him the best years of her life," "worked her
fingers to the bone." Like other clichés, these expressions were once forceful.
Now we should use them only when we can't possibly think of anything else.

Some pat expressions stand like a wall between the writer and thought.   32
Such a one is "the American way of life." Many student writers feel that when
they have said that something accords with the American way of life or does
not they have exhausted the subject. Actually, they have stopped at the highest
level of abstraction. The American way of life is the complicated set of bonds
between a hundred and eighty million ways. All of us know this when we think
about it, but the tag phrase too often keeps us from thinking about it.

So with many another phrase dear to the politician: "this great land of   33
ours," "the man in the street," "our national heritage." These may prove our
patriotism or give a clue to our political beliefs, but otherwise they add nothing to the paper except words.

Colorful Words

The writer builds with words, and no builder uses a raw material more slippery   34
and elusive and treacherous. A writer's work is a constant struggle to get the
right word in the right place, to find that particular word that will convey his
meaning exactly, that will persuade the reader or soothe him or startle or amuse
him. He never succeeds altogether — sometimes he feels that he scarcely succeeds at all — but such successes as he has are what make the thing worth doing.

There is no book of rules for this game. One progresses through ever-   35
lasting experiment on the basis of ever-widening experience. There are few

useful generalizations that one can make about words as words, but there are perhaps a few.

Some words are what we call "colorful." By this we mean that they are 36 calculated to produce a picture or induce an emotion. They are dressy instead of plain, specific instead of general, loud instead of soft. Thus, in place of "Her heart beat," we may write "Her heart *pounded, throbbed, fluttered, danced.*" Instead of "He sat in his chair," we may say, "He *lounged, sprawled, coiled.*" Instead of "It was hot," we may say, "It was *blistering, sultry, muggy, suffocating, steamy, wilting.*"

However, it should not be supposed that the fancy word is always bet- 37 ter. Often it is as well to write "Her heart beat" or "It was hot" if that is all it did or all it was. Ages differ in how they like their prose. The nineteenth century liked it rich and smoky. The twentieth has usually preferred it lean and cool. The twentieth-century writer, like all writers, is forever seeking the exact word, but he is wary of sounding feverish. He tends to pitch it low, to understate it, to throw it away. He knows that if he gets too colorful, the audience is likely to giggle.

See how this strikes you: "As the rich, golden glow of the sunset died away 38 along the eternal western hills, Angela's limpid blue eyes looked softly and trustingly into Montague's flashing brown ones, and her heart pounded like a drum in time with the joyous song surging in her soul." Some people like that sort of thing, but most modern readers would say, "Good grief," and turn on the television.

Colored Words

Some words we would call not so much colorful as colored — that is, loaded 39 with associations, good or bad. All words — except perhaps structure words — have associations of some sort. We have said that the meaning of a word is the sum of the contexts in which it occurs. When we hear a word, we hear with it an echo of all the situations in which we have heard it before.

In some words, these echoes are obvious and discussable. The word 40 *mother*, for example, has, for most people, agreeable associations. When you hear *mother* you probably think of home, safety, love, food, and various other pleasant things. If one writes, "She was like a mother to me," he gets an effect which he would not get in "She was like an aunt to me." The advertiser makes use of the associations of *mother* by working it in when he talks about his product. The politician works it in when he talks about himself.

So also with such words as *home, liberty, fireside, contentment, patriot,* 41 *tenderness, sacrifice, childlike, manly, bluff, limpid.* All of these words are loaded with favorable associations that would be rather hard to indicate in a straightforward definition. There is more than a literal difference between "They sat around the fireside" and "They sat around the stove." They might have been equally warm and happy around the stove, but *fireside* suggests leisure, grace, quiet tradition, congenial company, and *stove* does not.

Conversely, some words have bad associations. *Mother* suggests pleasant things, but *mother-in-law* does not. Many mothers-in-law are heroically lovable and some mothers drink gin all day and beat their children insensible, but these facts of life are beside the point. The thing is that *mother* sounds good and *mother-in-law* does not. 42

Or consider the word *intellectual*. This would seem to be a complimentary term, but in point of fact it is not, for it has picked up associations of impracticality and ineffectuality and general dopiness. So also with such words as *liberal, reactionary, Communist, Socialist, capitalist, radical, schoolteacher, truck driver, undertaker, operator, salesman, huckster, speculator*. These convey meanings on the literal level, but beyond that — sometimes, in some places — they convey contempt on the part of the speaker. 43

The question of whether to use loaded words or not depends on what is being written. The scientist, the scholar, try to avoid them; for the poet, the advertising writer, the public speaker, they are standard equipment. But every writer should take care that they do not substitute for thought. If you write, "Anyone who thinks that is nothing but a Socialist (or Communist or capitalist)" you have said nothing except that you don't like people who think that, and such remarks are effective only with the most naïve readers. It is always a bad mistake to think your readers more naïve than they really are. 44

Colorless Words

But probably most student writers come to grief not with words that are colorful or those that are colored but with those that have no color at all. A pet example is *nice*, a word we would find it hard to dispense with in casual conversation but which is no longer capable of adding much to a description. Colorless words are those of such general meaning that in a particular sentence they mean nothing. Slang adjectives, like *cool* ("That's real cool.") tend to explode all over the language. They are applied to everything, lose their original force, and quickly die. 45

Beware also of nouns of very general meaning, like *circumstances, cases, instances, aspects, factors, relationships, attitudes, eventualities*, etc. In most circumstances you will find that those cases of writing which contain too many instances of words like these will in this and other aspects have factors leading to unsatisfactory relationships with the reader resulting in unfavorable attitudes on his part and perhaps other eventualities, like a grade of D. Notice also what *etc.* means. It means "I'd like to make this list longer, but I can't think of any more examples." 46

■ **Thinking Critically about the Text**

In this essay, Roberts points out certain features, positive and negative, found in the work of many writers. Does your writing exhibit any of these features? How would you rate your writing with respect to each of these features?

■ Questions on Subject

1. What, for you, is the most important advice Roberts has to offer?
2. According to Roberts, what is the job of the writer? Why, in particular, is it difficult for college students to do this job well? Discuss how your college experience leads you to agree or disagree with Roberts.
3. The author offers several "tricks" or techniques of good writing in his essay. What are they? Do you find them more useful than other techniques? Explain.
4. If, according to Roberts, a good writer never uses unnecessary words, then what are the legitimate ways a student can reach the goal of the five-hundred-word essay?
5. According to Roberts, how has modern psychology made it more difficult to write well?

■ Questions on Strategy

1. What is Roberts's thesis in this essay? (Glossary: *Thesis*)
2. Make a scratch outline of Roberts's essay. What are the similarities between his organization of material and the process analysis he outlines for students? (Glossary: *Organization*) Explain.
3. What kind of information does the title of Roberts's essay lead you to expect? (Glossary: *Title*) Does the author deliver what the title promises? Why do you think he chose this title?
4. What are Roberts's main points? How do his examples help him explain and clarify his main points? (Glossary: *Illustration*)
5. Roberts's writing style is well suited to his student audience; he includes examples that would be familiar to many students. How would you describe his writing style? What are some of the ways he uses narration and illustration to make the process analysis easy to follow? (Glossary: *Illustration; Narration*)

■ Questions on Diction and Vocabulary

1. Roberts wrote this essay over fifty years ago, and at some points the facts he cites indicate this: For example, he gives the population of the United States as 180 million (paragraph 32), whereas today it is over 300 million. Is there anything in his diction or word choice that makes Roberts's writing seem dated, or does it sound contemporary? Choose examples from the text to support your answer. (Glossary: *Diction*)
2. What does Roberts mean by "colorful words," "colored words," and "colorless words"?
3. What is Roberts's tone in this essay? What words does he use to create this tone? Explain how the tone affects you as a reader. (Glossary: *Tone*)

▪ Classroom Activity Using Process Analysis

Before class, find a how-to article that interests you on the Web site for wikiHow at www.wikihow.com. Bring a copy of the article to class and be prepared to discuss why you think the article is incomplete or inaccurate and how you might revise it.

▪ Writing Suggestions

1. In paragraph 16, Roberts explains how a brief but good essay on college football might be written. He obeys a major rule of good writing — show, don't tell. Thus, instead of a dry string of words, his brief "essay" uses humor, exaggeration, and concrete details to breathe life into the football player. Review Roberts's strategies for good writing. Then choose one of the dull topics he suggests or one of your own, and following the steps he lays out, write a five-hundred-word essay.

2. Roberts's essay was first published in 1958 — before personal computers and word processing programs became ubiquitous. Write an essay in which you compare and contrast the process of writing an essay on a typewriter or by hand and on a computer. (Glossary: *Comparison and Contrast*) How is the process similar? How is it different? What equipment and supplies does each require? Which do you prefer? Why?

Eating Industrial Meat

MICHAEL POLLAN

Writer, journalist, and educator Michael Pollan was born in 1955 and grew up on Long Island. In 1977 he graduated from Bennington College. He attended Mansfield College, Oxford University, and received a master's in English from Columbia University in 1981. As a writer, Pollan is fascinated by food, agriculture, gardening, drugs, and architecture — those places where the human and natural worlds intersect. Running throughout Pollan's work is the belief that eating is our most deeply significant interaction with the natural world. His award-winning nonfiction books include *Second Nature: A Gardener's Education* (1991), *A Place of My Own: The Education of an Amateur Builder* (1997), *The Botany of Desire: A Plant's Eye View of the World* (2001), *The Omnivore's Dilemma: A Natural History of Four Meals* (2006), and *In Defense of Food: An Eater's Manifesto* (2008). Since 1987 Pollan has been a contributing writer to the *New York Times Magazine*, and his articles on various food-related topics have appeared in *Esquire*, *Harper's*, *Gourmet*, *Condé Nast Traveler*, *Mother Jones*, and *Vogue*. He has taught at the University of Pittsburgh and the University of Wisconsin and is currently the John S. and James L. Knight Professor of Journalism at the University of California, Berkeley, where he directs the Knight Program in Science and Environmental Journalism.

In the following selection, excerpted from *The Omnivore's Dilemma*, Pollan examines the process of bringing beef to market. His focus is one steer in particular, number 534, as it's being held in a feedlot in Kansas to gain weight before being slaughtered. As you read, pay special attention to the far-ranging connections and implications of what he's learned about the way we have industrialized cattle farming in this country.

■ Preparing to Read

Reflect on the origins of the food you eat. Do you know where it comes from? Do you have any sense of how it is farmed or manufactured? If you are a meat eater, do you ever think about what the creatures you eat have themselves eaten? If you know very little about the origins of the food you eat, does that lack of knowledge affect you?

My first impression of pen 63, where my steer [534] is spending his last five months, was, *Not a bad little piece of real estate, all considered.* The pen is far enough from the feed mill to be fairly quiet and it has a water   1 view of what I thought was a pond or reservoir until I noticed the brown scum. The body of water is what is known, in the geography of CAFOs,[1] as a manure lagoon. I asked the feedlot manager why they didn't just spray the liquefied manure on neighboring farms. The farmers don't want it, he explained. The nitrogen and phosphorus levels are so high that spraying the crops would kill them. He didn't say that feedlot wastes also contain heavy metals and hormone residues, persistent chemicals that end up in waterways downstream, where scientists have found fish and amphibians exhibiting abnormal sex characteristics. CAFOs like Poky transform what at the proper scale would be a precious source of fertility — cow manure — into toxic waste.

The pen 534 lives in is surprisingly spacious, about the size of a hockey rink, with a concrete feed bunk along the road, and a fresh water trough out back. I climbed over the railing and joined the ninety steers, which, en masse, retreated a few lumbering steps, and then stopped to see what I would do. 2

I had on the same carrot-colored sweater I'd worn to the ranch in South Dakota, hoping to elicit some glint of recognition from my steer. I couldn't find him at first; all the faces staring at me were either completely black or bore an unfamiliar pattern of white marks. And then I spotted him — the three white blazes — way off in the back. As I gingerly stepped toward him the quietly shuffling mass of black cowhide between us parted, and there stood 534 and I, staring dumbly at one another. Glint of recognition? None, none whatsoever. I told myself not to take it personally; 534 and his pen mates have been bred for their marbling, after all, not their ability to form attachments. 3

I noticed that 534's eyes looked a little bloodshot. Dr. Metzin had told me that some animals are irritated by feedlot dust. The problem is especially serious in the summer months, when the animals kick up clouds of the stuff and workers have to spray the pens with water to keep it down. I had to remind myself that this is not ordinary dirt dust, inasmuch as the dirt in a feedyard is not ordinary dirt; no, this is fecal dust. But apart from the air quality, how did feedlot life seem to be agreeing with 534? I don't know enough about the emotional life of a steer to say with confidence that 534 was miserable, bored, or indifferent, but I would not say he looked happy. 4

He's clearly eating well, though. My steer had put on a couple hundred pounds since we'd last met, and he looked it: thicker across the shoulder and round as a barrel through the middle. He carried himself more like a steer now than a calf, even though his first birthday was still two months away. Dr. Metzin complimented me on his size and conformation. "That's a handsome-looking beef you got there." (Shucks.) 5

---

[1]Concentrated Animal Feeding Operations—Ed.

> If I stared at my steer hard enough, I could imagine the white lines of the butcher's chart dissecting his black hide: rump roast, flank steak, standing rib, tenderloin, brisket.

If I stared at my steer hard enough, I could imagine the white lines of the butcher's chart dissecting his black hide: rump roast, flank steak, standing rib, tenderloin, brisket. One way of looking at 534 — the feedlot way, the industrial way — was as a most impressive machine for turning number 2 field corn into cuts of beef. Every day between now and his slaughter in six months, 534 will convert thirty-two pounds of feed into four pounds of gain — new muscle, fat, and bone. This at least is how 534 appears in the computer program I'd seen at the mill: the ratio of feed to gain that determines his efficiency. (Compared to other food animals, cattle are terribly inefficient: The ratio of feed to flesh in chicken, the most efficient animal by this measure, is two pounds of corn to one of meat, which is why chicken costs less than beef.) Poky Feeders is indeed a factory, transforming — as fast as bovinely possible — cheap raw materials into a less cheap finished product, through the mechanism of bovine metabolism. 6

Yet metaphors of the factory and the machine obscure as much as they reveal about the creature standing before me. He has, of course, another, quite different identity — as an animal, I mean, connected as all animals must be to certain other animals and plants and microbes, as well as to the earth and the sun. He's a link in a food chain, a thread in a far-reaching web of ecological relationships. Looked at from this perspective, everything going on in this cattle pen appears quite different, and not nearly as far removed from our world as this manure-encrusted patch of ground here in Nowhere, Kansas, might suggest. 7

For one thing, the health of these animals is inextricably linked to our own by that web of relationships. The unnaturally rich diet of corn that undermines a steer's health fattens his flesh in a way that undermines the health of the humans who will eat it. The antibiotics these animals consume with their corn at this very moment are selecting, in their gut and wherever else in the environment they end up, for new strains of resistant bacteria that will someday infect us and withstand the drugs we depend on to treat that infection. We inhabit the same microbial ecosystem as the animals we eat, and whatever happens in it also happens to us. 8

Then there's the deep pile of manure on which I stand, in which 534 sleeps. We don't know much about the hormones in it — where they will end up, or what they might do once they get there—but we do know something about the bacteria, which can find their way from the manure on the ground to his hide and from there into our hamburgers. The speed at which these 9 animals will be slaughtered and processed — four hundred an hour at the plant where 534 will go — means that sooner or later some of the manure caked on these hides gets into the meat we eat. One of the bacteria that almost certainly resides in the manure I'm standing in is particularly lethal to humans. *Escherichia coli* 0157:H7 is a relatively new strain of the common intestinal bacteria (no one had seen it before 1980) that thrives in feedlot cattle, 40 percent of which carry it in their gut. Ingesting as few as ten of these microbes can cause a fatal infection; they produce a toxin that destroys human kidneys.

Most of the microbes that reside in the gut of a cow and find their way   10
into our food get killed off by the strong acids in our stomachs, since they evolved to live in the neutral pH environment of the rumen. But the rumen of a corn-fed feedlot steer is nearly as acidic as our own stomachs, and in this new, man-made environment new acid-resistant strains of *E. coli*, of which 0157:H7 is one, have evolved — yet another creature recruited by nature to absorb the excess biomass coming off the Farm Belt. The problem with these bugs is that they can shake off the acid bath in our stomachs — and then go on to kill us. By acidifying the rumen with corn we've broken down one of our food chain's most important barriers to infection. Yet another solution turned into a problem.

We've recently discovered that this process of acidification can be reversed,   11
and that doing so can greatly diminish the threat from *E. coli* 0157:H7. Jim Russell, a USDA microbiologist on the faculty at Cornell, has found that switching a cow's diet from corn to grass or hay for a few days prior to slaughter reduces the population of *E. coli* 0157:H7 in the animal's gut by as much as 80 percent. But such a solution (*Grass?!*) is considered wildly impractical by the cattle industry and (therefore) by the USDA. Their preferred solution for dealing with bacterial contamination is irradiation — essentially, to try to sterilize the manure getting into the meat.

So much comes back to corn, this cheap feed that turns out in so many   12
ways to be not cheap at all. While I stood in pen 63 a dump truck pulled up alongside the feed bunk and released a golden stream of feed. The black mass of cowhide moved toward the trough for lunch. The $1.60 a day I'm paying for three meals a day here is a bargain only by the narrowest of calculations. It doesn't take into account, for example, the cost to the public health of antibiotic resistance or food poisoning by *E. coli* 0157:H7. It doesn't take into account the cost to taxpayers of the farm subsidies that keep Poky's raw materials cheap. And it certainly doesn't take into account all the many environmental costs incurred by cheap corn.

I stood alongside 534 as he lowered his big head into the stream of fresh   13
grain. How absurd, I thought, the two of us standing hock-deep in manure in this godforsaken place, overlooking a manure lagoon in the middle of nowhere somewhere in Kansas. Godforsaken perhaps, and yet not apart, I

realized, as I thought of the other places connected to this place by the river of commodity corn. Follow the corn from this bunk back to the fields where it grows and I'd find myself back in the middle of that 125,000-mile-square monoculture, under a steady rain of pesticide and fertilizer. Keep going, and I could follow the nitrogen runoff from that fertilizer all the way down the Mississippi into the Gulf of Mexico, adding its poison to an eight-thousand-square-mile zone so starved of oxygen nothing but algae can live in it. And then go farther still, follow the fertilizer (and the diesel fuel and the petrochemical pesticides) needed to grow the corn all the way to the oil fields of the Persian Gulf.

I don't have a sufficiently vivid imagination to look at my steer and see a   14 barrel of oil, but petroleum is one of the most important ingredients in the production of modern meat, and the Persian Gulf is surely a link in the food chain that passes through this (or any) feedlot. Steer 534 started his life part of a food chain that derived all of its energy from the sun, which nourished the grasses that nourished him and his mother. When 534 moved from ranch to feedlot, from grass to corn, he joined an industrial food chain powered by fossil fuel — and therefore defended by the U.S. military, another never-counted cost of cheap food. (One-fifth of America's petroleum consumption goes to producing and transporting our food.) After I got home from Kansas, I asked an economist who specializes in agriculture and energy if it might be possible to calculate precisely how much petroleum it will take to grow my steer to slaughter weight. Assuming 534 continues to eat twenty-five pounds of corn a day and reaches a weight of twelve hundred pounds, he will have consumed in his lifetime the equivalent of thirty-five gallons of oil — nearly a barrel.

So this is what commodity corn can do to a cow: industrialize the mir-   15 acle of nature that is a ruminant, taking this sunlight- and prairie grass-powered organism and turning it into the last thing we need: another fossil fuel machine. This one, however, is able to suffer.

Standing there in the pen alongside my steer, I couldn't imagine ever   16 wanting to eat the flesh of one of these protein machines. Hungry was the last thing I felt. Yet I'm sure that after enough time goes by, and the stink of this place is gone from my nostrils, I will eat feedlot beef again. Eating industrial meat takes an almost heroic act of not knowing or, now, forgetting. But I left Poky determined to follow this meat to a meal on a table somewhere, to see this food chain at least that far. I was curious to know what feedlot beef would taste like now, if I could taste the corn or even, since taste is as much a matter of what's in the head as it is about molecules dancing on the tongue, some hint of the petroleum. "You are what you eat" is a truism hard to argue with, and yet it is, as a visit to a feedlot suggests, incomplete, for you are what what you eat eats, too. And what we are, or have become, is not just meat but number 2 corn and oil.

■ **Thinking Critically about the Text**

Pollan writes at the beginning of his essay that his first impression of the feedlot was that it was *"Not a bad little piece of real estate, all considered."* What facts undermine his first impression?

■ **Questions on Subject**

1. Why don't farmers want the liquefied manure from feedlots? What does that fact tell you about industrialized beef?
2. A butcher might look at 534 as an array of cuts of meat. Identify some of the other perspectives by which farm animals such as 534 are viewed.
3. What discovery has recently been made regarding reversing the acidification of the rumen of steers? Explain how it works.
4. Why do the cattle industry and the USDA find feeding grass to cattle impractical?
5. Why does the cheap corn fed to cows turn out to be not cheap after all, according to Pollan?

■ **Questions on Strategy**

1. How does Pollan organize his essay? (Glossary: *Organization*). Explain why his organization seems most appropriate for his subject.
2. Explain the process by which bacteria enter cattle and end up in the hamburgers we eat.
3. Explain the process by which a natural barrier to infection is diminished by feeding corn to cows.
4. How has Pollan used transitions to move from paragraph to paragraph in his essay? (Glossary: *Transitions*) Cite several examples and explain how they work.
5. How does Pollan connect what's happening to 534 to the oil fields of the Persian Gulf?

■ **Questions on Diction and Vocabulary**

1. In paragraph 3 Pollan writes, "534 and his pen mates have been bred for their marbling, after all, not their ability to form attachments." What does he mean by *marbling*?
2. Pollan ends paragraph 5 with "(Shucks)." How are we meant to interpret that expression? (Glossary: *Irony*)
3. What does Pollan mean when he writes in paragraph 7, "Yet metaphors of the factory and the machine obscure as much as they reveal about the creature standing before me." (Glossary: *Figures of Speech*)

■ Classroom Activity Using Process Analysis

Most do-it-yourself jobs require that you follow a set process to achieve the best results. Make a list of the steps involved in accomplishing one of the following household tasks:

baking chocolate chip cookies

transplanting a plant

replacing a lock

packing a suitcase

mowing a lawn

washing a pile of dirty towels

Compare your list with those of other students who focused on the same task. How do the lists differ? What could be improved?

■ Writing Suggestions

1. In an essay, write, as Pollan does, about the web of interconnectedness among processes that might at first seem unrelated. Pollan writes, for example, about the unintended consequences that arise when we pursue food-production practices and processes that run counter to the laws of nature. For your essay, consider an entirely different arena — the world of the Internet, for example, and the unintended consequences of our pursuit of maximum technological connectivity.

2. **Writing with Sources.** Pollan focuses his attention on the processes by which we raise cattle and bring them to market. By explaining those processes as they are carried out by the large industrial meat producers, he intends to provide us with information we need in order to make decisions about our economy, our environment, and our health. Do some research on other areas of food production — fruit growing or milk production, for example — and explain the processes involved. Write an essay in which you describe what the implications of the process might be for our economy, environment, or health.

   For models of and advice on integrating sources, see Chapters 14–15.

▶ Young Love

Tiffany Sharples

 Tiffany Sharples was born in 1981 in New Haven, Connecticut. She earned a bachelor of arts degree from Colgate University and a master of science degree in journalism from the Medill School of Journalism at Northwestern University. As a head reporter for *Time* and Time.com, Sharples specializes in family, health, and social science issues; she has also been published on CNN.com, *Arthur Frommer's Budget Travel*, the *Santiago Times*, and *Chicago Parent*. When asked if she had any advice for young writers, she offered, "Don't expect to get everything right the first time. That's what revision is for."

In the following article, which first appeared on Time.com on January 17, 2008, Sharples writes, "Most Western romance research involves Western cultures, where things may move at a very different pace from that of, say, the Far East or the Muslim world. While not all of the studies yield universal truths, they all suggest that people are wired to pick up their love skills in very specific stages."

■ Preparing to Read

Do you remember the first time you fell in love? What was it like? Were you frightened? Intrigued? Exhilarated? Bewildered?

There's a very thin line between being thrilled and being terrified, and Candice Feiring saw both emotions on her son's face. The sixth grader had just gotten off the phone with a girl in his class who called to ask if he'd like to go to the movies — just the two of them. It sounded a whole lot like a date to him. "Don't I have something to do tomorrow?" he asked his mother. A psychologist and an editor of *The Development of Romantic Relationships in Adolescence*, Feiring was uniquely prepared to field that question and give her son the answer that, for now, he needed. "I think you're too young to go out one-on-one," she said. His face broke into a relieved grin.

A year later, even a month later, Feiring's adolescent son might have reacted very differently to being told he was not ready to date. That moment-to-moment mutability of his interest in — never mind his readiness for — courtship is only one tiny part of the exhilarating, exhausting, confounding path all humans travel as they make their halting way into the world of love. From the moment we're born — when the world is mostly sensation, and nothing much matters beyond a full belly, a warm embrace, and a clean diaper — until we finally emerge into adulthood and understand the rich mix of tactile, sexual, and emotional experiences that come with loving another adult, we are in a constant state of learning and rehearsing. Along with language, romance may be one of the hardest skills we'll ever be called on to acquire. But while we're more or less fluent in speech by the time we're five, romance takes a lot longer. Most Western romance research involves Western cultures, where things may move at a very different pace from that of, say, the Far East or the Muslim world. While not all of the studies yield universal truths, they all suggest that people are wired to pick up their love skills in very specific stages.

> Along with language, romance may be one of the hardest skills we'll ever be called on to acquire.

Infancy and Babyhood

Babies may not have much to do right after they're born, but the stakes are vitally high that they do it right. One of the first skills newborns must learn is how to woo the adults in their world. "For a baby literally you're going to be dead without love, so getting people around you to love you is a really good strategy," says Alison Gopnik, a cognitive psychologist at the University of California, Berkeley.

Babies do this much the way adults do: by flirting. Within a couple of months, infants may move and coo, bob, and blink in concert with anyone who's paying attention to them. Smiling is a critical and cleverly timed part of this phase. Babies usually manage a first smile by the time they're six weeks old, which, coincidentally or not, is about the time the novelty of a newborn has worn off and sleep-deprived parents are craving some peace. A smile can be a powerful way to win them back.

Even before we know how to turn on the charm, touch and chemistry are bonding us firmly to our parents — and bonding them to us. Oxytocin — a hormone sometimes called the cuddle chemical — surges in new mothers and, to a lesser extent, in new fathers, making their baby instantly irresistible to them. One thing grown-ups particularly can't resist doing is picking a baby up, and that, too, is a key to survival. "Babies need physical contact with human hands to grow and thrive," says Lisa Diamond, a psychologist at the University of Utah. Years of data have shown that premature babies who are regularly touched fare much better than those who aren't.

As babies seduce and adults respond, a sophisticated dynamic develops. Mothers learn to synch their behavior with their newborn's, so that they offer a smile when their baby smiles, food when their baby's hungry. That's a pleasingly reciprocal deal, and while adults are already aware that when you give pleasure and comfort, you get it in return, it's news for the baby. "Babies are building up ideas about how close relationships work," says Gopnik.

Toddlerhood and Preschool

When kids reach two, mom and dad aren't paying quite the same attention   7
they used to. You feed yourself, you play on your own, you get held less often. That's not to say you need your parents less — and you're not shy about letting them know it. Children from ages two to five have yet to develop what's known as a theory of mind — the understanding that other people have hidden thoughts that are different from yours and that you can conceal your thoughts, too. Without that knowledge, kids conceal nothing. "They love you," says Gopnik, "and they really, really express it."

At the same time, kids are learning something about sensual pleasures.   8
They explore their bodies more, discovering that certain areas yield more electrifying feelings than others. This simultaneous emotional development and physical experience can lead to surprising behavior. "Three- and four-year-olds are very sexual beings," says Gopnik, "and a lot of that is directed at their parents." Some of this can get generalized to other adults, too, as when a small child develops a crush on a teacher or seems to flirt with an aunt or uncle. While a number of things are at work when this happens, the most important is playacting and the valuable rehearsal for later life it provides. "Kids are trying to play out a set of roles and be more like adults," says psychologist Andrew Collins of the University of Minnesota's Institute of Child Development.

The same kind of training behavior can show up with playmates and friends,   9
often accompanied by unexpectedly powerful feelings. Social psychologist Elaine Hatfield of the University of Hawaii is best known for cocreating the Passionate Love Scale, a questionnaire with which she can gauge feelings of romantic connectedness in adults. She has modified the test to elicit similar information from children. In early work, she studied 114 boys and 122 girls, some as young as four, presenting them with statements like "I am always thinking about _____" or "I would rather be with _____ than anybody else." The kids filled in the name of someone they loved, and Hatfield asked them to rate the intensity of feelings with stacks of checkers: the higher the stack, the more they felt. In some instances, the kids became overwhelmed with emotion, as in the case of a five-year-old girl who wept at the thought of a boy she would never see again. "Little kids fall in love, too," Hatfield says plainly.

School Age and Puberty

As with so much else in childhood, things get more complicated once kids   10
reach the social incubator of elementary school. Nowhere near sexually mature,

they nonetheless become sexually active — in their own fashion. The opposite-sex teasing and chasing that are rife on playgrounds may give teachers headaches, but they teach boys and girls a lot. The games, after all, are about pursuit and emotional arousal, two critical elements of sex. "There are a lot of erotic forms of play," says Barrie Thorne, a sociologist at the University of California, Berkeley, and the author of *Gender Play: Boys and Girls in School.* "It can be titillating, and it may involve sexual meaning, but it comes and goes."

More enduring — for a while at least — is the gender segregation that begins   11
at this age. Boys and girls who once played in mixed groups at school begin to drift apart into single-sex camps, drawing social boundaries that will stay in place for years. In her 1986 study that is still cited today, Thorne looked at 802 elementary-school students from California and Massachusetts to determine just what goes on behind these gender fortifications and why they're established in the first place.

To no one's surprise, both groups spend a lot of time talking and thinking   12
about the opposite sex, but they do it in very different ways. Boys experiment more with sexually explicit vocabulary and, later, sexual fantasies. Girls focus more heavily — but hardly exclusively — on romantic fantasies. The two-gender world they'll eventually reenter will be a lot more complex than that, but for now, the boys are simply practicing being boys — albeit in a very rudimentary way — and the girls are practicing being girls. "Among the boys, for example, there's a lot of bragging talk," says Thorne. "You're supposed to be powerful and not vulnerable."

When puberty hits, the wall between the worlds begins to crumble — a bit.   13
Surging hormones make the opposite sex irresistible, but the rapprochement happens collectively, with single-gender groups beginning to merge into coed social circles within which individual boys and girls can flirt and experiment. Generally, kids who pair off with a love interest and begin dating will hold on to a return ticket to the mixed-gender group. Jennifer Connolly, a psychologist at York University in Toronto, studied 174 high school students in grades nine to eleven and found that when things go awry with couples, the kids are quickly absorbed back into the coed circle, with the old single-sex group increasingly eclipsed. "Once the progression has started," Connolly says, "we don't see kids retreating back into only same-gender interaction."

Almost all of these early relationships are, not surprisingly, short-lived —   14
and a good thing, too. If the purpose is to pick a mate for life, you're hardly likely to find a suitable one on your very first go. What's more, even if you did get lucky, you'd almost certainly not have the emotional wherewithal to keep the relationship going. Adults often lament the love they had and lost in high school and wonder what would have happened if they had met just a few years later. But the only way to acquire the skills to conduct a lifetime relationship is to practice on ones you may destroy in the process. "Kids

don't really have a sense of working to preserve a relationship," Connolly says. "Adolescence is a time for experimentation."

Sexual experimentation is a big part of that — and it's a part that's especially fraught. Pregnancy and sexually transmitted diseases are just two of the things that make sex perilous. There are also emotional conflicts kids bring into their early experiences with intimacy. Psychologists have long warned that children who grow up in a hostile home or one in which warmth is withheld are likelier to start having sex earlier and engage in it more frequently. In a [2008] study. . . , Trish Williams, a neuropsychology fellow at Alberta Children's Hospital, studied a group of 1,959 kids ages eleven to thirteen and did find a striking correlation between a volatile home and earlier sexual behavior. A few of the children had had intercourse at as young an age as twelve, and while the number of sexually active kids wasn't high — just 2 percent of the total — the cause was clear. "Hostile parenting is highly associated with problem behavior," says Williams.   15

Even kids without such emotional scarring can be pretty undiscriminating in their sexual choices. Two studies conducted by sociologist Wendy Manning in 2005 and 2006 showed that while 75 percent of kids have their first sexual experience with a partner they're dating — a figure that may bring at least some comfort to worried parents — more than 60 percent will eventually have sex with someone with whom they're not in any kind of meaningful dating relationship. Hooking up — very informal sex between two people with no intent of pursuing a deeper relationship — takes this casualness even further. A 2004 study Manning worked on showed that the overwhelming majority of hookups involve alcohol use — an impairer of sexual judgment if ever there was one — and according to the work of other researchers, more than half the times kids hook up, they do not use a condom. Manning's studies suggest that hooking up prevents kids from practicing the interpersonal skills they'll need in a permanent relationship and may lead to lowered expectations of what those relationships should be like — and a greater willingness to settle for less.   16

For all these perils, the fact is, most people manage to shake off even such high-stakes behavior and find a satisfying life partner, and that says something about the resilience of humans as romantic creatures. In the United States, by the time we're eighteen, about 80 percent of us have had at least one meaningful romantic relationship. As adults, up to 75 percent of us marry. Certainly, nature doesn't make things easy. From babyhood on, it equips us with the tools we'll need for the hardest social role we'll ever play — the role of romantic — and then chooses the moment when we're drunk on the hormones of adolescence and least confident in ourselves to push us on stage to perform. That we go on at all is a mark of our courage. That we learn the part so well is a mark of how much is at stake.   17

x

■ Thinking Critically about the Text

Respond to Sharples's statement in paragraph 2 that "romance may be one of the hardest skills we'll ever be called on to acquire." Explain why you agree or disagree.

■ Questions on Subject

1. What role does flirting play in all stages of human development? Why is it so important?
2. How do children rehearse for adult roles (paragraph 8)?
3. Why does Sharples say that romantic relationships in puberty are "almost all . . . , not surprisingly, short-lived — and a good thing, too" (paragraph 14)?
4. Men and women who "hook up" often use alcohol and fail to use condoms, according to researchers. What does hooking up also prevent kids from doing, according to Sharples (paragraph 16)?
5. What role does hostile parenting play in early sexual behavior, according to neuropsychologist Trish Williams (paragraph 15)?

■ Questions on Strategy

1. On what principle has Sharples organized her explanation of the process whereby we learn to love? (Glossary: *Organization*)
2. How effective is the beginning of Sharples's essay? Explain. (Glossary: *Beginnings/Endings*)
3. Comment on the author's use of research. Where and how has she used outside authorities to support her claims? (Glossary: *Evidence*) How have those outside sources enhanced her essay? Does she cite too many outside authorities? Explain.
4. Does the fact that many marriages end in divorce factor into the overall picture that Sharples paints regarding romantic love? Do you think she has purposely left divorce statistics out of the essay? Would such a discussion be appropriate given her title? Explain.
5. Do you think anything is lost — perhaps the mystery of love itself — in Sharples's objective analysis of the process we go through as we learn to love? Explain.

■ Questions on Diction and Vocabulary

1. Sharples uses the metaphor of life as a stage in her final paragraph. Is the metaphor an effective one, in your opinion? (Glossary: *Figures of Speech*)
2. How would you characterize Sharples's tone in this essay? Do you find it appropriate for her purpose and audience? Explain. (Glossary: *Audience; Tone*)

■ Classroom Activity Using Process Analysis

Perhaps one of the most universally memorable activities of childhood is making a paper airplane. Carefully read the instructions for making one at wikiHow: The How-to-Manual You Can Edit <www.wikiHow.com /Make-a-Paper-Airplane>. Then construct your own airplane, using the wikiHow instructions, and fly it. How far, if at all, did it fly? How helpful did you find the illustrations that accompany the written instructions? Based on your results, what revisions to the instructions would you make? Why?

■ Writing Suggestions

1. Write an essay using directional process analysis for a "simple" task that could prove disastrous if not explained precisely — for example, changing a tire, putting out a kitchen fire, driving a manual-transmission car, packing for a camping trip, or testing for and eliminating lead or radon in your home. Be sure to explain why your directions are the best and what could happen if readers don't follow them exactly.

2. **Writing with Sources.** How are love skills learned in non-Western cultures? Choose a non-Western culture that interests you — for example, Japanese, Afghan, or Turkish — and do some research on it. Then write an essay modeled on Sharples's that examines the process by which babies, children, and young adults learn their romantic roles in that society.

For models of and advice on integrating sources, see Chapters 14–15.

Campus Racism 101

NIKKI GIOVANNI

Yolanda Cornelia "Nikki" Giovanni was born in Knoxville, Tennessee, in 1943 and was raised in Ohio. After graduating from Fisk University, she organized the Black Arts Festival in Cincinnati and then entered graduate school at the University of Pennsylvania. Her first book of poetry, *Black Feeling, Black Talk*, was published in 1968 and began a lifetime of writing that reflects on the African American identity. Recent books of poetry include the anthologies *Selected Poems of Nikki Giovanni* (1996), *Love Poems* (1997), *Blues for All the Changes: New Poems* (1999), *Quilting the Black-Eyed Pea: Poems and Not Quite Poems* (2002), *The Collected Poetry of Nikki Giovanni* (2003), and *Acolytes: Poems* (2007). Her honors include the Langston Hughes Award for Distinguished Contributions to Arts and Letters in 1996, the NAACP Image Award for Literature in 1998, and Woman of the Year awards from several magazines, including *Essence, Mademoiselle*, and *Ladies Home Journal*. She is currently professor of English and Gloria D. Smith Professor of Black Studies at Virginia Tech.

The following selection, taken from her nonfiction work *Racism 101*, instructs black students about how to succeed at predominantly white colleges.

■ Preparing to Read

How would you characterize race relations at your school? How much do white and minority students interact, and what, in your experience, is the tone of those interactions? What is being done within the institution to address any problems or to foster greater respect and understanding?

There is a bumper sticker that reads: TOO BAD IGNORANCE ISN'T PAINFUL. I like   1
that. But ignorance is. We just seldom attribute the pain to it or even recognize it when we see it. Like the postcard on my corkboard. It shows a young man in a very hip jacket smoking a cigarette. In the background is a high school with the American flag waving. The caption says: "Too cool for school. Yet too stupid for the real world." Out of the mouth of the young man is a bubble enclosing the words "Maybe I'll start a band." There could be a postcard showing a jock in a uniform saying, "I don't need school. I'm going to the NFL or NBA." Or one showing a young man or woman studying and a group of young people saying, "So you want to be white." Or something equally demeaning. We need to quit it.

I am a professor of English at Virginia Tech. I've been here for four years, though for only two years with academic rank. I am tenured, which means I have a teaching position for life, a rarity on a predominantly white campus. Whether from malice or ignorance, people who think I should be at a predominantly Black institution will ask, "Why are you at Tech?" Because it's here. And so are Black students. But even if Black students weren't here, it's painfully obvious that this nation and this world cannot allow white students to go through higher education without interacting with Blacks in authoritative positions. It is equally clear that predominantly Black colleges cannot accommodate the numbers of Black students who want and need an education.

Is it difficult to attend a predominantly white college? Compared with what? Being passed over for promotion because you lack credentials? Being turned down for jobs because you are not college-educated? Joining the armed forces or going to jail because you cannot find an alternative to the streets? Let's have a little perspective here. Where can you go and what can you do that frees you from interacting with the white American mentality? You're going to interact; the only question is, will you be in some control of yourself and your actions, or will you be controlled by others? I'm going to recommend self-control.

What's the difference between prison and college? They both prescribe your behavior for a given period of time. They both allow you to read books and develop your writing. They both give you time alone to think and time with your peers to talk about issues. But four years of prison doesn't give you a passport to greater opportunities. Most likely that time only gives you greater knowledge of how to get back in. Four years of college gives you an opportunity not only to lift yourself but to serve your people effectively. What's the difference when you are called nigger in college from when you are called nigger in prison? In college you can, though I admit with effort, follow procedures to have those students who called you nigger kicked out or suspended. You can bring issues to public attention without risking your life. But mostly, college is and always has been the future.

> There are discomforts attached to attending predominantly white colleges, though no more so than living in a racist world.

We, neither less nor more than other people, need knowledge. There are discomforts attached to attending predominantly white colleges, though no more so than living in a racist world. Here are some rules to follow that may help:

Go to class. No matter how you feel. No matter how you think the professor feels about you. It's important to have a consistent presence in the classroom. If nothing else, the professor will know you care enough and are serious enough to be there.

Meet your professors. Extend your hand (give a firm handshake) and tell them your name. Ask them what you need to do to make an A. You may never make an A, but you have put them on notice that you are serious about getting good grades.

Do assignments on time. Typed or computer-generated. You have the 7
syllabus. Follow it, and turn those papers in. If for some reason you can't
complete an assignment on time, let your professor know before it is due and
work out a new due date — then meet it.

Go back to see your professor. Tell him or her your name again. If an 8
assignment received less than an A, ask why, and find out what you need to
do to improve the next assignment.

Yes, your professor is busy. So are you. So are your parents who are work- 9
ing to pay or help with your tuition. Ask early what you need to do if you feel
you are starting to get into academic trouble. Do not wait until you are failing.

Understand that there will be professors who do not like you; there may even 10
be professors who are racist or sexist or both. You must discriminate among
your professors to see who will give you the help you need. You may not simply
say, "They are all against me." They aren't. They mostly don't care. Since you are
the one who wants to be educated, find the people who want to help.

Don't defeat yourself. Cultivate your friends. Know your enemies. You can- 11
not undo hundreds of years of prejudicial thinking. Think for yourself and speak
up. Raise your hand in class. Say what you believe no matter how awkward you
may think it sounds. You will improve in your articulation and confidence.

Participate in some campus activity. Join the newspaper staff. Run for 12
office. Join a dorm council. Do something that involves you on campus. You
are going to be there for four years, so let your presence be known, if not felt.

You will inevitably run into some white classmates who are troubling because 13
they often say stupid things, ask stupid questions — and expect an answer. Here
are some comebacks to some of the most common inquiries and comments:

Q: What's it like to grow up in a ghetto? 14
A: I don't know. 15

Q: (from the teacher) Can you give us the Black perspective on Toni Mor- 16
rison, Huck Finn, slavery, Martin Luther King Jr., and others?
A: I can give you *my* perspective. (Do not take the burden of 22 million 17
people on your shoulders. Remind everyone that you are an individual,
and don't speak for the race or any other individual within it.)

Q: Why do all the Black people sit together in the dining hall? 18
A: Why do all the white students sit together? 19

Q: Why should there be an African American studies course? 20
A: Because white Americans have not adequately studied the contributions 21
of Africans and African Americans. Both Black and white students need
to know our total common history.

Q: Why are there so many scholarships for "minority" students? 22

A: Because they wouldn't give my great-grandparents their forty acres and 23
the mule.

Q: How can whites understand Black history, culture, literature, and so forth? 24

A: The same way we understand white history, culture, literature, and so 25
forth. That is why we're in school: to learn.

Q: Should whites take African American studies courses? 26

A: Of course. We take white-studies courses, though the universities don't 27
call them that.

Comment: When I see groups of Black people on campus, it's really 28
intimidating.

Comeback: I understand what you mean. I'm frightened when I see white 29
students congregating.

Comment: It's not fair. It's easier for you guys to get into college than for 30
other people.

Comeback: If it's so easy, why aren't there more of us? 31

Comment: It's not our fault that America is the way it is. 32

Comeback: It's not our fault, either, but both of us have a responsibility to 33
make changes.

It's really very simple. Educational progress is a national concern; educa- 34
tion is a private one. Your job is not to educate white people; it is to obtain
an education. If you take the racial world on your shoulders, you will not
get the job done. Deal with yourself as an individual worthy of respect, and
make everyone else deal with you the same way. College is a little like playing
grown-up. Practice what you want to be. You have been telling your parents
you are grown. Now is your chance to act like it.

■ Thinking Critically about the Text

Giovanni concludes her essay by pointing out the nature of the "job" black
students have undertaken, focusing on what it does *not* involve for them.
For you, does the "job" of being a student involve more than just getting
an education? If so, what other priorities do you have, and what additional
challenges do they present? If not, explain your situation. How well are you
able to put other things aside to achieve your educational goals?

■ Questions on Subject

1. Who is Giovanni's audience? Where does the intended audience first become clear? (Glossary: *Audience*)
2. Why does Giovanni dismiss the notion that it is difficult being a black student at a predominantly white college? What contexts does she use to support her contention?
3. The rules Giovanni presents to help black students succeed at white colleges offer a lot of sound advice for any student at any college. Why does Giovanni use what could be considered general information in her essay?
4. On what topic does Giovanni provide sample questions and answers for her readers? Why is the topic important to her readers?
5. In paragraph 34, Giovanni makes the point that there is a difference between "educational progress" and "education." What is that difference?

■ Questions on Strategy

1. What is Giovanni arguing for in this essay? (Glossary: *Argument*) What is her thesis? (Glossary: *Thesis*)
2. Giovanni begins her essay with staccato rhythm. Short sentences appear throughout the essay, but they are emphasized in the beginning. (Glossary: *Beginnings/Endings*) Reread paragraph 1. What does Giovanni accomplish with her rapid-fire delivery? Why is it appropriate for the subject matter?
3. What does Giovanni gain by including her short personal narrative in paragraph 2? (Glossary: *Narration*) Why is it necessary to know her personal history and current situation?
4. After beginning her essay with straight prose, Giovanni uses a list with full explanations and a series of Q&A examples to outline strategies to help black students cope at predominantly white colleges. Why did Giovanni use these techniques to convey her material? How might they add to the usefulness of the essay for the reader?
5. What does Giovanni mean when she says, "Educational progress is a national concern; education is a private one" (paragraph 34)? In what ways is this point important to her purpose? (Glossary: *Purpose*)

■ Questions on Diction and Vocabulary

1. How did you first react to Giovanni's title, "Campus Racism 101"? What did it connote to you? (Glossary: *Connotation/Denotation*) After reading the essay, do you think the title is appropriate? Explain your answer.
2. Giovanni uses the word *stupid* on two occasions. The first use (paragraph 1), "too stupid for the real world," provides a context for how she views the word, while the second characterizes what white students sometimes ask or say to black students. The second use (paragraph 13) is a little jarring — often these days the characterization is softened to "insensitive" or "thoughtless." The use of *stupid*

implies a more active ignorance on the part of the questioner. What does Giovanni gain by using the word? Do you think it is meant to be pejorative toward the white students? Explain your answer.
3. How would you describe the author's tone in this essay? (Glossary: *Tone*) Is it angry, firm, moderate, instructional, or something else? Explain.

■ Classroom Activity Using Process Analysis

After finishing the first draft of your process analysis essay, have some-one else in your writing class read it. If you are writing a directional analy-sis, ask your reader to follow the instructions and then tell you whether he or she was able to understand each step and, if possible, perform it satisfactorily. Was the desired result achieved? If not, examine your pro-cess step by step, looking for errors and omissions that would explain the unsatisfactory result.

■ Writing Suggestions

1. What specific strategies do you employ to do well in your classes? Do you ask the professor what is needed for an A and make sure you attend every class, as Giovanni suggests in her essay? Do you take meticulous notes, study every day, just cram the night before exams, or have a lucky shirt for test days? Write a process analysis in which you present your method for success in school in a way that others could emulate, should they so choose.

2. In Giovanni's Q&A section, she replies to the question, "Why are there so many scholarships for 'minority' students?" with the answer, "Because they wouldn't give my great-grandparents their forty acres and the mule" (paragraphs 22–23). Write an argumentative essay in which you react to both Giovanni's answer and the situation as a whole. Do you think qualified minority students should receive pref-erential treatment for admissions and financial aid? If you argue no, what other strategies would you support to address the current edu-cational inequities between whites and blacks?

3. **Writing with Sources.** Giovanni's essay covers a subject — African Amer-icans attending predominantly white colleges — that has a relatively short history in many areas of the country. Although African Americans have a long history of success in higher education in the Northeast, where they were admitted to some schools as early as the 1820s, it has only been in the last five decades that the final barriers to college attendance have been removed nationwide. The battle over edu-cation rights became one of the most important components of the civil rights movement and led to some of the most contentious showdowns.

The photograph on page 276 shows James Meredith as he at-tempts to become the first African American to enter the University of Mississippi on October 1, 1962. His efforts resulted in riots that caused two deaths and 160 injuries. Meredith graduated from Ole Miss in 1964 and then went on to Columbia University and earned a degree in law.

What evidence of determination do you see on the faces and in the body language of both those who wished to keep James Meredith from entering the university and those who were his supporters? Notice that the photograph reveals a sort of mirror image, with the opposing sides reflecting each other's confrontational attitudes.

Research the background and precipitating circumstances of Meredith's admittance to the University of Mississippi, and write an essay explaining the process he went through to make his case heard and accepted by authorities in the civil rights movement, the federal government, the state of Mississippi, and the university.

For models of and advice on integrating sources, see Chapters 14–15.

WRITING SUGGESTIONS FOR PROCESS ANALYSIS

1. Write a directional or evaluative process analysis on one of the following topics:

    a. how to copy a CD

    b. how to adjust bicycle brakes

    c. how to save photos you take on your smartphone

    d. how to throw a party

    e. how to use the memory function on a calculator

    f. how to add, drop, or change a course

    g. how to play a specific card game

    h. how to wash a sweater

    i. how to develop black-and-white film

    j. how to stop spam

    k. how to build a Web page

    l. how to select a major course of study

    m. how to safety dispose of old electronics

    n. how to rent an apartment

    o. how to develop confidence

    p. how to wrap a present

    q. how to change oil in a car

    r. how to do a magic trick

2. Think about your favorite pastime or activity. Write an essay in which you explain one or more of the processes you follow in participating in that activity. For example, if basketball is your hobby, how do you go about making a layup? If you are a photographer, how do you develop and print a picture? If you are an actor, how do you go about learning your lines? Do you follow standard procedures, or do you personalize the process in some way?

3. All college students have to register for courses each term. What is the registration process like at your college? Do you find any part of the process unnecessarily frustrating or annoying? In a letter to your campus newspaper or an appropriate administrator, evaluate your school's current registration procedure, offering suggestions for making the process more efficient and pleasurable.

4. Writing to a person who is a computer novice, explain how to do a Web search. Be sure to define key terms and to illustrate the steps in your process with screen shots of search directories and search results.

5. **Writing with Sources.** Do some research, and then write an informational or evaluative process analysis on one of the following topics:

   a. how your heart functions

   b. how a U.S. president is elected

   c. how ice cream is made

   d. how a hurricane forms

   e. how hailstones form

   f. how a volcano erupts

   g. how the human circulatory system works

   h. how a camera works

   i. how photosynthesis takes place

   j. how an atomic bomb or reactor works

   k. how fertilizer is made

   l. how a refrigerator works

   m. how water evaporates

   n. how flowers bloom

   o. how a recession occurs

   p. how an automobile is made

   q. how a bill becomes law in your state

   r. how a caterpillar becomes a butterfly

   For models and advice on integrating sources, see Chapters 14 and 15.

6. **Writing with Sources.** Although each of us hopes never to be in a natural disaster such as an earthquake or a major flood, many of us have been or will be, and it is important that people know what to do. Do some research on the topic, and then write an essay in which you explain the steps that a person should follow to protect life and property during and in the aftermath of a particular natural disaster.

   For models and advice on integrating sources, see Chapters 14 and 15.

7. **Writing with Sources.** If you are scientifically minded or simply want to know more about evolution, research some subprocesses that contribute to the evolutionary process, using books, journals, articles, videos, and online resources. Some of the subprocesses that you may want to pursue include adaptation, selection, divergence, genetic drift, natural selection, mutation, and bipedalism. Consider an educated, general-interest reader to be your audience, so be sure to define technical terms.

   For models and advice on integrating sources, see Chapters 14 and 15.

8. The poster reproduced on page 222 tells you how to "Cover your Cough" and protect yourself from the spread of germs. The diagram demonstrates a simple directional process analysis. Study the diagram and create a poster of your own, with both simple text and line drawings, that simplifies the process of one of the following common activities:

    a.   brushing your teeth

    b.   applying a bandage to a minor scratch or cut

    c.   washing your hands

    d.   applying suntan lotion

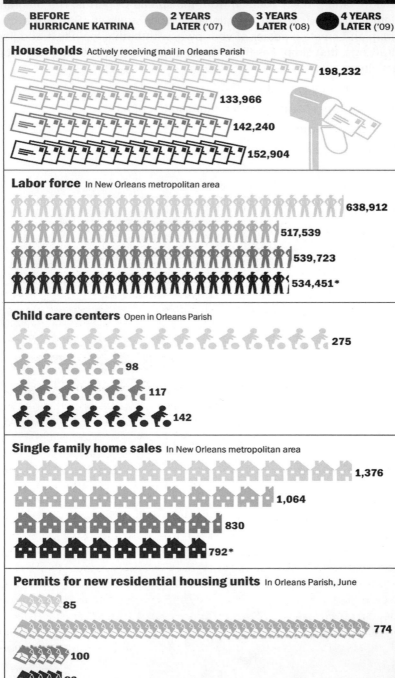

REBUILDING PROGRESS IN NEW ORLEANS

- **BEFORE HURRICANE KATRINA**
- **2 YEARS LATER** ('07)
- **3 YEARS LATER** ('08)
- **4 YEARS LATER** ('09)

Households Actively receiving mail in Orleans Parish

198,232
133,966
142,240
152,904

Labor force In New Orleans metropolitan area

638,912
517,539
539,723
534,451*

Child care centers Open in Orleans Parish

275
98
117
142

Single family home sales In New Orleans metropolitan area

1,376
1,064
830
792*

Permits for new residential housing units In Orleans Parish, June

85
774
100
89

*Preliminary

CHAPTER 8

Comparison and Contrast

What Are Comparison and Contrast?

A comparison presents two or more subjects (people, ideas, or objects), considers them together, and shows in what ways they are alike; a contrast shows how they differ. These two perspectives, apparently in contradiction to each other, actually work so often in conjunction that they are commonly considered a single strategy, called *comparison and contrast* or simply *comparison* for short.

Comparison and contrast are so much a part of daily life that we are often not aware of using them. Whenever you make a choice — what to wear, where to eat, what college to attend, what career to pursue — you implicitly use comparison and contrast to evaluate your options and arrive at your decision.

The graphic on the opposite page uses visual comparison and contrast to clearly demonstrate rebuilding progress in New Orleans after Hurricane Katrina. The chart establishes points or areas of comparison, such as "households receiving mail," "child care centers open," and "single family home sales." Then, using pre–Hurricane Katrina statistics as a baseline, the visual charts comparative statistics in each area for "2 years later ('07)," "3 years later ('08)," and "4 years later ('09)." Thus we can see that in the two years immediately following Katrina the number of households receiving mail dropped from 198,232 to 133,966. This number increased to 142,240 in 2008 and 152,904 in 2009 as residents moved back to Orleans Parish. In what other areas do you see progress being made? (Do you think the point of the graphic *is* that progress is being made?)

Comparison and Contrast in Written Texts

The strategy of comparison and contrast is most commonly used in writing when the subjects under discussion belong to the same class or general category: four makes of car, for example, or two candidates for Senate. (See Chapter 9, "Division and Classification," for a more complete discussion of classes.) Such subjects are said to be *comparable*, or to have a strong basis for comparison.

■ Point-by-Point and Block Comparison

There are two basic ways to organize comparison and contrast essays. In the first, *point-by-point comparison*, the author starts by comparing both subjects in terms of a particular point, then moves on to a second point and compares both subjects, then moves on to a third point, and so on. The other way to organize a comparison is called *block comparison*. In this pattern, the information about one subject is gathered into a block, which is followed by a block of comparable information about the second subject.

Each pattern of comparison has advantages and disadvantages. Point-by-point comparison allows the reader to grasp fairly easily the specific points of comparison the author is making; it may be harder, though, to pull together the details and convey a distinct impression of what each subject is like. The block comparison guarantees that each subject will receive a more unified discussion; however, the points of comparison between them may be less clear.

The first of the following two annotated passages illustrates a point-by-point comparison. This selection, a comparison of President Franklin Roosevelt and his vice-presidential running mate Harry Truman of Missouri, is from historian David McCullough's Pulitzer Prize–winning biography *Truman* (1992).

> Point-by-point comparison identifies central similarities between the two men.
>
> Point-by-point contrast introduces several differences, alternating between Roosevelt and Truman.

Both were men of exceptional determination, with great reserves of personal courage and cheerfulness. They were alike, too, in their enjoyment of people. (The human race, Truman once told a reporter, was an "excellent outfit.") Each had an active sense of humor and was inclined to be dubious of those who did not. But Roosevelt, who loved stories, loved also to laugh at his own, while Truman was more of a listener and laughed best when somebody else told "a good one." Roosevelt enjoyed flattery, Truman was made uneasy by it. Roosevelt loved the subtleties of human relations. He was a master of the circuitous solution to problems, of the pleasing if ambiguous answer to difficult questions. He was sensitive to nuances in a way Harry Truman never was and never would be. Truman, with his rural Missouri background, and partly, too, because of the

Development of key difference

limits of his education, was inclined to see things in far simpler terms, as right or wrong, wise or foolish. He dealt little in abstractions. His answers to questions, even complicated questions, were nearly always direct and assured, plainly said, and followed often by a conclusive "And that's all there is to it," an old Missouri expression, when in truth there may have been a great deal more "to it."

Point-by-point comparison and contrast— Roosevelt's and Truman's life struggles and experiences

Each of them had been tested by his own painful struggle, Roosevelt with crippling polio, Truman with debt, failure, obscurity, and the heavy stigma of the Pendergasts. Roosevelt liked to quote the admonition of his old headmaster at Groton, Dr. Endicott Peabody: "Things in life will not always run smoothly. Sometimes we will be rising toward the heights — then all will seem to reverse itself and start downward. The great fact to remember is that the trend of civilization is forever upward. . . . " Assuredly Truman would have subscribed to the same vision. They were two optimists at heart, each in his way faithful to the old creed of human progress. But there had been nothing in Roosevelt's experience like the night young Harry held the lantern as his mother underwent surgery, nothing like the Argonne, or Truman's desperate fight for political survival in 1940.

In the following example from *Harper's* magazine, Otto Friedrich uses a block format to contrast a newspaper story with a newsmagazine story.

Subjects of comparison: Newspaper story and magazine story belong to the same class.

There is an essential difference between a news story, as understood by a newspaperman or a wire-service writer, and a newsmagazine story. The chief purpose of the conventional news story is to tell what happened. It starts with the most important information and continues into increasingly inconsequential details, not only because the reader may not read beyond the first paragraph, but because an editor working on galley proofs a few minutes before press time likes to be able to cut freely from the end of the story.

Block comparison: Each paragraph deals with one type of story.

A newsmagazine is very different. It is written to be read consecutively from beginning to end, and each of its stories is designed, following the critical theories of Edgar Allan Poe, to create one emotional effect. The news, what happened that week, may be told in the beginning, the middle, or the end; for the purpose is not to throw information at the reader but to seduce him into reading the whole story, and into accepting the dramatic (and often political) point being made.

In this selection, Friedrich has two purposes: to offer information that explains the differences between a newspaper story and a newsmagazine story and to persuade readers that magazine stories tend to be more biased than newspaper stories.

■ Analogy: A Special Form of Comparison and Contrast

When the subject under discussion is unfamiliar, complex, or abstract, the resourceful writer may use a special form of comparison called *analogy* to help readers understand the difficult subject. Whereas most comparisons analyze items within the same class, analogies compare two largely dissimilar subjects to look for illuminating similarities. In addition, while the typical comparison seeks to illuminate specific features of both subjects, the primary purpose of analogy is to clarify one subject that is complex or unfamiliar by pointing out its similarities to a more familiar or concrete subject.

If, for example, your purpose were to explain the craft of fiction writing, you might note its similarities to the craft of carpentry. In this case, you would be drawing an analogy, because the two subjects clearly belong to different classes. You would be using the concrete work of the carpenter to help readers understand the more abstract work of the novelist. You can use analogy in one or two paragraphs to clarify a particular aspect of the larger topic, or you can use it as the organizational strategy for an entire essay.

In the following example from *The Mysterious Sky* (1960), observe how Lester Del Rey explains the functions of Earth's atmosphere (a subject that people have difficulty with because they can't "see" it) by making an analogy to an ordinary window.

> The atmosphere of Earth acts like any window in serving two very important functions. It lets light in and it permits us to look out. It also serves as a shield to keep out dangerous or uncomfortable things. A normal glazed window lets us keep our houses warm by keeping out cold air, and it prevents rain, dirt, and unwelcome insects and animals from coming in. As we have already seen, Earth's atmospheric window also helps to keep our planet at a comfortable temperature by holding back radiated heat and protecting us from dangerous levels of ultraviolet light.

You'll notice that Del Rey's analogy establishes no direct relationship between the subjects under comparison. The analogy is effective precisely because it enables the reader to visualize the atmosphere, which is unobservable, by comparing it to something quite different — a window — that is familiar and concrete.

Using Comparison and Contrast As a Writing Strategy

To compare one thing or idea with another, to discover the similarities and differences between them, is one of the most basic human strategies for learning, evaluating, and making decisions. Because it serves so many fundamental purposes, comparison and contrast is a particularly useful strategy for the writer. It may be the primary mode for essay writers who seek to educate or persuade the reader; to evaluate things, people, or events; and to differentiate between apparently similar subjects or to reconcile the differences between dissimilar ones.

Comparison and contrast may be combined readily with other writing strategies and often serves to sharpen, clarify, and add interest to essays written in a different primary mode. For example, an essay of argumentation gains credibility when the writer contrasts desirable and undesirable reasons or examples. In the Declaration of Independence (pages 513–16), Thomas Jefferson effectively contrasts the actual behavior of the English king with the ideals of a democratic society. In "I Have a Dream" (pages 525–28), Martin Luther King Jr. compares 1960s America with the promise of what it ought to be to argue that the realization of the dream of freedom for all American citizens is long overdue. Likewise, Richard Lederer, in "The Case for Short Words" (pages 519–22), uses comparison and contrast to showcase the virtues of one-syllable words when measured against their multisyllabic counterparts.

Many descriptive essays rely heavily on comparison and contrast; one of the most effective ways to describe any person, place, or thing is to show how it is like another model of the same class and how it differs. Robert Ramírez ("The Barrio," page 150) describes his Hispanic neighborhood as contrasted with "the harshness and the coldness of the Anglo world." Definition is also clarified and enriched by the use of comparison and contrast. Virtually all the essays in Chapter 10 employ this strategy to some degree.

Using Comparison and Contrast across the Disciplines

When writing essays in the academic disciplines, you will have many opportunities to use the strategy of comparison and contrast to both organize and strengthen the presentation of your ideas. To determine whether or not comparison and contrast is the right strategy for you in a particular paper, use the four-step method described in Chapter 2 (Determining a Strategy for Developing Your Essay, pages 25–26). Consider the following examples, which illustrate how this four-step method works for typical college papers.

Music

1. MAIN IDEA: The music of the Romantic period sharply contrasts with the music of the earlier Classical period.
2. QUESTION: What are the key differences between the music of the Romantic and the Classical periods?

3. STRATEGY: Comparison and Contrast. The direction words *contrasts* and *differences* call for a discussion distinguishing characteristics of the two periods in music history.

4. SUPPORTING STRATEGIES: Definition and Illustration. It might be helpful to define the key terms *romanticism* and *classicism* and to illustrate each of the differences with examples from representative Romantic composers (Brahms, Chopin, Schubert, and Tchaikovsky) and Classical composers (Beethoven, Haydn, and Mozart).

Political Science

1. MAIN IDEA: Though very different people, Winston Churchill and Franklin D. Roosevelt shared many larger-than-life leadership qualities during World War II, a period of doubt and crisis.

2. QUESTION: What are the similarities between Winston Churchill and Franklin D. Roosevelt as world leaders?

3. STRATEGY: Comparison and Contrast. The direction words *shared* and *similarities* require a discussion of the leadership traits displayed by both men.

4. SUPPORTING STRATEGY: Definition. It might prove helpful to define *leader* and/or *leadership* to establish a context for this comparison.

Physics

1. MAIN IDEA: Compare and contrast the three classes of levers — simple machines used to amplify force.

2. QUESTION: What are the similarities and differences among the three classes of levers?

3. STRATEGY: Comparison and Contrast. The direction words *compare, contrast, similarities,* and *differences* say it all.

4. SUPPORTING STRATEGY: Illustration. Readers will certainly appreciate familiar examples — pliers, nutcracker, and tongs — of the three classes of levers, examples that both clarify and emphasize the similarities and differences.

Sample Student Essay Using Comparison and Contrast As a Writing Strategy

A studio art major from Pittsburgh, Pennsylvania, Barbara Bowman has a special interest in photography. In her writing courses, Bowman has discovered many similarities between the writing process and the process that an artist follows. Her essay "Guns and Cameras," however, explores similarities of another kind: those between hunting with a gun and hunting with a camera.

Guns and Cameras
Barbara Bowman

Introduction of the objects being compared

Brief point-by-point contrast

Thesis

Block organization: first block about the hunter

Point A: equipment

Point B: stalking

Point C: the result

With a growing number of animals heading   1
toward extinction and with the idea of protecting such
animals on game reserves increasing in popularity,
photographic safaris are replacing hunting safaris.
This may seem odd because of the obvious differences
between guns and cameras. Shooting is aggressive,
photography is passive; shooting eliminates,
photography preserves. However, some hunters
are willing to trade their guns for cameras because
of similarities in the way the equipment is used, as
well as in the relationship among equipment, user,
and "prey."

The hunter has a deep interest in the   2
apparatus he uses to kill his prey. He carries various
types of guns, different kinds of ammunition,
and special sights and telescopes to increase his
chances of success. He knows the mechanics of
his guns and understands how and why they work.
This fascination with the hardware of his sport is
practical—it helps him achieve his goal—but it
frequently becomes an end, almost a hobby in itself.

Not until the very end of the long process of   3
stalking an animal does a game hunter use his gun.
First he enters into the animal's world. He studies his
prey, its habitat, its daily habits, its watering holes
and feeding areas, its migration patterns, its enemies
and allies, its diet and food chain. Eventually the
hunter himself becomes animal-like, instinctively
sensing the habits and moves of his prey. Of course,
this instinct gives the hunter a better chance of
killing the animal; he knows where and when he will
get the best shot. But it gives him more than that.
Hunting is not just pulling the trigger and killing
the prey. Much of it is a multifaceted and ritualistic
identification with nature.

After the kill, the hunter can do a number of   4
things with his trophy. He can sell the meat or eat it
himself. He can hang the animal's head on the wall

or lay its hide on the floor or even sell these objects. But any of these uses is a luxury, and its cost is high. An animal has been destroyed; a life has been eliminated.

Second block about the photographer

Point A: equipment

Like the hunter, the photographer has a great interest in the tools he uses. He carries various types of cameras, lenses, and film to help him get the picture he wants. He understands the way cameras work, the uses of telephoto and micro lenses, and often the technical procedures of printing and developing. Of course, the time and interest a photographer invests in these mechanical aspects of his art allow him to capture and produce the image he wants. But as with the hunter, these mechanics can and often do become fascinating in themselves.   5

Point B: stalking

The wildlife photographer also needs to stalk his "prey" with knowledge and skill in order to get an accurate "shot." Like the hunter, he has to understand the animal's patterns, characteristics, and habitat; he must become animal-like in order to succeed. And like the hunter's, his pursuit is much more prolonged and complicated than the shot itself. The stalking processes are almost identical and give many of the same satisfactions.   6

Point C: the result

The successful photographer also has something tangible to show for his efforts. A still picture of an animal can be displayed in a home, a gallery, a shop; it can be printed in a publication, as a postcard, or as a poster. In fact, a single photograph can be used in all these ways at once; it can be reproduced countless times. And despite all these ways of using his "trophies," the photographer continues to preserve his prey.   7

Conclusion: The two activities are similar and give the same satisfaction, so why kill?

Photography is obviously the less violent and to many the more acceptable method for obtaining a trophy of a wild animal. People no longer need to hunt in order to feed or clothe themselves, and hunting for "sport" seems to be barbaric. Luckily, the excitement of pursuing an animal, learning its habits and patterns, outsmarting it on its own level, and finally "getting" it can all be done with a camera. So why use guns?   8

**Analyzing Barbara Bowman's Comparison
and Contrast Essay: Questions for Discussion**

1. What is Bowman's thesis in this essay?

2. What are her main points of comparison between hunting with a gun and hunting with a camera?

3. How has Bowman organized her comparison? Why do you suppose she decided on this option? Explain.

4. How else could she have organized her essay? Would this alternative organization have been as effective as the one she used? Explain.

5. How does Bowman conclude her essay? In what ways is her conclusion a reflection of her thesis?

Suggestions for Using Comparison and Contrast As a Writing Strategy

As you plan, write, and revise your comparison and contrast essay, be mindful of the writing process guidelines described in Chapter 2 (see pages 16–40). Also, pay particular attention to the basic requirements and essential ingredients for this writing strategy.

■ Planning Your Comparison and Contrast Essay

Planning is an essential part of writing a good comparison and contrast essay. You can save yourself a great deal of aggravation by taking the time to think about the key components of your essay before you actually begin to write.

Many college assignments ask you to use the strategy of comparison and contrast. As you read an assignment, look for one or more of the words that suggest the use of this strategy. When you are asked to *compare* and *contrast* one item with another or to identify the *similarities* and *differences* between two items, you should use comparison and contrast. Other assignments might ask you to determine which of two options is *better* or to select the *best* solution to a particular problem. Again, the strategy of comparison and contrast will help you make this evaluation and arrive at a sound, logical conclusion.

As you start planning and writing a comparison and contrast essay, keep in mind the basic requirements of this writing strategy.

Compare Subjects from the Same Class.   Remember that the subjects of your comparison should be in the same class or general category so that you can establish a clear basis for comparison. (There are any number of possible classes, such as particular types of persons, places, and things, as well as occupations, activities, philosophies, points in history, and even concepts and ideas.) If your subject is difficult, complex, or unobservable, you may find that analogy, a special form of comparison, is the most effective strategy to explain that subject. Remember, also, that if the similarities and differences between the subjects are too obvious, your reader is certain to lose interest quickly.

Determine Your Purpose, and Focus on It. Suppose you choose to compare and contrast solar energy with wind energy. It is clear that both are members of the same class — energy — so there is a basis for comparing them; there also seem to be enough interesting differences to make a comparison and contrast possible. But before going any further, you must ask yourself why you want to compare and contrast these particular subjects. What audience do you seek to address? Do you want to inform, to emphasize, to explain, to evaluate, to persuade? Do you have more than one purpose? Whatever your purpose, it will influence the content and organization of your comparison.

In comparing and contrasting solar and wind energy, you will certainly provide factual information, yet you will probably also want to evaluate the two energy sources to determine whether either is a practical means of producing energy. You may also want to persuade your readers that one technology is superior to the other.

Formulate a Thesis Statement. Once you have your purpose clearly in mind, formulate a preliminary thesis statement. At this early stage in the writing process, the thesis statement is not cast in stone; you may well want to modify it later on, as a result of research and further consideration of your subject. A preliminary thesis statement has two functions: First, it fixes your direction so that you will be less tempted to stray into byways while doing research and writing drafts; second, establishing the central point of the essay makes it easier for you to gather supporting material and to organize your essay.

Suppose, for example, that you live in the Champlain Valley of Vermont, one of the cloudiest areas of the country, where the wind whistles along the corridor between the Green Mountains and the Adirondacks. If you were exploring possible alternative energy sources for the area, your purpose might be to persuade readers of a local environmental journal that wind is preferable to sun as a source of energy for this region. The thesis statement for this essay will certainly differ from that of a writer for a national newsmagazine whose goal is to offer general information about alternative energy sources to a broad readership.

Choose the Points of Comparison. *Points of comparison* are the qualities and features of your subjects on which you base your comparison.

For some comparisons, you will find the information you need in your own head; for others, you will have to search for that information in the library or on the Internet.

At this stage, if you know only a little about the subjects of your comparison, you may have only a few hazy ideas for points of comparison. Perhaps wind energy means no more to you than an image of giant windmills lined up on a California ridge, and solar energy brings to mind only the reflective, glassy roof on a Colorado ski lodge. Even so, it is possible to list points of comparison that will be relevant to your subjects and your purpose. Here, for example, are important points of comparison in considering energy sources:

Cost

Efficiency

Convenience

Environmental impact

A tentative list of points will help you by suggesting the kind of information you need to gather for your comparison and contrast. You should always remain alert, however, for other factors you may not have thought of. For example, as you conduct research, you may find that maintenance requirements are another important factor in considering energy systems, and thus you might add that point to your list.

■ Organizing and Writing Your Comparison and Contrast Essay

Choose an Organizational Pattern That Fits Your Material. Once you have gathered the necessary information, you should decide which organizational pattern, block or point-by-point, will best serve your purpose. In deciding which pattern to use, you may find it helpful to jot down a scratch outline before beginning your draft.

Block organization works best when the two objects of comparison are relatively straightforward and when the points of comparison are rather general, few in number, and can be stated succinctly. As a scratch outline illustrates, block organization makes for a unified discussion of each object, which can help your readers understand the information you have to give them.

Block Organization

BLOCK ONE   **Solar Energy**
    Point 1. Cost
    Point 2. Efficiency
    Point 3. Convenience
    Point 4. Maintenance requirements
    Point 5. Environmental impact

BLOCK TWO   **Wind Energy**
Point 1. Cost
Point 2. Efficiency
Point 3. Convenience
Point 4. Maintenance requirements
Point 5. Environmental impact

If your essay will be more than two or three pages long, however, block organization may be a poor choice: By the time your readers come to your discussion of the costs of wind energy, they may well have forgotten what you had to say about solar energy costs several pages earlier. In this case, you would do better to use point-by-point organization.

Point-by-Point Organization

POINT ONE   **Cost**
Subject 1. Solar energy
Subject 2. Wind energy

POINT TWO   **Efficiency**
Subject 1. Solar energy
Subject 2. Wind energy

POINT THREE   **Convenience**
Subject 1. Solar energy
Subject 2. Wind energy

POINT FOUR   **Maintenance Requirements**
Subject 1. Solar energy
Subject 2. Wind energy

POINT FIVE   **Environmental Impact**
Subject 1. Solar energy
Subject 2. Wind energy

Use Parallel Constructions for Emphasis.   Use parallel grammatical structures to emphasize the similarities and differences between the items being compared. Parallelism is the repetition of word order or grammatical form either within a single sentence or in several sentences that develop the same central idea. As a rhetorical device, parallel structure can aid coherence and add emphasis. Franklin Roosevelt's famous Depression-era statement "I see one-third of a nation *ill-housed, ill-clad,* and *ill-nourished*" illustrates effective parallelism. Look for opportunities to use parallel

E8

constructions with (1) paired items or items in a series, (2) correlative conjunctions, and (3) the words *as* or *than*.

Draw a Conclusion from Your Comparison. Only after you have gathered your information and made your comparisons will you be ready to decide on a conclusion. When drawing your essay to its conclusion, remember your purpose in writing, the claim made in your thesis statement, and your audience and emphasis.

Perhaps, having presented information about both technologies, your comparison shows that solar and wind energy are both feasible, with solar energy having a slight edge on most points. If your purpose has been evaluation for a general audience, you might conclude, "Both solar and wind energy are practical alternatives to conventional energy sources." If you asserted in your thesis statement that one of the technologies is superior to the other, your comparison will support a more persuasive conclusion. For the general audience, you might say, "While both solar and wind energy are practical technologies, solar energy now seems the better investment." However, for a readership made up of residents of the cloudy Champlain Valley, you might conclude, "While both solar and wind energy are practical technologies, wind energy makes more economic sense for investors in northwest Vermont."

■ Revising and Editing Your Comparison and Contrast Essay

Share Your Drafts with Others. Try sharing the drafts of your essays with other students in your writing class to make sure that your comparison and contrast works. Ask them if there are any parts of your essay that they do not understand. Have them tell you what they think your point is. If their answers differ from what you intended, have them tell you what led them to their interpretations so that you can revise accordingly. To maximize the effectiveness of conferences with your peers, use the guidelines presented on page 29. Feedback from these conferences often provides one or more places where you can start revising.

Question Your Own Work While Revising and Editing. Revision is best done by asking yourself key questions about what you have written. Begin by reading, preferably aloud, what you have written. Reading aloud forces you to pay attention to every single word, and you are more likely to catch lapses in the logical flow of thought. For help with twelve common writing problems, see Chapter 16, "Editing for Grammar, Punctuation, and Sentence Style."

After you have read your paper through, answer the questions for revising and editing on page 294 and make the necessary changes.

Questions for Revising and Editing: Comparison and Contrast

1. Are the subjects of my comparison comparable; that is, do they belong to the same class of items (for example, two cars, two advertisements, two landscape paintings) so that there is a clear basis for comparison?

2. Are there any complex or abstract concepts that might be clarified by using an analogy?

3. Is the purpose of my comparison clearly stated?

4. Have I presented a clear thesis statement?

5. Have I chosen my points of comparison well? Have I avoided obvious points of comparison, concentrating instead on similarities between obviously different items or differences between essentially similar items?

6. Have I developed my points of comparison in sufficient detail so that my readers can appreciate my thinking?

7. Have I chosen the best pattern — block or point-by-point — to organize my information?

8. Have I drawn a conclusion that is in line with my thesis and purpose?

9. Have I used parallel constructions correctly in my sentences?

10. Have I avoided other errors in grammar, punctuation, and mechanics? Is my sentence style as clear, smooth, and persuasive as possible?

E8

E1–12

Chinese in New York, American in Beijing

KIM HOANG

 Kim Hoang was born and raised in New York City. After graduating from Stuyvesant High School, she went to Wellesley College. In 2008 Hoang moved to Los Angeles, where she currently works in advertising and design. Hoang wrote the following essay when she was seventeen years old and had just returned from a trip to China. It first appeared in *New Youth Connections*, a magazine written by and for New York City teens, and was later anthologized in *Starting with "I": Personal Essays by Teenagers* (1997). Notice how Hoang uses her trip to China as a means to compare her life in America with her experience in China and thus come to a better understanding of herself.

■ **Preparing to Read**

If someone were to ask you who or what you are, how would you answer? How easy is it for you to come up with an answer? Does your answer depend on who is asking the question? Explain.

When I was growing up and people asked me what I was, I would immediately say that I was Chinese even though I was born and raised in New York City. I always acknowledged my Chinese roots, but sometimes. I felt stupid for not knowing more about my ancestry and about a culture that has, in fact, influenced the way I live and think.

I am American, but there are things about my life that are distinctly Chinese. I eat Chinese food every night with chopsticks. I can understand Cantonese Chinese although I cannot really speak it. I go to family weddings in which the bride usually wears a white wedding gown in the morning and a cheongsam, a traditional Chinese silk dress, at the evening banquet. I celebrate the annual Chinese New Year festival with friends and family, and watch the sidewalk dragon dances in Chinatown.

> I am American, but there are things about my life that are distinctly Chinese.

These things are part of my life that came from China, a place I knew very little about. I wanted to go there and see it for myself. I hoped a trip to China would bring me closer to my Chinese side. When I mentioned my interest in traveling to China, my mom agreed immediately. She's never forced me to learn Chinese traditions, but I knew she would be pleased that I was ready to learn more about where my ancestors came from. Besides, my older sister was already there studying and I could stay with her and our relatives.

As I left for China last summer, I hardly felt the emotions I thought I   4
would. I didn't cry when I said goodbye to my mother. I didn't cry when the plane took off, and I didn't even cry when I began to feel ill on the plane because of all the junky airline food.

But I did cry when we landed. I remember having this great feeling of awe   5
and excitement, and I couldn't contain it. I envisioned all the new things I was going to see and all the relatives I would finally meet. Landing was so final. There was no going back, and all I could do was soak up every ounce of culture I possibly could.

My sister picked me up at the airport in China's capital, Beijing, and   6
we boarded a minivan, China's cheaper version of a regular taxi. When we arrived at our relatives' apartment complex, I saw an eighty-year-old man and woman I vaguely remembered from photographs. They were my aunt and uncle on my father's side. It turned out that the last time they had seen me was when I was three and they were in America for a visit.

They went on and on about how I looked so much like my father. They   7
said this all in Chinese and I could understand every word of it. But I couldn't express my feelings. All I could do was nod and smile, and they laughed, knowing that I couldn't talk to them.

It was apparent from the first day I spent in Beijing that I had virtually   8
no chance of sneaking into the crowd and living like a native. The fact that I couldn't understand Mandarin Chinese blew my cover. (Although China has one written language, it has dozens of spoken languages. My mother taught us Cantonese, which sounds nothing like Mandarin.)

Everyone in Beijing spoke so fast and my sister, who was studying   9
Mandarin, had to translate everything for me. Not being able to speak the language meant I had no freedom. I couldn't buy my own clothes or order my own meal. I couldn't even buy my own water. I felt like a three-year-old who had to ask her mother for everything.

The funny thing is that when I'm in America, Chinese people on the   10
street ask me for directions in Chinese and expect me to answer them flawlessly in the same dialect. I feel bad when I can't answer them.

In China, however, people saw me and assumed that since I wore blue   11
jeans and Nikes and carried myself differently (staring at every building with amazement and looking at every passing bicycle and every person with genuine interest, like most tourists do), I couldn't possibly understand a word of Chinese or anything about China.

People were surprised that I could understand the simplest Mandarin   12
phrases (like "It's time for dinner" and "Did you have fun today?") without their having to translate for me. It's like I was living in two worlds and even though I was a part of both, I didn't fit into either of them perfectly. In America, I am Chinese but when I was in China, I was American.

What made matters worse was that my sister sometimes encouraged me to be silent so that we would get better rates for things. When we bought tickets to get into the Forbidden City (the ancient home of the emperors), for example, my sister told me not to say a word. She said that many museums and parks charge a higher admission price (sometimes three times higher than for a native) if they know you're a tourist. I never found out if this was legal, but it was widely done. 13

Keeping silent made me feel all the more foreign. It was a constant reminder that I could never fully assimilate into life there. I stuck out, and I began to feel extremely paranoid walking down the street. I felt like I had this big sign on my back that said, Kick Me, I'm an American. 14

Other times, though, I felt so connected to China. One night I looked out the window next to my bed. I saw the black sky and the bright stars and I felt like I was home. Other times I felt like I had been there before. I saw busy street markets with people haggling for the lowest prices. Traffic was horrible, and of course, almost every face you saw was Chinese. I had seen all of this in Chinatowns in New York, Boston, and Toronto. I was surprised at the similarities, but there were differences too: In America, I can always walk a few blocks or take the subway and once again mix with people of different races and cultures. 15

I visited many places while I was in China, but it was Tiananmen Square that had the biggest impact on me. This was where people gathered to listen to Mao Zedong's speeches as he spoke on a rostrum high above the square. (He was the founder of Communist China.) It was also the site of the 1989 Tiananmen Square Massacre, in which thousands of students demonstrating for democracy were killed after government troops opened fire. 16

The square is an open space where both tourists and natives hang out. Walking across the stone tiles, I remembered the news footage of Tiananmen Square, filled with tanks and chaos. I realized I was standing where many people had died for their cause, people who weren't that much older than I was. 17

One of the final things I did during my trip was talk to my uncle. Although I had been eager to chat with him, there never seemed to be enough time. (I was always sightseeing and he worked at a chemical company during the day.) I knew my uncle spoke fluent English, so talking wouldn't be a problem. (He had graduated from college in the United States before returning to his family in China.) 18

We talked for more than two hours, mostly about Tiananmen Square. My uncle said he thought that the students could have used a less dangerous method to obtain their goal and that they could have tried harder to work with the government. Although he still supports Communism, he thinks that all governments have their flaws and that there will be more demonstrations for freedom in China. 19

I wish I could've talked with my uncle longer. He has seen so many things in his lifetime — the end of the emperors, the birth of Communism — and I didn't have time to hear all that he had to say. But I was glad for what I did learn. Hearing his firsthand accounts made the recent events of Chinese history seem real to me. They weren't just facts in a book or images on a television screen anymore. 20

It's been a year since my trip to China, and the things I remember most   21
are not the big places but the small things. The hot buses that my sister and I
took to Tiananmen Square. The imitation Good Humor ice cream we bought
to cool down since many of the museums didn't have air conditioning.

I still want to know more about China and Chinese culture. It may be   22
a while before I have a chance to go back, but in the meantime I'm taking
Mandarin classes and I'm volunteering at New York's Chinatown History
Museum to learn more about the Chinese in America.

I had wanted China to bring me closer to the Chinese culture and herit-   23
age I knew so little about. But the trip brought into perspective the two sides
of my life. I can enjoy the freedoms I have in America, like the freedom of
speech. And I can also relate to the history of China and its customs. I now
realize that who I am is a combination of the two.

■ Thinking Critically about the Text

How did Hoang's understanding of herself change as a result of her trip to
China? Did you get the feeling that she was surprised by what she learned
there? Explain.

■ Questions on Subject

1. Why do you suppose Hoang answered "Chinese" and not "American"
   when asked what she was?
2. According to Hoang, what's "distinctly Chinese" (paragraph 2) about
   her life?
3. What hopes and expectations did Hoang have for her travel to China?
4. Even though she is Chinese, what prevented Hoang from blending
   into "the crowd and living like a native" (paragraph 8)? In what ways
   was she an American in China?
5. Why did Hoang's sister ask her to remain silent on several occasions?
   Even though she followed her sister's instructions, how did Hoang
   feel about keeping silent?
6. What impressed Hoang about Tiananmen Square? Why was it important that she talk with her eighty-year-old uncle?

■ Questions on Strategy

1. What is the purpose of Hoang's comparison and contrast? (Glossary:
   Purpose)
2. Why do you suppose Hoang devotes more space to establishing that
   she feels American in Beijing than that she feels Chinese in New York?
3. To what end does Hoang introduce her experiences with Chinatowns
   in New York, Boston, and Toronto in paragraph 15? Why do you think
   she was "surprised at the similarities"?

4. Identify an example of parallel construction in paragraph 4. (Glossary: *Parallelism*) How does Hoang use this parallel construction to transition to paragraph 5? (Glossary: *Transitions*)
5. For you, how effective is Hoang's conclusion? How is her conclusion related to her opening? (Glossary: *Beginnings/Endings*)

■ Questions on Diction and Vocabulary

1. How would you characterize Hoang's diction in this essay — formal or informal? (Glossary: *Diction*) Cite several examples of phrases or words that she uses that led you to this conclusion.
2. Identify the simile Hoang uses in paragraph 9. (Glossary: *Figures of Speech*) How well does it express her frustration at not being able to speak Chinese?
3. Refer to your desk dictionary to determine the meanings of the following words as Hoang uses them in this selection: *ancestry* (paragraph 1), *virtually* (8), *dialect* (10), *assimilate* (14), *paranoid* (14), *haggling* (15), *rostrum* (16), *perspective* (23).

■ Classroom Activity Using Comparison and Contrast

Consider the following topics for an essay of comparison and contrast:

1. two close friends
2. two entertainers
3. two professional athletes
4. *Time* and *Newsweek* magazines
5. two cities you have visited

Select one topic, then write out short answers to the following questions:

Who/what could I compare and contrast?

What is my purpose in this comparison and contrast?

Are the similarities or differences more interesting?

What specific points of comparison should I discuss?

What organizational pattern will best suit my purpose: point-by-point or block comparison?

What do your answers to these questions tell you about the importance of planning for any writing project? Compare your answers with those of your classmates, and discuss.

■ Writing Suggestions

1. While visiting China, where she hoped to learn more about her heritage and the Chinese culture, Hoang suddenly realized that "[she] was living in two worlds and even though [she] was a part of both,

[she] didn't fit into either of them perfectly" (paragraph 12). Have you ever felt like you were living in two worlds — socioeconomic, religious, ethnic, or educational, for example — and didn't fit into either well? Write an essay in which you compare and contrast your two worlds.

2. The United States contains members of nearly every ethnic and religious group on earth. What do you know about your roots? When and where did your family arrive in the United States? If asked who or what you are, how do you answer? How do you fit into American society? In what ways has your ancestry influenced the way you live and think? How much of a role has America played in establishing your identity? Write an essay in which you explore the question, Who or what am I?

Two Ways to Belong in America

Bharati Mukherjee

The prominent Indian American writer and university professor Bharati Mukherjee was born into a wealthy family in Calcutta (now Kolkata), India, in 1940. Shortly after India gained its independence, her family relocated to England. In the 1950s, she returned to India, where she earned her bachelor's degree at the University of Calcutta in 1959 and a master's degree from the University of Baroda in 1961. Later she pursued her long-held desire to become a writer by earning a master of fine arts degree at the University of Iowa and eventually a doctorate in English and comparative literature. After marrying an American, Clark Blaise, she moved with her husband to Canada, where they lived for fourteen years until legislation there against South Asians led them to move back to the United States.

Before joining the faculty at the University of California, Berkeley, Mukherjee taught at McGill University, Skidmore College, Queens College, and the City University of New York. Currently her work centers on writing and the theme of immigration, particularly as it concerns women; immigration policy; and cultural alienation. With her husband, she has authored *Days and Nights in Calcutta* (1977) and *The Sorrow and the Terror: The Haunting Legacy of the Air India Tragedy* (1987). In addition, she has published seven novels, including *The Tiger's Daughter* (1971), *Wife* (1975), *Darkness* (1985), *Jasmine* (1989), *The Holder of the World* (1993), and *The Tree Bride* (2004); two collections of short stories, *Darkness* (1985) and *The Middleman and Other Stories* (1988), for which she won the National Book Critics Circle Award; and two works of nonfiction, *Political Culture and Leadership in India* (1991) and *Regionalism in Indian Perspective* (1992).

The following essay was first published in the *New York Times* in 1996 in response to new legislation championed by then–vice president Al Gore, which provided for expedited routes to citizenship for legal immigrants living in the United States. As you read Mukherjee's essay, notice the way she has organized the contrasting views she and her sister have toward various aspects of living as either a legal immigrant or a citizen.

■ Preparing to Read

The word *immigrant* has many connotations. What associations does the word have for you? If you were to move to another country, how do you think it would feel to be considered an immigrant?

This is a tale of two sisters from Calcutta, Mira and Bharati, who have   1
lived in the United States for some thirty-five years, but who find themselves on different sides in the current debate over the status of immigrants.
I am an American citizen and she is not. I am moved that thousands of long-
term residents are finally taking the oath of citizenship. She is not.

Mira arrived in Detroit in 1960 to study child psychology and pre-   2
school education. I followed her a year later to study creative writing at the
University of Iowa. When we left India, we were almost identical in appearance and attitude. We dressed alike, in saris; we expressed identical views on
politics, social issues, love and marriage in the same Calcutta convent-school
accent. We would endure our two years in America, secure our degrees, then
return to India to marry the grooms of our father's choosing.

Instead, Mira married an Indian student in 1962 who was getting his business   3
administration degree at Wayne State University. They soon acquired the labor cer-
tifications necessary for the green card of hassle-free residence and employment.

Mira still lives in Detroit, works in the Southfield, Michigan, school   4
system, and has become nationally recognized for her contributions in the
fields of preschool education and parent-teacher relationships. After thirty-
six years as a legal immigrant in this country, she clings passionately to her
Indian citizenship and hopes to go home to India when she retires.

In Iowa City in 1963, I married a fellow student, an American of Ca-   5
nadian parentage. Because of the accident of his North Dakota birth, I
bypassed labor-certification requirements and the race-related "quota" system that favored the applicant's country of origin over his or her merit. I
was prepared for (and even welcomed) the emotional strain that came with
marrying outside my ethnic community. In thirty-three years of marriage,
we have lived in every part of North America. By choosing a husband who
was not my father's selection, I was opting for fluidity, self-invention, blue
jeans, and T-shirts, and renouncing three thousand years (at least) of caste-
observant, "pure culture" marriage in the Mukherjee family. My books have
often been read as unapologetic (and in some quarters overenthusiastic)
texts for cultural and psychological "mongrelization." It's a word I celebrate.

Mira and I have stayed sisterly close by phone. In our regular Sunday   6
morning conversations, we are unguardedly affectionate. I am her only blood
relative on this continent. We expect to see each other through the looming
crises of aging and ill health without being asked. Long before Vice President
Gore's "Citizenship USA" drive, we'd had our polite arguments over the ethics
of retaining an overseas citizenship while expecting the permanent protection and economic benefits that come with living and working in America.

Like well-raised sisters, we never said what was really on our minds, but   7
we probably pitied one another. She, for the lack of structure in my life, the
erasure of Indianness, the absence of an unvarying daily core. I, for the nar-
rowness of her perspective, her uninvolvement with the mythic depths or
the superficial pop culture of this society. But, now, with the scapegoating of

"aliens" (documented or illegal) on the increase, and the targeting of long-term legal immigrants like Mira for new scrutiny and new self-consciousness, she and I find ourselves unable to maintain the same polite discretion. We were always unacknowledged adversaries, and we are now, more than ever, sisters.

"I feel used," Mira raged on the phone the other night. "I feel manipu- 8 lated and discarded. This is such an unfair way to treat a person who was invited to stay and work here because of her talent. My employer went to the INS and petitioned for the labor certification. For over thirty years, I've invested my creativity and professional skills into the improvement of *this* country's preschool system. I've obeyed all the rules, I've paid my taxes, I love my work, I love my students, I love the friends I've made. How dare America now change its rules in midstream? If America wants to make new rules curtailing benefits of legal immigrants, they should apply only to immigrants who arrive after those rules are already in place."

> I embraced the demotion from expatriate aristocrat to immigrant nobody, surrendering those thousands of years of "pure culture," the saris, the delightfully accented English.

To my ears, it sounded like the description of 9 a long-enduring, comfortable yet loveless marriage, without risk or recklessness. Have we the right to demand, and to expect, that we be loved? (That, to me, is the subtext of the arguments by immigration advocates.) My sister is an expatriate, professionally generous and creative, socially courteous and gracious, and that's as far as her Americanization can go. She is here to maintain an identity, not to transform it.

I asked her if she would follow the example 10 of others who have decided to become citizens because of the anti-immigration bills in Congress. And here, she surprised me. "If America wants to play the manipulative game, I'll play it, too," she snapped. "I'll become a U.S. citizen for now, then change back to Indian when I'm ready to go home. I feel some kind of irrational attachment to India that I don't to America. Until all this hysteria against legal immigrants, I was totally happy. Having my green card meant I could visit any place in the world I wanted to and then come back to a job that's satisfying and that I do very well."

In one family, from two sisters alike as peas in a pod, there could not be 11 a wider divergence of immigrant experience. America spoke to me — I married it — I embraced the demotion from expatriate aristocrat to immigrant nobody, surrendering those thousands of years of "pure culture," the saris, the delightfully accented English. She retained them all. Which of us is the freak?

Mira's voice, I realize, is the voice not just of the immigrant South Asian 12 community but of an immigrant community of the millions who have stayed rooted in one job, one city, one house, one ancestral culture, one cuisine, for the entirety of their productive years. She speaks for greater numbers than I possibly can. Only the fluency of her English and the anger, rather than fear, born of confidence from her education, differentiate her from the seamstresses, the domestics, the technicians, the shop owners, the millions of hardworking but effectively silenced documented immigrants as well as their less fortunate "illegal" brothers and sisters.

Nearly twenty years ago, when I was living in my husband's ancestral 13 homeland of Canada, I was always well-employed but never allowed to feel part of the local Quebec or larger Canadian society. Then, through a Green Paper that invited a national referendum on the unwanted side effects of "nontraditional" immigration, the government officially turned against its immigrant communities, particularly those from South Asia.

I felt then the same sense of betrayal that Mira feels now. I will never for- 14 get the pain of that sudden turning, and the casual racist outbursts the Green Paper elicited. That sense of betrayal had its desired effect and drove me, and thousands like me, from the country.

Mira and I differ, however, in the ways in which we hope to interact with 15 the country that we have chosen to live in. She is happier to live in America as an expatriate Indian than as an immigrant American. I need to feel like a part of the community I have adopted (as I tried to feel in Canada as well). I need to put roots down, to vote and make the difference that I can. The price that the immigrant willingly pays, and that the exile avoids, is the trauma of self-transformation.

■ **Thinking Critically about the Text**

What do you think Mukherjee's sister means when she says in paragraph 10, "If America wants to play the manipulative game, I'll play it, too"? How do you react to her plans? Explain.

■ **Questions on Subject**

1. What is Mukherjee's thesis? (Glossary: *Thesis*) Where does she present it?
2. What arguments does Mukherjee make for becoming an American citizen? What arguments does her sister make for retaining Indian citizenship?
3. Why do you think Mukherjee's sister feels "used" by attempts to change American laws regarding benefits for legal noncitizens?
4. At the end of paragraph 11, Mukherjee asks a question. How does she answer it? How would you answer it?
5. What does Mukherjee mean when she says, "The price that the immigrant willingly pays, and that the exile avoids, is the trauma of self-transformation" (paragraph 15)?
6. In your eyes, which sister made the right decision? Explain.

■ Questions on Strategy

1. How has Mukherjee organized her essay? Is it block comparison, point-by-point comparison, or some combination of the two?
2. Why is the pattern of organization that Mukherjee uses appropriate for her subject and purpose? (Glossary: *Purpose; Subject*)
3. Mukherjee chooses to let her sister, Mira, speak for herself in this essay. What do you think would have been lost had Mukherjee simply reported what Mira felt and believed? Explain.

■ Questions on Diction and Vocabulary

1. Mukherjee uses the word *mongrelization* in paragraph 5. What do you think she means by this word, and why does she "celebrate" it?
2. Mukherjee uses quotation marks around a number of words — "quota" (paragraph 5), "pure culture" (5, 11), "aliens" (7), "illegal" (12), "nontraditional" (13). What does she gain by using the quotation marks?
3. How does Mukherjee use "marriage" to describe the essential differences between Mira's and her relationship to America?
4. Refer to your desk dictionary to determine the meanings of the following words as Mukherjee uses them in this selection: *caste* (paragraph 5), *ethics* (6), *scapegoating* (7), *subtext* (9), *expatriate* (15).

■ Classroom Activity Using Comparison and Contrast

Consider the following Charles Addams cartoon:

© Charles Addams. With permission from the Tee and Charles Addams Foundation.

"By George, you're right! I thought there was something familiar about it."

How is it possible for two people with similar backgrounds to have completely different views about something? And why are we so fascinated by differences when we were expecting similarities or by similarities when we were expecting differences? Explain.

■ Writing Suggestions

1. Mukherjee writes about her relationship with her sister by saying, "[W]e never said what was really on our minds, but we probably pitied one another" (paragraph 7). Such differences are often played out on a larger scale when immigrants who have transformed themselves into Americans are confronted by those who have chosen to retain their ethnic identity; these tensions can sometimes lead to name-calling and even aggressive prejudice within immigrant communities. Write an essay about an ethnic or cultural community you are familiar with, comparing and contrasting lifestyle choices its members make as they try to find a comfortable place in American society.

2. Mukherjee presents her sister's reasons for not becoming a citizen and supports them with statements that her sister has made. Imagine that you are Mira Mukherjee. Write a counterargument to the argument presented by Bharati, giving your reasons for remaining an Indian citizen. Remember that you have already broken with tradition by marrying a man not of your "father's choosing" and that the "trauma of self-transformation" that Bharati raises in the conclusion of her essay is much deeper and more complicated than she has represented it to be. Can you say that you are holding to tradition when you are not? Can you engage in a challenging self-transformation if it is not genuinely motivated?

Who Was More Important: Lincoln or Darwin?

MALCOLM JONES

Malcolm Jones was born in 1952 in Lancaster, South Carolina. When he was two, his family moved to Winston-Salem, North Carolina, where he attended public school through high school. Jones has fond memories of pounding away as a child on his uncle's Smith Corona typewriter (which he still owns). He attended New College in Sarasota, Florida, and graduated from Wake Forest University with a B.A. in 1974. While in college, he worked part-time at the *Winston-Salem Journal*, where upon graduation he went to work as an editorial writer. He also worked for newspapers in Durham and Greensboro, North Carolina, mostly as the editor of the book review section, before moving to the *St. Petersburg Times* to start that paper's book section, a job he held for five years. Jones joined *Newsweek* in 1989 as a book reviewer, where he now contributes to the arts and culture section, writing features, news, and reviews on all aspects of the arts. In 1985, Jones collaborated with the composer and songwriter Van Dyke Parks and the artist Barry Moser on *Jump!* — a retelling of several Brer Rabbit stories. In 2010, he published a memoir, *Little Boy Blues*, about growing up in the South in the 1950s and 1960s. Currently Jones is working on a book he calls *Erasures,* a series of related essays about how art changes with — and perceptions about art are changed by — time.

The following essay first appeared in the July 7–14, 2008, issue of *Newsweek*. Jones remembers, "[T]he question of who was more important was not mine — it was an editor who decided to cast the story in terms of who was more important. I had merely noticed the bizarre coincidence that both men were born on the same day in the same year, and this fact seemed to be worth fooling around with, since both men were so profoundly important, in such radically different ways, in shaping the modern world." As you read, notice how Jones creates interest by exploring the unexpected similarities that these two radically different men share and how his organizational plan leads the reader logically to his conclusion.

■ Preparing to Read

How much do you know about Charles Darwin and Abraham Lincoln? Based on what you know now, how would you answer the question asked by the title of this essay? Explain your answer.

How's this for a coincidence? Charles Darwin and Abraham Lincoln were born in the same year, on the same day: February 12, 1809. As historical facts go, it amounts to little more than a footnote. Still, while it's just a coincidence, it's a coincidence that's guaranteed to make you do a double take the first time you run across it. Everybody knows Darwin and Lincoln were near-mythic figures in the nineteenth century. But who ever thinks of them in tandem? Who puts the theory of evolution and the Civil War in the same sentence? Why would you, unless you're writing your dissertation on epochal events in the nineteenth century? But instinctively, we want to say that they belong together. It's not just because they were both great men, and not because they happen to be exact coevals. Rather, it's because the scientist and the politician each touched off a revolution that changed the world.

As soon as you do start comparing this odd couple, you discover there is more to this birthday coincidence than the same astrological chart (as Aquarians, they should both be stubborn, visionary, tolerant, free-spirited, rebellious, genial but remote and detached—hmmm, so far so good). As we approach their shared bicentennial, there is already one book that gives them double billing, historian David R. Contosta's *Rebel Giants*, with another coming . . . from *New Yorker* writer Adam Gopnik. Contosta's joint biography doesn't turn up anything new, but the biographical parallels he sets forth are enough to make us see each man afresh. Both lost their mothers in early childhood. Both suffered from depression (Darwin also suffered from a variety of crippling stomach ailments and chronic headaches), and both wrestled with religious doubt. Each had a strained relationship with his father, and each of them lost children to early death. Both spent the better part of their 20s trying to settle on a career, and neither man gave much evidence of his future greatness until well into middle age: Darwin published *The Origin of Species* when he was 50, and Lincoln won the presidency a year later. Both men were private and guarded. Most of Darwin's friendships were conducted through the mail, and after his five-year voyage on HMS *Beagle* as a young man, he rarely left his home in the English countryside. Lincoln, though a much more public man, carefully cultivated a bumpkin persona that encouraged both friends and enemies to underestimate his considerable, almost Machiavellian skill as a politician.

> It is a measure of their accomplishments, of how much they changed the world, that the era into which Lincoln and Darwin were born seems so strange to us now.

It is a measure of their accomplishments, of how much they changed the world, that the era into which Lincoln and Darwin were born seems so strange to us now. On their birth date, Thomas Jefferson had three weeks left in his second term as president. George III still sat on the throne of England. The Enlightenment was giving way to Romanticism. At the center of what people then believed, the tent poles of their reality were that God created the world and that man was the crown of creation. Well, some men, since the institution of slavery was still acceptable on both sides of the Mason-Dixon line — it would not be abolished in New York State, for example, until 1827, and while it had been illegal in England since 1772, it would not be abolished in English colonies until 1833. And Darwin, at least at the outset, was hardly even a scientist in the sense that we understand the term — a highly trained specialist whose professional vocabulary is so arcane that he or she can talk only to other scientists.

Darwin, the man who would almost singlehandedly redefine biological science, started out as an amateur naturalist, a beetle collector, a rockhound, a 22-year-old rich-kid dilettante who, after flirting with the idea of being first a physician and then a preacher, was allowed to ship out with the *Beagle* as someone who might supply good conversation at the captain's table. His father had all but ordered him not to go to sea, worrying that it was nothing more than one of Charles's lengthening list of aimless exploits — years before, Dr. Darwin had scolded his teenage son, saying, "You care for nothing but shooting, dogs, and rat catching, and you will be a disgrace to yourself and all your family." How could the father know that when the son came ashore after his five-year voyage, he would not only have shed his aimlessness but would have replaced it with a scientific sense of skepticism and curiosity so rigorous and abiding that he would be a workaholic almost to the day he died? Darwin was also in the grip of an idea so subversive that he would keep it under wraps for another two decades. But the crucial thing is that he did all this by himself. He became the very model of a modern major scientist without benefit of graduate school, grants, or even much peer review. (It's hard to get a sympathetic hearing when your work, if successful, is clearly going to knock the blocks out from under civilization.) Darwin may have been independently wealthy, but in terms of his vocation, he was a self-made man.

Lincoln was self-made in the more conventional sense — a walking, talking embodiment of the frontier myth made good. Like Darwin, Lincoln was not a quick study. Both men worked slowly to master a subject. But both had restless, hungry minds. After about a year of schooling as a boy — and that spread out in dribs and drabs of three months here and four months there — Lincoln taught himself. He mastered trigonometry (for work as a surveyor), he read Blackstone on his own to become a lawyer. He memorized swaths of the Bible and Shakespeare. At the age of 40, after he had already served a term in the U.S. House of Representatives, he undertook Euclidean geometry as a mental exercise. After a while, his myth becomes a little much — he actually was born in a log cabin with a dirt floor — so much that we begin looking for flaws, and they're there: the bad marriage, some maladroit comments on racial inferiority. Then there were those terrible jokes. But even there, dammit, he could be truly witty: "I have endured a great deal of ridicule without much malice; and have received a great deal of kindness, not quite free from ridicule. I am used to it."

Perhaps the most mysterious aspect of this riddlesome man was just how he managed, somewhere along the way, to turn himself into one of the best prose writers America has produced. Lincoln united the North behind him with an eloquence so timeless that his words remain fresh no matter how many times you read them. Darwin wrote one of the few scientific treatises, maybe the only one, worth reading as a work of literature. Both of them demand to be read in the original, not in paraphrase, because both men are so much in their prose. To read them is to know these elusive figures a little better. Given their influence on our lives, these are men you want to know.

Darwin seems to have been able to think only with a pen in his hand. He was a compulsive note taker and list maker. He made an extensive list setting down the pros and cons of marriage before he proposed to his future wife. His first published work, *The Voyage of the Beagle*, is a tidied-up version of the log he kept on the five-year trip around the world, and he is unflaggingly meticulous in his observations of the plant and animal life he saw or collected along the way. To live, for Darwin, meant looking and examining and then writing down what he saw and then trying to make sense of it.   7

In the *Beagle* log and his journals, Darwin is something like a cub reporter, asking questions, taking notes, delighting in the varieties of life he discovers, both alive and in the fossil record, in South America, Australia, or the Cape Verde Islands. With Darwin there is no Eureka moment when he suddenly discovers evolution. But by the time he left the *Beagle* in 1836, he was plainly becoming convinced that, contrary to the prevailing wisdom, life is not static — species change and evolve. Shortly before the voyage was over, he mulled over what he had seen on the Galápagos: "When I see these islands in sight of each other, and possessed of but a scanty stock of animals, tenanted by these birds, but slightly differing in structure and filling the same place in Nature, I must suspect they are only varieties. . . . If there is the slightest foundation for these remarks the zoology of the [Galápagos] will be well worth examining; for such facts would undermine the stability of Species." What he did not have was a controlling mechanism for this process. It was not until two years later that he conceived the idea of natural selection, after reading economist Thomas Malthus on the competition for resources among humans brought on by the inexorable demands of overpopulation. There he had it: a theory of everything that actually worked. Species evolve and the ones best adapted to their environment thrive and leave more offspring, crowding out the rest.   8

As delighted as he was with his discovery, Darwin was equally horrified, because he understood the consequences of his theory. Mankind was no longer the culmination of life but merely part of it; creation was mechanistic and purposeless. In a letter to a fellow scientist, Darwin wrote that confiding his theory was "like confessing a murder." Small wonder that instead of rushing to publish his theory, he sat on it — for 20 years. He started a series of notebooks in which he began refining his theory, recording the results of his research in fields as disparate as animal husbandry and barnacles. Over the next five or six years, he went through notebook after notebook, including one in which he began to pose metaphysical questions arising from his research. Do animals have consciences? Where does the idea of God come from?   9

This questioning spirit is one of the most appealing facets of Darwin's 10
character, particularly where it finds its way into his published work. Reading
The Origin of Species, you feel as though he is addressing you as an equal. He
is never autocratic, never bullying. Instead, he is always willing to admit what
he does not know or understand, and when he poses a question, he is never
rhetorical. He seems genuinely to want to know the answer. He's also a good
salesman. He knows that what he has to say will not only be troubling for a
general reader to take but difficult to understand — so he works very hard
not to lose his customer. The book opens not with theory but in the humblest
place imaginable: the barnyard, as Darwin introduces us to the idea of species
variation in a way we, or certainly his nineteenth-century audience, will easily
grasp — the breeding of domestic animals. The quality of Darwin's mind is in
evidence everywhere in this book, but so is his character — generous, open-
minded, and always respectful of those who he knew would disagree with him,
as you might expect of a man who was, after all, married to a creationist.

Like Darwin, Lincoln was a compulsive scribbler, forever jotting down 11
phrases, notes, and ideas on scraps of paper, then squirreling the notes away in
a coat pocket, a desk drawer — or sometimes his hat — where they would collect
until he found a use for them in a letter, a speech, or a document. He was also a
compulsive reviser. He knew that words heard are not the same as words read.
After delivering his emotional farewell speech in Springfield, Illinois, in 1861,
he boarded the train for Washington and, if the shakiness of his handwriting is
any indication, immediately began revising his remarks prior to publication.

The Gettysburg Address apparently gestated in a somewhat similar 12
fashion. The winter and spring of 1863 were one of the lowest points for
the Union. In the West, Grant was bogged down in his protracted siege of
Vicksburg. In the East, the South won decisively at Chancellorsville. Since
the Emancipation Proclamation had been issued on January 1, people in the
North were wondering aloud just what it was they were fighting for. Was it
to preserve the Union, or was it to abolish slavery? Lincoln was keenly aware
that he needed to clarify the issue. The Northern victory at Gettysburg in
early July gave him the occasion he was seeking.

Some witnesses at Gettysburg claimed to recall applause during the 13
speech, but most did not, and Lincoln was already taking his seat before many
in the audience realized he had finished. This was a time when speeches could
last for four hours. Edward Everett, who preceded the president on the program,
had confined his remarks to two hours. Lincoln said what he had to say in two
minutes. Brevity is only one of the several noteworthy aspects of what is surely
one of the greatest speeches ever made. Of much greater importance are what
the president said and how he said it.

With his first 29 words, Lincoln accomplished what he had come to 14
Gettysburg to do — he defined the purpose of the war for the Union: Four score
and seven years ago our fathers brought forth on this continent, a new nation,
conceived in Liberty, and dedicated to the proposition that all men are created

equal." He could have put this sentence in the form of an argument — the equality of all men was one of the things the war was about. Instead, he states his argument as fact: The nation was founded on the principle of equality; this is what we fight to preserve. There is a hint of qualification — but only a hint — in the word *proposition*: Equality is not a self-evident truth; it is what we believe in. In the next paragraph, he continues this idea of contingency: "Now we are engaged in a great civil war, testing whether that nation, or any nation so conceived and so dedicated, can long endure." In other words, republican democracy hangs in the balance. Before the speech, none of this was taken for granted, even in the North. In 272 words, he defined the national principle so thoroughly that today no one would think of arguing otherwise.

Lincoln's political genius stood on two pillars: He possessed an uncanny 15 awareness of what *could* be done at any given moment, and he had the ability to change his mind, to adapt to circumstances, to grow. This is Lincoln in 1838, addressing the Springfield Young Men's Lyceum on a citizen's obligations to the legal system with such lines as, "Let reverence for the laws, be breathed by every American mother, to the lisping babe, that prattles on her lap." Here he is not quite 30 years later in the Second Inaugural of 1865 (there's a mother and child in this one, too, but what a difference): "With malice toward none; with charity for all; with firmness in the right, as God gives us to see the right, let us strive on to finish the work we are in; to bind up the nation's wounds; to care for him who shall have borne the battle, and for his widow, and his orphan — to do all which may achieve and cherish a just, and a lasting peace, among ourselves, and with all nations."

This is the language of the Bible, and if the rhetoric does not convince 16 us of that, Lincoln mentions God six times in one paragraph. But what kind of God? Lincoln's religious history is perhaps the most tangled aspect of his life. His law partner, William Herndon, swore Lincoln was an atheist, and to be sure, there are plenty of boilerplate references to the Almighty scattered through Lincoln's speeches. But as the war wears on, and the speeches grow more spiritual, they become less conventional. Lincoln was a believer, but it is hard to say just what he believed. He speaks often of the will of God, but just as often adamantly refuses to decipher God's purpose. And he never, ever claims that God is on his side.

The God of the Second Inaugural is utterly inscrutable: "The Almighty 17 has His own purposes." One of those purposes, Lincoln then suggests, may be to punish both North and South for permitting the offense of slavery. Then he delivers what biographer David Herbert Donald has called "one of the most terrible statements ever made by an American public official": "Fondly do we hope, fervently do we pray, that this mighty scourge of war may speedily pass away. Yet, if God wills that it continue until all the wealth piled by the bondsman's two hundred and fifty years of unrequited toil shall be sunk, and until every drop of blood drawn with the lash shall be paid by another drawn with the sword, as was said three thousand years ago, so still it must be said 'the

judgments of the Lord are true and righteous altogether.'" It is here, just when he has brought his audience to the edge of the cliff, that Lincoln spins on his heel in one of the great rhetorical 180s of all time and concludes, "With malice toward none; with charity for all . . ." Even today, reading that conclusion after what's come before is like coming out of a tunnel into bright sunshine — or out of a war that claimed more than 600,000 lives. Lincoln understood that language could heal, and he knew when to use it.

Lincoln, no less than Mark Twain, forged what we think of today as the   18
American style: forthright, rhythmic, muscular, beautiful but never pretty. As Douglas L. Wilson observes in *Lincoln's Sword*, his brilliant analysis of the president's writing, Lincoln was political, not literary, but he was, every bit as much as Melville or Thoreau, "perfecting a prose that expressed a uniquely American way of apprehending and ordering experience." What Lincoln says and how he says it are one. You cannot imagine the Gettysburg Address or the Second Inaugural in words other than those in which they are conveyed.

Lincoln and Darwin were both revolutionaries, in the sense that both   19
men upended realities that prevailed when they were born. They seem — and sound — modern to us, because the world they left behind them is more or less the one we still live in. So, considering the joint magnitude of their contributions — and the coincidence of their conjoined birthdays — it is hard not to wonder: Who was the greater man? It's an apples-and-oranges — or Superman-vs.-Santa — comparison. But if you limit the question to influence, it bears pondering, all the more if you turn the question around and ask, what might have happened if one of these men had not been born? Very quickly the balance tips in Lincoln's favor. As much of a bombshell as Darwin detonated, and as great as his book on evolution is (E. O. Wilson calls it "the greatest scientific book of all time"), it does no harm to remember that he hurried to publish *The Origin of Species* because he thought he was about to be scooped by his fellow naturalist Alfred Russel Wallace, who had independently come up with much the same idea of evolution through natural selection. In other words, there was a certain inevitability to Darwin's theory. Ideas about evolution surfaced throughout the first part of the nineteenth century, and while none of them was as cogent as Darwin's — until Wallace came along — it was not as though he was the only man who had the idea.

Lincoln, in contrast, is sui generis. Take him out of the picture, and there   20
is no telling what might have happened to the country. True, his election to the presidency did provoke secession and, in turn, the war itself, but that war seems inevitable — not a question of if but when. Once in office, he becomes the indispensable man. As James McPherson demonstrates so well in *Tried by War: Abraham Lincoln as Commander in Chief*, Lincoln's prosecution of the war was crucial to the North's success — before Grant came to the rescue, Lincoln was his own best general. Certainly we know what happened

once he was assassinated: Reconstruction was administered punitively and then abandoned, leaving the issue of racial equality to dangle for another century. But here again, what Lincoln said and wrote matters as much as what he did. He framed the conflict in language that united the North — and inspires us still. If anything, with the passage of time, he only looms larger — more impressive, and also more mysterious. Other presidents, even the great ones, submit to analysis. Lincoln forever remains just beyond our grasp — though not for want of trying: It has been estimated that more books have been written about him than any other human being except Jesus.

If Darwin were not so irreplaceable as Lincoln, that should not gainsay his accomplishment. No one could have formulated his theory any more elegantly — or anguished more over its implications. Like Lincoln, Darwin was brave. He risked his health and his reputation to advance the idea that we are not over nature but a part of it. Lincoln prosecuted a war — and became its ultimate casualty — to ensure that no man should have dominion over another. Their identical birthdays afford us a superb opportunity to observe these men in the shared context of their time — how each was shaped by his circumstances, how each reacted to the beliefs that steered the world into which he was born, and ultimately how each reshaped his corner of that world and left it irrevocably changed.   21

■ Thinking Critically about the Text

Jones is particularly interested in how both Darwin and Lincoln wrote and used writing in their lives. What does he see as most striking about each man as a writer? What characteristics do they share? How are they different? Why do you suppose Jones spends as much space as he does — a full thirteen paragraphs — developing the comparison of the two men as writers? What does his analysis of their writing habits and style reveal about the men themselves?

■ Questions on Subject

1. What most interests Jones about Lincoln and Darwin, as men?
2. According to Jones, what personality traits did these men share? In what ways were they both self-made?
3. According to Jones, Darwin returned to England a changed man after his five-year voyage on the *Beagle*. What changes does Jones note? What do you think happened on the voyage that might account for these changes? Explain.

4. Why did Darwin leave his theory unpublished for twenty years? According to Jones, what "horrified" him about this theory? What ultimately pushed him to publish *The Origin of Species*?

5. How does Jones answer the question, "Who was the greater man?" Why do you suppose Jones limits the question to "influence"? In what ways is Jones's job made easier when he "turn[s] the question around and ask[s], what might have happened if one of these men had not been born?" (paragraph 19).

■ Questions on Strategy

1. What does Jones do in his introduction to grab your attention? (Glossary: *Beginnings/Endings*) In what way is his beginning related to his title? (Glossary: *Title*)

2. What function does paragraph 3 serve in the context of this essay?

3. How has Jones organized his comparison and contrast? (Glossary: *Organization*) You may find it helpful to make an outline of the essay to answer this question.

4. Jones quotes a number of sources in his essay. How does he introduce the quotations into his text? For what purpose does Jones use the quoted sources?

5. What techniques does Jones employ to make transitions from one paragraph to the next? (Glossary: *Transitions*)

6. How does Jones's conclusion serve to summarize his essay? How is it related to his opening paragraphs? (Glossary: *Beginnings/Endings*)

■ Questions on Diction and Vocabulary

1. How would you describe Jones's diction — formal or informal? Cite specific examples of word choice that led you to this conclusion. In what ways is his diction appropriate for his subject, purpose, and intended audience? (Glossary: *Audience, Purpose*)

2. At several points in his essay Jones sounds colloquial (e.g., "going to knock the blocks out from under civilization" (paragraph 4) and "dammit" (5). Cite other examples of colloquialisms that Jones uses. How do they affect you, the reader? Explain.

3. Refer to your desk dictionary to determine the meanings of the following words as Jones uses them in this selection: *tandem* (paragraph 1), *epochal* (1), *coevals* (1), *bumpkin* (2), *swaths* (5), *maladroit* (5), *inexorable* (8), *autocratic* (10), *squirreling* (11), *gestated* (12), *boilerplate* (16), *inscrutable* (17), *punitively* (20), *irrevocably* (21).

■ Classroom Activity Using Comparison and Contrast

Consider the following point-by-point comparison of Earth versus the sun, from NASA's Solar System Exploration site <solarsystem.nasa.gov /planets>.

Comparison: Earth vs. the Sun

This chart shows the differences between Earth and the Sun. To change the planets/moons being compared, change one or more of the form fields at the bottom and click **Refresh**.

	Earth	Sun
Discovered By	Known by the Ancients	Known by the Ancients
Date of Discovery	Unknown	Unknown
Equatorial Radius	6,378.14 km	695,500 km
Equatorial Circumference	40,075 km	4,379,000 km
Volume	1,083,200,000,000 km^3	1,412,200,000,000,000,000 km^3
Mass	5,973,700,000,000,000,000,000,000 kg	1,989,000,000,000,000,000,000,000,000,000 kg
Density	5.515 g/cm^3	1.409 g/cm^3
Surface Area	510,065,700 km^2	6,087,799,000,000 km^2
Equatorial Surface Gravity	9.766 m/s^2	274.0 m/s^2
Escape Velocity	40,248 km/h	2,223,720 km/h
Rotation Period (Length of Day)	0.99726968 sidereal days	25.38 sidereal days
Minimum/Maximum Surface Temperature	-88/58 (min/max) °C	5,500 °C

Why do you think NASA chose the points of comparison used for the chart? What do they help us understand about our solar system? What aspects did they leave out? What, if anything, do you think could be done to enhance the chart's effectiveness? Explain.

■ **Writing Suggestions**

1. Lincoln and Darwin were leaders in their respective worlds. From what Jones tells us, how would you say their leadership styles differed? What leadership styles have you observed in political, business, religious, science, or educational leaders? What impressed or failed to impress you about the different styles these people used? Write an essay comparing and contrasting two or more leadership styles, highlighting the strengths of each.

2. **Writing with Sources.** Write an essay in which you compare and contrast two world leaders, sports figures, or celebrities whose careers have at some point crossed in a dramatic or decisive way: Examples include Hillary Clinton and Barack Obama; Ronald Reagan and Mikhail Gorbachev; Andre Agassi and Roger Federer; Brad Pitt and Angelina Jolie; Marilyn Monroe and Joe DiMaggio; George W. Bush and Al Gore. Use library resources and the Internet to research your two famous people.

For models of and advice on integrating sources, see Chapters 14–15.

Neat People vs. Sloppy People

SUZANNE BRITT

 Born in Winston-Salem, North Carolina, Suzanne Britt now makes her home in Raleigh. She graduated from Salem College and Washington University, where she received her M.A. in English. A poet and essayist, Britt has been a columnist for the Raleigh *News and Observer* and *Stars and Stripes*, European edition. Her work appears regularly in *North Carolina Gardens and Homes*, the *New York Times*, *Newsweek*, and the *Boston Globe*. Her essays have been collected in two books, *Skinny People Are Dull and Crunchy Like Carrots* (1982) and *Show and Tell* (1982). She is the author of *A Writer's Rhetoric* (1988), a college textbook, and *Images: A Centennial Journey* (1991), a history of Meredith College, the small independent women's college in Raleigh where Britt teaches English and continues to write.

The following essay was taken from *Show and Tell*, a book Britt humorously describes as a report on her journey into "the awful cave of self: You shout your name and voices come back in exultant response, telling you their names." Here, mingling humor with a touch of seriousness, Britt examines the differences between neat and sloppy people and gives us some insights about several important personality traits.

■ Preparing to Read

Many people in our society are fond of comparing people, places, and things. Often, these comparisons are premature and even damaging. Consider the ways people judge others based on clothes, appearance, or hearsay. Write about a time in your life when you made such a comparison about someone or something. Did your initial judgment hold up? If not, why did it change?

I've finally figured out the difference between neat people and sloppy   1
people. The distinction is, as always, moral. Neat people are lazier and meaner than sloppy people.

Sloppy people, you see, are not really sloppy. Their sloppiness is   2
merely the unfortunate consequence of their extreme moral rectitude. Sloppy people carry in their mind's eye a heavenly vision, a precise plan, that is so stupendous, so perfect, it can't be achieved in this world or the next.

Sloppy people live in Never-Never Land. Someday is their métier.[1] Some-   3
day they are planning to alphabetize all their books and set up home catalogs.

> I've finally fig-
> ured out the dif-
> ference between
> neat people and
> sloppy people.
> The distinction
> is, as always,
> moral.

Someday they will go through their wardrobes and mark certain items for tentative mending and certain items for passing on to relatives of similar shape and size. Someday sloppy people will make family scrapbooks into which they will put newspaper clippings, postcards, locks of hair, and the dried corsage from their senior prom. Someday they will file everything on the surface of their desks, including the cash receipts from coffee purchases at the snack shop. Someday they will sit down and read all the back issues of *The New Yorker*.

For all these noble reasons and more, sloppy   4
people never get neat. They aim too high and wide. They save everything, planning someday to file, order, and straighten out the world. But while these ambitious plans take clearer and clearer shape in their heads, the books spill from the shelves onto the floor, the clothes pile up in the hamper and closet, the family mementos accumulate in every drawer, the surface of the desk is buried under mounds of paper and the unread magazines threaten to reach the ceiling.

Sloppy people can't bear to part with anything. They give loving atten-   5
tion to every detail. When sloppy people say they're going to tackle the surface of the desk, they really mean it. Not a paper will go unturned; not a rubber band will go unboxed. Four hours or two weeks into the excavation, the desk looks exactly the same, primarily because the sloppy person is meticulously creating new piles of papers with new headings and scrupulously stopping to read all of the old book catalogs before he throws them away. A neat person would just bulldoze the desk.

Neat people are bums and clods at heart. They have cavalier attitudes   6
toward possessions, including family heirlooms. Everything is just another dust-catcher to them. If anything collects dust, it's got to go and that's that. Neat people will toy with the idea of throwing the children out of the house just to cut down on the clutter.

Neat people don't care about process. They like results. What they want   7
to do is get the whole thing over with so they can sit down and watch the rasslin' on TV. Neat people operate on two unvarying principles: Never handle any item twice, and throw everything away.

The only thing messy in a neat person's house is the trash can. The   8
minute something comes to a neat person's hand, he will look at it, try to decide if it has immediate use and, finding none, throw it in the trash.

---

[1]Activity or work for which a person is especially suited. —Ed.

Neat people are especially vicious with mail. They never go through   9
their mail unless they are standing directly over a trash can. If the trash
can is beside the mailbox, even better. All ads, catalogs, pleas for charitable
contributions, church bulletins, and money-saving coupons go straight
into the trash can without being opened. All letters from home, postcards
from Europe, bills, and paychecks are opened, immediately responded to,
then dropped in the trash can. Neat people keep their receipts only for tax
purposes. That's it. No sentimental salvaging of birthday cards or the last
letter a dying relative ever wrote. Into the trash it goes.

Neat people place neatness above everything, even economics. They   10
are incredibly wasteful. Neat people throw away several toys every time
they walk through the den. I knew a neat person once who threw away
a perfectly good dish drainer because it had mold on it. The drainer was
too much trouble to wash. And neat people sell their furniture when they
move. They will sell a La-Z-Boy recliner while you are reclining in it.

Neat people are no good to borrow from. Neat people buy everything   11
in expensive little single portions. They get their flour and sugar in two-
pound bags. They wouldn't consider clipping a coupon, saving a leftover,
reusing plastic nondairy whipped cream containers, or rinsing off tin foil
and draping it over the unmoldy dish drainer. You can never borrow a neat
person's newspaper to see what's playing at the movies. Neat people have
the paper all wadded up and in the trash by 7:05 A.M.

Neat people cut a clean swath through the organic as well as the inor-   12
ganic world. People, animals, and things are all one to them. They are so
insensitive. After they've finished with the pantry, the medicine cabinet,
and the attic, they will throw out the red geranium (too many leaves), sell
the dog (too many fleas), and send the children off to boarding school (too
many scuff marks on the hardwood floors).

■ Thinking Critically about the Text

Suzanne Britt reduces people to two types: sloppy and neat. What does
she see as the defining characteristics of each type? Do you consider
yourself a sloppy or a neat person? Perhaps you are neither. If this is the
case, make up your own category, and explain why Britt's categories are
not broad enough.

■ Questions on Subject

1. Why do you suppose Britt characterizes the distinction between
   sloppy and neat people as a "moral" one (paragraph 1)? What is she
   really poking fun at with this reference? (Glossary: *Irony*)

2. In your own words, what is the "heavenly vision," the "precise plan," Britt refers to in paragraph 2? How does Britt use this idea to explain why sloppy people can never be neat?
3. Exaggeration, as Britt uses it, is only effective if it is based on some shared idea of the truth. What commonly understood ideas about sloppy and neat people does Britt rely on? Do you agree with her? Why or why not?

■ Questions on Strategy

1. Note Britt's use of transitions as she moves from trait to trait. (Glossary: *Transitions*) How well does she use transitions to achieve unity in her essay? Explain.
2. One of the ways Britt achieves a sense of the ridiculous in her essay is to switch the commonly accepted attributes of sloppy and neat people. Cite examples of this technique, and discuss the ways in which it adds to her essay. What does it reveal to the reader about her purpose in writing the essay? (Glossary: *Purpose*)
3. Britt uses block comparison to point out the differences between sloppy and neat people. Make a side-by-side list of the traits of sloppy and neat people. After reviewing your list, determine any ways in which sloppy and neat people may be similar. Why do you suppose Britt does not include any of the ways in which they are the same?
4. Why do you think Britt has chosen to use a block comparison? What would have been gained or lost had she used a point-by-point system of contrast?
5. Throughout the essay, Britt uses numerous examples to show the differences between sloppy and neat people. (Glossary: *Illustration*) Cite five examples that Britt uses to exemplify these points. How effective do you find Britt's use of examples? What do they add to her comparison and contrast essay?

■ Questions on Diction and Vocabulary

1. Cite examples of Britt's diction that indicate her change of tone when she is talking about either sloppy or neat people. (Glossary: *Diction; Tone*)
2. How would you characterize Britt's vocabulary in the essay — easy or difficult? What does her choice of vocabulary say about her intended audience? In which places does Britt use precise word choice to particularly good effect?
3. Refer to your desk dictionary to determine the meanings of the following words as Britt uses them in this selection: *rectitude* (paragraph 2), *tentative* (3), *meticulously* (5), *heirlooms* (6), *salvaging* (9), *swath* (12).

■ Classroom Activity Using Comparison and Contrast

Using the sample outlines on pages 291–92 as models, prepare both block and point-by-point outlines for one of the following topics:

1. dogs and cats as pets
2. print media and electronic media
3. an economy car and a luxury car
4. your local newspaper and the *New York Times*
5. a high school teacher and a college teacher

Explain any advantages of one organizational plan over the other.

■ Writing Suggestions

1. Write an essay in which you describe yourself as either sloppy or neat. In what ways does your behavior compare or contrast with the traits Britt offers? You may follow Britt's definition of sloppy and neat, or you may come up with your own.
2. Take some time to reflect on a relationship in your life — perhaps one with a friend, a family member, or a teacher. Write an essay in which you discuss what it is about you and that other person that makes the relationship work. You may find it helpful to think of a relationship that doesn't work to better understand why the relationship you're writing about does work. What discoveries about yourself did you make while working on this essay? Explain. (Glossary: *Description*)

Grant and Lee: A Study in Contrasts

BRUCE CATTON

Arguably the most prolific and popular Civil War historian, Bruce Catton (1899–1978) was born in Petoskey, Michigan, and attended Oberlin College. Early in his career, Catton worked as a reporter for various newspapers, among them the *Cleveland Plain Dealer*. His interest in history led him to write about the Civil War. His books on the subject include *Mr. Lincoln's Army* (1951), *Glory Road* (1952), *A Stillness at Appomattox* (1953), *This Hallowed Ground* (1956), *The Coming Fury* (1961), *Never Call Retreat* (1965), and *Gettysburg: The Final Fury* (1974). Catton won both the Pulitzer Prize and the National Book Award in 1954. A fellow historian once wrote, "there is a near-magic power of imagination in Catton's work that seem[s] to project him physically into the battlefields, along the dusty roads, and to the campfires of another age."

The following selection was included in *The American Story,* a collection of historical essays edited by Earl Schenk Miers. In this essay, Catton considers "two great Americans, Grant and Lee — very different, yet under everything very much alike."

■ **Preparing to Read**

What do you know about America's Civil War and the roles played by Ulysses S. Grant and Robert E. Lee in that monumental struggle? For you, what does each of these men represent? Do you consider either of them to be an American hero? Explain.

When Ulysses S. Grant and Robert E. Lee met in the parlor of a modest house at Appomattox Court House, Virginia, on April 9, 1865, to work out the terms for the surrender of Lee's Army of Northern Virginia, a great chapter in American life came to a close, and a great new chapter began. 1

These men were bringing the Civil War to its virtual finish. To be sure, other armies had yet to surrender, and for a few days the fugitive Confederate government would struggle desperately and vainly, trying to find some way to go on living now that its chief support was gone. But in effect it was all over when Grant and Lee signed the papers. And the little room where they wrote out the terms was the scene of one of the poignant, dramatic contrasts in American history. 2

They were two strong men, these oddly different generals, and they represented the strengths of two conflicting currents that, through them, had come into final collision. 3

> They were two strong men, these oddly different generals, and they represented the strengths of two conflicting currents that, through them, had come into final collision.

Back of Robert E. Lee was the notion that the old aristocratic concept might somehow survive and be dominant in American life. 4

Lee was tidewater Virginia, and in his background were family, culture, and tradition . . . the age of chivalry transplanted to a New World which was making its own legends and its own myths. He embodied a way of life that had come down through the age of knighthood and the English country squire. America was a land that was beginning all over again, dedicated to nothing much more complicated than the rather hazy belief that all men had equal rights and should have an equal chance in the world. In such a land Lee stood for the feeling that it was somehow of advantage to human society to have a pronounced inequality in the social structure. There should be a leisure class, backed by ownership of land; in turn, society itself should be keyed to the land as the chief source of wealth and influence. It would bring forth (according to this ideal) a class of men with a strong sense of obligation 5

Robert E. Lee

to the community; men who lived not to gain advantage for themselves, but to meet the solemn obligations which had been laid on them by the very fact that they were privileged. From them the country would get its leadership; to them it could look for the higher values — of thought, of conduct, of personal deportment — to give it strength and value.

Lee embodied the noblest elements of this aristocratic ideal. Through him, the landed nobility justified itself. For four years, the Southern states had fought a desperate war to uphold the ideals for which Lee stood. In the end, it almost seemed as if the Confederacy fought for Lee; as if he himself was the Confederacy . . . the best thing that the way of life for which the Confederacy stood could ever have to offer. He had passed into legend before Appomattox. Thousands of tired, underfed, poorly clothed Confederate soldiers, long since past the simple enthusiasm of the early days of the struggle, somehow considered Lee the symbol of everything for which they had been willing to die. But they could not quite put this feeling into words. If the Lost Cause, sanctified by so much heroism and so many deaths, had a living justification, its justification was General Lee.

Grant, the son of a tanner on the Western frontier, was everything Lee was not. He had come up the hard way and embodied nothing in particular except the eternal toughness and sinewy fiber of the men who grew up beyond the mountains. He was one of a body of men who owed reverence and obeisance to no one, who were self-reliant to a fault, who cared hardly anything for the past but who had a sharp eye for the future.

These frontier men were the precise opposite of the tidewater aristocrats. Back of them, in the great surge that had taken people over the Alleghenies and into the opening Western country, there was a deep, implicit dissatisfaction with a past that had settled into grooves. They stood for democracy, not from any reasoned conclusion about the proper ordering of human society, but simply because they had grown up in the middle of democracy and knew how it worked. Their society might have privileges, but they would be privileges each man had won for himself. Forms and patterns meant nothing. No man was born to anything, except perhaps to a chance to show how far he could rise. Life was competition.

Yet along with this feeling had come a deep sense of belonging to a national community. The Westerner who developed a farm, opened a shop, or set up in business as a trader, could hope to prosper only as his own community prospered — and his community ran from the Atlantic to the Pacific and from Canada down to Mexico. If the land was settled, with towns and highways and accessible markets, he could better himself. He saw his fate in terms of the nation's own destiny. As its horizons expanded, so did his. He had, in other words, an acute dollars-and-cents stake in the continued growth and development of his country.

And that, perhaps, is where the contrast between Grant and Lee becomes most striking. The Virginia aristocrat, inevitably, saw himself in relation to

Ulysses S. Grant

his own region. He lived in a static society which could endure almost anything except change. Instinctively, his first loyalty would go to the locality in which that society existed. He would fight to the limit of endurance to defend it, because in defending it he was defending everything that gave his own life its deepest meaning.

The Westerner, on the other hand, would fight with an equal tenacity   11
for the broader concept of society. He fought so because everything he lived by was tied to growth, expansion and a constantly widening horizon. What he lived by would survive or fall with the nation itself. He could not possibly stand by unmoved in the face of an attempt to destroy the Union. He would combat it with everything he had, because he could only see it as an effort to cut the ground out from under his feet.

So Grant and Lee were in complete contrast, representing two dia-   12
metrically opposed elements in American life. Grant was the modern man emerging; beyond him, ready to come on the stage, was the great age of steel and machinery, of crowded cities and a restless burgeoning vitality. Lee might have ridden down from the old age of chivalry, lance in hand, silken banner fluttering over his head. Each man was the perfect champion

of his cause, drawing both his strengths and his weaknesses from the people he led.

Yet it was not all contrast, after all. Different as they were — in back-   13
ground, in personality, in underlying aspiration — these two great soldiers had much in common. Under everything else, they were marvelous fighters. Furthermore, their fighting qualities were really very much alike.

Each man had, to begin with, the great virtue of utter tenacity and fidel-   14
ity. Grant fought his way down the Mississippi Valley in spite of acute personal discouragement and profound military handicaps. Lee hung on in the trenches at Petersburg after hope itself had died. In each man there was an indomitable quality . . . the born fighter's refusal to give up as long as he can still remain on his feet and lift his two fists.

Daring and resourcefulness they had, too; the ability to think faster   15
and move faster than the enemy. These were the qualities which gave Lee the dazzling campaigns of Second Manassas and Chancellorsville and won Vicksburg for Grant.

Lastly, and perhaps greatest of all, there was the ability, at the end, to turn   16
quickly from war to peace once the fighting was over. Out of the way these two men behaved at Appomattox came the possibility of a peace of reconciliation. It was a possibility not wholly realized, in the years to come, but which did, in the end, help the two sections to become one nation again . . . after a war whose bitterness might have seemed to make such a reunion wholly impossible. No part of either man's life became him more than the part he played in their brief meeting in the McLean house at Appomattox. Their behavior there put all succeeding generations of Americans in their debt. Two great Americans, Grant and Lee — very different, yet under everything very much alike. Their encounter at Appomattox was one of the great moments of American history.

■ **Thinking Critically about the Text**

Catton concludes with the claim that Grant and Lee's "encounter at Appomattox was one of the great moments of American history" (paragraph 16). How does Catton prepare readers for this claim? What, for Catton, do these two Civil War generals represent, and what does he see as the implications for the country of Lee's surrender?

■ **Questions on Subject**

1. In paragraphs 10–12, Catton discusses what he considers to be the most striking contrast between Grant and Lee. What is that difference?
2. List the similarities that Catton sees between Grant and Lee. Which similarity does Catton believe is most important? Why?

3. What attitudes and ideas does Catton describe to support his view that the culture of tidewater Virginia was a throwback to the "age of chivalry" (paragraph 5)?
4. Catton says that Grant was "the modern man emerging" (paragraph 12). How does he support that statement? Do you agree?

■ Questions on Strategy

1. What would have been lost had Catton looked at the similarities between Grant and Lee before looking at the differences? Would anything have been gained?
2. How does Catton organize the body of his essay (paragraphs 3–16)? When answering this question, you may find it helpful to summarize the point of comparison in each paragraph and to label whether the paragraph concerns Lee, Grant, or both. (Glossary: *Organization*)
3. Catton makes clear transitions between paragraphs. Identify the transitional devices he uses to lead readers from one paragraph to the next throughout the essay. As a reader, how do these transitions help you? (Glossary: *Transitions*) Explain.
4. How does Catton use both description and cause and effect analysis to enhance his comparison and contrast of Grant and Lee? In what ways does description serve to sharpen the differences between these generals? How does Catton use cause and effect analysis to explain their respective natures? Cite several examples of Catton's use of each strategy to illustrate your answer. (Glossary: *Cause and Effect Analysis; Description*)

■ Questions on Diction and Vocabulary

1. Identify at least two metaphors that Catton uses, and explain what each contributes to his comparison. (Glossary: *Figures of Speech*)
2. Refer to your desk dictionary to determine the meanings of the following words as Catton uses them in this selection: *poignant* (paragraph 2), *chivalry* (5), *sanctified* (6), *sinewy* (7), *obeisance* (7), *tidewater* (8), *tenacity* (11), *aspiration* (13).

■ Classroom Activity Using Comparison and Contrast

Carefully read and analyze the following paragraphs from Stephen E. Ambrose's book *Crazy Horse and Custer: The Parallel Lives of Two American Warriors* (1975). Then answer the questions that follow.

It was bravery, above and beyond all other qualities, that Custer and Crazy Horse had in common. Each man was an outstanding warrior in war-mad societies. Thousands upon thousands of Custer's fellow whites had as much opportunity as he did to demonstrate their courage, just as all of Crazy Horse's associates had countless opportunities to show that they equaled him in bravery. But no white warrior, save his younger brother, Tom, could outdo Custer, just as no Indian warrior, save his younger brother, Little Hawk, could outdo Crazy Horse. And for both white and red societies, no masculine virtue was more admired than bravery. To survive, both societies felt they had to have men willing to put their lives on the line. For men who were willing to do so, no reward was too great, even though there were vast differences in the way each society honored its heroes.

Beyond their bravery, Custer and Crazy Horse were individualists, each standing out from the crowd in his separate way. Custer wore outlandish uniforms, let his hair fall in long, flowing golden locks across his shoulders, surrounded himself with pet animals and admirers, and in general did all he could to draw attention to himself. Crazy Horse's individualism pushed him in the opposite direction—he wore a single feather in his hair when going into battle, rather than a war bonnet. Custer's vast energy set him apart from most of his fellows; the Sioux distinguished Crazy Horse from other warriors because of Crazy Horse's quietness and introspection. Both men lived in societies in which drugs, especially alcohol, were widely used, but neither Custer nor Crazy Horse drank. Most of all, of course, each man stood out in battle as a great risk taker.

What is Ambrose's point in these two paragraphs? How does he use comparison and contrast to make this point? How has he organized his paragraphs?

▪ Writing Suggestions

1. Catton gives readers few details of the physical appearance of Grant and Lee, but the portraits that accompany this essay do show us what these men looked like. (For a discussion of how to analyze photographs and other visual texts, see pages 11–14.) Write a brief essay in which you compare and contrast the men you see in the portraits. How closely does your assessment of each general match the "picture" Catton presents in his essay? How would you describe the appearance — both dress and posture — of these two generals? What details in the photographs are most telling for you? Explain why. In what ways can Grant and Lee be said to represent the way of life associated with the side each commanded? Explain.

2. In the persons of Grant and Lee, Catton sees the "final collision" (paragraph 3) between two ways of living and thinking — the "age of steel and machinery" (12) conquering the "age of chivalry" (5). What do you see as the dominant ways of living and thinking in the current "age of information"? Do today's lifestyles appear to be on a collision course with one another, or do you think they can all coexist? Write an essay in which you present your position and defend it using appropriate examples.

WRITING SUGGESTIONS FOR COMPARISON AND CONTRAST

1. Write an essay in which you compare and contrast two objects, people, or events to show at least one of the following.
   a. their important differences
   b. their significant similarities
   c. their relative value
   d. their distinctive qualities

2. Select a topic from the list that follows. Write an essay using comparison and contrast as your primary means of development. Be sure that your essay has a definite purpose and a clear direction.
   a. two methods of dieting
   b. two television situation comedies
   c. two types of summer employment
   d. two people who display different attitudes toward responsibility
   e. two restaurants
   f. two courses in the same subject area
   g. two friends who exemplify different lifestyles
   h. two network television or local news programs
   i. two professional quarterbacks
   j. two ways of studying for an exam
   k. two rooms in which you have classes
   l. two of your favorite magazines
   m. two attitudes toward death
   n. two ways to heat a home

3. Use one of the following "before and after" situations as the basis for an essay of comparison and contrast.
   a. before and after an examination
   b. before and after seeing a movie
   c. before and after reading an important book
   d. before and after dieting
   e. before and after a long trip

4. Most of us have seen something important in our lives — a person, place, or thing — undergo a significant change, either in the subject itself or in our own perception of it. Write an essay comparing and contrasting the person, place, or thing before and after the change.

There are many possibilities to consider. Perhaps a bucolic vista of open fields has become a shopping mall; perhaps a favorite athletic team has gone from glory to shame; perhaps a loved one has been altered by decisions, events, or illness.

5. Interview a professor who has taught for many years at your college or university. Ask the professor to compare and contrast the college as it was when he or she first taught there with the way it is now; encourage reminiscence and evaluation. Combine strategies of description, comparison and contrast, and possibly definition as you write your essay. (Glossary: *Definition; Description*)

6. **Writing with Sources.** Five of the essays in this book deal, more or less directly, with issues related to the definition, achievement, or nature of manhood in America. The essays are "How to Give Orders Like a Man" (page 192) by Deborah Tannen; "Grant and Lee: A Study in Contrasts" by Bruce Catton (page 323); "What does 'Boys Will Be Boys' Really Mean?" by Deborah M. Roffman (page 422); "How Boys Become Men" by Jon Katz (page 455); and "Shooting an Elephant" by George Orwell (page 615). Read these essays, and discuss with classmates the broad issues they raise. Choose one aspect of the topic of particular interest to you, and study the three or four essays that seem to bear most directly on this topic. Write an essay in which you compare, contrast, and evaluate the assertions in these essays.

7. **Writing with Sources.** Study the "Rebuilding Progress in New Orleans" chart reproduced at the beginning of this chapter (page 280). In what areas is the most progress being made? What areas seem to be lagging behind? What conclusions, if any, can you draw about New Orleans's recovery from Hurricane Katrina? After doing research in your library as well as on the Internet, write an essay in which you report on current efforts to revitalize New Orleans. What still needs to be done? What's being done to reduce or eliminate the chance of a Katrina-like catastrophe happening again?

Before starting your research and drafting your essay, you will find it helpful to become familiar with the materials found in Chapter 14, "Writing with Sources" and Chapter 15, "A Brief Guide to Researching and Documenting Essays."

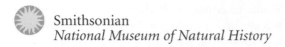

Smithsonian
National Museum of Natural History

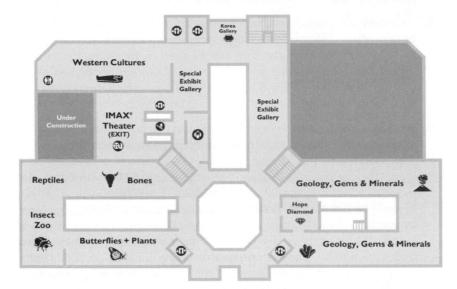

Second Floor

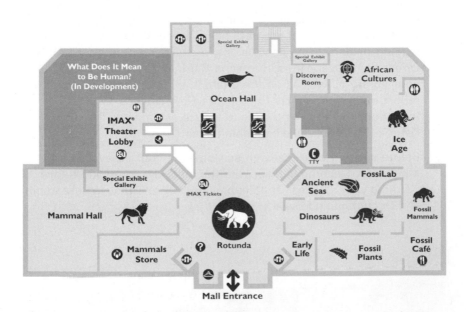

First Floor

CHAPTER 9

Division and Classification

What Are Division and Classification?

Like comparison and contrast, division and classification are separate yet closely related operations. Division involves breaking down a single large unit into smaller subunits or separating a group of items into discrete categories. Classification, on the other hand, entails placing individual items into established categories. Division, then, takes apart, whereas classification groups together. But even though the two processes can operate separately, they tend to be used together.

The floor plan of the National Museum of Natural History (opposite) illustrates division and classification at work. The museum has divided its floor space into sections—Western Cultures, African Cultures, Ocean Hall, Mammal Hall, Dinosaurs, and so forth—named for the categories its scientists have used to organize the gigantic inventory of natural specimens. Visitors to the museum can quickly glance at the depiction of the floor plan, get a simplified understanding of the natural world, and learn where to go to see representative examples of a particular class of objects from that world. The principles of division and classification have provided an easy way for museumgoers to make sense out of what would otherwise be an overwhelming conglomeration of objects.

Division and Classification in Written Texts

In writing, division can be the most effective method for making sense of one large, complex, or multifaceted entity. Consider, for example, the following passage from E. B. White's *Here is New York,* in which he discusses New Yorkers and their city.

Division into categories occurs in the opening sentence.
There are roughly three New Yorks. There is, first, the New York of the man or woman who was born here, who takes the city for granted and accepts its size and its turbulence as natural and inevitable. Second, there is the

New York of the commuter — the city that is devoured by locusts each day and spat out each night. Third, there is the New York of the person who was born somewhere else and came to New York in quest of something. Of these three trembling cities the greatest is the last — the city of final destination, the city that is a goal. It is this third city that accounts for New York's highstrung disposition, its poetical deportment, its dedication to the arts, and its incomparable achievements. Commuters give the city its tidal restlessness; natives give it solidarity and continuity; but the settlers give it passion. And whether it is a farmer arriving from Italy to set up a small grocery store in a slum, or a young girl arriving from a small town in Mississippi to escape the indignity of being observed by her neighbors, or a boy arriving from the Corn Belt with a manuscript in his suitcase and a pain in his heart, it makes no difference: each embraces New York with the intense excitement of first love, each absorbs New York with the fresh eyes of an adventurer, each generates heat and light to dwarf the Consolidated Edison Company.

Author explains the nature of people in each category.

In his opening sentences, White suggests a principle for dividing the population of New York, establishing his three categories on the basis of a person's relationship to the city. There is the New York of the native, the New York of the commuter, and the New York of the immigrant. White's divisions help him make a point about the character of New York City, depicting its restlessness, its solidarity, and its passion.

In contrast to breaking a large idea into parts, classification can be used to draw connections between disparate elements based on a common category — price, for example. Often, classification is used in conjunction with another rhetorical strategy, such as comparison and contrast. Consider, for example, how in the following passage from Toni Cade Bambara's "The Lesson" she classifies a toy in F.A.O. Schwarz and other items in the thirty-five-dollar category to compare the relative value of things in the life of two girls, Sylvia and Sugar.

Me and Sugar at the back of the train watchin the tracks whizzin by large then small then getting gobbled up in the dark. I'm thinkin about this tricky toy I saw in the store. A clown that somersaults on a bar then does chin-ups just cause you yank lightly at his leg. Cost $35. I could see me askin my mother for a $35 birthday clown. "You wanna who that costs what?" she'd say, cocking her head to the side to get a better view of the hole in my head. Thirty-five dollars could buy new bunk beds for Junior and Gretchen's boy. Thirty-five dollars and the whole household could go visit Grand-daddy Nelson in the country. Thirty-five dollars

Classification used along with comparison and contrast

would pay for the rent and the piano bill, too. Who are these people that spend that much for performing clowns and $1000 for toy sailboats? What kinda work they do and how they live and how come we ain't in on it?

Another example may help clarify how division and classification work hand in hand. Suppose a sociologist wants to determine whether the socioeconomic status of the people in a particular neighborhood has any influence on their voting behavior. Having decided on her purpose, the sociologist chooses as her subject the fifteen families living on Maple Street. Her goal then becomes to group these families in a way that will be relevant to her purpose: (1) according to socioeconomic status (low-income earners, middle-income earners, and high-income earners) and (2) according to voting behavior (voters and nonvoters).

In confidential interviews with each family, the sociologist begins to classify each family according to her established categories. Her work leads her to construct the following diagram, which allows her to visualize her division and classification system and its essential components: the subject, her bases or principles of division, the subclasses or categories that derive from these principles, and her conclusion.

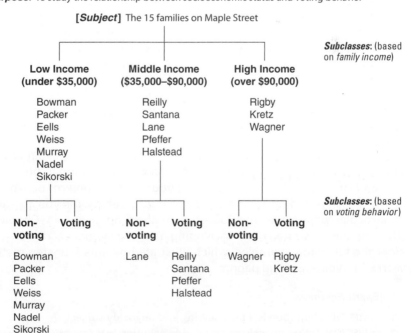

Purpose: To study the relationship between socioeconomic status and voting behavior

[Subject] The 15 families on Maple Street

			Subclasses: (based on *family income*)
Low Income (under $35,000)	**Middle Income ($35,000–$90,000)**	**High Income (over $90,000)**	
Bowman	Reilly	Rigby	
Packer	Santana	Kretz	
Eells	Lane	Wagner	
Weiss	Pfeffer		
Murray	Halstead		
Nadel			
Sikorski			

Subclasses: (based on *voting behavior*)

Non-voting	**Voting**	**Non-voting**	**Voting**	**Non-voting**	**Voting**
Bowman		Lane	Reilly	Wagner	Rigby
Packer			Santana		Kretz
Eells			Pfeffer		
Weiss			Halstead		
Murray					
Nadel					
Sikorski					

Conclusion: On Maple Street there seems to be a relationship between socioeconomic status and voting behavior: The low-income families are nonvoters.

Using Division and Classification As a Writing Strategy

As the work of the Maple Street sociologist shows, division and classification are used primarily to demonstrate a particular point about the subject under discussion. In a paper about the emphasis a television network places on reaching various audiences, you could begin by dividing prime-time programming into suitable subclasses: shows primarily for adults, shows for families, shows for children, and so forth. You could then classify each of that network's programs into one of these categories, analyze this data, and draw your conclusions about which audiences the network tries hardest to reach.

Another purpose of division and classification is to help writers and readers make choices. A voter may classify politicians on the basis of their attitudes toward nuclear energy or abortion; *Consumer Reports* classifies laptop computers on the basis of available memory, screen size, processor speed, repair record, and warranty; high school seniors classify colleges and universities on the basis of prestige, geographic location, programs available, and tuition fees. In such cases, division and classification have an absolutely practical end: making a decision about whom to vote for, which laptop to buy, and where to apply for admission to college.

Finally, writers use division and classification as a basic organizational strategy, one that brings a sense of order to a large amorphous whole. As you'll see later in this chapter, for example, Rosalind Wiseman's system of classification in "The Queen Bee and Her Court" establishes seven categories of roles played by young girls in school cliques to help us better understand how those cliques function.

Using Division and Classification across the Disciplines

When writing essays in the academic disciplines, you will have many opportunities to use the strategy of division and classification to both organize and strengthen the presentation of your ideas. To determine whether or not division and classification is the right strategy for you to use in a particular paper, use the four-step method described in Chapter 2 (Determining a Strategy for Developing Your Essay, pages 25–26). Consider the following examples, which illustrate how this four-step method works for typical college papers:

Earth Sciences

1. MAIN IDEA: Pollution is a far-reaching and unwieldy subject.
2. QUESTION: On what basis can we divide pollution into its various categories and what examples of pollution can we place into each category?

3. STRATEGY: Division and Classification. This strategy involves two activities: dividing into categories and placing items in their appropriate categories. The word *divide* signals the need to separate pollution into manageable groupings. The word *examples* and the phrase *place into each category* signal the need to classify types of pollution into appropriate categories.
4. SUPPORTING STRATEGY: Argumentation is often used to support both the rationale for categorization and classification itself.

Education

1. MAIN IDEA: Children's learning disabilities fall into three major groups.
2. QUESTION: What are the major types of learning disabilities into which children fall?
3. STRATEGY: Division and Classification. The words *major types* suggest the need to divide learning problems into major categories. The words *fall into* suggest that every learning disability can be classified into one of the three categories.
4. SUPPORTING STRATEGY: Argumentation could be used to persuade readers that the categories of problems discussed are major and to persuade them that a knowledge of these three major types of problems can be useful to teachers and parents in helping a child.

Political Science

1. MAIN IDEA: There are four types of U.S. presidents.
2. QUESTION: On what basis or bases do we group U.S. presidents?
3. STRATEGY: Division and Classification. The words *basis* or *bases* signals the need to establish criteria for dividing all our presidents. The word *group* suggests the need to classify the presidents according to the established groupings.
4. SUPPORTING STRATEGY: Illustration can be used to provide examples of various presidents.

Sample Student Essay Using Division and Classification As a Writing Strategy

Gerald Cleary studied mathematics as an undergraduate and later attended law school at Cornell University. He spent his last two years of high school in West Germany as a military dependent. During that time, Cleary sold stereo equipment at a large outlet. In this well-unified essay, Cleary has fun dividing and classifying the different types of customers he dealt with in his job.

How Loud? How Good? How Much? How Pretty?

Gerald Cleary

Thesis: Division
of stereo
buyers into four
categories

During my year as a stereo sales associate, 1
I waited on hundreds of customers, and it didn't
take long for me to learn that people buy stereos for
different reasons. Eventually, though, I was able to
divide all the stereo buyers into four basic categories:
the looks buyer, the wattage buyer, the price buyer,
and the quality buyer.

Organization:
Buyer who is
least appealing
to salesperson
is discussed.

The looks buyer cannot be bothered with the 2
question of how the stereo will sound. This buyer's
only concern is how the stereo looks, making him
or her least respected by the stereo salesperson. The
looks buyer has an irresistible attraction to flashing
lights, knobs, switches, and frivolous features.
Even the loudspeakers are chosen on the basis of
appearance—the looks buyer always removes the
grille to make sure a couple of knobs are present.

Illustration:
Typical
statement used
as example

Enjoyment for him is watching the output meters
flash or playing with the system's remote control. No
matter what the component, the looks buyer always
decides on the flashiest, exclaiming, "Wait 'til my
friends see this!"

Organization:
Second, more
appealing, buyer
is discussed.

Slightly more respected is the wattage buyer, 3
who is most easily identified by his trademark
question: "How many watts does it put out?" This
buyer will not settle for less than 100 watts from the
amp, and the speakers must be able to handle all this
power. The wattage buyer always turns the stereo up
loud—so loud that most would find it painful. This
buyer genuinely enjoys music—usually either rap
or heavy metal—at this volume and is proud of his
stereo's ability to put out deafening noise. As a result,
the wattage buyer usually becomes as well-known
to the neighbors as to the salesperson. The wattage

Illustration:
Typical
statement used
as example

buyer's competitive nature emerges as he pays for
his new system and says something along the lines
of, "Man, this is gonna blow Jones's stereo away!"

Organization:
Third, still more
appealing, buyer
is discussed.

In our money-conscious world, the price
buyer has the understanding, if not the respect, of

the salesperson. Often, this buyer is ashamed of his or her budget limitations and will try to masquerade as one of the other types of buyers, asking, "What's the loudest amp I can buy for $200?" Or, "What's the best CD player for under $300?" It is always obvious that price is this buyer's greatest worry—not getting the "loudest" or the "best" equipment. The price buyer can be spotted looking over the sale items or staring open-mouthed at the price tag of an expensive unit. After asking the salesperson where the best deal in the store can be found, this buyer cringes at the standard reply: "You usually get what you pay for." But the price buyer still picks the cheapest model, telling friends, "You won't believe the deal I got on this!"

4

Illustration: Typical statement used as example

Only one category remains: the quality buyer. This is the buyer most respected by the salesperson, although he or she is often not even in the store to buy and may simply want to listen to the new CD player tested in the latest reviews. The quality buyer never buys on impulse; he or she has already researched and read about most of the equipment in the store. The quality buyer is not always able to buy the best, however; he or she can often be seen fingering the price tag of a well-engineered but unaffordable noise-reduction unit or state-of-the-art set of headphones. This buyer never considers a cheaper model, preferring to save for the high standard of quality he demands. The quality buyer shuns salespeople, believing (often correctly) that their advice and information are unnecessary. Asking this buyer "May I help you?" is the greatest insult of all.

5

Organization: Fourth, and most appealing, buyer is discussed.

Recognizing the kinds of buyer I was dealing with helped me steer them to the right corner of the store. I took looks buyers to the visually dazzling working displays, and wattage buyers into the soundproof speaker rooms. I directed price buyers to the sale items and left quality buyers alone. By the end of the year, I was able to identify every buyer by type almost instantly. My expertise paid off, making me the most successful and efficient sales associate in the store.

6

Conclusion: How classifying buyers helped the author do his job

Analyzing Gerald Cleary's Division and Classification Essay: Questions for Discussion

1. What categories does Cleary use to classify his subject? Brainstorm about other categories of stereo shoppers that might exist. Could these alternate categories be used to make a similar point?

2. How did Cleary organize the categories in his essay? Is his organization effective, or could he have chosen a better way?

3. What other strategies might Cleary have used to strengthen his essay? Be specific about the benefits of each strategy.

Suggestions for Using Division and Classification As a Writing Strategy

As you plan, write, and revise your division and classification essay, be mindful of the writing process guidelines described in Chapter 2. Pay particular attention to the basic requirements and essential ingredients of this writing strategy.

■ Planning Your Division and Classification Essay

Planning is an essential part of writing a good division and classification essay. You can save yourself a great deal of trouble by taking the time to think about the key building blocks of your essay before you actually begin to write.

Determine Your Purpose, and Focus on It. The principle you use to divide your subject into categories depends on your larger purpose. It is crucial, then, that you determine a clear purpose for your division and classification before you begin to examine your subject in detail. For example, in studying the student body at your school, you might have any number of purposes, such as discovering how much time your classmates spend in the library during the week, explaining how financial aid is distributed, discussing the most popular movies or music on campus, or describeing styles of dorm-room decor. The categories into which you divide the student body will vary according to your purpose.

Let's say, for example, that you are in charge of writing an editorial for your school newspaper that will make people aware of how they might reduce the amount of trash going to the landfill. Having established your purpose, your next task might be to identify the different ways objects could be handled to avoid sending them to the landfill. For instance, you might decide that there are four basic ways to prevent things from ending up in the trash. Then, you could establish a sequence or order of importance in which they should be addressed. Your first draft might start something like the following:

Over the course of the last semester, more trash was removed from our campus than in any semester in history. But was it all trash that had to go to the landfill? For example, many of us love to wear fleece vests, but did you know that they are made from recycled plastic bottles? Much of what is considered trash need not go to the landfill at all. There are four ways we can prevent trash from being sent to the landfill. I call them the four R's. First, we can all reduce the amount of individually packaged goods that we send to the landfill by buying frequently used items in family-size or bulk containers. Next, we can reuse those containers, as well as other items, either for their original purpose or for another. Be creative. After a while, though, things will wear out after repeated use. Then it's a good time to try to restore them. If that, too, can no longer be done, then they should be recycled. Only after these options have failed should items be considered "real" trash and be removed to the landfill. Using the four R's—Reduce, Reuse, Restore, Recycle—we can reduce the amount of trash our campus sends to the landfill every semester.

This introduction clearly expresses the purpose of the editorial: to change readers' behavior regarding the amount of "trash" they throw out.

As this example shows, classification and division can be used to persuade readers toward or away from certain types of actions. As we will see in the essay "The Ways of Meeting Oppression" later in this chapter, Martin Luther King Jr., by identifying three categories of protest, is able to cite historical precedents to argue against violent forms of protest and in favor of nonviolent ones. (Argumentation, one of the most powerful rhetorical modes, will be explained in detail in Chapter 12.)

Formulate a Thesis Statement. When writing a division and classification essay, be sure that your thesis statement clearly presents the categories that you will be using to make your point. Here are two examples from this chapter.

- "Eventually, though, I was able to divide all the stereo buyers into four basic categories: the looks buyer, the wattage buyer, the price buyer, and the quality buyer." This thesis statement, from the annotated student essay by Gerald Cleary, presents the subject — stereo buyers — and the four different categories into which they fall.

- "Because girls' social hierarchies are complicated and overwhelming in their detail, I'm going to take you through a general breakdown of the different positions in the clique." This thesis statement is from Rosalind Wiseman's "The Queen Bee and Her Court" later in this chapter. From this opening statement, the reader knows exactly what Wiseman intends to discuss and how.

When you begin to formulate your thesis statement, keep these examples in mind. You could also look for other examples of thesis statements in the essays throughout this book. As you begin to develop your thesis statement, ask yourself the following questions: "What is my point?," "What categories will be most useful in making my point?" If you can't answer these questions, write some ideas down, and try to determine your main point from these ideas.

Once you have settled on an idea, go back to the two questions above, and write down your answers to them. Then combine the answers into a single thesis statement. (Your thesis statement does not necessarily have to be one sentence; making it one sentence, though, can be an effective way of focusing both your point and your categories.)

■ Organizing and Writing Your Division and Classification Essay

Establish Valid Categories. When establishing categories, make sure that they meet three criteria:

- *The categories must be appropriate to your purpose.* In determining the factors affecting financial aid distribution among students at a particular school, you might consider family income, academic major, and athletic participation, but obviously you would not consider style of dress or preferred brand of toothpaste.

- *The categories must be consistent and mutually exclusive.* For example, dividing the student body into the classes of men, women, and athletes would be illogical because athletes can be either male or female. Instead, you could divide the student body into male athletes, female athletes, male nonathletes, and female nonathletes.

- *The categories must be complete, and they must account for all the members or aspects of your subject.* In dividing the student body according to place of birth, it would be inaccurate to consider only states in the United States; such a division would not account for foreign students or citizens born outside the country.

You may often find that a diagram (such as the one of families on Maple Street, shown on page 335), a chart, or a table can help you visualize your organization and help you make sure that your categories are appropriate, mutually exclusive, and complete.

Division and classification essays, when sensibly planned, can generally be organized with little trouble; the essay's chief divisions will reflect the classes into which you have divided the subject. A scratch outline can help you see those divisions and plan your presentation. For example, here is an outline of student Gerald Cleary's essay "How Loud? How Good? How Much? How Pretty?"

Four Types of Stereo Shoppers

1. The Looks Buyer
   a. Least respected by salespeople
   b. Appearance of stereo paramount

2. The Wattage Buyer
   a. More respected
   b. Volume level capability paramount

3. The Price Buyer
   a. Not respected but understood
   b. Cost concerns paramount

4. The Quality Buyer
   a. Most respected
   b. Quality and sound reproduction paramount

Such an outline clearly reveals the essay's overall structure.

State Your Conclusion.   Your essay's purpose will determine the kinds of conclusions you reach. For example, a study of the student body of your college might show that 35 percent of male athletes are receiving scholarships, compared with 20 percent of female athletes, 15 percent of male nonathletes, and 10 percent of female nonathletes. These facts could provide a conclusion in themselves, or they might be the basis for a more controversial assertion about your school's athletic program. A study of dorm-room decor might conclude with the observation that juniors and seniors tend to have more elaborate rooms than first-year students. Your conclusion will depend on the way you work back and forth between the various classes you establish and the individual items available for you to classify.

■ Revising and Editing Your Division and Classification Essay

Listen to What Your Classmates Have to Say.   The importance of student peer conferences cannot be stressed enough, particularly as you revise and edit your essay. Often, others in your class will immediately see problems that you can't see yourself because you are too close to your essay: For example, they might see that the basis for your classification needs adjustment, that there are inconsistencies in your categories, that you need more and better transitions to link the discussions of your categories, or that you may need more examples. So take advantage of suggestions where you judge them to be valid, and make revisions accordingly. For questions on peer conferences, see page 29.

Question Your Own Work While Revising and Editing.   Revision is best done by asking yourself key questions about what you have written. Begin by reading, preferably aloud, what you have written. Reading aloud forces you to pay attention to every single word, and you are more likely to catch lapses in the logical flow of thought. After you have read your paper through, answer the following questions for revising and editing and make the necessary changes.

For help with twelve common writing problems, see Chapter 16, "Editing for Grammar, Punctuation, and Sentence Style."

Questions for Revising and Editing: Division and Classification

1. Is my subject a coherent entity that readily lends itself to analysis by division and classification?

2. Does the manner in which I divide my subject into categories help me achieve my purpose in writing the essay?

3. Does my thesis statement clearly identify the number and type of categories I will be using in my essay?

4. Do I stay focused on my subject and stay within the limits of my categories throughout my essay?

5. Do my categories meet the following three criteria: Are they appropriate to my purpose, consistent and mutually exclusive, and complete?

6. Have I organized my essay in a way that makes it easy for the reader to understand my categories and how they relate to my purpose?

7. Are there other rhetorical strategies that I can use to help me achieve my purpose?

8. Is my use of headings and subheadings consistent? Could I use headings and subheadings to clarify the organization of my essay?

9. Does my paper contain any errors in grammar, punctuation, or mechanics? Is my sentence style as clear, smooth, and persuasive as possible?

The Queen Bee and Her Court

ROSALIND WISEMAN

Rosalind Wiseman was born in 1969 in Philadelphia, Pennsylvania. She received her B.A. in political science from Occidental College in Los Angeles, California, in 1988. Wiseman is the cofounder and president of the Empower Program, a nonprofit organization certified through the Program for Young Negotiators at Harvard University, whose mission is "to work with youth to end the culture of violence." Wiseman's articles have appeared in *Principal Leadership* magazine, *Educational Digest*, and *New York Newsday*, and she has spoken extensively in the media about young people and violence. Her books include *Defending Ourselves: A Guide to Prevention, Self-Defense, and Recovery from Rape* (1995); *Queen Bees and Wannabees: Helping Your Daughter Survive Cliques, Gossip, Boyfriends, and Other Realities of Adolescence* (2002), on which the film *Mean Girls* (2004) is based; and *Queen Bee Moms and Kingpin Dads* (2007), a book about the social pecking orders of parents.

In "The Queen Bee and Her Court," an excerpt from *Queen Bees and Wannabees,* Wiseman divides and classifies young schoolgirls into various hierarchical social classes dominated by the "Queen Bee."

■ Preparing to Read

How did the various cliques work in your elementary school and high school? What roles did you play within those cliques? Did the existence of cliques bother you, or did you regard them as merely a reflection of society as a whole?

We need to give girls credit for the sophistication of their social struc-   1 tures. Our best politicians and diplomats couldn't do better than a teen girl does in understanding the social intrigue and political landscape that lead to power. Cliques are sophisticated, complex, and multilayered, and every girl has a role within them. However, positions in cliques aren't static. Especially from the sixth to eighth grade, a girl can lose her position to another girl, and she can move up and down the social totem pole. Also, your daughter doesn't have to be in the "popular" group to have these roles within her group of friends. Because girls' social hierarchies are complicated and overwhelming in their detail, I'm going to take you through a general breakdown of the different positions in the clique. However, when you talk

> Our best politicians and diplomats couldn't do better than a teen girl does in understanding the social intrigue and political landscape that lead to power.

to your daughter about cliques, encourage her to come up with her own names and create roles she thinks I've missed. If you can answer yes to the majority of items for each role, you've identified your daughter. So, here are the different roles that your daughter and her friends might play:

Queen Bee

Sidekick

Banker

Floater

Torn Bystander

Pleaser/Wannabe/Messenger

Target

The Queen Bee

For the girl whose popularity is based on fear and control, think of a combination of the Queen of Hearts in *Alice in Wonderland* and Barbie. I call her the Queen Bee. Through a combination of charisma, force, money, looks, will, and manipulation, this girl reigns supreme over the other girls and weakens their friendships with others, thereby strengthening her own power and influence. Indeed, she appears omnipotent. Never underestimate her power over other girls (and boys as well). She can and will silence her peers with a look. If your daughter's the Queen Bee and you could spy on her, you would (or should) be mortified by how she treats other girls.   2

Your Daughter Is a Queen Bee If . . .

- Her friends do what she wants to do.   3

- She isn't intimidated by any other girl in her class.

- Her complaints about other girls are limited to the lame things they did or said.

- When she's young, you have to convince her to invite everyone to her birthday party. When she does invite everyone you want, she ignores and excludes some of her guests. (When she's older, you lose your privilege to tell her who she can invite.)

- She can persuade her peers to do just about anything she wants.

- She can argue anyone down, including friends, peers, teachers, and parents.

- She's charming to adults, a female Eddie Haskell.

- She can make another girl feel "anointed" by declaring her a special friend.

- She's affectionate, but often that affection is deployed to demonstrate her rejection of another girl. For example, she sees two girls in her group, one she's pleased with and one she isn't. When she sees them, she'll throw her arms around one and insist that they sit together and barely say anything to the other.

- She won't (or is very reluctant to) take responsibility when she hurts someone's feelings.

- If she thinks she's been wronged she feels she has the right to seek revenge. She has an eye-for-an-eye worldview.

4   She thinks she's better than everyone else. She's in control, intimidating, smart, caring, and has the power to make others feel good or bad. She'll make stuff up about people and everyone will believe her.

— ANNE, 15

5   Who was the Queen Bee in your junior and/or high school? (If you were the Queen Bee, it's okay to admit it.) Remember how much power she had? Keep in mind that Queen Bees are good at slipping under adults' radar (including parents, teachers, and myself). Some of the nicest girls in my classes, who speak the most eloquently about how terrible they feel when girls are mean to each other, turn out to be the most cruel.

6   We're like an army.

— AMANDA, 13

7   Most Queen Bees aren't willing to recognize the cruelty of their actions. They believe their behavior is justified because of something done to them first. Justifications usually begin with, "For no reason, this girl got really upset about not being in the group. I mean we told her nicely and she just wasn't getting the hint. We tried to be nice but she just wasn't listening." When a Queen Bee does this, she's completely bypassing what she did and defining right and wrong by whether the individual was loyal (i.e., not challenging her authority).

8   If that sinking feeling in your stomach is because you just realized your daughter is a Queen Bee, congratulate yourself. Honesty is the first step to parenting an adolescent successfully.

What Does She Gain by Being a Queen Bee?

9   She feels power and control over her environment. She's the center of attention and people pay homage to her.

What Does She Lose by Being a Queen Bee?

A real sense of self. She's so busy maintaining her image that she loses herself   10
in the process. She can be incredibly cynical about her friendships with both
boys and girls ("They're only sucking up to me because I'm popular; they
don't really like me."). She's vulnerable to having intimate relationships where
she believes her image is dependent on the relationship. She may easily feel
that she can't admit to anyone when she's in over her head because her reputation dictates that she always has everything and everyone in control.

The Sidekick

She's the lieutenant or second in command, the girl who's closest to the Queen   11
Bee and will back her no matter what because her power depends on the confidence she gets from the Queen Bee. All girls in a clique tend to dress similarly,
but the Sidekick wears the most identical clothes and shares the mannerisms
and overall style closest to the Queen Bee. Together they appear to other girls as
an impenetrable force. They commonly bully and silence other girls to forward
their own agenda. These girls are usually the first to focus on boys and are often
attracted to older boys. This is particularly true in seventh and eighth grade (and
their behavior is even worse if they're physically mature and going to high school
parties). The difference between the two is if you separate the Sidekick from the
Queen Bee, the Sidekick can alter her behavior for the better, while the Queen
Bee would be more likely to find another Sidekick and begin again.

Your Daughter Is a Sidekick If . . .

- She has a best friend (the Queen Bee) who tells her what to do, think,   12
  dress, etc.

- The best friend is your daughter's authority figure, not you.

- She feels like it's the two of them and everyone else is a Wannabe.

- You think her best friend pushes her around.

> She notices everything about the Queen Bee. She will do   13
> everything the Queen Bee says and wants to be her. She lies for the
> Queen Bee but she isn't as pretty as the Queen Bee.
> —Madeline, 14

What Does She Gain by Being a Sidekick?

Power over other girls that she wouldn't have without the Queen Bee. She also   14
gains a close friend (whom you may not like) who makes her feel popular and
included.

What Does She Lose by Being a Sidekick?

The right to express her personal opinions. If she sticks around the Queen   15
Bee too long, she may forget she even has her own opinion.

The Banker

Information about each other is currency in Girl World. The Banker cre-   16
ates chaos everywhere she goes by banking information about girls in her
social sphere and dispensing it at strategic intervals for her own benefit. For
instance, if a girl has said something negative about another girl, the Banker
will casually mention it to someone in conversation because she knows it's
going to cause a conflict and strengthen her status as someone "in the know."
She can get girls to trust her because when she pumps them for information
it doesn't seem like gossip; instead, she does it in an innocent, I'm-trying-to-
be-your-friend way.

> Her power lies in getting girls to confide in her. Once they   17
> figure out she can't be trusted, it's too late because she already
> has information on them, and in order to keep her from revealing
> things, girls will be nice to her.
>
> —LEIGH, 17

The Banker is almost as powerful as the Queen Bee, but it's easy to mistake   18
her for the Messenger. She's usually quiet and withdrawn in front of adults
and can be physically immature in comparison to her friends. This is the girl
who sneaks under adult radar all the time because she seems so cute and
harmless.

Your Daughter Is a Banker If . . .

- She is extremely secretive.   19

- She thinks in complex, strategic ways.

- She seems to be friends with everyone; some girls even treat her like
  a pet.

- She's rarely the subject of fights.

- She's rarely excluded from the group.

What Does She Gain by Being a Banker?

Power and security. The Banker is very confusing to other girls because she   20
seems harmless and yet everyone is afraid of her.

What Does She Lose by Being a Banker?

Once other girls figure out what she's doing, they don't trust her. With her utilitarian mind-set, she can forget to look to other girls as a trusted resource. 21

> The girls can't oust the Banker from the clique because she 22
> has information on everyone and could make or break reputations
> based on the information she knows.
> — CHARLOTTE, 15

The Floater

You can usually spot this girl because she doesn't associate with only one 23
clique. She has friends in different groups and can move freely among them.
She usually has protective characteristics that shield her from other girls'
cruelty — for example, she's beautiful but not too beautiful, nice, not terribly sophisticated, and avoids conflicts. She's more likely to have higher self-esteem because she doesn't base her self-worth on how well she's accepted by one group. Because she has influence over other girls but doesn't use it to make them feel bad, I call her the Floater. Girls want to be the Floater because she has confidence, people genuinely like her, and she's nice to everyone. She has the respect of other girls because she doesn't rule by meanness. When backed into a corner, the Floater is one of the few girls who will actually stand up to the Queen Bee. While Floaters have some power, they don't have the same influence and impact as Queen Bees. Why? Because Floaters don't gain anything by sowing seeds of discontent and insecurity among the other girls; Queen Bees do.

> I have always felt that many potential Floaters are either swal- 24
> lowed up by the popular crowd or choose not to identify with popu-
> lar people at all and instead create their own groups. In every girl
> there is a Floater who wants to get out.
> — JOANNA, 17

> I don't think there are *real* Floaters. Maybe I'm just bitter, but 25
> most of the time they are too good to be true.
> — LIZA, 17

Your Daughter Is a Floater If . . .

- She doesn't want to exclude people; you aren't always having fights with her about spending time with people she considers "losers." 26

- Her friends are comfortable around her and don't seem intimidated; she's not "winning" all the conversations.

- She's not exclusively tied to one group of friends; she may have a jock group she hangs with, then the kids in the band, then her friends in the neighborhood.

- She can bring another person into a group on her own with some success.

What Does She Gain by Being a Floater?

Her peers like her for who she is as a person. She'll be less likely to sacrifice herself to gain and keep social status. 27

What Does She Lose by Being a Floater?

Nothing! Count yourself truly blessed that she's your daughter. 28

If you're thinking this is your daughter, wait. It isn't that I don't believe you, but please read all the roles before making your final decision. We all want to believe the best about the people we love, but sometimes our love blinds us to reality. I've met countless parents who truly believe their daughters are Floaters, and they're not. It should go without saying that just because your daughter isn't a Floater doesn't mean she won't become an amazing young woman and/or that you haven't done a good job raising her. But if you insist on seeing her in a way that she isn't, you won't be able to be as good a parent as she needs you to be. 29

The Torn Bystander

She's constantly conflicted between doing the right thing and her allegiance to the clique. As a result, she's the one most likely to be caught in the middle of a conflict between two girls or two groups of girls. She'll often rationalize or apologize for the Queen Bee and Sidekick's behavior, but she knows it's wrong. She often feels more uncomfortable around boys, but can be very easily influenced by the clique to do what it wants (for example, getting together with a boy they decide is right for her). The status she gets from the group is very important, and the thought of standing up to the more powerful girls in the clique is terrifying. She's honest enough with herself (and maybe with you as well) to know that she doesn't like what the Queen Bee does but feels powerless to stop it. 30

Your Daughter Is a Torn Bystander If . . .

- She's always finding herself in situations where she has to choose between friends. 31

- She tries to accommodate everyone.

- She's not good at saying no to her friends.

- She wants everyone "to get along."

- She can't imagine standing up to anyone she has a conflict with; she goes along to get along.

> She's confused and insecure because her reputation is over if   32
> she doesn't stick with the Queen Bee, but she can be really cool
> when she's alone.
>
> —ANNE, 13

What Does She Gain by Being a Torn Bystander?

By associating herself with more powerful girls, she has access to popularity,   33
high social status, and boys.

What Does She Lose by Being a Torn Bystander?

She has to sacrifice a great deal. She may not try new things or she may stop   34
doing things she's interested in (plays, band, "geeky" clubs, etc.) because her
friends make fun of her. She may dumb herself down to get along with others. This doesn't mean her grades will suffer, although they could. Lots of girls
hide their academic accomplishments from their peers for this reason. ("I
know I totally failed that test.") It more likely means that she presents herself
as less intelligent than she is. This is merely irritating when she's a teen, but
literally stupid when she's an adult in a job interview.

The Pleaser/Wannabe/Messenger

Almost all girls are pleasers and wannabes; some are just more obvious than   35
others. This is one of the more fascinating roles. She can be in the clique or on
the perimeter trying to get in. She will do anything to be in the good graces
of the Queen Bee and the Sidekick. She'll enthusiastically back them up no
matter what. She'll mimic their clothes, style, and anything else she thinks
will increase her position in the group. She's a careful observer, especially of
the girls in power. She's motivated above all else to please the person who's
standing above her on the social totem pole. She can easily get herself into
messy conflicts with other people because she'll change her mind depending
on who she's interacting with.

As a Pleaser/Wannabe/Messenger her security in the clique is pre-   36
carious and depends on her doing the Queen Bee's "dirty work," such as
spreading gossip about a Target. While the Banker gathers information to
further her own causes, the Pleaser/Wannabe/Messenger does it to service
the Queen Bee and get in her good graces and feel important. But she can
easily be dropped and ridiculed if she's seen as trying too hard to fit in. (One
of the worst accusations you can make of a teen is to say she's trying too

hard. In Girl World, all actions must appear effortless.) The Queen Bee and Sidekick enjoy the convenience of making her their servant, but they love talking behind her back. ("Can you believe what a suck-up she is? That's so pathetic.")

When there's a fight between two girls or two groups of girls, she often 37 serves as a go-between. Her status immediately rises when she's in active duty as a Messenger. It's also the most powerful position she can attain, which means she has a self-interest in creating and maintaining conflicts between girls so she doesn't get laid off.

Your Daughter Is a Pleaser/Wannabe/ Messenger If . . .

- Other girls' opinions and wants are more important than her own. 38

- Her opinions on dress, style, friends, and "in" celebrities constantly change.

- She can't tell the difference between what she wants and what the group wants.

- She's desperate to have the "right" look (clothes, hair, etc.).

- She'll stop doing things she likes because she fears the clique's disapproval.

- She's always in the middle of a conflict.

- She feels better about herself when the other girls are coming to her for help, advice, or when she's doing their dirty work.

- She loves to gossip — the phone and e-mail are her lifeline.

What Does She Gain by Being a Pleaser?

The feeling that she belongs; she's in the middle of the action and has power 39 over girls.

What Does She Lose by Being a Pleaser?

Personal authenticity — she hasn't figured out who she is or what she values. 40 She's constantly anticipating what people want from her and doesn't ask herself what she wants in return. She feels insecure about her friendships — do girls really like her, or do they only value her for the gossip she trades in? She has trouble developing personal boundaries and the ability to communicate them to others.

She's insecure and you can't trust her. 41

— CARRIE, 14

The Target

She's the victim, set up by the other girls to be humiliated, made fun of, 42
excluded. Targets are assumed to be out of the clique, one of the class "losers." While this is sometimes true, it's not always the case. Just because a girl is
in the clique doesn't mean she can't be targeted by the other members. Often
the social hierarchy of the clique is maintained precisely by having someone
clearly at the bottom of the group's totem pole. Girls outside the clique tend
to become Targets because they've challenged the clique or because their
style of dress, behavior, and such are outside the norms acceptable to the
clique. Girls inside the clique tend to become Targets if they've challenged
someone higher on the social totem pole (i.e., the Queen Bee, Sidekick, or
Banker) and need to be taken down a peg.

Your Daughter Is a Target If . . .

- She feels helpless to stop the girls' behavior. 43

- She feels she has no allies. No one will back her up.

- She feels isolated.

- She can mask her hurt by rejecting people first, saying she doesn't like
  anyone.

This role can be harder to figure out than you would think, and your daugh- 44
ter may be too embarrassed to tell you. She might admit she feels excluded, or
she might just withdraw from you and "not want to talk about it."

> Targets don't want to tell their parents because they don't want 45
> their parents to think they're a loser or a nobody.
>
> — JENNIFER, 16

What Does She Gain by Being a Target?

This may seem like an odd question, but being a Target can have some hid- 46
den benefits. There's nothing like being targeted to teach your daughter about
empathy and understanding for people who are bullied and/or discriminated
against. Being a Target can also give her objectivity. She can see the costs of
fitting in and decide she's better off outside the clique because at least she can
be true to herself and/or find good friends who like her for who she is, not
for her social standing.

What Does She Lose by Being a Target?

She feels totally helpless in the face of other girls' cruelty. She feels ashamed 47
of being rejected by the other girls because of who she is. She'll be tempted
to change herself in order to fit in. She feels vulnerable and unable to affect

the outcome of her situation. She could become so anxious that she can't concentrate on schoolwork.

> I didn't understand why I was so unhappy in sixth grade. I couldn't have told my parents that girls were being mean to me.
>
> —ERIN, 17

48

> Girls will almost always withdraw instead of telling a parent.
>
> —CLAIRE, 14

49

> If a girl's stuck in a degrading clique, it's the same as when she's later in a bad relationship. She doesn't expect to be treated any better.
>
> —ELLEN, 15

50

OK, now you know the different roles girls play in cliques. The next questions are: How were these roles created in the first place? Who and what determine these positions and power plays? Why are girls able to get away with treating each other so badly?

51

It isn't really that big a secret. As girls become teens, the world becomes a much bigger, scarier place. Many girls go from a small elementary school to a much larger, more impersonal institutional school.

52

In elementary school, students are usually based in one room, with one teacher. The principal sees them on a daily basis and parents are often active in the school's activities, going on field trips, bringing food for bake sales, and volunteering in after-school programs. By the end of fifth or sixth grade, girls are beginning to prepare to leave this safe, comfy haven of elementary school. They alternatively look forward to and dread moving on to middle school or junior high.

53

Then comes the first day at the middle school or junior high — and everything changes. Adults, in our profound wisdom, place them in a setting where they're overwhelmed by the number of students, and they become nameless faces with ID security cards. If you ever want to remember what it feels like, go to your daughter's school and hang out in the hall when the bell rings right before a lunch period (you probably have lots of times to choose from since most schools have so many students that they need multiple lunch periods, which means some students eat their midday meal at ten A.M.). When the bell rings, walk from one end of the hall to the other. It's hard enough simply navigating through this noisy throng. Now imagine navigating the same hallway and caring what each person thinks of you as you walk by.

54

We put our girls in this strange new environment at exactly the same time that they're obsessively microanalyzing social cues, rules, and regulations and therefore are at their most insecure. Don't underestimate how difficult and frightening this is for girls, and give your daughter credit for getting out of bed in the morning.

55

■ Thinking Critically about the Text

How real for you is the social classification system that Wiseman establishes in this selection? If you are a woman, where would you place your younger self in the hierarchy? Were you a Queen Bee, a Banker, a Floater? If you are a young man, do you think a similar classification would work for boys as well? Explain.

■ Questions on Subject

1. What characteristics does the Queen Bee possess, according to Wiseman? Would you agree or disagree with her assessment of the girl at the top of the social totem pole? Would you add or subtract any characteristics? Explain.
2. Throughout her essay, Wiseman includes quoted passages in which young girls offer their own accounts of the characters. How effective do you find these passages? What do they add, if anything, to Wiseman's classification system?
3. For every character type Wiseman includes a formulaic set of questions: "What does she gain by being an X?" and "What does she lose by being an X?" Why do you suppose she uses that formula? (Glossary: *Cause and Effect Analysis*)
4. Wiseman states that each character in the hierarchy gains from her position — even the Target. Do you agree? Explain.
5. What explanation does Wiseman give for the development of cliques? (Glossary: *Cause and Effect Analysis*)

■ Questions on Strategy

1. What does Wiseman mean when she writes that "cliques are sophisticated, complex, and multilayered, and every girl has a role within them" (paragraph 1)? Is that statement her thesis? (Glossary: *Thesis*)
2. What does Wiseman hope to gain when she advises that "when you talk to your daughter about cliques, encourage her to come up with her own names and create roles she thinks I've missed" (paragraph 1)? Why is her advice a useful strategy, given her subject and audience? (Glossary: *Audience; Subject*)
3. Into what classes does Wiseman divide all young girls in her classification system?
4. Explain how Wiseman has organized her essay. (Glossary: *Organization*) Is that organizational pattern effective? Explain.
5. Wiseman's division and classification is supported by her use of definition, illustration, and comparison and contrast. (Glossary: *Comparison and Contrast; Definition; Illustration*) How do these supporting strategies strengthen Wiseman's essay?

■ Questions on Diction and Vocabulary

1. How effective is Wiseman's title? (Glossary: *Title*) How effective are the names she gives each class in her classification? Would you change any of those names? If so, why?
2. What is Wiseman's attitude toward cliques? (Glossary: *Attitude*) What in her diction indicates that attitude? (Glossary: *Diction*)
3. Refer to your desk dictionary to determine the meanings of the following words as Wiseman uses them in this selection: *clique* (paragraph 1), *omnipotent* (2), *mortified* (2), *anointed* (3), *cynical* (10), *agenda* (11), *utilitarian* (21), *oust* (22), *rationalize* (30), *perimeter* (35), *precarious* (36).

■ Classroom Activity Using Division and Classification

Think about how you might classify people in one of the following groups:

athletes

dieters

television viewers

sports fans

college students

Compare your method of classification with the method used by others in your class who chose the same category. What conclusions can you draw from the differences?

■ Writing Suggestions

1. Rosalind Wiseman offers her classification system for the roles that young girls play in cliques. Her system is based on interviews with young girls, their friends, their teachers, and their mothers. But girls are not the only ones who belong to cliques. What about boys' cliques? Write a classification essay in which you divide and classify schoolboys on the basis of their behavioral characteristics and the roles they play within cliques. Review Wiseman's organization. Model your organization on hers, modify her design, or create an entirely new approach.
2. What about parents? Can we classify them into some recognizable and meaningful classes and subclasses? Jim Faye of the Love and Logic Institute in Boulder, Colorado, thinks so. He classifies parents into three groups: the Consultant who "provides guidance," the Helicopter "who hovers over children and rescues them from the hostile world in which they live," and the Drill Sargeant "who commands and directs the lives of children." Think about your parents and talk to your friends, the students in your class, and others to gather opinions

about the various parenting approaches that people demonstrate. Use the information to write an essay in which you classify parents. Be sure to define each class clearly and provide examples of their members' behavior. (Glossary: *Definition; Illustration*)

3. The photograph below depicts a common scene of a group of girls sitting, talking, and passing the time together. How do you "read" this photograph? What might the girls' facial expressions, body language, hairstyles, and dress tell you about them as individuals? As members of the group? What does their configuration on the steps tell you about the girls as a group? About their roles in the group? Write an essay in which you analyze the photograph and theorize about this group of girls and the dynamics that may hold them together as well as separate them.

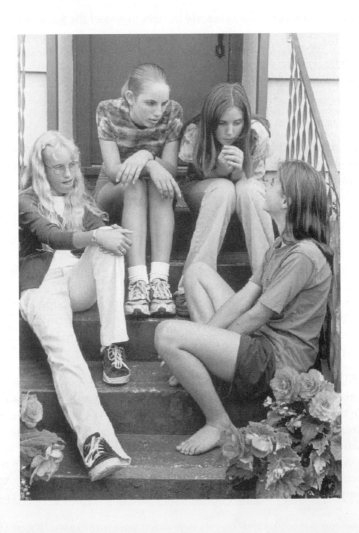

The Psychology of Persuasive Messaging

JIM KITCHENS

Jim Kitchens, founder of the Orlando-based public opinion research firm the Kitchens Group, is an attitude and mass persuasion specialist with a Ph.D. in political communication from the University of Florida. He received his degree at twenty-four and was a professor from 1975 to 1979, first at the University of Alabama and then at Texas Christian University. In 1979 Kitchens became an independent pollster and consultant and was hired in 1980 by U.S. House majority leader Jim Wright to study the propaganda techniques of right-leaning organizations, such as the Moral Majority, and to design a counterstrategy. Since then, Kitchens has served as a pollster and strategist for campaigns at all levels of American politics, advising more than forty members of the U.S. House of Representatives and executing national policy polls for the House Democratic Caucus.

Kitchens's knowledge of the American public derives from interviews with more than a million Americans on topics ranging from environmental concerns to attitudes about professional sports. He is an expert on land-conservation attitudes and has worked with the Nature Conservancy in more than thirty states; his work on referenda campaigns has resulted in more than one billion dollars earmarked for conservation throughout the country. Kitchens has also guest lectured at a number of universities and political conferences and has authored numerous articles for such publications as *Southern Speech Communication Journal*, *Kentucky Journal of Communication Arts*, *Communication Quarterly*, *Campaign & Elections*, and *Communication Research Reports*.

In the following essay, first published in the May 2006 issue of *Campaign & Elections*, Kitchens examines what he deems the four pillars of the collective American psyche, which need to be considered to ensure a successful mass-persuasion campaign.

■ Preparing to Read

Why do you think some political messages work and others fail? Is the problem the messenger, the delivery, failure to understand the intended audience, or some other problem?

There are some political messages that resonate with voters, while others fall on deaf ears. To understand why certain messages appeal to voters — and to develop effective political communication — one must first understand the

"Four Pillars of the American Psyche." These pillars, or attitudinal anchors, consist of four psychological states: fear, narcissism, consumerism, and religiosity.

An effective message should engage voters in several attitudinal anchors   2
simultaneously. Whether you're running a national or local campaign, whether you're developing direct mail pieces or television commercials, incorporating the four pillars into the messaging plan will result in persuasive, effective communication.

Fear

The first, and perhaps most dominant, pillar is fear. While president   3
Franklin D. Roosevelt famously stated, "We have nothing to fear but fear itself," the fact is Americans do possess a variety of fears.

Polls clearly indicate that Americans believe there will be another act of   4
extreme terrorism within the next year.

Hurricane Katrina still haunts the national conscience as well, even in   5
areas not typically affected by devastating hurricanes. In a recent survey of New England coastal residents conducted by my company, nearly 60 percent of respondents fear their region — the upper Northeast — will be desolated by a Katrina-like hurricane within the next 5 to 10 years.

In addition, economic fears consume Americans. We're terrified of los-   6
ing our jobs, we're scared that Social Security is going to fail retirees, we fear the results of a stock market crash.

Be it weather, terrorism, or the economy, fear drives American attitudes   7
and actions. It has dominated the rhetoric surrounding the Patriot Act — fear of the government knowing too much versus fear of the government not knowing enough. Supporters and opponents have incorporated this pillar into their key messages, resulting in passionate, persuasive arguments from both sides. Likewise, since 2001, Republicans have effectively integrated fear into their communication, affecting outcomes at the polls. The Bush campaign was victorious in 2004 partially because it portrayed John Kerry as soft on terrorism, implying he was the candidate most favored by terrorists.

Fear is one of the dominant components of the American psyche.   8
Campaign messages playing on this attitudinal anchor (for example, threat of destructive hurricanes, threat of illegal immigrants taking "our" jobs, or threat of preventing future terrorist attacks) will resonate with the American public.

Narcissism

How does the electorate decide who to vote for? Do people consider the   9
impact of politicians' economic and social beliefs on a macro level (the country or state) or a micro level (each individual situation)? Politics have transformed into an exercise in self-expression.

To understand this evolution, just compare John F. Kennedy's verbiage to   10
that of Ronald Reagan 20 years later. In Kennedy's 1961 inaugural address, he
said, "Ask not what your country can do for you — ask what you can do for
your country." Two decades later, Reagan illustrated the narcissism of politics
when he asked, "Are you better off than you were four years ago?" He didn't
ask voters about their towns, states, or country; instead, he asked about their
individual situations.

Narcissism encompasses extreme patriotism, self-involvement, and self-   11
importance. Campaign messages should come from this mindset, relating on
a micro level to the voters. National campaigns should incorporate messaging at a community level, while messages for grass-roots campaigns should
speak to voters on a personal level.

In 2005, senator Barack Obama spoke at the AFL-CIO national conven-   12
tion. His opening statement demonstrated a perfect understanding of the current narcissistic mindset: "We meet here at a challenging time for the labor
movement. And I can imagine that many of you are anxious not only about
labor's future, but yours. You're wondering 'Will I be able to leave my children
a better world than I was given? Will I be able to save enough to send them to
college or plan for a secure retirement? Will my job even be there tomorrow?'"

With just these few sentences, Obama conveyed his understanding of the   13
union members' personal challenges, their desire to provide for their children and concerns about personal job security.

Consumerism

Many Americans are consumers; we want big houses, luxury cars, trendy   14
clothes, and exotic vacations. From an economic standpoint, consumer spending strengthens the economy. Republicans have controlled this conversation
for the better part of the last decade providing tax cuts and other incentives to
encourage spending.

Because we want more of, well, everything, voters elect leaders who   15
keep money in the pockets of the people, not the government's coffers. For
Republicans, this equates to tax cuts. For Democrats, this means a sticky situation. Pegged as the party that wants to raise taxes, Democrats are forced
to explain how, in the long run, their plan is better for the country. (This
goes against the narcissism pillar, making the situation incredibly difficult.)
As campaign managers and message developers, we need to remember that
people want material possessions; they want wealth. Frame your message from
that perspective. Will your plan increase property values? Diminish government spending? Increase personal income? These messages persuade voters.

Just weeks after the attacks of September 11, 2001, in a speech at O'Hare   16
International Airport, Bush asked the American public to "get on board. Fly
and enjoy America's great destination spots. Get down to Disney World in

Florida. Take your families and enjoy life, the way we want it to be enjoyed." His goal: to instill confidence by triggering one of the dominant components of the American psyche. Bush's implied message was that returning to a high level of consumerism would provide a sense of normalcy to the general public, still reeling from the terrorist attacks.

Fear, narcissism, consumerism, and religiosity shape our perception and understanding of public communication.

Religiosity

There isn't a standard for involving religion in politics. But know that when incorporated correctly, it can be very effective. Hinting at religion or openly discussing religious topics can convey moral standards or draw sharp attention to a specific issue, as illustrated by senator Hillary Clinton, Democrat–New York, in March. Knowing that a recently introduced immigration bill was very complicated, and that Americans were divided about the issue, Clinton used a religious metaphor to rally support for amending the bill, specifically the criminal penalties for providing assistance to illegal immigrants. She said, "This bill would literally criminalize the good Samaritan and probably even Jesus himself." That simple statement garnered nationwide media coverage and helped communicate what Clinton and others believe to be cause for concern in the legislation. She knew that this would be an effective way to simplify a complicated piece of legislation. Americans, who overwhelmingly profess a strong belief in God, would not support legislation that would theoretically punish his son. 17

Religious beliefs shape the debate about a number of hot-button issues in today's political landscape, including abortion, gay rights, and medical research. When developing campaign messages, remember that religion, especially as it pertains to morality, is a significant influencing factor. More than 90 percent of respondents to a 2004 Fox News poll said they believe in God. As the fourth pillar of the country's collective psyche, religiosity consequently impacts how we perceive and choose our leaders. 18

Best Message Wins

Political campaigns are won or lost on effective messaging. You can have the most qualified candidate, but if the campaign has a weak message, odds are it will fail. Conversely, if you take that same candidate (or even a lesser one) and communicate a strong message, the campaign will likely be victorious. 19

Create that persuasive message by incorporating the four pillars of the American psyche. Fear, narcissism, consumerism, and religiosity shape our perception and understanding of public communication. ■ 20

■ Thinking Critically about the Text

Noticeably absent from Kitchens's pillars is honesty. Why do you suppose he has not made it a fifth pillar or replaced one of the others with honesty?

■ Questions on Subject

1. Do you agree with Kitchens's choice for the "Four Pillars of the American Psyche"? Would you make different choices? Explain.
2. Why is it important for a creator of political messages to have some idea of what the pillars of the American psyche are?
3. In paragraph 19, Kitchens talks about the relative impact of weak and strong messages on the success of weak and strong candidates. Do you agree with his assessment? Explain.
4. In your own words, explain what trend Kitchens sees represented in the differences between John F. Kennedy's 1961 inaugural address and Ronald Reagan's question two decades later, "Are you better off than you were four years ago?" In your estimation, has the trend become stronger or weaker in recent years?
5. How would you counter the charge that the advice Kitchens provides is manipulative and cynical and may be one reason Americans are so distrustful of their political leaders?

■ Questions on Strategy

1. What is Kitchens's purpose in this essay? (Glossary: *Purpose*) In your opinion, did he accomplish his purpose? Why, or why not?
2. How does Kitchens use division and classification in this essay? Do you see any problems with his division and classification? Explain.
3. Are the "Four Pillars of the American Psyche" a matter of audience awareness? (Glossary: *Audience*) Explain.
4. What does Kitchens advise communicators to do when dealing with the "sticky situation" he reveals in paragraph 15? How does he illustrate his advice? (Glossary: *Illustration*)
5. Kitchens advises clients on how to communicate most effectively. How would you evaluate his skill in communicating his message? Was his message clear and direct? How and where might he have improved it, if at all?
6. Examine the illustration on page 364. How effective is it at conveying Kitchens's ideas about the "Four Pillars of the American Psyche" and their interconnectedness?

■ Questions on Diction and Vocabulary

1. Is Kitchens's use of the word *narcissism* clear to you? Would it have been better, worse, or about the same if he had used the term *self-interest*? Do the two words have the same meaning? Explain.

FOUR PILLARS OF THE AMERICAN PSYCHE

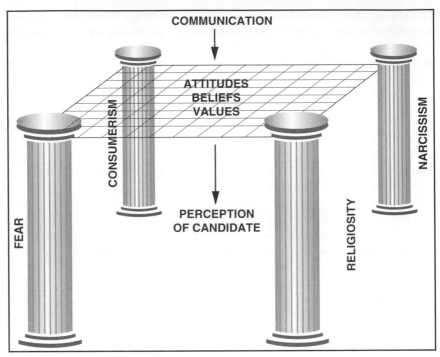

2. What is Kitchens's tone in this essay? (Glossary: *Tone*) Given that he is a consultant for the Democratic Party, does he seem to favor Democrats and their positions or is he objective in his diction and tone? Explain, being sure to cite examples from the essay as evidence.

■ Classroom Activity Using Division and Classification

Visit a local supermarket and select one of the many product areas (frozen foods, dairy products, cereals, soft drinks, meat, produce) for an exercise in classification. First, establish the general class of products in the area you have selected by determining the features that distinguish one subclass from another. Next, place the products from your selected area in appropriate subclasses within your classification system. Finally, share your classification system and how it works with members of your class. Finally, be prepared to answer questions your classmates may have about the decisions you made.

■ Writing Suggestions

1. Kitchens has been quite successful in advising individuals and organizations on how best to communicate their messages. His four pillars of the American psyche—fear, narcissism, consumerism, and

religiosity—are derived from his research, and he advises his clients to shape their messages accordingly. You do not have the same experience in detecting what other "pillars" exist within the American psyche but you probably have some ideas about them. Write an essay in which you put forth your own classification system of the pillars of the American psyche and your advice on how to use them in mass-marketing messages. Illustrate your points by providing examples, as Kitchens has done in his essay.

2. Kitchens's method is, of course, a form of market-based advertising in which the messenger uses what works to strengthen a given message and leaves out or reshapes what doesn't. Write an essay in which you argue against such appeals because they are deceitful and, ultimately, not in the public's best interest.

3. Given what you have learned from Kitchens's essay, how might you approach a campus political campaign or an effort to win acceptance for, say, an environmental initiative, a public-safety issue, or some other important campus-wide concern? Use as many of Kitchens's "four pillars" as you think appropriate and write a brochure directed at students and/or other college stakeholders explaining the issue you are advancing and why your audience should adopt your position.

The Truth about Lying

JUDITH VIORST

Judith Viorst, poet, journalist, author of children's books, and novelist, was born in 1931. She has chronicled her life in such books as *It's Hard to Be Hip Over Thirty and Other Tragedies of Married Life* (1968), *How Did I Get to Be Forty and Other Atrocities* (1976), and *When Did I Stop Being Twenty and Other Injustices: Selected Prose from Single to Mid-Life* (1987). In 1981, she went back to school, taking courses at the Washington Psychoanalytic Institute. This study, along with her personal experience of psychoanalysis, helped to inspire *Necessary Losses* (1986), a popular and critical success. Combining theory, poetry, interviews, and anecdotes, Viorst approaches personal growth as a shedding of illusions. Her recent work includes *I'm Too Young to Be Seventy: And Other Delusions* (2005).

In this essay, first published in the March 1981 issue of *Redbook*, the author approaches lying with delicacy and candor as she carefully classifies the different types of lies we all encounter.

■ Preparing to Read

Lying happens every day in our society, whether it is a politician hiding behind a subtly worded statement or a guest fibbing to a host about the quality of a meal. What, for you, constitutes lying? Are all lies the same? In other words, are there different degrees or types of lying?

I've been wanting to write on a subject that intrigues and challenges me: the   1
subject of lying. I've found it very difficult to do. Everyone I've talked to has a quite intense and personal but often rather intolerant point of view about what we can — and can never *never* — tell lies about. I've finally reached the conclusion that I can't present any ultimate conclusions, for too many people would promptly disagree. Instead, I'd like to present a series of moral puzzles, all concerned with lying. I'll tell you what I think about them. Do you agree?

Social Lies

Most of the people I've talked with say that they find social lying acceptable   2
and necessary. They think it's the civilized way for folks to behave. Without these little white lies, they say, our relationships would be short and brutish

and nasty. It's arrogant, they say, to insist on being so incorruptible and so brave that you cause other people unnecessary embarrassment or pain by compulsively assailing them with your honesty. I basically agree. What about you?

Will you say to people, when it simply isn't true, "I like your new hairdo," "You're looking much better," "It's so nice to see you," "I had a wonderful time"?   3

Will you praise hideous presents and homely kids?   4

Will you decline invitations with "We're busy that night — so sorry we can't come," when the truth is you'd rather stay home than dine with the So-and-sos?   5

And even though, as I do, you may prefer the polite evasion of "You really cooked up a storm" instead of "The soup" — which tastes like warmed-over coffee — "is wonderful," will you, if you must, proclaim it wonderful?   6

There's one man I know who absolutely refuses to tell social lies. "I can't play that game," he says; "I'm simply not made that way." And his answer to the argument that saying nice things to someone doesn't cost anything is, "Yes, it does — it destroys your credibility." Now, he won't, unsolicited, offer his views on the painting you just bought, but you don't ask his frank opinion unless you want *frank*, and his silence at those moments when the rest of us liars are muttering, "Isn't it lovely?" is, for the most part, eloquent enough. My friend does not indulge in what he calls "flattery, false praise, and mellifluous comments." When others tell fibs he will not go along. He says that social lying is lying, that little white lies are still lies. And he feels that telling lies is morally wrong. What about you?   7

Peace-Keeping Lies

Many people tell peace-keeping lies; lies designed to avoid irritation or argument; lies designed to shelter the liar from possible blame or pain; lies (or so it is rationalized) designed to keep trouble at bay without hurting anyone.   8

I tell these lies at times, and yet I always feel they're wrong. I understand why we tell them, but still they feel wrong. And whenever I lie so that someone won't disapprove of me or think less of me or holler at me, I feel I'm a bit of a coward, I feel I'm dodging responsibility, I feel . . . guilty. What about you?   9

Do you, when you're late for a date because you overslept, say that you're late because you got caught in a traffic jam?   10

Do you, when you forget to call a friend, say that you called several times but the line was busy?   11

Do you, when you didn't remember that it was your father's birthday, say that his present must be delayed in the mail?   12

And when you're planning a weekend in New York City and you're not in the mood to visit your mother, who lives there, do you conceal — with a lie, if you must — the fact that you'll be in New York? Or do you have the courage — or is it the cruelty? — to say, "I'll be in New York, but sorry — I don't plan on seeing you"? 13

(Dave and his wife Elaine have two quite different points of view on this very subject. He calls her a coward. She says she's being wise. He says she must assert her right to visit New York sometimes and not see her mother. To which she always patiently replies: "Why should we have useless fights? My mother's too old to change. We get along much better when I lie to her.") 14

Finally, do you keep the peace by telling your husband lies on the subject of money? Do you reduce what you really paid for your shoes? And in general do you find yourself ready, willing and able to lie to him when you make absurd mistakes or lose or break things? 15

"I used to have a romantic idea that part of intimacy was confessing every dumb thing that you did to your husband. But after a couple of years of that," says Laura, "have I changed my mind!" 16

And having changed her mind, she finds herself telling peace-keeping lies. And yes, I tell them, too. What about you? 17

Protective Lies

Protective lies are lies folks tell — often quite serious lies — because they're convinced that the truth would be too damaging. They lie because they feel there are certain human values that supersede the wrong of having lied. They lie, not for personal gain, but because they believe it's for the good of the person they're lying to. They lie to those they love, to those who trust them most of all, on the grounds that breaking this trust is justified. 18

They may lie to their children on money or marital matters. 19

They may lie to the dying about the state of their health. 20

They may lie about adultery, and not — or so they insist — to save their own hide, but to save the heart and the pride of the men they are married to. 21

They may lie to their closest friend because the truth about her talents or son or psyche would be — or so they insist — utterly devastating. 22

I sometimes tell such lies, but I'm aware that it's quite presumptuous to claim I know what's best for others to know. That's called playing God. That's called manipulation and control. And we never can be sure, once we start to juggle lies, just where they'll land, exactly where they'll roll. 23

And furthermore, we may find ourselves lying in order to back up the lies that are backing up the lie we initially told. 24

And furthermore — let's be honest — if conditions were reversed, we certainly wouldn't want anyone lying to us. 25

Yet, having said all that, I still believe that there are times when protec- 26
tive lies must nonetheless be told. What about you?

If your Dad had a very bad heart and you had to tell him some bad fam- 27
ily news, which would you choose: to tell him the truth or lie?

If your former husband failed to send his monthly child-support check 28
and in other ways behaved like a total rat, would you allow your children — who believed he was simply wonderful — to continue to believe that
he was wonderful?

If your dearly beloved brother selected a wife whom you deeply disliked, 29
would you reveal your feelings or would you fake it?

And if you were asked, after making love, "And how was that for you?" 30
would you reply, if it wasn't too good, "Not too good"?

Now, some would call a sex lie unimportant, little more than social lying, 31
a simple act of courtesy that makes all human intercourse run smoothly. And
some would say all sex lies are bad news and unacceptably protective. Because,
says Ruth, "a man with an ego that fragile doesn't need your lies — he needs a
psychiatrist." Still others feel that sex lies are indeed protective lies, more serious than simple social lying, and yet at times they tell them on the grounds
that when it comes to matters sexual, everybody's ego is somewhat fragile.

"If most of the time things go well in sex," says Sue, "I think you're allowed 32
to dissemble when they don't. I can't believe it's good to say, 'Last night was
four stars, darling, but tonight's performance rates only a half.'"

I'm inclined to agree with Sue. What about you? 33

Trust-Keeping Lies

Another group of lies are trust-keeping lies, lies that involve triangulation, 34
with *A* (that's you) telling lies to *B* on behalf of *C* (whose trust you'd promised to keep). Most people concede that once you've agreed not to betray a
friend's confidence, you can't betray it, even if you must lie. But I've talked
with people who don't want you telling them anything that they might be
called on to lie about.

"I don't tell lies for myself," says Fran, "and I don't want to have to tell 35
them for other people." Which means, she agrees, that if her best friend is
having an affair, she absolutely doesn't want to know about it.

"Are you saying," her best friend asks, "that if I went off with a lover and I 36
asked you to tell my husband I'd been with you, that you wouldn't lie for me,
that you'd betray me?"

Fran is very pained but very adamant. "I wouldn't want to betray you, 37
so . . . don't ask me."

Fran's best friend is shocked. What about you? 38

Do you believe you can have close friends if you're not prepared to 39
receive their deepest secrets?

Do you believe you must always lie for your friends? 40

Do you believe, if your friend tells a secret that turns out to be 41
quite immoral or illegal, that once you've promised to keep it, you must
keep it?

And what if your friend were your boss — if you were perhaps one of the 42
President's men — would you betray or lie for him over, say, Watergate?

As you can see, these issues get terribly sticky. 43

It's my belief that once we've promised to keep a trust, we must tell lies to 44
keep it. I also believe that we can't tell Watergate lies. And if these two statements strike you as quite contradictory, you're right — they're quite contradictory. But for now they're the best I can do. What about you?

Some say that truth will out and thus you might as well tell the 45
truth. Some say you can't regain the trust that lies lose. Some say that
even though the truth may never be revealed, our lies pervert and damage our relationships. Some say . . . well, here's what some of them have
to say.

"I'm a coward," says Grace, "about telling close people important, dif- 46
ficult truths. I find that I'm unable to carry it off. And so if something is
bothering me, it keeps building up inside till I end up just not seeing them
anymore."

"I lie to my husband on sexual things, but I'm furious," says Joyce, "that 47
he's too insensitive to know I'm lying."

"I suffer most from the misconception that children can't take the truth," 48
says Emily. "But I'm starting to see that what's harder and more damaging for
them is being told lies, is not being told the truth."

"I'm afraid," says Joan, "that we often wind up feeling a bit of contempt 49
for the people we lie to."

> I'm willing to
> lie. But just as a
> last resort — the
> truth's always
> better.

And then there are those who have no talent 50
for lying.

"Over the years, I tried to lie," a friend of mine 51
explained, "but I always got found out and I always
got punished. I guess I gave myself away because I
feel guilty about any kind of lying. It looks as if I'm
stuck with telling the truth."

For those of us, however, who are good at 52
telling lies, for those of us who lie and don't get
caught, the question of whether or not to lie can be a hard and serious moral
problem. I liked the remark of a friend of mine who said, "I'm willing to lie.
But just as a last resort — the truth's always better."

"Because," he explained, "though others may completely accept the lie 53
I'm telling, I don't."

I tend to feel that way, too. 54

What about you? ■ 55

■ Thinking Critically about the Text

The title of the essay plays with the relationship between lies and the truth. Viorst discusses lies that help to conceal the truth, but she's quick to point out that not all lies are malicious. Look at her subsections about "protective lies" (paragraphs 18–33) and "trust-keeping lies" (34–44). Do you think that these lies are necessary, or would it be easier to tell the truth? Explain.

■ Questions on Subject

1. Why is Viorst wary of giving advice on the subject of lying?
2. Viorst admits to contradicting herself in her section on "trust-keeping lies." Where else do you see her contradicting herself?
3. In telling a "protective lie," what assumption about the person hearing the lie does Viorst make? Would you make the same assumption? Why or why not?
4. What's the difference between a "peace-keeping lie" and a "protective lie"?

■ Questions on Strategy

1. Into what main categories does Viorst divide lying? Do you agree with her division, or do some of her categories seem to overlap? Explain.
2. Viorst recognizes that many people have steadfast views on lying. What accommodations does she make for this audience? (Glossary: *Audience*) How does she challenge this audience?
3. There are at least two parties involved in a lie — the liar and the listener. How much significance does the author give to each of these parties? How does she make the distinction?
4. Viorst presents the reader with a series of examples or moral puzzles. How do these puzzles encourage further thought on the subject of lying? Are they successful? Why or why not?
5. Viorst chooses an unconventional way to conclude her essay by showing different people's opinions of lying. What do you think she's doing in this last section, beginning in paragraph 45? Does this ending intensify any of the points she has made? Explain. (Glossary: *Beginnings/Endings*)
6. Viorst wants us to see that a lie is not a lie is not a lie is not a lie (i.e., that not all lies are the same). To clarify the various types of lies, she uses division and classification. She also uses illustration to show the reasons people lie. (Glossary: *Illustration*) Using several of the examples that work best for you, discuss how Viorst's use of illustration strengthens and enhances her classification.

■ Questions on Diction and Vocabulary

1. How would you characterize Viorst's diction in this essay? (Glossary: *Diction*) Consider the essay's subject and audience. (Glossary: *Audience;*

Subject) Cite specific examples of her word choice to support your conclusions.

2. Refer to your desk dictionary to determine the meanings of the following words as Viorst uses them in this selection: *mellifluous* (paragraph 7), *supersede* (18), *dissemble* (32).

■ Classroom Activity Using Division and Classification

Consider the following classes of items and determine at least two principles of division that could be used for each class. Then write a paragraph or two in which you classify one of the groups of items according to a single principle of division. For example, in discussing crime one could use the seriousness of the crime or the type of crime as principles of division. If the seriousness of the crime were used, this might yield two categories: felonies and misdemeanors. If the types of crime were used, this would yield categories such as burglary, murder, larceny, and embezzlement.

movies

college professors

social sciences

roommates

professional sports

■ Writing Suggestions

1. Viorst wrote this essay for *Redbook*, which is usually considered a women's magazine. If you were writing this essay for a male audience, would you change the examples? If so, how would you change them? If not, why not? Do you think men are more likely to tell lies of a certain category? Explain. Write an essay in which you discuss whether men and women share similar perspectives about lying. (Glossary: *Comparison and Contrast*)

2. Write an essay of division and classification on the subject of friends. How many different types of friends do you recognize? On what basis do you differentiate them? Do you make distinctions among them on the basis of gender? Are some friends more important, more useful, more intimate, more convenient, more trustworthy, more reliable, more supportive, more lasting than others? Are you more willing to share your most personal thoughts and feelings with some friends than with others? Be sure to establish a context for why you are writing about friends and putting forth an essay that divides and classifies them. Conclude with an insightful statement drawn from your thesis, the division and classification you establish, and the examples you provide.

The American Dream for Sale: Ethnic Images in Magazines

AMY RASHAP

 Amy Rashap, who earned a B.A. in anthropology from Cornell University and a Ph.D. in cultural anthropology from the University of Pennsylvania, spent fourteen years as director of marketing for various academic publishing houses, among them Syracuse University Press and Rutgers University Press, before leaving to teach ESL (English as a second language) in Singapore. She became the director of an English-language school and authored three ESL textbooks along the way. In 2010, Rashap and two partners started an English-language school in Singapore.

Asked why she wrote "The American Dream for Sale: Ethnic Images in Magazines," Rashap comments, "I wrote the article when I was working as a graduate student at the University of Pennsylvania, studying folklore and folk life. I was working at the Balch Institute of Ethnic Studies in Philadelphia and the museum was mounting an exhibit on ethnic images in advertising. As a graduate student in folklore, I was becoming increasingly aware that what interested me was not traditional 'folk cultures,' for example, Appalachian pottery or Irish step dancing or Celtic music, but the cultural aspects of modern society. It's not just 'they' that are the 'folk'—'we' are the folk. Important cultural messages are embedded in modern culture and need to be revealed. So I wrote the essay for the Balch Institute's exhibit catalog. . . ." As you read, notice the way Rashap divides and classifies ethnic advertisements in magazines.

■ Preparing to Read

We usually think of advertisements as a means of selling goods and services, but ads can also reveal a lot about our culture at a given time in history. What important information do you think we can learn from such ads?

"Promise—large promise—is the soul of advertising," wrote Dr. Samuel Johnson in the eighteenth century. His dictum has remained remarkably accurate during the last two hundred and fifty years. Advertisements tell the viewer much more than the merits of a particular product. From the glossy and colorful pages of magazines, catalogs, and newspaper supplements the reader can extract images of how to live the perfect American life. This exhibit shows how the depiction of ethnic groups has changed radically in the advertisements of nationally distributed magazines over the last century. The pictures tell a complex tale of economic power and mobility; of conflicting attitudes toward one's ethnic heritage and toward Anglo American culture.

The development of modern advertising, with its sophisticated use of imagery and catchy phrases, grew hand in hand with the advent of the affordable monthly and weekly magazines. By the 1880s factories were churning out a plethora of ready-made goods, and the expanded system of railways and roads linked producer and consumer into a national network. During this period magazine production rose apace. Due to a variety of factors, ranging from improved type-setting techniques and low postal rates to the utilization of increasingly sophisticated photoengraving processes, publishers began to produce low-priced, profusely illustrated magazines fashioned to appeal to a national audience. The contents of the magazines, such as *Collier's*, the *Saturday Evening Post*, and the *Ladies Home Journal*, covered a wide variety of topics: from homemaking to current events, new inventions to briskly paced fiction. By 1905 twenty general monthlies, each with a circulation of over 100,000, were in existence. Ranging in price from 10 to 15¢, easily within the budget of tens of thousands of Americans, they were an ideal vehicle for carrying the manufacturer's messages to a national audience.

> Advertisers devised images that tapped into deeply held beliefs and myths of an "all-American" lifestyle—one that didn't just sell a product, but a way of life.

What were the implications of advertising for the masses? As advertisers targeted their products toward a mass audience, the need arose to create an "average person," a type who embodied the qualities and attitudes of many others. Advertisers devised images that tapped into deeply held beliefs and myths of an "all-American" lifestyle — one that didn't just sell a product, but a way of life that people could buy.

The very nature of the advertising medium itself necessitates the use of symbols and character types that could be understood at a glance. If the advertisement was to be effective, its message had to be quickly absorbed and understood. Thus, in their depiction of ethnic groups, advertisers often used commonly held stereotypes. Within these stock images, however, one can observe various levels of complexity.

When the N.H.M. Hotels ad in figure 1 appeared in 1936, the nation was still in the midst of the Great Depression. The black railroad porter, with his knowledge of the rails and reputation for prompt and courteous service, was an effective spokesman for a hotel chain dependent for its livelihood upon Americans getting back on the move. The portrayal of the porter is interesting in this ad, for, beyond the obvious fact that the only blacks present are in service roles, the spokesman's subservience is visually reinforced by his deferential smile, slight stoop, and bent knees. As porters, blacks could assist in the resurgence of the American economy, but not fully participate in its benefits.

Figure 1: *Magazine advertisement, 1936* (Courtesy Balch Institute/Historical Society of Pennsylvania)

An advertisement for the Milwaukee Railroad from a 1945 *National Geographic* (figure 2) reveals another way in which ethnic groups are shown as outsiders — at the service of American culture while not actively participating in it. Here is the Noble Savage, not as the representative of any particular group of Native Americans, but as the symbol for the railroad itself, barely visible in the advertisement. In both the visuals and the copy the sale is made through stock images and associations. He is as familiar as a dime-store Indian; a reassuring and time-honored part of the American landscape. However, while the Indian shown here still brandishes his bow and arrow, he has been tamed. He gazes mutely over the changed landscape, another symbol of technological domination.

Figure 2: National Geographic *advertisement, July 1945 (*Courtesy Balch Institute/Historical Society of Pennsylvania)

In a 1949 ad in *American Home* (figure 3), Chiquita Banana entices us to buy her goods. Wearing a traditional ruffled skirt and fruit-laden hat, she embodies the stereotypical, fun-loving, gay Hispanic woman. While she occasionally doffs the more demure chef's hat, her smile and pert manner never waver. Her basic message is one of festivity, tempered with the American housewife's concern for nutrition: while bananas are good for you, they can be fun, too! They make mealtimes a party. In the later television ads of the 1960s, Chiquita Banana was transformed into a more overtly sexual figure doing the

Figure 3: *American Home* advertisement, 1949 The Museum of Modern Mythology

rumba. Singing her famous "I'm Chiquita Banana . . . " song in a Spanish accent, the advertisement's emphasis was more on festivity than wholesomeness.

The use of simple external attributes to symbolize ethnic identification has   8
long been a favorite technique of advertisers. In a Royal Crown Cola advertisement of 1938, the reader was urged to be like the thrifty "Scotchman" and buy the economical refreshment. Presenting its Scotsman with a broad grin and conspiratorial, chummy wink, the ad pokes gentle fun at the Scottish reputation for miserliness. Whether the character in Scottish garb is Scottish or not is incidental, for the white American can easily put on this ethnic persona without compromising or jeopardizing his identity. The Scottish stereotype can be invoked by using a few external character traits; the image does not extend beyond that initial statement. The black stereotype represented in the N.H.M. Hotel ad, however, reflects more deeply held attitudes toward cultural differences. [If we were to] compare the closeness of the two men in the RC Cola ad with the black porter and the white traveler in figure 1, [we would note that] even the spacing between the characters in both ads is significant: While the men in the RC Cola ad display an easy intimacy, the black porter stands deferentially apart from the white traveler.

Advertisements were not the only medium that reflected the subservi-   9
ent role certain ethnic groups occupied within mainstream American culture. Magazine fiction, too, depicted a world in which white, Anglo-Americans were getting most of the world's material goods and occupying the more powerful roles in most human relationships. In story after story the heroes and heroines were of northern European stock, and in many cases when the protagonists were nominally foreign, their visual portrayal and characterization would belie the differences. This tendency is illustrated in a 1913 cover of the *Sunday Magazine of the Philadelphia Press*, which shows a pretty young Serbian dancer smiling languidly out at the viewer (figure 4). In her colorful native costume and dance pose, she plays her role of "old country" ethnic. But while her dress presents an image of quaint and wholesome rusticity, her features bear a reassuringly western European stamp. She satisfied an American need for foreign experience and armchair travel without really challenging any assumptions about significant cultural variation.

Until the advent of the civil rights movement of the 1950s and '60s,   10
American businessmen and advertisers assumed, on the whole, that the best way to sell their products was to address their advertisements to the white Anglo American. Hence magazine stories and ads were geared toward appealing to . . . them. In recent years, however, though advertisers have become increasingly concerned with the purchasing power of the different ethnic groups, the images they use continue to reassure the consumer that the group's "foreignness" is carefully controlled. Their cultural identity is often reduced to a few superficial symbols.

A Sprite ad [that appeared in *Newsweek*, among other places, in 1983]   11
reveals a group of smiling Americans of all different lineages brandishing

SUNDAY MAGAZINE
Of the PHILADELPHIA PRESS

PHILADELPHIA, PA.
NOVEMBER 9, 1913

PART 3
20 PAGES

DANCES OF THE
NATIONS—Servian

Figure 4: *Magazine cover: November 9, 1913* (Courtesy Balch Institute/Historical Society of Pennsylvania)

their favorite brand of soda. Yet while different ethnic groups are shown, they are all of the wholesome "all-American" type. The advertisement's point is that the "you"—the American youth, who choose Sprite, now includes Asians, Hispanics, and blacks.

Advertisements that have appeared in nationally distributed magazines   12
targeted at specific ethnic groups also need mentioning. Until the civil rights
movement gave many groups the impetus to speak out in their own voices,
many of the advertisements in such magazines showed them displaying all
the accoutrements and mannerisms of white, middle-class Americans. Thus
the Ballantine Beer ad (figure 5) in a 1955 issue of *Ebony* portrays a group of

Figure 5: Ebony *advertisement, January 1955* (Courtesy of Pabst Brewing Co., San Antonio, TX)

thoroughly Anglicized and fair-complexioned black people. In black society light skin often gave a person enhanced prestige and eased acceptance into white American culture.

Today agencies have been formed to deal exclusively with advertisements 13 targeted towards specific minority groups. Many of these more recent ads reveal the complex negotiations involved in attempting to reconcile indigenous cultural needs with societal acceptance: a crucial issue facing many ethnic Americans today. ■

■ Thinking Critically about the Text

The advertisers whose ads Rashap comments on drew on stereotypes to promote products. How much do you think those advertisements reinforced such stereotypes? Was any real ethnic and cultural understanding advanced?

■ Questions on Subject

1. What examples can you provide to support the idea that advertising not only attempts to sell a product but also a way of life? What lifestyle do most beer ads reflect and promote, for example?
2. What characterizes the growth of modern advertising beginning in the late 1880s, according to Rashap?
3. What is the irony that Rashap points to in the Sprite advertisement she discusses in paragraph 11? (Glossary: *Irony*)
4. Are the historical examples Rashap provides clear to the contemporary reader? Did you have trouble understanding any of the references? For example, is the statement "In the later television ads of the 1960s, Chiquita Banana was transformed into a more overtly sexual figure doing the rumba" (paragraph 7) clear enough as Rashap presents it or do you need more context? Explain.
5. Examine Figure 5 closely. What "accoutrements and mannerisms" (paragraph 12) can you see in the advertisement for Ballantine Ale?

■ Questions on Strategy

1. What do you think Rashap hoped to achieve in writing her essay for the Balch Institute exhibit? (Glossary: *Purpose*)
2. What is Rashap's thesis in the essay? (Glossary: *Thesis*) Where does she state it?
3. Why is it important for Rashap to give a history of magazine publishing in America before proceeding to her division and classification of the advertisements in the exhibit?

4. How has Rashap made use of division and classification in her essay? Is the illustration she provides for each category she discusses sufficient for your understanding of that category? Explain.
5. Rashap's essay was written for a museum exhibit catalog. What demands and what restrictions did that medium likely make on her as a writer? (Glossary: *Audience; Purpose*)

■ Questions on Diction and Vocabulary

1. Evaluate Rashap's diction in this selection. On a spectrum from academic to colloquial, where would you say her diction falls? Choose one or two of her discussions of particular advertisements and explain how the language she uses supports your claim.
2. Consult your desk dictionary for the meanings of the following words and phrases as they are used in this selection: *dictum* (1), *plethora* (2), *stock images* (4), *railroad porter* (5), *subservience* (5), *demure* (7), *deferentially* (8), *languidly* (9), *rusticity* (9), *lineages* (11), *accoutrements* (12).

■ Classroom Activity Using Division and Classification

Divide each item in the following list into at least three different categories, and be prepared to explain your principle of division. For example, newspapers can be divided by: the time of the day they are published (morning or evening); how conventional they are (mainstream or alternative); the coverage they give (national or local, or both); their cost (more or less than a dollar); their degree of specialization (sports, foreign language); and so forth.

    instructors

    restaurants

    writers

    coaches

■ Writing Suggestions

1. Advertisers use a variety of ploys to win you over, including the use of statistics and other information (or misinformation), enticing images, clever language devices, side-by-side comparisons, music, logical argumentation, and so on. Watch an hour or so of television, and note the techniques used in various commercials. Then write a division and classification essay in which you present the different types of techniques you have observed and describe how advertisers use them.

2. Reread paragraph 13 in Rashap's essay. Write an essay in which you examine one or more contemporary magazines aimed at minority groups for what Rashap terms the "complex negotiations involved in attempting to reconcile indigenous cultural needs with societal acceptance." Consider examining *Jet, Ebony, Hispanic Business, Hispanic, Essence, Latina, Vanidades, Cosmopolitan en Español, AsianWoman,* or a magazine of your own choosing.

The Ways of Meeting Oppression

MARTIN LUTHER KING JR.

 Martin Luther King Jr. (1929–1968) was the son of a Baptist minister. Ordained at the age of eighteen, King went on to study at Morehouse College, Crozer Theological Seminary, Boston University, and Chicago Theological Seminary. He came to prominence in 1955 in Montgomery, Alabama, when he led a successful boycott against the city's segregated bus system. A powerful orator and writer, King went on to become the leading spokesperson for the civil rights movement during the 1950s and 1960s. In 1964, he was awarded the Nobel Peace Prize for his policy of nonviolent resistance to racial injustice, a policy that he explains in the following selection. King was assassinated in April 1968 after speaking at a rally in Memphis, Tennessee.

This selection is excerpted from the book *Stride Toward Freedom* (1958). Notice how King classifies the three ways oppressed people throughout history have reacted to their oppressors and how his organization prepares the reader for his conclusion.

■ Preparing to Read

Summarize what you know about the civil rights movement of the late 1950s and early 1960s. What were the movement's goals? What tactics did its leaders use? How successful were those tactics? How did this movement change American society?

Oppressed people deal with their oppression in three characteristic ways. 1
One way is acquiescence: The oppressed resign themselves to their doom. They tacitly adjust themselves to oppression, and thereby become conditioned to it. In every movement toward freedom some of the oppressed prefer to remain oppressed. Almost 2,800 years ago Moses set out to lead the children of Israel from the slavery of Egypt to the freedom of the promised land. He soon discovered that slaves do not always welcome their deliverers. They become accustomed to being slaves. They would rather bear those ills they have, as Shakespeare pointed out, than flee to others that they know not of. They prefer the "fleshpots of Egypt" to the ordeals of emancipation.

There is such a thing as the freedom of exhaustion. Some people are so 2
worn down by the yoke of oppression that they give up. A few years ago in the slum areas of Atlanta, a Negro guitarist used to sing almost daily: "Been down so long that down don't bother me." This is the type of negative freedom and resignation that often engulfs the life of the oppressed.

But this is not the way out. To accept passively an unjust system is to cooperate with that system; thereby the oppressed become as evil as the oppressor. Noncooperation with evil is as much a moral obligation as is cooperation with good. The oppressed must never allow the conscience of the oppressor to slumber. Religion reminds every man that he is his brother's keeper. To accept injustice or segregation passively is to say to the oppressor that his actions are morally right. It is a way of allowing his conscience to fall asleep. At this moment the oppressed fails to be his brother's keeper. So acquiescence — while often the easier way — is not the moral way. It is the way of the coward. The Negro cannot win the respect of his oppressor by acquiescing; he merely increases the oppressor's arrogance and contempt. Acquiescence is interpreted as proof of the Negro's inferiority. The Negro cannot win the respect of the white people of the south or the peoples of the world if he is willing to sell the future of his children for his personal and immediate comfort and safety. 3

> The problem is not a purely racial one, with Negroes set against whites. In the end, it's not a struggle between people at all, but a tension between justice and injustice.

A second way that oppressed people sometimes deal with oppression is to resort to physical violence and corroding hatred. Violence often brings about momentary results. Nations have frequently won their independence in battle. But in spite of temporary victories, violence never brings permanent peace. It solves no social problem; it merely creates new and more complicated ones. 4

Violence as a way of achieving racial justice is both impractical and immoral. It is impractical because it is a descending spiral ending in destruction for all. The old law of an eye for an eye leaves everybody blind. It is immoral because it seeks to humiliate the opponent rather than win his understanding; it seeks to annihilate rather than to convert. Violence is immoral because it thrives on hatred rather than love. It destroys community and makes brotherhood impossible. It leaves society in monologue rather than dialogue. Violence ends by defeating itself. It creates bitterness in the survivors and brutality in the destroyers. A voice echoes through time saying to every potential Peter, "Put up your sword." History is cluttered with the wreckage of nations that failed to follow this command. 5

If the American Negro and other victims of oppression succumb to the temptation of using violence in the struggle for freedom, future generations will be the recipients of a desolate night of bitterness, and our chief legacy to them will be an endless reign of meaningless chaos. Violence is not the way. 6

The third way open to oppressed people in their quest for freedom is the way of nonviolent resistance. Like the synthesis in Hegelian philosophy, the principle of nonviolent resistance seeks to reconcile the truths of two opposites — the acquiescence and violence — while avoiding the extremes and 7 immoralities of both. The nonviolent resister agrees with the person who acquiesces that one should not be physically aggressive toward his opponent; but he balances the equation by agreeing with the person of violence that evil must be resisted. He avoids the nonresistance of the former and the violent resistance of the latter. With nonviolent resistance, no individual or group need submit to any wrong, nor need anyone resort to violence in order to right a wrong.

It seems to me that this is the method that must guide the actions of   8
the Negro in the present crisis in race relations. Through nonviolent resistance the Negro will be able to rise to the noble height of opposing the unjust system while loving the perpetrators of the system. The Negro must work passionately and unrelentingly for full stature as a citizen, but he must not use inferior methods to gain it. He must never come to terms with falsehood, malice, hate, or destruction.

Nonviolent resistance makes it possible for the Negro to remain in the South   9
and struggle for his rights. The Negro's problem will not be solved by running away. He cannot listen to the glib suggestion of those who would urge him to migrate en masse to other sections of the country. By grasping his great opportunity in the South he can make a lasting contribution to the moral strength of the nation and set a sublime example of courage for generations yet unborn.

By nonviolent resistance, the Negro can also enlist all men of good will in   10
his struggle for equality. The problem is not a purely racial one, with Negroes set against whites. In the end, it is not a struggle between people at all, but a tension between justice and injustice. Nonviolent resistance is not aimed against oppressors but against oppression. Under its banner consciences, not racial groups, are enlisted.

■ Thinking Critically about the Text

Find the definition of *oppress* or *oppression* in the dictionary. Exactly what does King mean when he speaks of people being "oppressed" in the South in twentieth-century America? Do you think that people are still being oppressed in America today? Explain.

■ Questions on Subject

1. What does King mean by the phrase "freedom of exhaustion" (paragraph 2)? Why is he scathing in his assessment of people who succumb to such a condition in response to oppression?
2. According to King, what is the role of religion in the battle against oppression?
3. Why does King advocate the avoidance of violence in fighting oppression, despite the short-term success violence often achieves for the victors? How do such victories affect the future?

4. According to King, how does nonviolent resistance transform a racial issue into one of conscience?

■ Questions on Strategy

1. King's essay is easy to read and understand, and everything in it relates to his purpose. (Glossary: *Purpose*) What is that purpose? Summarize how each paragraph supports his purpose. How does the essay's organization help King achieve his purpose? (Glossary: *Organization*)

2. King says that "nonviolent resistance is not aimed against oppressors but against oppression" (paragraph 10). What does he mean by this? Why does he deflect anger and resentment away from a concrete example, the oppressors, to an abstract concept, oppression? (Glossary: *Concrete/Abstract*) How does this choice support his purpose? (Glossary: *Purpose*)

3. King evokes the names of Moses, Shakespeare, and Hegel in his essay. What does this tell you about his intended audience? (Glossary: *Audience*) Why does King address the audience in this way?

4. King uses division and classification to help him argue his point in this essay. What other rhetorical strategies does King use? How does each strategy, including division and classification and argument, contribute to the effectiveness of the essay?

■ Questions on Diction and Vocabulary

1. In his discussion about overcoming oppression with violence, King says that "future generations will be the recipients of a desolate night of bitterness" (paragraph 6). What image do his words evoke for you? Why do you think he chooses to use a striking metaphor here, instead of a less poetic statement? (Glossary: *Figures of Speech*)

2. King urges Negroes to avoid "falsehood, malice, hate, or destruction" (paragraph 8) in their quest to gain full stature as citizens. How does each of these terms relate to his earlier argument about avoiding violence? How does each enhance or add new meaning to his earlier argument?

3. Refer to your desk dictionary to determine the meanings of the following words as King uses them in this selection: *acquiescence* (paragraph 1), *tacitly* (1), *yoke* (2), *perpetrators* (8), *glib* (9), *sublime* (9).

■ Classroom Activity Using Division and Classification

Be prepared to discuss in class why you believe division and classification are important strategies or ways of thinking in everyday life. Explain, for example, how useful the two complementary strategies are for you as you go shopping in the supermarket for items on your shopping list or look for particular textbooks in your college bookstore.

■ Writing Suggestions

1. Write a division and classification essay in which you follow King's model. Identify three methods that you can use to achieve a goal — study for a test, apply to graduate school, or interview for a job, for example. Choose one method to advocate; then frame your essay so that the division and classification strategy helps you make your point.

2. Toward the end of his essay, King states, "By grasping his great opportunity in the South [the Negro] can make a lasting contribution to the moral strength of the nation and set a sublime example of courage for generations yet unborn" (paragraph 9). With your classmates, discuss whether the movement that King led achieved its goal of solving many of the underlying racial tensions and inequities in the United States. In terms of equality, what has happened in the United States since King's famous "I Have a Dream" speech (page 525)? Write a paper in which you argue for or against the idea that King's "dream" is still intact. (Glossary: *Argument*)

WRITING SUGGESTIONS FOR DIVISION AND CLASSIFICATION

1. To write a meaningful classification essay, you must analyze a body of unorganized material, arranging it for a particular purpose. (Glossary: *Purpose*) For example, to identify for a buyer the most economical cars currently on the market, you might initially determine which cars can be purchased for under $20,000 and which cost between $20,000 and $30,000. Then, using a second basis of selection — fuel economy — you could determine which cars have the best gas mileage within each price range.

   Select one of the following subjects, and write a classification essay. Be sure that your purpose is clearly explained and that your bases of selection are chosen and ordered in accordance with your purpose.

   a. attitudes toward physical fitness

   b. contemporary American music

   c. reading materials

   d. reasons for going to college

   e. attitudes toward the religious or spiritual side of life

   f. choosing a hobby

   g. television comedies

   h. college professors

   i. local restaurants

   j. choosing a career

   k. college courses

   l. recreational activities

   m. ways of financing a college education

   n. parties or other social events

2. We sometimes resist classifying other people because it can seem like "pigeonholing" or stereotyping individuals unfairly. In an essay, compare and contrast two or more ways of classifying people, including at least one that you would call legitimate and one that you would call misleading. (Glossary: *Comparison and Contrast*) What conclusions can you draw about the difference between useful classifications and damaging stereotypes?

3. Use division and classification to explain your school or town. What categories might you use? Would you divide your subject into different types of people? Would you classify people by their spending habits? What are the other ways in which you might explain your school or town? What other rhetorical strategies might you incorporate to

strengthen your presentation? You might want to look at the Web site of your school or town to find out what categories it uses to present itself.

4. The cartoon below was created by Bernard Schoenbaum and first appeared in the *New Yorker* on September 19, 1994.

While it's meant to be amusing, the cartoon's classification of books according to reader's attention span does provide more than a moment's comic relief: Readers usually do prefer certain types of books, from more to less challenging, depending on what they hope to achieve by reading. Write an essay in which you divide and classify book readers according to a system of your own devising.

5. **Writing with Sources.** Do some research on the last presidential election or another political campaign that interests you. Reread or watch online major news coverage of the last days of the election, and identify at least three qualities that were mentioned most often for the two final contenders. What categories or classes do these qualities belong to? Write an essay in which you discuss how this division and classification of the candidates' qualities might have contributed to the winner's victory. Also consider who did the dividing: Was it the media? The public?

For models of and advice on integrating sources, see Chapters 14–15.

Espresso
[ess-press-oh]

Espresso Macchiato
[ess-press-oh mock-e-ah-toe]

Espresso con Panna
[ess-press-oh kon pawn-nah]

Caffé Latte
[caf-ay lah-tey]

Flat White

Cafe Breve
[caf-ay brev-ay]

Cappuccino
[kap-oo-chee-noh]

Caffé Mocha
[caf-ay moh-kuh]

Americano
[uh-mer-i-kan-oh]

CHAPTER 10

Definition

What Is Definition?

If you have ever used a dictionary, you are already familiar with the concept of definition. The job of explaining the meanings of words and phrases is not limited to the dictionary alone, however: We use definition all the time in our everyday lives to make our points clearer. How often have you been asked what you mean when a word or phrase you're using is ambiguous, unusual, or simply unfamiliar to your listener? We can only communicate with one another clearly and effectively when we all define the words we use in the same way — and that is not always easy.

Visuals can come to our aid in definition, as the chart on the page opposite shows. While we could certainly define the various coffee drinks using words alone, the illustration gives a quick, at-a-glance indication of their basic components. A chart like this one displayed at a specialty coffee shop would eliminate all ambiguity in ordering.

Definition in Written Texts

Unlike the relative proportions of coffee, milk, and water in various coffee drinks, understanding and explaining complex concepts is often impossible without using precise, detailed, verbal definitions. These definitions can take on many different forms depending, in part, on the purpose of the definition and on what is being defined.

For example, let's look at how Robert Keith Miller attempts to define *discrimination* in his essay called "Discrimination Is a Virtue," which first appeared in *Newsweek*.

> We have a word in English which means "the ability to tell differences." That word is *discrimination*. But within the last [50] years, this word has been so frequently misused that an entire generation has grown up believing that "discrimination" means "racism."

People are always proclaiming that "discrimination" is something that should be done away with. Should that ever happen, it would prove to be our undoing.

Discrimination means discernment; it means the ability to perceive the truth, to use good judgment and to profit accordingly. The *Oxford English Dictionary* traces this meaning of the word back to 1648 and demonstrates that for the next 300 years, "discrimination" was a virtue, not a vice. Thus, when a character in a nineteenth-century novel makes a happy marriage, Dickens has another character remark, "It does credit to your discrimination that you should have found such a very excellent young woman."

Of course, "the ability to tell differences" assumes that differences exist, and this is unsettling for a culture obsessed with the notion of equality. The contemporary belief that discrimination is a vice stems from the compound "discriminate against." What we need to remember, however, is that some things deserve to be judged harshly: We should not leave our kingdoms to the selfish and the wicked.

Discrimination is wrong only when someone or something is discriminated against because of prejudice. But to use the word in that sense, as so many people do, is to destroy its true meaning. If you discriminate against something because of general preconceptions rather than particular insights, then you are not discriminating—bias has clouded the clarity of vision that discrimination demands.

How does Miller define *discrimination*? He mainly uses a technique called *extended definition,* a definition that requires a full discussion. This is only one of many types of definition that you could use to explain what a word or an idea means to you. The following paragraphs identify and explain several other types.

A *formal definition*—a definition such as that found in a dictionary — explains the meaning of a word by assigning it to a class and then differentiating it from other members of that class.

Term		**Class**	**Differentiation**
Music	is	sound	made by voices or instruments and characterized by melody, harmony, or rhythm.

Note how crucial the differentiation is here: There are many sounds — from the roar of a passing jet airplane to the fizz of soda in a glass — that must be excluded for the definition to be precise and useful. Dictionary entries often follow the class-differentiation pattern of the formal definition.

A *synonymous definition* explains a word by pairing it with another word of similar but perhaps more limited meaning.

Music is melody.

Synonymous definition is almost never as precise as formal definition because few words share exactly the same meaning. But when the word being defined is reasonably familiar and somewhat broad, a well-chosen synonym can provide readers with a surer sense of its meaning in context.

A *negative definition* explains a word by saying what it does not mean.

> Music is not silence, and it is not noise.

Such a definition must obviously be incomplete: There are sounds that are neither silence nor noise and yet are not music — quiet conversation, for example. But specifying what something is *not* often helps to clarify other statements about what it is.

An *etymological definition* also seldom stands alone, but by tracing a word's origins it helps readers understand its meaning. *Etymology* itself is defined as the study of the history of a linguistic form — the history of words.

> Music is descended from the Greek word *mousikē*, meaning literally "the art of the Muse."

The Muses, according to Greek mythology, were deities and the sources of inspiration in the arts. Thus the etymology suggests why we think of music as an art and as the product of inspiration. Etymological definitions often reveal surprising sources that suggest new ways of looking at ideas or objects.

A *stipulative definition* is a definition invented by a writer to convey a special or unexpected sense of an existing and often familiar word.

> Music is a language, but a language of the intangible, a kind of soul-language.
>
> — EDWARD MACDOWELL

> Music is the arithmetic of sounds.
>
> — CLAUDE DEBUSSY

Although these two examples seem to disagree with each other, and perhaps also with your idea of what music is, note that neither is arbitrary. (That is, neither assigns to the word *music* a completely foreign meaning, as Humpty Dumpty did in *Through the Looking-Glass* when he defined *glory* as "a nice knock-down argument.") The stipulative definitions by MacDowell and Debussy help explain each composer's conception of the subject and can lead, of course, to further elaboration. Stipulative definitions almost always provide the basis for a more complex discussion. These definitions are often the subjects of an extended definition.

Extended definition, like the definition of *discrimination* given by Robert Keith Miller on pages 393–94, is used when a word, or the idea it stands for, requires more than a sentence of explanation. *Extended definition* may employ any of the definition techniques mentioned above, as well as the strategies discussed in other chapters. For example, an extended definition of music might provide *examples*, ranging from African drumming to a Bach fugue to a Bruce Springsteen song, to develop a fuller and more vivid sense of what music is. A writer might *describe* music in detail by showing its characteristic features, or explain the *process* of composing music, or *compare and contrast* music with language (according to MacDowell's stipulative definition) or arithmetic (according to Debussy's). Each of these strategies helps make the meaning of a writer's words and ideas clear.

In his extended definition of the word *discrimination*, Miller uses a very brief formal definition of *discrimination* [term]: "the ability [class] to tell differences [differentiation]." He then offers a negative definition (discrimination is not racism) and a synonymous definition (discrimination is discernment). Next he cites the entry in a great historical dictionary of English to support his claim, and he quotes an example to illustrate his definition. He concludes by contrasting the word *discrimination* with the compound "discriminate against." Each of these techniques helps make the case that the most precise meaning of *discrimination* is in direct opposition to its common usage today.

Using Definition As a Writing Strategy

Since most readers have dictionaries, it might seem that writers would hardly ever have to define their terms with formal definitions. In fact, writers don't necessarily do so all the time, even when using an unusual word like *tergiversation*, which few readers have in their active vocabularies; if readers don't know it, the reasoning goes, let them look it up. But there are times when a formal definition is quite necessary. One of these times is when a writer uses a word so specialized or so new that it simply won't be in dictionaries; another is when a writer must use a number of unfamiliar technical terms within only a few sentences. Also, when a word has several different meanings or may mean different things to different people, writers will often state exactly the sense in which they are using the word. In each of these cases, definition serves the purpose of achieving clarity.

But writers also sometimes use definition, particularly extended definition, to explain the essential nature of the things and ideas they write about. For example, consider E. B. White's definition of *democracy,* which first appeared in the *New Yorker* on July 3, 1943.

> We received a letter from the Writers' War Board the other day asking for a statement on "The Meaning of Democracy." It presumably is our duty to comply with such a request, and it is certainly our pleasure.
>
> Surely the Board knows what democracy is. It is the line that forms on the right. It is the *don't* in "don't shove." It is the hole in the stuffed shirt through which the sawdust slowly trickles; it is the dent in the high hat. Democracy is the recurrent suspicion that

more than half of the people are right more than half of the time. It is the feeling of privacy in the voting booths, the feeling of communion in the libraries, the feeling of vitality everywhere. Democracy is a letter to the editor. Democracy is the score at the beginning of the ninth. It is an idea which hasn't been disproved yet, a song the words of which have not gone bad. It's the mustard on the hot dog and the cream in the rationed coffee. Democracy is a request from a War Board, in the middle of a morning in the middle of a war, wanting to know what democracy is.

Such writing goes beyond answering the question, "What does _____ mean exactly?" to tackle the much broader and deeper question "What is _____, and what does it represent?"

Although exploring a term and what it represents is often the primary object of such a definition, sometimes writers go beyond giving a formal definition; they also use extended definitions to make persuasive points. Take the Miller essay, for example (pages 393–94). The subject of Miller's extended definition is clearly the word *discrimination.* His purpose, however, is less immediately obvious. At first it appears that he wants only to explain what the word means. But by the third sentence he is distinguishing what it does not mean, and at the end it's clear he's trying to persuade readers to use the word correctly and thus to discriminate more sharply and justly themselves.

Using Definition across the Disciplines

When writing essays in the academic disciplines, you will have many opportunities to use the strategy of definition to both organize and strengthen the presentation of your ideas. To determine whether or not definition is the right strategy for you in a particular paper, use the four-step method described in Chapter 2 (Determining a Strategy for Developing Your Essay, pages 25–26). Consider the following examples, which illustrate how this four-step method works for typical college papers:

Philosophy

1. MAIN IDEA: A person of integrity is more than just an honest person.
2. QUESTION: What does it mean to have *integrity?*
3. STRATEGY: Definition. The direction words *mean* and *is more than* call for a complete explanation of the meaning of the word *integrity.*
4. SUPPORTING STRATEGY: Comparison and Contrast. To clarify the definition of *integrity*, it might be helpful to differentiate a person of integrity from a moral person or an ethical person.

Economics

1. MAIN IDEA: One way to understand the swings in the United States economy is to know the meaning of inflation.

2. QUESTION: What is inflation?
3. STRATEGY: Definition. The direction words *meaning* and *is* point us toward the strategy of definition—the word *inflation* needs to be explained.
4. SUPPORTING STRATEGY: Cause and Effect Analysis. In explaining the meaning of *inflation*, it would be interesting to explore economic factors that cause inflation as well as the effects of inflation on the economy.

Astronomy

1. MAIN IDEA: With the demotion of Pluto from planet to asteroid, astronomers have given new attention to the definition of *planet*.
2. QUESTION: What is a planet?
3. STRATEGY: Definition. The direction words *definition* and *is* call for an extended definition of the word *planet*. For clarification purposes, it would be helpful to define *asteroid* as well.
4. SUPPORTING STRATEGIES: Illustration and Cause and Effect Analysis. The definition of *planet* could be supported with several concrete examples of planets as well as an explanation of why astronomers thought a new definition was necessary.

Sample Student Essay Using Definition As a Writing Strategy

Originally a native of New York City, Howard Solomon Jr. studied in France as part of the American Field Services Intercultural Program in high school, and he majored in French at the University of Vermont. Solomon's other interests include foreign affairs, languages, photography, and cycling; in his wildest dreams, he imagines becoming an international lawyer. For the following essay, Solomon began by interviewing twenty students in his dormitory, collecting information and opinions that he eventually brought together with his own experiences to develop a definition of *best friends.*

Best Friends
Howard Solomon Jr.

Introduction: Writer provides brief definition of *best friend.*

Best friends, even when they are not a part of people's day-to-day lives, are essential to their well-being. They supply the companionship, help, security, and love that all people need. It is not

1

easy to put into words exactly what a best friend is, because the matter is so personal. People can benefit, however, from thinking about their best friends—who they are, what characteristics they share, and why they are so important—in order to gain a better understanding of themselves and their relationships.

When interviewed for their opinions about the qualities they most valued in their own best friends, twenty people in a University of Vermont dormitory agreed on three traits: reciprocity, honesty, and love. Reciprocity means that one can always rely on a best friend in times of need. A favor doesn't necessarily have to be returned, but best friends will return it anyway, because they want to. Best friends are willing to help each other for the sake of helping and not just for personal gain. One woman interviewed said that life seemed more secure because she knew her best friend was there if she ever needed help.

Honesty in a best friendship is the sharing of feelings openly and without reserve. All people interviewed said they could rely on their best friends as confidants: They could share problems with their best friends and ask for advice. They also felt that, even if best friends were critical of each other, they would never be hurtful or spiteful.

Love is probably the most important quality of a best friend relationship, according to the interview group. They very much prized the affection and enjoyment they felt in the company of their best friends. One man described it as a "gut reaction," and all said it was a different feeling from being with other friends. Private jokes, looks, and gestures create personal communication between best friends that is at a very high level—many times one person knows what the other is thinking without anything being said. The specifics differ, but almost everyone agreed that a special feeling exists, which is best described as love.

When asked who could be a best friend and who could not, most of those interviewed

Purpose: In defining *best friend,* writer comes to new understanding of self and relationships.

Organization: Sequence of interview questions

Three-part answer to question 1: What qualities do you value in a best friend?

Defines reciprocity between best friends

Defines honesty between best friends

Describes feelings of love between best friends

Answers to question 2: Who can be a best friend?

2

3

4

5

stated that it was impossible for parents, other relatives, and people of the opposite sex (especially husbands or wives) to be best friends. One woman said such people were "too inhibitive." Only two of those interviewed, both of whom were men, disagree—each had a female best friend. However, they seem to be an exception. Most of the people interviewed thought that their best friends were not demanding, while relatives and partners of the opposite sex can be very demanding.

> Interprets informants' responses

To the question of how many best friends one can have, about half of the sample responded that it is possible to have several best friends, although very few people can do so; others said it was possible to have only a very few best friends; and still others felt they could have just one. It was interesting to see how ideas varied on this question. Although best friends may be no less special for one person than another, people do define the concept differently.

> Answers to question 3: How many best friends can a person have?

Regarding how long it takes to become best friends and how long the relationship lasts, all were in agreement. "It is a long hard process which takes a lot of time," one woman explained. "It isn't something that can happen overnight," suggested another. One man said, "You usually know the person very well before you consider him your best friend. In fact you know everything about him, his bad points as well as his good points, so there is little likelihood that you can come into conflict with him." In addition, everyone thought that once a person has become a best friend, he or she remains so for the rest of one's life.

> Answers to question 4: How long does it take to become a best friend?

> Quotes informants to capture their thoughts and feelings accurately

During the course of the interviews one important and unexpected difference emerged between men and women. The men all said that a best friend usually possessed one quality that stood out above all others—an easygoing manner or humor or sympathy, for example. One of them said that he looked not for loyalty but for honesty, for someone who was truthful, because it was so rare

> Writer highlights an important difference in responses from men and women.

6

7

8

to find this quality in anyone. The women, however, all responded that they looked for a well-rounded person who had many good qualities. One woman said that a person who had just one good quality and not several would be "too boring to associate with." If this difference holds true beyond my sample, it means that men and women have quite different definitions of their best friends.

Personal example: Writer tells what he learned about best friends at the time of his father's death.

On a personal note, I have always wondered why my own best friends were so important to me; it wasn't until recently that something happened to make me really understand my relationship with them. My father died, and this was a crisis for me. Most of my friends gave me their condolences, but my best friends did more than that: They actually supported me. They called long distance to see how I was and what I needed, to try to help me work out my problems, or simply to talk. Two of my best friends even took time from their spring break and, along with two other best friends, attended my father's memorial service. None of my other friends came. Since then, these are the only people who have continued to worry about me and talk to me about my father. I know that whenever I need someone they will be there and willing to help me. I know also that whenever they need help I will be ready to do the same for them.

Conclusion: Writer gives personal definition of *best friend.*

Thesis

Yet, like the people I interviewed, I don't value my best friends just for what they do for me. I simply enjoy their company more than anyone else's. We talk, joke, play sports, and do all kinds of things when we are together. I never feel ill at ease with them, even after we've been apart for a while. As with virtually all of those I interviewed, the most important thing for me about best friends is the knowledge that I am never alone, that there are others in the world who care about my well-being as much as I do about theirs. Viewed in this light, having a best friend seems more like a necessity than it does a luxury reserved for the lucky few.

9

10

Analyzing Howard Solomon Jr.'s Definition Essay: Questions for Discussion

1. How does Solomon define *best friend* in his opening paragraph?

2. According to the people Solomon surveyed, what three qualities are valued most in a best friend?

3. Which of these qualities is considered the most important? Why?

4. How do men's and women's definitions of *best friend* differ? Do you agree with Solomon's interviewees?

5. In what ways do Solomon's interviews enhance his own definition of *best friend*?

6. In the final analysis, why does Solomon think people value their best friends so much?

Suggestions for Using Definition As a Writing Strategy

As you plan, write, and revise your definition essay, be mindful of the writing process guidelines described in Chapter 2. Also, pay particular attention to the basic requirements and essential ingredients for this writing strategy.

■ Planning Your Definition Essay

Planning is an essential part of writing a good definition essay. You can save yourself a great deal of work by taking the time to think about the key components of your essay before you actually begin to write.

Determine Your Purpose. Whatever your subject, make sure you have a clear sense of your purpose. Why are you writing a definition? If it's only to explain what a word or phrase means, you'll probably run out of things to say in a few sentences, or you'll find that a good dictionary has already said them for you. An effective extended definition should attempt to explain the essential nature of a thing or an idea, whether it be *photosynthesis* or *spring fever* or *Republicanism* or *prison* or *common sense*.

Often the challenge of writing a paper using the rhetorical strategy of definition is in getting your audience to understand your particular perception of the term or idea you are trying to define and explain. Take, for example, the selection on page 403 from a student essay. For many years, the citizens of Quebec, one of Canada's ten provinces, have been debating and voting on the issue of secession from Canada. At the core of this volatile issue is the essential question of Canadian identity. As you will see from the student's introduction, the Quebecois define Canadian identity very differently from the way other Canadians define it.

Quebecois Are Canadians

The peaceful formation of Canada as an independent nation has led to the current identity crisis in Quebec. The Quebecois perceive themselves to be different from all other Canadians because of their French ancestry and their unique history as both rulers and minorities in Canada. In an attempt to create a unified Canada the government has tried to establish a common Canadian culture through the building of a transcontinental railroad, a nationalized medical system, a national arts program, a national agenda, and the required use of both French and English in all publications and on all signs. As the twenty-first century begins, however, Canadians, especially the Quebecois, continue to grapple with the issue of what it means to be a Canadian, and unless some consensus can be reached on the definition of the Canadian identity, Quebec's attempt to secede from Canada may succeed.

This introductory paragraph establishes the need to define the terms *Canadians* and *Quebecois*. The emphasis on these two terms implies that another rhetorical strategy—comparison and contrast—will likely come into play. The writer might go on to use other strategies, such as description or illustration, to highlight common characteristics or differences between the Canadians and Quebecois. Judging from the title, it is clear that an argument will be made that Quebecois are Canadians.

When you decide on your topic, consider an idea or term that you would like to clarify or explain to someone. For example, Howard Solomon Jr. hit on the idea of defining what a best friend is. He recalls that "a friend of mine had become a best friend, and I was trying to figure out what had happened, what was different. So I decided to explore what was on my mind." At the beginning, you should have at least a general idea of what your subject means to you, as well as a sense of the audience you are writing your definition for and the impact you want your definition to achieve. The following advice will guide you as you plan and draft your essay.

Formulate a Thesis Statement.   A strong, clear thesis statement is critical in any essay. When writing an essay using extended definition, you should formulate a thesis statement that states clearly both the word or idea that you want to define or explain and the way in which you are going to present your thoughts. Here are two examples from this chapter.

Thesis   We have a word in English which means "the ability to tell differences." That word is *discrimination*. But within the last [fifty] years, this word has been so frequently misused that an entire generation has grown up believing that "discrimination" means "racism."

[Robert Keith Miller's thesis statement tells us that he will be discussing the word *discrimination* and how it is not the same as racism.]

Thesis   As the twenty-first century begins, however, Canadians, especially the Quebecois, continue to grapple with the issue of what it means to be a Canadian, and unless some consensus can be reached on the definition of the Canadian identity, Quebec's attempt to secede from Canada may succeed.

[The student writer makes it clear that the identity of both the Canadians and the Quebecois will be defined. The thesis statement also conveys a sense of the urgency of discussing these definitions.]

As you begin to develop your thesis statement, ask yourself, "What is my point?" Next ask yourself, "What types of definitions will be most useful in making my point?" If you can't answer these questions yet, write some ideas down and try to determine your main point from these ideas.

Once you have settled on an idea, go back to the two questions above and write down your answers to them. Then combine the answers into a single-sentence thesis statement. Your eventual thesis statement does not have to be one sentence, but this exercise can be an effective way of focusing your point.

Consider Your Audience.   What do your readers know? If you're an economics major in an undergraduate writing course, you can safely assume that you know your subject better than most of your readers do, and so you will have to explain even very basic terms and ideas. If, however, you're writing a paper for your course in econometrics, your most important reader — the one who grades your paper — won't even slow down at your references to *monetary aggregates* and *Philips Curves* — provided, of course, that you use them correctly, showing that you know what they mean.

Choose a Type of Definition That Fits Your Subject.   How you choose to develop your definition depends on your subject, your purpose, and your readers. Many inexperienced writers believe that any extended definition, no matter what the subject, should begin with a formal "dictionary" definition. This is not necessarily so; you will find that few of the essays in this chapter include formal definitions.

Instead, their authors assume that their readers have dictionaries and know how to use them. If, however, you think your readers do require a formal definition at some point, don't simply quote from a dictionary. Unless you have some very good reason for doing otherwise, put the definition into your own words — words that suit your approach and the probable readers of your essay. (Certainly, in an essay about photosynthesis, non-scientists would be baffled by an opening such as this: "The dictionary defines *photosynthesis* as 'the process by which chlorophyll-containing cells in green plants convert incident light to chemical energy and synthesize organic compounds from inorganic compounds, especially carbohydrates from carbon dioxide and water, with the simultaneous release of oxygen.'") There's another advantage to using your own words: You won't have to write "The dictionary defines . . ." or "According to *Webster's* . . ."; stock phrases like these almost immediately put the reader's mind to sleep.

Certain concepts, such as *liberalism* and *discrimination*, lend themselves to different interpretations, depending on the writer's point of view. While readers may agree in general about what such subjects mean, there will be much disagreement over particulars and therefore room for you to propose and defend your own definitions.

Solomon remembers the difficulties he had getting started with his essay on best friends:

> The first draft I wrote was nothing. I tried to get a start with the dictionary definition, but it didn't help—it just put into two words what really needs hundreds of words to explain, and the words it used had to be defined, too. My teacher suggested I might get going better if I talked about my topic with other people. I decided to make it semiformal, so I made up a list of a few specific questions—five questions—and went to twenty people I knew and asked them questions like, "What qualities do your best friends have?" and "What are some of the things they've done for you?" I took notes on the answers, and I was surprised when so many of them agreed. It isn't a scientific sampling, but the results helped me get started.

■ Organizing and Writing Your Definition Essay

Develop an Organizational Plan.   Once you have gathered all the information you will need for your extended definition essay, you will want to settle on an organizational plan that suits your purpose and your materials. If you want to show that one definition of *family* is better than others, for example, you might want to lead with the definitions you plan to discard and end with the one you want your readers to accept.

Howard Solomon Jr. can trace several distinct stages that his paper went through before he settled on the plan of organizing his examples around the items on his interview questionnaire.

> Doing this paper showed me that writing isn't all that easy. Boy, I went through so many drafts—adding some things, taking out some things, reorganizing. At one point half the paper was a definition of

friends, so I could contrast them with the definition of *best friends.* That wasn't necessary. Then the personal stuff came in late. In fact, my father died after I'd begun writing the paper, so that paragraph came in almost last of all. On the next-to-last draft everything was there, but it was put together in a sort of random way—not completely random, one idea would lead to the next and then the next—but there was a lot of circling around. My teacher pointed this out and suggested I outline what I'd written and work on the outline. So I tried it, and I saw what the problem was and what I had to do. It was just a matter of getting my examples into an order that corresponded to my interview questions.

Use Other Rhetorical Strategies to Support Your Definition. Although definition can be used effectively as a separate rhetorical strategy, it is generally used alongside other writing strategies. Photosynthesis, for example, is a natural process, so one logical strategy for defining it would be *process analysis*; readers who know little about biology may better understand photosynthesis if you draw an *analogy* with the eating and breathing of human beings. *Common sense* is an abstract concept, so its meaning could certainly be *illustrated* with concrete *examples*; in addition, its special nature might emerge more sharply through *comparison and contrast* with other ways of thinking. To define a salt marsh, you might choose a typical marsh and *describe* it. To define economic inflation or a particular disease, you might discuss its *causes and effects*. In the end, only one requirement limits your choice of supporting strategy: The strategy must help you define your term.

As you read the essays in this chapter, consider all of the writing strategies that the authors have used to support their definitions. Solomon, for example, builds his definition essay around the many examples he garnered from his interviews with other students and from his own personal experiences. As you read the other essays and note the supporting strategies authors use when defining their subjects, ask yourself the following: How do you think these other strategies have added to or changed the style of the essay? Are there strategies that you might have added or taken out? What strategies, if any, do you think you might use to strengthen your definition essay?

■ Revising and Editing Your Definition Essay

Share Your Drafts with Others.   Try sharing the drafts of your essay with other students in your writing class to make sure that your definition works. Ask them if there are any parts that they do not understand. Have them tell you what they think is the point of your essay. If their answers differ from what you intended, have them indicate the passages that led them to their interpretations so that you can change your text accordingly. To maximize the effectiveness of conferences with your peers, use the guidelines presented on page 29. Feedback from these conferences often provides one or more places where you can start revising.

Select Words That Accurately Denote and Connote What You Want to Say.   The *denotation* of a word is its literal meaning or dictionary definition. Most of the time you will have no trouble with denotation, but problems can occur when words are close in meaning or sound a lot alike.

accept	*v.*, to receive
except	*prep.*, to exclude
affect	*v.*, to influence
effect	*n.*, the result; v., to produce, bring into existence
anecdote	*n.*, a short narrative
antidote	*n.*, a medicine for countering effects of poison
coarse	*adj.*, rough; crude
course	*n.*, a route, a program of instruction
disinterested	*adj.*, free of self-interest or bias
uninterested	*adj.*, without interest
eminent	*adj.*, outstanding, as in reputation
immanent	*adj.*, remaining within, inherent
imminent	*adj.*, about to happen
principal	*n.*, a school official; in finance, a capital sum; adj., most important
principle	*n.*, a basic law or rule of conduct
than	*conj.*, used in comparisons
then	*adv.*, at that time

Consult your desk dictionary if you are not sure you are using the correct word.

Words have connotative values as well as denotative meanings. *Connotations* are the associations or emotional overtones that words have acquired. For example, the word *hostage* denotes a person who is given or held as security for the fulfillment of certain conditions or terms, but it connotes images of suffering, loneliness, torture, fear, deprivation, starvation, anxiety, as well as other images based on our individual associations. Because many words in English are synonyms or have the same meanings — *strength, potency, force*, and *might* all denote "power" — your task as a writer in any given situation is to choose the word with the connotations that best suit your purpose.

Use Specific and Concrete Words.   Words can be classified as relatively general or specific, abstract or concrete. *General words* name groups or classes of objects, qualities, or actions. *Specific words* name individual objects, qualities, or actions within a class or group. For example, *dessert* is more specific than *food*, but more general than *pie*. And *pie* is more general than *blueberry pie*.

Abstract words refer to ideas, concepts, qualities, and conditions — *love, anger, beauty, youth, wisdom, honesty, patriotism,* and *liberty,* for example. *Concrete words,* on the other hand, name things you can see, hear, taste, touch, or smell. *Cornbread, rocking chair, sailboat, nitrogen, computer, rain, horse,* and *coffee* are all concrete words.

General and abstract words generally fail to create in the reader's mind the kind of vivid response that concrete, specific words do. Always question the words you choose. Notice how Jo Goodwin Parker uses concrete, specific diction in the opening sentences of many paragraphs in her essay "What Is Poverty?" to paint a powerful verbal picture of what poverty is:

> Poverty is getting up every morning from a dirt- and illness-stained mattress.
> Poverty is being tired.
> Poverty is dirt.
> Poverty is staying up all night on cold nights to watch the fire, knowing one spark on the newspaper covering the walls means your sleeping children die in flames.
>
> — JO GOODWIN PARKER
> "What Is Poverty?," pages 410–13

Collectively, these specific and concrete words create a memorable definition of the abstraction *poverty.*

Question Your Own Work While Revising and Editing. Revision is best done by asking yourself key questions about what you have written. Begin by reading, preferably aloud, what you have written. Reading aloud forces you to pay attention to every single word, and you are more likely to catch lapses in the logical flow of thought. After you have read your paper through, answer the following questions for revising and editing, and make the necessary changes.

For help with twelve common writing problems, See Chapter 16, "Editing for Grammar, Punctuation, and Sentence Style."

Questions for Revising and Editing: Definition

1. Have I selected a subject in which there is some controversy or at least a difference of opinion about the definitions of key words?

2. Is the purpose of my definition clearly stated?

3. Have I presented a clear thesis statement?

4. Have I considered my audience? Do I oversimplify material for knowledgeable people or complicate material for beginners?

5. Have I used the types of definitions (*formal definition, synonymous definition, negative definition, etymological definition, stipulative definition,* and *extended definition*) that are most useful in making my point?

6. Is my definition essay easy to follow? That is, is there a clear organizational principle (chronological or logical, for example)?

7. Have I used other rhetorical strategies — such as illustration, comparison and contrast, and cause and effect analysis — as needed and appropriate to enhance my definition?

8. Does my conclusion stem logically from my thesis statement and purpose?

9. Have I used precise language to convey my meaning? Have I used words that are specific and concrete?

10. Have I avoided errors in grammar, punctuation, and mechanics? Is my sentence style as clear, smooth, and persuasive as possible? E1–12

What Is Poverty?

Jo Goodwin Parker

All we know about Jo Goodwin Parker comes from the account of professor George Henderson, who received the following essay from Parker while he was compiling a selection of readings intended for future educators planning to teach in rural communities. This selection, which Henderson subsequently included in *America's Other Children: Public Schools Outside Suburbs* (1971), has been identified as the text of a speech given in De Land, Florida, on December 27, 1965. Although Henderson has not shared any biographical information on the author, it may be useful to consider her identity. While Parker may be who she claims to be—one of the rural poor who eke out a difficult living just beyond view of America's middle-class majority—it is also possible that she is instead a spokesperson for these individuals, families, and communities, writing not from her own experience, but from long and sympathetic observation. In either case, her definition of *poverty* is so detailed and forceful that it conveys, even to those who have never known it, the nature of poverty.

■ Preparing to Read

What does it mean to you to be poor? What do you see as some of the effects of poverty on people?

You ask me what is poverty? Listen to me. Here I am, dirty, smelly, and with 1 no "proper" underwear on and with the stench of my rotting teeth near you. I will tell you. Listen to me. Listen without pity. I cannot use your pity. Listen with understanding. Put yourself in my dirty, worn-out, ill-fitting shoes, and hear me.

Poverty is getting up every morning from a dirt- and illness-stained mat- 2 tress. The sheets have long since been used for diapers. Poverty is living in a smell that never leaves. This is a smell of urine, sour milk, and spoiling food sometimes joined with the strong smell of long-cooked onions. Onions are cheap. If you have smelled this smell, you did not know how it came. It is the smell of the outdoor privy. It is the smell of young children who cannot walk the long dark way in the night. It is the smell of the mattresses where years of "accidents" have happened. It is the smell of the milk which has gone sour because the refrigerator long has not worked, and it costs money to get it fixed. It is the smell of rotting garbage. I could bury it, but where is the shovel? Shovels cost money.

Poverty is being tired. I have always been tired. They told me at the hos- 3 pital when the last baby came that I had chronic anemia caused from poor diet, a bad case of worms, and that I needed a corrective operation. I listened politely—the poor are always polite. The poor always listen. They don't say that there is no money for iron pills, or better food, or worm medicine. The

Poverty is getting up every morning from a dirt- and illness-stained mattress. The sheets have long since been used for diapers. Poverty is living in a smell that never leaves.

idea of an operation is frightening and costs so much that, if I had dared, I would have laughed. Who takes care of my children? Recovery from an operation takes a long time. I have three children. When I left them with "Granny" the last time I had a job, I came home to find the baby covered with fly specks, and a diaper that had not been changed since I left. When the dried diaper came off, bits of my baby's flesh came with it. My other child was playing with a sharp bit of broken glass, and my oldest was playing alone at the edge of a lake. I made twenty-two dollars a week, and a good nursery school costs twenty dollars a week for three children. I quit my job.

Poverty is dirt. You say in your clean clothes coming from your clean house, "Anybody can be clean." Let me explain about housekeeping with no money. For breakfast I give my children grits with no oleo or cornbread without eggs and oleo. This does not use up many dishes. What dishes there are, I wash in cold water and with no soap. Even the cheapest soap has to be saved for the baby's diapers. Look at my hands, so cracked and red. Once I saved for two months to buy a jar of Vaseline for my hands and the baby's diaper rash. When I had saved enough, I went to buy it and the price had gone up two cents. The baby and I suffered on. I have to decide every day if I can bear to put my cracked, sore hands into the cold water and strong soap. But you ask, why not hot water? Fuel costs money. If you have a wood fire it costs money. If you burn electricity, it costs money. Hot water is a luxury. I do not have luxuries. I know you will be surprised when I tell you how young I am. I look so much older. My back has been bent over the wash tubs for so long, I cannot remember when I ever did anything else. Every night I wash every stitch my school-age child has on and just hope her clothes will be dry by morning. 4

Poverty is staying up all night on cold nights to watch the fire, knowing one spark on the newspaper covering the walls means your sleeping children die in flames. In summer poverty is watching gnats and flies devour your baby's tears when he cries. The screens are torn and you pay so little rent you know they will never be fixed. Poverty means insects in your food, in your nose, in your eyes, and crawling over you when you sleep. Poverty is hoping it never rains because diapers won't dry when it rains and soon you are using newspapers. Poverty is seeing your children forever with runny noses. Paper handkerchiefs cost money and all your rags you need for other things. Even more costly are antihistamines. Poverty is cooking without food and cleaning without soap. 5

Poverty is asking for help. Have you ever had to ask for help, knowing your children will suffer unless you get it? Think about asking for a loan from a relative, if this is the only way you can imagine asking for help. I will 6 tell you how it feels. You find out where the office is that you are supposed to visit. You circle that block four or five times. Thinking of your children, you go in. Everyone is very busy. Finally, someone comes out and you tell her that you need help. That never is the person you need to see. You go see another person, and after spilling the whole shame of your poverty all over the desk between you, you find that this isn't the right office after all — you must repeat the whole process, and it never is any easier at the next place.

You have asked for help, and after all it has a cost. You are again told to 7 wait. You are told why, but you don't really hear because of the red cloud of shame and the rising black cloud of despair.

Poverty is remembering. It is remembering quitting school in junior 8 high because "nice" children had been so cruel about my clothes and my smell. The attendance officer came. My mother told him I was pregnant. I wasn't but she thought that I could get a job and help out. I had jobs off and on, but never long enough to learn anything. Mostly I remember being married. I was so young then. I am still young. For a time, we had all the things you have. There was a little house in another town, with hot water and everything. Then my husband lost his job. There was unemployment insurance for a while and what few jobs I could get. Soon, all our nice things were repossessed and we moved back here. I was pregnant then. This house didn't look so bad when we first moved in. Every week it gets worse. Nothing is ever fixed. We now had no money. There were a few odd jobs for my husband, but everything went for food then, as it does now. I don't know how we lived through three years and three babies, but we did. I'll tell you something, after the last baby I destroyed my marriage. It had been a good one, but could you keep on bringing children in this dirt? Did you ever think how much it costs for any kind of birth control? I knew my husband was leaving the day he left, but there were no good-byes between us. I hope he has been able to climb out of this mess somewhere. He never could hope with us to drag him down.

That's when I asked for help. When I got it, you know how much it was? 9 It was, and is, seventy-eight dollars a month for the four of us; that is all I ever can get. Now you know why there is no soap, no needles and thread, no hot water, no aspirin, no worm medicine, no hand cream, no shampoo. None of these things forever and ever and ever. So that you can see clearly, I pay twenty dollars a month rent, and most of the rest goes for food. For grits and cornmeal, and rice and milk and beans. I try my best to use only the minimum electricity. If I use more, there is that much less for food.

Poverty is looking into a black future. Your children won't play with my 10 boys. They will turn to other boys who steal to get what they want. I can already see them behind the bars of their prison instead of behind the bars of my poverty. Or they will turn to the freedom of alcohol or drugs, and find themselves enslaved. And my daughter? At best, there is for her a life like mine.

But you say to me, there are schools. Yes, there are schools. My children 11 have no extra books, no magazines, no extra pencils, or crayons, or paper and the most important of all, they do not have health. They have worms, they have infections, they have pinkeye all summer. They do not sleep well on the floor, or with me in my one bed. They do not suffer from hunger, my seventy-eight dollars keeps us alive, but they do suffer from malnutrition. Oh yes, I do remember what I was taught about health in school. It doesn't do much good. In some places there is a surplus commodities program. Not here. The county said it cost too much. There is a school lunch program. But I have two children who will already be damaged by the time they get to school.

But, you say to me, there are health clinics. Yes, there are health clinics and 12
they are in the towns. I live out here eight miles from town. I can walk that far (even if it is sixteen miles both ways), but can my little children? My neighbor will take me when he goes; but he expects to get paid, *one way or another.* I bet you know my neighbor. He is that large man who spends his time at the gas station, the barbershop, and the corner store complaining about the government spending money on the immoral mothers of illegitimate children.

Poverty is an acid that drips on pride until all pride is worn away. Poverty 13
is a chisel that chips on honor until honor is worn away. Some of you say that you would do *something* in my situation, and maybe you would, for the first week or the first month, but for year after year after year?

Even the poor can dream. A dream of a time when there is money. Mo- 14
ney for the right kinds of food, for worm medicine, for iron pills, for tooth-brushes, for hand cream, for a hammer and nails and a bit of screening, for a shovel, for a bit of paint, for some sheeting, for needles and thread. Money to pay *in money* for a trip to town. And, oh, money for hot water and money for soap. A dream of when asking for help does not eat away the last bit of pride. When the office you visit is as nice as the offices of other governmental agencies, when there are enough workers to help you quickly, when workers do not quit in defeat and despair. When you have to tell your story to only one person, and that person can send you for other help and you don't have to prove your poverty over and over and over again.

I have come out of my despair to tell you this. Remember I did not come 15
from another place or another time. Others like me are all around you. Look at us with an angry heart, anger that will help you help me. Anger that will let you tell of me. The poor are always silent. Can you be silent, too?

▪ Thinking Critically about the Text

Throughout the essay, Parker describes the feelings and emotions associated with her poverty. Have you ever witnessed or observed people in Parker's situation? What was your reaction?

▪ Questions on Subject

1. Why didn't Parker have the operation that was recommended for her? Why did she quit her job?

2. In Parker's view, what makes asking for help such a difficult and painful experience? What compels her to do so anyway?

3. Why did Parker's husband leave her? How does she justify her attitude toward his leaving? (Glossary: *Attitude*)

4. In paragraph 12, Parker says the following about a neighbor giving her a ride to the nearest health clinic: "My neighbor will take me when he goes; but he expects to get paid, *one way or another*. I bet you know my neighbor." What is she implying in these sentences and in the rest of the paragraph?

5. What are the chances that the dreams described in paragraph 14 will come true? What do you think Parker would say?

■ Questions on Strategy

1. What is Parker's purpose in defining poverty as she does? (Glossary: *Purpose*) Why has she cast her essay in the form of an extended definition? What effect does this have on the reader?

2. What techniques of definition does Parker use? What is missing that you would expect to find in a more general and impersonal definition of poverty? Why does Parker leave such information out?

3. Parker repeats words and phrases throughout this essay. Choose several examples, and explain their impact on you. (Glossary: *Coherence*)

4. In depicting poverty, Parker uses description to create vivid verbal pictures, and she illustrates the various aspects of poverty with examples drawn from her experience. (Glossary: *Description; Illustration*) What are the most striking details she uses? How do you account for the emotional impact of the details and images she has selected? In what ways do description and illustration enhance her definition of poverty?

■ Questions on Diction and Vocabulary

1. Although her essay is written for the most part in simple, straightforward language, Parker does make use of an occasional striking figure of speech. (Glossary: *Figures of Speech*) Identify at least three such figures — you might begin with those in paragraph 13 (for example, "Poverty is an acid") — and explain their effect on the reader.

2. In paragraph 10, Parker states that "poverty is looking into a black future." How does this language characterize her children's future?

3. How would you characterize Parker's tone and her style? (Glossary: *Style; Tone*) How do you respond to her use of the pronoun *you*? Point to specific examples of her diction and descriptions as support for your view. (Glossary: *Diction*)

4. Refer to your desk dictionary to determine the meanings of the following words as Parker uses them in this selection: *chronic* (paragraph 3), *anemia* (3), *grits* (4), *oleo* (4), *antihistamines* (5).

■ Classroom Activity Using Definition

Without consulting a dictionary, try writing a formal definition for one of the following terms by putting it in a class and then differentiating it from other words in the class. (See page 394 for a discussion of formal definitions together with examples.)

tortilla chips	trombone
psychology	*American Idol*
robin	Catholicism
anger	secretary

Once you have completed your definition, compare it with the definition found in a dictionary. What conclusions can you draw? Explain.

■ Writing Suggestions

1. Using Parker's essay as a model, write an extended definition of a topic about which you have some expertise. Choose as your subject a particular environment (suburbia, the inner city, a dormitory, a shared living area), a way of living (as the child of divorce, as a person with a disability, as a working student), or a topic of your own choosing. If you prefer, you can adopt a persona instead of writing from your own perspective.

2. **Writing with Sources.** Write a proposal or a plan of action that will make people aware of poverty or some other social problem in your community. How do you define the problem? What needs to be done to increase awareness of it? What practical steps would you propose be undertaken once the public is made aware of the situation? You will likely need to do some research in the library or online in order to garner support for your proposal.

For models of and advice on integrating sources, see Chapters 14–15.

Steal This MP3 File: What Is Theft?

G. ANTHONY GORRY

G. Anthony Gorry is a medical educator and information technology specialist. He received his B.S. from Yale University in 1962 and pursued graduate study at the University of California–Berkeley, where he earned his M.S. in chemical engineering in 1964, and at MIT, where he received his Ph.D. in computer science in 1967. Gorry has taught at Baylor College of Medicine and is the Friedkin Professor of Management and a professor of computer science at Rice University. He is the author of numerous journal articles on management information systems and problem identification. Since 1997 he has served as a director for Arc Pharmaceuticals, Inc.

In the following article, which first appeared in the *Chronicle of Higher Education* on May 23, 2003, Gorry recounts an experience he had in one of his information technology courses in order to demonstrate how technology might be shaping the attitude of today's youth. He senses that the meaning of *theft* may be shifting in our ever-changing world.

■ Preparing to Read

What for you constitutes theft? Do you recall ever stealing anything? Did you get caught? Did you have to return the item or make restitution? How did you feel about the incident at the time? How do you feel about it now?

Sometimes when my students don't see life the way I do, I recall the com- 1
plaint from *Bye Bye Birdie*, "What's the matter with kids today?" Then I remember that the "kids" in my class are children of the information age. In large part, technology has made them what they are, shaping their world and what they know. For my students, the advance of technology is expected, but for me, it remains both remarkable and somewhat unsettling.

In one course I teach, the students and I explore the effects of informa- 2
tion technology on society. Our different perspectives on technology lead to engaging and challenging discussions that reveal some of the ways in which technology is shaping the attitudes of young people. An example is our discussion of intellectual property in the information age, of crucial importance to the entertainment business.

In recent years, many users of the Internet have launched an assault 3
on the music business. Armed with tools for "ripping" music from compact

discs and setting it "free" in cyberspace, they can disseminate online countless copies of a digitally encoded song. Music companies, along with some
artists, have tried to stop this perceived pillaging of intellectual property
by legal and technical means. The industry has had some success with legal
actions against companies that provide the infrastructure for file sharing,
but enthusiasm for sharing music is growing, and new file-sharing services
continue to appear.

4   The Recording Industry Association of America . . . filed lawsuits against
four college students, seeking huge damages for "an emporium of music piracy"
run on campus networks. However, the industry settled those lawsuits less
than a week after a federal judge in California ruled against the association in
another case, affirming that two of the Internet's most popular music-swapping
services are not responsible for copyright infringements by their users. (In the
settlement, the students admitted no wrongdoing but agreed to pay amounts
ranging from $12,000 to $17,500 in annual installments over several years and
to shut down their file-sharing systems.)

> [I]n the case
> of digital
> music, where
> the material is
> disconnected
> from the physical
> moorings of
> conventional
> stores and
> copying is so
> easy, many of my
> students see mat-
> ters differently.

5   With so many Internet users currently sharing music, legal maneuvers alone seem unlikely
to protect the industry's way of doing business.
Therefore, the music industry has turned to the
technology itself, seeking to create media that
cannot be copied or can be copied only in prescribed circumstances. Finding the right technology for such a defense, however, is not easy.
Defensive technology must not prevent legitimate uses of the media by customers, yet it must
somehow ward off attacks by those seeking to
"liberate" the content to the Internet. And each
announcement of a defensive technology spurs
development of means to circumvent it.

6   In apparent frustration, some companies
have introduced defective copies of their music
into the file-sharing environment of the Internet,
hoping to discourage widespread downloading
of music. But so far, the industry's multifaceted defense has failed. Sales of CDs
continue to decline. And now video ripping and sharing has emerged on the
Internet, threatening to upset another industry in the same way.

7   Music companies might have more success if they focused on the users
instead of the courts and technology. When they characterize file sharing as
theft, they overlook the interplay of technology and behavior that has altered
the very idea of theft, at least among young people. I got a clear demonstration
of that change in a class discussion that began with the matter of a stolen book.

8   During the '60s, I was a graduate student at a university where student
activism had raised tensions on and around the campus. In the midst of debates,

demonstrations, and protests, a football player was caught leaving the campus store with a book he had not bought. Because he was well known, his misadventure made the school newspaper. What seemed to be a simple case of theft, however, took on greater significance. A number of groups with little connection to athletics rose to his defense, claiming that he had been entrapped: The university required that he have the book, the publisher charged an unfairly high price, and the bookstore put the book right in front of him, tempting him to steal it. So who could blame him?

Well, my students could. They thought it was clear that he had stolen the book. But an MP3 file played from my laptop evoked a different response. Had I stolen the song? Not really, because a student had given me the file as a gift. Well, was that file stolen property? Was it like the book stolen from the campus bookstore so many years ago? No again, because it was a copy, not the original, which presumably was with the student. But then what should we make of the typical admonition on compact-disc covers that unauthorized duplication is illegal? Surely the MP3 file was a duplication of the original. To what extent is copying stealing? 9

The readings for the class amply demonstrated the complexity of the legal, technical, and economic issues surrounding intellectual property in the information age and gave the students much to talk about. Some students argued that existing regulations are simply inadequate at a time when all information "wants to be free" and when liberating technology is at hand. Others pointed to differences in the economics of the music and book businesses. In the end, the students who saw theft in the removal of the book back in the '60s did not see stealing in the unauthorized copying of music. For me, that was the most memorable aspect of the class because it illustrates how technology affects what we take to be moral behavior. 10

The technology of copying is closely related to the idea of theft. For example, my students would not take books from a store, but they do not consider photocopying a few pages of a book to be theft. They would not copy an entire book, however, perhaps because they vaguely acknowledge intellectual-property rights but probably more because copying would be cumbersome and time-consuming. They would buy the book instead. In that case, the very awkwardness of the copying aligns their actions with moral guidelines and legal standards. 11

But in the case of digital music, where the material is disconnected from the physical moorings of conventional stores and copying is so easy, many of my students see matters differently. They freely copy and share music. And they copy and share software, even though such copying is often illegal. If their books were digital and thus could be copied with comparable ease, they most likely would copy and share them. 12

Of course, the Digital Millennium Copyright Act, along with other laws, prohibits such copying. So we could just say that theft is theft, and complain with the song, "Why can't they be like we were, perfect in every way? . . . Oh, 13 what's the matter with kids today?" But had we had the same digital technology when we were young, we probably would have engaged in the same copying and sharing of software, digital music, and video that are so common among students today. We should not confuse lack of tools with righteousness.

The music industry would be foolish to put its faith in new protective   14
schemes and devices alone. Protective technology cannot undo the changes that previous technology has caused. Should the industry aggressively pursue legal defenses like the suits against the four college students? Such highly publicized actions may be legally sound and may even slow music sharing in certain settings, but they cannot stop the transformation of the music business. The technology of sharing is too widespread, and my students (and their younger siblings) no longer agree with the music companies about right and wrong. Even some of the companies with big stakes in recorded music seem to have recognized that lawsuits and technical defenses won't work. Sony, for example, sells computers with "ripping and burning" capabilities, MP3 players, and other devices that gain much of their appeal from music sharing. And the AOL part of AOL Time Warner is promoting its new broadband service for faster downloads, which many people will use to share music sold by the Warner part of the company.

The lesson from my classroom is that digital technology has unalter-   15
ably changed the way a growing number of customers think about recorded music. If the music industry is to prosper, it must change, too — perhaps offering repositories of digital music for downloading (like Apple's . . . iTunes Music Store), gaining revenue from the scope and quality of its holdings, and from a variety of new products and relationships, as yet largely undefined. Such a transformation will be excruciating for the industry, requiring the abandonment of previously profitable business practices with no certain prospect of success. So it is not surprising that the industry has responded aggressively, with strong legal actions, to the spread of file sharing. But by that response, the industry is risking its relationship with a vital segment of its market. Treating customers like thieves is a certain recipe for failure.

▪ Thinking Critically about the Text

Where do you stand on file sharing? Like Gorry's students, do you freely copy and share music or software? Do you consider all such sharing acceptable, or is there some point where it turns into theft? Explain.

▪ Questions on Subject

1. What is intellectual property, and how is it different from other types of property?
2. How has the music industry tried to stop "music piracy" on the Internet? What has been the success of their efforts?

3. Do you think the football player caught leaving the campus store with a book was guilty of stealing, or are you persuaded by the argument that "he had been entrapped" (paragraph 8)? Explain.
4. What does Gorry mean when he says that "the technology of copying is closely related to the idea of theft" (11)?
5. What advice do Gorry and his students have for the music industry? Is this advice realistic? Explain. What suggestions would you like to add?

■ Questions on Strategy

1. What is Gorry's thesis, and where is it stated? (Glossary: *Thesis*)
2. Gorry's purpose is to show that there has recently been a shift in what the Internet generation believes constitutes theft. (Glossary: *Purpose*) How well does he accomplish his purpose?
3. What examples does Gorry use to develop his definition of theft? (Glossary: *Illustration*) How does he use these examples to illustrate the shift in meaning that he believes has occurred?
4. With what authority does Gorry write on the subjects of intellectual property, technology, and theft?
5. Gorry uses lyrics from the movie *Bye Bye Birdie* to introduce his essay and start his conclusion. (Glossary: *Beginnings/Endings*) Are these just gimmicky quotations, or do they contribute to the substance of Gorry's essay?
6. Gorry ends paragraph 8 with the question "So who could blame him?" and then begins paragraph 9 with the response "Well, my students could," thus making a smooth transition from one paragraph to the next. (Glossary: *Transitions*) What other transitional devices does Gorry use to add coherence to his essay? (Glossary: *Coherence*)

■ Questions on Diction and Vocabulary

1. Who is Gorry's intended audience? (Glossary: *Audience*) To whom does the pronoun *we* in paragraph 13 refer? What other evidence in Gorry's diction do you find to support your conclusion about his audience?
2. How would you describe Gorry's diction — formal, objective, conversational, jargon-filled? (Glossary: *Technical Language*) Point out specific words and phrases that led you to this conclusion.
3. Refer to your desk dictionary to determine the meanings of the following words as Gorry uses them in this selection: *disseminate* (paragraph 3), *encoded* (3), *emporium* (4), *infringements* (4), *repositories* (15).

■ Classroom Activity Using Definition

Definitions are often dependent on one's perspective, as Gorry illustrates with the word *theft* in his essay. Discuss with your classmates other words or terms — such as *success, failure, wealth, poverty, cheap, expensive, happiness, loneliness, want, need*—whose definitions often are dependent on one's perspective. Write brief definitions for several of these words from your perspective. Share your definitions with other members of your class. What differences in perspective, if any, are apparent in the definitions?

■ Writing Suggestions

1. Although it is not always immediately apparent, English is constantly changing because it is a living language. New words come into the lexicon, and others become obsolete. Some words like *theft* change over time to reflect society's thinking and behavior. Another word whose definition has ignited recent debate is *marriage.* Using Gorry's essay as a model, write a paper in which you define a word whose meaning has changed over the past decade.

2. Gorry is very aware of how information technology is shaping our attitudes about the world. We're living at a time when digital technology makes it not only possible but also surprisingly easy for us to copy and share software, music, e-books, and video. Gorry does not condemn such behavior out of hand; instead, he warns that "we should not confuse lack of tools with righteousness" (paragraph 13). Write an essay in which you explore some of the ways today's technology has shaped your attitudes, especially as it "affects what we take to be moral behavior" (10). Be sure to support your key points with examples from your own reading or experience. (Glossary: *Illustration*)

What Does "Boys Will Be Boys" Really Mean?

DEBORAH M. ROFFMAN

A nationally certified sexuality and family life educator, Deborah M. Roffman was born in 1947 in Baltimore, Maryland. She graduated from Goucher College in 1968 and later received an M.S. in community health education from Towson University. Since 1975, Roffman has worked with scores of public and private schools on curriculum, faculty development, and parent education issues. Her articles on health and sex education have been featured in the *New York Times, Baltimore Sun, Chicago Tribune, Boston Globe, Los Angeles Times, Education Week, Teacher* magazine, and *Parents* magazine. A former associate editor of the *Journal of Sex Education and Therapy*, she has appeared on an HBO special on parenting, on National Public Radio, on *The Early Show*, and on the *O'Reilly Factor*. In addition, Roffman was featured, in December of 2002, in a story on teenage sexuality on ABC's *20/20*. In 2001 Roffman published her first book, *Sex and Sensibility: The Thinking Parent's Guide to Talking Sense about Sex*. This was followed by *But How Did I Get in There in the First Place?: The Thinking Parent's Guide to Talking to Young Children about Sex* (2002). Of the latter book, one reviewer wrote, "Roffman is a powerful advocate for children, understanding that in a society that gives confusing and exploitative messages about sexuality, children are desperate for communication from the caring adults in their lives." Currently Roffman lives in Baltimore, where she teaches human sexuality education in grades 4 through 12 in an effort to combat "American popular culture," which she believes "is becoming unhealthier and unhealthier for our kids all the time."

The following essay was first published in the *Washington Post* on February 5, 2006. Roffman reports that the reaction to this article was overwhelming. "Many people thanked me for underscoring the point that boys and men are also treated disrespectfully in our culture and in some ways even more disrespectfully than girls and women, because of the gender-role stereotyping that defines them in even animalistic terms." Here she takes a common expression — "boys will be boys" — and asks us to think about what it really means and how that message affects boys in our society. Her conclusions will surprise those who have come to take the meaning of the expression for granted.

■ Preparing to Read

When you hear the expression "boys will be boys," what comes to mind? What traits or characteristics about boys and men does the expression imply for you?

Three of my seventh-grade students asked the other week if we might view a recent episode of the Fox TV cartoon show *Family Guy* in our human sexuality class. It's about reproduction, they said, and besides, it's funny. Not having seen it, I said I'd have to check it out. 1

Well, there must be something wrong with my sense of humor because most of the episode made me want to alternately scream and cry. 2

It centers on Stewie, a sexist, foul-mouthed preschooler who hates his mother, fantasizes killing her off in violent ways, and wants to prevent his parents from making a new baby — until he realizes that he might get to have a sibling as nasty as he is. Then he starts encouraging his parents' lovemaking. At one point he peers into their room and tells his dad to "Give it to her good, old man." When his father leaves the bed he orders him to "Come here this instant you fat [expletive] and do her!" 3

Of course I know that this is farce, but I announced the next day that no, we wouldn't be taking class time to view the episode, titled "Emission Impossible." When I asked my students why they thought that was, they guessed: The language? The women dressed like "bimbos"? The implied sexual acts? The mistreatment of the mother? 4

> It's not so much that the boy is always *being* bad — sometimes that sort of thing can seem so outrageous it's funny. It's the underlying assumption ... that boys, by nature, are bad.

Nope, nope, nope, I replied. I didn't love any of that, either, but it was the less obvious images and messages that got my attention, the ones that kids your age *are* less likely to notice. It's not so much that the boy is always *being* bad — sometimes that sort of thing can seem so outrageous it's funny. It's the underlying assumption in the show, and often in our society, that boys, by nature, are bad. 5

I said I thought the "boys will be bad" message of the show was a terribly disrespectful one, and I wouldn't use my classroom in any way to reinforce it. It was a good moment: Recognizing for the first time the irony that maybe it was they who were really being demeaned, some of the boys got mad, even indignant. 6

You can hear and see evidence of this long-standing folk "wisdom" about boys almost everywhere, from the gender-typed assumptions people make about young boys to the resigned attitude or 7 blind eye adults so often turn to disrespectful or insensitive male behavior. Two years ago, when Justin Timberlake grabbed at Janet Jackson's breast during the Super Bowl halftime, he got a free pass while she was excoriated. As the mother of two sons and teacher of thousands of boys, the reaction to that incident made me furious, but perhaps not for the reason you may think: I understood it paradoxically as a twisted kind of compliment to women and a hidden and powerful indictment of men. Is the female in such instances the only one from whom we think we can expect responsible behavior?

That incident and so many others explain why, no matter how demeaning   8 today's culture may seem toward girls and women, I've always understood it to be fundamentally more disrespectful of boys and men—a point that escapes many of us because we typically think of men as always having the upper hand.

Consider, though, what "boys will be boys" thinking implies about the true   9 nature of boys. I often ask groups of adults or students what inherent traits or characteristics the expression implies. The answers typically are astonishingly negative: Boys are messy, immature, and selfish; hormone-driven and insensitive; irresponsible and troublemaking; rebellious, rude, aggressive, and disrespectful—even violent, predatory, and animal-like.

Is this a window into what we truly think, at least unconsciously, of the   10 male of the species? Is it possible that deep inside we really think they simply can't be expected to do any better than this? How else to explain the very low bar we continue to set for their behavior, particularly when it comes to girls, women, and sex? At a talk I gave recently, a woman in the audience asked, only half in jest, "Is it okay to instruct my daughters that when it comes to sex, teenage boys are animals?" Do we stop to think how easily these kinds of remarks can become self-fulfilling prophecies or permission-giving of the worst kind?

Thanks to popular culture, unfortunately, it only gets worse. Not too   11 long ago, I confiscated a hat from a student's head that read, "I'm a Pimp." This once-derogatory term is a complimentary handle these days for boys whom girls consider "hot." I asked the boy whether he would wear a hat that said "I'm a Rapist." Totally offended, he looked at me as if I had three heads. "Duh," I said. "Do you have any idea what real pimps do to keep their 'girls' in line?" Yet the term—like "slut" for girls—has been glamorized and legitimized by TV, movies, and popular music to such an extent that kids now bandy it about freely.

Just as fish don't know they're in water, young people today, who've been   12 swimming all their formative years in the cesspool that is American popular culture, are often maddeningly incapable of seeing how none of this is in their social, sexual, or personal best interest.

Adults I work with tend to be a lot less clueless. They are sick and tired of   13 watching the advertising and entertainment industries shamelessly pimp the increasingly naked bodies of American women and girls to sell everything from Internet service to floor tiles (I've got the ads to prove it).

Yet from my perspective, these same adults aren't nearly as clued in about how destructive these ubiquitous images and messages can be for boys. It, too, often takes patient coaching for them to see "boys will be boys" for what it is — an insidious and long-neglected character issue: People who think of and treat others as objects, in any way, are not kind, decent people. It's bad enough that boys are being trained by the culture to think that behaving in these ways is "cool"; it's outrageous and much more disturbing that many of the immediate adults in their lives can't see it, and may even buy into it.

The "boys will be bad" stereotype no doubt derives from a time when men were the exclusively entitled gender: Many did behave badly, simply because they could. (Interestingly, that's pretty much how Bill Clinton in hindsight ultimately explained his poor behavior in the Lewinsky affair.) For today's boys, however, the low expectations set for them socially and sexually have less to do with any real entitlement than with the blinders we wear to these antiquated and degrading gender myths.

I think, too, that the staying power of these myths has to do with the fact that as stereotypes go, they can be remarkably invisible. I've long asked students to bring in print advertisements using sex to sell products or showing people as sex objects. No surprise that in the vast majority of ads I receive, women are the focus, not men.

And yet, as I try to teach my students, there's always at least one invisible man present — looking at the advertisement. The messages being delivered to and/or about him are equally if not more powerful.

In one of my least favorite examples, a magazine ad for a video game (brought to me by a sixth-grade boy) depicts a highly sexualized woman with a dominatrix air brandishing a weapon. The heading reads, "Bet you'd like to get your hands on these!," meaning her breasts, er, the game controllers. And the man or boy not in the picture but looking on? The ad implies that he's just another low-life guy who lives and breathes to ogle and grab every large-breasted woman he sees.

Many boys I've talked with are pretty savvy about the permission-giving that "boys will be bad" affords and use it to their advantage in their relationships with adults. "Well, they really don't expect as much from us as they do from girls," said one tenth-grade boy. "It makes it easier to get away with a lot of stuff."

Others play it sexually to their advantage, knowing that in a system where boys are expected to want sex but not necessarily to be responsible about it, the girl will probably face the consequences if anything happens. As long as girls can still be called sluts, the sexual double standard — and its lack of accountability for boys — will rule.

Most boys I know are grateful when they finally get clued in to all this. A fifth-grade boy once told me that the worst insult anyone could possibly give him would be to call him a girl. When I walked him through what he seemed to be saying — that girls are inferior to him — he was suddenly ashamed that he could have thought such a thing. "I'm a better person than that," he said.

Just as we've adjusted the bar for girls in academics and athletics, we 22 need to let boys know that, in the sexual and social arenas, we've been short-changing them by setting the bar so low. We need to explain why the notion that "boys will be boys" embodies a bogus and ultimately corrupting set of expectations that are unacceptable.

We'll know we've succeeded when girls and boys better recognize sexual 23 and social mistreatment and become angry and personally offended whenever anyone dares use the word *slut* against any girl, call any boy a *pimp*, or suggest that anyone reduce themselves or others to a sexual object.

We'll also know when boys call one another more often on disrespectful 24 behavior, instead of being congratulatory, because they will have the self-respect and confidence that comes with being held to and holding themselves to high standards.

■ Thinking Critically about the Text

Why is it important that Roffman ask her readers to think about what the expression "boys will be boys" really means? What does she think the expression means? What does she mean when she says, "We need to explain why the notion that 'boys will be boys' embodies a bogus and ultimately corrupting set of expectations that are unacceptable" (paragraph 22)?

■ Questions on Subject

1. Why did Roffman's students think she did not want to show the episode of *Family Guy* in class? How does she respond to their answers? What about the show does Roffman find objectionable?
2. How did some of the boys react when Roffman revealed her reason for not viewing the show in class? In what ways was it "a good moment" (paragraph 6)?
3. In paragraph 7, Roffman uses the now infamous Justin Timberlake and Janet Jackson "wardrobe malfunction" incident during the Super Bowl halftime festivities as an example of "this longstanding folk 'wisdom' about boys." In what ways does she find this episode demeaning and disrespectful of boys and men? Do you agree?
4. What about America's advertising and entertainment industries does Roffman find objectionable? What does she find disturbing about adult responses to the images and messages in so much current advertising and entertainment?
5. What does Roffman see as the source of the "boys will be bad" stereotype? Why does she believe this stereotype has such staying power?

■ Questions on Strategy

1. Roffman opens her essay with an anecdote about seventh-graders asking to view and discuss an episode of *Family Guy* in their human sexuality class. How effective did you find this introduction? (Glossary: *Beginnings/Endings*)
2. What is Roffman's purpose in writing this essay? (Glossary: *Purpose*)
3. In paragraph 10, Roffman asks a series of questions. How do these questions function in the context of her essay? How did you answer these questions when you first read them?
4. Identify the analogy that Roffman uses in paragraph 12. (Glossary: *Analogy*) How does this strategy help her explain the plight of today's young people? Explain.

■ Questions on Diction and Vocabulary

1. Who is Roffman's intended audience? (Glossary: *Audience*) To whom do the pronouns *you* in paragraph 7 and *us* and *we* in paragraph 8 refer? What other evidence in Roffman's diction do you find to support your conclusion about her audience?
2. In paragraph 9, Roffman lists the negative traits and characteristics of boys suggested by the expression "boys will be boys." What connotations do you associate with each of the descriptors? (Glossary: *Connotation/Denotation*) What order, if any, do you see in her list? Explain.
3. Refer to your desk dictionary to determine the meanings of the following words as Roffman uses them in this selection: *sibling* (paragraph 3), *expletive* (3), *farce* (4), *irony* (6), *excoriated* (7), *paradoxically* (7), *bandy* (11), *cesspool* (12), *ubiquitous* (14), *insidious* (14).

■ Classroom Activity Using Definition

Consider the following *Grand Avenue* strip by Steve Breen and Mike Thompson.

What insights into the nature of definition does the cartoon give you? If you were asked to help Michael, what advice or suggestions would you give him?

▪ Writing Suggestions

1. When discussing people, we often resort to personality labels to identify or define them — *leader, procrastinator, workaholic, obsessive-compulsive, liar, addict, athlete, genius, mentor,* and so on. But such labels can be misleading because one person's idea of what a leader or a workaholic is doesn't necessarily match another person's idea.Write an essay in which you explain the defining characteristics for one of these personality types or for one personality type of your own choosing. Be sure to use examples to illustrate each of the defining characteristics.

2. **Writing with Sources.** In analyzing "print advertisements using sex to sell products or showing people as sex objects" (paragraph 16), Roffman recounts how she and her students discovered that, while most of the ads focused on women, "there's always at least one invisible man present — looking at the advertisement" (17). They conclude that what these ads say or imply about this invisible man is not very flattering. Collect several print advertisements that use sex to promote products or show women or men as sex objects, and analyze one of them. What insights, if any, does this advertisement offer about how popular culture portrays and defines both men and women? How do you think Roffman would interpret or analyze your advertisement? Write a paper in which you report your findings and conclusions.

For models of and advice on integrating sources, see Chapters 14–15.

Ain't I a Woman?

SOJOURNER TRUTH

Sojourner Truth was born into slavery and named Isabella in Ulster County, New York, in 1797. After her escape from slavery in 1827, she went to New York City and underwent a profound religious transformation. She worked as a domestic servant, and as an evangelist she tried to reform prostitutes. Adopting the name Sojourner Truth in 1843, she became a traveling preacher and abolitionist, frequently appearing with Frederick Douglass. Although she never learned to write, Truth's compelling presence gripped her audience as she spoke eloquently about emancipation and women's rights. After the Civil War and until her death in 1883, she worked to provide education and employment for emancipated slaves.

At the Women's Rights Convention in Akron, Ohio, in May 1851, Truth extemporaneously delivered the following speech to a nearly all-white audience. The version we reprint was transcribed by Elizabeth Cady Stanton.

■ Preparing to Read

What comes to mind when you hear the word *speech*? Have you ever attended a rally or convention and heard speeches given on behalf of a social cause or political issue? What were your impressions of the speakers and their speeches?

Well, children, where there is so much racket there must be something out of kilter. I think that 'twixt the Negroes of the South and the women of the North, all talking about rights, the white men will be in a fix pretty soon. But what's all this here talking about? 1

> Nobody ever helps me into carriages, or over mud-puddles, or gives me any best place!

That man over there says that women need to be helped into carriages, and lifted over ditches, and to have the best place everywhere. Nobody ever helps me into carriages, or over mud-puddles, or gives me any best place! And ain't I a woman? Look at me! Look at my arm! I have ploughed and planted, and gathered into barns, and no man could head me! And ain't I a woman? I could work as much and eat as much as a man — when I could get it — and bear the lash as 2 well! And ain't I a woman? I have borne thirteen children, and seen them most all sold off to slavery, and when I cried out with my mother's grief, none but Jesus heard me! And ain't I a woman?

Then they talk about this thing in the head; what's this they call it? 3 [Intellect, someone whispers.] That's it, honey. What's that got to do with women's rights or negro's rights? If my cup won't hold but a pint, and yours holds a quart, wouldn't you be mean not to let me have my little half-measure full?

Then that little man in black there, he says women can't have as much 4 rights as men, 'cause Christ wasn't a woman! Where did your Christ come from? Where did your Christ come from? From God and a woman! Man had nothing to do with Him.

If the first woman God ever made was strong enough to turn the world 5 upside down all alone, these women together ought to be able to turn it back, and get it right side up again! And now they is asking to do it, the men better let them.

Obliged to you for hearing me, and now old Sojourner ain't got nothing 6 more to say.

■ Thinking Critically about the Text

What are your immediate impressions of Truth's speech? Now take a minute to read her speech again, this time aloud. What are your impressions now? Are they different, and if so, how and why? What aspects of her speech are memorable?

■ Questions on Subject

1. What does Truth mean when she says, "Where there is so much racket there must be something out of kilter" (paragraph 1)? Why does Truth believe that white men are going to find themselves in a "fix" (1)?
2. What does Truth put forth as her "credentials" as a woman?
3. How does Truth counter the argument that "women can't have as much rights as men, 'cause Christ wasn't a woman" (paragraph 4)?

■ Questions on Strategy

1. What is Truth's purpose in this essay? (Glossary: *Purpose*) Why is it important for her to define what a woman is for her audience? (Glossary: *Audience*)
2. How does Truth use the comments of "that man over there" (paragraph 2) and "that little man in black" (4) to help her establish her definition of *woman*?

3. What, for you, is the effect of Truth's repetition of the question "And ain't I a woman?" four times? (Glossary: *Rhetorical Question*) What other questions does she ask? Why do you suppose Truth doesn't provide answers to the questions in paragraph 3, but does for the question in paragraph 4?
4. How would you characterize Truth's tone in this speech? (Glossary: *Tone*) What phrases in the speech suggest that tone to you?
5. Explain how Truth uses comparison and contrast to help establish her definition of *woman*, especially in paragraph 2. (Glossary: *Comparison and Contrast*)

■ Questions on Diction and Vocabulary

1. How would you describe Truth's diction in this speech? What does her diction reveal about her character and background?
2. Refer to your desk dictionary to determine the meanings of the following words as Truth uses them in this selection: *kilter* (paragraph 1), *ditches* (2), *intellect* (3), *obliged* (6).

■ Classroom Activity Using Definition

In a letter to the editor of the *New York Times*, Nancy Stevens, president of a small New York City advertising agency, argues against using the word *guys* to address women. She believes that the "use of *guy* to mean 'person' is so insidious that I'll bet most women don't notice they are being called 'guys,' or, if they do, find it somehow flattering to be one of them." Do you find such usage objectionable? Why, or why not? How is the use of *guy* to mean "person" different from using *gal* to mean "person"? How do you think Truth would react to the use of the word *guys* to refer to women? What light does your dictionary shed on this issue of definition?

■ Writing Suggestions

1. Sojourner Truth spoke out against the injustice she saw around her. In arguing for the rights of women, she found it helpful to define *woman* in order to make her point. What social cause do you find most compelling today? Human rights? AIDS awareness? Domestic abuse? Alcoholism? Gay marriage? Racism? Select an issue about which you have strong feelings. Now carefully identify all key terms that you must define before arguing your position. Write an essay in which you use definition to make your point convincingly.

2. Sojourner Truth's speech holds out hope for the future. She envisions a future in which women join together to take charge and "turn [the world] back, and get it right side up again" (paragraph 5). What she envisioned has, to some extent, come to pass. For example, today the

distinction between "women's work" and "men's work" has blurred or even vanished in some fields. Write an essay in which you speculate about how Truth would react to the world as we know it, and, more specifically, to the world depicted in the photograph above. What do you think would please her? What would disappoint her? What do you think she would want to change about our society? Explain your reasoning.

The Odyssey Years

DAVID BROOKS

Political pundit and cultural commentator David Brooks was born in Toronto, Ontario, Canada, in 1961 and grew up in New York City. After receiving his B.A. in history from the University of Chicago in 1983, Brooks served as an editorial writer and movie reviewer for the *Washington Times*, as a reporter and op-ed editor for the *Wall Street Journal*, as a senior editor at the *Weekly Standard*, as a contributing editor at *Newsweek* and the *Atlantic Monthly*, and as a commentator and analyst on National Public Radio's *All Things Considered*. Brooks's articles have appeared in the *New Yorker*, the *New York Times Magazine*, *Forbes*, and the *Washington Post*. In 1996 he edited the anthology *Backward and Upward: The New Conservative Writing*. He has written two books of cultural commentary — *Bobos in Paradise: The New Upper Class and How They Got There* (2000) and *On Paradise Drive: How We Live Now (and Always Have) in the Future Tense* (2004). Currently, Brooks is a columnist for the *New York Times* and a commentator on *PBS NewsHour*.

"The Odyssey Years" first appeared on the op-ed page of the *New York Times* on October 9, 2007. Notice how Brooks uses examples and comparison and contrast to develop his definition of this new and "least understood" life phase: the "odyssey" years.

■ Preparing to Read

Are you planning to graduate from college in four years, or do you see yourself taking some time off along the way? What are your plans after graduation: Will you take a job immediately or would you like to travel or pursue some other interest?

There used to be four common life phases: childhood, adolescence, adult-   1
hood, and old age. Now, there are at least six: childhood, adolescence, odyssey, adulthood, active retirement, and old age. Of the new ones, the least understood is odyssey, the decade of wandering that frequently occurs between adolescence and adulthood.

During this decade, 20-somethings go to school and take breaks from   2
school. They live with friends and they live at home. They fall in and out of love. They try one career and then try another.

Their parents grow increasingly anxious. These parents understand that   3
there's bound to be a transition phase between student life and adult life. But

when they look at their own grown children, they see the transition stretching five years, seven, and beyond. The parents don't even detect a clear sense of direction in their children's lives. They look at them and see the things that are being delayed.

> It's possible to see that this period of improvisation is a sensible response to modern conditions.

They see that people in this age bracket are delaying marriage. They're delaying having children. They're delaying permanent employment. People who were born before 1964 tend to define adulthood by certain accomplishments — moving away from home, becoming financially independent, getting married, and starting a family.

In 1960, roughly 70 percent of 30-year-olds had achieved these things. By 2000, fewer than 40 percent of 30-year-olds had done the same.

Yet with a little imagination it's possible even for baby boomers to understand what it's like to be in the middle of the odyssey years. It's possible to see that this period of improvisation is a sensible response to modern conditions.

Two of the country's best social scientists have been trying to understand this new life phase. William Galston of the Brookings Institution has recently completed a research project for the Hewlett Foundation. Robert Wuthnow of Princeton has just published a tremendously valuable book, *After the Baby Boomers*, that looks at young adulthood through the prism of religious practice.

Through their work, you can see the spirit of fluidity that now characterizes this stage. Young people grow up in tightly structured childhoods, Wuthnow observes, but then graduate into a world characterized by uncertainty, diversity, searching, and tinkering. Old success recipes don't apply, new norms have not been established, and everything seems to give way to a less permanent version of itself.

Dating gives way to Facebook and hooking up. Marriage gives way to cohabitation. Church attendance gives way to spiritual longing. Newspaper reading gives way to blogging. (In 1970, 49 percent of adults in their 20s read a daily paper; now it's at 21 percent.)

The job market is fluid. Graduating seniors don't find corporations offering them jobs that will guide them all the way to retirement. Instead they find a vast menu of information economy options, few of which they have heard of or prepared for.

Social life is fluid. There's been a shift in the balance of power between the genders. Thirty-six percent of female workers in their 20s now have a college degree, compared with 23 percent of male workers. Male wages have stagnated over the past decades, while female wages have risen.

This has fundamentally scrambled the courtship rituals and decreased the pressure to get married. Educated women can get many of the things they want (income, status, identity) without marriage, while they find it harder (or, if they're working-class, next to impossible) to find a suitably accomplished mate.

The odyssey years are not about slacking off. There are intense competitive pressures as a result of the vast numbers of people chasing relatively few opportunities. Moreover, surveys show that people living through these years have highly traditional aspirations (they rate parenthood more highly than their own parents did) even as they lead improvising lives.   13

Rather, what we're seeing is the creation of a new life phase, just as adolescence came into being a century ago. It's a phase in which some social institutions flourish—knitting circles, Teach for America—while others—churches, political parties—have trouble establishing ties.   14

But there is every reason to think this phase will grow more pronounced in the coming years. European nations are traveling this route ahead of us, Galston notes. Europeans delay marriage even longer than we do and spend even more years shifting between the job market and higher education.   15

And as the new generational structure solidifies, social and economic entrepreneurs will create new rites and institutions. Someday people will look back and wonder at the vast social changes wrought by the emerging social group that saw their situations first captured by *Friends* and later by *Knocked Up*.   16

■ **Thinking Critically about the Text**

In discussing the odyssey years, Brooks says that "[i]t's possible to see that this period of improvisation is a sensible response to modern conditions" (paragraph 6). Do you consider the odyssey years "a sensible response" or do you think this "period of improvisation" is better characterized as laziness or drifting? Explain.

■ **Questions on Subject**

1. According to Brooks, what are the four common or traditional life phases? What new phases does he identify that bring the total to six?
2. How does Brooks define the *odyssey phase*? What is it? What is it not?
3. For Brooks, what distinguishes today's parents from their twenty-something children? From your own experience or observations, do you agree with his assessment?
4. Brooks believes that a "spirit of fluidity" characterizes the "odyssey" stage. What do you suppose he means by "spirit of fluidity" (paragraph 8)? What specifically does he think is fluid in the lives of twenty-somethings?

■ Questions on Strategy

1. What rhetorical strategies does Brooks utilize to define the odyssey years? Point out examples of comparison and contrast, division and classification, and cause and effect analysis. (Glossary: *Cause and Effect Analysis; Classification; Comparison and Contrast; Division*)
2. In paragraph 4, Brooks gives a definition of *adulthood* that most people born before 1964 would subscribe to. What function does this definition serve in the context of his essay? Explain.
3. Cite several places where Brooks uses parallel constructions in his essay. (Glossary: *Parallelism*) How do these constructions add coherence and emphasis to his content?
4. Brooks cites the work of William Galston of the Brookings Institution and Robert Wuthnow of Princeton University, two eminent social scientists who have studied this new life phase. In what ways does their work enhance Brooks's definition of *odyssey* and your understanding of this life phase?
5. Brooks uses transitions adeptly to link sentences and paragraphs together. Identify several of the different transitional devices he uses. (Glossary: *Transitions*) In what ways does his essay benefit from these devices?

■ Questions on Diction and Vocabulary

1. How appropriate is the label *odyssey* for the new life phase Brooks discusses? What else might Brooks have called this period?
2. How would you describe Brooks's diction — formal, objective, conversational, jargon-filled? Point out specific words and phrases that led you to this conclusion.
3. Refer to your desk dictionary to determine the meanings of the following words as Brooks uses them in this selection: *odyssey* (paragraph 1), *improvisation* (6), *prism* (7), *tinkering* (8), *blogging* (9), *stagnated* (11), *aspirations* (13), *entrepreneurs* (16).

■ Classroom Activity Using Definition

One approach to defining something is through negative definition — explaining a word or phrase by what it does *not* mean. For example, in paragraph 13 notice how Brooks uses negative definition to eliminate misunderstandings about what the odyssey years are not, thus clarifying and emphasizing his statements about what they are.

Try your hand at negative definition, using one or more of the following words. Be sure that when you specify what something is *not*, you help clarify what it *is*.

freedom	patriotism	friendship	secret
marriage	trust	loyalty	lie

■ Writing Suggestions

1. In paragraph 15, Brooks claims that "there is every reason to think this phase will grow more pronounced in the coming years." Do you think his assessment is correct, or do you see the "odyssey years" as a passing phase, one that will be forgotten by the time you and your peers graduate and are ready to join the working world? Write an essay in which you present your position and defend it.

2. **Writing with Sources**. In his conclusion, Brooks suggests that the television series *Friends* and the movie *Knocked Up* first captured the emergence of the social group that gave shape and substance to the life phase he calls *odyssey*. Watch several episodes of *Friends* and/or the movie *Knocked Up*. To what extent do you think the lives of the characters in these shows illustrate what Brooks is talking about in this essay? Write an essay in which you analyze one or two episodes of the television series or the movie through the lens of Brooks's definition and discussion of the odyssey years.

For models of and advice on integrating sources, see Chapters 14–15.

||||||||||||||||||||||||||||||||||||||||||||||||||||||||||||||||||||||||||||||||||||||||||||||||||||||||||||||||||||||||||||||||||||||||||||||||||||||||||||||||

WRITING SUGGESTIONS FOR DEFINITION

1. Some of the most pressing social issues in American life today are further complicated by imprecise definitions of critical terms. Various medical cases, for example, have brought worldwide attention to the legal and medical definitions of the word *death*. Debates continue about the meanings of other controversial words, such as these:

a.	values	i.	remedial
b.	minority (ethnic)	j.	insanity
c.	alcoholism	k.	forgiveness
d.	cheating	l.	sex
e.	pornography	m.	success
f.	kidnapping	n.	happiness
g.	lying	o.	life
h.	censorship	p.	equality

   Select one of these words, and write an essay in which you discuss not only the definition of the term but also the problems associated with defining it.

2. Write an essay in which you define one of the words listed below by telling not only what it is, but also what it is *not*. (For example, one could say that "poetry is that which cannot be expressed in any other way.") Remember, however, that defining by negation does not relieve you of the responsibility of defining the term in other ways as well.

a.	intelligence	g.	family
b.	leadership	h.	style
c.	fear	i.	loyalty
d.	patriotism	j.	selflessness
e.	wealth	k.	creativity
f.	failure	l.	humor

3. *Marriage* is a word that often means different things to different people. What does *marriage* mean to you? How would you define it? Write a definition essay to explain your understanding of marriage and what it means to be married. To make your definition clearer to your reader, you might consider describing a marriage with which you are personally familiar. Perhaps it would be helpful to compare and contrast two or more different marriages. (Glossary: *Comparison and Contrast*) You could also incorporate some narration or illustration to make your definition more powerful. (Glossary: *Illustration; Narration*)

4. Consider the sample introduction to the essay defining Quebecois and Canadian identity (page 403). Think about your school, town,

or country's identity. How would you define its essential character? Choose a place that is important in your life, and write an essay defining its character and its significance to you.

5. **Writing with Sources.** Karl Marx defined *capitalism* as an economic system in which the bourgeois owners of the means of production exploit the proletariat for their own selfish gain. How would you define *capitalism*? Write an essay defining *capitalism* that includes all six types of definition: formal, synonymous, negative, etymological, stipulative, and extended. Do some research in the library or online to help you with your definitions.

For models of and advice on integrating sources, see Chapters 14–15.

6. **Writing with Sources.** In discussing the power of labels that define identity, psychiatrist Thomas Szasz once wrote:

> The struggle for definition is veritably the struggle for life itself. In the typical western two men fight desperately for the possession of a gun that has been thrown to the ground: Whoever reaches the weapon first, shoots and lives; his adversary is shot and dies. In ordinary life, the struggle is not for guns but for words: Whoever first defines the situation is the victor; his adversary, the victim. . . . In short, he who first seizes the word imposes reality on the other; he who defines thus dominates and lives; and he who is defined is subjugated and may be killed.
>
> — FROM *THE SECOND SIN*

Take some time to think about words like *gay, retarded,* or *jock,* whose meaning in our culture has become contested — that is, challenged by some who are offended by the way(s) in which those words are used (for information on campaigns that attempt to educate the public on these issues, see thinkb4youspeak.com and r-word.org). What other defining labels have you encountered or observed? After doing some research in your library as well as on the Internet, write an essay in which you explore the power of labels to define. Before starting your research and drafting your essay, you will find it helpful to become familiar with Chapter 14, "Writing with Sources" and Chapter 15, "A Brief Guide for Researching and Documenting Essays."

WHERE
DID ALL THE MONEY GO
?

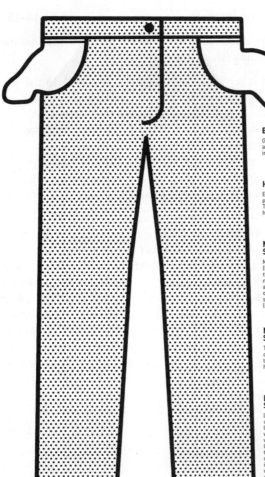

Easy Credit

Growing foreign capital fueled a demand for new investment, in turn creating easy credit.

↓

Housing Boom

Easy credit meant more people could buy houses. The increased demand drove house prices up.

↓

Mortgage Securitization

Mortgage-backed securities (MBS's) grew in demand on the stock market. Virtually all mortgages were securitized and traded. Banks could take old loans off their balance sheets and acquire new ones (making money on the fees).

↓

Market Saturation

The easy credit allowed everyone who wanted a house to get one. MBS's still were in high demand as "safe bets."

↓

Lowered Loan Standards

Lenders had to find a way to create yet more loans, so they lowered the requirements for who could get one. The loans were quickly sold off, so the lender did not bear any risk in the case of a default. It did not matter whom they were lending to or whether the money would be repaid. The lenders and brokers just collected their fees and created the MBS's for the market demand.

Global Economic Downturn

Lack of credit caused a mad cycle of stock selloffs, bankruptcies, cutbacks, higher unemployment, lower spending & production. The global economy shrunk. There was less money to go around.

↑

Credit Crisis

Toxic assets, toxic companies, and panic virtually stopped global lending. Some lenders ceased out of fear: scared that they would never get their money back. Others (such as major banks) could no longer afford to lend. They had lost too much capital and had nothing to lend out.

↑

Subprime Crisis

Throughout the housing boom, the financial market operated with the assumption that house prices would not fall. Assets that were thought to be safe were only safe because they were backed by houses of increasing value. When the prices did fall, the entire system was turned on its head.

↑

House Prices Fall

The average household income did not increase as house prices soared. Even with the easy loans, people could not afford houses anymore and stopped buying. More houses were still being built so the supply kept growing, but the demand dropped. House prices fell. Drastically.

↑

CHAPTER 11

Cause and Effect Analysis

What Is Cause and Effect Analysis?

People exhibit their natural curiosity about the world by asking questions. These questions represent a fundamental human need to find out how things work. Whenever a question asks *why*, answering it will require discovering a *cause* or a series of causes for a particular *effect*; whenever a question asks *what if*, its answer will point out the effect or effects that can result from a particular cause. Cause and effect analysis, then, explores the relationship between events or circumstances and the outcomes that result from them.

The illustration opposite is an excerpt from an analysis that attempts to explain a persistent question people have about the United States' current economic woes: Where did all the money go? The complex causal chain that "turned our country's pockets inside out" is represented with a combination of text and graphics explaining that easy credit, the initial cause, led to a chain of events culminating in the global economic downturn, with its multitude of disastrous consequences that Americans and people around the world are now feeling in all aspects of their lives.

Cause and Effect Analysis in Written Texts

You will have frequent opportunity to use cause and effect analysis in your college writing. For example, a history instructor might ask you to explain the causes of the Six-Day War between Israel and its neighbors. In a paper for an American literature course, you might try to determine why *Huckleberry Finn* has sparked so much controversy in a number of schools and communities. On an environmental studies exam, you might have to speculate about the long-term effects acid rain will have on the ecology of northeastern Canada and the United States. Demonstrating an understanding of cause and effect is crucial to the process of learning.

One common use of the strategy is for the writer to identify a particular causal agent or circumstance and then discuss the consequences or effects it has had or may have. In the following passage from *Telephone* by John Brooks, it is clear from the first sentence that the author is primarily concerned with the effects that the telephone has had or may have had on modern life.

First sentence establishes purpose in the form of a question.

What has the telephone done to us, or for us, in the hundred years of its existence? A few effects suggest themselves at once. It has saved lives by getting rapid word of illness, injury, or famine from remote places. By joining with the elevator to make possible the multistory residence or office building, it has made possible — for better or worse — the modern city. By bringing about a quantum leap in the speed and ease with which information moves from place to place,

A series of effects with the telephone as cause.

it has greatly accelerated the rate of scientific and technological change and growth in industry. Beyond doubt it has crippled if not killed the ancient art of letter writing. It has made living alone possible for persons with normal social impulses; by so doing, it has played a role in one of the greatest social changes of this century, the breakup of the multigenerational household. It has made the waging of war chillingly more efficient than formerly. Perhaps (though not provably) it has prevented wars that might have arisen out of international misunderstanding caused by written communication. Or perhaps — again not provably — by magnifying and extending irrational personal conflicts based on voice contact, it has caused wars. Certainly it has extended the scope of human conflicts, since it impartially disseminates the useful knowledge of scientists and the babble of bores, the affection of the affectionate and the malice of the malicious.

The bulk of Brooks's paragraph is devoted to answering the very question he poses in his opening sentence: "What has the telephone done to us, or for us, in the hundred years of its existence?" Notice that even though many of the effects Brooks discusses are verifiable or probable, he is willing to admit that he is speculating about those effects that he cannot prove.

A second common use of the strategy is to reverse the forms by first examining the effect; the writer describes an important event or problem (effect) and then examines the possible reasons (causes) for it. For example, experts might trace the causes of poverty to any or all of the following: poor education, a nonprogressive tax system, declining commitment to social services, inflation, discrimination, or even the welfare system that is designed to help those most in need.

A third use of the strategy is for the writer to explore a complex causal chain. In this selection from his book *The Politics of Energy,* Barry Commoner examines the series of malfunctions that led to the near disaster at the Three Mile Island nuclear facility in Harrisburg, Pennsylvania.

On March 28, 1979, at 3:53 A.M., a pump at the Harrisburg plant failed. Because the pump failed, the reactor's heat was not drawn off in the heat exchanger and the very hot water in the primary loop overheated. The pressure in the loop increased, opening a release valve that was supposed to counteract such an event. But the valve stuck open and the primary loop system lost so much water (which ended up as a highly radioactive pool, six feet deep, on the floor of the reactor building) that it was unable to carry off all the heat generated within the reactor core. Under these circumstances, the intense heat held within the reactor could, in theory, melt its fuel rods, and the resulting "meltdown" could then carry a hugely radioactive mass through the floor of the reactor. The reactor's emergency cooling system, which is designed to prevent this disaster, was then automatically activated, but when it was, apparently, turned off too soon, some of the fuel rods overheated. This produced a bubble of hydrogen gas at the top of the reactor. (The hydrogen is dissolved in the water in order to react with oxygen that is produced when the intense reactor radiation splits water molecules into their atomic constituents. When heated, the dissolved hydrogen bubbles out of the solution.) This bubble blocked the flow of cooling water so that despite the action of the emergency cooling system the reactor core was again in danger of melting down. Another danger was that the gas might contain enough oxygen to cause an explosion that could rupture the huge containers that surround the reactor and release a deadly cloud of radioactive material into the surrounding countryside. Working desperately, technicians were able to gradually reduce the size of the gas bubble using a special apparatus brought in from the atomic laboratory at Oak Ridge, Tennessee, and the danger of a catastrophic release of radioactive materials subsided. But the sealed-off plant was now so radioactive that no one could enter it for many months – or, according to some observers, for years – without being exposed to a lethal dose of radiation.

Tracing a causal chain, as Commoner does here, is similar to narration. The writer must organize the events sequentially to show clearly how each event leads to the next.

In a causal chain, an initial cause brings about a particular effect, which in turn becomes the immediate cause of a further effect, and so on, bringing about a series of effects that also act as new causes. The so-called domino effect is a good illustration of the idea of a causal chain; the simple tipping over of a domino (initial cause) can result in the toppling of any number of dominoes down the line (series of effects). For example, before a salesperson approaches an important client about a big sale, she prepares extensively for the meeting (initial cause). Her preparation causes her to impress the client (effect A), which guarantees her the big sale (effect B), which in turn results in her promotion to district sales manager (effect C). The sale she made is the most immediate and the most obvious cause of her promotion, but it is possible to trace the chain back to its more essential cause: her hard work preparing for the meeting.

While the ultimate purpose of cause and effect analysis may seem simple — to know or to understand why something happens — determining causes and effects is often a thought-provoking and complex strategy. One reason for this complexity is that some causes are less obvious than others. *Immediate causes* are readily apparent because they are closest in time to the effect; the immediate cause of a flood, for example, may be the collapse of a dam. However, *remote causes* may be just as important, even though they are not as apparent and are perhaps even hidden. The remote (and, in fact, primary) cause of the flood might have been an engineering error or the use of substandard building materials or the failure of personnel to relieve the pressure on the dam caused by unseasonably heavy rains. In many cases, it is necessary to look beyond the most immediate causes to discover the true underlying sources of an event.

A second reason for the complexity of this strategy is the difficulty of distinguishing between possible and actual causes, as well as between possible and actual effects. An upset stomach may be caused by spoiled food, but it may also be caused by overeating, by flu, by nervousness, by pregnancy, or by a combination of factors. Similarly, an increase in the cost of electricity may have multiple effects: higher profits for utility companies, fewer sales of electrical appliances, higher prices for other products that depend on electricity in their manufacture, even the development of alternative sources of energy. Making reasonable choices among the various possibilities requires thought and care.

Using Cause and Effect Analysis As a Writing Strategy

Writers may use cause and effect analysis for three essential purposes: to inform, to speculate, and to argue. Most commonly, they will want to inform — to help their readers understand some identifiable fact. A state wildlife biologist, for example, might wish to tell the public about the effects severe winter weather has had on the state's deer herds. Similarly, in a newsletter, a member of Congress might explain to his or her constituency the reasons changes are being made in the Social Security system.

Cause and effect analysis may also allow writers to speculate — to consider what might be or what might have been. To satisfy the board of trustees, for example, a university treasurer might discuss the impact an increase in tuition will have on the school's budget. A columnist for *People* magazine might speculate about the reasons for a new singer's sudden popularity. Similarly, pollsters estimate the effects that various voter groups will have on future elections, and historians evaluate how the current presidency will continue to influence American government in the coming decades.

Finally, cause and effect analysis provides an excellent basis from which to argue a given position or point of view. An editorial writer, for example, could argue that bringing a professional basketball team into the area would have many positive effects on the local economy and on the community as a whole. Educators who think that video games are a cause of delinquency and poor school performance have argued in newspapers and professional journals against the widespread acceptance of such games.

Using Cause and Effect Analysis across the Disciplines

When writing essays in the academic disciplines, you will have many opportunities to use the strategy of cause and effect analysis to both organize and strengthen the presentation of your ideas. To determine whether or not cause and effect analysis is the right strategy for you in a particular paper, use the four-step method described in Chapter 2 (Determining a Strategy for Developing Your Essay, pages 25–26). Consider the following examples, which illustrate how this four-step method works for typical college papers:

Native American History

1. MAIN IDEA: Treaties between Native American groups and the U.S. government had various negative effects on the Native Americans involved.
2. QUESTION: What have been some of the most harmful results for Native Americans of treaties between Native American groups and the U.S. government?
3. STRATEGY: Cause and Effect Analysis. The word *results* signals that this study needs to examine the harmful effects of the provisions of the treaties.
4. SUPPORTING STRATEGY: Illustration. Examples need to be given of both treaties and their consequences.

Nutrition

1. MAIN IDEA: A major factor to be considered when examining why people suffer from poor nutrition is poverty.
2. QUESTION: What is the relationship between poverty and nutrition?
3. STRATEGY: Cause and Effect Analysis. The word *relationship* signals a linkage between poverty and nutrition. The writer has to determine what is meant by poverty and poor nutrition in this country or in the countries examined.

4. SUPPORTING STRATEGY: Definition. Precise definitions will first be necessary in order for the writer to make valid judgments concerning the causal relationship in question.

Nursing

1. MAIN IDEA: Alzheimer's disease is the progressive loss of brain nerve cells, causing gradual loss of memory, concentration, understanding, and in some cases sanity.
2. QUESTION: What role does the overproduction of a protein that destroys nerve cells play in the development of Alzheimer's disease, and what causes the overproduction in the first place?
3. STRATEGY: Cause and Effect Analysis. The words *role*, *play*, and *causes* signal that the issue here is determining and explaining how Alzheimer's disease originates.
4. SUPPORTING STRATEGY: Process Analysis. Describing how Alzheimer's operates will be essential to making the reader understand its causes and effects.

Sample Student Essay Using Cause and Effect Analysis As a Writing Strategy

Born in Brooklyn, New York, Kevin Cunningham spent most of his life in Flemington, New Jersey. While enrolled in the mechanical engineering program at the University of Vermont, Cunningham shared an apartment near the Burlington waterfront with several other students. There he became interested in the effects that upscale real estate development — or gentrification — would have on his neighborhood. Such development is not unique to Burlington; it is happening in the older sections of cities across the country. After gathering information for his essay by talking with people who live in the neighborhood, Cunningham found it useful to discuss both the causes and the effects of gentrification in his well-unified essay.

Gentrification

Kevin Cunningham

*Epigraph sets
forth theme*

I went back to Ohio, and my city was gone. . . .
—Chrissie Hynde, of the Pretenders

My city is in Vermont, not Ohio, but soon my
city might be gone, too. Or maybe it's I who will be

1

gone. My street, Lakeview Terrace, lies unobtrusively in the old northwest part of Burlington and is notable, as its name suggests, for spectacular views of Lake Champlain framed by the Adirondacks. It's not that the neighborhood is going to seed, though—quite the contrary. Recently it has been discovered, and now it is on the verge of being gentrified. For some of us who live here, that's bad.

Thesis

Well-organized and unified paragraph: Description of life cycle of city neighborhoods

Cities are often assigned human characteristics, one of which is a life cycle: They have a birth, a youth, a middle age, and an old age. A neighborhood is built and settled by young, vibrant people, proud of their sturdy new homes. Together, residents and houses mature, as families grow larger and extensions get built on. Eventually, though, the neighborhood begins to show its age. Buildings sag a little, houses aren't repainted as quickly, and maintenance slips. The neighborhood may grow poorer, as the young and upwardly mobile find new jobs and move away, while the older and less successful inhabitants remain.

2

Decay, renewal, or redevelopment awaits aging neighborhoods.

One of three fates awaits the aging neighborhood. Decay may continue until the neighborhood becomes a slum. It may face urban renewal, with old buildings being razed, and ugly, new apartment houses taking their place. Finally, it may undergo redevelopment, in which government encourages the upgrading of existing housing stock by offering low-interest loans or outright grants. This last possibility would mean that the original character of the neighborhood may be retained or restored, allowing the city to keep part of its identity.

3

Organization: Example of Hoboken, New Jersey

Effects of redevelopment on Hoboken

An example of redevelopment at its best is Hoboken, New Jersey. In the early 1970s Hoboken was a dying city, with rundown housing and many abandoned buildings. However, low-interest loans enabled some younger residents to begin to refurbish their homes, and soon the area began to show signs of renewed vigor. Outsiders moved in and rebuilt some of the abandoned houses. Today, whole blocks

4

have been restored, and neighborhood life is active again. The city does well, too, because property values are higher and so are property taxes. There, at least for my neighborhood, is the rub.

Transition: Writer moves from example of Hoboken to his Lakeview Terrace neighborhood.

Lakeview Terrace is a demographic potpourri   5
of students and families, young professionals and elderly retirees, homeowners and renters. It's a quiet street where kids can play safely and the neighbors know each other. Most of the houses are fairly old and look it, but already some redevelopment has begun. Recently, several old houses were bought by a real estate company, rebuilt, and sold as condominiums; the new residents drive BMWs and keep to themselves. The house where I live is owned by a young professional couple—he's an architect—and they have renovated the place to what it must have looked like when it was new. They did a nice job, too. These two kinds of development are the main forms of gentrification, and so far they have done no real harm.

Describes "gentrification" to date

The city is about to start a major property tax   6
reappraisal, however. Because of the renovations, the houses on Lakeview Terrace are currently worth more than they used to be; soon there will be a big jump in property taxes. That's when a lot of people will be hurt—possibly even evicted from their own neighborhood.

Redevelopment causes property values to increase, which will cause property taxes to rise.

Clem is a retired General Electric employee   7
who has lived on Lakeview for over thirty years and who owns his home. About three years ago some condos were built on the lot next door, which didn't please Clem—he says they just don't fit in. With higher property taxes, however, it may be Clem who no longer fits in. At the very least, since he's on a fixed income, he will have to make sacrifices in order to stay. Ryan works as a mailman and also owns his Lakeview Terrace home, which is across the street from the houses that were converted into condos: same cause, same effect.

Organization: Effects of gentrification on local property owners

Then there are those who rent. As   8
landlords have to pay higher property taxes, they will naturally raise rents at least as much

Organization: Effects of gentrification on renters

(and maybe more, if they've spent money on renovations of their own). Some renters won't be able to afford the increase and will have to leave. "Some renters" almost certainly includes me, as well as others who have lived on Lakeview Terrace much longer than I have. In fact, the exodus has already begun, with the people who were displaced by the condo conversions.

Conclusion

Of course, many people would consider what's happening on Lakeview Terrace a genuine improvement in every way, resulting not only in better-looking houses but also in a better class of people. I dispute that. The new people may be more affluent than those they displace, but certainly not "better," not by any standard that matters. Gentrification may do wonders for a neighborhood's aesthetics, but it certainly can be hard on its soul.

Restatement of thesis

9

Analyzing Kevin Cunningham's Cause and Effect Analysis: Questions for Discussion

1. According to Cunningham, in what way are cities like humans? What does he describe as the three possible outcomes for aging neighborhoods?

2. Cunningham presents this causal chain: Redevelopment (cause) increases property values (effect), which in turn increases property taxes upon reassessment by the city (effect), which leads to the displacement of poorer residents (effect). What other effects of redevelopment can you think of?

3. Cunningham decries the gentrification of his neighborhood, but a neighborhood descending into disrepair is not a desirable alternative. What do you think Cunningham would like to see happen on Lakeview Terrace? How can a neighborhood fend off decay while still maintaining its "soul"?

4. Would the essay have benefited if Cunningham had proposed and speculated about a viable alternative to gentrification? Explain.

Suggestions for Using Cause and Effect Analysis As a Writing Strategy

As you plan, write, and revise your cause and effect analysis, be mindful of the writing process guidelines described in Chapter 2. Pay particular attention to the basic requirements and essential ingredients of this writing strategy.

■ Planning Your Cause and Effect Analysis

Establish Your Focus.   Decide whether your essay will propose causes, talk about effects, or analyze both causes and effects. Any research you do and any questions you ask will depend on how you wish to concentrate your attention. For example, let's say that as a reporter for the school paper, you are writing a story about a fire that destroyed an apartment building in the neighborhood, killing four people. In planning your story, you might focus on the cause of the fire: Was there more than one cause? Was carelessness to blame? Was the fire of suspicious origin? You might focus on the effects of the fire: How much damage was done to the building? How many people were left homeless? What was the impact on the families of the four victims? Or you might cover both the reasons for this tragic event and its ultimate effects, setting up a sort of causal chain. Such focus is crucial as you gather information. For example, student Kevin Cunningham decided early on that he wanted to explore what would happen to his neighborhood (the effects) if gentrification continued.

Determine Your Purpose.   Once you begin to draft your essay and as you continue to refine it, make sure your purpose is clear. Do you wish your cause and effect analysis to be primarily informative, speculative, or argumentative? An informative essay allows readers to say, "I learned something from this. I didn't know that the fire was caused by faulty wiring." A speculative essay suggests to readers new possibilities: "That never occurred to me before. The apartment house could indeed be replaced by an office building." An argumentative essay convinces readers that some sort of action should be taken: "I have to agree — fire inspections should occur more regularly in our neighborhood." In his essay on gentrification, Cunningham uses cause and effect analysis to question the value of redevelopment by examining what it does to the soul of a neighborhood. Whatever your purpose, be sure to provide the information necessary to carry it through.

Formulate a Thesis Statement.   All essays need a strong, clear thesis statement. When you are writing an essay using cause and effect, your thesis statement should clearly present either a cause and its effect(s) or an effect and its cause(s). As a third approach, your essay could focus on a complex causal chain of events. Here are a few examples from this chapter:

- "What has the telephone done to us, or for us, in the hundred years of its existence?" John Brooks's opening sentence makes it easy for the reader to know that he has chosen the telephone as his cause and that he will be exploring its effects in the essay.

- "On March 28, 1979, at 3:53 A.M., a pump at the Harrisburg plant failed." Here, Barry Commoner has chosen the failure of the pump to introduce the causal chain of events that led to the near–nuclear disaster at Three Mile Island.

- "Recently [our neighborhood] has been discovered, and now it is on the verge of being gentrified. For some of us who live here, that's bad."

When you begin to formulate your thesis statement, keep these examples in mind. You can find other examples of thesis statements in the essays throughout this book. As you begin to develop your thesis statement, ask yourself, "What is my point?" Next, ask yourself, "What approach to a cause and effect essay will be most useful in making my point?" If you can't answer these questions yet, write some ideas down and try to determine your main point from these ideas.

■ Organizing and Writing Your Cause and Effect Analysis

Avoid Oversimplification and Errors of Logic.   Sound and thoughtful reasoning, while present in all good writing, is central to any analysis of cause and effect. Writers of convincing cause and effect analysis must examine their material objectively and develop their essays carefully, taking into account any potential objections that readers might raise. Therefore, do not jump to conclusions or let your prejudices interfere with the logic of your interpretation or the completeness of your presentation. In gathering information for his essay, Kevin Cunningham discovered that he had to distinguish between cause and effect and mere coincidence:

> You have to know your subject, and you have to be honest. For example, my downstairs neighbors moved out last month because the rent was raised. Somebody who didn't know the situation might say, "See? Gentrification." But that wasn't the reason—it's that heating costs went up. This is New England, and we had a cold winter; gentrification had nothing to do with it. It's something that is just beginning to happen, and it's going to have a big effect, but we haven't actually felt many of the effects here yet.

Be sure that you do not oversimplify the cause and effect relationship you are writing about. A good working assumption is that most important matters cannot be traced to a single verifiable cause; similarly, a cause or set of causes rarely produces a single isolated effect. To be believable, your analysis of your topic must demonstrate a thorough understanding of the surrounding circumstances; there is nothing less convincing than the single-minded determination to show one particular connection. For example, someone writing about how the passage of a tough new crime bill (cause) has led to a decrease in arrests in a particular area (effect) will have little credibility unless other possible causes — socioeconomic conditions, seasonal fluctuations in crime, the size and budget of the police force, and so on — are also examined and taken into account. Of course, to achieve coherence, you will want to emphasize the important causes or the most significant effects: just be careful not to lose your reader's trust by insisting on an oversimplified "X leads to Y" relationship.

The other common problem in cause and effect analysis is lack of evidence in establishing a cause or an effect. This error is known as the "after this, therefore because of this" fallacy (in Latin, *post hoc, ergo propter hoc*). In attempting to discover an explanation for a particular event or circumstance, a writer may point to something that merely preceded it in time, assuming a causal connection where none has in fact been proven. For example, if you have dinner out one evening and the next day come down with stomach cramps, you may blame your illness on the restaurant where you ate the night before; you do so without justification, however, if your only proof is the fact that you ate there beforehand. More evidence would be required to establish a causal relationship. The *post hoc, ergo propter hoc* fallacy is often harmlessly foolish ("I failed the exam because I lost my lucky key chain"). It can, however, lead writers into serious errors of judgment and blind them to more reasonable explanations of cause and effect. And, like oversimplification, such mistakes in logic can undercut a reader's confidence. Make sure that the causal relationships you cite are, in fact, based on demonstrable evidence and not merely on a temporal connection.

Use Other Rhetorical Strategies.   Although cause and effect analysis can be used effectively as a separate writing strategy, it is more common for essays to combine different strategies. For example, in an essay about a soccer team's victories, you might use comparison and contrast to highlight the differences between the team's play in the two losses and in five victories. Narration from interviews might also be used to add interest and color. An essay about the Internet might incorporate the strategy of argumentation as well as definition to defend the openness and effectiveness of the Internet. The argument could analyze exactly how the benefits outweigh the drawbacks, while definition could be used to focus the subject matter to better achieve your purpose. By combining strategies, you can gain both clarity and forcefulness in your writing.

Be aware, however, that you must always keep the purpose of your essay and the tone you wish to adopt in the front of your mind when combining strategies. Without careful planning, using more than one rhetorical strategy can alter both the direction and the tone of your essay in ways that detract from, rather than contribute to, your ability to achieve your purpose.

As you read the essays in this chapter, consider all of the writing strategies the authors have used to support their cause and effect analysis. How have these other strategies added to or changed the style of the essay? Are there strategies that you might have added or taken out? What strategies, if any, do you think you might use to strengthen your cause and effect essay?

■ Revising and Editing Your Cause and Effect Analysis

Select Words That Strike a Balanced Tone.   Be careful to neither overstate nor understate your position. Avoid exaggerations like "there can be no question" and "the evidence speaks for itself." Such diction is usually annoying and undermines your interpretation. Instead, allow your analysis of the facts to convince readers of the cause and effect relationship you wish to suggest. At the same time, no analytical writer convinces by continually understating or qualifying information with words and phrases such as *it seems that, perhaps, maybe, I think, sometimes, most often, nearly always,* or *in my opinion.* While it may be your intention to appear reasonable, overusing such qualifying words can make you sound unclear or indecisive, and it renders your analysis less convincing. Present your case forcefully, but do so honestly and sensibly.

Share Your Draft with Others.   Try sharing the draft of your essay with other students in your writing class to make sure that your analysis makes sense. Ask them if there are any parts that they do not understand. Have them tell you what they think is the point of your analysis. If their answers differ from what you intended, have them indicate the passages that led them to their interpretations so that you can change your text accordingly. To maximize the effectiveness of conferences with your peers, use the guidelines presented on page 29. Feedback from these conferences often provides one or more places where you can start revising.

Question Your Own Work While Revising and Editing.   Revision is best done by asking yourself key questions about what you have written. Begin by reading, preferably aloud, what you have written. Reading aloud forces you to pay attention to every word, and you are more likely to catch lapses in the logic. After you have read your paper through, answer the questions for revising and editing on the following page, and make the necessary changes.

For help with twelve common writing problems, see, Chapter 16, "Editing for Grammar, Punctuation, and Sentence Style."

Questions for Revising and Editing: Cause and Effect Analysis

1. Why do I want to use cause and effect: to inform, to speculate, or to argue? Does my analysis help me achieve my purpose?

2. Is my topic manageable for the essay I wish to write? Have I effectively established my focus?

3. Does my thesis statement clearly state either the cause and its effects or the effect and its causes?

4. Have I identified the nature of my cause and effect scenario? Is there a causal chain? Have I identified immediate and remote causes? Have I distinguished between possible and actual causes and effects?

5. Have I been able to avoid oversimplifying the cause and effect relationship I am writing about? Are there any errors in my logic?

6. Is my tone balanced, neither overstating nor understating my position?

7. Is there another rhetorical strategy that I can use with cause and effect to assist me in achieving my purpose? If so, have I been able to implement it with care so that I have not altered either the direction or the tone of my essay?

8. Have I taken every opportunity to use words and phrases that signal cause and effect relationships?

9. Have I used *affect* and *effect* properly?

10. Have I avoided the phrase *the reason is because*?

11. Have I avoided errors in grammar, punctuation, and mechanics? Is my sentence style as clear, smooth, and persuasive as possible?

E1–12

How Boys Become Men

JON KATZ

Journalist and novelist Jon Katz was born in 1947. He writes with a keen understanding of life in contemporary suburban America. Each of his four mystery novels is a volume in the Suburban Detective Mystery series: *The Family Stalker* (1994), *Death by Station Wagon* (1994), *The Father's Club* (1996), and *The Last Housewife* (1996). The best known of these novels, *The Last Housewife*, won critical praise for its insights into the pressures and conflicts experienced by young professional couples in their efforts to achieve the American dream. Katz is also the author of *Media Rants: Postpolitics in the Digital Nation* (1997), a collection of his newspaper columns dealing primarily with the role and influence of the media in the public life of modern America; *Virtuous Reality: How Americans Surrendered Discussion of Moral Values to Opportunists, Nitwits, and Blockheads Like William Bennett* (1998); and *Geeks: How Two Lost Boys Rode the Internet Out of Idaho* (2000). Since 2000, he has written six books about dogs.

In the following essay, first published in January 1993 in *Glamour*, Katz explains why many men appear insensitive.

■ Preparing to Read

How important are childhood experiences to the development of identity? How do the rituals of the playground, the slumber party, and the neighborhood gang help mold us as men and women? Write about one or two examples from your own experience.

Two nine-year-old boys, neighbors and friends, were walking home from 1 school. The one in the bright blue windbreaker was laughing and swinging a heavy-looking book bag toward the head of his friend, who kept ducking and stepping back. "What's the matter?" asked the kid with the bag, whooshing it over his head. "You chicken?"

His friend stopped, stood still, and braced himself. The bag slammed into 2 the side of his face, the thump audible all the way across the street where I stood watching. The impact knocked him to the ground, where he lay mildly stunned for a second. Then he struggled up, rubbing the side of his head. "See?" he said proudly. "I'm no chicken."

No. A chicken would probably have had the sense to get out of the 3 way. This boy was already well on the road to becoming a *man*, having learned one of the central ethics of his gender: Experience pain rather than show fear.

Women tend to see men as a giant problem in need of solution.

Women tend to see men as a giant problem 4 in need of solution. They tell us that we're remote and uncommunicative, that we need to demonstrate less machismo and more commitment, more humanity. But if you don't understand something about boys, you can't understand why men are the way we are, why we find it so difficult to make friends or to acknowledge our fears and problems.

Boys live in a world with its own Code of Conduct, a set of ruthless, 5 unspoken, and unyielding rules:

> Don't be a goody-goody.
> Never rat. If your parents ask about bruises, shrug.
> Never admit fear. Ride the roller coaster, join the fistfight, do what you have to do. Asking for help is for sissies.
> Empathy is for nerds. You can help your best buddy, under certain circumstances. Everyone else is on his own.
> Never discuss anything of substance with anybody. Grunt, shrug, dump on teachers, laugh at wimps, talk about comic books. Anything else is risky.

Boys are rewarded for throwing hard. Most other activities — reading, 6 befriending girls, or just thinking — are considered weird. And if there's one thing boys don't want to be, it's weird.

More than anything else, boys are supposed to learn how to handle them- 7 selves. I remember the bitter fifth-grade conflict I touched off by elbowing aside a bigger boy named Barry and seizing the cafeteria's last carton of chocolate milk. Teased for getting aced out by a wimp, he had to reclaim his place in the pack. Our fistfight, at recess, ended with my knees buckling and my lip bleeding while my friends, sympathetic but out of range, watched resignedly.

When I got home, my mother took one look at my swollen face and 8 screamed. I wouldn't tell her anything, but when my father got home I cracked and confessed, pleading with them to do nothing. Instead, they called Barry's parents, who restricted his television for a week.

The following morning, Barry and six of his pals stepped out from behind 9 a stand of trees. "It's the rat," said Barry.

I bled a little more. *Rat* was scrawled in crayon across my desk. 10

They were waiting for me after school for a number of afternoons to 11 follow. I tried varying my routes and avoiding bushes and hedges. It usually didn't work.

I was as ashamed for telling as I was frightened. "You did ask for it," said 12 my best friend. Frontier Justice has nothing on Boy Justice.

In panic, I appealed to a cousin who was several years older. He followed   13
me home from school, and when Barry's gang surrounded me, he came bar-
reling toward us. "Stay away from my cousin," he shouted, "or I'll kill you."

After they were gone, however, my cousin could barely stop laughing.   14
"You were afraid of *them*?" he howled. "They barely came up to my waist."

Men remember receiving little mercy as boys; maybe that's why it's   15
sometimes difficult for them to show any.

"I know lots of men who had happy childhoods, but none who have   16
happy memories of the way other boys treated them," says a friend. "It's a
macho marathon from third grade up, when you start butting each other in
the stomach."

"The thing is," adds another friend, "you learn early on to hide what you   17
feel. It's never safe to say, 'I'm scared.' My girlfriend asks me why I don't talk
more about what I'm feeling. I've gotten better at it, but it will *never* come
naturally."

You don't need to be a shrink to see how the lessons boys learn affect   18
their behavior as men. Men are being asked, more and more, to show sensitivity, but they dread the very word. They struggle to build their increasingly uncertain work lives but will deny they're in trouble. They want love,
affection, and support but don't know how to ask for them. They hide their
weaknesses and fears from all, even those they care for. They've learned to be
wary of intervening when they see others in trouble. They often still balk at
being stigmatized as weird.

Some men get shocked into sensitivity — when they lose their jobs, their   19
wives, or their lovers. Others learn it through a strong marriage, or through
their own children.

It may be a long while, however, before male culture evolves to the point   20
that boys can learn more from one another than how to hit curve balls. Last
month, walking my dog past the playground near my house, I saw three boys
encircling a fourth, laughing and pushing him. He was skinny and rumpled,
and he looked frightened. One boy knelt behind him while another pushed
him from the front, a trick familiar to any former boy. He fell backward.

When the others ran off, he brushed the dirt off his elbows and walked   21
toward the swings. His eyes were moist and he was struggling for control.

"Hi," I said through the chain-link fence. "How ya doing?"   22

"Fine," he said quickly, kicking his legs out and beginning his swing.   ■ 23

■ Thinking Critically about the Text

Do you agree with Katz that men in general are less communicative, less
sensitive, and less sympathetic in their behavior than women? Why, or
why not? Where does "Boy Justice" originate?

■ Questions on Subject

1. Why, according to Katz, do "women tend to see men as a giant problem in need of solution" (paragraph 4)?
2. In paragraph 3, Katz states that one of the "central ethics" of his gender is "Experience pain rather than show fear." Would you agree with Katz?
3. What is it that boys are supposed to learn "more than anything else" (paragraph 7)? What do you think girls are supposed to learn more than anything else?
4. In paragraph 12, what does Katz mean when he says, "Frontier Justice has nothing on Boy Justice"?
5. How, according to Katz, do some men finally achieve sensitivity? Can you think of other softening influences on adult males?

■ Questions on Strategy

1. This essay was originally published in *Glamour* magazine. Can you find any places where Katz addresses himself specifically to an audience of young women? Where? (Glossary: *Audience*)
2. Early in the essay, Katz refers to men as "we," but later he refers to men as "they." What is the purpose of this change?
3. Notice that in paragraphs 16 and 17, Katz quotes two friends on the nature of male development. Why is the location of these quotes crucial to the structure of the essay?
4. Katz illustrates his thesis with three anecdotes. Identify each of them. Where in the essay is each located? How do they differ? How does each enhance the author's message? (Glossary: *Narration*)
5. What irony is expressed by the boy's answer "Fine" in paragraph 23? (Glossary: *Irony*)

■ Questions on Diction and Vocabulary

1. In paragraph 3, Katz identifies what he describes as "one of the central ethics" of his gender. Why does he call it an ethic rather than a rule?
2. What connotations do the words *chicken* and *weird* have for you? (Glossary: *Connotation/Denotation*)
3. Are you familiar with the word *rat* as Katz uses it? What does it mean? Check your desk dictionary for what it says about *rat* as a noun and as a verb.

■ Classroom Activity Using Cause and Effect Analysis

Think about what might be necessary to write an essay similar to Katz's but entitled "How Girls Become Women." If we assume, as Katz does, that who men are is the product of their early experiences as boys, what in a woman's character might be caused by the experiences girls have growing up in our society? Share your response with others in your class.

■ Writing Suggestions

1. Write an essay patterned on "How Boys Become Men," showing the causes and effects surrounding females growing up in American culture. In preparing to write, it may be helpful to review your response to the Preparing to Read prompt as well as ideas generated by the Classroom Activity for this selection. You might come to the conclusion that women do not have a standard way of growing up; you could also write a cause and effect essay supporting this idea. Either way, be sure to include convincing examples.

2. **Writing with Sources**. The subject of the differences between men and women perpetually spawns discussion and debate, and a spate of recently published and widely read books have commented seriously on relationship issues. Read one of these books. (*Men Are from Mars, Women Are from Venus* by John Gray and *You Just Don't Understand* by Deborah Tannen are good examples.) Write a review presenting and evaluating the major thesis of the book you have chosen. What issues make male-female relations so problematic? What can be done to bridge the "gender gap" that so many experts, books, and teachers struggle to explain?

For models of and advice on integrating sources, see Chapters 14–15.

Here's Looking at You, Kids

JENNIE YABROFF

 Jennie Yabroff writes frequently for *Newsweek,* where she is a staff writer for the arts section. She was born in San Francisco in 1973 and earned her B.A. degree at the University of California–Santa Cruz in 1994. In 2006 she earned an M.F.A. in writing from Columbia University. Yabroff has also worked for the *San Francisco Chronicle* and *Wired* magazine. About the craft of writing and reporting, Yabroff offered the following: "The best piece of advice I've heard on writing is to talk to as many people as possible about the piece as you're writing it. The fact or anecdote you tell them first is probably your lede." (Notice that Yabroff uses a variant spelling of *lead* to refer to the opening of an essay or article intended to hook the reader.)

In the following article, first published in the March 24, 2008, issue of *Newsweek,* Yabroff reports on the "Look at Me" generation, people born after 1982. No group has been more documented than this one, and sociologists and other culture watchers have begun to study the effects of this documentation on the lives of the young people at its center. Do we know better who they are as a result of it? More important, do *they* know better who they are?

■ Preparing to Read

Are you signed onto Facebook, MySpace, YouTube, Twitter, or another social-networking site? If so, do you always feel comfortable on such sites, or do you worry sometimes that you have become "overexposed," or made too public, through your participation? In general, are you willing to trade privacy for social involvement? Explain.

When filmmaker Caroline Suh decided to make a documentary about   1
the student-council election at New York's Stuyvesant High School, she was concerned about how the kids would react to the camera. It's an understandable fear: For those of us of Suh's age — she's 37 — and older, the introduction of a movie camera has traditionally turned people into either hams mouthing "Hi, Mom!" or zombies frozen stiff with anxiety. "When I was in high school, if someone was making a film, it would have been this glamorous, exciting thing," Suh says. Turns out she needn't have worried. During the year Suh spent making *Frontrunners*, two other journalists were

also documenting Stuyvesant's kids: one for a book about the school's academic pressures, another for a magazine cover story on the sexual mores of contemporary youth. And the kids, Suh says, were unfazed by the scrutiny. "They've all seen reality TV. They make movies with their cell phones," she says. "Being under the microscope is just part of their lives."

> "They've all seen reality TV. They make movies with their cell phones," she says. "Being under the microscope is just part of their lives."

The kids in *Frontrunners* are the leading edge of what's being called the millennials — the cohort born after 1982 — but you might call them the Look at Me Generation. Thanks to *The Real World*, *Laguna Beach*, and the like, they've been documented like no group before them, most especially by themselves: on their blogs, their MySpace, Facebook, and Flickr pages, and on YouTube. And now the artistes are taking their turn, with a new wave of reality series, films, and books examining the documentation generation. But are we seeing real people, or personas? Listen to girls talk about their roles in the WE series *High School Confidential*, and they sound like eerily polished publicists — for themselves. Flip through the photo book *One Hundred Young Americans*, and you see a collection of pretty young things prepping for fame, not life, such as Jake, who says, "The whole MySpace thing is a good warm-up for when I'm really famous." It's not just the entertainment that can feel hollow. Sociologists have begun to question the effect of all this exhibitionism on young people. Can they form durable identities off camera, or are they so used to producing their images for outside consumption that images have replaced their essences? Will a generation for whom all secrets are fair game and every private moment can become public trust each other and form intimate relationships? 2

To trace the roots of this culture of overexposure, consider two of the forerunners of reality programming: the BBC's *Up* series, which followed a group of 7-year-olds starting in 1964, and the five Loud children in the PBS series *An American Family*, from 1973. It's amazing how artless the subjects are in their self-presentation, and how conflicted they are about their participation in the projects. In the *Up* series, a few of the children even express annoyance at the camera's presence and wonder what the point is of being filmed. Contemporary documentaries such as *American Teen*, *Frontrunners*, and *High School Confidential* have the unvarnished appearance of authenticity — all those handheld cameras and dodgy lighting — but the subjects seem to take for granted that their lives are documentary worthy. In fact, being filmed often takes on an air of community service. "I had moments of feeling like what I was going through was private, and you don't want the world to know you," says Jessi, who had a miscarriage and struggled with depression during 3 the filming of *High School Confidential*, which followed a group of high school girls in Kansas over four years. "At the same time, other girls are going through those things, and maybe it will help them to see they're not alone. I saw it as an opportunity." The only time Jessi asked the director to stop filming was when she auditioned for an acting school. Did she fear coming off as too real when she's acting, or not real enough?

You can really see how blurry the lines between reality and "reality"   4 have become in a typical meta-moment: when the girls from *High School Confidential* did a taping recently of *The Tyra Banks Show*. They were seated in a row onstage, acting like spokeswomen for the issues they expected to represent: Cate is the anorexic wrist-cutter, Cappie is the party girl, Jessi the suicidal depressive. It's hard not to think that the girls have learned their roles, at least in part, from *The Hills* and *The Real World*, where subjects craft their identities for maximum screen time. "There is some savviness of trying to fit some position on the show," says Jon Murray, one of the creators of *The Real World*. "The persona might be, I'm the fun-loving frat guy, I'm the dark-poet type. I'm the say-anything crazy person." And if you have to endure the embarrassment of having the topless photo you sent to your boyfriend forwarded to your entire school — and then endure it again as a major plot point in *American Teen* — so be it. No pain, no gain, which is the prime lesson of MTV's *The Hills*, where Lauren Conrad has parlayed her tragic love life into B-level stardom. "With Lauren, it was like we had a reality house with Angelina Jolie," says Murray.

One of the ironies of the Look at Me Generation is that many young   5 people believe they are masters of their own images, only to discover, like the topless girl in *American Teen*, they can't control anything. "Every decision you make can be so regrettable now, because technology can be so much more vicious," says Nanette Burstein, the film's director. Online gossip sites such as juicycampus.com exacerbate the problem by making it possible for kids to post rumors about each other anonymously, with little recourse for the victims. "What is different is there are these digital footprints," says C. J. Pascoe, a sociologist studying how teens use new media. One kid she studied had broken up with his girlfriend a year earlier, but he still had her name as part of his MySpace page address, the virtual equivalent of having SUZY FOREVER tattooed on his arm.

At the extreme, consider Errol Morris's upcoming *Standard Operating*   6 *Procedure*, about the torture scandals at Iraq's Abu Ghraib prison. In the film we see the dozens of photos the soldiers — most of whom were in their teens and early 20s at the time — took of the prisoners they abused, and of each other, posing and goofing around. In some of the shots with the prisoners, other soldiers' cameras are visible as well. Their eagerness to document themselves seemed to blind them to the consequences of creating a record of their actions. The pictures not only resulted in the guards' downfall — without the photos, there would have been almost no proof of crimes — but they may have fed their ugliest impulses. As Morris says, "I often think that if cameras had not been present, these events would not have occurred."

It's probably too soon to weigh the implication of all this publicization   7 on teens' abilities to have meaningful experiences off camera. In order to form intimate relationships, they will need to trust each other, and not view friendships and romances — not to mention guarding prisoners — as one more arena for MySpace-worthy performances. But instant trust via a blog or Facebook page can be misleading, says Kate Helienga, a psychology professor at San Francisco State who has studied intimacy and online behavior. "There's a difference between spewing a lot of 'content' between two people and true knowledge of another person," she says. "There isn't a lot of room for trust and earnestness because of the younger generation's constant awareness of self-presentation." Some young people are aware of this conundrum. Looking at a portrait of himself taken by Dawoud Bey "feels strange because I am trying to extract a private memory from an image that is now public," writes one of Bey's subjects in the foreword to *Class Pictures*, a book of photos of high school kids across the country. It seems contradictory: one thing you can say for the Look at Mes is that they won't suffer the collective amnesia of their boomer elders, who often boast about being too stoned during their youth to remember it. But this generation may have something else in common with boomers: They are so busy documenting their experiences, and being documented, that they may end up with postcards from a trip they have no memory of taking. ■

■ Thinking Critically about the Text

Consider the statement by Errol Morris about the filming of incidents of prisoner abuse at Abu Ghraib prison in Iraq: "I often think that if cameras had not been present, these events would not have occurred" (paragraph 6). What does he mean?

■ Questions on Subject

1. Who are the "millennials," according to Yabroff? Why are they called *millennials* and what's different about them?
2. Yabroff writes, "[I]t's probably too soon to weigh the implication of all this publicization on teens' abilities to have meaningful experiences off camera" (paragraph 7). What are some concerns that sociologists have about the millennials?
3. What are "digital footprints"?
4. What is a major difference between the millennials and their boomer elders? How are the two generations similar, according to Yabroff?

5. What does Yabroff mean when she writes in paragraph 3 that "being filmed often takes on an air of community service?"

▪ Questions on Strategy

1. What is Yabroff's thesis in this essay and where does she state it? (Glossary: *Thesis*)
2. Is Yabroff's essay more about causes or effects? Explain.
3. Yabroff points to the irony inherent in young peoples' desire to be documented through movies and photos while they are unable to "form durable identities off camera" (paragraph 2). (Glossary: *Irony*) Why is this situation ironic?
4. Yabroff cites a number of reality shows in her essay. (Glossary: *Evidence*) Are you familiar with any (or all) of them? Does your level of familiarity with them enhance or hinder your understanding of the issues she presents? Explain.
5. Yabroff's title repeats a toast that Humphrey Bogart gives Ingrid Bergman several times in the movie *Casablanca*. (Glossary: *Title*) It reflects his love for her, memories of the past, and some say, his concerns about the future. Is Yabroff's title appropriate for the essay she's written? What additional meanings does it carry for her and for her readers?

▪ Questions on Diction and Vocabulary

1. In paragraph 2, Yabroff asks, "But are we seeing real people, or personas?" What is a *persona*? Using your desk dictionary, find out where the term originates.
2. How would you characterize Yabroff's tone in this essay? (Glossary: *Tone*) How does she create that tone?

▪ Classroom Activity Using Cause and Effect Analysis

Discuss at least six possible effects stemming from any one of the following innovations:

laser surgery

smartphones

blogs

magnetic resonance imaging (MRI)

YouTube

Hubble telescope

▪ Writing Suggestions

1. Yabroff presents some complex, perhaps daunting, questions regarding the millennials she discusses. Some might argue, however, that

they are still in many respects like all young people in previous generations. Write an essay in which you take the position that there is, in fact, nothing new about the "Look at Me" generation's fears, apprehensions, aspirations, and pursuit of happiness.

2. Popular media today often refer disparagingly to the influence of the Internet on the way many of us think and communicate. This influence is usually blamed for a tendency to present information in sound bites and to analyze and discuss it superficially. Do you feel comfortable with the frenetic pace of communication these days? Write an essay in which you explore how new ways of communicating affect thinking and writing.

iPod World: The End of Society?

ANDREW SULLIVAN

 Andrew Sullivan was born in 1963 in South Godstone, Surrey, England, to Irish parents. He earned his B.A. degree in modern history at Magdalene College, Oxford, and his master's degree and Ph.D. in government at Harvard. Sullivan began his career in journalism at the *New Republic* and later wrote for the *New York Times Magazine*. A gay, Catholic, conservative, and often controversial commentator, Sullivan has made history as a blogger. His *The Daily Dish* blog became very popular post–9/11 and was receiving over 50,000 hits a day by 2005. After nearly five years of blogging and writing books and articles, however, Sullivan decided to take a break from journalism. In 2007 he accepted an editorial position with the *Atlantic*. Sullivan has written several books: *Virtually Normal: An Argument about Homosexuality* (1995); *Love Undetectable: Notes on Friendship, Sex and Survival* (1998); and *The Conservative Soul: How We Lost It, How to Get It Back* (2006).

In "iPod World: The End of Society?," which was first published in the *New York Times Magazine* on February 20, 2005, Sullivan examines the effects, both positive and negative, of the proliferation of iPods in our society.

■ Preparing to Read

If you are an iPod owner, what is attractive to you about the device? What does it allow you to do? What does it prevent you from having to do? Do you feel any sense of isolation when using your iPod? Do you think that your use of an iPod represents anything unique in our history? If so, what? If you do not have an iPod, what has prevented you from entering "iPod World"?

I was visiting New York City last week and noticed something I'd never thought I'd say about the big city. Yes, nightlife is pretty much dead (and I'm in no way the first to notice that). But daylife — that insane mishmash of yells, chatter, clatter, hustle, and chutzpah that makes New York the urban equivalent of methamphetamine — was also a little different. It was just a little quieter. Yes, the suburbanization of Manhattan is now far-gone, its downtown a Disney-like string of malls, riverside parks, and pretty upper-middle-class villages. But there was something else as well. And as I looked across the throngs on the pavements, I began to see why. There were little white wires hanging down from their ears, tucked into pockets or purses or jackets. The eyes were a little vacant. Each was in his or her own little musical world, walking to their own soundtrack, stars in their own music video, almost oblivious to the world around them. These are the iPod people.

> Even without the white wires, you can tell who they are. They walk down the street in their own MP3 cocoon, bumping into others, deaf to small social cues, shutting out anyone not in their bubble.

Even without the white wires, you can tell who they are. They walk down the street in their own MP3 cocoon, bumping into others, deaf to small social cues, shutting out anyone not in their bubble. Every now and again, some start unconsciously emitting strange tuneless squawks, like a badly-tuned radio, and their fingers snap or their arms twitch to some strange soundless rhythm. When others say, "Excuse me," there's no response. "Hi." Ditto. It's strange to be among so many people and hear so little. Except that each one is hearing so much.

Yes, I might as well fess up. I'm one of them. I witnessed the glazed New York looks through my own glazed pupils, my own white wires peeping out of my eardrums. I joined the cult a few years ago: the sect of the little white box worshippers. Every now and again, I go to church — those huge, luminous Apple stores, pews in the rear, the clerics in their monastic uniforms all bustling around, or sitting behind the "Genius Bars," like priests waiting to hear confessions. Others began, like I did, with a Walkman — and then another kind of clunkier MP3 player. But the sleekness of the iPod won me over. Unlike previous models, it actually gave me my entire musical collection to rearrange as I saw fit — on the fly, in my pocket. What was once an occasional musical diversion became a compulsive obsession. Now I have my iTunes in my iMac for my iPod in my iWorld. It's Narcissus's heaven: We've finally put the "i" into Me.

And, like all addictive cults, it's spreading. There are now 22 million iPod owners in the United States and Apple is now becoming a mass market company for the first time. Walk through any U.S. airport these days, and you will see person after person gliding through the social ether as if on autopilot. Get on a subway, and you're surrounded by a bunch of Stepford commuters, all sealed off from each other, staring into mid-space as if anesthetized by technology. Don't ask, don't tell, don't overhear, don't observe. Just tune in and tune out.

It wouldn't be so worrisome if it weren't part of something even bigger. Americans are beginning to narrowcast their own lives. You get your news from your favorite blogs, the ones that won't challenge your own view of the world. You tune in to a paid satellite radio service that also aims directly at a small market — for New Age fanatics, or liberal talk, or Christian rock. Television is all cable. Culture is all subculture. Your cell phones can receive e-mail feeds of your favorite blogger's latest thoughts — seconds after he has posted them — or sports scores for your own team, or stock quotes of just your portfolio. Technology has given us finally a universe entirely for ourselves — where the serendipity of meeting a new stranger, or hearing a piece of music we would never choose for ourselves, or an opinion that might actually force us to change our mind about something are all effectively banished. Atomization by little white boxes and cell phones. Society without the social. Others who are chosen — not met at random.

Human beings have never lived like this before. Yes, we have always had homes or retreats or places where we went to relax or unwind or shut the world out. But we didn't walk around the world like hermit crabs with our isolation surgically attached. Music in particular was once the preserve of the living room or the concert hall. It was sometimes solitary but it was primarily a shared experience, something that brought people together, gave them the comfort of knowing that others too understood the pleasure of that Brahms symphony or that Beatles album. 6

But music is as atomized now as living is. And it's also secret. That bloke next to you on the bus could be listening to heavy metal or Gregorian chant. You'll never know. And so, bit by bit, you'll never really know him. And by his very white wires, he is indicating he doesn't really want to know you. 7

What do we get from this? The awareness of more music, more often. The chance to slip away for a while from everydayness, to give our lives our own sound track, to still the monotony of the commute, to listen more closely and carefully to music that can lift you up and keep you going. We become masters of our own interests, more connected to people like us over the Internet, more instantly in touch with anything we want or need or think we want and think we need. Ever tried a stairmaster in silence? And why not listen to a Haydn trio while in line at Tesco? 8

But what are we missing? That hilarious shard of an overheard conversation that stays with you all day; the child whose chatter on the sidewalk takes you back to your own early memories; birdsong; weather; accents; the laughter of others; and those thoughts that come not by filling your head with selected diversion, but by allowing your mind to wander aimlessly through the regular background noise of human and mechanical life. External stimulation can crowd out the interior mind. Even the boredom that we flee has its uses. We are forced to find our own means to overcome it. And so we enrich our life from within, rather than from the static of white wires. 9

It's hard to give up, though, isn't it? Not so long ago, I was on a trip and realized I had left my iPod behind. Panic. But then something else. I noticed the rhythms of others again, the sound of the airplane, the opinions of the cabby, the small social cues that had been obscured before. I noticed how others related to each other. And I felt just a little bit connected again. And a little more aware. Try it. There's a world out there. And it has a sound track all its own. ■ 10

■ Thinking Critically about the Text

Sullivan's title asks whether "iPod world" represents the end of society. Do you think Sullivan answers his own question? If so, how and where in the text does he do so? If not, why might Sullivan have left the question for us to answer? Explain.

■ Questions on Subject

1. What is Sullivan's thesis in this essay? (Glossary: *Thesis*)
2. What does Sullivan see as the benefits of iPod world? What does he see as the drawbacks?
3. What does Sullivan mean when he writes in paragraph 5, "Culture is all subculture"?
4. What suggestion does Sullivan make at the conclusion of his essay? Is his suggestion an appropriate conclusion for his essay? (Glossary: *Beginnings/Endings*)

■ Questions on Strategy

1. What particular features of the iPod lead to the effects Sullivan points out?
2. In paragraph 3, Sullivan equates iPod world to a cult or religion. How does his analogy work? (Glossary: *Analogy*)
3. Sullivan writes in paragraph 6, "Human beings have never lived like this before." How does he use comparison and contrast to help make his point? (Glossary: *Comparison and Contrast*)
4. Cite several examples where Sullivan uses irony in his essay. (Glossary: *Irony*) To what effect does he use this rhetorical device?
5. In his final paragraph Sullivan gives us a brief example of cause and effect at work. What happens when he forgets to take his iPod on a trip?

■ Questions on Diction and Vocabulary

1. Reread paragraph 7. If you didn't already know that Sullivan was an Englishman, would you be able to tell from his diction in this paragraph? Explain.
2. Sullivan uses the words *atomization* (paragraph 5) and *atomized* (7). What does he mean by their use and why do these words work so well for him?
3. How would you characterize Sullivan's style in this essay? Is it formal or informal, chatty or preachy, journalistic or academic, or something else? Support your answer with examples from the text. (Glossary: *Style*)

■ Classroom Activity Using Cause and Effect Analysis

In preparation for a classroom discussion, use your iPod or MP3 player for a morning as you go about your daily campus activities. In the afternoon, do not use the device at all. Make a brief list of the effects of both using and not using the device as a prompt for your later classroom discussion.

▪ Writing Suggestions

1. Study the photo below. It is one of a series of poster advertisements for the iPod on which someone has written an interpretation of the meaning of the *i* in *iPod*. Write an argument for or against the idea expressed in the graffit: "The *i* stands for ISOLATION." Feel free to use the ideas and statements that Andrew Sullivan uses in his essay as prompts, quotations, and evidence in your own work, but do not simply parrot what Sullivan has to say. Reach out in new and creative ways to express the causal relationship between the iPod and isolation.

2. Every time a new technological advance has been made that is widely accepted — telephone, radio, television, video, DVDs, cell phones, and similar devices — there are those who decry the innovation as the end of society as we know it. Write an essay in which you argue either that the iPod is just such a device or that it is different from the others in significant ways. Be sure to include clear explanations that are based in cause and effect analysis.

3. An underlying concern, and perhaps a theme, in Sullivan's essay is that music plays a vital role in our sense of well-being. Each person with an iPod plays, in effect, a personally programmed and designed sound track for his or her life. Write an essay in which you examine music as a cause in your life and the way it affects you.

The Real Computer Virus

CARL M. CANNON

 Carl M. Cannon was born in San Francisco and majored in journalism at the University of Colorado. For twenty years he worked on a number of newspapers covering local and state politics, education, crime, and race relations. His reporting was instrumental in securing the freedom of a man in Georgia and a man in California who had both been wrongly convicted of murder. In 1989 Cannon's reporting on the Loma Prieta earthquake for the *San Jose Mercury* won him a Pulitzer Prize. Since 1998, Cannon has been a staff writer for the prestigious *National Journal,* where he is now the White House correspondent. Cannon's books include *Boy Genius* (2003), a biography of George W. Bush's advisor Karl Rove, which he wrote with Lou Dubose and Jan Reid; and *The Pursuit of Happiness in Times of War* (2003), which examines the meaning and history of Thomas Jefferson's influential and quintessentially American phrase.

In the following excerpt from "The Real Computer Virus," which first appeared in *American Journalism Review* in April 2001, Cannon writes about the problems of obtaining accurate information on the Internet and correcting the misinformation frequently found and spread there.

■ Preparing to Read

How do you go about fact-checking information from the Internet? Do you check to see who writes or sponsors the Web sites you visit? Do you use more than one or two sources for the information you need? Have you ever had reason to doubt the accuracy of information you have used in an assignment?

The Internet is an invaluable information-gathering tool for journalists. It also has an unmatched capacity for distributing misinformation, which all too often winds up in the mainstream media. 1

To commemorate Independence Day last year, *Boston Globe* columnist Jeff Jacoby came up with an idea that seemed pretty straightforward. Just explain to his readers what happened to the brave men who signed the Declaration of Independence. 2

This column caused big trouble for Jacoby when it was discovered that he had lifted the idea and some of its language from a ubiquitous e-mail 3 making the rounds. It touched a particular nerve at the *Globe*, which had recently forced two well-regarded columnists to resign for making up quotes and characters. Jacoby was suspended for four months without pay, generating a fair amount of controversy, much of it because he was the primary conservative voice at an identifiably liberal paper.

But there was a more fundamental issue at play than Jacoby's failure to attribute the information in the column: Much of what the e-mail contained was factually incorrect. To his credit, Jacoby recognized this flaw and tried, with some success, to correct it. Ann Landers, however, didn't. She got the same e-mail and simply ran it verbatim in her column.   4

Passing along what she described as a "perfect" Independence Day column sent to her from "Ellen" in New Jersey, Ann Landers's epistle began this way: 5

Have you ever wondered what happened to the 56 men who signed the Declaration of Independence?   6

Mark Twain supposedly said . . . that a lie can make it halfway 'round the world before the truth gets its boots on. The Internet gives untruth a head start it surely never needed.

Five signers were captured by the British as traitors and tortured before they died. Twelve had their homes ransacked and burned. Two lost their sons who served in the Revolutionary Army. . . . Nine of the 56 fought and died from wounds or hardships of the Revolutionary War. They pledged their lives, their fortunes, and their sacred honor.   7

Landers's column — like Ellen's e-mail — goes on from that point to list names and explain the purported fates of many of the men. But this was not the "perfect" column Landers thought it was, for the simple reason that much of the information in it is simply false — as any Revolutionary War scholar would know readily.   8

I know because I interviewed some of them. R. J. Rockefeller, director of reference services at the Maryland State Archives, reveals that none of the signers was tortured to death by the British. E. Brooke Harlowe, a political scientist at the College of St. Catherine in St. Paul, Minnesota, reports that 2 of the 56 were wounded in battle, rather than 9 being killed. Brown University historian Gordon S. Wood points out that although the e-mail claims that for signer Thomas McKean "poverty was his reward," McKean actually ended up being governor of Pennsylvania and lived in material comfort until age 83.   9

And so on. What Landers was passing along was a collection of myths and partial truths that had been circulating since at least 1995, and which has made its way into print in newspaper op-eds and letters-to-the-editor pages and onto the radio airwaves many times before. Mark Twain supposedly said, in a less technologically challenging time, that a lie can make   10 it halfway 'round the world before the truth gets its boots on. The Internet gives untruth a head start it surely never needed. And what a head start: If an e-mailer sends a message to 10 people and each person who receives it passes it on to 10 more, by the ninth transmission this missive could reach a billion people.

This is the real computer virus: misinformation. Despite years of warnings, this malady keeps creeping its way into the newsprint and onto the airwaves of mainstream news outlets.   11

One of the things that makes the Internet so appealing is that anyone can pull things off of it. The other side of the coin is that anyone can put anything on it. This poses a particular challenge for reporters who are taught in journalism school to give more weight to the written word (get the official records!) than to something they hear — say, word-of-mouth at the corner barber shop. But the Web has both official documents and idle gossip, and reporters using it as a research tool — or even a tip sheet — do not always know the difference.   12

"Journalists should be really skeptical of everything they read online," says Sreenath Sreenivasan, a professor at the Columbia University Graduate School of Journalism. "They should be very aware of where they are on the Web, just the way they would be if they were on the street."   13

They aren't always.   14

In November 1998, the *New York Times* pulled off the Web — and published — a series of riotously funny Chinese translations of actual Hollywood hits. *The Crying Game* became "Oh No! My Girlfriend Has a Penis!" *My Best Friend's Wedding* became "Help! My Pretend Boyfriend Is Gay." *Batman and Robin* was "Come to My Cave and Wear this Rubber Codpiece, Cute Boy."   15

If those seemed, in the old newsroom phrase, too good to check, it's because they were. They came from an irreverent Web site called TopFive .com, which bills itself as offering "dangerously original humor."   16

But even after the *Times* issued a red-faced correction, the "translations" kept showing up. On January 5, 1999, Peter Jennings read the spoof of the title of the movie *Babe* ("The Happy Dumpling–To Be Who Talks and Solves Agricultural Problems") as if it were factual. Jennings issued a correction 13 days later for his *World News Tonight* gaffe, but that didn't stop things. On April 16, 1999, some of the bogus translations showed up on CNN's *Showbiz Today*. On June 10, a *Los Angeles Times* staff writer threw one of the TopFive.com titles into his sports column. In Hong Kong, he claimed, the title *Field of Dreams* was "Imaginary Dead Ballplayers in a Cornfield."   17

"What journalists need to do is learn to distinguish between the crap on the Web and the good stuff," says Yale University researcher and lecturer Fred Shapiro. "It's a crucial skill and one that some journalists need to be taught."   18

Even before President Clinton stirred up controversy with a slew of late-term pardons and commutations, I researched and wrote a 4,000-word article on the historical and legal underpinnings of a U.S. president's power to grant pardons, commutations, and clemency orders. One pertinent constitutional question was whether there are any real restrictions on the presidential pardon authority.   19

Logging onto Lexis-Nexis, I found several relevant, in-depth law review articles. Some of them cited Internet links to the original cases being cited. In fact these were highlighted "hyperlinks," meaning that with a single click of my mouse I was able to read the controlling Supreme Court cases dating back to Reconstruction. Within seconds of clicking on those Supreme Court links, I was gazing at the actual words of Salmon P. Chase, the chief justice appointed by Abraham Lincoln. Justice Chase answered my question rather unequivocally: "To the executive alone is entrusted the power of pardon," he wrote with simple eloquence, "and it is granted without limit."   20

This is not an isolated example. I cover the White House for *National Journal* and, like many of my colleagues, I have developed an utter reliance on the Internet. I do research and interviews online, find phone numbers, check facts and spellings, and research the clips. I can read court cases online, check presidential transcripts, find the true source of quotes, and delve into history.   21

Some days this is a tool that feels like a magic wand. The riches of the Web are as vast as the journalist's imagination.   22

The point of these examples is that the Internet has rapidly become such a valuable research tool that it's hard to remember how we did our jobs without it. Need that killer Shakespeare reference to truth-telling from *As You Like It* to spice up that Clinton legacy piece? Log on and find it. Fact-checking the Bible verses slung around by the candidates during the 2000 presidential election? The Bible is not only on the Web but is searchable with a couple of keystrokes. Attorney general John Ashcroft's Senate voting record is there, too, along with his controversial interview with *Southern Partisan* magazine.   23

Yet in recent months I have found myself quietly checking the validity of almost everything I find in cyberspace and whenever possible doing it the old-fashioned way: consulting reference books in libraries, calling professors or original sources on the phone, double-checking everything. I don't trust the information on the Net very much anymore. It turns out the same technology that gives reporters access to the intellectual richness of the ages also makes misinformation ubiquitous. It shouldn't come as a surprise, but a tool this powerful must be handled with care.   24

These problems are only going to get worse unless Net users — and journalists — get a whole lot more careful. According to the Nielsen/NetRatings released on February 15, 168 million Americans logged onto the Web in the first month of the new millennium.   25

Seven years ago, *American Journalism Review* warned that an over-reliance on Lexis-Nexis was leading to a "misinformation explosion." Since that time, the number of journalists using the data retrieval service has increased exponentially; at many news organizations, libraries have been phased out and reporters do their own searches. This has led, predictably, to an entire subgenre of phony quotes and statistics that won't die. 26

Sometimes the proliferation of errors carries serious implications. A couple of years ago, Diane Sawyer concluded a *PrimeTime Live* interview with Ellen DeGeneres the night her lesbian television character "came out" by reciting what Sawyer called "a government statistic": gay teenagers are "three times as likely to attempt suicide" as straight teenagers. 27

This factoid, which Sawyer said was provided to her by DeGeneres, is a crock. 28

Sleuthing by a diligent reporter named Delia M. Rios of Newhouse News Service revealed that this figure is not a government statistic, but rather the opinion of a single San Francisco social worker. In fact, a high-level interagency panel made up of physicians and researchers from the U.S. Department of Health and Human Services, the Centers for Disease Control, the National Institute of Mental Health, and other organizations concluded that there is no evidence that "sexual orientation and suicidality are linked in some direct or indirect manner." 29

Yet, the bogus stat is still routinely cited by certain gay-rights activists, and thanks to Internet-assisted databases, has made its way into the *New York Times*, the *Chicago Tribune*, the *Los Angeles Times* — and onto prime time network television. 30

Joyce Hunter, onetime president of the National Lesbian and Gay Health Association, insists that the available evidence suggests that both gay and straight teens are, instead, emotionally resilient people who "go on to develop a positive sense of self and who go on with their lives." Other clinicians fear that this misinformation could turn into a self-fulfilling prophecy. Peter Muehrer of the National Institutes of Health says he worries that a public hysteria over gay-teen suicide could contribute to "suicide contagion," in which troubled gay teens come to see suicide as a practical, almost normal, way out of their identity struggles. 31

Junk science on the Web — or junk history — has a way of oozing into the mainstream media, often because it proves irresistible to disc jockeys and radio talk-show hosts. The same is true of conspiracy theories and faulty understanding of the law, particularly when the incendiary subject of race relations is involved. 32

An e-mail marked "URGENT! URGENT! URGENT!" flew like the wind through the African American community for more than two years. It warned that blacks' "right to vote" will expire in 2007. The impetus for the e-mail was the impending expiration of the Voting Rights Act, which has 33 since been renewed and, in any event, no longer has anything to do with guaranteeing anyone the right to vote.

Nonetheless, the preposterous claim was reiterated by callers to African American radio talk shows. Eventually, it prompted an official rebuttal by the Justice Department and a public disavowal by the Congressional Black Caucus. "The Web has good, useful information," observes David Bositis, senior political analyst for the Joint Center for Political and Economic Studies. "But it also has a lot of garbage." 34

This particular cyberrumor was eventually traced to a naive but well-intentioned college student from Chicago, who toured the South on a promotional trip sponsored by the NAACP. The mistaken notion that blacks' right to vote depends on the whims of Congress was given wide circulation in a guest column in *USA Today* by Camille O. Cosby, wife of entertainer Bill Cosby. 35

"Congress once again will decide whether African Americans will be allowed to vote," she wrote, echoing the e-mail. "No other Americans are subjected to this oppressive nonsense." 36

Black leaders went to great lengths to dispel this hoax, but it energized black voters. The ensuing higher-than-normal black turnout in the 1998 midterm elections helped Democrats at the polls, led to House Speaker Newt Gingrich's demise, and may have saved Bill Clinton's job. Could the e-mail hoax have played a role? 37

Other hoaxes are not so accidental. Last year, as the presidential campaign began heating up, I received an e-mail from a fellow journalist alerting me to an anti–Al Gore Web site she thought contained valuable information. It included a litany of silly statements attributed to Gore. Some of them were accurate, but several of them I recognized as being utterances of former vice president Dan Quayle. Others were statements never said by either Gore or Quayle. 38

On October 3, 1999, when liberal movie star Warren Beatty spoke to Americans for Democratic Action about his political views, he said that he wasn't the only one who worried that corporations were a threat to democracy. Beatty said that Abraham Lincoln himself had warned that corporations are "more despotic than monarchy," adding that Lincoln also said "the money power preys upon the nation in times of peace, and it conspires against it in times of adversity." Beatty's populist version of Lincoln hardly squares with his career as a corporate attorney — he represented Illinois Central Railroad before he ran for public office — but that didn't faze modern journalists. "That Lincoln stuff just amazed me," gushed *Newsweek*'s Jonathan Alter on *Rivera Live*. Alter wrote that Beatty's "harshest attacks . . . were actually quotes from a speech by Abraham Lincoln." 39

Actually, they weren't. Lincoln's official biographer once called the quote "a bold, unblushing forgery." And in a piece for History News Service, 40 an online site that often debunks faulty history, Lincoln scholar Matthew Pinsker said this particular fake Lincoln citation has been around since 1896. In his speech at the 1992 Republican National Convention, Ronald Reagan attributed phony conservative sentiments to Honest Abe, including, "You cannot help the weak by punishing the strong," and "You cannot help the poor by destroying the rich."

This example underscores a couple of important caveats about the Web. First, bogus quotes were around a long time before the Internet. Moreover, the Net itself is often a useful tool for those trying to correct canards.   41

A postscript: Three years ago, while discussing with reporters the pitfalls of the Internet, Hillary Rodham Clinton employed the line often attributed to Twain — and cited earlier in this piece — about a lie making its way halfway 'round the world before the truth could get its boots on. "Well, today," she added, "the lie can be twice around the world before the truth gets out of bed to find its boots." While fact-checking this article, I had reason to call Fred Shapiro at Yale. Perhaps because Mrs. Clinton never mentioned Twain — she attributed it to an "old saying" — my interest was piqued, and I asked Shapiro if he'd ever heard the aphorism. "I have just been intensively researching Twain quotes, and didn't come across this one," he replied. "I would assume that Twain did not say it."   42

Uh-oh. That sent me back into research mode. What I found is that the "Twain" quote has been around. According to a 1996 article by James Bennet of the *New York Times*, Mrs. Clinton (and Al Gore as well) used the line, with attribution to Twain. Other politicians have credited it to Twain as well. Clintonite Paul Begala, writing last year in the *Orlando Sentinel*, used it, giving Twain full credit. So did Republican stalwart Haley Barbour in a *Roll Call* op-ed. In a 1999 column in the *Chattanooga Times*, a writer named L. M. Boyd gave credit for the quote to "the sage Israel Zangwill," adding that famed CBS newsman Edward R. Murrow used it all the time.   43

On the Internet, the responses were even more varied. Several Web sites credited Twain while others attributed the quote to Will Rogers; Reagan-era interior secretary James Watt; Winston Churchill; another former British prime minister, James Callaghan; and, in one case, merely to "a French proverb."   44

Possibly all of these sources uttered it at one time or another. Callaghan seems to have done so on November 1, 1976, in an address to the House of Commons. But he attributed the line to the man who is probably its rightful author: a Baptist preacher from England named Charles Haddon Spurgeon, a contemporary of Twain who, according to *Benham's Book of Quotations*, wrote this line: "A lie travels 'round the world, while Truth is putting on her boots."   45

Amen. ■   46

■ Thinking Critically about the Text

In paragraph 12, Cannon states, "One of the things that makes the Internet so appealing is that anyone can pull things off of it. The other side of the coin is that anyone can put anything on it." Do you agree? Why, or why not?

■ Questions on Subject

1. Cannon writes that one cause of journalists' errors is that they don't have much time to check their sources for accuracy. How do you respond?
2. What false understanding of the law in a cyberrumor led to a great deal of anxiety among African Americans?
3. What are the causes of errors in the information found on the Internet, according to Cannon?
4. If, as Cannon argues, the Web is a terrible source for accurate information, what can be done about the increasing numbers of people who have come to rely on it?
5. Have Cannon's ideas about the accuracy of information retrieved from the Web altered your own research methods? Why, or why not?

■ Questions on Strategy

1. What is Cannon arguing for in this essay? (Glossary: *Argument*) What is his thesis? (Glossary: *Thesis*)
2. What evidence does Cannon cite to support the fact that misinformation on the Internet can be downright dangerous? (Glossary: *Evidence*; *Illustration*)
3. How does Cannon use cause and effect analysis in his essay? Cite several examples.
4. Cannon begins with the story of Jeff Jacoby and the *Boston Globe*. Why is this a particularly good example for the beginning of his article? (Glossary: *Beginnings/Endings*)
5. Cannon ends with a postscript about the quotation falsely attributed to Mark Twain: "A lie can make it halfway 'round the world before the truth gets its boots on." Why is this an apt way of ending his essay? (Glossary: *Beginnings/Endings*)

■ Questions on Diction and Vocabulary

1. How appropriate is "The Real Computer Virus" as a title? (Glossary: *Title*) Is the comparison of misinformation to a computer virus appropriate? (Glossary: *Analogy*) Why or why not?
2. What is Cannon's tone in this essay? (Glossary: *Tone*) What evidence do you have for your assessment?
3. Cannon labels paragraphs 42–46 "A postscript." Why is that label appropriate?

▪ Classroom Activity Using Cause and Effect Analysis

In preparation for writing a cause and effect analysis, list two effects on society and two effects on personal behavior for one of the following items: television talk shows, online shopping, all-sports channels, reality television programs, television advertising, fast food, or an other item of your choosing. For example, a cell phone could be said to have the following effects:

Society

Fewer highway fatalities due to quicker response to accidents

Expansion of the economy

Personal Behavior

Higher personal phone bills

Risks to driving safety (where cell phone use is allowed)

Be prepared to discuss your answers with the class.

▪ Writing Suggestions

1. "According to the Nielsen/NetRatings released on February 15, 168 million Americans logged on to the Web in the first month of the new millennium" (paragraph 25). Why does Cannon cite this figure? (Glossary: *Evidence*) What does he mean when he says "These problems are only going to get worse unless Net users — and journalists — get a whole lot more careful" (25)? Write an essay in which you discuss possible effects of misinformation on an increasingly Web-savvy and Web-dependent public. How do incidents of incorrect reporting, such as those Cannon discusses, affect public trust of the media? What skills will people need to better judge what they read both online and off? What measures could be implemented to ensure that information is accurate and reliable? What would the other effects of such measures be?

2. Cannon discusses how the Internet, electronic databases, and e-mail can be used to spread *misinformation* and *disinformation*. What do these two terms mean? (Glossary: *Definition*) What examples does Cannon cite as evidence of each? (Glossary: *Evidence; Illustration*) Write an essay in which you explore the differences between misinformation and disinformation. (Glossary: *Comparison and Contrast*) In your opinion, which poses the greater threat? Why?

▶ The Downside of Diversity

Michael Jonas

Michael Jonas, who has worked in journalism since the early 1980s, is executive editor of *CommonWealth* magazine, a quarterly focused on politics, ideas, and civic life in Massachusetts. Jonas was born in 1959 in Ann Arbor, Michigan, and received his B.A. in history from Hampshire College in 1981. Before joining the *CommonWealth* staff in 2001, Jonas was a contributing writer for the magazine. His cover story for *CommonWealth*'s Fall 1999 issue on youth antiviolence workers was selected for a PASS (Prevention for a Safer Society) Award from the National Council on Crime and Delinquency. His 2009 article on the centralization of power in the Massachusetts House of Representatives won an award for commentary and analysis from Capitolbeat, the national organization of state capitol reporters and editors.

In the following article, first published August 5, 2007, on Boston .com, the Web presence of the *Boston Globe*, Jonas reports on a Harvard political scientist who finds that diversity hurts civic life. "Be fearless in your willingness to probe difficult questions and write uncomfortable truths," comments Jonas. "Not only do I hope my article does this, but it is, in many ways, what Robert Putnam, the Harvard scholar whose study I write about, confronted himself in publishing research results that are at odds with what he would have hoped to find."

■ Preparing to Read

Do you think that people who live in ethnically diverse communities demonstrate stronger or weaker civic engagement and interconnectedness than people who live in homogeneous communities? What are your reasons for thinking as you do?

It has become increasingly popular to speak of racial and ethnic diversity   1
as a civic strength. From multicultural festivals to pronouncements from
political leaders, the message is the same: Our differences make us stronger.

But a massive new study, based on detailed interviews of nearly 30,000   2
people across America, has concluded just the opposite. Harvard political
scientist Robert Putnam — famous for *Bowling Alone*, his 2000 book
on declining civic engagement — has found that the greater the diversity
in a community, the fewer people vote and the less they volunteer, the less
they give to charity and work on community projects. In the most diverse

communities, neighbors trust one another about half as much as they do in the most homogeneous settings. The study, the largest ever on civic engagement in America, found that virtually all measures of civic health are lower in more diverse settings.

"The extent of the effect is shocking," says Scott Page, a University of Michigan political scientist.   3

The study comes at a time when the future of the American melting pot is   4
the focus of intense political debate, from immigration to race-based admissions to schools, and it poses challenges to advocates on all sides of the issues. The study is already being cited by some conservatives as proof of the harm large-scale immigration causes to the nation's social fabric. But with demographic trends already pushing the nation inexorably toward greater diversity, the real question may yet lie ahead: how to handle the unsettling social changes that Putnam's research predicts.

> **Birds of different feathers may sometimes flock together, but they are also less likely to look out for one another.**

"We can't ignore the findings," says Ali Noorani,   5
executive director of the Massachusetts Immigrant and Refugee Advocacy Coalition. "The big question we have to ask ourselves is, what do we do about it; what are the next steps?"

The study is part of a fascinating new portrait   6
of diversity emerging from recent scholarship. Diversity, it shows, makes us uncomfortable— but discomfort, it turns out, isn't always a bad thing. Unease with differences helps explain why teams of engineers from different cultures may be ideally suited to solve a vexing problem. Culture clashes can produce a dynamic give-and-take, generating a solution that may have eluded a group of people with more similar backgrounds and approaches. At the same time, though, Putnam's work adds to a growing body of research indicating that more diverse populations seem to extend themselves less on behalf of collective needs and goals.

His findings on the downsides of diversity have also posed a challenge for   7
Putnam, a liberal academic whose own values put him squarely in the pro-diversity camp. Suddenly finding himself the bearer of bad news, Putnam has struggled with how to present his work. He gathered the initial raw data in 2000 and issued a press release the following year outlining the results. He then spent several years testing other possible explanations.

When he finally published a detailed scholarly analysis in June in the jour-   8
nal *Scandinavian Political Studies*, he faced criticism for straying from data into advocacy. His paper argues strongly that the negative effects of diversity can be remedied and says history suggests that ethnic diversity may eventually fade as a sharp line of social demarcation.

"Having aligned himself with the central planners intent on sustaining such social engineering, Putnam concludes the facts with a stern pep talk," wrote conservative commentator Ilana Mercer, in a recent *Orange Country Register* op-ed titled "Greater diversity equals more misery."

9

Putnam has long staked out ground as both a researcher and a civic player, someone willing to describe social problems and then have a hand in addressing them. He says social science should be "simultaneously rigorous and relevant," meeting high research standards while also "speaking to concerns of our fellow citizens." But on a topic as charged as ethnicity and race, Putnam worries that many people hear only what they want to.

10

"It would be unfortunate if a politically correct progressivism were to deny the reality of the challenge to social solidarity posed by diversity," he writes in the new report. "It would be equally unfortunate if an ahistorical and ethnocentric conservatism were to deny that addressing that challenge is both feasible and desirable."

11

Putnam is the nation's premier guru of civic engagement. After studying civic life in Italy in the 1970s and 1980s, Putnam turned his attention to the United States, publishing an influential journal article on civic engagement in 1995 that he expanded five years later into the best-selling *Bowling Alone*. The book sounded a national wake-up call on what Putnam called a sharp drop in civic connections among Americans. It won him audiences with presidents Bill Clinton and George W. Bush and made him one of the country's best-known social scientists.

12

Putnam claims the United States has experienced a pronounced decline in *social capital*, a term he helped popularize. Social capital refers to the social networks—whether friendships or religious congregations or neighborhood associations—that he says are key indicators of civic well-being. When social capital is high, says Putnam, communities are better places to live. Neighborhoods are safer; people are healthier; and more citizens vote.

13

The results of his new study come from a survey Putnam directed among residents in 41 U.S. communities, including Boston. Residents were sorted into the four principal categories used by the U.S. Census: black, white, Hispanic, and Asian. They were asked how much they trusted their neighbors and those of each racial category and questioned about a long list of civic attitudes and practices, including their views on local government, their involvement in community projects, and their friendships. What emerged in more diverse communities was a bleak picture of civic desolation, affecting everything from political engagement to the state of social ties.

14

Putnam knew he had provocative findings on his hands. He worried about coming under some of the same liberal attacks that greeted Daniel Patrick

15

Moynihan's landmark 1965 report on the social costs associated with the breakdown of the black family. There is always the risk of being pilloried as the bearer of "an inconvenient truth," says Putnam.

After releasing the initial results in 2001, Putnam says he spent time "kick- 16
ing the tires really hard" to be sure the study had it right. Putnam realized, for instance, that more diverse communities tended to be larger, have
greater income ranges, higher crime rates, and more mobility among their
residents—all factors that could depress social capital independent of any
impact ethnic diversity might have.

"People would say, 'I bet you forgot about X,'" Putnam says of the string of 17
suggestions from colleagues. "There were 20 or 30 Xs."

But even after statistically taking them all into account, the connection 18
remained strong: Higher diversity meant lower social capital. In his findings, Putnam writes that those in more diverse communities tend to "distrust their neighbors, regardless of the color of their skin, to withdraw even
from close friends, to expect the worst from their community and its leaders, to volunteer less, give less to charity and work on community projects
less often, to register to vote less, to agitate for social reform more but have
less faith that they can actually make a difference, and to huddle unhappily
in front of the television."

"People living in ethnically diverse settings appear to 'hunker down'—that 19
is, to pull in like a turtle," Putnam writes.

In documenting that hunkering down, Putnam challenged the two domi- 20
nant schools of thought on ethnic and racial diversity, the "contact" theory
and the "conflict" theory. Under the contact theory, more time spent with
those of other backgrounds leads to greater understanding and harmony
between groups. Under the conflict theory, that proximity produces tension
and discord.

Putnam's findings reject both theories. In more diverse communities, 21
he says, there were neither great bonds formed across group lines nor
heightened ethnic tensions, but a general civic malaise. And in perhaps
the most surprising result of all, levels of trust were not only lower
between groups in more diverse settings, but even among members of
the same group.

"Diversity, at least in the short run," he writes, "seems to bring out the turtle 22
in all of us."

The overall findings may be jarring during a time when it's become com- 23
monplace to sing the praises of diverse communities, but researchers in the
field say they shouldn't be.

"It's an important addition to a growing body of evidence on the challenges created by diversity," says Harvard economist Edward Glaeser. 24

In a recent study, Glaeser and colleague Alberto Alesina demonstrated that roughly half the difference in social welfare spending between the United States and Europe — Europe spends far more — can be attributed to the greater ethnic diversity of the U.S. population. Glaeser says lower national social welfare spending in the United States is a "macro" version of the decreased civic engagement Putnam found in more diverse communities within the country. 25

Economists Matthew Kahn of UCLA and Dora Costa of MIT reviewed 15 recent studies in a 2003 paper, all of which linked diversity with lower levels of social capital. Greater ethnic diversity was linked, for example, to lower school funding, census response rates, and trust in others. Kahn and Costa's own research documented higher desertion rates in the Civil War among Union Army soldiers serving in companies whose soldiers varied more by age, occupation, and birthplace. 26

Birds of different feathers may sometimes flock together, but they are also less likely to look out for one another. "Everyone is a little self-conscious that this is not politically correct stuff," says Kahn. 27

So how to explain New York, London, Rio de Janeiro, Los Angeles — the great melting-pot cities that drive the world's creative and financial economies? 28

The image of civic lassitude dragging down more diverse communities is at odds with the vigor often associated with urban centers, where ethnic diversity is greatest. It turns out there is a flip side to the discomfort diversity can cause. If ethnic diversity, at least in the short run, is a liability for social connectedness, a parallel line of emerging research suggests it can be a big asset when it comes to driving productivity and innovation. In high-skill workplace settings, says Scott Page, the University of Michigan political scientist, the different ways of thinking among people from different cultures can be a boon. 29

"Because they see the world and think about the world differently than you, that's challenging," says Page, author of *The Difference: How the Power of Diversity Creates Better Groups, Firms, Schools, and Societies*. "But by hanging out with people different than you, you're likely to get more insights. Diverse teams tend to be more productive." 30

In other words, those in more diverse communities may do more bowling alone, but the creative tensions unleashed by those differences in the workplace may vault those same places to the cutting edge of the economy and of creative culture. 31

Page calls it the "diversity paradox." He thinks the contrasting positive and negative effects of diversity can coexist in communities, but "there's got to be a limit." If civic engagement falls off too far, he says, it's easy to imagine the positive effects of diversity beginning to wane as well. "That's what's unsettling about his findings," Page says of Putnam's new work. 32

Meanwhile, by drawing a portrait of civic engagement in which more homogeneous communities seem much healthier, some of Putnam's worst fears about how his results could be used have been realized. A stream of conservative commentary has begun—from places like the Manhattan Institute and the *American Conservative*—highlighting the harm the study suggests will come from large-scale immigration. But Putnam says he's also received hundreds of complimentary e-mails laced with bigoted language. "It certainly is not pleasant when David Duke's Web site hails me as the guy who found out racism is good," he says. 33

In the final quarter of his paper, Putnam puts the diversity challenge in a broader context by describing how social identity can change over time. Experience shows that social divisions can eventually give way to "more encompassing identities" that create a "new, more capacious sense of 'we,'" he writes. 34

Growing up in the 1950s in a small midwestern town, Putnam knew the religion of virtually every member of his high school graduating class because, he says, such information was crucial to the question of "who was a possible mate or date." The importance of marrying within one's faith, he says, has largely faded since then, at least among many mainline Protestants, Catholics, and Jews. 35

While acknowledging that racial and ethnic divisions may prove more stubborn, Putnam argues that such examples bode well for the long-term prospects for social capital in a multiethnic America. 36

In his paper, Putnam cites the work done by Page and others, and uses it to help frame his conclusion that increasing diversity in America is not only inevitable, but ultimately valuable and enriching. As for smoothing over the divisions that hinder civic engagement, Putnam argues that Americans can help that process along through targeted efforts. He suggests expanding support for English-language instruction and investing in community centers and other places that allow for "meaningful interaction across ethnic lines." 37

Some critics have found his prescriptions underwhelming. And in offering ideas for mitigating his findings, Putnam has drawn scorn for stepping out of the role of dispassionate researcher. "You're just supposed to tell your peers what you found," says John Leo, senior fellow at the Manhattan Institute, a conservative think tank. "I don't expect academics to fret about these matters." 38

But fretting about the state of American civic health is exactly what   39
Putnam has spent more than a decade doing. While continuing to research
questions involving social capital, he has directed the Saguaro Seminar,
a project he started at Harvard's Kennedy School of Government that
promotes efforts throughout the country to increase civic connections in
communities.

"Social scientists are both scientists and citizens," says Alan Wolfe, direc-   40
tor of the Boisi Center for Religion and American Public Life at Boston
College, who sees nothing wrong in Putnam's efforts to affect some of the
phenomena he studies.

Wolfe says what is unusual is that Putnam has published findings as a social   41
scientist that are not the ones he would have wished for as a civic leader.
There are plenty of social scientists, says Wolfe, who never produce research
results at odds with their own worldview.

"The problem too often," says Wolfe, "is people are never uncomfortable   42
about their findings."

X

■ Thinking Critically about the Text

If ethnic diversity seems to be a liability, at least in the short term, why does
Putnam think it's "ultimately valuable and enriching"? (paragraph 37)

■ Questions on Subject

1. What are the effects of greater social diversity that Putnam's research
   reveals? What's being lost and gained? How serious are the losses, as
   Putnam sees them?
2. Putnam coined the term *social capital*. What does he mean by the
   term? (Glossary: *Definition*)
3. Why did Putnam worry about the effects that his research might have
   on his fellow social scientists and on the public at large?
4. What evidence related to the world's most vibrant cities seems to con-
   tradict the findings in Putnam's study? (Glossary: *Evidence*)
5. What are Putnam's suggestions for increasing social capital within
   diverse ethnic communities? Do you think those efforts are worthwhile? Why, or why not?

■ Questions on Strategy

1. How does cause and effect work in Jonas's essay? Does it work only
   on the level of diversity and its effects?

2. In paragraph 38, conservative think-tank fellow John Leo is scornful of Putnam's role as an advocate for diversity. Do you agree with Leo's criticism of Putnam? Why, or why not?

3. Jonas uses a number of very short, one- or two-sentence paragraphs. Examine several of them and explain why you think he uses them. Could Jonas have combined these short paragraphs with other paragraphs? Explain.

4. Examine Jonas's essay for examples of his use of outside authorities and evidence. How have these outside sources helped him to provide perspective on the issues he discusses? (Glossary: *Evidence*)

5. Is Jonas objective about the results and implications of Putnam's research, or does he reveal his own attitude about them? (Glossary: *Attitude*) Explain.

■ Questions on Diction and Vocabulary

1. One of Putnam's earlier works was *Bowling Alone*, a book that studied the gradual change from earlier decades in American culture, in which bowling was a very social activity, to more recent times, in which bowling has become one primarily engaged in by solitary individuals. Why was that metaphor a good one for the loss of social capital he wrote about? (Glossary: *Figures of Speech*)

2. Putnam says in paragraph 19 that "people living in ethnically diverse settings appear to 'hunker down'—that is, to pull in like a turtle." What figure of speech does his statement contain and what does it mean? (Glossary: *Figures of Speech*)

■ Classroom Activity Using Cause and Effect Analysis

Determining causes and effects requires careful thought. Establishing a causal chain of events is no less demanding, but it can also bring clarity and understanding to many complex issues. Consider the following example involving the H1N1 virus, or swine flu:

ultimate cause　According to the Centers for Disease Control (CDC), this virus was originally referred to as "swine flu" because laboratory testing showed that many of the genes in this new virus were very similar to influenza viruses that normally occur in pigs (swine) in North America. But further study has shown that this new virus is very different from what normally circulates in North American pigs. It has two genes from flu viruses that normally circulate in pigs in Europe and Asia and bird (avian) genes and human genes. Scientists call this a "quadruple reassortant" virus.

immediate cause　Contact with surfaces that have the flu virus on them and then touching the mouth or nose or eyes.

effect	Influenza (fever, cough, sore throat, runny or stuffy nose, body aches, headache, chills and fatigue, possible vomiting and diarrhea)
effect	Possible death; possible pandemic

Develop a causal chain for each of the cause and effect pairs listed below. Then mix two of the pairs (for example, develop a causal chain for vacation/anxiety). Be prepared to discuss your answers with the class.

terror/alert

vacation/relaxation

making a speech/anxiety

climate change/technological innovation

■ Writing Suggestions

1. In the note that precedes this selection, Jonas suggests that you "be fearless in your willingness to probe difficult questions and write uncomfortable truths." Write an essay in which you examine more deeply the implications of Jonas's advice. Why does he consider it good and necessary advice to follow? What might be the difficult-to-deal-with effects of following that advice? Before writing, you may wish to read Steven Pinker's "In Defense of Dangerous Ideas" (page 531) for examples of what Jonas means and for a source of probing ideas about this topic.

2. Write an essay in which you examine your own ideas about diversity at all levels. What do you think its benefits and its negative aspects are? How might we as Americans work to achieve more social integration and understanding? In thinking about your topic you might want to consider the lessons that American history has taught us about how waves of immigrants gradually learned to live in mutually beneficial settings. Consider as well the measures that have been taken legally, socially, economically, and in other ways to maintain respect for diversity as well as social cohesion.

WRITING SUGGESTIONS FOR CAUSE AND EFFECT ANALYSIS

1. Write an essay in which you analyze the most significant reasons for your decision to attend college. You may wish to discuss your family background, your high school experience, people and events that influenced your decision, and your goals in college as well as in later life.

2. It is interesting to think of ourselves in terms of the influences that have caused us to be who we are. Write an essay in which you discuss two or three of what you consider the most important influences on your life. Following are some areas you may wish to consider in planning and writing your paper.

   a. a parent

   b. a book or movie

   c. a member of the clergy

   d. a teacher

   e. a friend

   f. a hero

   g. a youth organization

   h. a coach

   i. your neighborhood

   j. your ethnic background

3. Write an essay about a recent achievement of yours or about an important achievement in your community. Explain the causes of this success. Look at all of the underlying elements involved in the accomplishment, and explain how you selected the one main cause or the causal chain that led to the achievement. To do this, you will probably want to use the rhetorical strategy of comparison and contrast. You might also use exemplification and process analysis to explain the connection between your cause and its effect.

4. **Writing with Sources.** Decisions often involve cause and effect relationships; that is, a person usually weighs the possible results of an action before deciding to act. Write an essay in which you consider the possible effects that would result from one decision or another in one of the following controversies. You will need to do some research in the library or online in order to support your conclusions.

   a. taxing cars on the basis of fuel consumption

   b. reinstituting the military draft

   c. legalizing marijuana

    d. mandatory licensing of handguns

    e. raising the mandatory fuel efficiency rating of cars

    f. cloning humans

    g. abolishing grades for college courses

    h. raising the minimum wage

    i. mandatory community service (one year) for all eighteen-year-olds

    j. banning the use of pesticides on produce

    k. requiring an ethics course in college

For models of and advice on integrating sources, see Chapters 14–15.

5. **Writing with Sources.** Review the graphic that opens this chapter (page 440). Take any one of the topics in the causal chain put forth in the graphic—for example, the housing boom, mortgage securitization, subprime crisis, or global economic downturn—and write an essay in which you dig deeper into the topic, exploring further causes and effects. For example, what caused "easy credit" to become available? How did foreign investors infuse our financial institutions with money? In examining mortgage securitization further, what did banks do that so destabilized the mortgage system as we know it? What checks and balances or regulations did the government provide in this area of banking? Why did they fail? What causes (immediate and ultimate), effects, and causal chains do you see in the events?

    For any of these topics you will need to do further research in print and online sources to understand and report on your findings.

For models of and advice on integrating sources, see Chapters 14–15.

Ignoring global warming won't make it go away.
worldwildlife.org/globalwarming

CHAPTER 12

Argumentation

What Is Argumentation?

The word *argument* probably first brings to mind disagreements and disputes. Occasionally, such disputes are constructive. More often, though, disputes like these are inconclusive and result only in anger over your opponent's stubbornness or in the frustration of realizing that you have failed to make your position understood.

Reasoned argument is something else again entirely. In reasoned argument, we attempt to convince listeners or readers to agree with a particular point of view, to make a particular decision, or to pursue a particular course of action. Such arguments involve the presentation of well-chosen evidence and the artful control of language or other persuasive tools. Arguments need not be written to be effective, however; oral argument, if well planned and well delivered, can be equally effective, as can primarily visual arguments.

For an example of argument that combines text and visuals, consider the public service advertisement opposite. This ad, which was sponsored by the U.S. arm of the World Wildlife Fund, uses an arresting image and a single line of text to make its argument: Global warming is real, and refusing to acknowledge the threat it poses won't save us from its dire effects. The pathos generated by the image of the Little Leaguer up to his shoulders in water, but bravely ready to bat, is meant to impel us to action — if not for our sake, then for the sake of the generation to come.

Argument in Written Texts

Written arguments must be carefully planned. The writer must settle in advance on a specific thesis or proposition rather than grope toward one, as in a dispute. There is a greater need for organization, for choosing the most effective types of evidence from all that is available, for determining the strategies of rhetoric, language, and style that will best suit the argument's subject, purpose, thesis, and effect on the intended audience.

Most strong arguments are constructed around an effective thesis statement. Take, for example, the following opening to the essay "The Case for Short Words" by Richard Lederer (page 519).

> When you speak and write, there is no law that says you have to use big words. Short words are as good as long ones, and short, old words — like *sun* and *grass* and *home* — are [Thesis statement] best of all. A lot of small words, more than you might think, can meet your needs with a strength, grace, and charm that large words do not have.
>
> [Several examples support the thesis.] Big words can make the way dark for those who read what you write and hear what you say. Small words cast their clear light on big things — night and day, love and hate, war and peace, and life and death. Big words at times seem strange to the eye and the ear and the mind and the heart. Small words are the ones we seem to have known from the time we were born, like the hearth fire that warms the home.

Note how Lederer uses examples to support his thesis statement. When you read the whole essay, you will want to check whether Lederer's argument is well reasoned and carefully organized. You will also want to check that his argument is logical and persuasive. A strong argument will have all of these qualities.

■ Persuasive and Logical Argument

Most people who specialize in the study of argument identify two essential categories: persuasion and logic.

Persuasive argument relies primarily on appeals to emotion, to the subconscious, even to bias and prejudice. These appeals involve diction, slanting, figurative language, analogy, rhythmic patterns of speech, and a tone that encourages a positive, active response. Examples of persuasive argument are found in the claims of advertisers and in the speech making of politicians and social activists.

Logical argument, on the other hand, appeals primarily to the mind — to the audience's intellectual faculties, understanding, and knowledge. Such appeals depend on the reasoned movement from assertion to evidence to conclusion and on an almost mathematical system of proof and counterproof. Logical argument, unlike persuasion, does not normally impel its audience to action. Logical argument is commonly found in scientific or philosophical articles, in legal decisions, and in technical proposals.

Most arguments, however, are neither purely persuasive nor purely logical in nature. A well-written newspaper editorial that supports a controversial piece of legislation or that proposes a solution to a local problem, for example, will rest on a logical arrangement of assertions and evidence but will employ striking diction and other persuasive patterns of language to make it more effective. Thus the kinds of appeals a writer emphasizes depend on the nature of the topic, the thesis or proposition of the argument, the various kinds of support (e.g., evidence, opinions, examples, facts, statistics) offered, and a thoughtful consideration of the audience. Knowing the differences between persuasive and logical arguments is, then, essential in learning both to read and to write arguments.

Some additional types of arguments that are helpful in expanding your understanding of this strategy are described below.

■ Informational, or Exploratory, Argument

It is often useful to provide a comprehensive review of the various facets of an issue. This is done to inform an audience, especially one that may not understand why the issue is controversial in the first place, and to help that audience take a position. An example of this kind of argument is Steven Pinker's "In Defense of Dangerous Ideas" (page 531). The writer of this type of argument does not take a position but aims, instead, to render the positions taken by the various sides in accurate and clear language. Your instructors may occasionally call for this kind of argumentative writing as a way of teaching you to explore the complexity of a particular issue.

■ Focused Argument

This kind of argument has only one objective: to change the audience's mind about a controversial issue. Barbara Ehrenreich, in "This Land Is Their Land" (page 541), focuses on her concern that the rich are monopolizing natural resources in the United States. Being comprehensive or taking the broad view is not the objective here. If opposing viewpoints are considered, it is usually to show their inadequacies and thereby to strengthen the writer's own position. This kind of argument is what we usually think of when we think of traditional argument.

■ Action-Oriented Argument

This type of argument is highly persuasive and attempts to accomplish a specific task. This is the loud car salesperson on your television, the over-the-top subscription solicitation in your mail, the vote-for-me-because-I-am-the-only-candidate-who-can-lower-your-taxes type of argument. The language is emotionally charged, and buzzwords designed to arouse the emotions of the audience may even be used, along with such propaganda devices as glittering generalities (broad, sweeping statements) and bandwagonism ("Everyone else is voting for me — don't be left out").

▪ Quiet, or Subtle, Argument

Some arguments do not immediately appear to the audience to be arguments at all. They set out to be informative and objective, but when closely examined, they reveal that the author has consciously, or perhaps subconsciously, shaped and slanted the evidence in such a manner as to favor a particular position. Such shaping may be the result of choices in diction that bend the audience to the writer's perspective, or they may be the result of decisions not to include certain types of evidence while admitting others. Such arguments can, of course, be quite convincing, as there are always those who distrust obvious efforts to convince them, preferring to make their own decisions on the issues. This category probably best describes the *New York Times*: *Room for Debate* discussions of a recent Pew Research Center study on so-called Alpha Wives (see page 572).

▪ Reconciliation Argument

Increasingly popular today is a form of argument in which the writer attempts to explore all facets of an issue to find common ground or areas of agreement. Of course, one way of viewing that common ground is to see it as a new argumentative thrust, a new assertion, about which there may yet be more debate. The object, nevertheless, is to lessen stridency and the hardening of positions and to mediate opposing views into a rational and, where appropriate, even practical outcome. Martin Luther King Jr.'s speech "I Have a Dream" (page 525) is perhaps the greatest example of a reconciliation argument of the past century.

Using Argumentation As a Writing Strategy

Reasoned arguments are limited to assertions about which there is a legitimate and recognized difference of opinion. It is unlikely that anyone will ever need to convince a reader that falling in love is a rare and intense experience, that crime rates should be reduced, or that computers are changing the world. Not everyone would agree, however, that women experience love more intensely than men do, that the death penalty reduces the incidence of crime, or that computers are changing the world for the worse; these assertions are arguable and admit differing perspectives. Similarly, a leading heart specialist might argue in a popular magazine that too many doctors are advising patients to have pacemakers implanted when they are not necessary; the editorial writer for a small-town newspaper could urge that a local agency supplying food to poor families be given a larger percentage of the town's budget; and in a lengthy and complex book, a foreign-policy specialist might attempt to prove that the current administration exhibits no consistent policy in its relationship with other countries and that the State Department is in need of overhauling.

No matter what forum it uses and no matter what its structure, an argument has as its chief purpose the detailed setting forth of a particular point of view and the rebuttal of any opposing views.

■ The Classical Appeals

Classical thinkers believed that there are three key components in all rhetorical situations or attempts to communicate: the *speaker* (and for us the *writer*) who comments about a *subject* to an *audience*. For purposes of discussion we can isolate each of these three entities, but in actual rhetorical situations they are inseparable, each inextricably tied to and influencing the other two. The ancients also recognized the importance of qualities attached to each of these components that are especially significant in the case of argumentation: *ethos*, which is related to the speaker; *logos*, which is related to the subject; and *pathos*, which is related to the audience. Let's look a little closer at each of these.

Ethos (Greek for "character") has to do with the authority, the credibility, and, to a certain extent, the morals of the speaker or writer. In other words, *ethos* is the speaker's character as perceived by the audience, often based on shared values. Aristotle and Cicero, classical rhetoricians, believed that it was important for the speaker to be credible and to argue for a worthwhile cause. Putting one's argumentative skills in the service of a questionable cause was simply not acceptable. But how did one establish credibility? Sometimes it was gained through achievements outside the rhetorical arena. That is, the speaker had experience with an issue, had argued the subject before, and had been judged to be sincere and honest.

In the case of your own writing, establishing such credentials is not always possible, so you will need to be more concerned than usual with presenting your argument reasonably, sincerely, and in language untainted by excessive emotionalism. Finally, it is well worth remembering that you should always show respect for your audience in your writing.

Logos (Greek for "word"), related as it is to the subject, is the effective presentation of the argument itself. It refers to the speaker's grasp of the subject — his or her knowledge. Is the thesis or claim a worthwhile one? Is it logical, consistent, and well buttressed by supporting evidence? Is the evidence itself factual, reliable, and convincing? Finally, is the argument so thoughtfully organized and so clearly presented that it has an impact on the audience and could change opinions? Indeed, this aspect of argumentation is the most difficult to accomplish but is, at the same time, the most rewarding.

Pathos (Greek for "emotion") has the most to do with the audience. The essential question is, How does the speaker or writer present an argument or a persuasive essay to maximize its appeal for a given audience? One way, of course, is to appeal to the audience's emotions through the artful and strategic use of well-crafted language. Certain buzzwords, slanted diction, or emotionally loaded language may become either rallying cries or causes of resentment in an argument.

■ Considering Audience

It is worth remembering at this point that you can never be certain who your audience is; readers range along a spectrum from extremely friendly and sympathetic to extremely hostile and resistant, with a myriad of possibilities in between. The friendly audience will welcome new information and support the writer's position; the hostile audience will look for just the opposite: flaws in logic and examples of dishonest manipulation. With many arguments, there is the potential for a considerable audience of interested parties who are uncommitted. If the targeted audience is judged to be friendly, then the writer needs to be logical, but should feel free to use emotional appeals. If the audience is thought to be hostile, the *logos* must be the writer's immediate concern, and the language should be straightforward and objective. The greatest caution, subtlety, and critical thinking must be applied to the attempt to win over an uncommitted audience.

■ Argumentation and Other Rhetorical Strategies

In general, writers of argument are interested in explaining aspects of a subject as well as in advocating a particular view. Consequently, they frequently use the other rhetorical strategies in a supportive role. In your efforts to argue convincingly, you may find it necessary to define, to compare and contrast, to analyze causes and effects, to classify, to describe, and to narrate. (For more information on the use of other strategies in argumentation, see Use Other Rhetorical Strategies, page 510.) Nevertheless, it is the writer's attempt to convince, not explain, that is of primary importance in an argumentative essay. In this respect, it is helpful to know that there are two basic patterns of thinking and of presenting our thoughts that are followed in argumentation: *induction* and *deduction*.

■ Inductive and Deductive Reasoning

Inductive reasoning moves from a set of specific examples to a general statement or principle. As long as the evidence is accurate, pertinent, complete, and sufficient to represent the assertion, the conclusion of an inductive argument can be regarded as valid; if, however, you can spot inaccuracies in the evidence or can point to contrary evidence, you have good reason to doubt the assertion as it stands. Inductive reasoning is the most common of argumentative structures.

    Deductive reasoning, more formal and complex than inductive reasoning, moves from an overall premise, rule, or generalization to a more specific conclusion. Deductive logic follows the pattern of the *syllogism*, a simple three-part argument consisting of a major premise, a minor premise, and a conclusion. For example, notice how the following syllogism works.

   a. All humans are mortal. (*Major premise*)

   b. Catalina is a human. (*Minor premise*)

   c. Catalina is mortal. (*Conclusion*)

The conclusion here is true because both premises are true and the logic of the syllogism is valid.

Obviously, a syllogism will fail to work if either of the premises is untrue.

   a. All living creatures are mammals. (*Major premise*)

   b. A lobster is a living creature. (*Minor premise*)

   c. A lobster is a mammal. (*Conclusion*)

The problem is immediately apparent. The major premise is obviously false: There are many living creatures that are not mammals, and a lobster happens to be one of them. Consequently, the conclusion is invalid.

Syllogisms, however, can fail in other ways, even if both premises are objectively true. Such failures occur most often when the arguer jumps to a conclusion without taking obvious exceptions into account.

   a. All college students read books. (*Major premise*)

   b. Larry reads books. (*Minor premise*)

   c. Larry is a college student. (*Conclusion*)

Both the premises in this syllogism are true, but the syllogism is still invalid because it does not take into account that other people besides college students read books. The problem is in the way the major premise has been interpreted: If the minor premise were instead "Larry is a college student," then the valid conclusion "Larry reads books" would logically follow.

It is fairly easy to see the problems in a deductive argument when its premises and conclusion are rendered in the form of a syllogism. It is often more difficult to see errors in logic when the argument is presented discursively, or within the context of a long essay. If you can reduce the argument to its syllogistic form, however, you will have much less difficulty testing its validity. Similarly, if you can isolate and examine out of context the evidence provided to support an inductive assertion, you can more readily evaluate the written inductive argument.

Consider this excerpt from "The Draft: Why the Country Needs It," an article by James Fallows that first appeared in the *Atlantic* in 1980:

> The Vietnam draft was unfair racially, economically, educationally. By every one of those measures, the volunteer Army is less representative still. Libertarians argue that military service should be a matter of choice, but the plain fact is that service in the volunteer force is too frequently dictated by economics. Army enlisted ranks E1 through E4,

the privates and corporals, the cannon fodder, the ones who will fight and die, are 36 percent black now. By the Army's own projections, they will be 42 percent black in three years. When other "minorities" are taken into account, we will have, for the first time, an army whose fighting members are mainly "non-majority," or more bluntly, a black and brown army defending a mainly white nation. The military has been an avenue of opportunity of many young blacks. They may well be first-class fighting men. They do not represent the nation.

Such a selective sharing of the burden has destructive spiritual effects in a nation based on the democratic creed. But its practical implications can be quite as grave. The effect of a fair, representative draft is to hold the public hostage to the consequences of its decisions, much as the children's presence in the public schools focuses parents' attention on the quality of the schools. If the citizens are willing to countenance a decision that means that someone's child may die, they may contemplate more deeply if there is the possibility that the child will be theirs. Indeed, I would like to extend this principle even further. Young men of nineteen are rightly suspicious of the congressmen and columnists who urge them to the fore. I wish there were a practical way to resurrect provisions of the amended Selective Service Act of 1940, which raised the draft age to forty-four. Such a gesture might symbolize the desire to offset the historic injustice of the Vietnam draft, as well as suggest the possibility that, when a bellicose columnist recommends dispatching the American forces to Pakistan, he might also realize that he could end up as a gunner in a tank.

Here Fallows presents an inductive argument against the volunteer army and in favor of reinstating a draft. His argument can be summarized as follows:

Assertion: The volunteer army is racially and economically unfair.

Evidence: He points to the disproportionate percentage of blacks in the army, as well as to projections indicating that, within three years of the article's publication, more than half of the army's fighting members will be nonwhite.

Conclusion: "Such a selective sharing of the burden has destructive spiritual effects in a nation based on the democratic creed." Not until there is a fair, representative draft will the powerful majority be held accountable for any decision to go to war.

Fallows's inductive scheme here is, in fact, very effective. The evidence is convincing, and the conclusion is strong. But his argument also depends on a more complicated deductive syllogism.

a. The democratic ideal requires equal representation in the responsibilities of citizenship. (*Major premise*)

b. Military service is a responsibility of citizenship. (*Minor premise*)

    c. The democratic ideal requires equal representation in military service. (*Conclusion*)

To attack Fallows's argument, it would be necessary to deny one of his premises.

Fallows also employs a number of other persuasive techniques, including an analogy: "The effect of a fair, representative draft is to hold the public hostage to the consequences of its decisions, much as the children's presence in the public schools focuses parents' attention on the quality of the schools." The use of such an analogy proves nothing, but it can force readers to reconsider their viewpoint and can make them more open-minded. The same is true of Fallows's almost entirely unserious suggestion about raising the draft age to forty-four. Like most writers, Fallows uses persuasive arguments to complement his more important logical ones.

Using Argumentation across the Disciplines

When writing essays in the academic disciplines, you will have many opportunities to use the strategy of argumentation to both organize and strengthen the presentation of your ideas. To determine whether or not argumentation is the right strategy for you in a particular paper, use the four-step method described in Chapter 2 (Determining a Strategy for Developing Your Essay, pages 25–26). Consider the following examples, which illustrate how this four-step method works for typical college papers:

Ethics

1. MAIN IDEA: Suicide is an end-of-life option.
2. QUESTION: Should a person be allowed to end his or her life when no longer able to maintain an acceptable quality of life?
3. STRATEGY: Argumentation. The question "Should a person be allowed" triggers a pro/con argument. The writer argues for or against laws that allow physician-assisted suicide, for example.
4. SUPPORTING STRATEGY: Definition should be used to clarify what is meant by the expression "quality of life." Cause and effect analysis should be used to determine, for example, at what point a person has lost a desirable "quality of life."

Environmental Studies

1. MAIN IDEA: The burning of fossil fuels is creating greenhouse gas emissions that are, in turn, causing global warming.
2. QUESTION: What can we do to reduce emissions from the burning of fossil fuels?
3. STRATEGY: Argumentation. The question "What can we do?" suggests an answer in the form of an argument. The writer might want to argue for higher taxes on fossil fuels, or for the installation of smokestack scrubbers.

4. SUPPORtING STRATEGY: Cause and effect analysis will be necessary to show how burning fossil fuels increases greenhouse emissions and how higher taxes and smokestack scrubbers will work to reduce harmful gases.

Biology

1. MAIN IDEA: The use of animals in biomedical research is crucial.
2. QUESTION: Should there be a ban on the use of animals in biomedical research?
3. STRATEGY: Argumentation. The word *should* signals a pro/con debate: Animals should/should not be used in biomedical research.
4. SUPPORtING STRATEGY: Comparison and contrast might be used to help make the case that alternatives to the use of animals are better/worse than using animals.

Sample Student Essay Using Argumentation As a Writing Strategy

Mark Jackson wrote the following essay while a student at the University of Cincinnati. Jackson's essay explores a number of arguments made in favor of a liberal arts education. In the course of the essay, Jackson rejects some of these arguments, such as the idea that a liberal arts education makes students well-rounded. He does, however, support the argument that a liberal arts education fosters critical-thinking skills, and he comes to the conclusion that the ideal education would balance practical or vocational training and a grounding in the liberal arts.

The Liberal Arts:
A Practical View
Mark Jackson

Title hints at writer's position.

Many students question the reasoning behind a liberal arts education. But even though they may have been forced to swallow liberal arts propaganda since junior high, students seldom receive a good explanation for why they should strive to be "well-rounded." They are told that they should value the accumulation of knowledge for its own sake, yet this argument does not convince those who believe that knowledge must have some practical value or material benefit to be worth seeking

Writer identifies central problem: liberal arts inadequately explained.

1

In "What Is an Idea?" Wayne Booth and Marshall Gregory argue convincingly that "a liberal education is an education in ideas—not merely memorizing them, but learning to move among them, balancing one against the other, negotiating relationships, accommodating new arguments, and returning for a closer look" (17). These writers propose that a liberal arts education is valuable to students because it helps to develop their analytical-thinking skills and writing skills. This is, perhaps, one of the best arguments for taking a broad range of classes in many different subjects.

First argument for liberal arts education

2

Other, more radical arguments in favor of the liberal arts are less appealing. Lewis Thomas, a prominent scientist and physician, believes that classical Greek should form the backbone of a college student's education. This suggestion seems extreme. It is more reasonable to concentrate on the English language, since many students do not have a firm grasp of basic reading and writing skills. Freshman English and other English courses serve as a better foundation for higher education than classical Greek could.

Another, less convincing argument

3

The opposition to a liberal arts curriculum grows out of the values that college-bound students learn from their parents and peers: They place an immeasurable value on success and disregard anything that is not pertinent to material achievements. Students often have trouble seeing what practical value studying a particular discipline can have for them. Teenagers who are headed for the world of nine-to-five employment tend to ignore certain studies in their haste to succeed.

4

My parents started discussing the possibility of college with me when I was in the sixth grade. They didn't think that it was important for me to go to college to become a more fulfilled human being. My mom and dad wanted me to go to college so that I might not have to live from paycheck to paycheck as they do. Their reason for wanting me to go to college has become my primary motivation for pursuing a college degree.

Writer links personal experience to his attitude toward liberal arts.

5

I remember getting into an argument with my high school counselor because I didn't want to take a third year of Spanish. I was an A student in Spanish II, but I hated every minute of the class. My counselor noticed that I didn't sign up for Spanish III, so he called me into his office to hassle me. I told him that I took two years of a foreign language so that I would be accepted to college, but that I did not want to take a third year. Mr. Gallivan told me that I needed a third year of a foreign language to be a "well-rounded" student. My immediate response was "So what?!" I hated foreign languages, and no counselor was going to make me take something that I didn't want or need. I felt Spanish was a waste of time.

I frequently asked my high school counselor why I needed to take subjects like foreign languages and art. He never really gave me an answer (except for the suggestion that I should be "well-rounded"). Instead, Mr. Gallivan always directed my attention to a sign on the wall of his office which read, "THERE'S NO REASON FOR IT. IT'S JUST OUR POLICY!" I never found that a satisfactory explanation.

Norman Cousins, however, does offer a more reasonable explanation for the necessity of a liberal education. In his essay "How to Make People Smaller than They Are," Cousins points out how valuable the humanities are for career-minded people. He says, "The irony of the emphasis being placed on careers is that nothing is more valuable for anyone who has had a professional or vocational education than to be able to deal with abstractions or complexities, or to feel comfortable with subtleties of thought or language, or to think sequentially" (15). Cousins reminds us that technical or vocational knowledge alone will not make one successful in a chosen profession: Unique problems and situations may arise daily in the context of one's job, so an employee must be able to think creatively and deal with events that no textbook ever discussed. The workers who get the promotions and advance to high positions are the ones who can "think on their feet" when they are faced with a complex problem.

6

7

8

Writer points to value of communication skills learned through liberal arts.

Cousins also suggests that the liberal arts teach students communication skills that are critical for success. A shy, introverted person who was a straight-A student in college would not make a very good public relations consultant, no matter how keen his or her intellectual abilities. Employees who cannot adequately articulate their ideas to a client or an employer will soon find themselves unemployed, even if they have brilliant ideas. Social integration into a particular work environment would be difficult without good communication skills and a wide range of interests and general knowledge. The broader a person's interests, the more compatible he or she will be with other workers.

9

Thesis: Writer calls for balance of liberal arts courses and professional courses.

Though it is obvious that liberal arts courses do have considerable practical value, a college education would not be complete without some job training. The liberal arts should be given equal billing in the college curriculum, but by no means should they become the focal point of higher education. If specialization is outlawed in our institutions of higher learning, then college students might lose their competitive edge. Maxim Gorky has written that "any kind of knowledge is useful" (22), and, of course, most knowledge is useful; but it would be misguided to structure the college curriculum around an overview of all disciplines instead of allowing a student to master one subject or profession. Universities must seek to maintain an equilibrium between liberal and specialized education. A liberal arts degree without specialization or intended future specialization (such as a master's degree in a specific field) is useless unless one wants to be a professional game-show contestant.

10

Plan of action for college students

Students who want to make the most of their college years should pursue a major course of study while choosing electives or a few minor courses of study from the liberal arts. In this way, scholars can become experts in a profession and still have a broad enough background to ensure versatility, both within and outside the field. In a university's quest to produce "well-rounded" students, specialization must not come to be viewed as an evil practice.

11

Writer calls for education to better articulate the value of the liberal arts.

If educators really want to increase the number 12 of liberal arts courses that each student takes, they must first increase the popularity of such studies. It is futile to try to get students to learn something just for the sake of knowing it. They must be given examples, such as those already mentioned, of how a liberal education will further their own interests. Instead of telling students that they need to be "well-rounded," counselors and professors should point out the practical value and applications of a broad education in the liberal arts. It is difficult to persuade some college students that becoming a better person is an important goal of higher education. Many students want a college education so that they can make more money and have more power. This is the perceived value of a higher education in their world.

Works Cited

Booth, Wayne, and Marshall Gregory. "What Is an Idea?" *The Harper and Row Reader.* 2nd ed. New York: Harper, 1988. Print.

Cousins, Norman. "How to Make People Smaller than They Are." *The Saturday Review* Dec. 1978: 15. Print.

Gorky, Maxim. "How I Studied." *On Literature.* Trans. Julius Katzer. Seattle: U of Washington P, 1973. 9-22. Print.

Thomas, Lewis. "Debating the Unknowable." *Atlantic Monthly* July 1981: 49-52. Print.

Analyzing Mark Jackson's Argumentation Essay: Questions for Discussion

1. Why did Jackson refuse to take Spanish III? How does his personal experience with Spanish and with his guidance counselor relate to his argument?

2. What is Jackson's thesis? Where and how does he present it?

3. Jackson employs several arguments in favor of liberal arts education. How does he classify them? What does he accomplish by including a variety of rationales regarding the validity of a "well-rounded" education?

Suggestions for Using Argumentation As a Writing Strategy

As you plan, write, and revise your argumentation essay, be mindful of the writing process guidelines described in Chapter 2. Pay particular attention to the basic requirements and essential ingredients of this writing strategy.

■ Planning Your Argumentation Essay

Writing an argument can be very rewarding. By its nature, an argument must be carefully reasoned and thoughtfully structured to have maximum effect. In other words, the *logos* of the argument must be carefully tended. Allow yourself, therefore, enough time to think about your thesis, to gather the evidence you need, and to draft, revise, edit, and proofread your essay. Sloppy thinking, confused expression, and poor organization will be immediately evident to your reader and will make for weaker arguments.

For example, you might be given an assignment in your history class to write a paper explaining what you think was the main cause of the Civil War. How would you approach this topic? First, it would help to assemble a number of possible interpretations of the causes of the Civil War and to examine them closely. Once you have determined what you consider to be the main cause, you will need to develop points that support your position. Then you will need to explain why you did not choose other possibilities, and you will have to assemble reasons that refute them. For instance, you might write an opening similar to this example.

The Fugitive Slave Act Forced the North to Go to War

While the start of the Civil War can be attributed to many factors—states' rights, slavery, a clash between antithetical economic systems, and westward expansion—the final straw for the North was the Fugitive Slave Act. This act, more than any other single element of disagreement between the North and the South, forced the North into a position in which the only option was to fight.

Certainly, slavery and the clash over open lands in the West contributed to the growing tensions between the two sides, as did the economically incompatible systems of production—plantation and manufacture—but the Fugitive Slave Act required the North either to actively support slavery or to run the risk of becoming a criminal in defiance of it. The North chose not to support the Fugitive Slave Act and was openly angered by the idea that it should be required to do so by law. This anger and open defiance led directly to the Civil War.

In these opening paragraphs, the author states the main argument for the cause of the Civil War and sets up, in addition, the possible alternatives to this view. The points outlined in the introduction would lead, one by one, to a logical argument asserting that the Fugitive Slave Act was responsible for the onset of the Civil War and refuting the other interpretations.

This introduction is mainly a logical argument. As was mentioned before, writers often use persuasive, or emotional, arguments along with logical ones. Persuasive arguments focus on issues that appeal to people's subconscious or emotional nature, along with their logical powers and intellectual understanding. Such arguments rely on powerful and charged language, and they appeal to the emotions. Persuasive arguments can be especially effective but should not be used without a strong logical backing. Indeed, this is the only way to use emotional persuasion ethically. Emotional persuasion, when not in support of a logical point, can be dangerous in that it can make an illogical point sound appealing to a listener or reader.

Determine Your Thesis or Proposition.   Begin by determining a topic that interests you and about which there is some significant difference of opinion or about which you have a number of questions. Find out what's in the news, what people are talking about, what authors and instructors are emphasizing as important intellectual arguments. As you pursue your research, consider what assertion you can make about the topic you chose. The more specific this thesis or proposition, the more directed your research can become and the more focused your ultimate argument will be. While researching your topic, however, be aware that the information may point you in new directions. Don't hesitate at any point to modify or even reject an initial or preliminary thesis as continued research warrants.

A thesis can be placed anywhere in an argument, but it is probably best while learning to write arguments to place the statement of your controlling idea somewhere near the beginning of your composition. Explain the importance of the thesis, and make clear to your reader that you share a common concern or interest in this issue. You may wish to state your central assertion directly in your first or second paragraph so that there is no possibility for your reader to be confused about your position. You may also wish to lead off with a particularly striking piece of evidence to capture your reader's interest.

Consider Your Audience.   It is well worth remembering that in no other type of writing is the question of audience more important than in argumentation. Here again, the *ethos* and *pathos* aspects of argumentation come into play. The tone you establish, the type of diction you choose, the kinds of evidence you select to buttress your assertions, and indeed the organizational pattern you design and follow will all influence your audience's perception of your trustworthiness and believability. If you make good judgments about the nature of your audience, respect its knowledge of the subject, and correctly envision whether it is likely to be hostile, neutral, complacent, or receptive, you will be able to tailor the various aspects of your argument appropriately.

Gather Supporting Evidence.   For each point of your argument, be sure to provide appropriate and sufficient supporting evidence: verifiable facts and statistics, illustrative examples and narratives, or quotations from authorities. Don't overwhelm your reader with evidence, but don't skimp either; it is important to demonstrate your command of the topic and your control of the thesis by choosing carefully from all the evidence at your disposal. If there are strong arguments on both sides of the issue, you will need to take this into account while making your choices. (See the Consider Refutations to Your Argument section below.)

■ Organizing and Writing Your Argumentation Essay

Choose an Organizational Pattern.   Once you think that you have sufficient evidence to make your assertion convincing, consider how best to organize your argument. To some extent, your organization will depend on your method of reasoning: inductive, deductive, or a combination of the two. For example, is it necessary to establish a major premise before moving on to discuss a minor premise? Should most of your evidence precede or follow your direct statement of an assertion? Will induction work better with the particular audience you have targeted?

As you present your primary points, you may find it effective to move from those that are least important to those that are most important or from those that are least familiar to those that are most familiar. A scratch outline can help, but it is often the case that a writer's most crucial revisions in an argument involve rearranging its components into a sharper, more coherent order. It is often difficult to tell what that order should be until the revision stage of the writing process.

Consider Refutations to Your Argument.   As you proceed with your argument, you may wish to take into account well-known and significant opposing arguments. To ignore them would be to suggest to your readers any one of the following: You don't know about them, you know about them and are obviously and unfairly weighting the argument in your favor, or you know about them and have no reasonable answers to them. Grant the validity of the opposing argument or refute it, but respect your readers' intelligence by addressing the problems. Your readers will in turn respect you for doing so.

To avoid weakening your thesis, you must be very clear in your thinking and presentation. It must remain apparent to your readers why your argument is superior to opposing points of view. If you feel that you cannot introduce opposing arguments because they will weaken rather than strengthen your thesis, you should probably reassess your thesis and the supporting evidence.

Use Other Rhetorical Strategies.   Although argument is one of the most powerful single rhetorical strategies, it is almost always strengthened by incorporating other strategies. In every professional selection in this chapter, you will find a number of rhetorical strategies at work.

Combining strategies is probably not something you want to think about when you first try to write an argument. Instead, let the strategies develop naturally as you organize, draft, and revise your essay. As you develop your argument essay, use the following chart as a reminder of what the eight strategies covered previously can do for you.

Strategies for Development	
Narration	Telling a story or giving an account of an event
Description	Presenting a picture in words
Illustration	Using examples to illustrate a point or an idea
Process Analysis	Explaining how something is done or happens
Comparison and Contrast	Demonstrating likenesses and differences
Division and Classification	Separating a subject into its parts and placing them in appropriate categories
Definition	Explaining what something is or means
Cause and Effect Analysis	Explaining why something happens or the ramifications of an action

As you draft your essay, look for places where you can use the above strategies to strengthen your argument. For example, do you need a more convincing example, a term defined, a process explained, or the likely effects of an action detailed?

Conclude Forcefully.   In the conclusion of your essay, be sure to restate your position in different language, at least briefly. Besides persuading your reader to accept your point of view, you may also want to encourage some specific course of action. Above all, your conclusion should not introduce new information that may surprise your reader; it should seem to follow naturally, almost seamlessly, from the series of points that have been carefully established in the body of the essay.

■ Revising and Editing Your Argumentation Essay

Avoid Faulty Reasoning. Have someone read your argument, checking sentences for errors in judgment and reasoning. Sometimes others can see easily what you can't because you are so intimately tied to your assertion. Review the following list of errors in reasoning, making sure that you have not committed any of them.

Oversimplification – a foolishly simple solution to what is clearly a complex problem. *The reason we have a balance-of-trade deficit is that foreigners make better products than we do.*

Hasty generalization – in inductive reasoning, a generalization that is based on too little evidence or on evidence that is not representative. *It was the best movie I saw this year, and so it should get an Academy Award.*

Post hoc, ergo propter hoc ("after this, therefore because of this") – confusing chance or coincidence with causation. The fact that one event comes after another does not necessarily mean that the first event caused the second. *Every time I wear my orange Syracuse sweater to a game, we win.*

Begging the question – assuming in a premise something that needs to be proven. *Parking fines work because they keep people from parking illegally.*

False analogy – making a misleading analogy between logically connected ideas. *Of course he'll make a fine coach. He was an all-star basketball player.*

Either/or thinking – seeing only two alternatives when there may in fact be other possibilities. *Either you love your job or you hate it.*

Non sequitur ("it does not follow") – an inference or conclusion that is not clearly related to the established premises or evidence. *She is very sincere; she must know what she is talking about.*

Name-Calling – linking a person to a negative idea or symbol. The hope is that by invoking the name the user will elicit a negative reaction without the necessary evidence. *Senator Jones is a bleeding heart.*

Share Your Drafts with Others. Try sharing the drafts of your essay with other students in your writing class to make sure that your argument works, that it makes its point. Ask them if there are any parts that they do not understand. Have them restate your thesis in their own words. Ask them if you have overlooked any opposing arguments that you should consider and if you have provided enough evidence for your side of the argument to be convincing. If their answers differ from what you intended, have them point to the troublesome parts of your essay and discuss what you can do to improve your argument. If you find their suggestions valid, revise your text accordingly. To maximize the effectiveness of conferences with your peers, use the guidelines presented on page 29. Feedback from these conferences often provides one or more places where you can start revising.

Question Your Own Work While Revising and Editing.   Revision is best done by asking yourself key questions about what you have written. Begin by reading, preferably aloud, what you have written. Reading aloud forces you to pay attention to every single word, and you are more likely to catch lapses in the logical flow of thought. After you have read your paper through, answer the following questions for revising and editing, and make the necessary changes.

For help with twelve common writing problems, see Chapter 16, "Editing for Grammar, Punctuation, and Sentence Style."

Questions for Revising and Editing: Argumentation

1. Is my thesis or proposition focused? Do I state my thesis well?

2. Assess the different kinds of arguments. Am I using the right technique to argue my thesis? Does my strategy fit my subject matter and audience?

3. Does my presentation include enough evidence to support my thesis? Do I acknowledge opposing points of view in a way that strengthens, rather than weakens, my argument?

4. Have I chosen an appropriate organizational pattern that makes it easy to support my thesis?

5. Have I avoided faulty reasoning within my essay? Have I had a friend read the essay to help me find problems in my logic?

6. Is my conclusion forceful and effective?

7. Have I thought about or attempted to combine rhetorical strategies to strengthen my argument? If so, is the combination of strategies effective? If not, what strategy or strategies would help my argument?

8. Have I used a variety of sentences to enliven my writing? Have I avoided wordiness?

E11–12

E1–10

9. Have I avoided errors in grammar, punctuation, and mechanics?

The Declaration of Independence

THOMAS JEFFERSON

President, governor, statesman, diplomat, lawyer, architect, philosopher, thinker, and writer, Thomas Jefferson (1743–1826) is one of the most important figures in U.S. history. He was born in Albemarle County, Virginia, and attended the College of William and Mary. After being admitted to law practice in 1767, he began a long and illustrious career of public service to the colonies and, later, the new republic.

Jefferson drafted the Declaration of Independence in 1776. Although it was revised by Benjamin Franklin and his colleagues in the Continental Congress, in its sound logic and forceful, direct style the document retains the unmistakable qualities of Jefferson's prose.

■ Preparing to Read

What, for you, is the meaning of democracy? Where do your ideas about democracy come from?

When in the course of human events, it becomes necessary for one people to dissolve the political bonds which have connected them with another, and to assume among the Powers of the earth, the separate and equal station to which the Laws of Nature and of Nature's God entitle them, a decent respect to the opinions of mankind requires that they should declare the causes which impel them to the separation. 1

We hold these truths to be self-evident, that all men are created equal, that they are endowed by their Creator with certain unalienable Rights, that among these are Life, Liberty and the pursuit of Happiness.— That to secure these rights, Governments are instituted among Men, deriving their just powers from the consent of the governed, — That whenever any Form of Government becomes destructive of these ends, it is the Right of the People to alter or to abolish it, and to institute new Government, laying its foundation on such principles and organizing its powers in such form, as to them shall seem most likely to effect their Safety and Happiness. Prudence, indeed, will dictate that Governments long established should not be changed for light and transient causes; and accordingly all experience hath shewn, that mankind are more disposed to suffer, while evils are sufferable, than to right themselves by abolishing the forms to which they are accustomed. But when a long train of abuses and usurpations, pursuing invariably the same Object evinces a design to reduce them under absolute Despotism, it is their right, it is their duty, to throw off such 2

Government, and to provide new Guards for their future security.—Such has been the patient sufferance of these Colonies; and such is now the necessity which constrains them to alter their former Systems of Government. The history of the present King of Great Britain is a history of repeated injuries and usurpations, all having in direct object the establishment of an absolute Tyranny over these States. To prove this, let Facts be submitted to a candid world.

He has refused his Assent to Laws, the most wholesome and necessary 3 for the public good.

We hold these truths to be self-evident, that all men are created equal, that they are endowed by their Creator with certain unalienable Rights, that among these are Life, Liberty and the pursuit of Happiness.

He has forbidden his Governors to pass Laws 4 of immediate and pressing importance, unless suspended in their operation till his Assent should be obtained; and when so suspended, he has utterly neglected to attend to them.

He has refused to pass other Laws for the ac- 5 commodation of large districts of people, unless those people would relinquish the right of Representation in the Legislature, a right inestimable to them and formidable to tyrants only.

He has called together legislative bodies at places 6 unusual, uncomfortable, and distant from the depository of their public Records, for the sole purpose of fatiguing them into compliance with his measures.

He has dissolved Representative Houses re- 7 peatedly, for opposing with manly firmness his invasions on the rights of the people.

He has refused for a long time, after such dis- 8 solutions, to cause others to be elected; whereby the Legislative powers, incapable of Annihilation, have returned to the People at large for their exercise; the State remaining in the mean time exposed to all the dangers of invasion from without, and convulsions within.

He has endeavoured to prevent the population of these States; for that 9 purpose obstructing the Laws of Naturalization of Foreigners; refusing to pass others to encourage their migration hither, and raising the conditions of new Appropriations of Lands.

He has obstructed the Administration of Justice, by refusing his Assent 10 to Laws for establishing Judiciary Powers.

He has made Judges dependent on his Will alone, for the tenure of their 11 offices, and the amount and payment of their salaries.

He has erected a multitude of New Offices, and sent hither swarms of 12 Officers to harass our People, and eat out their substance.

He has kept among us, in times of peace, Standing Armies without the 13 Consent of our legislatures.

He has affected to render the Military independent of and superior to 14 the Civil power.

He has combined with others to subject us to a jurisdiction foreign to   15
our constitution, and unacknowledged by our laws; giving his Assent to their
Acts of pretended Legislation:

For quartering large bodies of armed troops among us: 16

For protecting them, by a mock Trial, from punishment for any Murders   17
which they should commit on the Inhabitants of these States:

For cutting off our Trade with all parts of the world: 18

For imposing Taxes on us without our Consent: 19

For depriving us in many cases, of the benefits of Trial by Jury: 20

For transporting us beyond Seas to be tried for pretended offenses: 21

For abolishing the free System of English Laws in a neighbouring Province,   22
establishing therein an Arbitrary government, and enlarging its Boundaries so
as to render it at once an example and fit instrument for introducing the same
absolute rule into these Colonies:

For taking away our Charters, abolishing our most valuable Laws, and   23
altering fundamentally the Forms of our Governments:

For suspending our own Legislatures, and declaring themselves invested   24
with power to legislate for us in all cases whatsoever.

He has abdicated Government here, by declaring us out of his Protection   25
and waging War against us.

He has plundered our seas, ravaged our Coasts, burnt our towns, and   26
destroyed the lives of our people.

He is at this time transporting large Armies of foreign Mercenaries to   27
compleat works of death, desolation and tyranny already begun with circumstances of Cruelty & perfidy scarcely paralleled in the most barbarous ages,
and totally unworthy the Head of a civilized nation.

He has constrained our fellow Citizens taken Captive on the high Seas to   28
bear Arms against their Country, to become the executioners of their friends
and Brethren, or to fall themselves by their Hands.

He has excited domestic insurrections amongst us, and has endeavoured   29
to bring on the inhabitants of our frontiers, the merciless Indian Savages,
whose known rule of warfare, is an undistinguished destruction of all ages,
sexes and conditions.

In every stage of these Oppressions We Have Petitioned for Redress in   30
the most humble terms: Our repeated Petitions have been answered only by
repeated injury. A Prince, whose character is thus marked by every act which
may define a Tyrant, is unfit to be the ruler of a free people.

Nor have We been wanting in attention to our Brittish brethren. We have   31
warned them from time to time of attempts by their legislature to extend an
unwarrantable jurisdiction over us. We have reminded them of the circumstances of our emigration and settlement here. We have appealed to their
native justice and magnanimity, and we have conjured them by the ties of
our common kindred to disavow these usurpations, which, would inevitably
interrupt our connections and correspondence. They too have been deaf to

the voice of justice and of consanguinity. We must, therefore, acquiesce in the necessity, which denounces our Separation, and hold them, as we hold the rest of mankind, Enemies in War, in Peace Friends.

We, therefore, the Representatives of the united States of America, in General Congress, Assembled, appealing to the Supreme Judge of the world for the rectitude of our intentions, do, in the Name, and by Authority of the good People of these Colonies, solemnly publish and declare, That these United Colonies are, and of Right ought to be Free and Independent States; that they are Absolved from all Allegiance to the British Crown, and that all political connection between them and the State of Great Britain, is and ought to be totally dissolved; and that as Free and Independent States, they have full Power to levy War, conclude Peace, contract Alliances, establish Commerce, and to do all other Acts and Things which Independent States may of right do. And for the support of this Declaration, with a firm reliance on the protection of divine Providence, we mutually pledge to each other our Lives, our Fortunes and our sacred Honor.

32

■ Thinking Critically about the Text

Why do you think the Declaration of Independence is still such a powerful and important document more than two hundred years after it was written? Do any parts of it seem more memorable than others? Did any part surprise you in this reading?

■ Questions on Subject

1. Where, according to Jefferson, do rulers get their authority? What does Jefferson believe is the purpose of government?
2. What argument does the Declaration of Independence make for overthrowing any unacceptable government? What assumptions underlie this argument?
3. In paragraphs 3–29, Jefferson lists the many ways King George has wronged the colonists. Which of these "injuries and usurpations" (paragraph 2) do you feel are just cause for the colonists to declare their independence?
4. According to the Declaration of Independence, how did the colonists try to persuade the English king to rule more justly?
5. What are the specific declarations that Jefferson makes in his final paragraph?

■ Questions on Strategy

1. The Declaration of Independence is a deductive argument; it is therefore possible to present it in the form of a syllogism. What is the major premise, the minor premise, and the conclusion of Jefferson's argument? (Glossary: *Syllogism*)

2. In paragraph 2, Jefferson presents certain "self-evident" truths. What are these truths, and how are they related to the intent of his argument?
3. The list of charges against the king is given as evidence in support of Jefferson's minor premise. Does he offer any evidence in support of his major premise? Why, or why not? (Glossary: *Evidence*)
4. What organizational pattern do you see in the list of grievances in paragraphs 3–29? (Glossary: *Organization*) Describe the cumulative effect of this list on you as a reader.
5. Explain how Jefferson uses cause and effect thinking to justify the colonists' argument in declaring their independence. (Glossary: *Cause and Effect Analysis*)

■ Questions on Diction and Vocabulary

1. Who is Jefferson's audience, and in what tone does he address this audience? Discuss why this tone is or isn't appropriate for this document. (Glossary: *Audience*)
2. Is the language of the Declaration of Independence coolly reasonable or emotional, or does it change from one to the other? Give examples to support your answer.
3. Paraphrase the following excerpt, and comment on Jefferson's diction and syntax: "They too have been deaf to the voice of justice and of consanguinity. We must, therefore, acquiesce in the necessity, which denounces our Separation, and hold them, as we hold the rest of mankind, Enemies in War, in Peace Friends" (paragraph 31). Describe the author's tone in these two sentences. (Glossary: *Diction; Tone*)

■ Classroom Activity Using Argumentation

Use the following test, developed by William V. Haney, to determine your ability to analyze accurately evidence that is presented to you. After completing Haney's test, discuss your answers with other members of your class, and then compare them to the correct answers printed at the end of the test.

THE UNCRITICAL INFERENCE TEST

Directions

1. You will read a brief story. Assume that all of the information presented in the story is definitely accurate and true. Read the story carefully. You may refer back to the story whenever you wish.

2. You will then read statements about the story. Answer them in numerical order. *Do not go back* to fill in answers or to change answers. This will only distort your test score.

3. After you read each statement carefully, determine whether the statement is:

   a. "T" — meaning: On the basis of the information presented in the story the statement is *definitely true*.

b. "F" — meaning: On the basis of the information presented in the story the statement is *definitely false*.

c. "?" —The statement *may* be true (or false) but on the basis of the information presented in the story you cannot be definitely certain. (If any part of the statement is doubtful, mark the statement "?".)

4. Indicate your answer by circling either "T" or "F" or "?" opposite the statement.

The Story

Babe Smith has been killed. Police have rounded up six suspects, all of whom are known gangsters. All of them are known to have been near the scene of the killing at the approximate time that it occurred. All had substantial motives for wanting Smith killed. However, one of these suspected gangsters, Slinky Sam, has positively been cleared of guilt.

Statements about the Story

1. Slinky Sam is known to have been near the scene of the killing of Babe Smith.   T   F   ?
2. All six of the rounded-up gangsters were known to have been near the scene of the murder.   T   F   ?
3. Only Slinky Sam has been cleared of guilt.   T   F   ?
4. All six of the rounded-up suspects were near the scene of Smith's killing at the approximate time that it took place.   T   F   ?
5. The police do not know who killed Smith.   T   F   ?
6. All six suspects are known to have been near the scene of the foul deed.   T   F   ?
7. Smith's murderer did not confess of his own free will.   T   F   ?
8. Slinky Sam was not cleared of guilt.   T   F   ?
9. It is known that the six suspects were in the vicinity of the cold-blooded assassination.   T   F   ?

¿ˈ6 Ⅎˈ8 ¿ˈ7 ¿ˈ9 ¿ˈ5 Tˈ4 ¿ˈ3 ¿ˈ2 Tˈ1

■ Writing Suggestions

1. To some people, the Declaration of Independence still accurately reflects America's political philosophy and way of life; to others, it does not. What is your position on this issue? Discuss your analysis of the Declaration of Independence's contemporary relevance, and try to persuade others to accept your position.

2. **Writing with Sources.** How does a monarchy differ from American democracy? Write an essay in which you compare and contrast a particular monarchy and the presidency. How are they similar? You might also consider comparing the presidency with the British monarchy of 1776. Do some research online or in the library to support your analysis.

For models of and advice on integrating sources, see Chapters 14–15.

The Case for Short Words

RICHARD LEDERER

Born in 1938, Richard Lederer has been a lifelong student of language. He holds degrees from Haverford College, Harvard University, and the University of New Hampshire. For twenty-seven years he taught English at St. Paul's School in Concord, New Hampshire. Anyone who has read one of his more than thirty books will understand why he has been referred to as "Conan the Grammarian" and "America's wittiest verbalist." Lederer loves language and enjoys writing about its richness and usage by Americans. His books include *Anguished English* (1987), *Crazy English* (1989), *Adventures of a Verbivore* (1994), *Nothing Risque, Nothing Gained* (1995), *A Man of My Words: Reflections on the English Language* (2003), and *Word Wizard: Super Bloopers, Rich Reflections, and Other Acts of Word Magic* (2006). In addition to writing books, Lederer pens a weekly syndicated column called "Looking at Language" for newspapers and magazines throughout the country. He is the "Grammar Grappler" for *Writer's Digest*, the language commentator for National Public Radio, and the cohost of *A Way with Words*, a weekly radio program out of San Diego, California.

In the following selection, a chapter from *The Miracle of Language* (1990), Lederer sings the praises of short words and reminds us that well-chosen monosyllabic words can be a writer's best friends because they are functional and often pack a powerful punch. Note the clever way in which he uses short words throughout the essay itself to support his argument.

■ Preparing to Read

Find a paragraph you like in a book that you enjoyed reading. What is it that appeals to you? What did the author do to make the writing so appealing? Do you like the vocabulary, the flow of the words, the imagery it presents, or something else?

When you speak and write, there is no law that says you have to use big 1
words. Short words are as good as long ones, and short, old words — like *sun* and *grass* and *home* — are best of all. A lot of small words, more than you might think, can meet your needs with a strength, grace, and charm that large words do not have.

Big words can make the way dark for those who read what you write and 2
hear what you say. Small words cast their clear light on big things — night and day, love and hate, war and peace, and life and death. Big words at times

seem strange to the eye and the ear and the mind and the heart. Small words are the ones we seem to have known from the time we were born, like the hearth fire that warms the home.

Short words are bright like sparks that glow in the night, prompt like the dawn that greets the day, sharp like the blade of a knife, hot like salt tears that scald the cheek, quick like moths that flit from flame to flame, and terse like the dart and sting of a bee.   3

> A lot of small words, more than you might think, can meet your needs with a strength, grace, and charm that large words do not have.

Here is a sound rule: Use small, old words where you can. If a long word says just what you want to say, do not fear to use it. But know that our tongue is rich in crisp, brisk, swift, short words. Make them the spine and the heart of what you speak and write. Short words are like fast friends. They will not let you down.   4

The title of this chapter and the four paragraphs that you have just read are wrought entirely of words of one syllable. In setting myself this task, I did not feel especially cabined, cribbed, or confined. In fact, the structure helped me to focus on the power of the message I was trying to put across.   5

One study shows that twenty words account for twenty-five percent of all spoken English words, and all twenty are monosyllabic. In order of frequency they are: *I, you, the, a, to, is, it, that, of, and, in, what, he, this, have, do, she, not, on,* and *they.* Other studies indicate that the fifty most common words in written English are each made of a single syllable.   6

For centuries our finest poets and orators have recognized and employed the power of small words to make a straight point between two minds. A great many of our proverbs punch home their points with pithy monosyllables: "Where there's a will, there's a way," "A stitch in time saves nine," "Spare the rod and spoil the child," "A bird in the hand is worth two in the bush."   7

Nobody used the short word more skillfully than William Shakespeare, whose dying King Lear laments: 8

> And my poor fool is hang'd! No, no, no life!
> Why should a dog, a horse, a rat have life,
> And thou no breath at all? . . .
> Do you see this? Look on her; look, her lips.
> Look there, look there!

Shakespeare's contemporaries made the King James Bible a centerpiece of short words — "And God said, Let there be light: and there was light. And God saw the light, that it was good." The descendants of such mighty lines live on in the twentieth century. When asked to explain his policy to Parliament, Winston Churchill responded with these ringing monosyllables: "I will say: 9

It is to wage war, by sea, land, and air, with all our might and with all the strength that God can give us." In his "Death of the Hired Man" Robert Frost observes that "Home is the place where, when you have to go there, / They have to take you in." And William H. Johnson uses ten two-letter words to explain his secret of success: "If it is to be, / It is up to me."

You don't have to be a great author, statesman, or philosopher to tap the   10 energy and eloquence of small words. Each winter I ask my ninth graders at St. Paul's School to write a composition composed entirely of one-syllable words. My students greet my request with obligatory moans and groans, but, when they return to class with their essays, most feel that, with the pressure to produce high-sounding polysyllables relieved, they have created some of their most powerful and luminous prose. Here are submissions from two of my ninth graders:

> What can you say to a boy who has left home? You can say that he has done wrong, but he does not care. He has left home so that he will not have to deal with what you say. He wants to go as far as he can. He will do what he wants to do.
>
> This boy does not want to be forced to go to church, to comb his hair, or to be on time. A good time for this boy does not lie in your reach, for what you have he does not want. He dreams of ripped jeans, shorts with no starch, and old socks.
>
> So now this boy is on a bus to a place he dreams of, a place with no rules. This boy now walks a strange street, his long hair blown back by the wind. He wears no coat or tie, just jeans and an old shirt. He hates your world, and he has left it.
>
> — Charles Shaffer

> For a long time we cruised by the coast and at last came to a wide bay past the curve of a hill, at the end of which lay a small town. Our long boat ride at an end, we all stretched and stood up to watch as the boat nosed its way in.
>
> The town climbed up the hill that rose from the shore, a space in front of it left bare for the port. Each house was a clean white with sky blue or grey trim; in front of each one was a small yard, edged by a white stone wall strewn with green vines.
>
> As the town basked in the heat of noon, not a thing stirred in the streets or by the shore. The sun beat down on the sea, the land, and the back of our necks, so that, in spite of the breeze that made the vines sway, we all wished we could hide from the glare in a cool, white house. But, as there was no one to help dock the boat, we had to stand and wait.
>
> At last the head of the crew leaped from the side and strode to a large house on the right. He shoved the door wide, poked his head through the gloom, and roared with a fierce voice. Five or six men

came out, and soon the port was loud with the clank of chains and creak of planks as the men caught ropes thrown by the crew, pulled them taut, and tied them to posts. Then they set up a rough plank so we could cross from the deck to the shore. We all made for the large house while the crew watched, glad to be rid of us.

— CELIA WREN

You, too, can tap into the vitality and vigor of compact expression. Take a suggestion from the highway department. At the boundaries of your speech and prose place a sign that reads "Caution: Small Words at Work." | 11

■ Thinking Critically about the Text

Reread a piece of writing you turned in earlier this year for any class. Analyze your choice of words, and describe your writing vocabulary. Did you follow Lederer's admonition to use short words whenever they are appropriate, or did you tend to use longer, more important-sounding words? Is Lederer's essay likely to change the way you write papers in the future? Why, or why not?

■ Questions on Subject

1. What rule does Lederer present for writing? What does he do to demonstrate the feasibility of this rule?
2. Lederer states that the twenty words that account for a quarter of all spoken English words are monosyllabic. So are the fifty most common written words. Why, then, do you think Lederer felt it was necessary to argue that people should use them? Who is his audience? (Glossary: *Audience*)
3. How do his students react to the assignment he gives them requiring short words? How do their essays turn out? What does the assignment teach them?
4. In paragraph 10, Lederer refers to the relief his students feel when released from "the pressure to produce high-sounding polysyllables." Where does this pressure come from? How does it relate to the central purpose of his essay?
5. Do you think Lederer's argument will change the way you write? Explain.

■ Questions on Strategy

1. As you read Lederer's essay for the first time, were you surprised by his announcement in paragraph 5 that the preceding four paragraphs contained only single-syllable words? If not, when were you first aware of what he was doing? What does Lederer's strategy tell you about small words?

2. Lederer starts using multisyllabic words when discussing the process of writing with single-syllable words. Why do you think he abandons his single-syllable presentation? Does it diminish the strength of his argument? Explain.
3. Lederer provides two long examples of writing by his own students. What does he accomplish by using these examples along with ones from famous authors? (Glossary: *Illustration*)
4. Lederer illustrates his argument with examples from several prominent authors as well as from students. (Glossary: *Illustration*) Which of these examples did you find the most effective? Why? Provide an example from your own reading that you think is effective in illustrating Lederer's argument.
5. How does Lederer's final paragraph serve to close the essay effectively? (Glossary: *Beginnings/Endings*)

■ Questions on Diction and Vocabulary

1. Lederer uses similes to help the reader form associations and images with short words. (Glossary: *Figures of Speech*) What are some of these similes? Do you find the similes effective in the context of Lederer's argument? Explain.
2. In paragraph 9, Lederer uses such terms as *mighty* and *ringing monosyllables* to describe the passages he gives as examples. Do you think such descriptions are appropriate? Why do you think he includes them?
3. Carefully analyze the two student essays that Lederer presents. In particular, circle all the main verbs that each student uses. (Glossary: *Verb*) What, if anything, do these verbs have in common? What conclusions can you draw about verbs and strong, powerful writing?

■ Classroom Activity Using Argumentation

One strategy in developing a strong argument that most people find convincing is illustration. As Lederer demonstrates, an array of examples, both brief and extended, has a remarkable ability to convince readers of the truth of a proposition. While it is possible to argue a case with one specific example that is both appropriate and representative, most writers find that a varied set of examples often makes a more convincing case. Therefore, it is important to identify your examples before starting to write.

As an exercise in argumentation, choose one of the following position statements:

a. More parking spaces should be provided on campus for students.

b. Children's television programs are marked by a high incidence of violence.

c. Capital punishment is a relatively ineffective deterrent to crime.

d. More computer stations should be provided on campus for students.

e. In-state residency requirements for tuition are unfair at my school.

Make a list of the examples — types of information and evidence — you would need to write an argumentative essay on the topic you choose. Indicate where and how you might obtain this information. Finally, share your list of examples with other students in your class who chose the same topic.

■ Writing Suggestions

1. People tend to avoid single-syllable words because they are afraid they will look inadequate and that their writing will lack sophistication. Are there situations in which demonstrating command of a large vocabulary is desirable? If you answer yes, present one situation, and argue that the overuse of short words in that situation is potentially detrimental. If you answer no, defend your reasoning. How can the use of short words convey the necessary style and sophistication in all situations?

2. Advertising is an industry that depends on efficient, high-impact words. Choose ten advertising slogans and three jingles that you find effective. For example, "Just Do It" and "Think Different" are two prominent slogans. Analyze the ratio of short to long words in the slogans and jingles, and write an essay in which you present your findings. What is the percentage of short words? Argue that the percentage supports or contradicts Lederer's contention that short words are often best for high-impact communicating.

I Have a Dream

MARTIN LUTHER KING JR.

 Civil rights leader Martin Luther King Jr. (1929–1968) was the son of a Baptist minister in Atlanta, Georgia. Ordained at the age of eighteen, King went on to earn academic degrees from Morehouse College, Crozer Theological Seminary, Boston University, and Chicago Theological Seminary. He came to prominence in 1955 in Montgomery, Alabama, when he led a successful boycott against the city's segregated bus system. The first president of the Southern Christian Leadership Conference, King became the leading spokesperson for the civil rights movement during the 1950s and 1960s, espousing a consistent philosophy of nonviolent resistance to racial injustice. He also championed women's rights and protested the Vietnam War. Named *Time* magazine's Man of the Year in 1963, King was awarded the Nobel Peace Prize in 1964. King was assassinated in April 1968 after speaking at a rally in Memphis, Tennessee.

"I Have a Dream," the keynote address for the March on Washington in 1963, has become one of the most renowned and recognized speeches of the past century. Delivered from the steps of the Lincoln Memorial to commemorate the centennial of the Emancipation Proclamation, King's speech resonates with hope even as it condemns racial oppression.

▪ Preparing to Read

Most Americans have seen film clips of King delivering the "I Have a Dream" speech. What do you know of the speech? What do you know of the events and conditions under which King presented it?

Five score years ago, a great American, in whose symbolic shadow we 1 stand, signed the Emancipation Proclamation. This momentous decree came as a great beacon light of hope to millions of Negro slaves who had been seared in the flames of withering injustice. It came as a joyous daybreak to end the long night of captivity.

But one hundred years later, we must face the tragic fact that the Negro is 2 still not free. One hundred years later, the life of the Negro is still sadly crippled by the manacles of segregation and the chains of discrimination. One hundred years later, the Negro lives on a lonely island of poverty in the midst of a vast ocean of material prosperity. One hundred years later, the Negro is still languishing in the corners of American society and finds himself an exile in his own land. So we have come here today to dramatize an appalling condition.

In a sense we have come to our nation's Capitol to cash a check. When the 3
architects of our republic wrote the magnificent words of the Constitution and
the Declaration of Independence, they were signing a promissory note to which
every American was to fall heir. This note was a promise that all men would be
guaranteed the unalienable rights of life, liberty, and the pursuit of happiness.

It is obvious today that America has defaulted on this promissory note 4
insofar as her citizens of color are concerned. Instead of honoring this sacred
obligation, America has given the Negro people a bad check; a check which
has come back marked "insufficient funds." But we refuse to believe that the
bank of justice is bankrupt. We refuse to believe that there are insufficient
funds in the great vaults of opportunity of this nation. So we have come to
cash this check — a check that will give us upon demand the riches of freedom and the security of justice. We have also come to this hallowed spot
to remind America of the fierce urgency of *now*. This is no time to engage
in the luxury of cooling off or to take the tranquilizing drug of gradualism.
Now is the time to make real the promises of Democracy. *Now* is the time
to rise from the dark and desolate valley of segregation to the sunlit path of
racial justice. *Now* is the time to open the doors of opportunity to all of God's
children. *Now* is the time to lift our nation from the quicksands of racial
injustice to the solid rock of brotherhood.

It would be fatal for the nation to overlook the urgency of the moment 5
and to underestimate the determination of the Negro. This sweltering summer
of the Negro's legitimate discontent will not pass until there is an invigorating
autumn of freedom and equality. Nineteen sixty-three is not an end, but a
beginning. Those who hope that the Negro needed to blow off steam and will
now be content will have a rude awakening if the nation returns to business as
usual. There will be neither rest nor tranquility in America until the Negro is
granted his citizenship rights. The whirlwinds of revolt will continue to shake
the foundations of our nation until the bright day of justice emerges.

But there is something I must say to my people who stand on the warm 6
threshold which leads into the palace of justice. In the process of gaining
our rightful place we must not be guilty of wrongful deeds. Let us not seek
to satisfy our thirst for freedom by drinking from the cup of bitterness and
hatred. We must forever conduct our struggle on the high plane of dignity
and discipline. We must not allow our creative protest to degenerate into
physical violence. Again and again we must rise to the majestic heights of
meeting physical force with soul force. The marvelous new militancy which
has engulfed the Negro community must not lead us to a distrust of all white
people, for many of our white brothers, as evidenced by their presence here
today, have come to realize that their destiny is tied up with our destiny and
their freedom is inextricably bound to our freedom. We cannot walk alone.

And as we walk, we must make the pledge that we shall march ahead. We 7
cannot turn back. There are those who are asking the devotees of civil rights,
"When will you be satisfied?" We can never be satisfied as long as the Negro

is the victim of the unspeakable horrors of police brutality. We can never be satisfied as long as our bodies, heavy with the fatigue of travel, cannot gain lodging in the motels of the highways and the hotels of the cities. We cannot be satisfied as long as the Negro's basic mobility is from a smaller ghetto to a larger one. We can never be satisfied as long as a Negro in Mississippi cannot vote and a Negro in New York believes he has nothing for which to vote. No, no, we are not satisfied, and we will not be satisfied until justice rolls down like waters and righteousness like a mighty stream.

8   I am not unmindful that some of you have come here out of great trials and tribulations. Some of you have come fresh from narrow jail cells. Some of you have come from areas where your quest for freedom left you battered by the storms of persecution and staggered by the winds of police brutality. You have been the veterans of creative suffering. Continue to work with the faith that unearned suffering is redemptive.

> I have a dream that my four little children will one day live in a nation where they will not be judged by the color of their skin but by the content of their character.

9   Go back to Mississippi, go back to Alabama, go back to South Carolina, go back to Georgia, go back to Louisiana, go back to the slums and ghettoes of our northern cities, knowing that somehow this situation can and will be changed. Let us not wallow in the valley of despair.

10   I say to you today, my friends, that in spite of the difficulties and frustrations of the moment I still have a dream. It is a dream deeply rooted in the American dream.

11   I have a dream that one day this nation will rise up and live out the true meaning of its creed: "We hold these truths to be self-evident; that all men are created equal."

12   I have a dream that one day on the red hills of Georgia the sons of former slaves and the sons of former slaveowners will be able to sit down together at the table of brotherhood.

13   I have a dream that the state of Mississippi, a desert state sweltering with the heat of injustice and oppression, will be transformed into an oasis of freedom and justice.

14   I have a dream that my four little children will one day live in a nation where they will not be judged by the color of their skin but by the content of their character.

15   I have a dream today.

16   I have a dream that the state of Alabama, whose governor's lips are presently dripping with the words of interposition and nullification, will be transformed into a situation where little black boys and black girls will be able to join hands with little white boys and white girls and walk together as sisters and brothers.

17   I have a dream today.

I have a dream that one day every valley shall be exalted, every hill and 18
mountain shall be made low, the rough places will be made plain, and the
crooked places will be made straight, and the glory of the Lord shall be
revealed, and all flesh shall see it together.

This is our hope. This is the faith with which I return to the South. With 19
this faith we will be able to hew out of the mountain of despair a stone of hope.
With this faith we will be able to transform the jangling discords of our nation
into a beautiful symphony of brotherhood. With this faith we will be able to
work together, to pray together, to struggle together, to go to jail together, to
stand up for freedom together, knowing that we will be free one day.

This will be the day when all of God's children will be able to sing with 20
new meaning.

> My country, 'tis of thee
> Sweet land of liberty,
>   Of thee I sing:
> Land where my fathers died,
> Land of the pilgrims' pride,
> From every mountainside
>   Let freedom ring.

And if America is to be a great nation this must become true. So let 21
freedom ring from the prodigious hilltops of New Hampshire. Let freedom
ring from the mighty mountains of New York. Let freedom ring from the
heightening Alleghenies of Pennsylvania!

Let freedom ring from the snowcapped Rockies of Colorado! 22

Let freedom ring from the curvaceous peaks of California! 23

But not only that; let freedom ring from Stone Mountain of Georgia! 24

Let freedom ring from Lookout Mountain of Tennessee! 25

Let freedom ring from every hill and molehill of Mississippi. From every 26
mountainside, let freedom ring.

When we let freedom ring, when we let it ring from every village and every 27
hamlet, from every state and every city, we will be able to speed up that day when
all of God's children, black men and white men, Jews and Gentiles, Protestants
and Catholics, will be able to join hands and sing in the words of the old Negro
spiritual, "Free at last! free at last! thank God almighty, we are free at last!"

■ Thinking Critically about the Text

King portrayed an America in 1963 in which there was still systematic
oppression of African Americans. What is oppression? Have you ever
felt yourself — or have you known others — to be oppressed or part of a
group that is oppressed? Who are the oppressors? How can oppression
be overcome?

■ Questions on Subject

1. Why does King say that the Constitution and the Declaration of Independence act as a "promissory note" (paragraph 3) to the American people? In what way has America "defaulted" (4) on its promise?
2. What does King mean when he says that in gaining a rightful place in society "we must not be guilty of wrongful deeds" (paragraph 6)? Why is the issue so important to him?
3. When *will* King be satisfied in his quest for civil rights?
4. What, in a nutshell, is King's dream? What vision does he have for the future?
5. How do you personally respond to the argument King puts forth?

■ Questions on Strategy

1. King delivered his address to two audiences: the huge audience that listened to him in person, and another, even larger audience. (Glossary: *Audience*) What is that larger audience? What did King do in his speech to catch its attention and to deliver his point?
2. Explain King's choice of a title. (Glossary: *Title*) Why is the title particularly appropriate given the context in which the speech was delivered? What other titles might he have used?
3. Examine the speech, and determine how King organized his presentation. (Glossary: *Organization*) What are the main sections of the speech and what is the purpose of each? How does the organization serve King's overall purpose? (Glossary: *Purpose*)
4. Review King's opening paragraph. What happened "Five score years ago" and what purpose does King have in invoking its memory? (Glossary: *Beginnings/Endings*)
5. In his final paragraph, King claims that by freeing the Negro we will all be free. What exactly does he mean? Is King simply being hyperbolic or does his claim embody an undeniable truth? Explain.

■ Questions on Diction and Vocabulary

1. King uses parallel constructions and repetition throughout his speech. Identify the phrases and words that he emphasizes. Explain what these techniques add to the persuasiveness of his argument.
2. King makes liberal use of metaphor — and metaphorical imagery — in his speech. (Glossary: *Figures of Speech*) Choose a few examples, and examine what they add to the speech. How do they help King engage his listeners' feelings of injustice and give them hope for a better future?
3. Comment on King's diction. Choose a half dozen words as evidence that his diction is well-chosen and rich.

■ Classroom Activity Using Argumentation

As Martin Luther King Jr.'s speech well demonstrates, the effectiveness of a writer's argument depends in large part on the writer's awareness of audience. For example, if a writer wished to argue for the use of more technology to solve our pressing environmental problems, that argument to a group of environmentalists would need to convince them that the technology would not cause as many environmental problems as it solves, while an argument designed for a group of industrialists might argue that the economic opportunity in developing new technologies is as important as the environmental benefits.

Consider the following proposition:

The university mascot should be changed to reflect the image of our school today.

How would you argue this proposition to the following audiences?

a. the student body

b. the faculty

c. the alumni

d. the administration

As a class, discuss how the consideration of audience influences the purpose and content of an argument.

■ Writing Suggestions

1. King's language is powerful and his imagery is vivid, but the effectiveness of any speech partially depends on its delivery. If read in monotone, King's use of repetition and parallel language would sound almost redundant rather than inspiring. Keeping presentation in mind, write a short speech that argues a point of view about which you feel strongly. Use King's speech as a model, and incorporate imagery, repetition, and metaphor to communicate your point. Read your speech aloud to a friend to see how it flows and how effective your use of language is. Refine your presentation — both your text and how you deliver it — and then present your speech to your class.

2. King uses a variety of metaphors in his speech, but a single encompassing metaphor can be useful to establish the tone and purpose of an essay. Write a description based on a metaphor that conveys an overall impression from the beginning. Try to avoid clichés ("My dorm is a beehive," "My life is an empty glass"), but make your metaphor readily understandable. For example, you could say, "A police siren is a lullaby in my neighborhood," or "My town is a car that has gone 15,000 miles since its last oil change." Carry the metaphor through the entire description.

In Defense of Dangerous Ideas

STEVEN PINKER

 Internationally recognized language and cognition scholar and researcher Steven Pinker was born in Montreal, Quebec, Canada, in 1954. He immigrated to the United States shortly after receiving his B.A. from McGill University in 1976. After earning a doctorate from Harvard University in 1979, Pinker taught psychology at Stanford University and the Massachusetts Institute of Technology, where he directed the Center for Cognitive Neuroscience. Currently, he is professor of psychology at Harvard University. Pinker has written extensively on language development in children, starting with *Language Learnability and Language Development* (1984). He has what one critic writing in the *New York Times Book Review* calls "that facility, so rare among scientists, of making the most difficult material . . . accessible to the average reader." Pinker's books, *The Language Instinct* (1994), *How the Mind Works* (1997), *Words and Rules: The Ingredients of Language* (1999), *The Blank Slate: The Modern Denial of Human Nature* (2002), and *The Stuff of Thought: Language as a Window into Human Nature* (2007), all attest to the public's interest in human language and the world of ideas.

The following article was first published as the preface to *What Is Your Dangerous Idea? Today's Leading Thinkers on the Unthinkable* (2006, edited by John Brockman) and later posted at *Edge* <www.edge.com>. In this essay Steven Pinker explores what makes an idea "dangerous" and argues that "important ideas need to be aired," especially in academia, no matter how discomfiting people find them. Notice how Pinker uses a number of examples from a wide range of academic disciplines to illustrate his points about dangerous ideas and the need to discuss them.

■ Preparing to Read

What did you think when you first read the title to Pinker's essay? For you, what would make an idea dangerous? Do any issues or questions make you uncomfortable or unwilling to discuss them? Explain.

In every age, taboo questions raise our blood pressure and threaten moral panic. But we cannot be afraid to answer them.   1

Do women, on average, have a different profile of aptitudes and emotions than men?   2

Were the events in the Bible fictitious — not just the miracles, but those involving kings and empires?   3

Has the state of the environment improved in the last fifty years?   4

Do most victims of sexual abuse suffer no lifelong damage?   5

Did Native Americans engage in genocide and despoil the landscape?   6

Do men have an innate tendency to rape?   7

Did the crime rate go down in the 1990s because two decades earlier   8
poor women aborted children who would have been prone to violence?

Are suicide terrorists well-educated, mentally healthy, and morally   9
driven?

Would the incidence of rape go down if prostitution were legalized?   10

Do African American men have higher levels of testosterone, on average,   11
than white men?

Is morality just a product of the evolution of our brains, with no inherent   12
reality?

Would society be better off if heroin and cocaine were legalized?   13

Is homosexuality the symptom of an infectious disease?   14

Would it be consistent with our moral principles to give parents the   15
option of euthanizing newborns with birth defects that would consign them
to a life of pain and disability?

Do parents have any effect on the character or intelligence of their children?   16

Have religions killed a greater proportion of people than Nazism?   17

Would damage from terrorism be reduced if the police could torture   18
suspects in special circumstances?

Would Africa have a better chance of rising out of poverty if it hosted   19
more polluting industries or accepted Europe's nuclear waste?

Is the average intelligence of Western nations declining because duller   20
people are having more children than smarter people?

Would unwanted children be better off if there were a market in adop-   21
tion rights, with babies going to the highest bidder?

Would lives be saved if we instituted a free market in organs for trans-   22
plantation?

Should people have the right to clone themselves, or enhance the genetic   23
traits of their children?

Perhaps you can feel your blood pressure rise as you read these questions.   24
Perhaps you are appalled that people can so much as think such things. Perhaps
you think less of me for bringing them up. These are dangerous ideas — ideas that
are denounced not because they are self-evidently false, nor because they advocate
harmful action, but because they are thought to corrode the prevailing moral order.

Think about It

By "dangerous ideas" I don't have in mind harmful technologies, like those   25
behind weapons of mass destruction, or evil ideologies, like those of racist,
fascist, or other fanatical cults. I have in mind statements of fact or policy
that are defended with evidence and argument by serious scientists and

thinkers but which are felt to challenge the collective decency of an age. The ideas listed above, and the moral panic that each one of them has incited during the past quarter century, are examples. Writers who have raised ideas like these have been vilified, censored, fired, threatened, and in some cases physically assaulted.

> **Dangerous ideas are likely to confront us at an increasing rate, and we are ill-equipped to deal with them.**

Every era has its dangerous ideas. For millennia, the monotheistic religions have persecuted countless heresies, together with nuisances from science such as geocentrism, biblical archeology, and the theory of evolution. We can be thankful that the punishments have changed from torture and mutilation to the canceling of grants and the writing of vituperative reviews. But intellectual intimidation, whether by sword or by pen, inevitably shapes the ideas that are taken seriously in a given era, and the rear-view mirror of history presents us with a warning. 26

Time and again, people have invested factual claims with ethical implications that today look ludicrous. The fear that the structure of our solar system has grave moral consequences is a venerable example, and the foisting of "intelligent design" on biology students is a contemporary one. These travesties should lead us to ask whether the contemporary intellectual mainstream might be entertaining similar moral delusions. Are we enraged by our own infidels and heretics whom history may some day vindicate? 27

Unsettling Possibilities

Dangerous ideas are likely to confront us at an increasing rate, and we are ill-equipped to deal with them. When done right, science (together with other truth-seeking institutions, such as history and journalism) characterizes the world as it is, without regard to whose feelings get hurt. Science in particular has always been a source of heresy, and today the galloping advances in touchy areas like genetics, evolution, and the environment sciences are bound to throw unsettling possibilities at us. Moreover, the rise of globalization and the Internet are allowing heretics to find one another and work around the barriers of traditional media and academic journals. I also suspect that a change in generational sensibilities will hasten the process. The term "political correctness" captures the 1960s conception of moral rectitude that we baby boomers brought with us as we took over academia, journalism, and government. In my experience, today's students — black and white, male and female — are bewildered by the idea, common among their parents, that certain scientific opinions are immoral or certain questions too hot to handle. 28

What makes an idea "dangerous"? One factor is an imaginable train of events in which acceptance of the idea could lead to an outcome recognized as harmful. In religious societies, the fear is that if people ever stopped 29 believing in the literal truth of the Bible they would also stop believing in the authority of its moral commandments. That is, if today people dismiss the part about God creating the earth in six days, tomorrow they'll dismiss the part about "Thou shalt not kill." In progressive circles, the fear is that if people ever were to acknowledge any differences between races, sexes, or individuals, they would feel justified in discrimination or oppression. Other dangerous ideas set off fears that people will neglect or abuse their children, become indifferent to the environment, devalue human life, accept violence, and prematurely resign themselves to social problems that could be solved with sufficient commitment and optimism.

All these outcomes, needless to say, would be deplorable. But none of them   30 actually follows from the supposedly dangerous idea. Even if it turns out, for instance, that groups of people are different in their averages, the overlap is certainly so great that it would be irrational and unfair to discriminate against individuals on that basis. Likewise, even if it turns out that parents don't have the power to shape their children's personalities, it would be wrong on grounds of simple human decency to abuse or neglect one's children. And if currently popular ideas about how to improve the environment are shown to be ineffective, it only highlights the need to know what would be effective.

Another contributor to the perception of dangerousness is the intellec-   31 tual blinkers that humans tend to don when they split into factions. People have a nasty habit of clustering in coalitions, professing certain beliefs as badges of their commitment to the coalition and treating rival coalitions as intellectually unfit and morally depraved. Debates between members of the coalitions can make things even worse, because when the other side fails to capitulate to one's devastating arguments, it only proves they are immune to reason. In this regard, it's disconcerting to see the two institutions that ought to have the greatest stake in ascertaining the truth — academia and government — often blinkered by morally tinged ideologies. One ideology is that humans are blank slates and that social problems can be handled only through government programs that especially redress the perfidy of European males. Its opposite number is that morality inheres in patriotism and Christian faith and that social problems may be handled only by government policies that punish the sins of individual evildoers. New ideas, nuanced ideas, hybrid ideas — and sometimes dangerous ideas — often have trouble getting a hearing against these group-bonding convictions.

The conviction that honest opinions can be dangerous may even arise   32 from a feature of human nature. Philip Tetlock and Alan Fiske have argued that certain human relationships are constituted on a basis of unshakable convictions. We love our children and parents, are faithful to our spouses, stand by our friends, contribute to our communities, and are loyal to our coalitions not because we continually question and evaluate the merits of these commitments but because we feel them in our bones. A person who spends too much time pondering whether logic and fact really justify a commitment to one of these relationships is seen as just not "getting it." Decent people don't carefully weigh the advantages and disadvantages of selling their children or selling out their friends or their spouses or their colleagues or their country. They reject these possibilities outright; they "don't go there." So the taboo on questioning sacred values makes sense in the context of personal relationships. It makes far less sense in the context of discovering how the world works or running a country.

Explore All Relevant Ideas

Should we treat some ideas as dangerous? Let's exclude outright lies, deceptive propaganda, incendiary conspiracy theories from malevolent crackpots, and technological recipes for wanton destruction. Consider only ideas about the truth of empirical claims or the effectiveness of policies that, if they turned out to be true, would require a significant rethinking of our moral sensibilities. And consider ideas that, if they turn out to be false, could lead to harm if people believed them to be true. In either case, we don't know whether they are true or false a priori, so only by examining and debating them can we find out. Finally, let's assume that we're not talking about burning people at the stake or cutting out their tongues but about discouraging their research and giving their ideas as little publicity as possible. There is a good case for exploring all ideas relevant to our current concerns, no matter where they lead. The idea that ideas should be discouraged a priori is inherently self-refuting. Indeed, it is the ultimate arrogance, as it assumes that one can be so certain about the goodness and truth of one's own ideas that one is entitled to discourage other people's opinions from even being examined. 33

Also, it's hard to imagine any aspect of public life where ignorance or delusion is better than an awareness of the truth, even an unpleasant one. Only children and madmen engage in "magical thinking," the fallacy that good things can come true by believing in them or bad things will disappear by ignoring them or wishing them away. Rational adults want to know the truth, because any action based on false premises will not have the effects they desire. Worse, logicians tell us that a system of ideas containing a contradiction can be used to deduce any statement whatsoever, no matter how absurd. Since ideas are connected to other ideas, sometimes in circuitous and unpredictable ways, choosing to believe something that may not be true, or even maintaining walls of ignorance around some topic, can corrupt all of intellectual life, proliferating error far and wide. In our everyday lives, would we want to be lied to, or kept in the dark by paternalistic "protectors," when it comes to our health or finances or even the weather? In public life, imagine someone saying that we should not do research into global warming or energy shortages because if it found that they were serious the consequences for the economy would be extremely unpleasant. Today's leaders who tacitly 34 take this position are rightly condemned by intellectually responsible people. But why should other unpleasant ideas be treated differently?

There is another argument against treating ideas as dangerous. Many of our moral and political policies are designed to preempt what we know to be the worst features of human nature. The checks and balances in a democracy, for instance, were invented in explicit recognition of the fact that human leaders will always be tempted to arrogate power to themselves. Likewise, our sensitivity to racism comes from an awareness that groups of humans, left to their own devices, are apt to discriminate and oppress other groups, often in ugly ways. History also tells us that a desire to enforce dogma and suppress heretics is a recurring human weakness, one that has led to recurring waves of gruesome oppression and violence. A recognition that there is a bit of Torquemada[1] in everyone should make us wary of any attempt to enforce a consensus or demonize those who challenge it. 35

"Sunlight is the best disinfectant," according to Justice Louis Brandeis's famous case for freedom of thought and expression. If an idea really is false, only by examining it openly can we determine that it is false. At that point we will be in a better position to convince others that it is false than if we had let it fester in private, since our very avoidance of the issue serves as a tacit acknowledgment that it may be true. And if an idea is true, we had better accommodate our moral sensibilities to it, since no good can come from sanctifying a delusion. This might even be easier than the ideaphobes fear. The moral order did not collapse when the earth was shown not to be at the center of the solar system, and so it will survive other revisions of our understanding of how the world works. 36

Dangerous to Air Dangerous Ideas?

In the best Talmudic tradition of arguing a position as forcefully as possible and then switching sides, let me now present the case for discouraging certain lines of intellectual inquiry. . . . [Alison] Gopnik and [W. Daniel] Hillis offer as their "dangerous idea" the exact opposite of [Daniel] Gilbert's: They say that it's a dangerous idea for thinkers to air their dangerous ideas. How might such an argument play out? 37

First, one can remind people that we are all responsible for the foreseeable consequences of our actions, and that includes the consequences of our public statements. Freedom of inquiry may be an important value, according to this argument, but it is not an absolute value, one that overrides all others. We know that the world is full of malevolent and callous people who will use any pretext to justify their bigotry or destructiveness. We must expect that they will seize on the broaching of a topic that seems in sympathy with their beliefs as a vindication of their agenda. 38

---

[1] *Torquemada:* Tomás de Torquemada (1420–1498), Spanish grand inquisitor.

Not only can the imprimatur of scientific debate add legitimacy to toxic ideas, but the mere act of making an idea common knowledge can change its effects. Individuals, for instance, may harbor a private opinion on differences between genders or among ethnic groups but keep it to themselves because of its opprobrium. But once the opinion is aired in public, they may be emboldened to act on their prejudice — not just because it has been publicly ratified but because they must anticipate that everyone else will act on the information. Some people, for example, might discriminate against the members of an ethnic group despite having no pejorative opinion about them, in the expectation that their customers or colleagues will have such opinions and that defying them would be costly. And then there are the effects of these debates on the confidence of the members of the stigmatized groups themselves.

Of course, academics can warn against these abuses, but the qualifications and nitpicking they do for a living may not catch up with the simpler formulations that run on swifter legs. Even if they did, their qualifications might be lost on the masses. We shouldn't count on ordinary people to engage in the clear thinking — some would say the hair-splitting — that would be needed to accept a dangerous idea but not its terrible consequence. Our overriding precept, in intellectual life as in medicine, should be "First, do no harm."

We must be especially suspicious when the danger in a dangerous idea is to someone other than its advocate. Scientists, scholars, and writers are members of a privileged elite. They may have an interest in promulgating ideas that justify their privileges, that blame or make light of society's victims, or that earn them attention for cleverness and iconoclasm. Even if one has little sympathy for the cynical Marxist argument that ideas are always advanced to serve the interest of the ruling class, the ordinary skepticism of a tough-minded intellectual should make one wary of "dangerous" hypotheses that are no skin off the nose of their hypothesizers. (The mind-set that leads us to blind review, open debate, and statements of possible conflicts of interest.)

But don't the demands of rationality always compel us to seek the complete truth? Not necessarily. Rational agents often choose to be ignorant. They may decide not to be in a position where they can receive a threat or be exposed to a sensitive secret. They may choose to avoid being asked an incriminating question, where one answer is damaging, another is dishonest, and a failure to answer is grounds for the questioner to assume the worst (hence the Fifth Amendment protection against being forced to testify against oneself). Scientists test drugs in double-blind studies in which they keep themselves from knowing who got the drug and who got the placebo, and they referee manuscripts anonymously for the same reason. Many people rationally choose not to know the gender of their unborn child, or whether they carry a gene for Huntington's disease, or whether their nominal father is genetically related to them. Perhaps a similar logic would call for keeping socially harmful information out of the public sphere.

Intolerance of Unpopular Ideas

As for restrictions on inquiry, every scientist already lives with them. They   43
accede, for example, to the decisions of committees for the protection of
human subjects and to policies on the confidentiality of personal information. In 1975, biologists imposed a moratorium on research on recombinant
DNA pending the development of safeguards against the release of dangerous microorganisms. The notion that intellectuals have carte blanche in conducting their inquiry is a myth.

Though I am more sympathetic to the argument that important ideas be   44
aired than to the argument that they should sometimes be suppressed, I think it
is a debate we need to have. Whether we like it or not, science has a habit of turning up discomfiting thoughts, and the Internet has a habit of blowing their cover.

Tragically, there are few signs that the debates will happen in the place where   45
we might most expect it: academia. Though academics owe the extraordinary
perquisite of tenure to the ideal of encouraging free inquiry and the evaluation
of unpopular ideas, all too often academics are the first to try to quash them.
The most famous recent example is the outburst of fury and disinformation that
resulted when Harvard president Lawrence Summers gave a measured analysis of the multiple causes of women's underrepresentation in science and math
departments in elite universities and tentatively broached the possibility that discrimination and hidden barriers were not the only cause.

But intolerance of unpopular ideas among academics is an old story.   46
Books like Morton Hunt's *The New Know-Nothings* and Alan Kors and Harvey
Silverglate's *The Shadow University* have depressingly shown that universities cannot be counted on to defend the rights of their own heretics and that
it's often the court system or the press that has to drag them into policies of
tolerance. In government, the intolerance is even more frightening, because
the ideas considered there are not just matters of intellectual sport but have
immediate and sweeping consequences. Chris Mooney, in *The Republican War
on Science*, joins Hunt in showing how corrupt and demagogic legislators are
increasingly stifling research findings they find inconvenient to their interests.

■ **Thinking Critically about the Text**

What do you think is Pinker's purpose in defending dangerous ideas?
What does he want his readers to do after reading this essay? Did he
achieve his purpose, in your case? Explain.

■ **Questions on Subject**

1. Pinker starts his essay with a list of twenty-two questions, each an
   example of a "dangerous" idea. What were you thinking as you read
   Pinker's list? Which questions touched a sensitive nerve for you?
   Explain.

2. Reread paragraph 32. Pinker writes that "the taboo on questioning sacred values makes sense in the context of personal relationships." Do you agree? Why do you think that Pinker believes that "[i]t makes far less sense in the context of discovering how the world works or running a country" (paragraph 32)?
3. What does Pinker mean when he says in paragraph 33, "The idea that ideas should be discouraged a priori is inherently self-refuting"?
4. How does Pinker's discussion of rational thinking help to support the ideas presented in the introduction to this chapter on argumentation?
5. In paragraph 46 Pinker writes, "But intolerance of unpopular ideas among academics is an old story." Why is the situation he points to ironic? (Glossary: *Irony*)

■ Questions on Strategy

1. How does Pinker define "dangerous idea"? (Glossary: *Definition*) Do you agree with his definition?
2. According to Pinker, fear is one of the main factors that contribute to the perception of dangerousness. What examples of fears does Pinker use to illustrate his claim? What other factors contribute to the perception of dangerousness? (Glossary: *Illustration*)
3. According to Pinker, what is the "case for discouraging certain lines of intellectual inquiry" (paragraph 37)? What evidence does he present to support this side of the issue? (Glossary: *Evidence*)
4. How does Pinker support his claim that "intolerance of unpopular ideas among academics is an old story" (paragraph 46)?
5. Pinker concludes his essay in paragraph 46 with a reference to Chris Mooney's *The Republican War on Science*. Is this a partisan reference? If so, does it damage Pinker's analysis and purpose in this essay? Would you have ended the essay in a different manner? (Glossary: *Beginnings/Endings*) Explain.

■ Questions on Diction and Vocabulary

1. In paragraph 36 Pinker uses the term *ideaphobes*. What does the term mean?
2. What is the "magical thinking" that Pinker discusses in paragraph 34? Can you think of any examples of magical thinking that have currency today?

■ Classroom Activity Using Argumentation

Consider the following paragraph from the rough draft of a student paper on Americans' obsession with losing weight. The student writer wanted to show the extreme actions that people sometimes take to improve their appearance.

Americans have long been obsessed with thinness — even at the risk of dying. In the 1930s, people took di-nitrophenol, an industrial poison, to lose weight. It boosted metabolism but caused blindness and some deaths. Since that time, dieters have experimented with any number of bizarre schemes that seem to work wonders in the short term but often end in disappointment or disaster in the long term. Some weight-loss strategies have even led to life-threatening eating disorders.

Try your hand at revising this paragraph, supplying specific examples of "bizarre schemes" or "weight-loss strategies" that you have tried, observed, or read about. Share your examples with others in your class. Which examples best illustrate and support the central idea contained in the writer's topic sentence?

■ Writing Suggestions

1. Reread the list of twenty-two questions at the beginning of Pinker's essay. After giving them some thought, select one to use as a central example in an essay about the need to debate important ideas no matter how uncomfortable those ideas might make us. Before you start writing, consider the following questions: What about the question I've chosen makes me or others uncomfortable? What are some of the idea's implications if we find it to be true? What if we find it false? What would happen if we simply ignore this question?

2. In a case involving freedom of thought and expression, Justice Louis Brandeis said, "Sunlight is the best disinfectant" (paragraph 36). What do you think he meant? How do you think Justice Brandeis would respond to the proposition that "it's a dangerous idea for thinkers to air their dangerous ideas"? How do you respond to this proposition? Write an essay in which you present your position, and support that position with clear examples from your own experiences or reading.

This Land Is Their Land: How the Rich Confiscate Natural Beauty from the Public

Barbara Ehrenreich

Barbara Ehrenreich was born in 1941 in Butte, Montana, and is a feminist, social activist, political activist, columnist, essayist, and author of over twenty books. She graduated from Reed College and earned her Ph.D. in biology from Rockefeller University in 1968. She has contributed to many prominent magazines, among them *Ms.*, *Mother Jones*, *Esquire*, *Vogue*, the *New York Times Magazine*, the *Progressive*, and *Time.* Among her books are *The American Health Empire: Power, Profits, and Politics* (with John Ehrenreich and Health PAC) (1971); *Fear of Falling: The Inner Life of the Middle Class* (1989); *The Worst Years of Our Lives: Irreverent Notes from a Decade of Greed* (1990); *The Snarling Citizen: Essays* (1995); *Nickel and Dimed: On (Not) Getting By in America* (2001); *Bait and Switch: The (Futile) Pursuit of the American Dream* (2005); *Dancing in the Street: A History of Collective Joy* (2007); and *Bright-Sided: How the Relentless Promotion of Positive Thinking Has Undermined America* (2009). In reflecting on what prepared her for a career as a writer, she wrote, "Probably the main thing was that I've always been a big reader. By reading 'the classics' while I was growing up and good fiction ever since, I developed an ear for the language and what can be done with it. Then, too, science played a role: One thing I learned in my dilettantish bopping around from one scientific discipline to another is that I can learn almost anything if I try hard enough. So I've never been afraid to take on any assignment that came my way."

In the following essay, taken from *This Land Is Their Land: Reports from a Divided Nation* (2008), Ehrenreich argues against the takeover of America's "beautiful places" by the wealthy, who, in her view, are illegitimately forcing everyone else to the fringes, where it costs less to live.

■ Preparing to Read

What role do beautiful scenic areas and vistas play in your life? Do such views give you satisfaction? What is it that many people find so appealing about vast mountain ranges and lush green valleys? Is it the peacefulness they promise, the solitude of their primitiveness, or the way they remind us of our place in the natural order? How would you feel if you were not able to enjoy such sights? Would anything be missing in your life?

I took a little vacation recently — nine hours in Sun Valley, Idaho, before an   1
evening speaking engagement. The sky was deep blue, the air crystalline,
the hills green and not yet on fire. Strolling out of the Sun Valley Lodge, I
found a tiny tourist village, complete with Swiss-style bakery, multistar restaurant, and "opera house." What luck — the boutiques were displaying outdoor racks of summer clothing on sale! Nature and commerce were conspir-
ing to make this the perfect microvacation.

But as I approached the stores things started to get a little sinister —   2
maybe I had wandered into a movie set or Paris Hilton's closet? — because
even at a 60 percent discount, I couldn't find a sleeveless cotton shirt for less
than $100. These items shouldn't have been outdoors; they should have been
in locked glass cases.

Then I remembered the general rule, which has been in effect since   3
sometime in the 1990s: If a place is truly beautiful, you can't afford to be
there. All right, I'm sure there are still exceptions — a few scenic spots not yet
eaten up by mansions. But they're going fast.

> And if your heart doesn't bleed for the dishwasher or landscaper who commutes two to four hours a day, at least shed a tear for the wealthy vacationer who gets stuck in the ensuing traffic.

About ten years ago, for example, a friend and   4
I rented a snug, inexpensive one-bedroom house
in Driggs, Idaho, just over the Teton Range from
wealthy Jackson Hole, Wyoming. At that time,
Driggs was where the workers lived, driving over
the Teton Pass every day to wait tables and make
beds on the stylish side of the mountains. The point
is, we low-rent folks got to wake up to the same
scenery the rich people enjoyed and hike along the
same pine-shadowed trails.

But the money was already starting to pour   5
into Driggs — Paul Allen of Microsoft, August
Busch III of Anheuser-Busch, Harrison Ford —
transforming family potato farms into vast dynas-
tic estates. I haven't been back, but I understand
Driggs has become another unaffordable Jackson
Hole. Where the wait staff and bed-makers live today I do not know.

I witnessed this kind of deterioration up close in Key West, Florida,   6
where I first went in 1986, attracted not only by the turquoise waters and
frangipani-scented nights but by the fluid, egalitarian social scene. At a typical party you might find literary stars like Alison Lurie, Annie Dillard, and
Robert Stone, along with commercial fishermen, waitresses, and men who
risked their lives diving for treasure (once a major blue-collar occupation).
Then, at some point in the '90s, the rich started pouring in. You'd see them
on the small planes coming down from Miami — taut-skinned, linen-clad,
and impatient. They drove house prices into the seven-figure range. They
encouraged restaurants to charge upward of $30 for an entree. They tore
down working-class tiki bars to make room for their waterfront "condotels."

Of all the crimes of the rich, the aesthetic deprivation of the rest of us   7
may seem to be the merest misdemeanor. Many of them owe their wealth
to the usual tricks: squeezing their employees, overcharging their customers, and polluting any land they're not going to need for their third or fourth
homes. Once they've made (or inherited) their fortunes, the rich can bid up
the price of goods that ordinary people also need—housing, for example.
Gentrification is dispersing the urban poor into overcrowded suburban ranch
houses, while billionaires' horse farms displace rural Americans into trailer
homes. Similarly, the rich can easily fork over annual tuitions of $50,000 and
up, which has helped make college education a privilege of the upper classes.

There are other ways, too, that the rich are robbing the rest of us of   8
beauty and pleasure. As the bleachers in stadiums and arenas are cleared to
make way for skybox "suites" costing more than $100,000 for a season, going
out to a ballgame has become prohibitively expensive for the average family.
At the other end of the cultural spectrum, superrich collectors have driven
up the price of artworks, leading museums to charge ever rising prices for
admission.

It shouldn't be a surprise that the Pew Research Center finds happiness   9
to be unequally distributed, with 50 percent of people earning more than
$150,000 a year describing themselves as "very happy," compared with only
23 percent of those earning less than $20,000. When nations are compared,
inequality itself seems to reduce well-being, with some of the most equal
nations—Iceland and Norway—ranking highest, according to the United
Nations' Human Development Index. We are used to thinking that poverty
is a "social problem" and wealth is only something to celebrate, but extreme
wealth is also a social problem, and the superrich have become a burden on
everyone else.

If Edward O. Wilson is right about "biophilia"—an innate human need   10
to interact with nature—there may even be serious mental health consequences to letting the rich hog all the good scenery. I know that if I don't
get to see vast expanses of water, 360-degree horizons, and mountains pierc-
ing the sky for at least a week or two of the year, chronic, cumulative claus-
trophobia sets in. According to evolutionary psychologist Nancy Etcoff, the
need for scenery is hardwired into us. "People like to be on a hill, where they
can see a landscape. And they like somewhere to go where they can *not* be
seen themselves," she told *Harvard Magazine* last year. "That's a place desirable to a predator who wants to avoid becoming prey." We also like to be able
to see water (for drinking), low-canopy trees (for shade), and animals (whose
presence signals that a place is habitable).

Ultimately, the plutocratic takeover of rural America has a downside for   11
the wealthy, too. The more expensive a resort town gets, the farther its workers have to commute to keep it functioning. And if your heart doesn't bleed
for the dishwasher or landscaper who commutes two to four hours a day,
at least shed a tear for the wealthy vacationer who gets stuck in the ensuing

traffic. It's bumper to bumper westbound out of Telluride, Colorado, every day at 5, or eastbound on Route 1 out of Key West, for the Lexuses as well as the beat-up old pickup trucks.

Or a place may simply run out of workers. Monroe County, which includes Key West, has seen more than 2,000 workers leave since the 2000 Census, a loss the *Los Angeles Times* calls "a body blow to the service-oriented economy of a county with only 75,000 residents and 2.25 million overnight visitors a year." Among those driven out by rents of more than $1,600 for a one-bedroom apartment are many of Key West's wait staff, hotel housekeepers, gardeners, plumbers, and handymen. No matter how much money you have, everything takes longer — from getting a toilet fixed to getting a fish sandwich at Pepe's.

Then there's the elusive element of charm, which quickly drains away in a uniform population of multimillionaires. The Hamptons had their fishermen. Key West still advertises its "characters" — sun-bleached, weather-beaten misfits who drifted down for the weather or to escape some difficult situation on the mainland. But the fishermen are long gone from the Hamptons and disappearing from Cape Cod. As for Key West's characters — with the traditional little conch houses once favored by shrimpers flipped into million-dollar second homes, these human sources of local color have to be prepared to sleep with the scorpions under the highway overpass.

In Telluride even a local developer is complaining about the lack of affordable housing. "To have a real town," he told the *Financial Times*, "Telluride needs some locals hanging out" — in old-fashioned diners, for example, where you don't have to speak Italian to order a cup of coffee.

When I was a child, I sang "America the Beautiful" and meant it. I was born in the Rocky Mountains and raised, at various times, on the coasts. The Big Sky, the rolling surf, the jagged, snowcapped mountains — all this seemed to be my birthright. But now I flinch when I hear Woody Guthrie's line "This land was made for you and me." Somehow, I don't think it was meant to be sung by a chorus of hedge-fund operators.

▪ Thinking Critically about the Text

Ehrenreich writes at the end of paragraph 9, "We are used to thinking that poverty is a 'social problem' and wealth is only something to celebrate, but extreme wealth is also a social problem, and the superrich have become a burden on everyone else." How might you support Ehrenreich's claims using your personal experience?

▪ Questions on Subject

1. Does Ehrenreich dislike the rich in general or just because they deprive others of the aesthetic enjoyment of scenic beauty? Explain.

2. According to Ehrenreich, how are wealthy people, themselves, deprived by the "plutocratic takeover of rural America" (paragraph 11)?
3. As evidence of the negative impact of the superrich taking over, Ehrenreich writes, "Then there's the elusive element of charm, which quickly drains away in a uniform population of multimillionaires" (paragraph 13). Are you comfortable with that statement? Does she want "characters" around for "local color" only?
4. Does Ehrenreich offer any solutions for the problem she sees? If so, what are they? If not, why not?
5. Ehrenreich is a successful professional speaker and widely published author. Might she, in fact, be one of the people she is decrying? Explain.

■ Questions on Strategy

1. What is Ehrenreich's thesis? (Glossary: *Thesis*) Where in the essay does she offer her thesis?
2. How has Ehrenreich used personal experience to support her claim that the rich deprive others of the opportunity to enjoy nature's riches? Do you find those examples effective? Explain.
3. How has Ehrenreich used evidence from experts to support her claims? (Glossary: *Evidence*) Discuss several examples that you find effective.
4. Ehrenreich cites the expert testimony of evolutionary psychologist Nancy Etcoff regarding an innate human need for natural scenery. Do we have enough information to judge the validity of the evidence? Does Etcoff's claim convince you?
5. In your judgment, how effective is Ehrenreich's title? (Glossary: *Title*)

■ Questions on Diction and Vocabulary

1. Ehrenreich refers to Nancy Etcoff as an evolutionary psychologist. What is an *evolutionary psychologist*? Use your library or the Internet to find out.
2. Ehrenreich's tone is informal. Cite six examples of diction that contribute to her tone. (Glossary: *Diction; Tone*)

■ Classroom Activity Using Argumentation

An excellent way to gain some experience in formulating an argumentative position on an issue, and perhaps to establish a thesis, is to engage in a debate with someone who is on the other side of the question. When we listen to arguments and think of refutations and counterarguments, we have a chance to make a rehearsal and revision of our position before it is put in written form.

To try this out, use Ehrenreich's argument against wealthy people monopolizing scenic beauty as the subject for class debate. Divide the class into pro and con sides. Each side should elect a spokesperson to present its arguments before the class. Finally, have the class make some estimate of the success of each side in (1) articulating its position, (2) presenting ideas and evidence to support that position, and (3) convincing the audience of its position. The exercise should give you a good idea of the kind of work that's involved in preparing a written argument.

■ Writing Suggestions

1. **Writing with Sources.** Write an argument in favor of regional, city, and town planning as ways of combating the problems that Ehrenreich argues are created by wealthy landowners and developers. If you are not familiar with community efforts to promote more socially conscious and sustainable living arrangements, do some background reading of both print and online sources to familiarize yourself with their history and with their successes and failures. Also, feel free to cite whichever aspects of Ehrenreich's arguments you find useful as a base from which to argue.

   For models of and advice on integrating sources, see Chapters 14–15.

2. **Writing with Sources.** One promising solution to the problems of gentrification that Ehrenreich discusses is the rise of community land trusts. Write an essay in favor of land trusts: First, define the concept, citing examples of how land trusts work, and then explain how such an arrangement might benefit your community or how a community without one is being threatened by powerful interests.

   In order to write this essay, you will likely have to do research on the topic online or in the library.

   For models of and advice on integrating sources, see Chapters 14–15.

ARGUMENT TRIO: ON BLOGGING

When blogging began, many people used their blogs to share experiences and keep their friends updated. Now, with the advent of the popular social-networking Web sites Facebook and Twitter, many believe that blogging is becoming passé. While there might be some truth in that assessment, by some measures the breadth and depth of the blogosphere has never been greater, numbering as it does untold millions of people engaged in self-reflection and in sharing information, news, and opinions on subjects as varied as politics, education, health, technology, recreation, games, art, music, business, travel, medicine, religion, science, and much more. The accelerating growth in blogging and the seemingly untamed nature of its development have given rise to questions about its unique character, the directions it has taken, and the changes it has brought to institutions as we have known them.

We begin this trio of argumentative essays on the topic with Andrew Sullivan's "Why I Blog." As one of the medium's most insightful and articulate practitioners, Sullivan makes a strong case for considering blogging a special form of writing, characterized in part by its lack of extensive revision, its backward-in-time order of presentation, its palpable immediacy, and what Sullivan calls its "inherent humanity." Andrew Keen, the author of "Web 2.0," is a thoughtful and outspoken critic of not only blogging but also most other forms of communication that have emerged in the world of Web 2.0. Keen sees this world as "flattened," where everyone is a writer, a composer, an artist, a singer, a dancer, a critic, and a jazz trumpeter — just not very good ones. The absence of filters and the authority and knowledge of critics is nothing short of the beginning of the end for Keen. His argument, while perhaps difficult to countenance for many of us who feel at home in Web 2.0, is nevertheless as compelling in some respects as Sullivan's. Finally, in "Blogworld and Its Gravity," Matt Welch jumps into the long-running debate about blogging's effect on journalism and the newspaper industry. For some years, journalists and critics have complained that blogging is not journalism, in large part because it is not vetted by editors, fact checkers, or copyeditors. To such critics, blogging represents the Wild West of journalism. Shedding new light on a world that he knows well from years of practical experience both here and abroad, Welch offers hope for traditional journalists in a rapidly changing media environment.

■ Preparing to Read

Are you a blogger? If you are, what do you gain from blogging? In what ways does it differ from traditional forms of writing? Does blogging have any shortcomings for you? If you are not a blogger, what keeps you from participating? Do you regularly read any blogs? What is there about them that keeps you engaged?

Why I Blog

ANDREW SULLIVAN

Andrew Sullivan was born in 1963 in South Godstone, Surrey, England, to Irish parents. He earned his B.A. in modern history at Magdalene College, Oxford, and his master's and Ph.D. in government at Harvard University. Sullivan began his journalism career at the *New Republic* and later wrote for the *New York Times Magazine*. A gay, Catholic, conservative, and often controversial commentator, Sullivan has made history as a blogger. His blog, *The Daily Dish*, became very popular post–9/11 and was receiving over 50,000 hits a day by 2005. After nearly five years of blogging and writing books and articles, however, Sullivan took a break from his feverish journalistic activity. In 2007, Sullivan accepted an editorial position with the *Atlantic*, where he moved his blog <andrewsullivan.theatlantic.com>. Sullivan has written several books: *Virtually Normal: An Argument about Homosexuality* (1995); *Love Undetectable: Notes on Friendship, Sex and Survival* (1998); and *The Conservative Soul: How We Lost It, How to Get It Back* (2006).

In "Why I Blog," first published in the *Atlantic* online in November 2008, Sullivan offers insights on blogging and why he finds the form revolutionary. Contrary to charges that blogging is unprofessional and sloppy, he claims that it is anything but because of the instantaneous and brutally frank scrutiny that floods in from readers. He writes, "Alone in front of a computer, at any moment, are two people: a blogger and a reader. The proximity is palpable, the moment human — whatever authority a blogger has is derived not from the institution he works for but from the humanness he conveys. This is writing with emotion not just under but always breaking through the surface. It renders a writer and a reader not just connected but linked in a visceral, personal way. The only term that really describes this is *friendship*. And it is a relatively new thing to write for thousands and thousands of friends."

The word *blog* is a conflation of two words: *Web* and *log*. It contains in its four letters a concise and accurate self-description: It is a log of thoughts and writing posted publicly on the World Wide Web. In the monosyllabic vernacular of the Internet, *Web log* soon became the word *blog*.

This form of instant and global self-publishing, made possible by technology widely available only for the past decade or so, allows for no retroactive editing (apart from fixing minor typos or small glitches) and removes from the act of writing any considered or lengthy review. It is the spontaneous expression of instant thought—impermanent beyond even the ephemera of daily journalism. It is accountable in immediate and unavoidable ways to readers and other bloggers, and linked via hypertext to continuously multiplying references and sources. Unlike any single piece of print journalism, its borders are extremely porous and its truth inherently transitory. The consequences of this for the act of writing are still sinking in.

A ship's log owes its name to a small wooden board, often weighted with 3 lead, that was for centuries attached to a line and thrown over the stern. The weight of the log would keep it in the same place in the water, like a provisional anchor, while the ship moved away. By measuring the length of line used up in a set period of time, mariners could calculate the speed of their journey (the rope itself was marked by equidistant "knots" for easy measurement). As a ship's voyage progressed, the course came to be marked down in a book that was called a log.

In journeys at sea that took place before radio or radar or satellites or 4 sonar, these logs were an indispensable source for recording what actually happened. They helped navigators surmise where they were and how far they had traveled and how much longer they had to stay at sea. They provided accountability to a ship's owners and traders. They were designed to be as immune to faking as possible. Away from land, there was usually no reliable corroboration of events apart from the crew's own account in the middle of an expanse of blue and gray and green; and in long journeys, memories always blur and facts disperse. A log provided as accurate an account as could be gleaned in real time.

As you read a log, you have the curious sense of moving backward in 5 time as you move forward in pages — the opposite of a book. As you piece together a narrative that was never intended as one, it seems — and is — more truthful. Logs, in this sense, were a form of human self-correction. They amended for hindsight, for the ways in which human beings order and tidy and construct the story of their lives as they look back on them. Logs require a letting-go of narrative because they do not allow for a knowledge of the ending. So they have plot as well as dramatic irony — the reader will know the ending before the writer did.

> Blogging is to writing what extreme sports are to athletics: more free-form, more accident-prone, less formal, more alive. It is, in many ways, writing out loud.

Anyone who has blogged his thoughts for 6 an extended time will recognize this world. We bloggers have scant opportunity to collect our thoughts, to wait until events have settled and a clear pattern emerges. We blog now — as news reaches us, as facts emerge. This is partly true for all journalism, which is, as its etymology suggests, daily writing, always subject to subsequent revision. And a good columnist will adjust position and judgment and even political loyalty over time, depending on events. But a blog is not so much daily writing as hourly writing. And with that level of timeliness, the provisionality of every word is even more pressing — and the risk of error or the thrill of prescience that much greater.

No columnist or reporter or novelist will have his minute shifts or   7
constant small contradictions exposed as mercilessly as a blogger's are. A columnist can ignore or duck a subject less noticeably than a blogger committing thoughts to pixels several times a day. A reporter can wait — must wait — until every source has confirmed. A novelist can spend months or years before committing words to the world. For bloggers, the deadline is always now. Blogging is therefore to writing what extreme sports are to athletics: more free-form, more accident-prone, less formal, more alive. It is, in many ways, writing out loud.

You end up writing about yourself, since you are a relatively fixed point   8
in this constant interaction with the ideas and facts of the exterior world. And in this sense, the historic form closest to blogs is the diary. But with this difference: A diary is almost always a private matter. Its raw honesty, its dedication to marking life as it happens and remembering life as it was, makes it a terrestrial log. A few diaries are meant to be read by others, of course, just as correspondence could be — but usually posthumously, or as a way to compile facts for a more considered autobiographical rendering. But a blog, unlike a diary, is instantly public. It transforms this most personal and retrospective of forms into a painfully public and immediate one. It combines the confessional genre with the log form and exposes the author in a manner no author has ever been exposed before.

I remember first grappling with what to put on my blog. It was the spring   9
of 2000 and, like many a freelance writer at the time, I had some vague notion that I needed to have a presence "online." I had no clear idea of what to do, but a friend who ran a Web-design company offered to create a site for me, and, since I was technologically clueless, he also agreed to post various essays and columns as I wrote them. Before too long, this became a chore for him, and he called me one day to say he'd found an online platform that was so simple I could henceforth post all my writing myself. The platform was called Blogger.

As I used it to post columns or links to books or old essays, it occurred   10
to me that I could also post new writing — writing that could even be exclusive to the blog. But what? Like any new form, blogging did not start from nothing. It evolved from various journalistic traditions. In my case, I drew on my mainstream-media experience to navigate the virgin sea. I had a few early inspirations: the old Notebook section of the *New Republic*, a magazine that, under the editorial guidance of Michael Kinsley, had introduced a more English style of crisp, short commentary into what had been a more high-minded genre of American opinion writing. The *New Republic* had also pioneered a Diarist feature on the last page, which was designed to be a more personal, essayistic, first-person form of journalism. Mixing the two genres, I did what I had been trained to do — and improvised.

I'd previously written online as well, contributing to a listserv for gay 11
writers and helping Kinsley initiate a more discursive form of online writing for *Slate*, the first magazine published exclusively on the Web. As soon
as I began writing this way, I realized that the online form rewarded a colloquial, unfinished tone. In one of my early Kinsley-guided experiments, he
urged me not to think too hard before writing. So I wrote as I'd write an
e-mail — with only a mite more circumspection. This is hazardous, of course,
as anyone who has ever clicked Send in a fit of anger or hurt will testify. But
blogging requires an embrace of such hazards, a willingness to fall off the
trapeze rather than fail to make the leap.

From the first few days of using the form, I was hooked. The simple 12
experience of being able to directly broadcast my own words to readers was
an exhilarating literary liberation. Unlike the current generation of writers,
who have only ever blogged, I knew firsthand what the alternative meant. I'd
edited a weekly print magazine, the *New Republic*, for five years, and written countless columns and essays for a variety of traditional outlets. And in
all this, I'd often chafed, as most writers do, at the endless delays, revisions,
office politics, editorial fights, and last-minute cuts for space that dead-tree
publishing entails. Blogging — even to an audience of a few hundred in the
early days — was intoxicatingly free in comparison. Like taking a narcotic.

It was obvious from the start that it was revolutionary. Every writer 13
since the printing press has longed for a means to publish himself and
reach — instantly — any reader on Earth. Every professional writer has paid
some dues waiting for an editor's nod, or enduring a publisher's incompetence, or being ground to literary dust by a legion of fact-checkers and copy
editors. If you added up the time a writer once had to spend finding an outlet, impressing editors, sucking up to proprietors, and proofreading edits,
you'd find another lifetime buried in the interstices. But with one click of the
Publish Now button, all these troubles evaporated.

Alas, as I soon discovered, this sudden freedom from above was imme- 14
diately replaced by insurrection from below. Within minutes of my posting something, even in the earliest days, readers responded. E-mail seemed
to unleash their inner beast. They were more brutal than any editor, more
persnickety than any copy editor, and more emotionally unstable than any
colleague.

Again, it's hard to overrate how different this is. Writers can be sensitive, 15
vain souls, requiring gentle nurturing from editors, and oddly susceptible
to the blows delivered by reviewers. They survive, for the most part, but the
thinness of their skins is legendary. Moreover, before the blogosphere, reporters and columnists were largely shielded from this kind of direct hazing. Yes,
letters to the editor would arrive in due course and subscriptions would be
canceled. But reporters and columnists tended to operate in a relative sanc-
tuary, answerable mainly to their editors, not readers. For a long time, columns were essentially monologues published to applause, muffled murmurs,

silence, or a distant heckle. I'd gotten blowback from pieces before—but in an amorphous, time-delayed, distant way. Now the feedback was instant, personal, and brutal.

And so blogging found its own answer to the defensive counterblast from   16
the journalistic establishment. To the charges of inaccuracy and unprofessionalism, bloggers could point to the fierce, immediate scrutiny of their readers. Unlike newspapers, which would eventually publish corrections in a box of printed spinach far from the original error, bloggers had to walk the walk of self-correction in the same space and in the same format as the original screwup. The form was more accountable, not less, because there is nothing more conducive to professionalism than being publicly humiliated for sloppiness. Of course, a blogger could ignore an error or simply refuse to acknowledge mistakes. But if he persisted, he would be razzed by competitors and assailed by commenters and abandoned by readers. In an era when the traditional media found itself beset by scandals as disparate as Stephen Glass, Jayson Blair, and Dan Rather, bloggers survived the first assault on their worth. In time, in fact, the high standards expected of well-trafficked bloggers spilled over into greater accountability, transparency, and punctiliousness among the media powers that were. Even *New York Times* columnists were forced to admit when they had been wrong.

The blog remained a *superficial* medium, of course. By superficial, I   17
mean simply that blogging rewards brevity and immediacy. No one wants to read a 9,000-word treatise online. On the Web, one-sentence links are as legitimate as thousand-word diatribes—in fact, they are often valued more. And, as Matt Drudge told me when I sought advice from the master in 2001, the key to understanding a blog is to realize that it's a broadcast, not a publication. If it stops moving, it dies. If it stops paddling, it sinks.

But the superficiality masked considerable depth—greater depth, from   18
one perspective, than the traditional media could offer. The reason was a single technological innovation: the hyperlink. An old-school columnist can write 800 brilliant words analyzing or commenting on, say, a new think-tank report or scientific survey. But in reading it on paper, you have to take the columnist's presentation of the material on faith, or be convinced by a brief quotation (which can always be misleading out of context). Online, a hyperlink to the original source transforms the experience. Yes, a few sentences of bloggy spin may not be as satisfying as a full column, but the ability to read the primary material instantly—in as careful or shallow a fashion as you choose—can add much greater context than anything on paper. Even a blogger's chosen pull quote, unlike a columnist's, can be effortlessly checked against the original. Now this innovation, predating blogs but popularized by them, is increasingly central to mainstream journalism.

A blog, therefore, bobs on the surface of the ocean but has its anchorage   19
in waters deeper than those print media is technologically able to exploit. It disempowers the writer to that extent, of course. The blogger can get away

with less and afford fewer pretensions of authority. He is — more than any writer of the past — a node among other nodes, connected but unfinished without the links and the comments and the track-backs that make the blogosphere, at its best, a conversation, rather than a production.

A writer fully aware of and at ease with the provisionality of his own   20
work is nothing new. For centuries, writers have experimented with forms that suggest the imperfection of human thought, the inconstancy of human affairs, and the humbling, chastening passage of time. If you compare the meandering, questioning, unresolved dialogues of Plato with the definitive, logical treatises of Aristotle, you see the difference between a skeptic's spirit translated into writing and a spirit that seeks to bring some finality to the argument. Perhaps the greatest single piece of Christian apologetics, Pascal's *Pensées*, is a series of meandering, short, and incomplete stabs at arguments, observations, insights. Their lack of finish is what makes them so compelling — arguably more compelling than a polished treatise by Aquinas.

Or take the brilliant polemics of Karl Kraus, the publisher of and main   21
writer for *Die Fackel*, who delighted in constantly twitting authority with slashing aphorisms and rapid-fire bursts of invective. Kraus had something rare in his day: the financial wherewithal to self-publish. It gave him a fearlessness that is now available to anyone who can afford a computer and an Internet connection.

But perhaps the quintessential blogger *avant la lettre* was Montaigne.   22
His essays were published in three major editions, each one longer and more complex than the previous. A passionate skeptic, Montaigne amended, added to, and amplified the essays for each edition, making them three-dimensional through time. In the best modern translations, each essay is annotated, sentence by sentence, paragraph by paragraph, by small letters (A, B, and C) for each major edition, helping the reader see how each rewrite added to or subverted, emphasized or ironized, the version before. Montaigne was living his skepticism, daring to show how a writer evolves, changes his mind, learns new things, shifts perspectives, grows older — and that this, far from being something that needs to be hidden behind a veneer of unchanging authority, can become a virtue, a new way of looking at the pretensions of authorship and text and truth. Montaigne, for good measure, also peppered his essays with myriads of what bloggers would call external links. His own thoughts are strewn with and complicated by the aphorisms and anecdotes of others. Scholars of the sources note that many of these "money quotes" were deliberately taken out of context, adding layers of irony to writing that was already saturated in empirical doubt.

To blog is therefore to let go of your writing in a way, to hold it at arm's   23
length, open it to scrutiny, allow it to float in the ether for a while, and to let others, as Montaigne did, pivot you toward relative truth. A blogger will notice this almost immediately upon starting. Some e-mailers, unsurprisingly, know more about a subject than the blogger does. They will send links,

stories, and facts, challenging the blogger's view of the world, sometimes outright refuting it, but more frequently adding context and nuance and complexity to an idea. The role of a blogger is not to defend against this but to embrace it. He is similar in this way to the host of a dinner party. He can provoke discussion or take a position, even passionately, but he also must create an atmosphere in which others want to participate.

That atmosphere will inevitably be formed by the blogger's personality. 24 The blogosphere may, in fact, be the least veiled of any forum in which a writer dares to express himself. Even the most careful and self-aware blogger will reveal more about himself than he wants to in a few unguarded sentences and publish them before he has the sense to hit Delete. The wise panic that can paralyze a writer — the fear that he will be exposed, undone, humiliated — is not available to a blogger. You can't have blogger's block. You have to express yourself now, while your emotions roil, while your temper flares, while your humor lasts. You can try to hide yourself from real scrutiny, and the exposure it demands, but it's hard. And that's what makes blogging as a form stand out: it is rich in personality. The faux intimacy of the Web experience, the closeness of the e-mail and the instant message, seeps through. You feel as if you know bloggers as they go through their lives, experience the same things you are experiencing, and share the moment. When readers of my blog bump into me in person, they invariably address me as Andrew. Print readers don't do that. It's Mr. Sullivan to them.

On my blog, my readers and I experienced 9/11 together, in real time. I can 25 look back and see not just how I responded to the event, but how I responded to it at 3:47 that afternoon. And at 9:46 that night. There is a vividness to this immediacy that cannot be rivaled by print. The same goes for the 2000 recount, the Iraq War, the revelations of Abu Ghraib, the death of John Paul II, or any of the other history-making events of the past decade. There is simply no way to write about them in real time without revealing a huge amount about yourself. And the intimate bond this creates with readers is unlike the bond that the the *Times*, say, develops with its readers through the same events. Alone in front of a computer, at any moment, are two people: a blogger and a reader. The proximity is palpable, the moment human — whatever authority a blogger has is derived not from the institution he works for but from the humanness he conveys. This is writing with emotion not just under but always breaking through the surface. It renders a writer and a reader not just connected but linked in a visceral, personal way. The only term that really describes this is *friendship*. And it is a relatively new thing to write for thousands and thousands of friends.

These friends, moreover, are an integral part of the blog itself — sources 26 of solace, company, provocation, hurt, and correction. If I were to do an inventory of the material that appears on my blog, I'd estimate that a good third of it is reader-generated, and a good third of my time is spent absorbing readers' views, comments, and tips. Readers tell me of breaking stories, new perspectives, and counterarguments to prevailing assumptions. And this is what blogging, in turn, does to reporting. The traditional method involves a journalist searching for key sources, nurturing them, and sequestering them from his rivals. A blogger splashes gamely into a subject and dares the sources to come to him.

Some of this material — e-mails from soldiers on the front lines, from   27 scientists explaining new research, from dissident Washington writers too scared to say what they think in their own partisan redoubts — might never have seen the light of day before the blogosphere. And some of it, of course, is dubious stuff. Bloggers can be spun and misled as easily as traditional writers — and the rigorous source assessment that good reporters do can't be done by e-mail. But you'd be surprised by what comes unsolicited into the in-box, and how helpful it often is.

Not all of it is mere information. Much of it is also opinion and scholar-   28 ship, a knowledge base that exceeds the research department of any news-paper. A good blog is your own private Wikipedia. Indeed, the most plea-sant surprise of blogging has been the number of people working in law or government or academia or rearing kids at home who have real literary talent and real knowledge, and who had no outlet — until now. There is a distinction here, of course, between the edited use of e-mailed sources by a careful blogger and the often mercurial cacophony on an unmediated comments section. But the truth is out there — and the miracle of e-mail allows it to come to you.

Fellow bloggers are always expanding this knowledge base. Eight years   29 ago, the blogosphere felt like a handful of individual cranks fighting with one another. Today, it feels like a universe of cranks, with vast, pulsating readerships, fighting with one another. To the neophyte reader, or blogger, it can seem overwhelming. But there is a connection between the intimacy of the early years and the industry it has become today. And the connection is human individuality.

The pioneers of online journalism — *Slate* and *Salon* — are still very pop-   30 ular, and successful. But the more memorable stars of the Internet — even within those two sites — are all personally branded. *Daily Kos*, for example, is written by hundreds of bloggers, and amended by thousands of commenters. But it is named after Markos Moulitsas, who started it, and his own prose still provides a backbone to the front-page blog. The biggest news-aggregator site in the world, the Drudge Report, is named after its founder, Matt Drudge, who somehow conveys a unified sensibility through his selection of links, images, and stories. The vast, expanding universe of *The Huffington Post* still finds some semblance of coherence in the Cambridge-Greek twang of Arianna; the entire world of online celebrity gossip circles the drain of *Perez Hilton;* and the investigative journalism, reviewing, and commentary of *Talking Points Memo* is still tied together by the tone of Josh Marshall. Even *Slate* is unimaginable without Mickey Kaus's voice.

What endures is a human brand. Readers have encountered this phe- 31
nomenon before—*I.F. Stone's Weekly* comes to mind—but not to this extent.
It stems, I think, from the conversational style that blogging rewards. What
you want in a conversationalist is as much character as authority. And if you
think of blogging as more like talk radio or cable news than opinion magazines or daily newspapers, then this personalized emphasis is less surprising.
People have a voice for radio and a face for television. For blogging, they have
a sensibility.

But writing in this new form is a collective enterprise as much as it is an 32
individual one—and the connections between bloggers are as important as
the content on the blogs. The links not only drive conversation, they drive
readers. The more you link, the more others will link to you, and the more
traffic and readers you will get. The zero-sum game of old media—in which
Time benefits from *Newsweek*'s decline and vice versa—becomes win-win.
It's great for *Time* to be linked to by *Newsweek* and the other way round.
One of the most prized statistics in the blogosphere is therefore not the total
number of readers or page views, but the "authority" you get by being linked
to by other blogs. It's an indication of how central you are to the online conversation of humankind.

The reason this open-source market of thinking and writing has such 33
potential is that the always adjusting and evolving collective mind can rapidly filter out bad arguments and bad ideas. The flip side, of course, is that
bloggers are also human beings. Reason is not the only fuel in the tank. In a
world where no distinction is made between good traffic and bad traffic, and
where emotion often rules, some will always raise their voice to dominate
the conversation; others will pander shamelessly to their readers' prejudices;
others will start online brawls for the fun of it. Sensationalism, dirt, and the
ease of formulaic talking points always beckon. You can disappear into the
partisan blogosphere and never stumble onto a site you disagree with.

But linkage mitigates this. A Democratic blog will, for example, be forced 34
to link to Republican ones, if only to attack and mock. And it's in the interests
of both camps to generate shared traffic. This encourages polarized slugfests.
But online, at least you see both sides. Reading the *Nation* or *National Review*
before the Internet existed allowed for more cocooning than the wide-open
online sluice gates do now. If there's more incivility, there's also more fluidity. Rudeness, in any case, isn't the worst thing that can happen to a blogger.
Being ignored is. Perhaps the nastiest thing one can do to a fellow blogger is
to rip him apart and fail to provide a link.

A successful blog therefore has to balance itself between a writer's own 35
take on the world and others. Some bloggers collect, or "aggregate," other
bloggers' posts with dozens of quick links and minimalist opinion topspin:
Glenn Reynolds at Instapundit does this for the right-of-center; Duncan
Black at Eschaton does it for the left. Others are more eclectic, or aggregate
links in a particular niche, or cater to a settled and knowledgeable reader

base. A *blogroll* is an indicator of whom you respect enough to keep in your galaxy. For many years, I kept my reading and linking habits to a relatively small coterie of fellow political bloggers. In today's blogosphere, to do this is to embrace marginality. I've since added links to religious blogs and literary ones and scientific ones and just plain weird ones. As the blogosphere has expanded beyond anyone's capacity to absorb it, I've needed an assistant and interns to scour the Web for links and stories and photographs to respond to and think about. It's a difficult balance, between your own interests and obsessions, and the knowledge, insight, and wit of others — but an immensely rich one. There are times, in fact, when a blogger feels less like a writer than an online disc jockey, mixing samples of tunes and generating new melodies through mashups while also making his own music. He is both artist and producer — and the beat always goes on.

If all this sounds postmodern, that's because it is. And blogging suffers 36 from the same flaws as postmodernism: a failure to provide stable truth or a permanent perspective. A traditional writer is valued by readers precisely because they trust him to have thought long and hard about a subject, given it time to evolve in his head, and composed a piece of writing that is worth their time to read at length and to ponder. Bloggers don't do this and cannot do this — and that limits them far more than it does traditional long-form writing.

A blogger will air a variety of thoughts or facts on any subject in no partic- 37 ular order other than that dictated by the passing of time. A writer will instead use time, synthesizing these thoughts, ordering them, weighing which points count more than others, seeing how his views evolved in the writing process itself, and responding to an editor's perusal of a draft or two. The result is almost always more measured, more satisfying, and more enduring than a blizzard of posts. The triumphalist notion that blogging should somehow replace traditional writing is as foolish as it is pernicious. In some ways, blogging's gifts to our discourse make the skills of a good traditional writer much more valuable, not less. The torrent of blogospheric insights, ideas, and arguments places a greater premium on the person who can finally make sense of it all, turning it into something more solid, and lasting, and rewarding.

The points of this essay, for example, have appeared in shards and frag- 38 ments on my blog for years. But being forced to order them in my head and think about them for a longer stretch has helped me understand them better, and perhaps express them more clearly. Each week, after a few hundred posts, I also write an actual newspaper column. It invariably turns out to be more considered, balanced, and evenhanded than the blog. But the blog will always inform and enrich the column, and often serve as a kind of free-form, free-associative research. And an essay like this will spawn discussion best handled on a blog. The conversation, in other words, is the point, and the different idioms used by the conversationalists all contribute something of value to it. And so, if the defenders of the old media once viscerally regarded blogging as some kind of threat, they are starting to see it more as a portal, and a spur.

There is, after all, something simply irreplaceable about reading a piece   39
of writing at length on paper, in a chair or on a couch or in bed. To use an
obvious analogy, jazz entered our civilization much later than composed, formal music. But it hasn't replaced it; and no jazz musician would ever claim
that it could. Jazz merely demands a different way of playing and listening,
just as blogging requires a different mode of writing and reading. Jazz and
blogging are intimate, improvisational, and individual — but also inherently
collective. And the audience talks over both.

The reason they talk while listening, and comment or link while reading,   40
is that they understand that this is a kind of music that needs to be engaged
rather than merely absorbed. To listen to jazz as one would listen to an aria is
to miss the point. Reading at a monitor, at a desk, or on an iPhone provokes
a querulous, impatient, distracted attitude, a demand for instant, usable
information, that is simply not conducive to opening a novel or a favorite
magazine on the couch. Reading on paper evokes a more relaxed and medi-
tative response. The message dictates the medium. And each medium has its
place—as long as one is not mistaken for the other.

In fact, for all the intense gloom surrounding the newspaper and maga-   41
zine business, this is actually a golden era for journalism. The blogosphere
has added a whole new idiom to the act of writing and has introduced an
entirely new generation to nonfiction. It has enabled writers to write out loud
in ways never seen or understood before. And yet it has exposed a hunger
and need for traditional writing that, in the age of television's dominance,
had seemed on the wane.

Words, of all sorts, have never seemed so now.   ▪   42

▪ Thinking Critically about the Text

Sullivan says that hypertext (internal links to related online data) changed
everything. Here's how he put it in paragraph 19:

> A blog, therefore, bobs on the surface of the ocean but has its
> anchorage in waters deeper than those print media is technologi-
> cally able to exploit. It disempowers the writer to that extent, of
> course. The blogger can get away with less and afford fewer preten-
> sions of authority. He is — more than any writer of the past — a node
> among other nodes, connected but unfinished without the links and
> the comments and the track backs that make the blogosphere, at its
> best, a conversation, rather than a production.

What does Sullivan mean when he says, "a conversation, rather
than a production"?

■ Examining the Issue

1. Sullivan uses an analogy between a ship's log and blogging to introduce his essay. How does this analogy work? (Glossary: *Analogy*) How does the analogy deepen your understanding of the unique experience of blogging?

2. A blog is like a diary but different, according to Sullivan. What does he mean?

3. Sullivan writes in paragraphs 13–15 that the unique experience of blogging cuts through all the procedural problems of getting published the traditional way but also opens new challenges for the blogger: in particular, "insurrection from below." What does he mean?

4. Another comparison that Sullivan makes in paragraph 17 came from blogger Matt Drudge, who advised him, "[T]he key to understanding a blog is to realize that it's a broadcast, not a publication. If it stops moving, it dies. If it stops paddling, it sinks." Why doesn't a blog enjoy the same longevity as a print article?

5. Sullivan claims that a blogger and his or her reader form a visceral relationship: They become friends. Can the same be said for the relationship between a conventional writer and reader? Explain.

6. Why is the number of links you get as a blogger one of the most prized statistics in the blogosphere, according to Sullivan?

7. For a blogger, what lessens the danger of getting lost in partisanship?

8. In a final analogy, Sullivan compares blogging to jazz. How does that analogy work? Is it a useful analogy for you?

9. In his conclusion, Sullivan makes several important claims: "The blogosphere has added a whole new idiom to the act of writing and has introduced an entirely new generation to nonfiction," and "it has exposed a hunger and need for traditional writing." Does he support these claims in his essay? Are you convinced? Explain.

WEB 2.0

ANDREW KEEN

 Andrew Keen — writer, media personality, and Silicon Valley entrepreneur — is noted for his provocative analysis and commentary on technology, media, and culture. Born in London in 1960, Keen graduated from the University of London with a degree in modern history, after which he did graduate work at the University of California–Berkeley. He entered the Internet boom (and bust) in the mid-1990s with his own start-up, AudioCafe.com, which lasted until 2000. He is the founder and host of *AfterTV*, a podcast chat show, whose guests "excavate the social, cultural, and political consequences of the digital revolution." Keen's commentaries can be read on sites such as *ZDNet*, *Britannica* online, and *iHollywood News*; he is a frequent guest on television and radio news programs (both fake and real), such as *The Colbert Report*, *PBS NewsHour*, *The Today Show*, *Fox News*, *CNN International*, and National Public Radio's *Weekend Edition*. His articles have appeared in numerous publications, including the *Los Angeles Times*, the *San Francisco Chronicle*, the *Wall Street Journal*, *Forbes*, *Entertainment Weekly*, *Fast Company*, and the *Weekly Standard*. Keen blogs about media, culture, and politics at TheGreatSeduction.com.

The following article, which first appeared in the *Weekly Standard* on February 15, 2006, compares Web 2.0 to Marxism and has brought Keen considerable notoriety. The article became the basis for his 2007 book, *The Cult of the Amateur: How the Internet Is Killing Our Culture*, which is described by *New York Times* book critic Michiko Kakutani as "a shrewdly argued jeremiad against the digerati effort to dethrone cultural and political gatekeepers and replace experts with the 'wisdom of the crowd.'"

THE SECOND GENERATION OF THE INTERNET HAS ARRIVED. IT'S WORSE THAN YOU THINK.

The ancients were good at resisting seduction. Odysseus fought the seductive song of the Sirens by having his men tie him to the mast of his ship as it sailed past the Siren's Isle. Socrates was so intent on protecting citizens from the seductive opinions of artists and writers, that he outlawed them from his imaginary republic.

We moderns are less nimble at resisting great seductions, particularly those utopian visions that promise grand political or cultural salvation. From the

French and Russian revolutions to the countercultural upheavals of the '60s and the digital revolution of the '90s, we have been seduced, time after time and text after text, by the vision of a political or economic utopia.

Rather than Paris, Moscow, or Berkeley, the grand utopian movement of our contemporary age is headquartered in Silicon Valley, whose great seduction is actually a fusion of two historical movements: the countercultural utopianism of the '60s and the techno-economic utopianism of the '90s. Here in Silicon Valley, this seduction has announced itself to the world as the "Web 2.0" movement.   3

Last week, I was treated to lunch at a fashionable Japanese restaurant in Palo Alto by a serial Silicon Valley entrepreneur who, back in the dot-com boom, had invested in my start-up Audiocafe.com. The entrepreneur, like me a Silicon Valley veteran, was pitching me his latest start-up: a technology platform that creates easy-to-use software tools for online communities to publish weblogs, digital movies, and music. It is technology that enables anyone with a computer to become an author, a film director, or a musician. This Web 2.0 dream is Socrates' nightmare: technology that arms every citizen with the means to be an opinionated artist or writer.   4

"This is historic," my friend promised me. "We are enabling Internet users to author their own content. Think of it as empowering citizen media. We can help smash the elitism of the Hollywood studios and the big record labels. Our technology platform will radically democratize culture, build authentic community, create citizen media." Welcome to Web 2.0.   5

> This Web 2.0 dream is Socrates' nightmare: technology that arms every citizen with the means to be an opinionated artist or writer.

Buzzwords from the old dot-com era—like "cool," "eyeballs," or "burn-rate"—have been replaced in Web 2.0 by language which is simultaneously more militant and absurd: *Empowering citizen media, radically democratize, smash elitism, content redistribution, authentic community* . . . . This sociological jargon, once the preserve of the hippie counterculture, has now become the lexicon of new media capitalism.   6

Yet this entrepreneur owns a $4 million house a few blocks from Steve Jobs's house. He vacations in the South Pacific. His children attend the most exclusive private academy on the peninsula. But for all of this he sounds more like a cultural Marxist — a disciple of Gramsci or Herbert Marcuse — than a capitalist with an M.B.A. from Stanford.   7

In his mind, "big media" — the Hollywood studios, the major record labels, and international publishing houses — really did represent the enemy. The promised land was user-generated online content. In Marxist terms, the traditional media had become the exploitative "bourgeoisie," and citizen media, those heroic bloggers and podcasters, were the "proletariat."   8

This outlook is typical of the Web 2.0 movement, which fuses '60s radi- 9
calism with the utopian eschatology of digital technology. The ideological
outcome may be trouble for all of us.

So what, exactly, is the Web 2.0 movement? As an ideology, it is based upon 10
a series of ethical assumptions about media, culture, and technology. It
worships the creative amateur: the self-taught filmmaker, the dorm-room
musician, the unpublished writer. It suggests that everyone — even the most
poorly educated and inarticulate amongst us — can and should use digital
media to express and realize themselves. Web 2.0 "empowers" our creativity, it "democratizes" media, it "levels the playing field" between experts and
amateurs. The enemy of Web 2.0 is "elitist" traditional media.

Empowered by Web 2.0 technology, we can all become citizen journal- 11
ists, citizen videographers, citizen musicians. Empowered by this technology,
we will be able to write in the morning, direct movies in the afternoon, and
make music in the evening. . . .

The consequences of Web 2.0 are inherently dangerous for the vitality of 12
culture and the arts. Its empowering promises play upon that legacy of the
'60s — the creeping narcissism that Christopher Lasch described so presci-
ently, with its obsessive focus on the realization of the self.

Another word for narcissism is *personalization*. Web 2.0 technology per- 13
sonalizes culture so that it reflects ourselves rather than the world around us.
Blogs personalize media content so that all we read are our own thoughts.
Online stores personalize our preferences, thus feeding back to us our own
taste. Google personalizes searches so that all we see are advertisements for
products and services we already use.

Instead of Mozart, Van Gogh, or Hitchcock, all we get with the Web 2.0 14
revolution is more of ourselves. . . .

Traditional "elitist" media is being destroyed by digital technologies. 15
Newspapers are in free fall. Network television, the modern equivalent of the
dinosaur, is being shaken by TiVo's overnight annihilation of the 30-second
commercial. The iPod is undermining the multibillion-dollar music industry. Meanwhile, digital piracy, enabled by Silicon Valley hardware and justified by Silicon Valley intellectual-property communists such as Larry Lessig,
is draining revenue from established artists, movie studios, newspapers,
record labels, and songwriters.

Is this a bad thing? The purpose of our media and culture indus- 16
tries — beyond the obvious need to make money and entertain people — is
to discover, nurture, and reward elite talent. Our traditional mainstream
media has done this with great success over the last century. Consider Alfred
Hitchcock's masterpiece *Vertigo* and a couple of other brilliantly talented works
of the same name: the 1999 book called *Vertigo*, by Anglo-German writer W. G.
Sebald, and the 2004 song "Vertigo," by Irish rock star Bono. Hitchcock could
never have made his expensive, complex movies outside the Hollywood studio

system. Bono would never have become Bono without the music industry's super-heavyweight marketing muscle. And W. G. Sebald, the most obscure of this trinity of talent, would have remained an unknown university professor had a high-end publishing house not had the good taste to discover and distribute his work. Elite artists and an elite media industry are symbiotic. If you democratize media, then you end up democratizing talent. The unintended consequence of all this democratization, to misquote Web 2.0 apologist Thomas Friedman, is cultural "flattening." No more Hitchcocks, Bonos, or Sebalds. Just the flat noise of opinion — Socrates' nightmare.

While Socrates correctly gave warning about the dangers of a society infatu-   17
ated by opinion in Plato's *Republic*, more modern dystopian writers—Huxley, Bradbury, and Orwell — got the Web 2.0 future exactly wrong. Much has been made, for example, of the associations between the all-seeing, all-knowing qualities of Google's search engine and the Big Brother in *Nineteen Eighty-Four*. But Orwell's fear was the disappearance of the individual right to self-expression. Thus Winston Smith's great act of rebellion in *Nineteen Eighty-Four* was his decision to pick up a rusty pen and express his own thoughts:

> The thing that he was about to do was open a diary. This was not illegal, . . . but if detected it was reasonably certain that it would be punished by death. . . . Winston fitted a nib into the penholder and sucked it to get the grease off. . . . He dipped the pen into the ink and then faltered for just a second. A tremor had gone through his bowels. To mark the paper was the decisive act.

In the Web 2.0 world, however, the nightmare is not the scarcity, but the   18
overabundance of authors. Since everyone will use digital media to express themselves, the only decisive act will be to *not* mark the paper. *Not writing* as rebellion sounds bizarre—like a piece of fiction authored by Franz Kafka. But one of the unintended consequences of the Web 2.0 future may well be that everyone is an author, while there is no longer any audience.

Speaking of Kafka, on the back cover of the January 2006 issue of *Poets and*   19
Writers magazine, there is a seductive Web 2.0 style advertisement which reads: "Kafka toiled in obscurity and died penniless. If only he'd had a Web site. . . ."

Presumably, if Kafka had had a Web site, it would be located at kafka.com,   20
which is today an address owned by a mad left-wing blog called The Biscuit Report. The front page of this site quotes some words written by Kafka in his diary:

> I have no memory for things I have learned, nor things I have read, nor things experienced or heard, neither for people nor events; I feel that I have experienced nothing, learned nothing, that I actually know less than the average schoolboy, and that what I do know is superficial, and that every second question is beyond me. I am

incapable of thinking deliberately; my thoughts run into a wall. I can grasp the essence of things in isolation, but I am quite incapable of coherent, unbroken thinking. I can't even tell a story properly; in fact, I can scarcely talk . . .

One of the unintended consequences of the Web 2.0 movement may well 21 be that we fall, collectively, into the amnesia that Kafka describes. Without an elite mainstream media, we will lose our memory for things learned, read, experienced, or heard. The cultural consequences of this are dire, requiring the authoritative voice of at least an Allan Bloom, if not an Oswald Spengler. But here in Silicon Valley, on the brink of the Web 2.0 epoch, there no longer are any Blooms or Spenglers. All we have is the great seduction of citizen media, democratized content, and authentic online communities. And weblogs, of course. Millions and millions of blogs.

■ Thinking Critically about the Text

Is Keen simply a cranky critic of Web 2.0, or is there substance to his arguments about the dangers of the decline of an elite mainstream media? Explain.

■ Examining the Issue

1. What does Silicon Valley represent in American culture? What are the various interpretations of its influence and worth?
2. What is so seductive about Silicon Valley and its productions?
3. What does Keen think his friend who "sounds more like a cultural Marxist" has against "big media"?
4. Why would Web 2.0 be Socrates' nightmare, as Keen writes in paragraph 4?
5. Is Keen an elitist? Why, or why not?
6. In paragraph 3 Keen says Web 2.0 fuses "the countercultural utopianism of the '60s and the techno-economic utopianism of the '90s." What does he mean?
7. Do you believe, as Keen does, that with Web 2.0, wherein everyone is a musician, an artist, and a journalist, it's unlikely that the world will produce more Mozarts, Van Goghs, or Hitchcocks? Why, or why not?

Blogworld and Its Gravity: The New Amateur Journalists Weigh In

MATT WELCH

Matt Welch is a blogger, journalist, pundit, and writer who was born in Bellflower, California, in 1968 and grew up in Long Branch, California. He attended the University of California–Santa Barbara before becoming a journalist abroad. Welch was the assistant editorial-page editor of the *Los Angeles Times* and is now the editor in chief of *Reason* magazine, a monthly libertarian journal. His writing has appeared in *Salon*, the *American Spectator*, the *Washington Post*, *Orange County Register*, *LA Weekly*, ESPN.com, *Wired*, the *Pittsburgh Post-Gazette*, *AlterNet*, and Canada's *National Post*, among many other publications, both here and abroad. Welch has also written *McCain: The Myth of a Maverick* (2007), a libertarian portrayal of former presidential candidate John McCain. Welch maintains a popular blog at mattwelch.com and makes his home in Washington, D.C.

In the following excerpt from "Blogworld and Its Gravity," which first appeared in the September/October 2003 issue of the *Columbia Journalism Review*, Welch examines the blogosphere and answers the questions: "Is journalism being produced by blogs, is it interesting, and how should journalists react to it?"

L ike just about everything else, blogging changed forever on September 11, 2001. The destruction of the World Trade Center and the attack on the Pentagon created a huge appetite on the part of the public to be part of The Conversation, to vent and analyze and publicly ponder or mourn. Many, too, were unsatisfied with what they read and saw in the mainstream media. Glenn Reynolds, proprietor of the wildly popular InstaPundit.com blog, thought the mainstream analysis was terrible. "All the talking heads . . . kept saying that 'we're gonna have to grow up, we're gonna have to give up a lot of our freedoms,'" he says. "Or it was the 'Why do they hate us' sort of teeth-gnashing. And I think there was a deep dissatisfaction with that." The daily op-ed diet of Column Left and Column Right often fell way off the mark. "It's time for the United Nations to get the hell out of town. And take with it CNN war-slut Christiane Amanpour" the *New York Post*'s Andrea Peyser seethed on September 21. "We forgive you; we reject vengeance," Colman McCarthy whimpered to the terrorists in the *Los Angeles Times*

September 17. September 11 was the impetus for my own blog <mattwelch .com/warblog.html>. Jeff Jarvis, who was trapped in the WTC dust cloud on September 11, started his a few days later. "I had a personal story I needed to tell," said Jarvis, a former *San Francisco Examiner* columnist, founding editor of *Entertainment Weekly,* and current president and creative director of Advance.net, which is the Internet wing of the Condé Nast empire. "Then lo and behold! I discovered people were linking to me and talking about my story, so I joined this great conversation." . . .

What's the Point?

So what have these people contributed to journalism? Four things: personality, eyewitness testimony, editorial filtering, and uncounted gigabytes of new knowledge. 2

"Why are weblogs popular?" asks Jarvis, whose company has launched four dozen of them, ranging from beachcams on the Jersey shore to a temporary blog during the latest Iraq war. "I think it's because they have something to say. In a media world that's otherwise leached of opinions and life, there's so much life in them." 3

> So what have these people contributed to journalism? Four things: personality, eyewitness testimony, editorial filtering, and uncounted gigabytes of new knowledge.

For all the history made by newspapers between 1960 and 2000, the profession was also busy contracting, standardizing, and homogenizing. Most cities now have their monopolist daily, their alt weekly or two, their business journal. Journalism is done a certain way, by a certain kind of people. Bloggers are basically oblivious to such traditions, so reading the best of them is like receiving a bracing slap in the face. It's a reminder that America is far more diverse and iconoclastic than its newsrooms. 4

After two years of reading weblogs, my short list of favorite news commentators in the world now includes an air force mechanic (Paul Palubicki of sgtstryker.com), a punk rock singer-songwriter (Dr. Frank of doktorfrank.com), a twenty-four-year-old Norwegian programmer (Bjorn Staerk of http://bearstrong.net /warblog/index.html), and a cranky libertarian journalist from Alberta, Canada (Colby Cosh). Outsiders with vivid writing styles and unique viewpoints have risen to the top of the blog heap and begun vaulting into mainstream media. Less than two years ago, Elizabeth Spiers was a tech-stock analyst for a hedge fund who at night wrote sharp-tongued observations about Manhattan life on her personal blog; now she's the It Girl of New York media, lancing her colleagues at Gawker.com, while doing freelance work for the *Times,* the *New York Post, Radar,* and other publications. Salam Pax, 5 a pseudonymous young gay Iraqi architect who made hearts flutter with his idiosyncratic personal descriptions of Baghdad before and after the war, now writes columns for the *Guardian* and in July signed a book deal with Grove/Atlantic. Steven Den Beste, a middle-aged unemployed software engineer in San Diego, has been spinning out thousands of words of international analysis most every day for the last two years; recently he has been seen in the online edition of the *Wall Street Journal*.

6   With personality and an online audience, meanwhile, comes a kind of reader interaction far more intense and personal than anything comparable in print. Once, when I had the poor taste to mention in my blog that I was going through a rough financial period, readers sent me more than $1,000 in two days. Far more important, the intimacy and network effects of the blogworld enable you to meet people beyond your typical circle and political affiliation, sometimes with specialized knowledge of interest to you. "It exposes you to worlds that most people, let alone reporters, never interact with," says Jarvis, whose personal blog <buzzmachine.com> has morphed into a one-stop shop for catching up on Iranian and Iraqi bloggers, some of whom he has now met online or face to face.

7   Such specialization and filtering is one of the form's key functions. Many bloggers, like the estimable Jim Romenesko, with his popular journalism forum on Poynter's site, focus like a laser beam on one microcategory, and provide simple links to the day's relevant news. There are scores dealing with ever-narrower categories of media alone, from a site that obsesses over the *San Francisco Chronicle* <ChronWatch.com>, to one that keeps the heat on newspaper ombudsmen <OmbudsGod.blogspot.com>. Charles Johnson, a Los Angeles Web designer, has built a huge and intensely loyal audience by spotting and vilifying venalities in the Arab press <littlegreenfootballs.com /weblog>. And individual news events, such as the Iraq War, spark their own temporary group blogs, where five or ten or more people all contribute links to minute-by-minute breaking news. Sometimes the single most must-see publication on a given topic will have been created the day before.

8   Besides introducing valuable new sources of information to readers, these sites are also forcing their proprietors to act like journalists: choosing stories, judging the credibility of sources, writing headlines, taking pictures, developing prose styles, dealing with readers, building audience, weighing libel considerations, and occasionally conducting informed investigations on their own.

9   Thousands of amateurs are learning how we do our work, becoming in the process more sophisticated readers and sharper critics. For lazy columnists and defensive gatekeepers, it can seem as if the hounds from a mediocre hell have been unleashed. But for curious professionals, it is a marvelous opportunity and entertaining spectacle; they discover what the audience finds important and encounter specialists who can rip apart the work of many a generalist. More than just A. J. Liebling–style press criticism, journalists

finally have something approaching real peer review, in all its brutality. If they truly value the scientific method, they should rejoice. Blogs can bring a collective intelligence to bear on a question.

And when the decentralized fact-checking army kicks into gear, it can be an impressive thing to behold. On March 30, veteran British war correspondent Robert Fisk, who has been accused so often of anti-American bias and sloppiness by bloggers that his last name has become a verb (meaning, roughly, "to disprove loudly, point by point"), reported that a bomb hitting a crowded Baghdad market and killing dozens must have been fired by U.S. troops because of some Western numerals he found on a piece of twisted metal lying nearby. Australian blogger Tim Blair, a freelance journalist, reprinted the partial numbers and asked his military-knowledgeable readers for insight. Within twenty-four hours, more than a dozen readers with specialized knowledge (retired air force, former Naval Air Systems Command employees, others) had written in describing the weapon (U.S. high-speed antiradiation missile), manufacturer (Raytheon), launch point (F-16), and dozens of other minute details not seen in press accounts days and weeks later. Their conclusion, much as it pained them to say so: Fisk was probably right. 10

In December 2001 a University of New Hampshire economics and women's studies professor named Marc Herold published a study, based mostly on press clippings, that estimated 3,767 civilians had died as a result of American military action in Afghanistan. Within a day, blogger Bruce Rolston, a Canadian military reservist, had already shot holes through Herold's methodology, noting that he conflated "casualties" with "fatalities," double counted single events, and depended heavily on dubious news sources. Over the next two days, several other bloggers cut Herold's work to ribbons. Yet for the next month, Herold's study was presented not just as fact, but as an understatement, by the *Guardian*, as well as the *New Jersey Star-Ledger*, the *Hartford Courant*, and several other newspapers. When news organizations on the ground later conducted their surveys of Afghan civilian deaths, most set the number at closer to 1,000. 11

But the typical group fact-check is not necessarily a matter of war. Bloggers were out in the lead in exposing the questionable research and behavior of gun-studying academics Michael Bellesiles and John Lott Jr. (the former resigned last year from Emory University after a blogger-propelled investigation found that he falsified data in his antigun book, *Arming America*; the latter, author of the pro-gun book *More Guns, Less Crime*, was forced by bloggers to admit that he had no copies of his own controversial self-defense study he had repeatedly cited as proving his case, and that he had masqueraded in online gun-rights discussions as a vociferous John Lott supporter named "Mary Rosh." The fact-checking bloggers have uncovered misleading use of quotations by opinion columnists, such as Maureen Dowd, and jumped all over the inaccurate or irresponsible comments of various 2004 presidential candidates. They have become part of the journalism conversation. 12

Breathing in Blogworld

Which is not to say that 90 percent of news-related blogs aren't crap. First of all, 90 percent of any new form of expression tends to be mediocre (think of band demos, or the cringe-inducing underground papers of years gone by), and judging a medium by its worst practitioners is not very sporting. Still, almost every criticism about blogs is valid — they often are filled with cheap shots, bad spelling, the worst kind of confirmation bias, and an extremely off-putting sense of self-worth (one that this article will do nothing to alleviate). But the "blogosphere," as many like to pompously call it, is too large and too varied to be defined as a single thing, and the action at the top 10 percent is among the most exciting new trends the profession has seen in a while. Are bloggers journalists? Will they soon replace newspapers?

13

The best answer to those two questions is: Those are two really dumb questions; enough hot air has been expended in their name already.

14

A more productive, tangible line of inquiry is: Is journalism being produced by blogs, is it interesting, and how should journalists react to it? The answers, by my lights, are "yes," "yes," and "in many ways." After a slow start, news organizations are beginning to embrace the form. . . . Tech journalists, such as the *San Jose Mercury News*'s Dan Gillmor, launched weblogs long before *blogger* was a household word. Beat reporting is a natural fit for a blog — reporters can collect standing links to sites of interest, dribble out stories and anecdotes that don't necessarily belong in the paper, and attract a specific like-minded readership. One of the best such sites going is the recently created California Insider blog by the *Sacramento Bee*'s excellent political columnist, Daniel Weintraub, who has been covering the state's wacky recall news like a blanket. Blogs also make sense for opinion publications, such as the *National Review*, the *American Prospect*, and my employer, *Reason*, all of which have lively sites.

15

For those with time to notice, blogs are also a great cheap farm system for talent. You've got tens of thousands of potential columnists writing for free, fueled by passion, operating in a free market where the cream rises quickly.

16

Best of all, perhaps, the phenomenon is simply entertaining. When do you last recall reading some writer and thinking "damn, he sure looks like he's having fun"? It's what buttoned-down reporters thought of their longhaired brethren back in the 1960s. The 2003 version may not be so immediately identifiable on sight — and that may be the most promising development of all. ■

17

■ **Thinking Critically about the Text**

What is Welch's purpose in this argument? (Glossary: *Purpose*) What audience do you think he had in mind? Why did he believe those readers would be interested in what he had to say? (Glossary: *Audience*)

▪ Examining the Issue

1. On what grounds were people dissatisfied with what they saw and read in the mainstream media after September 11, 2001, according to Welch?

2. Welch refers to the "great conversation" that occurred post–9/11. What does he mean by that term?

3. What, according to Welch, have bloggers contributed to journalism as a profession?

4. Welch writes that "reading the best of [journalistic blogs] is like receiving a bracing slap in the face. It's a reminder that America is far more diverse and iconoclastic than its newsrooms" (paragraph 4). On what evidence does he base his assessment?

5. Welch claims in paragraph 7 that the "specialization and filtering" that goes on in some blogs "is one of the form's key functions." What does he mean by *specialization* and *filtering*?

6. What evidence does Welch provide in paragraph 10 for his claim that the decentralized fact-checking that takes place with regard to information provided in blogs "can be an impressive thing to behold"?

7. Despite Welch's praise for what bloggers have brought to journalism, he freely admits in paragraph 13 that 90 percent of news-related blogs may be "crap." Why doesn't he consider that a bad thing? How does his concession on this point further support his argument for what's worthwhile in news-related blogs?

▪ Making Connections: Writing and Discussion Suggestions for "On Blogging"

The following questions are offered to help you start making meaningful connections among the three articles in this section. If you are writing an essay, be sure to make specific references to at least one of the articles. With several of the questions, some additional research may be required.

1. If you are a blogger, write an essay arguing against Andrew Keen's objections to Web 2.0. You may want to review Andrew Sullivan's arguments in favor of blogging as a new art form, unique in its context, style, and audience. Consider the following while planning your essay: Why do you blog? What does blogging allow you to do? What benefits have you derived from blogging? Has it taught you to be a better writer? What have you heard from those who read your blog, and what influence, if any, do their comments have on what you write and how you write it? Sullivan uses a jazz analogy to characterize blogging. Is there an analogy to another art form that might help characterize blogging for your readers?

2. Write an essay responding more generally to Andrew Keen's criticisms of Web 2.0. In what ways has Web 2.0 allowed you to be creative? In

what ways has Web 2.0 hampered your creativity? Has Web 2.0 been a positive or a negative force in developing your powers of critical thinking? Write an essay arguing for your point of view. You may wish to consult Keen's fuller argument against Web 2.0 in *The Cult of the Amateur: How the Internet Is Killing Our Culture* (2007).

3. If you aspire to be a news reporter or a journalist in some other capacity, does the current upheaval in the industry cause you concern or encourage you in your career goals? What effect do Matt Welch's views have on you?

4. Matt Welch argues that the feedback of vast audiences enjoyed by some bloggers tends to take the place of traditional fact-checking. Others have responded that false reporting is, in fact, very difficult to correct and that it is far better to be accurate from the start. (The same debate rages around the value of Wikipedia, another Web 2.0 institution.) Write an argument on the question of fact-checking and accuracy for both online and print-based publications.

5. **Writing with Sources.** Some have argued that Web 2.0 and blogging, in particular, have threatened the existence of newspapers. Do you agree, or might there be other reasons for the decline of newspapers? Do you believe that Americans have lost interest in the news? Research the subject and write an argumentative essay based on your findings. For documentation models and advice on working with sources, see Chapters 14 and 15.

ARGUMENT ROUNDTABLE: ALPHA WIVES: THE TREND AND THE TRUTH

When World War II began, American women entered the workforce in larger numbers than ever, taking the places of men who had gone off to serve in the armed forces. Most of the jobs held by these women were manual or clerical in nature, not what we would today call careers. After the war ended and the modern women's movement began in the 1960s, women were encouraged to take their rightful places alongside men by pursuing college educations, taking advanced degrees, and entering professional schools. Women pursued careers in business, law, health sciences, finance, engineering, research, and corporate management, and they worked long hours, traveled, were away from home for days or weeks, and discussed work-related issues over lunch or dinner with their associates much the same way men had been doing for as long as anyone could remember.

The world was clearly different for these women than it had been for their mothers and grandmothers. Those who were married and had families were challenged as they had never been before. They wanted to hold down responsible professional positions but still carry on the traditional duties of wives and mothers. As the popular expression has it, "They wanted it all."

Sociological studies that have appeared in the past forty years have documented those changes. Stresses have undoubtedly been put on many marriages, and the divorce rate has increased. How to explain this? Greater earning power has meant that some women are no longer trapped economically in unhappy marriages. Some men have become resentful of spouses who earn more than they do. Some women have become dissatisfied with mates who have not exhibited the same ambition and energy as they have or who are not willing to adjust to a new set of dynamics. Some men who think that household chores are not their responsibility have become unhappy with less-than-tidy homes but have not changed their own attitudes and behavior with respect to housework. Whether two-career couples will continue to struggle with this transition from "traditional" family roles remains to be seen.

On January 19, 2010, Richard Fry and D'Vera Cohn of the Pew Research Center published "Women, Men and the New Economics of Marriage," a research report on recent trends in marriage. (You can read the study in full at pewsocialtrends.org.) The report states that "in recent decades women have outpaced men in education and earnings growth" and the "unequal gains have been accompanied by gender role reversals in both the spousal characteristics and the economic benefits of marriage." In the past, the study continues, women benefited economically from marriage more than men did; in the last two decades, however, the economic gains of marriage have been "greater for men than women."

A week after the Pew report was published, the *New York Times* asked the following experts to comment on the study's findings in its *Room for Debate* blog:

- Stephanie Coontz, historian

- Claudia Goldin, professor of economics, Harvard University

- Ralph Richard Banks, professor at Stanford Law School

- Andrew J. Cherlin, professor of sociology, Johns Hopkins University

- Janet Reibstein, professor of psychology and author of *The Best Kept Secret* (a study of successful couples)

- Kathleen Gerson, professor of sociology, New York University

- Barbara Dafoe Whitehead, Institute for American Values

We present, as did the *Times*, the comments of these seven experts as a roundtable discussion, hoping that they encourage questions, arguments, and counterarguments, and thereby enlarge and enhance the discussion that should naturally follow from the report's findings.

▶ Women Finally Start to Catch Up

Stephanie Coontz

Stephanie Coontz teaches history at the Evergreen State College in Olympia, Washington. Her new book, *A Strange Stirring: The Feminine Mystique and American Women at the Dawn of the 1960s*, will be published by Basic Books in January 2011.

Women are not taking over the economy. Since 1970, the antidiscrimination laws won by the women's movement have allowed women to make real progress toward equality in wages with men. In the 1960s, the average woman with a college degree earned less than the average man with a high school degree. By 1990 female college grads finally earned more than men with only a high school degree. 1

But not until 2000 did the average earnings of female college graduates outpace the average earnings of men with SOME college education. Since more women have been getting college degrees in recent years, some women have begun to earn more than their husbands or other men their own age, but most wives do not earn more than their husbands. 2

> **Women today are far less likely than their forerunners in the Great Depression to consider it "unmanly" if their husband can't support his family.**

It is unfortunate — but not women's fault — that they have been catching up with a wage system that has, for most workers, essentially been standing still. 3

Over the past 30 years women's work has provided the margin of difference that allowed family income to keep expanding over the past 20 years, despite that overall stagnation. And with recent heavy losses in traditional male jobs, women have become the main earners in a significant minority of families. 4

Far from hurting men, the gains of the women's movement have helped families cope with tough economic trends that started long before this recession. And though economic stress coupled with rapid changes in marital roles can lead to tensions, most families know better than to start a gender war. 5

Women today are far less likely than their forerunners in the Great Depression to consider it "unmanly" if their husband can't support his 6 family on his own wages. And men today are far more likely to pitch in at home when their wives go to work.

Researchers have long noted this trend among educated husbands, but it is now spreading to other sectors of the population. In fact, a paper now being prepared by the researcher Oriel Sullivan for the April conference of the Council on Contemporary Families will show that in dual earner couples, husbands with the lowest educational levels now do as much if not more housework than their more educated counterparts.   7

There are lots of people or trends we might want to blame for our economic stresses. But women and the women's movement should not be included in that list, and most men know it.   8

The Benefits of the Breadwinning Wife

Claudia Goldin

Claudia Goldin is a professor of economics at Harvard University. She is the author, most recently, of *The Race Between Education and Technology*, with Lawrence F. Katz (2008).

Females have been the majority of college graduates ever since 1980. Yes, for *30 years*. It's not too surprising that the average wife is now more educated than her husband and that many wives are the main breadwinners. After all, women's labor force participation rates soared until the 1990s, even for those with infants, and unemployment rates are now higher for men.   1

> **More educated women are healthier, live longer, have healthier children, more stable marriages, and higher incomes.**

Why did women become more educated than men? Girls began to do better in high school math and science classes beginning in the 1970s and took more of them. Why that happened concerns changed expectations of their future employment, what I termed the "quiet revolution."   2

Girls performed better than boys in high school throughout U.S. history. The playing field became more level in the 1970s so they went to   3

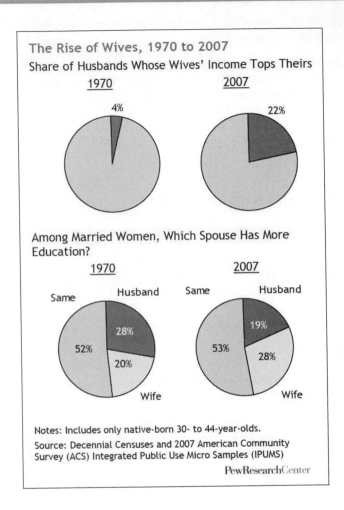

The Rise of Wives, 1970 to 2007
Share of Husbands Whose Wives' Income Tops Theirs

1970 — 4%

2007 — 22%

Among Married Women, Which Spouse Has More Education?

1970

Same — 52%
Husband — 28%
Wife — 20%

2007

Same — 53%
Husband — 19%
Wife — 28%

Notes: Includes only native-born 30- to 44-year-olds.

Source: Decennial Censuses and 2007 American Community Survey (ACS) Integrated Public Use Micro Samples (IPUMS)

PewResearchCenter

college at greater rates, did better there as well, and took more career-relevant courses.

The financial benefits from college are not much greater for females than they are for males, but women find it easier to do well in school. And for some women, especially those from more disadvantaged backgrounds, college provides added security for themselves and their children. Women, particularly those with kids, still earn less than men. A college education catapults even women into the upper middle class.   4

So, if these trends have continued for decades with deep historical roots, what's newsworthy? The implication of having more wives with greater education and earning power than their husbands holds interest.   5

I can foresee only beneficial effects. More educated women are healthier, live longer, have healthier children, more stable marriages, and higher incomes. Wives with more education and employment opportunities have greater bargaining power in the home (yes, men are doing a lot more at home). In the first half of the previous century women were more educated than were men but they did not have equality in the marketplace. Now they have both (or nearly so). Hurrah.

6

▶ The Marriage Decline

Ralph Richard Banks

Ralph Richard Banks is a professor at Stanford Law School and the author of the forthcoming book *Is Marriage for White People?*

The report by the Pew Research Center identifies a fundamental reconfiguration of marriage: As a consequence of increased education and greater access to high-paying jobs, wives are more likely than ever before to earn more and to be better educated than their husbands.

1

The increased percentage of wives who outearn their husbands signals the advent of more egalitarian marriages, a development that we should applaud. But if the experience of African Americans is any guide, the shifting relative status of men and women may also portend a threat to the stability and centrality of marriage in American society. The lingering discomfort among the couple, friends, or family with role reversal marriages is not the only or even primary difficulty in such relationships.

2

As I have discovered in the course of research for my forthcoming book, dramatic disparities in earnings and education often signify differences in values, a divide that is deeper and more intractable than any rift created simply by the fact that her paycheck is bigger than his. Attitudes toward education, how to spend money, goals for one's children, even leisure time activities — all reflect values that are shaped in part by one's educational experiences and professional environment.

3

Among African Americans, the group most likely to have role reversal marriages, such relationships often are conflict ridden and more likely to end in divorce than marriages where the partners are more economically

4

and educationally compatible. That role reversal marriages among African Americans have not worked is reflected, in part, in the fact that black married couples across the socioeconomic spectrum are more likely to divorce, by far, than any other group.

> Middle class black women are more unmarried than at any time since slavery and, as a result, have fewer children than any other group of women in our society.

The Pew report identifies another consequence   5 of the economic and educational ascendance of women relative to men: the decline in marriage. This change, too, is more stark among African Americans. While white Americans are much less likely to be married now than in 1970, what is most striking is that black women are only half as likely as white women to be married. According to the Pew Report fewer than one-third of black women between 30–44 years old are married.

The African American marriage decline is not   6 limited to the poor or economically marginal. Middle class black women are more unmarried than at any time since slavery and, as a result, have fewer children than any other group of women in our society. Black men, too, including those who are the best educated and most financially secure, are more likely than ever to be unmarried.

The causes of these shifts are complicated, and their consequences for African   7 Americans far-reaching. They also highlight a question that implicates us all: whether marriage will remain a bedrock social institution or whether African Americans are the canary in the coal mine heralding not just the reconfiguration but the reevaluation of marriage itself, the slow withering away of what we have always assumed to be a universal institution.

x

▶ The Housewife Anomaly

Andrew J. Cherlin

Andrew J. Cherlin is professor of sociology and public policy at Johns Hopkins University. He is the author, most recently, of *The Marriage-Go-Round*.

As with any major change, it will take some time for   1 Americans to adjust to the growth of marriages in which wives outearn their husbands. Initially, we will

> We are returning to the more typical kind of family in which women's work of all sorts — which now includes earning money — is crucial.

see some husbands with bruised egos, some wives who are anxious about their new status, and some marriages that cannot survive the reversal of roles. But the adjustment is likely to be easier and quicker than you might think.

First, the most unusual division of work between husbands and wives is not what is emerging today but rather what we celebrated in the 1950s.

The iconic breadwinner-homemaker marriage, which you can still view on YouTube videos of *Father Knows Best* episodes, was a new development in family life. In earlier times, when most people lived on farms, both the wife and husband did many kinds of important work. Husbands may have plowed the fields and built the barns, but their wives tended the vegetable gardens, milked the cows, helped with the harvests, and made everyone's clothes. Men knew that they could not lead a good life without a woman who shared the hard work.

The idea of a "housewife" who exclusively cared for the children and the home only emerged in the twentieth century as Americans migrated to cities and as factories replaced farms. What's happening today is that we are returning to the more typical kind of family in which women's work of all sorts — which now includes earning money—is crucial. That kind of family was fully accepted until the mid-twentieth century, and there is no reason to think it will be rejected now.

Second, the new stereotype of marriages in which the wife earns more than the husband — think of a hard-charging female corporate vice president married to a mildly successful office manager — is inaccurate. The Pew Center report released on January 19 shows that it's more common for wives to outearn husbands among couples where neither spouse has a college degree.

The typical case is more likely to be a female home health-care aide married to an intermittently employed construction worker. In marriages such as these, wives' earnings may exceed their husbands' but rarely by a huge amount. Both spouses will be at the mercy of an unreliable job market.

The result will be marriages in which wives and husbands share decision-making power rather than ones in which wives dominate. To be sure, our marriage culture needs to catch up to this change, but most men will eventually adapt to families in which father and mother jointly know best.

▶ It's about Respect

Janet Reibstein

Janet Reibstein is a professor of psychology at the University of Exeter in Britain. Her research and clinical work specializes in couples. She is the author of *The Best Kept Secret,* a study of resilience and success in couples published by Bloomsbury.

As women's economic and social standing has changed, so have their heterosexual relationships. Women want men "who will grow with them," in the words of Syreeta McFadden. But in the United States, Europe, and the rest of the developed word, fewer such men are developing in tandem with them.

Our now dominant model of marriage makes a priority of friendship, intimacy, and a more equal exchange of domestic labor and, crucially, respect. Research indicates that equality in a number of areas is associated with today's successful relationships: background, social class, and educational level among them. Respect for each other easily flows when these things roughly match.

> As the powerful woman becomes more common, she may be alluring to some men, but to other men this is a problem if it leads to an inequality of respect.

But women's increased economic power and social status has also led to the delay of first marriage, the rise in divorces, and a preference among both women and men not to get married at all, or cohabit, often serially. The reasons women who can be self-supporting might choose to be in a heterosexual relationship have changed from those of two generations ago: They want companionship, intimacy, and reliable support for the joint enterprise of living together.

A major sticking point arises when there are unequal sources of respect. Great differences within a couple in levels of education, social status, or income, for instance, thus pose problems. Additionally, men and women — even today — derive status and prestige differently. Today women can get it from jobs and also from being good mothers, being attractive, running efficient homes. Men's source of status and prestige is singular: their jobs. As the powerful woman becomes more common, she may be alluring to some men, but to other men this is a problem if it leads to an inequality of respect. Indeed, the decline in the number of marriages in some countries, the still high number of divorces, and the acceptability of serial cohabitations and singlehood (to a lesser extent, as both sexes still wish for committed relationships) have arisen in part because these can seem better choices for some women than picking men for whom respect will erode.

For couples in which the woman is the successful breadwinner, it is important to develop alternative sources of respect. The man who stays at home may be prized, for instance, if he has unusual powers and talents of empathy, a culturally valued quality. 5

The shift poses a larger question: Can we make the next cultural shift demanded by the effects of feminism? Can we now value in men what we also value in women? If we cannot, powerful women will lose their attraction to men, and women will be less likely to tolerate men who become potentially "lesser." 6

▶ No Role Reversals

Kathleen Gerson

Kathleen Gerson is a professor of sociology and Collegiate Professor of Arts and Science at New York University. She is the author of *The Unfinished Revolution: How a New Generation Is Reshaping Family, Work, and Gender in America.*

Every few years, a report reminds us that conventional wisdom is wrong. The "news" that more wives are outearning their husbands may surprise those who like to think that women are reluctant workers who are opting out and heading home. 1

Yet those who keep close track of the trends know that today's women, whether married or single, are shouldering more economic responsibilities for their families than ever before. Amid the recession — which some have called a "mancession" — women now make up close to half of all workers. Whatever term we choose, it's clear that the gender revolution is here to stay. Like water drawing back to reveal the shore before a tidal wave hits, uncertain economic times have made more visible what has been building for years. 2

Whether or not the decline of the traditional couple is "new" news, is it bad news or good? Many worry that the rise of women workers undermines men's sense of self and pushes them to leave women in the lurch. While this sometimes happens, such a scenario underestimates the resilience and flexibility of women and men alike. 3

New economic realities may be one factor driving changes in intimate relationships, but another is the strong and growing desire among new generations for equality and balance in marriage. Countless studies, including my own, find that most young people, regardless of gender, race, or the kind of family in which they grew up, support working mothers, want to balance work and caretaking, and hope to create an enduring egalitarian relationship.   4

> If we fail to help women and men create shared lives that integrate family and work in a flexible, egalitarian way, our worst fears may be realized.

If there is bad news here, it rests not with the values of today's young adults, but with the obstacles they face to achieving these ideals. Young women are more determined than ever to build careers and self-reliant lives, and young men now look to women to share in the financial responsibilities of family life, but everyone worries that dwindling job opportunities, time-greedy workplaces, and a dearth of child-rearing supports will put these goals out of reach.   5

Despite the obstacles, we can take heart in knowing that gender equality and family well-being are not in conflict. In a world where families increasingly depend on the earnings of women, the best way to promote family cohesion and satisfying marital relationships is to jettison outdated ideas about rigid gender differences and create the social supports that will allow new generations to bridge the work-family divide. If we fail to help women and men create shared lives that integrate family and work in a flexible, egalitarian way, our worst fears may be realized.   6

▶ Separate and Unequal Mating Markets

Barbara Dafoe Whitehead

Barbara Dafoe Whitehead directs the John Templeton Center for Thrift and Generosity at the Institute for American Values and is the coeditor of *Franklin's Thrift: The Lost History of an American Virtue.*

The Pew report sheds light on what is happening in two separate and unequal mating markets: the mating market for college-educated women and the mating market for   1 noncollege women. Virtually all of the media attention thus far has focused on what the report tells us about college women. But the more important story is what's going on with noncollege women.

It is certainly true that the percentage of young women with a college degree now exceeds the percentage of young men with a college degree. Some of these women are marrying down the educational ladder. Nevertheless, the fact remains that college-educated women are only a minority of all younger women, and of course, college-educated men are an even smaller minority of all younger men. Thus, of these two mating markets, the one that holds the much larger share of the younger generation is the noncollege market.

> For noncollege-educated women, marriage is becoming the exception rather than the rule.

For noncollege women, marriage is becoming the exception rather than the rule. Their mating pool consists mainly of noncollege men. And noncollege men are not attractive as prospective husbands for reasons that are already familiar. Their ability to support a wife and family has been declining for more than three decades, and public policies have done little to reverse this. Moreover, these men may be increasingly reluctant to take on the commitment to marry in the first place.

The ability to marry and stay married is a source of economic advantage. However, as the report demonstrates, this advantage has been moving beyond the reach of the nation's noncollege majority.

■ Thinking Critically about the Texts

1. Why did the *New York Times* ask this collection of authors to respond to the issues raised in the Pew Research study?
2. Do the respondents represent a real spectrum of possible perspectives on the issues? Explain.
3. Are some perspectives left out of the discussion? If so, what are those perspectives?
4. To what argument is Stephanie Coontz offering a counterargument in her last sentence?
5. What does Claudia Goldin mean by "the quiet revolution"?
6. If, as Claudia Goldin says, the trends reported in the Pew study have been present for decades, what's newsworthy?
7. For Ralph Richard Banks, "role reversal marriages [are] not the only or even primary difficulty in such relationships." What is, in his opinion? On what segment of the population is his opinion based?

8. Andrew J. Cherlin writes that the Pew study's "new stereotype of marriages in which the wife earns more than the husband — think of a hard-charging female corporate vice president married to a mildly successful office manager — is inaccurate" (paragraph 5). Why?

9. Janet Reibstein writes, "The reasons women who can be self-supporting might choose to be in a heterosexual relationship have changed from those of two generations ago" (paragraph 3). What does she mean by this? Do you agree with her? Why, or why not?

10. Kathleen Gerson asks whether the "news" in the Pew study is good or bad. What does she conclude? Do you agree?

11. What is Barbara Dafoe Whitehead's thesis? How do her comments refocus the discussion?

■ Examining the Issues

The writers who responded to the Pew study have touched on a number of issues related to the rise of the so-called Alpha Wife and the present state of American marriages. Now it's time for you to enter the conversation. Begin by recording your views in writing on any of the following:

- College-educated women and men make up a minority of the married couples in America.

- A man may/may not resent that his spouse earns more money than he does.

- Economic advantage for a woman or a man may be less important/more important now than ever before.

- The rise of feminism has strengthened/weakened marriage.

- Cultural differences between a man and a woman are more important to the success of a marriage than the earning power of a spouse is.

- Most women do not earn more than their husbands.

- Feminism and the women's movement have caused a "mancession."

- Men today contribute more, less, or about the same to household chores.

- Role-reversal marriages are more common among African Americans.

- Fewer black women (between 30–44 years old) and men are married than ever before since the time of slavery.

- Marriage among all segments of the population is a faltering institution.

- More Americans are college-educated than ever before, with women showing a greater percentage increase than men since 1970.

Now, imagine that you are going to submit your thoughts for publication on the *New York Times*: *Room for Debate* blog. Revise your draft so that your piece could take its place alongside the work of Coontz, Banks, Whitehead, and the rest.

WRITING SUGGESTIONS FOR ARGUMENTATION

1. Think of a product that you like and want to use even though it has an annoying feature. Write a letter of complaint in which you attempt to persuade the manufacturer to improve the product. Your letter should include the following points:

   a. A statement concerning the nature of the problem

   b. Evidence supporting or explaining your complaint

   c. Suggestions for improving the product

2. Select one of the position statements that follow, and write an argumentative essay in which you defend that statement.

   a. Living in a dormitory is (or is not) as desirable as living off campus.

   b. Student government shows (or does not show) that the democratic process is effective.

   c. America should (or should not) be a refuge for the oppressed.

   d. School spirit is (or is not) as important as it ever was.

   e. Interest in religion is (or is not) increasing in the United States.

   f. We have (or have not) brought air pollution under control in the United States.

   g. The need to develop alternative energy sources is (or is not) serious.

   h. America's great cities are (or are not) thriving.

   i. Fraternities and sororities do (or do not) build character.

   j. We have (or have not) found effective means to dispose of nuclear or chemical wastes.

   k. Fair play is (or is not) a thing of the past.

   l. Human life is (or is not) valued in a technological society.

   m. The consumer does (or does not) need to be protected.

   n. The family farm in America is (or is not) in danger of extinction.

   o. Grades do (or do not) encourage learning.

   p. America is (or is not) a violent society.

   q. Television is (or is not) a positive cultural force in America.

   r. America should (or should not) feel a commitment to the starving peoples of the world.

   s. The federal government should (or should not) regulate all utilities.

   t. Money is (or is not) the path to happiness.

   u. Animals do (or do not) have rights.

   v. Competition is (or is not) killing us.

   w. America is (or is not) becoming a society with deteriorating values.

3. Think of something on your campus or in your community that you would like to see changed. Write a persuasive argument that explains what is wrong and how you think it ought to be changed. Make sure you incorporate other writing strategies into your essay — for example, description, narration, or illustration — to increase the effectiveness of your persuasive argument. (Glossary: *Description; Illustration; Narration*)

4. Read some articles in the editorial section of today's paper, and pick one with which you agree or disagree. Write a letter to the editor that presents your point of view. Use a logical argument to support or refute the editorial's assertions. Depending on the editorial, you might choose to use different rhetorical strategies to reach your audience. (Glossary: *Audience*) You might use cause and effect, for example, to show the correct (or incorrect) connections made by the editorial. (Glossary: *Cause and Effect Analysis*)

5. **Writing with Sources.** Working with a partner, choose a controversial topic like the legalization of medical marijuana or any of the topics in writing suggestion 2. Each partner should argue one side of the issue. Decide who is going to write on which side of the issue, and keep in mind that there are often more than two sides to an issue. Then each of you should write an essay trying to convince your partner that your position is the most logical and correct.

   You'll both need to do research online or in the library to find support for your position. For advice on and documentation models for working with sources, see Chapters 14 and 15.

6. Take a close look at the public service advertisement in page 492. What kind of an argument does it represent? Is it effective, in your opinion? Why, or why not? If you were going to create an ad responding to this one — or an ad similarly warning against global warming — what would it look like?

7. Read or reread Michael Jonas's essay "The Downside of Diversity" on page 480 and discuss its relationship to the issues Steven Pinker raises in his essay "In Defense of Dangerous Ideas." Write an argument in which you make the case that Jonas supports Pinker's thesis that dangerous ideas need to be brought out into the open and discussed.

I was raised to believe that milk was part of a healthy diet. Then I discovered that to increase production, many dairy companies inject cows with hormones and antibiotics that we end up drinking. And that cows are kept "artificially" pregnant so they'll produce milk all year long. So I scrapped my milk mustache for a soy one. It's healthier for me AND the cows.

WHY MILK ?
Try soy instead.

CHAPTER 13

Combining Strategies

What Does It Mean to Combine Strategies?

Each of the preceding chapters of *Subject & Strategy* emphasizes a particular writing strategy: narration, description, illustration, process analysis, and so forth. The essays and selections within each of these chapters use the given strategy as the dominant method of development. It is important to remember, however, that the *dominant* strategy is rarely the *only* one used to develop a piece of writing. To fully explore their topics, writers often use other strategies in combination with the dominant strategy.

To highlight and reinforce this point, we focus on the use of multiple strategies in the Questions on Strategy section following each professional selection. In this chapter on combining strategies, we offer a collection of essays that make notable use of several different strategies. You will encounter such combinations of strategies in the reading and writing you do in other college courses. Beyond the classroom, you might write a business proposal using both description and cause and effect to make an argument for a new marketing plan, or you might use narration, description, and illustration to write a news story for a company newsletter or a letter to the editor of your local newspaper.

For an example of a visual text that combines strategies, see the advertisement on the opposite page. Few ad campaigns have been more successful than the California Milk Processor Board's "Got Milk?" promotion initiated in 1993. That campaign's use of celebrities, serial format, striking visuals, and pared-down, direct language made it instantly recognizable, and, inevitably, widely imitated. Among its many imitators is this Adbusters parody ad, "Why Milk?," which seeks to promote soy milk as a healthier alternative to cow's milk. While the Adbusters ad is primarily an argument for drinking soy milk and avoiding cow's milk, the ad copy and image of the soy-milk lover also implicitly rely for their impact on the strategies of narration, illustration, comparison and contrast, and cause and effect analysis.

Combining Strategies in Written Texts

The following essay by Sydney Harris reveals how several strategies can be used effectively, even in a brief piece of writing. Although primarily a work of definition, notice how "A Jerk" also uses illustration and personal narrative to engage the reader and achieve Harris's purpose.

A JERK

I don't know whether history repeats itself, but biography certainly does. The other day, Michael came in and asked me what a "jerk" was – the same question Carolyn put to me a dozen years ago.

At that time, I fluffed her off with some inane answer, such as "A jerk isn't a very nice person," but both of us knew it was an unsatisfactory reply. When she went to bed, I began trying to work up a suitable definition.

It is a marvelously apt word, of course. Until it was coined, not more than 25 years ago, there was really no single word in English to describe the kind of person who is a jerk – "boob" and "simp" were too old hat, and besides they really didn't fit, for they could be lovable, and a jerk never is.

Thinking it over, I decided that a jerk is basically a person without insight. He is not necessarily a fool or a dope, because some extremely clever persons can be jerks. In fact, it has little to do with intelligence as we commonly think of it; it is, rather, a kind of subtle but persuasive aroma emanating from the inner part of the personality.

I know a college president who can be described only as a jerk. He is not an unintelligent man, nor unlearned, nor even unschooled in the social amenities. Yet he is a jerk *cum laude*, because of a fatal flaw in his nature – he is totally incapable of looking into the mirror of his soul and shuddering at what he sees there.

A jerk, then, is a man (or woman) who is utterly unable to see himself as he appears to others. He has no grace, he is tactless without meaning to be, he is a bore even to his best friends, he is an egotist without charm. All of us are egotists to some extent, but most of us – unlike the jerk – are perfectly and horribly aware of it when we make asses of ourselves. The jerk never knows.

Essays that employ thoughtful combinations of rhetorical strategies have some obvious advantages for the writer and the reader. By reading the work of professional writers, you can learn how multiple strategies can be used to your advantage — how a paragraph of narration, a vivid description, a clarifying instance of comparison and contrast, or a clear definition can help convey your purpose and thesis.

For example, let's suppose you wanted to write an essay on the slang you hear on campus. You might find it helpful to use a variety of strategies.

Definition — to explain what slang is

Illustration — to give examples of slang

Comparison and contrast — to differentiate slang from other types of speech, such as idioms or technical language

Division and classification — to categorize different types of slang or different topics that slang terms are used for, such as courses, students, food, grades

Or let's say you wanted to write a paper on the Japanese Americans who were sent to internment camps during World War II while the United States was at war with Japan. The following strategies would be available to you.

Illustration — to illustrate several particular cases of families that were sent to internment camps

Narration — to tell the stories of former camp residents, including their first reaction to their internment and their actual experiences in the camps

Cause and effect — to examine the reasons why the United States government interned Japanese Americans and the long-term effects of this policy

When you rely on a single mode or approach to an essay, you lose the opportunity to come at your subject from a number of different angles, all of which complete the picture and any one of which might be the most insightful or engaging and, therefore, the most memorable for the reader. This is particularly the case with essays that attempt to persuade or argue. The task of changing readers' beliefs and thoughts is so difficult that writers look for any combination of strategies that will make their arguments more convincing.

Sample Student Essay Using a Combination of Strategies

While a senior at the University of Vermont, English major Tara E. Ketch took a course in children's literature and was asked to write a term paper on some aspect of the literature she was studying. She knew that she would soon be looking for a teaching position and realized that any teaching job she accepted would bring her face-to-face with the difficult task of selecting appropriate reading materials. Ketch understood, as well, that she would have to confront criticism of her choices, so she decided to delve a little deeper into the subject of censorship, particularly of literature for children and adolescents. She was interested in learning more about why people want to censor certain books so that she could consider an appropriate response to their efforts. In a way, she wanted to begin to develop her own teaching philosophy with respect to text selection. Her essay naturally incorporated several rhetorical modes working in combination. As you read Ketch's essay, notice how naturally she has used the supporting strategies of definition, cause and effect, and illustration to enhance the dominant strategy of argumentation.

Kids, You Can't Read That Book!
Tara E. Ketch

Definition of censorship and suggestion of cause and effect

Censorship is the restriction or suppression of speech or writing. In schools, debates about censorship arise when school officials, librarians, parents, or other adults in the community attempt to keep students from gaining access to particular books. Such attempts present serious questions for educators. How should educators decide what materials are fit for American schoolchildren? On what basis should they decide? A review of the reasons for challenges to books suggests that educators might forestall outright bans on books by paying more attention to age-appropriateness and to the kinds of guidance given to students who are reading challenging material. 1

Argument: Educators need to take steps to forestall outright censorship.

Illustration: Supreme Court decisions

The federal government has not set clear limits on censorship in the schools. In the 1968 case of *Epperson v. Arkansas*, the Supreme Court stated, "Public education in our Nation is committed to the control of state and local authorities. Courts do not and cannot intervene in the resolution of conflicts which arise in the daily operation of school systems and which do not directly and sharply implicate basic constitutional values" (Reichman 3). Yet in 1982, the Supreme Court ruled that "local school boards may not remove books from school library shelves simply because they dislike the ideas contained in those books and seek 2

Cause and effect: consequences of decisions

by their removal to prescribe what shall be orthodox in politics, nationalism, religion, or other matters of opinion" (Reichman 4). Different interpretations of rulings such as these have led to frequent efforts to ban children's books in school systems for a wide variety of reasons. Generally speaking, most attempts to ban books from school systems stem from the perception that the books offend community, family, or religious values.

Cause and effect: first ground for bans

Examples of challenges based on language

Challenges based on "offensive" or profane language are especially common in the area of adolescent literature. In the American Library Association's Office for Intellectual Freedom's (OIF) list of the most frequently challenged books from 1990–2000, J. D. Salinger's 1951 novel *Catcher in the Rye*, a perennial target of would-be censors, took the number thirteen slot, largely because of objections to its language, including the "F-word" (Office for Intellectual Freedom). In a debate about Katherine Paterson's 1977 novel *Bridge to Terabithia* (number nine on the OIF's list), one Lincoln, Nebraska, parent protested the use of the words *snotty* and *shut up* along with *Lord* and *damn*, saying, "Freedom of speech was not intended to guarantee schools the right to intrude on traditional family values without warning and regardless of the availability of nonoffensive alternatives" (Reichman 47–48). The school board in this case decided that the book had a value that transcended the use of offensive language.

3

Cause and effect: second ground for bans

Examples of challenges based on sexual content

Other challenges come from adults' idea that children should be protected from sexual content. Maya Angelou's 1969 autobiographical novel *I Know Why the Caged Bird Sings* (number three on the OIF's list) portrays rape, among other frankly sexual topics, and has since publication been banned from many school libraries and curricula. On what some would consider the opposite end of the spectrum, Maurice Sendak's 1970 illustrated book *In the Night Kitchen* (number twenty-five on the OIF list) shows a naked little boy, and although there is no explicit sexual content, many people have found the book offensive. According to an online exhibit at the site of the

4

University of Virginia Libraries, "[i]n Springfield, Missouri, the book was expurgated by drawing shorts on the nude boy" ("Through the Eyes"). In New York, in 1990, parents tried to have the book removed from an elementary school, and in Maine, a parent wanted the book removed because she felt it encouraged child molestation (Foerstel 201).

Additional examples

Many of Judy Blume's books have likewise come under fire for their portrayal of sexual themes: In fact, Blume has authored a total of five of the books on the OIF's top 100 list. *Are You There, God? It's Me, Margaret* (number sixty-two) has been banned for its frank discussion of menstruation and adolescent development. *Forever*, which discusses intercourse and abortion, comes in at number eight. These topics are clearly disturbing to many adults who grew up in environments where sex was not openly discussed and who may worry that these books will encourage sexual activity.

Cause and effect: clarification of reasoning underlying bans based on sexual content

A related source of debate is gay and lesbian content. (The OIF categorizes challenges based on homosexual content separately from those based on sexual explicitness.) Two children's books designed to explain gay lifestyles to children, Michael Willhoite's *Daddy's Roommate* and Leslea Newman's *Heather Has Two Mommies*, rank as number two and number eleven, respectively, on the OIF list. Henry Reichman writes that in 1990, Frank Mosca's *All-American Boys* (1983) and Nancy Garden's *Annie on My Mind* (1982), two books with gay themes, were donated to high schools in Contra Costa, California; at three of these high schools, the books were seized by administrators and then "lost" (53).

Cause and effect: third ground for bans

Examples of challenges based on gay/lesbian content

Religion, not surprisingly, has been the focus of many challenges to literature in the schools. The Bible's presence in the classroom has generated criticism from both religious and nonreligious groups: Those arguing from a religious perspective have objected when the Bible has been taught as literature, rather than as a sacred text, and those arguing from a secular perspective have objected to its being taught on any basis (Burress 219). Some

Cause and effect: fourth ground for bans

5

6

7

Examples of books banned on religious grounds

critics speaking from a religious perspective object to portrayals of the occult in books. The Harry Potter series (collectively number seven on the OIF list) is perhaps the most famous recent target of such objections, the latest of which was leveled by a Gwinnett County, Georgia, parent in 2005, whose lawsuit to have the books removed from county schools was dismissed in 2007 ("Harry Potter").

Cause and effect: fifth ground for bans

Example of challenge based on racism

Presentation of counter-argument

Another frequently cited reason for challenges to books is their portrayal of content considered to be racist or sexist. Mark Twain's *Adventures of Huckleberry Finn* (number five on the OIF list), the source of perhaps the most heated controversy of this type, has often been challenged and banned outright because of its use of racist language. Defenders of the text point out that such criticism ignores context and intent—Twain was writing specifically to draw negative attention to the South's racist attitudes and practices. Nevertheless, some critics claim that *any* use of such offensive terms, particularly in a text presented as a classic, can do more harm than good.

8

Argument: Age-appropriateness needs more attention from educators.

This brief review of some of the reasons used to ban children's books leaves us with the questions "How should educators decide what materials are fit for American schoolchildren?" and "On what basis should they decide?" It might be that the issue of age-appropriateness—the third most frequent reason given for challenges to books over the last decade and a half, according to the OIF—requires more attention than it gets from educators. A relatively large number of concerned adults seem interested not in banning books, necessarily, but in ensuring that the right books reach the right audiences in our schools.

9

Argument: appeals to common ground

Most educators likely agree that it is possible to identify age-appropriate (and age-inappropriate) themes in many of the books under discussion. Most would probably agree that elementary school children should not be exposed to the issues of rape and abortion present in some young-adult fiction. Many would rightly question whether young adults

10

should be exposed to extremely violent novels such as Anthony Burgess's *A Clockwork Orange*, given that they are still too young to put what they read into proper context. Does this mean, however, that such books should be removed altogether from school libraries? Perhaps not.

Argument (assumption): Censorship is contrary to aims of education.

Libraries and classrooms should be resources for children to broaden their horizons. Students need to learn about the range of human experience in order to make judgments about it; leaving them guessing, or gleaning what information they can from schoolyard conversations, will lead to misunderstood, or perhaps worse, half-understood "facts" of life. As Natalie Goldberg writes, "When we know the name of something . . . [i]t takes the blur out of our mind" (5)—and isn't that the purpose of an education?

11

Argument: Educators need to guide children in selecting and understanding material.

Support (expert opinion)

While outright censorship defeats the purpose of an education, educators must guide children in choosing age-appropriate material and then aid them in understanding material that might prove challenging. As Diane Ravitch writes, "Teachers have a responsibility to choose readings for their students based on their professional judgment of what students are likely to understand and what they need to learn" (506). If a child independently seeks out a controversial novel, educators should oversee the process, in order to give context to what might otherwise be a bewildering experience. In the case of a novel like *Catcher in the Rye,* which most critics agree has literary merit, but whose message is couched in profanity, it is the job of school educators to teach students how to read such literature critically and to understand the distance between the world of the novel and the student's own reality.

12

Examples of appropriate introduction of controversial literature

Similarly, novels like Maya Angelou's *I Know Why the Caged Bird Sings,* which have strong sexual content, need to be introduced to students old enough to understand something about mature sexual behavior, and discussion needs to focus on the meaning of the content within the world of the novel. Books with content deemed racist or

13

sexist should likewise not automatically be banned: Provided they have intrinsic merit, such books can be useful tools for increasing understanding in our society. Finally, while volatile religious topics are possibly best left outside of classroom discussion, children should have access to religious materials in school libraries in order to allow them to explore various systems of belief.

Conclusion   The efforts to censor what children read   14
can generate potentially explosive conflicts within schools and communities. Understanding the reasons that people seek to censor what children are reading in school will better prepare educators to respond to those efforts in a sensitive and reasonable manner. More importantly, educators will be able to provide the best learning environment for children, one that neither overly restricts the range of their reading nor exposes them, unaided, to material they have neither the experience nor the intellectual maturity to understand.

Works Cited

Burress, Lee. *Battle of the Books: Literary Censorship in the Public Schools, 1950-1985*. Metuchen: Scarecrow, 1989. Print.

Foerstel, Herbert N. *Banned in the USA: A Reference Guide to Book Censorship in Schools and Public Libraries*. Revised and expanded edition. London: Greenwood, 2002. Print.

Goldberg, Natalie. "Be Specific." *Language Awareness*. Ed. Paul Eschholz, Alfred Rosa, and Virginia Clark. 10th ed. Boston: Bedford, 2009. 4-5. Print.

"Harry Potter to Remain on Gwinnett County School Library Shelves." *School Library Journal* 31 May 2007: n. pag. Web. 23 Apr. 2008.

Office for Intellectual Freedom. "The 100 Most Frequently Challenged Books of 1990-2000 and Challenges by Initiator, Institution, Type, and Year." *ALA*. American Library Association, 2008. Web. 23 Apr. 2008.

Ravitch, Diane. "The Language Police." *Language Awareness*. Ed. Paul Eschholz, Alfred Rosa, and Virginia Clark. 10th ed. Boston: Bedford, 2009. 506–17. Print.

Reichman, Henry. *Censorship and Selection: Issues and Answers for Schools*. 3rd ed. Chicago: American Library Association, 2001. Print.

"Through the Eyes of a Child." *Censorship: Wielding the Red Pen*. The University of Virginia Libraries, 2000. Web. 23 Apr. 2008.

Analyzing Tara E. Ketch's Essay: Questions for Discussion

1. What is Ketch's thesis?

2. How do the two rulings of the U.S. Supreme Court on educational decisions within communities conflict with each other?

3. What reasons does Ketch give for the banning of children's and adolescents' books in schools?

4. How does Ketch answer the question "Should we censor children's books?" Do you agree with her?

Suggestions for Using a Combination of Strategies in an Essay

As you plan, write, and revise your essay using a combination of strategies, be mindful of the writing process guidelines described in Chapter 2. Pay particular attention to the basic requirements and essential ingredients of this writing strategy.

▪ Planning Your Combined Strategies Essay

Planning is an essential part of writing any good essay. You can save yourself a great deal of trouble by taking the time to think about the key building blocks of your essay before you actually begin to write. Before you can start combining strategies in your writing, it's essential that you have a firm understanding of the purposes and workings of each strategy. Once you become familiar with how the strategies work, you should be able to recognize ways to use and combine them in your writing.

Sometimes you will find yourself using a particular strategy almost intuitively. When you encounter a difficult or abstract term or concept — *liberal,* for example — you will define it almost as a matter of course. If you become perplexed because you are having trouble getting your readers to appreciate the severity of a problem, a quick review of the strategies will remind you that you could also use description and illustration.

Knowledge of the individual strategies is crucial because there are no formulas or prescriptions for combining strategies. The more you write and the more aware you are of the options available to you, the more skillful you will become at thinking critically about your topic, developing your ideas, and conveying your thoughts to your readers.

Determine Your Purpose.   The most common purposes in nonfiction writing are (1) to express your thoughts and feelings about a life experience, (2) to inform your readers by explaining something about the world around them, and (3) to persuade readers to embrace some belief or action. Your purpose will determine the dominant strategy you use in your essay.

If your major purpose is to tell a story of a river-rafting trip, you will primarily use narration. If you wish to re-create the experience of a famous landmark for the first time, you may find description most helpful. If you wish to inform your readers, you may find definition, cause and effect, process analysis, comparison and contrast, and/or division and classification to be best suited to your needs. If you wish to convince your readers of a certain belief or course of action, argumentation is an obvious choice.

Formulate a Thesis Statement.   Regardless of the purpose you have set for yourself in writing an essay, it is essential that you commit to a thesis statement, usually a one- or two-sentence statement giving the main point of your essay.

> Party primaries are an indispensable part of the American political process.

> Antibiotic use must be curtailed; because they have been overprescribed, antibiotics are not nearly as effective as they once were at combating infections among humans.

A question is not a thesis statement. If you find yourself writing a thesis statement that asks a question, answer the question first and then turn your answer into a thesis statement. A thesis statement can be presented anywhere in an essay, but usually it is presented at the beginning of a composition, sometimes after a few introductory sentences that set a context for it.

■ Organizing Your Combined Strategies Essay

Determine Your Dominant Strategy. Depending on your purpose for writing, your thesis statement, and the kinds of information you have gathered in preparing to write your essay, you may use any of the following strategies as the dominant strategy for your essay: narration, description, illustration, process analysis, comparison and contrast, division and classification, definition, cause and effect analysis, or argumentation.

Determine Your Supporting Strategies. The questions listed below — organized by rhetorical strategy — will help you decide which strategies will be most helpful to you in the service of the dominant strategy you have chosen for your essay and in achieving your overall purpose.

Narration. Are you trying to report or recount an anecdote, an experience, or an event? Does any part of your essay include the telling of a story (something that happened to you or to a person you include in your essay)?

Description. Does a person, a place, or an object play a prominent role in your essay? Would the tone, pacing, or overall purpose of your essay benefit from sensory details?

Illustration. Are there examples — facts, statistics, cases in point, personal experiences, interview quotations — that you could add to help you achieve the purpose of your essay?

Process analysis. Would any part of your essay be clearer if you included concrete directions about a certain process? Are there processes that readers would like to understand better? Are you evaluating any processes?

Comparison and contrast. Does your essay contain two or more related subjects? Are you evaluating or analyzing two or more people, places, processes, events, or things? Do you need to establish the similarities and differences between two or more elements?

Division and classification. Are you trying to explain a broad and complicated subject? Would it benefit your essay to reduce this subject to more manageable parts to focus your discussion?

Definition. Who is your audience? Does your essay focus on any abstract, specialized, or new terms that need further explanation so readers understand your point? Does any important word in your essay have many meanings and need to be clarified?

Cause and effect analysis. Are you examining past events or their outcomes? Is your purpose to inform, speculate, or argue about why an identifiable fact happens the way it does?

Argumentation. Are you trying to explain aspects of a particular subject, and are you trying to advocate a specific opinion on this subject or issue in your essay?

▪ Revising and Editing Your Combined Strategies Essay

Listen to What Your Classmates Have to Say. The importance of student peer conferences cannot be stressed enough, particularly as you revise and edit your essay. Others in your class will often see, for example, that the basis for your classification needs adjustment or that there are inconsistencies in your division categories that can easily be corrected — problems that you can't see yourself because you are too close to your essay. To maximize the effectiveness of work with your classmates, use the guidelines on page 29. Take advantage of suggestions when you know them to be valid, and make revisions accordingly.

Question Your Own Work While Revising and Editing. Revision is best done by asking yourself key questions about what you have written. Begin by reading, preferably aloud, what you have written. Reading aloud forces you to pay attention to every single word, and you are more likely to catch lapses in the logical flow of thought. After you have read your paper through, answer the following questions for revising and editing and make the necessary changes.

For help with twelve common writing problems, see Chapter 16, "Editing for Grammar, Punctuation, and Sentence Style."

Questions for Revising and Editing: Combining Strategies

1. Do I have a purpose for my essay?

2. Is my thesis statement clear?

3. Does my dominant strategy reflect my purpose and my thesis statement?

4. Do my subordinate strategies effectively support the dominant strategy of my essay?

5. Are my subordinate strategies woven into my essay in a natural manner?

6. Have I revised and edited my essay to avoid wordiness?   ＼E11

7. Have I used a variety of sentences to enliven my writing?   ＼E12

8. Have I avoided errors in grammar, punctuation, and mechanics?   ＼E1–10

On Dumpster Diving

LARS EIGHNER

Born in Texas in 1948, Lars Eighner attended the University of Texas–Austin. After graduation, he wrote essays and fiction, and several of his articles were published in magazines like *Threepenny Review*, the *Guide*, and *Inches*. A volume of short stories, *Bayou Boy and Other Stories*, was published in 1985. Eighner became homeless in 1988 when he left his job as an attendant at a mental hospital. The following piece, which appeared in the *Utne Reader*, is an abridged version of an essay that first appeared in *Threepenny Review*. The piece eventually became part of Eighner's startling account of the three years he spent as a homeless person, *Travels with Lizbeth* (1993). His publications include the novels *Pawn to Queen Four* (1995) and *Whispered in the Dark* (1996) and the nonfiction book *Gay Cosmos* (1995).

Eighner uses a number of rhetorical strategies in "On Dumpster Diving," but pay particular attention to how his process analysis of the "stages that a person goes through in learning to scavenge" contributes to the success of the essay as a whole.

■ Preparing to Read

Are you a pack rat, or do you get rid of what is not immediately useful to you? Outside of the usual kitchen garbage and empty toothpaste tubes, how do you make the decision to throw something away?

I began Dumpster diving about a year before I became homeless. 1

I prefer the term *scavenging*. I have heard people, evidently meaning to 2 be polite, use the word *foraging*, but I prefer to reserve that word for gathering nuts and berries and such, which I also do, according to the season and opportunity.

I like the frankness of the word *scavenging*. I live from the refuse of others. 3 I am a scavenger. I think it a sound and honorable niche, although if I could I would naturally prefer to live the comfortable consumer life, perhaps — and only perhaps — as a slightly less wasteful consumer owing to what I have learned as a scavenger.

Except for jeans, all my clothes come from Dumpsters. Boom boxes, 4 candles, bedding, toilet paper, medicine, books, a typewriter, a virgin male love doll, coins sometimes amounting to many dollars: All came from Dumpsters. And, yes, I eat from Dumpsters, too.

There is a predictable series of stages that a person goes through in learning to scavenge. At first the new scavenger is filled with disgust and self-loathing. He is ashamed of being seen.   5

This stage passes with experience. The scavenger finds a pair of running shoes that fit and look and smell brand-new. He finds a pocket calculator in perfect working order. He finds pristine ice cream, still frozen, more than he can eat or keep. He begins to understand: People do throw away perfectly good stuff, a lot of perfectly good stuff.   6

At this stage he may become lost and never recover: All the Dumpster divers I have known come to the point of trying to acquire everything they touch. Why not take it, they reason, it is all free. This is, of course, hopeless, and most divers come to realize that they must restrict themselves to items of relatively immediate utility.   7

> I live from the refuse of others. I am a scavenger.

The finding of objects is becoming something of an urban art. Even respectable, employed people will sometimes find something tempting sticking out of a Dumpster or standing beside one. Quite a number of people, not all of them of the bohemian type, are willing to brag that they found this or that piece in the trash.   8

But eating from Dumpsters is the thing that separates the dilettanti from the professionals. Eating safely involves three principles: using the senses and common sense to evaluate the condition of the found materials; knowing the Dumpsters of a given area and checking them regularly; and seeking always to answer the question "Why was this discarded?"   9

Yet perfectly good food can be found in Dumpsters. Canned goods, for example, turn up fairly often in the Dumpsters I frequent. I also have few qualms about dry foods such as crackers, cookies, cereal, chips, and pasta if they are free of visible contaminants and still dry and crisp. Raw fruits and vegetables with intact skins seem perfectly safe to me, excluding, of course, the obviously rotten. Many are discarded for minor imperfections that can be pared away.   10

A typical discard is a half jar of peanut butter — though nonorganic peanut butter does not require refrigeration and is unlikely to spoil in any reasonable time. One of my favorite finds is yogurt — often discarded, still sealed, when the expiration date has passed — because it will keep for several days, even in warm weather.   11

No matter how careful I am I still get dysentery at least once a month, oftener in warm weather. I do not want to paint too romantic a picture. Dumpster diving has serious drawbacks as a way of life.   12

I find from the experience of scavenging two rather deep lessons. The first is to take what I can use and let the rest go. I have come to think th there is no value in the abstract. A thing I cannot use or make useful, perhaps by trading, has no value, however fine or rare it may be.

The second lesson is the transience of material being. I do not suppose that ideas are immortal, but certainly they are longer-lived than material objects. 14

The things I find in Dumpsters, the love letters and rag dolls of so many lives, remind me of this lesson. Now I hardly pick up a thing without envisioning the time I will cast it away. This, I think, is a healthy state of mind. Almost everything I have now has already been cast out at least once, proving that what I own is valueless to someone. 15

I find that my desire to grab for the gaudy bauble has been largely sated. I think this is an attitude I share with the very wealthy — we both know there is plenty more where whatever we have came from. Between us are the rat-race millions who have confounded their selves with the objects they grasp and who nightly scavenge the cable channels for they know not what. 16

I am sorry for them. ■ 17

■ **Thinking Critically about the Text**

In paragraph 15, Eighner writes, "I hardly pick up a thing without envisioning the time I will cast it away. This, I think, is a healthy state of mind." React to this statement. Do you think such an attitude is healthy or defeatist? If many people thought this way, what impact would it have on our consumer society?

■ **Questions on Subject**

1. What stages do beginning Dumpster divers go through before they become what Eighner terms "professionals" (paragraph 9)? What examples does Eighner use to illustrate the passage through these stages? (Glossary: *Illustration*)
2. What three principles does one need to follow in order to eat safely from Dumpsters? What foods are best to eat from Dumpsters? What are the risks?
3. What two lessons has Eighner learned from his Dumpster diving experiences? Why are they significant to him?
4. Dumpster diving has had a profound effect on Eighner and the way he lives. How do his explanations of choices he makes, such as deciding which items to keep, enhance his presentation of the practical art of Dumpster diving?
5. How do you respond to Eighner's Dumpster-diving practices? Are you shocked? Bemused? Accepting? Challenged?

■ Questions on Strategy

1. Eighner's essay deals with both the immediate, physical aspects of Dumpster diving, such as what can be found in a typical Dumpster and the physical price one pays for eating out of them, and the larger, abstract issues that Dumpster diving raises, such as materialism and the transience of material objects. (Glossary: *Concrete/Abstract*) Why does he describe the concrete things before he discusses the abstract issues raised by their presence in Dumpsters? What does he achieve by using both types of elements?

2. Eighner's account of Dumpster diving focuses primarily on the odd appeal and interest inherent in the activity. Paragraph 12 is his one disclaimer, in which he states, "I do not want to paint too romantic a picture." Why does Eighner include this disclaimer? How does it add to the effectiveness of his piece? Why do you think it is so brief and abrupt?

3. Eighner uses many rhetorical techniques in his essay, but its core is a fairly complete process analysis of how to Dumpster dive. (Glossary: *Process Analysis*) Summarize this process analysis. Why do you think Eighner did not title the essay "How to Dumpster Dive"?

4. Discuss how Eighner uses illustration to bring the world of Dumpster diving to life. (Glossary: *Illustration*) What characterizes the examples he uses?

5. Writers often use process analysis in conjunction with other strategies, especially argument, to try to improve the way a process is carried out. (Glossary: *Argument; Process Analysis*) In this essay, Eighner uses a full process analysis to lay out his views on American values and materialism. How is this an effective way to combine strategies? Think of other arguments that could be strengthened if they included elements of process analysis.

■ Questions on Diction and Vocabulary

1. Eighner says he prefers the word *scavenging* to *Dumpster diving* or *foraging*. What do those three terms mean to him? Why do you think he finds the discussion of the terms important enough to include it at the beginning of his essay? (Glossary: *Diction*)

2. According to Eighner, "eating from Dumpsters is the thing that separates the dilettanti from the professionals" (paragraph 9). What do the words *dilettante* and *professional* connote to you? (Glossary: *Connotation/Denotation*) Why does Eighner choose to use them instead of the more straightforward *casual* and *serious*?

3. Eighner says, "The finding of objects is becoming something of an urban art" (paragraph 8). What does this sentence mean to you? Based on the essay, do you find his use of the word *art* appropriate when discussing any aspect of Dumpster diving? Why or why not?

▪ Classroom Activity for Combining Strategies

As a class, discuss the strategies that Eighner uses in his essay: narration, process analysis, cause and effect, illustration, and definition, for example. Where in the essay has he used each strategy and to what end? Has he used any other strategies not mentioned above? Explain.

▪ Writing Suggestions

1. Write a process analysis in which you relate how you acquire a consumer item of some importance or expense to you. (Glossary: *Process Analysis*) Do you compare brands, store prices, and so on? (Glossary: *Comparison and Contrast*) What are your priorities — must the item be stylish or durable, offer good overall value, give high performance? How do you decide to spend your money? In other words, what determines which items are worth the sacrifice?

2. In paragraph 3 Eighner states that he "live[s] from the refuse of others." How does his confession affect you? Do you think that we have become a throwaway society? If so, how? How do Eighner's accounts of homelessness and Dumpster diving make you feel about your own consumerism and trash habits? Write an essay in which you examine the things you throw away in a single day. What items did you get rid of? Why? Could those items be used by someone else? Have you ever felt guilty about throwing something away? If so, what was it and why?

3. One person's treasure is another person's trash. That is especially true around college campuses, when students who are moving often throw away their large — but frequently still useful — personal possessions. In the photograph on page 607 by Christopher S. Johnson, taken in Cambridge, Massachusetts, the college Dumpsters have obviously become points of interest for others in the community. Some view this as the purest form of recycling, and it underscores the transient nature of our material possessions. Choose a theme derived from the photograph and Eighner's essay — for example, the treasure/trash statement above or the transience of material goods — and write an essay developed by using at least three different strategies in combination.

On Not Winning the Nobel Prize

Doris Lessing

Doris Lessing is one of the most prolific writers of our time: She has written novels, short stories, poems, nonfiction, and science fiction, as well as plays, operas, essays, and reviews. She was born in Persia (present-day Iran) in 1919 to British parents who later settled in Rhodesia (present-day Zimbabwe) hoping to make their fortune raising maize. According to Lessing, she had few pleasures as a child, endured a stifling education, and finally in her teens rejected formal schooling in favor of self-education. She never went to college, preferring instead a series of practical jobs before beginning her professional writing career. Among her works are *The Grass Is Singing* (1950); *Martha Quest* (1952), the first of her five-volume Children of Violence series; *African Stories* (1964); *Briefing for a Descent into Hell* (1971); *Memoirs of a Survivor* (1974); *Shikasta* (1979), the first of her five-book science fiction series, Canopus in Argos: Archives; and *Under My Skin* (1994).

The Golden Notebook (1962) brought her instant fame and was quickly championed by feminists, recognition that made Lessing uneasy. Rather than a feminist tract, she avowed, the book was about personal struggles with society and freedom. Unmistakably, however, the work broke new ground with its female narrator's analysis of love, sex, maternity, politics, Africa, and the Communist Party and with its inventive structure and provocative style.

Lessing has won every major literary honor that Europe has to offer. In 2007 she was awarded the Nobel Prize for Literature, the oldest person, and the eleventh woman, to be so honored. In announcing the prize, the selection committee referred to Lessing as "that epicist of the female experience who with skepticism, fire, and visionary power has subjected a divided civilization to scrutiny."

Lessing makes her home in London, and though she is considered an English author, she continues to nurture her abiding passion for Africa and its peoples.

The following selection is an excerpt from Lessing's Nobel Prize acceptance speech. In the first part of her speech, Lessing describes Africans' thirst for books, focusing on a man who teaches himself to read using the labels on jars and cans and on others who, having received some books, are afraid to read them because they will become worn out and may not be replaced. This situation, which Lessing uses to represent that of all third world countries, stands in sharp contrast to the opportunities people in the West have to read, to write, and to connect with what Lessing refers to as the Great Tradition of cultural transmission and artistic inspiration. Lessing dedicates her title, "On Not Winning the Nobel Prize," to all those who will never win a prize for writing, either because they have been denied opportunities or because they are oblivious to the literary riches that surround them. In the part of the speech we have included here, Lessing tells a simple but profound story that bears witness to Africans' thirst for knowledge and the hope it represents.

■ Preparing to Read

Africa is a continent with fifty-three countries and over a billion people who speak approximately two thousand languages. What does Africa mean to you? Have you traveled there? Would you like to? Are you more intrigued or distressed by its people and its problems — the AIDS epidemic, for example, or its seemingly endless struggles for democracy and stability? How much do you know about Africa right now? Do you feel you ought to know more?

We are in a fragmenting culture, where our certainties of even a few decades ago are questioned and where it is common for young men and women, who have had years of education, to know nothing of the world, to have read nothing, knowing only some speciality or other, for instance, computers. 1

What has happened to us is an amazing invention — computers and the Internet and TV. It is a revolution. This is not the first revolution the human race has dealt with. The printing revolution, which did not take place in a matter of a few decades, but took much longer, transformed our minds and ways of thinking. A foolhardy lot, we accepted it all, as we always do, never asked, What is going to happen to us now, with this invention of print? In the same way, we never thought to ask, How will our lives, our way of thinking, be changed by this Internet, which has seduced a whole generation with its inanities so that even quite reasonable people will confess that once they are hooked, it is hard to cut free, and they may find a whole day has passed in blogging, etc. 2

Very recently, anyone even mildly educated would respect learning, education, and our great store of literature. Of course, we all know that when this happy state was with us, people would pretend to read, would pretend respect for learning. But it is on record that working men and women longed for books, and this is evidenced by the founding of working men's libraries and institutes, the colleges of the eighteenth and nineteenth centuries. 3

Reading, books, used to be part of a general education. 4

Older people, talking to young ones, must understand just how much of an education reading was, because the young ones know so much less. And if children cannot read, it is because they have not read. 5

We all know this sad story.   6

But we do not know the end of it.   7

We think of the old adage, "Reading maketh a full man" — and forgetting   8
about jokes to do with overeating — reading makes a woman and a man full
of information, of history, of all kinds of knowledge.

But we in the West are not the only people in the world. . . .   9

I would like you to imagine yourselves somewhere in southern Africa, stand-   10
ing in an Indian store, in a poor area, in a time of bad drought. There is a line
of people, mostly women, with every kind of container for water. This store
gets a bowser of precious water every afternoon from the town, and here the
people wait.

> **It is our stories that will re-create us, when we are torn, hurt, even destroyed.**

The Indian is standing with the heels of his   11
hands pressed down on the counter, and he is
watching a black woman, who is bending over a
wadge of paper that looks as if it has been torn
from a book. She is reading *Anna Karenina*. . . .

She is reading slowly, mouthing the words.   12
It looks a difficult book. This is a young woman
with two little children clutching at her legs. She
is pregnant. The Indian is distressed, because the
young woman's headscarf, which should be white, is yellow with dust. Dust
lies between her breasts and on her arms. This man is distressed because
of the lines of people, all thirsty. He doesn't have enough water for them.
He is angry because he knows there are people dying out there, beyond the
dust clouds. His older brother had been here holding the fort, but he had
said he needed a break, had gone into town, really rather ill, because of the
drought.

This man is curious. He says to the young woman, "What are you   13
reading?"

"It is about Russia," says the girl.   14

"Do you know where Russia is?" He hardly knows himself.   15

The young woman looks straight at him, full of dignity, though her eyes   16
are red from dust. "I was best in the class. My teacher said I was best."

The young woman resumes her reading. She wants to get to the end of   17
the paragraph.

The Indian looks at the two little children and reaches for some Fanta,   18
but the mother says, "Fanta makes them thirstier."

The Indian knows he shouldn't do this but he reaches down to a great   19
plastic container beside him, behind the counter, and pours out two mugs of
water, which he hands to the children. He watches while the girl looks at her
children drinking, her mouth moving. He gives her a mug of water. It hurts
him to see her drinking it, so painfully thirsty is she.

Now she hands him her own plastic water container, which he fills. The 20
young woman and the children watch him closely so that he doesn't spill any.

She is bending again over the book. She reads slowly. The paragraph fas- 21
cinates her and she reads it again.

> Varenka, with her white kerchief over her black hair, surrounded
> by the children and gaily and good-humoredly busy with them, and
> at the same visibly excited at the possibility of an offer of marriage
> from a man she cared for, looked very attractive. Koznyshev walked
> by her side and kept casting admiring glances at her. Looking at her,
> he recalled all the delightful things he had heard from her lips, all the
> good he knew about her, and became more and more conscious that
> the feeling he had for her was something rare, something he had felt
> but once before, long, long ago, in his early youth. The joy of being
> near her increased step by step, and at last reached such a point that,
> as he put a huge birch mushroom with a slender stalk and up-curling
> top into her basket, he looked into her eyes and, noting the flush of
> glad and frightened agitation that suffused her face, he was confused
> himself, and in silence gave her a smile that said too much.

This lump of print is lying on the counter, together with some old cop- 22
ies of magazines, some pages of newspapers with pictures of girls in bikinis.

It is time for the woman to leave the haven of the Indian store, and set off 23
back along the four miles to her village. Outside, the lines of waiting women
clamor and complain. But still the Indian lingers. . . .

She sends a thankful look to the Indian, whom she knew liked her and 24
was sorry for her, and she steps out into the blowing clouds.

The children are past crying, and their throats are full of dust. 25

This was hard, oh yes, it was hard, this stepping, one foot after another, 26
through the dust that lay in soft deceiving mounds under her feet. Hard, but
she was used to hardship, was she not? Her mind was on the story she had been
reading. She was thinking, She is just like me, in her white headscarf, and she is
looking after children, too. I could be her, that Russian girl. And the man there,
he loves her and will ask her to marry him. She had not finished more than
that one paragraph. Yes, she thinks, a man will come for me, and take me away
from all this, take me and the children, yes, he will love me and look after me.

She steps on. The can of water is heavy on her shoulders. On she goes. 27
The children can hear the water slopping about. Half way she stops, sets
down the can.

Her children are whimpering and touching it. She thinks that she cannot 28
open it, because dust would blow in. There is no way she can open the can
until she gets home.

"Wait," she tells her children, "wait." 29

She has to pull herself together and go on. 30

She thinks, My teacher said there is a library, bigger than the supermar- 31
ket, a big building and it is full of books. The young woman is smiling as she
moves on, the dust blowing in her face. I am clever, she thinks. Teacher said
I am clever. The cleverest in the school — she said I was. My children will be
clever, like me. I will take them to the library, the place full of books, and they
will go to school, and they will be teachers — my teacher told me I could be
a teacher. My children will live far from here, earning money. They will live
near the big library and enjoy a good life.

You may ask how that piece of the Russian novel ever ended up on that 32
counter in the Indian store.

It would make a pretty story. Perhaps someone will tell it. 33

On goes that poor girl, held upright by thoughts of the water she will give 34
her children once home, and drink a little of herself. On she goes, through
the dreaded dusts of an African drought. . . .

We are a jaded lot, we in our threatened world. We are good for irony and even 35
cynicism. Some words and ideas we hardly use, so worn out have they become.
But we may want to restore some words that have lost their potency.

We have a treasure-house of literature, going back to the Egyptians, the 36
Greeks, the Romans. It is all there, this wealth of literature, to be discovered
again and again by whoever is lucky enough to come upon it. A treasure.
Suppose it did not exist. How impoverished, how empty we would be.

We own a legacy of languages, poems, histories, and it is not one that will 37
ever be exhausted. It is there, always.

We have a bequest of stories, tales from the old storytellers, some of 38
whose names we know, but some not. The storytellers go back and back, to
a clearing in the forest where a great fire burns, and the old shamans dance
and sing, for our heritage of stories began in fire, magic, the spirit world. And
that is where it is held, today.

Ask any modern storyteller and they will say there is always a moment 39
when they are touched with fire, with what we like to call inspiration, and
this goes back and back to the beginning of our race, to the great winds that
shaped us and our world.

The storyteller is deep inside every one of us. The story maker is always with 40
us. Let us suppose our world is ravaged by war, by the horrors that we all of us
easily imagine. Let us suppose floods wash through our cities, the seas rise. But
the storyteller will be there, for it is our imaginations which shape us, keep us,
create us — for good and for ill. It is our stories that will re-create us, when we are
torn, hurt, even destroyed. It is the storyteller, the dream maker, the mythmaker,
that is our phoenix, that represents us at our best, and at our most creative.

That poor girl trudging through the dust, dreaming of an education for 41
her children, do we think that we are better than she is — we, stuffed full of
food, our cupboards full of clothes, stifling in our superfluities?

I think it is that girl . . . that may yet define us. 42

▪ Thinking Critically about the Text

Lessing tells of a woman struggling to read. What do you think we in the West can take away from her story?

▪ Questions on Subject

1. What does Lessing mean when she writes, "We are in a fragmenting culture" (paragraph 1)? Do you agree? Explain.
2. What does Lessing seem to think about the Internet and computers? What do you think her reasoning is? Explain.
3. Why does Lessing include the passage the African woman is reading from Tolstoy's novel *Anna Karenina*?
4. Do you think children are reading less today, as Lessing contends? If so, what is preventing them from reading?
5. What is the relationship between the young African woman and the Indian who runs the store? How, if at all, is that relationship tied to the passage from *Anna Karenina* that Lessing quotes?
6. Is Lessing generally pessimistic or optimistic about our future? Explain.

▪ Questions on Strategy

1. What is Lessing arguing for in her acceptance speech? (Glossary: *Argument*)
2. What patterns of development does Lessing use to make her argument? Explain how she combines those patterns.
3. On which of the three elements of argument — ethos, pathos, or logos — does Lessing's speech most heavily depend? Explain. (Glossary: *Ethos; Logos; Pathos*)
4. Does Lessing's title work? What does it mean? (Glossary: *Irony; Title*)

▪ Questions on Diction and Vocabulary

1. Refer to your desk dictionary to determine the meanings of the following words as they are used in this selection: *inanities* (paragraph 2), *bowser* (10), *wadge* (11), *haven* (23), *clamor* (23), *potency* (35), *phoenix* (40), *superfluities* (41).
2. In awarding Lessing the Nobel Prize, the Swedish Academy referred to her as an *epicist*. What did they mean by the term?

▪ Classroom Activity for Combining Strategies

Choose a local newspaper editorial dealing with a controversial social or educational problem. Outline the issues involved. Assuming that you have been given equal space in the newspaper to present an opposing viewpoint, make notes for a rebuttal argument and for the development strategies—say, narration, process analysis, comparison and contrast, and illustration—you might use to support it.

■ Writing Suggestions

1. Lessing argues for the importance of reading, writing, and acquiring knowledge. Write an essay in which you make your own case for the importance of connecting to the "great tradition" that she champions. In your response, try to situate the Internet and other newer technologies in relation to this tradition. In your opinion, do computers threaten the kinds of knowledge Lessing prizes, or should computers be considered part of the evolution of knowledge?

2. In her speech, Lessing makes a strong case for storytelling, an activity that many regard as entertainment. Write an essay that advocates for storytelling as more than more entertainment. What are the components of storytelling? How does storytelling reinforce cultural values and goals? How, for example, does storytelling teach about the past and the future; warn or encourage us; or help establish morals? What's lost when a culture stops telling stories? What's lost when a culture is too preoccupied to listen to or read its own stories?

Shooting an Elephant

GEORGE ORWELL

George Orwell (1903–1950) was capable of capturing the reader's imagination as few writers have ever done. Born in Bengal, India, but raised and educated in England, he chose to work as a civil servant in the British colonies after his schooling and was sent to Burma at nineteen as an assistant superintendent of police. Disillusioned by his firsthand experiences of public life under British colonial rule, he resigned in 1929 and returned to England to begin a career in writing. He captured the exotic mystery of life in the colonies, along with its many injustices and ironies, in such works as *Down and Out in Paris and London* (1933) and *The Road to Wigan Pier* (1937). His most famous books are *Animal Farm* (1945), a satire on the Russian Revolution, and *1984* (1949), a chilling novel set in an imagined totalitarian state of the future. Orwell maintained a lifelong interest in international social and political issues.

"Shooting an Elephant" was published in the British magazine *New Writing* in 1936. Adolf Hitler, Benito Mussolini, and Joseph Stalin were in power, building the "younger empires" that Orwell refers to in the second paragraph, and the old British Empire was soon to decline, as Orwell predicted. In this essay, Orwell tells of a time when, in a position of authority, he found himself compelled to act against his convictions.

■ Preparing to Read

Have you ever acted against your better judgment to save face with your friends or relatives? What motivated you to take the action that you did, and what did you learn from the experience?

In Moulmein, in Lower Burma, I was hated by large numbers of people — the   1
only time in my life that I have been important enough for this to happen to me. I was subdivisional police officer of the town, and in an aimless, petty kind of way anti-European feeling was very bitter. No one had the guts to raise a riot, but if a European woman went through the bazaars alone somebody would probably spit betel juice[1] over her dress. As a police officer I was an

---

1. The juice of an Asiatic plant whose leaves are chewed to induce narcotic effects. (Ed.)

obvious target and was baited whenever it seemed safe to do so. When a nimble Burman tripped me up on the football field and the referee (another Burman) looked the other way, the crowd yelled with hideous laughter. This happened more than once. In the end the sneering yellow faces of young men that met me everywhere, the insults hooted after me when I was at a safe distance, got badly on my nerves. The young Buddhist priests were the worst of all. There were several thousands of them in the town and none of them seemed to have anything to do except stand on street corners and jeer at Europeans.

All this was perplexing and upsetting. For at that time I had already made up my mind that imperialism was an evil thing and the sooner I chucked up my job and got out of it the better. Theoretically—and secretly, of course—I was all for the Burmese and all against the oppressors, the British. As for the job I was doing, I hated it more bitterly than I can perhaps make clear. In a job like that you see the dirty work of Empire at close quarters. The wretched prisoners huddling in the stinking cages of the lockups, the grey, cowed faces of the long-term convicts, the scarred buttocks of the men who had been flogged with bamboos—all these oppressed me with an intolerable sense of guilt. But I could get nothing into perspective. I was young and ill-educated and I had had to think out my problems in the utter silence that is imposed on every Englishman in the East. I did not even know that the British Empire is dying, still less did I know that it is a great deal better than the younger empires that are going to supplant it. All I knew was that I was stuck 2

> When I pulled the trigger I did not hear the bang or feel the kick—one never does when a shot goes home— but I heard the devilish roar of glee that went up from the crowd.

between my hatred of the empire I served and my rage against the evil-spirited little beasts who tried to make my job impossible. With one part of my mind I thought of the British Raj[2] as an unbreakable tyranny, as something clamped down, in *saecula saeculorum,*[3] upon the will of prostrate peoples; with another part I thought that the greatest joy in the world would be to drive a bayonet into a Buddhist priest's guts. Feelings like these are the normal byproducts of imperialism; ask any Anglo-Indian official, if you can catch him off duty.

One day something happened which in a roundabout way was enlightening. It was a tiny incident in itself, but it gave me a better glimpse than I had had before of the real nature of imperialism — the real motives for which despotic governments act. Early one morning the subinspector at a police station the other end of town rang me up on the phone and said that an elephant was ravaging the bazaar. Would I please come and do something about it? 3

---

2. British rule, especially in India.—Ed.
3. From time immemorial.—Ed.

I did not know what I could do, but I wanted to see what was happening and I got on to a pony and started out. I took my rifle, an old .44 Winchester and much too small to kill an elephant, but I thought the noise might be useful *in terrorem.* Various Burmans stopped me on the way and told me about the elephant's doings. It was not, of course, a wild elephant, but a tame one which had gone "must."[4] It had been chained up, as tame elephants always are when their attack of "must" is due, but on the previous night it had broken its chain and escaped. Its mahout,[5] the only person who could manage it when it was in that state, had set out in pursuit, but had taken the wrong direction and was now twelve hours' journey away, and in the morning the elephant had suddenly reappeared in the town. The Burmese population had no weapons and were quite helpless against it. It had already destroyed somebody's bamboo hut, killed a cow and raided some fruit stalls and devoured the stock; also it had met the municipal rubbish van and, when the driver jumped out and took to his heels, had turned the van over and inflicted violences upon it.

The Burmese subinspector and some Indian constables were waiting for me in the quarter where the elephant had been seen. It was a very poor quarter, a labyrinth of squalid bamboo huts, thatched with palmleaf, winding all over a steep hillside. I remember that it was a cloudy, stuffy morning at the beginning of the rains. We began questioning the people as to where the elephant had gone and, as usual, failed to get any definite information. That is invariably the case in the East; a story always sounds clear enough at a distance, but the nearer you get to the scene of events the vaguer it becomes. Some of the people said that the elephant had gone in one direction, some said that he had gone in another, some professed not even to have heard of any elephant. I had almost made up my mind that the whole story was a pack of lies, when we heard yells a little distance away. There was a loud, scandalized cry of "Go away, child! Go away this instant!" and an old woman with a switch in her hand came round the corner of a hut, violently shooing away a crowd of naked children. Some more women followed, clicking their tongues and exclaiming; evidently there was something that the children ought not to have seen. I rounded the hut and saw a man's dead body sprawling in the mud. He was an Indian, a black Dravidian coolie,[6] almost naked, and he could not have been dead many minutes. The people said that the elephant had come suddenly upon him round the corner of the hut, caught him with its trunk, put its foot on his back and ground him into the earth. This was the rainy season and the ground was soft, and his face had scored a trench a foot deep and a couple of yards long. He was lying on his belly with arms crucified and head sharply twisted to one side. His face was coated with mud, the eyes

4

---

4. That is, gone into an uncontrollable frenzy.—Ed.
5. The keeper and driver of an elephant.—Ed.
6. An unskilled laborer.—Ed.

wide open, the teeth bared and grinning with an expression of unendurable agony. (Never tell me, by the way, that the dead look peaceful. Most of the corpses I have seen looked devilish.) The friction of the great beast's foot had stripped the skin from his back as neatly as one skins a rabbit. As soon as I saw the dead man I sent an orderly to a friend's house nearby to borrow an elephant rifle. I had already sent back the pony, not wanting it to go mad with fright and throw me if it smelled the elephant.

The orderly came back in a few minutes with a rifle and five cartridges, 5 and meanwhile some Burmans had arrived and told us that the elephant was in the paddy fields below, only a few hundred yards away. As I started forward practically the whole population of the quarter flocked out of the houses and followed me. They had seen the rifle and were all shouting excitedly that I was going to shoot the elephant. They had not shown much interest in the elephant when he was merely ravaging their homes, but it was different now that he was going to be shot. It was a bit of fun to them, as it would be to an English crowd; besides they wanted the meat. It made me vaguely uneasy. I had no intention of shooting the elephant — I had merely sent for the rifle to defend myself if necessary — and it is always unnerving to have a crowd following you. I marched down the hill, looking and feeling a fool, with the rifle over my shoulder and an ever-growing army of people jostling at my heels. At the bottom, when you got away from the huts, there was a metalled road[7] and beyond that a miry waste of paddy fields a thousand yards across, not yet ploughed but soggy from the first rains and dotted with coarse grass. The elephant was standing eight yards from the road, his left side towards us. He took not the slightest notice of the crowd's approach. He was tearing up bunches of grass, beating them against his knees to clean them and stuffing them into his mouth.

I had halted on the road. As soon as I saw the elephant I knew with 6 perfect certainty that I ought not to shoot him. It is a serious matter to shoot a working elephant — it is comparable to destroying a huge and costly piece of machinery — and obviously one ought not to do it if it can possibly be avoided. And at that distance, peacefully eating, the elephant looked no more dangerous than a cow. I thought then and I think now that his attack of "must" was already passing off; in which case he would merely wander harmlessly about until the mahout came back and caught him. Moreover, I did not in the least want to shoot him. I decided that I would watch him for a little while to make sure that he did not turn savage again, and then go home.

But at that moment, I glanced round at the crowd that had followed 7 me. It was an immense crowd, two thousand at the least and growing every minute. It blocked the road for a long distance on either side. I looked at the sea of yellow faces above the garish clothes — faces all happy and excited over

---

7. A road made of broken or crushed stone.—Ed.

this bit of fun, all certain that the elephant was going to be shot. They were watching me as they would watch a conjuror about to perform a trick. They did not like me, but with the magical rifle in my hands I was momentarily worth watching. And suddenly I realized that I should have to shoot the elephant after all. The people expected it of me and I had got to do it; I could feel their two thousand wills pressing me forward, irresistibly. And it was at this moment, as I stood there with the rifle in my hands, that I first grasped the hollowness, the futility of the white man's dominion in the East. Here was I, the white man with his gun, standing in front of the unarmed native crowd — seemingly the leading actor of the piece; but in reality I was only an absurd puppet pushed to and fro by the will of those yellow faces behind. I perceived in this moment that when the white man turns tyrant it is his own freedom that he destroys. He becomes a sort of hollow, posing dummy, the conventionalized figure of a sahib.[8] For it is the condition of his rule that he shall spend his life in trying to impress the "natives," and so in every crisis he has got to do what the "natives" expect of him. He wears a mask, and his face grows to fit it. I had got to shoot the elephant. I had committed myself to doing it when I sent for the rifle. A sahib has got to act like a sahib; he has got to appear resolute, to know his own mind and do definite things. To come all that way, rifle in hand, with two thousand people marching at my heels, and then to trail feebly away, having done nothing — no, that was impossible. The crowd would laugh at me. And my whole life, every white man's life in the East, was one long struggle not to be laughed at.

But I did not want to shoot the elephant. I watched him beating his   8
bunch of grass against his knees, with that preoccupied grandmotherly air that elephants have. It seemed to me that it would be murder to shoot him. At that age I was not squeamish about killing animals, but I had never shot an elephant and never wanted to. (Somehow it always seems worse to kill a *large* animal.) Besides, there was the beast's owner to be considered. Alive, the elephant was worth at least a hundred pounds; dead, he would only be worth the value of his tusks, five pounds, possibly. But I had got to act quickly. I turned to some experienced-looking Burmans who had been there when we arrived, and asked them how the elephant had been behaving. They all said the same thing: He took no notice of you if you left him alone, but he might charge if you went too close to him.

It was perfectly clear to me what I ought to do. I ought to walk up to   9
within, say, twenty-five yards of the elephant and test his behavior. If he charged, I could shoot; if he took no notice of me, it would be safe to leave him until the mahout came back. But also I knew that I was going to do no such thing. I was a poor shot with a rifle and the ground was soft mud into which one would sink at every step. If the elephant charged and I missed him,

---

8. A title of respect when addressing Europeans in colonial India.—Ed.

I should have about as much chance as a toad under a steamroller. But even then I was not thinking particularly of my own skin, only of the watchful yellow faces behind. For at that moment, with the crowd watching me, I was not afraid in the ordinary sense, as I would have been if I had been alone. A white man mustn't be frightened in front of "natives"; and so, in general, he isn't frightened. The sole thought in my mind was that if anything went wrong those two thousand Burmans would see me pursued, caught, trampled on, and reduced to a grinning corpse like that Indian up the hill. And if that happened it was quite probable that some of them would laugh. That would never do. There was only one alternative. I shoved the cartridges into the magazine and lay down on the road to get a better aim.

The crowd grew very still, and a deep, low, happy sigh, as of people who   10
see the theater curtain go up at last, breathed from innumerable throats. They were going to have their bit of fun after all. The rifle was a beautiful German thing with cross-hair sights. I did not then know that in shooting an elephant one would shoot to cut an imaginary bar running from ear-hole to ear-hole. I ought, therefore, as the elephant was sideways on, to have aimed straight at his ear-hole; actually I aimed several inches in front of this, thinking the brain would be further forward.

When I pulled the trigger I did not hear the bang or feel the kick — one   11
never does when a shot goes home — but I heard the devilish roar of glee that went up from the crowd. In that instant, in too short a time, one would have thought, even for the bullet to get there, a mysterious, terrible change had come over the elephant. He neither stirred nor fell, but every line of his body had altered. He looked suddenly stricken, shrunken, immensely old, as though the frightful impact of the bullet had paralyzed him without knocking him down. At last, after what seemed a long time — it might have been five seconds, I dare say — he sagged flabbily to his knees. His mouth slobbered. An enormous senility seemed to have settled upon him. One could have imagined him thousands of years old. I fired again into the same spot. At the second shot he did not collapse but climbed with desperate slowness to his feet and stood weakly upright, with legs sagging and head drooping. I fired a third time. That was the shot that did for him. You could see the agony of it jolt his whole body and knock the last remnant of strength from his legs. But in falling he seemed for a moment to rise, for as his hind legs collapsed beneath him he seemed to tower upward like a huge rock toppling, his trunk reaching skywards like a tree. He trumpeted, for the first and only time. And then down he came, his belly towards me, with a crash that seemed to shake the ground even where I lay.

I got up. The Burmans were already racing past me across the mud. It   12
was obvious that the elephant would never rise again, but he was not dead. He was breathing very rhythmically with long rattling gasps, his great mound of a side painfully rising and falling. His mouth was wide open. I could see far down into caverns of pale pink throat. I waited a long time for him to die,

but his breathing did not weaken. Finally I fired my two remaining shots into the spot where I thought his heart must be. The thick blood welled out of him like red velvet, but still he did not die. His body did not even jerk when the shots hit him, the tortured breathing continued without a pause. He was dying, very slowly and in great agony, but in some world remote from me where not even a bullet could damage him further. I felt I had got to put an end to that dreadful noise. It seemed dreadful to see the great beast lying there, powerless to move and yet powerless to die, and not even to be able to finish him. I sent back for my small rifle and poured shot after shot into his heart and down his throat. They seemed to make no impression. The tortured gasps continued as steadily as the ticking of a clock.

In the end I could not stand it any longer and went away. I heard later 13
that it took him half an hour to die. Burmans were bringing dahs[9] and baskets even before I left, and I was told they had stripped his body almost to the bones by the afternoon.

Afterwards, of course, there were endless discussions about the shooting 14
of the elephant. The owner was furious, but he was only an Indian and could do nothing. Besides, legally I had done the right thing, for a mad elephant has to be killed, like a mad dog, if its owner fails to control it. Among the Europeans opinion was divided. The older men said I was right, the younger men said it was a damn shame to shoot an elephant for killing a coolie, because the elephant was worth more than any damn Coringhee coolie. And afterwards I was very glad that the coolie had been killed; it put me legally in the right and it gave me sufficient pretext for shooting the elephant. I often wondered whether any of the others grasped that I had done it solely to avoid looking a fool. ◾

---

9. Heavy knives.—Ed.

◾ Thinking Critically about the Text

Even though Orwell does not want to shoot the elephant, he does. How does he rationalize his behavior? On what grounds was Orwell legally in the right? What alternatives did he have? What do you think Orwell learned from this incident?

◾ Questions on Subject

1. What do you suppose would have happened had Orwell not sent for an elephant rifle?
2. What is imperialism, and what discovery about imperialism does Orwell make during the course of the event he narrates?

3. What does Orwell mean when he says, "I was very glad that the coolie had been killed" (paragraph 14)?
4. What is the point of Orwell's final paragraph? How does that paragraph affect your response to the whole essay?
5. Orwell wrote "Shooting an Elephant" some years after the event occurred. What does his account of the event gain with the passage of time? Explain.

■ Questions on Strategy

1. Why do you think Orwell is so meticulous in establishing the setting for his essay in paragraphs 1 and 2?
2. What do you think was Orwell's purpose in telling this story? (Glossary: *Purpose*) Cite evidence from the text that indicates to you that purpose. Does he accomplish his purpose?
3. Orwell is quick to capitalize on the ironies of the circumstances surrounding the events he narrates. (Glossary: *Irony*) Identify any circumstances you found ironic, and explain what this irony contributes to Orwell's overall purpose.
4. What part of the essay struck you most strongly? The shooting itself? Orwell's feelings? The descriptions of the Burmese and their behavior? What is it about Orwell's prose that enhances the impact of that passage for you? Explain.
5. "Shooting an Elephant" is, first of all, a narrative; Orwell has a story to tell. (Glossary: *Narration*) But Orwell uses other strategies in support of narration to help develop and give meaning to his story. Identify passages in which Orwell uses description, illustration, and cause and effect analysis, and explain how each enhances the incident he narrates. (Glossary: *Cause and Effect Analysis; Description; Illustration*)

■ Questions on Diction and Vocabulary

1. A British citizen, Orwell uses British English. Cite several examples of this British diction. How might an American say the same thing?
2. Identify several of the metaphors and similes that Orwell uses, and explain what each adds to his descriptions in this essay. (Glossary: *Figures of Speech*)
3. As a writer, Orwell always advocated using strong action verbs because they are vivid and eliminate unnecessary modification. (Glossary: *Verb*) For example, in paragraph 1 he uses the verb *jeer* instead of the verb *yell* plus the adverb *derisively*. Identify other strong verbs that you found particularly striking. What do these strong verbs add to Orwell's prose style?

■ Classroom Activity for Combining Strategies

Orwell's argument is couched in a very moving and affecting narrative replete with powerful descriptions. Think about how you might use narration to enhance an argument you have already written or are planning to write. How might your case, in effect, be made by telling a story — by showing rather than telling? Think about whether it would be more effective in your case to present your argument in one long narrative or to use several episodes to make your point. Discuss your approach with other members of your class to get their responses to your plans.

■ Writing Suggestions

1. Write an essay recounting a situation in which you felt compelled to act against your convictions. (Glossary: *Narration*) Before you start writing, you may find it helpful to consider one or more of the following questions and to review your Preparing to Read response for this essay. How can you justify your action? How much freedom of choice did you actually have, and what were the limits on your freedom? On what basis can you refuse to subordinate your convictions to others' or to society's?

2. Consider situations in which you have been a leader, like Orwell, or a follower. As a leader, what was your attitude toward your followers? As a follower, what did you feel toward your leader? Using Orwell's essay and your own experiences, what conclusions can you draw about leaders and followers? Write an essay in which you explore the relationship between leaders and followers.

A Modest Proposal

JONATHAN SWIFT

 One of the world's great satirists, Jonathan Swift was born in 1667 to English parents in Dublin, Ireland, and was educated at Trinity College. When his early efforts at a literary career in England met no success, he returned to Ireland in 1694 and was ordained an Anglican clergyman. From 1713 until his death in 1745, he was dean of Dublin's St. Patrick's Cathedral. A prolific chronicler of human folly, Swift is best known as the author of *Gulliver's Travels* and of the work included here, "A Modest Proposal."

In the 1720s Ireland had suffered several famines, but the English gentry, who owned most of the land, did nothing to alleviate the suffering of tenant farmers and their families; nor would the English government intervene. A number of pamphlets were circulated proposing solutions to the Irish problem.

"A Modest Proposal," published anonymously in 1729, was Swift's ironic contribution to the discussion.

■ Preparing to Read

Satire is a literary and dramatic art form wherein the shortcomings, foibles, abuses, and idiocies of both people and institutions are accented and held up for ridicule in order to shame their perpetrators into reforming themselves. Perhaps the very easiest way to see satire around us today is in the work of our political cartoonists. Think of individuals and institutions both here and abroad who today might make good subjects for satire.

> FOR PREVENTING THE CHILDREN OF POOR PEOPLE IN IRELAND
> FROM BEING A BURDEN TO THEIR PARENTS OR COUNTRY, AND
> FOR MAKING THEM BENEFICIAL TO THE PUBLIC

It is a melancholy object to those who walk through this great town[1] or travel in the country, when they see the streets, the roads, and cabin doors, crowded with beggars of the female sex, followed by three, four, or six children, all in rags and importuning every passenger for an alms. These mothers, instead of being able to work for their honest livelihood, are forced to

1

---

1. Dublin.—Ed.

employ all their time in strolling to beg sustenance for their helpless infants, who, as they grow up, either turn thieves for want of work, or leave their dear native country to fight for the Pretender in Spain, or sell themselves to the Barbadoes.[2]

2   I think it is agreed by all parties that this prodigious number of children in the arms, or on the backs, or at the heels of their mothers, and frequently of their fathers, is in the present deplorable state of the kingdom a very great additional grievance; and therefore whoever could find out a fair, cheap, and easy method of making these children sound, useful members of the commonwealth would deserve so well of the public as to have his statue set up for a preserver of the nation.

3   But my intention is very far from being confined to provide only for the children of professed beggars; it is of a much greater extent, and shall take in the whole number of infants at a certain age who are born of parents in effect as little able to support them as those who demand our charity in the streets.

4   As to my own part, having turned my thoughts for many years upon this important subject, and maturely weighed the several schemes of other projectors,[3] I have always found them grossly mistaken in their computation. It is true, a child just dropped from its dam may be supported by her milk for a solar year, with little other nourishment; at most not above the value of two shillings, which the mother may certainly get, or the value in scraps, by her lawful occupation of begging; and it is exactly at one year old that I propose to provide for them in such a manner as instead of being a charge upon their parents or the parish, or wanting food and raiment for the rest of their lives, they shall on the contrary contribute to the feeding, and partly to the clothing, of many thousands.

5   There is likewise another great advantage in my scheme, that it will prevent those voluntary abortions, and that horrid practice of women murdering their bastard children, alas, too frequent among us, sacrificing the poor innocent babes, I doubt, more to avoid the expense than the shame, which would move tears and pity in the most savage and inhuman breast.

6   The number of souls in this kingdom[4] being usually reckoned one million and a half, of these I calculate there may be about two hundred thousand couples whose wives are breeders; from which number I subtract thirty thousand couples who are able to maintain their own children, although I apprehend there cannot be so many under the present distresses of the kingdom; but this being granted, there will remain an hundred and seventy thousand

---

2. Many Irish Catholics were loyal to James Stuart, a claimant (or "pretender") to the English crown, and followed him into exile. Others, stricken by poverty, sold themselves into virtual slavery in order to escape to British colonies (like Barbadoes) in the New World.—Ed.

3. Proposers of solutions.—Ed.

4. Ireland.—Ed.

breeders. I again subtract fifty thousand for those women who miscarry, or whose children die by accident or disease within the year. There only remain an hundred and twenty thousand children of poor parents annually born. The question therefore is, how this number shall be reared and provided for, which, as I have already said, under the present situation of affairs, is utterly impossible by all the methods hitherto proposed. For we can neither employ them in handicraft or agriculture; we neither build houses (I mean in the country) nor cultivate land. They can very seldom pick up a livelihood by stealing till they arrive at six years old, except where they are of towardly parts;[5] although I confess they learn the rudiments much earlier, during which time they can however be looked upon only as probationers, as I have been informed by a principal gentleman in the county of Cavan, who protested to me that he never knew above one or two instances under the age of six, even in a part of the kingdom so renowned for the quickest proficiency in that art.

> A young healthy child well nursed is at a year old a most delicious, nourishing, and wholesome food, whether stewed, roasted, baked, or boiled. . . .

I am assured by our merchants that a boy or a girl before twelve years old is no salable commodity; and even when they come to this age they will not yield above three pounds, or three pounds and half a crown at most on the Exchange; which cannot turn to account either to the parents or the kingdom, the charge of nutriment and rags having been at least four times that value.   7

I shall now therefore humbly propose my own thoughts, which I hope will not be liable to the least objection.   8

I have been assured by a very knowing American of my acquaintance in London, that a young healthy child well nursed is at a year old a most delicious, nourishing, and wholesome food, whether stewed, roasted, baked, or boiled; and I make no doubt that it will equally serve in a fricassee or a ragout.[6]   9

I do therefore humbly offer it to public consideration that of the hundred and twenty thousand children, already computed, twenty thousand may be reserved for breed, whereof only one fourth part to be males, which is more than we allow to sheep, black cattle, or swine; and my reason is that these children are seldom the fruits of marriage, a circumstance not much regarded by our savages, therefore one male will be sufficient to serve four females. That the remaining hundred thousand may at a year old be offered in sale to the persons of quality and fortune through the kingdom, always advising the mother to let them suck plentifully in the last month, so as to render them plump and fat for a good table. A child will make two dishes at   10

---

5. Or "advanced for their age."—Ed.
6. Types of stews.—Ed.

an entertainment for friends; and when the family dines alone, the fore or hind quarter will make a reasonable dish, and seasoned with a little pepper or salt will be very good boiled on the fourth day, especially in winter.

I have reckoned upon a medium that a child just born will weigh twelve 11 pounds, and in a solar year if tolerably nursed increaseth to twenty-eight pounds.

I grant this food will be somewhat dear, and therefore very proper for 12 landlords, who, as they have already devoured most of the parents, seem to have the best title to the children.

Infant's flesh will be in season throughout the year, but more plentiful in 13 March, and a little before and after. For we are told by a grave author, an eminent French physician,[7] that fish being a prolific diet, there are more children born in Roman Catholic countries about nine months after Lent than at any other season; therefore, reckoning a year after Lent, the markets will be more glutted than usual, because the number of popish infants is at least three to one in this kingdom; and therefore it will have one other collateral advantage, by lessening the number of papists among us.

I have already computed the charge of nursing a beggar's child (in which 14 list I reckon all cottagers, laborers, and four fifths of the farmers) to be about two shillings per annum, rags included; and I believe no gentleman would repine to give ten shillings for the carcass of a good fat child, which, as I have said, will make four dishes of excellent nutritive meat, when he hath only some particular friend or his own family to dine with him. Thus the squire will learn to be a good landlord, and grow popular among the tenants; the mother will have eight shillings net profit, and be fit for work till she produces another child.

Those who are more thrifty (as I must confess the times require) may flay 15 the carcass; the skin of which artificially[8] dressed will make admirable gloves for ladies, and summer boots for fine gentlemen.

As to our city of Dublin, shambles[9] may be appointed for this purpose in 16 the most convenient parts of it, and butchers we may be assured will not be wanting; although I rather recommend buying the children alive, and dressing them hot from the knife as we do roasting pigs.

A very worthy person, a true lover of his country, and whose virtues 17 I highly esteem, was lately pleased in discoursing on this matter to offer a refinement upon my scheme. He said that many gentlemen of this kingdom, having of late destroyed their deer, he conceived that the want of venison might be well supplied by the bodies of young lads and maidens, not exceeding fourteen years of age nor under twelve, so great a number of both sexes

---

7. François Rabelais (c. 1494–1553), a French satirist—not at all "grave"—whom Swift admired for his broad humor and sharp wit.—Ed.
8. Skillfully, artfully.—Ed.
9. Slaughterhouses.—Ed.

in every county being now ready to starve for want of work and service; and these to be disposed of by their parents, if alive, or otherwise by their nearest relations. But with due deference to so excellent a friend and so deserving a patriot, I cannot be altogether in his sentiments; for as to the males, my American acquaintance assured me from frequent experience that their flesh was generally tough and lean, like that of our schoolboys, by continual exercise, and their taste disagreeable; and to fatten them would not answer the charge. Then as to the females, it would, I think with humble submission, be a loss to the public, because they soon would become breeders themselves: and besides, it is not improbable that some scrupulous people might be apt to censure such a practice (although indeed very unjustly) as a little bordering upon cruelty; which, I confess, hath always been with me the strongest objection against any project, how well soever intended.

But in order to justify my friend, he confessed that this expedient was put 18 into his head by the famous Psalmanazar,[10] a native of the island Formosa, who came from thence to London above twenty years ago, and in conversation told my friend that in his country when any young person happened to be put to death, the executioner sold the carcass to persons of quality as a prime dainty; and that in his time the body of a plump girl of fifteen, who was crucified for an attempt to poison the emperor, was sold to his Imperial Majesty's prime minister of state, and other great mandarins of the court, in joints from the gibbet, at four hundred crowns. Neither indeed can I deny that if the same use were made of several plump young girls in this town, who without one single groat to their fortunes cannot stir abroad without a chair, and appear at the playhouse and assemblies in foreign fineries which they never will pay for, the kingdom would not be the worse.

Some persons of a desponding spirit are in great concern about that vast 19 number of poor people who are aged, diseased, or maimed, and I have been desired to employ my thoughts what course may be taken to ease the nation of so grievous an encumbrance. But I am not in the least pain upon that matter, because it is very well known that they are every day dying and rotting by cold and famine, and filth and vermin, as fast as can be reasonably expected. And as to the younger laborers, they are now in almost as hopeful a condition. They cannot get work, and consequently pine away for want of nourishment to a degree that if at any time they are accidentally hired to common labor, they have not strength to perform it; and thus the country and themselves are happily delivered from the evils to come.

I have too long digressed, and therefore shall return to my subject. I 20 think the advantages by the proposal which I have made are obvious and many, as well as of the highest importance.

---

10. George Psalmanazar (c. 1679–1763), a French imposter who fooled London society with his tales of human sacrifice and cannibalism on Formosa.—Ed.

For first, as I have already observed, it would greatly lessen the number of Papists, with whom we are yearly overrun, being the principal breeders of the nation as well as our most dangerous enemies; and who stay at home on purpose to deliver the kingdom to the Pretender, hoping to take their advantage by the absence of so many good Protestants, who have chosen rather to leave their country than stay at home and pay tithes against their conscience to an Episcopal curate. 21

Secondly, the poorer tenants will have something valuable of their own, which by law may be made liable to distress,[11] and help to pay their landlord's rent, their corn and cattle being already seized and money a thing unknown. 22

Thirdly, whereas the maintenance of an hundred thousand children, from two years old and upwards, cannot be computed at less than ten shillings a piece per annum, the nation's stock will be thereby increased fifty thousand pounds per annum, besides the profit of a new dish introduced to the tables of all gentlemen of fortune in the kingdom who have any refinement in taste. And the money will circulate among ourselves, the goods being entirely of our own growth and manufacture. 23

Fourthly, the constant breeders, besides the gain of eight shillings sterling per annum by the sale of their children, will be rid of the charge of maintaining them after the first year. 24

Fifthly, this food would likewise bring great custom to taverns, where the vintners will certainly be so prudent as to procure the best receipts for dressing it to perfection, and consequently have their houses frequented by all the fine gentlemen, who justly value themselves upon their knowledge in good eating; and a skillful cook, who understands how to oblige his guests, will contrive to make it as expensive as they please. 25

Sixthly, this would be a great inducement to marriage, which all wise nations have either encouraged by rewards or enforced by laws and penalties. It would increase the care and tenderness of mothers toward their children, when they were sure of a settlement for life to the poor babes, provided in some sort by the public, to their annual profit instead of expense. We should see an honest emulation among the married women, which of them could bring the fattest child to the market. Men would become as fond of their wives during the time of their pregnancy as they are now of their mares in foal, their cows in calf, or sows when they are ready to farrow; nor offer to beat or kick them (as is too frequent a practice) for fear of a miscarriage. 26

Many other advantages might be enumerated. For instance, the addition of some thousand carcasses in our exportation of barreled beef, the propagation of swine's flesh, and improvement in the art of making good bacon, so much wanted among us by the great destruction of pigs, too frequent at 27

---

11. Subject to seizure by creditors.—Ed.

our tables, which are no way comparable in taste or magnificence to a well-grown, fat, yearling child, which roasted whole will make a considerable figure at a lord mayor's feast or any other public entertainment. But this and many others I omit, being studious of brevity.

Supposing that one thousand families in this city would be constant customers for infants' flesh, besides others who might have it at merry meetings, particularly weddings and christenings, I compute that Dublin would take off annually about twenty thousand carcasses, and the rest of the kingdom (where probably they will be sold somewhat cheaper) the remaining eighty thousand. **28**

I can think of no one objection that will possibly be raised against this proposal, unless it should be urged that the number of people will be thereby much lessened in the kingdom. This I freely own, and it was indeed one principal design in offering it to the world. I desire the reader will observe, that I calculate my remedy for this one individual kingdom of Ireland and for no other that ever was, is, or I think ever can be upon earth. Therefore let no man talk to me of other expedients: of taxing our absentees at five shillings a pound: of using neither clothes nor household furniture except what is of our own growth and manufacture: of utterly rejecting the materials and instruments that promote foreign luxury: of curing the expensiveness of pride, vanity, idleness, and gaming in our women: of introducing a vein of parsimony, prudence, and temperance: of learning to love our country, in the want of which we differ even from Laplanders and the inhabitants of Topinamhoo:[12] of quitting our animosities and factions, nor acting any longer like the Jews, who were murdering one another at the very moment their city was taken:[13] of being a little cautious not to sell our country and conscience for nothing: of teaching landlords to have at least one degree of mercy toward their tenants: lastly, of putting a spirit of honesty, industry, and skill into our shopkeepers; who, if a resolution could now be taken to buy only our native goods, would immediately unite to cheat and exact upon us in the price, the measure, and the goodness, nor could ever yet be brought to make one fair proposal of just dealing, though often and earnestly invited to it. **29**

Therefore I repeat, let no man talk to me of these and the like expedients, till he hath at least some glimpse of hope that there will ever be some hearty and sincere attempt to put them in practice. **30**

But as to myself, having been wearied out for many years with offering vain, idle, visionary thoughts, and at length utterly despairing of success, I fortunately fell upon this proposal, which, as it is wholly new, so it hath **31**

---

12. In other words, even from Laplanders who love their icy tundra and primitive Brazilian tribes who love their jungle.—Ed.

13. Swift refers to the Roman siege of Jerusalem in A.D. 70; the inhabitants lost the city because they dissolved into violent factions.—Ed.

something solid and real, of no expense and little trouble, full in our own power, and whereby we can incur no danger in disobliging England. For this kind of commodity will not bear exportation, the flesh being of too tender a consistence to admit a long continuance in salt, although perhaps I could name a country which would be glad to eat up our whole nation without it.

After all, I am not so violently bent upon my own opinion as to reject any 32 offer proposed by wise men, which shall be found equally innocent, cheap, easy, and effectual. But before something of that kind shall be advanced in contradiction to my scheme, and offering a better, I desire the author or authors will be pleased maturely to consider two points. First, as things now stand, how they will be able to find food and raiment for an hundred thousand useless mouths and backs. And secondly, there being a round million of creatures in human figure throughout this kingdom, whose sole subsistence put into a common stock would leave them in debt two millions of pounds sterling, adding those who are beggars by profession to the bulk of farmers, cottagers, and laborers, with their wives and children who are beggars in effect; I desire those politicians who dislike my overture, and may perhaps be so bold to attempt an answer, that they will first ask the parents of these mortals whether they would not at this day think it a great happiness to have been sold for food at a year old in the manner I prescribe, and thereby have avoided such a perpetual scene of misfortunes as they have since gone through by the oppression of landlords, the impossibility of paying rent without money or trade, the want of common sustenance, with neither house nor clothes to cover them from the inclemencies of the weather, and the most inevitable prospect of entailing the like or greater miseries upon their breed forever.

I profess, in the sincerity of my heart, that I have not the least personal 33 interest in endeavoring to promote this necessary work, having no other motive than the public good of my country, by advancing our trade, providing for infants, relieving the poor, and giving some pleasure to the rich. I have no children by which I can propose to get a single penny; the youngest being nine years old, and my wife past childbearing.

■ **Thinking Critically about the Text**

Satire often has a "stealth quality" about it; that is, the audience for it often does not realize at first that the author of the satire is not being serious. At some point in the satire the audience usually catches on and then begins to see the larger issue at the center of the satire. At what point in your reading did you begin to catch on to Swift's technique and larger, more important, message?

▪ Questions on Subject

1. What problem is being addressed in this essay? Describe the specific solution being proposed. What are the proposal's "advantages" (paragraph 20)?
2. What "other expedients" (29) are dismissed as "vain, idle, visionary thoughts" (31)? What do paragraphs 29 through 31 tell you about Swift's purpose? (Glossary: *Purpose*)
3. Describe the "author" of the proposal. Why does Swift choose such a character to present this plan? When can you detect Swift's own voice coming through?
4. What is the meaning and the significance of the title? (Glossary: *Title*)
5. In paragraph 2 Swift talks of making Ireland's "children sound, useful members of the commonwealth." In what way is this statement ironic? Cite several other examples of Swift's irony. (Glossary: *Irony*)

▪ Questions on Strategy

1. Toward what belief and/or action is Swift attempting to persuade his readers? How does he go about doing so? For example, did you feel a sense of outrage at any point in the essay? Did you feel that the essay was humorous at any point? If so, where and why?
2. What is the effect of the first paragraph of the essay? How does it serve to introduce the proposal? (Glossary: *Beginnings/Endings*)
3. What strategies does Swift use in this essay to make his proposer sound like an authority? Explain how this sense of authority relates to Swift's real purpose.
4. In what ways can the argument presented in this essay be seen as logical? What is the effect, for example, of the complicated calculations in paragraph 6?
5. What strategies, in addition to argumentation, does Swift use to develop his satire? Cite examples to support your answer. (Glossary: *Argument*)

▪ Questions on Diction and Vocabulary

1. It is not easy to summarize Swift's tone in a single word, but how would you describe the overall tone he establishes? Point to specific passages in the essay where you find his language particularly effective.
2. What is Swift's intent in using the term *modest*? (Glossary: *Purpose*)
3. In paragraph 6 Swift refers to women as "breeders." In terms of his proposal, why is the diction appropriate? (Glossary: *Diction*) Cite other examples of such diction used to describe the poor people of Ireland.

▪ Classroom Activity for Combining Strategies

Imagine that you will write a satire based on the model of Swift's "A Modest Proposal." Think in terms of attacking the foolish thinking or absurdity of a situation you find on the national, state, or local level and how your satire will get people to think about that issue in productive ways. What additional strategies might you employ to accomplish your satire? Discuss your possible approaches to this assignment with other members of your class.

▪ Writing Suggestions

1. **Writing with Sources.** Write a modest proposal of your own to solve a difficult social or political problem of the present day or, on a smaller scale, a problem you see facing your school or community. Do some research on your topic in the library or online.

   For models of and advice on integrating sources, see Chapters 14–15.

2. **Writing with Sources.** What is the most effective way to bring about social change and to influence societal attitudes? Would Swift's methods work today, or would they have to be significantly modified? Concentrating on the sorts of changes you have witnessed over the last ten years, write an essay in which you describe how best to influence public opinion. Do some research on your topic in the library or online.

   For models of and advice on integrating sources, see Chapters 14–15.

WRITING SUGGESTIONS FOR COMBINING STRATEGIES

1. Select a piece you have written for this class in which you used one primary writing strategy, and rewrite it using another. For example, choose a description you wrote and redraft it as a process analysis. Remember that the choice of a writing strategy influences the writer's "voice" — a descriptive piece might be lyrical, while a process analysis might be straightforward. How does your voice change along with the strategy? Does your assumed audience change as well? (Glossary: *Audience*)

    If time allows, exchange a piece of writing with a partner, and rewrite it using a different strategy. Discuss the choices you each made.

2. Select an essay you have written this semester, either for this class or another class. What was the primary writing strategy you used? Build on this essay by integrating another strategy. For example, if you wrote an argument paper for a political science class, you might try using narrative to give some historical background to the paper. (Glossary: *Argument; Narration*) For a paper in the natural sciences, you could use subjective description to open the paper up to non-scientists. (Glossary: *Objective/Subjective*) When you're finished ask yourself: How did use of the new strategy affect your paper?

3. The choice of a writing strategy reflects an author's voice — the persona he or she assumes in relation to the reader. Read back through any personal writing you've done this semester — a journal, letters to friends, e-mail. Can you identify the strategies you use outside of formal academic writing, as part of your natural writing voice? Write a few pages analyzing these strategies and your writing voice, using one of the rhetorical strategies studied this term. For example, you could compare and contrast your e-mail postings to your letters home. (Glossary: *Comparison and Contrast*) Or you could do a cause and effect analysis of how being at college has changed the tone or style of your journal writing. (Glossary: *Cause and Effect Analysis*)

4. **Writing with Sources.** Review the "Why Milk?" ad that opens this chapter (page 588). Write an essay in which you discuss the ad and the issues that underlie it. As you work, consider these questions: What are the potentially harmful effects of producing milk by using hormones and antibiotics? Of drinking such milk? If you agree that change is needed, explain what you would change and how. If you disagree with the ad, respond to the implicit claims of those who *do* call for change. Consider placing your argument in the context of economic, social, scientific, ethical, or ideological discussions of modern agriculture, the environment, health, diet, capitalism, advertising, political correctness, or another related topic that interests you.

    You will need to do some research to bolster your claims. For advice about and models of writing with sources, see Chapters 14 and 15.

CHAPTER 14

Writing with Sources

What Does It Mean to Write with Sources?

Many of your college assignments will call upon you to do research and write using information from sources. In order to do this effectively, you will have to learn some basic research practices — locating and evaluating print and online sources, taking notes from those sources, and documenting those sources. (For help with these basics, see Chapter 15, "A Brief Guide to Researching and Documenting Essays," pages 682–705.) Even more fundamental than this, however, is to understand what it *means* to do research and to write with sources.

Your purpose in writing with sources is not to present a collection of quotations that report what others have said about your topic. Rather, your goal is to *analyze*, *evaluate*, and *synthesize* the materials you have researched so that you become a full-fledged participant in the conversation about your topic. In order to enter into this conversation with authority, you will have to learn how to use soures both ethically and effectively. To help you on your way, this chapter provides advice on summarizing, paraphrasing, and quoting sources, on integrating sources, and on avoiding plagiarism. In addition, two student papers and two professional essays model different ways of engaging meaningfully with sources and of reflecting that engagement in writing.

Writing with Sources

Outside sources can be used to:

- Support your thesis and points with statements from noted authorities
- Offer memorable wording of key terms or ideas
- Extend your ideas by introducing new information
- Articulate opposing positions for you to argue against

Consider Sharon Begley's use of an outside source in the following paragraph from her *Newsweek* essay "Praise the Humble Dung Beetle":

> Of all creatures great and small, it is the charismatic megafauna — tigers and rhinos and gorillas and pandas and other soulful-eyed, warm, and fuzzy animals — that personify endangered species. That's both a shame and a dangerous bias. "Plants and invertebrates are the silent majority which feed the entire planet, stabilize the soil, and make all life possible," says Kiernan Suckling, cofounder of the Center for Biological Diversity. They pollinate crops and decompose carcasses, filter water and, lacking weapons like teeth and claws, brew up molecules to defend themselves that turn out to be remarkably potent medicines: The breast-cancer compound taxol comes from a yew tree, and a leukemia drug from the rosy periwinkle. Those are tricks that, Suckling dryly notes, "polar bears and blue whales haven't mastered yet."

Here Begley quotes Kiernan Suckling, a biologist specializing in biodiversity, to support her contention that it's "both a shame and a dangerous bias" to have tigers, polar bears, and other photogenic mammals be the headliners for all endangered species.

In the following passage from "Blaming the Family for Economic Decline," Stephanie Coontz uses outside sources to present the position that she will argue against.

> The fallback position for those in denial about the socioeconomic transformation we are experiencing is to admit that many families are in economic stress but to blame their plight on divorce and unwed motherhood. Lawrence Mead of New York University argues that economic inequalities stemming from differences in wages and employment patterns "are now trivial in comparison to those stemming from family structure." David Blankenhorn claims that the "primary fault line" dividing privileged and nonprivileged Americans is no longer "race, religion, class, education, or gender" but family structure. Every major newspaper in the country has published editorials and opinion pieces along these lines. This "new consensus" produces a delightfully simple, inexpensive solution to the economic ills of America's families. From Republican Dan Quayle to the Democratic Party's Progressive Policy Institute, we hear the same words: "Marriage is the best antipoverty program for children."
>
> Now I am as horrified as anyone by irresponsible parents who yield to the temptations of our winner-take-all society and abandon their family obligations. But we are kidding ourselves if we think the solution to the economic difficulties of America's children lies in getting their parents back together. Single-parent families, it is true, are five to six times more likely to be poor than two-parent ones. But correlations are not the same as causes. The association between poverty and single parenthood has several different

sources, suggesting that the battle to end child poverty needs to be fought on a number of different fronts.

By letting the opposition articulate their own position, Coontz reduces the possibility of being criticized for misrepresenting her opponents; at the same time, she sets herself up to give strong voice to her thesis.

Learning to Summarize, Paraphrase, and Quote from Your Sources

When taking notes from your sources, you must decide whether to summarize, paraphrase, or quote directly. The approach you take is largely determined by the content of the source passage and the way you envision using it in your paper. Be aware, however, that making use of all three of these techniques — rather than relying on only one or two — will keep your text varied and interesting.

Learning to summarize, paraphrase, and quote effectively and correctly is essential for the writing you'll do in school, at work, and in everyday life. The following sections will help you understand how the three techniques differ, when to use these techniques, and how to make them work within the context of your writing.

■ Summarizing

When you *summarize* material from one of your sources, you use your own words to capture in condensed form the essential idea of a passage, article, or entire chapter. Summaries are particularly useful when you are working with lengthy, detailed arguments or long passages of narrative or descriptive background information not germane to the overall thrust of your paper. You simply want to capture the essence of the passage while dispensing with the details because you are confident that your readers will readily understand the point being made or will not need to be convinced about the validity of the point. Because you are distilling information, a summary is always shorter than the original; often a chapter or more can be reduced to a paragraph, or several paragraphs to a sentence or two. Remember, in writing a summary you should use your own words.

Consider the following paragraphs in which Richard Lederer compares big words with small words.

> When you speak and write, there is no law that says you have to use big words. Short words are as good as long ones, and short, old words — like *sun* and *grass* and *home* — are best of all. A lot of small words, more than you might think, can meet your needs with a strength, grace, and charm that large words do not have.
> Big words can make the way dark for those who read what you write and hear what you say. Small words cast their clear light on

big things—night and day, love and hate, war and peace, and life and death. Big words at times seem strange to the eye and the ear and the mind and the heart. Small words are the ones we seem to have known from the time we were born, like the hearth fire that warms the home.

— RICHARD LEDERER,
"The Case for Short Words," pages 519–20

A student wishing to capture the gist of Lederer's point without repeating his detail wrote the following summary:

Lederer favors short words for their clarity, familiarity, durability, and overall usefulness (519–20).

■ Paraphrasing

When you *paraphrase* a source, you restate the information in your own words instead of quoting directly. Unlike a summary, which gives a brief overview of the essential information in the original, a paraphrase seeks to maintain the same level of detail as the original to aid readers in understanding or believing the information presented. A summary, then, condenses the original material, while a paraphrase presents the original information in approximately the same number of words as the original.

Paraphrase can be thought of as a sort of middle ground between summary and quotation, but beware: While a paraphrase should closely parallel the presentation of ideas in the original it should not use the same words or sentence structure as the original. Even though you are using your own words in a paraphrase, it's important to remember that you are borrowing ideas and therefore must acknowledge the source of these ideas with a citation.

How would you paraphrase the following passage from a speech by Martin Luther King Jr.?

But one hundred years later [after the Emancipation Proclamation], we must face the tragic fact that the Negro is still not free. One hundred years later, the life of the Negro is still sadly crippled by the manacles of segregation and the chains of discrimination. One hundred years later, the Negro lives on a lonely island of poverty in the midst of a vast ocean of material prosperity. One hundred years later, the Negro is still languishing in the corners of American society and finds himself an exile in his own land.

— MARTIN LUTHER KING JR.,
"I Have a Dream," page 525

The following illustrates how one student paraphrased the passage from King's speech.

Speaking on the one hundredth anniversary of the Emancipation Proclamation, King observed that African Americans still found themselves a marginalized people. He contended that African Americans did not experience the freedom that other Americans did—in a land of opportunity and plenty, racism and poverty affected the way they lived their lives, separating them from mainstream society (525).

In most cases, it is better to summarize or paraphrase materials — which by definition means using your own words — instead of quoting verbatim (word for word). Capturing an idea in your own words ensures that you have thought about and understood what your source is saying.

■ Using Direct Quotation

You should reserve direct quotation for important ideas stated memorably, for especially clear explanations by authorities, and for arguments by proponents of a particular position. Consider, for example, how author Malcolm Jones captures Charles Darwin's mixed emotions upon realizing the impact his theory of evolution would have on the world:

> As delighted as he was with his discovery, Darwin was equally horrified, because he understood the consequences of his theory. Mankind was no longer the culmination of life but merely part of it; creation was mechanistic and purposeless. In a letter to a fellow scientist, Darwin wrote that confiding his theory was "like confessing a murder." Small wonder that instead of rushing to publish his theory, he sat on it—for 20 years.
>
> —MALCOLM JONES,
> "Who Was More Important: Lincoln or Darwin?," page 307

The skillful prose Jones uses to describe Darwin's state of mind makes this passage well worth quoting in full, rather than summarizing or paraphrasing it.

On occasion, you'll find a useful passage with some memorable phrases in it. Avoid the temptation to quote the whole passage; instead you can combine summary or paraphrase with direct quotation. Consider, for example, the following paragraph from Rosalind Wiseman's essay on schoolgirls' roles in cliques.

> Information about each other is currency in Girl World. The Banker creates chaos everywhere she goes by banking information about girls in her social sphere and dispensing it at strategic intervals for her own benefit. For instance, if a girl has said something negative about another girl, the Banker will casually mention it to someone in conversation because she knows it's going to cause a conflict and strengthen her status as someone "in the know." She can get girls to trust her because when she pumps them for information it doesn't seem like gossip; instead, she does it in an innocent, I'm-trying-to-be-your-friend way.
>
> — ROSALIND WISEMAN,
> "The Queen Bee and Her Court," page 349

Note how one student cited this passage using paraphrase *and* quotation.

> In Wiseman's schema, the most dangerous character in the clique
> is the Banker, who "creates chaos everywhere she goes by banking
> information about girls in her social sphere and dispensing it at strate-
> gic intervals for her own benefit" (349). The Banker spreads gossip freely
> in order to cement her position as someone "'in the know'" (349).

Be sure that when you directly quote a source, you copy the words *exactly* and put quotation marks around them. Check and double-check your copy for accuracy, whether it's handwritten, transcribed, or cut-and-pasted from the original source.

■ Integrating Borrowed Material into Your Text

Whenever you use borrowed material, be it a quotation, paraphrase, or summary, your goal is to integrate it smoothly and logically so as not to disrupt the flow of your paper or to confuse your readers. It is best to introduce such material with a *signal phrase*, which alerts readers that borrowed information is about to be presented. A signal phrase minimally consists of the author's name and a verb (e.g., *Michael Pollan contends*).

How well you integrate a quote, paraphrase, or summary into your paper depends partly on varying your signal phrases and, in particular, choosing verbs for these signal phrases that accurately convey the tone and intent of the writers you are citing. Signal phrases help readers better follow your train of thought. If a writer is arguing, use the verb *argues* (or *asserts*, *claims*, or *contends*); if the writer is contesting a particular position or fact, use the verb *contests* (or *denies*, *disputes*, *refutes*, or *rejects*). In using verbs that are specific to the situation in your paper, you bring your readers into the intellectual debate as well as avoid the monotony of repeating such all-purpose verbs as *says* or *writes*.

The following are just a few examples of how you can vary signal phrases to add interest to your paper.

> Malcolm X confesses that . . .

> As professor of linguistics at Georgetown University Deborah Tannen
> has observed . . .

> Bruce Catton, noted Civil War historian, emphasizes . . .

> Rosalind Wiseman rejects the widely held belief that . . .

> Robert Ramírez enriches our understanding of . . .

> Carolina A. Miranda, a Latina living and working in New York City,
> explores . . .

Here are other verbs that you might use when constructing signal phrases.

acknowledges	declares	points out
adds	endorses	reasons
admits	grants	reports
believes	implies	responds
compares	insists	suggests
confirms		

Signal phrases also let your reader know exactly where your ideas end and someone else's begin. Never confuse your reader by inserting a quotation that appears suddenly without introduction in your paper. Unannounced quotations leave your reader wondering how the quoted material relates to the point you are trying to make.

Unannounced Quotation

It's no secret that digital technology is having profound effects on American society, often shaping our very attitudes about the world. We're living at a time when this technology makes it not only possible, but also surprisingly easy for us to copy and share software, music, and video. Is this a good situation? Software and music companies see such copying as theft or a violation of copyright law. "[M]any of my students see matters differently. They freely copy and share music. And they copy and share software, even though such copying is often illegal" (418).

In the following revision, the student integrated the quotation from Gorry's essay by giving the name of the writer being quoted, referring to his authority on the subject, noting that the writer is speaking from experience, and using the verb *counters*.

Integrated Quotation

It's no secret that digital technology is having profound effects on American society, often shaping our very attitudes about the world. We're living at a time when this technology makes it not only possible, but also surprisingly easy for us to copy and share software, music, and video. Is this a good situation? Software and music companies see such copying as theft or a violation of copyright law. "[M]any of my students see matters differently," counters information technology specialist and Rice University professor G. Anthony Gorry. "They freely copy and share music. And they copy and share software, even though such copying is often illegal" (418).

Avoiding Plagiarism

The importance of honesty and accuracy in doing library research can't be stressed enough. Any material borrowed word for word must be placed within quotation marks and properly cited; any idea, explanation, or argument you have paraphrased or summarized must be documented, and it must be clear where the paraphrased material begins and ends. In short, to use someone else's ideas, whether in their original form or in an altered form, without proper acknowledgment is to be guilty of plagiarism.

You must acknowledge and document the source of your information whenever you do any of the following:

- Quote a source word for word.

- Refer to information and ideas from another source that you present in your own words, as either a paraphrase or a summary.

- Cite statistics, tables, charts, graphs, or other visuals.

You do not need to document the following types of information:

- Your own observations, experiences, ideas, and opinions

- Factual information available in a number of sources (information known as "common knowledge")

- Proverbs, sayings, or familiar quotations

For a discussion of MLA-style in-text documentation, see pages 694–95.

The Council of Writing Program Administrators offers the following helpful definition of *plagiarism* in academic settings for administrators, faculty, and students: "In an instructional setting, plagiarism occurs when a writer deliberately uses someone else's language, ideas, or other (not common knowledge) material without acknowledging its source." Note, however, that accusations of plagiarism can be substantiated even if plagiarism is accidental. A little attention and effort at the note-taking stage can go a long way toward eliminating the possibility of such inadvertent plagiarism. While taking notes, check all direct quotations against the wording of the original, and double-check your paraphrases to be sure that you have not used the writer's wording or sentence structure. It is easy to forget to put quotation marks around material taken verbatim or to use the same sentence structure and most of the same words — substituting a synonym here and there — and record it as a paraphrase. In working closely with the ideas and words of others, intellectual honesty demands that we distinguish between what we borrow — and therefore acknowledge in a citation — and what is our own.

While writing your paper, be careful whenever you incorporate one of your notes into your paper: Make sure that you put quotation marks around material taken verbatim, and double-check your text against your notes — or, better yet, against the original if you have it on hand — to make sure that your quotations are accurate and that all paraphrases and summaries are really in your own words.

To learn more about how you can avoid plagiarism, go to the "Tutorial on Avoiding Plagiarism" at bedfordstmartins.com/plagiarismtutorial. There you will find information on the consequences of plagiarism, tutorials explaining what sources to acknowledge, how to keep good notes, how to organize your research, and how to appropriately integrate sources. Exercises are included throughout the tutorial to help you practice skills like integrating sources and recognizing acceptable paraphrases and summaries.

■ Using Quotation Marks for Language Borrowed Directly

Whenever you use another person's exact words or sentences, you must enclose the borrowed language in quotation marks. Without quotation marks you give your reader the impression that the wording is your own. Even if you cite the source, you are guilty of plagiarism if you fail to use quotation marks. The following example demonstrates both plagiarism and a correct citation for a direct quotation.

Original Source

> On my father's side, I figured, high cheekbones and almond eyes probably showed evidence of native-Andean blood. The aquiline profiles and curly hair on my mother's side, on the other hand, are common on Mediterranean shores. My best guess: I was mostly European, a bit of native South American and perhaps a dash of Middle Eastern.
>
> — CAROLINA A. MIRANDA,
> "Diving into the Gene Pool," *Time* 20 Aug. 2006, page 64

Plagiarism

> On my father's side, I figured, high cheekbones and almond eyes probably showed evidence of native-Andean blood, confesses Carolina A. Miranda. The aquiline profiles and curly hair on my mother's side, on the other hand, are common on Mediterranean shores. My best guess: I was mostly European, a bit of native South American and perhaps a dash of Middle Eastern (64).

Correct Citation of Borrowed Words In Quotation Marks

> "On my father's side, I figured, high cheekbones and almond eyes probably showed evidence of native-Andean blood," confesses Carolina A. Miranda. "The aquiline profiles and curly hair on my mother's side, on the other hand, are common on Mediterranean shores. My best guess: I was mostly European, a bit of native South American and perhaps a dash of Middle Eastern" (64).

■ Using Your Own Words and Word Order When Summarizing and Paraphrasing

When summarizing or paraphrasing a source, you need to use your own language. Pay particular attention to word choice and word order, especially if you are paraphrasing. Remember, it is not enough simply to use a synonym here or there and think you have paraphrased the source; you *must* restate the idea from the original in your own words, using your own style and sentence structure. In the following example, notice how plagiarism can occur when care is not taken in the wording or sentence structure of a paraphrase. Notice that in the acceptable paraphrase, the student writer uses her own language and sentence structure.

Original Source

> Stereotypes are a kind of gossip about the world, a gossip that makes us prejudge people before we ever lay eyes on them. Hence it is not surprising that stereotypes have something to do with the dark world of prejudice. Explore most prejudices (note that the word means prejudgment) and you will find a cruel stereotype at the core of each one.
>
> — ROBERT L. HEILBRONER,
> "Don't Let Stereotypes Warp Your Judgments," *Think* magazine
> June 1961, page 43

Unacceptably Close Wording

> According to Heilbroner, we prejudge other people even before we have seen them when we think in stereotypes. That stereotypes are related to the ugly world of prejudice should not surprise anyone. If you explore the heart of most prejudices, beliefs that literally prejudge, you will discover a mean stereotype lurking (43).

Unacceptably Close Sentence Structure

> Heilbroner believes that stereotypes are images of people, images that enable people to prejudge other people before they have seen them. Therefore, no one should find it surprising that stereotypes are somehow related to the ugly world of prejudice. Examine most prejudices (the word literally means prejudgment) and you will uncover a vicious stereotype at the center of each (43).

Acceptable Paraphrase

> Heilbroner believes that there is a link between stereotypes and the hurtful practice of prejudice. Stereotypes make for easy conversation, a kind of shorthand that enables us to find fault with people before ever meeting them. If you were to dissect most human prejudices, you would likely discover an ugly stereotype lurking somewhere inside it (43).

Preventing Plagiarism

Questions to Ask about Direct Quotations

▸ Do quotation marks clearly indicate the language that I borrowed verbatim?

▸ Is the language of the quotation accurate, with no missing or misquoted words or phrases?

▸ Do brackets or ellipsis marks clearly indicate any changes or omissions I have introduced?

▸ Does a signal phrase naming the author introduce each quotation? Does the verb in the signal phrase help establish a context for each quotation?

▸ Does a parenthetical page citation follow each quotation?

Questions to Ask about Summaries and Paraphrases

▸ Is each summary and paraphrase written in my own words and style?

▸ Does each summary and paraphrase accurately represent the opinion, position, or reasoning of the original writer?

▸ Does each summary and paraphrase start with a signal phrase so that readers know where my borrowed material begins?

▸ Does each summary and paraphrase conclude with a parenthetical page citation?

Questions to Ask about Facts and Statistics

▸ Do I use a signal phrase or some other marker to introduce each fact or statistic that is not common knowledge so that readers know where the borrowed material begins?

▸ Is each fact or statistic that is not common knowledge clearly documented with a parenthetical page citation?

Finally, as you proofread your final draft, check all your citations one last time. If at any time while you are taking notes or writing your paper you have a question about plagiarism, consult your instructor for clarification and guidance before proceeding.

Sample Student Essay Using Library and Internet Sources

Christine Olson was born in Jacksonville, Arkansas. She wrote the following essay while a student at Central Washington University in Ellensburg, Washington, where she majored in Law and Justice with the intent to go on to law school. The essay grew out of her course work for a class called Crime and the Media. After viewing a television program in class about how events in Mogadishu, Somalia, in early October 1993 were misrepresented in the media, Olson became interested in exploring distortions in today's media.

Olson began by brainstorming about her topic, listing recent news stories that had received a great deal of attention and that she thought might have been misreported. She then went to her college library and searched the Internet, where she located additional information on these stories from a number of credible sources. After carefully reading her sources and taking notes, she identified four major ways the media can distort news reports and decided to organize her essay around these four key points.

Olson's essay is annotated so that you can readily see how she has effectively integrated sources into her paper and has used them to establish, explore, and support her key points.

Distortions in the Media

Christine Olson

1

Writer sets context for discussion and makes first general claim: Today's media often fails to provide accurate, unbiased, objective reporting.

We are living in what has been called the information age, a time when we are bombarded with what seems like an endless stream of information. Ever-more-advanced communication technologies mean that the average person can access and share news and opinion faster than ever before, through a dizzying array of outlets. Many people have not adjusted their old-media expectations, however: While most people are wary of information that comes from anonymous or doubtful sources, when it comes to receiving information from other media outlets, the public still expects the information to be not only factual but also researched and unbiased. Are such expectations in fact realistic? Unfortunately, the answer is no:

High standards for factual accuracy and unbiased, objective reporting are often not met these days, even by supposedly reputable mainstream sources.

Writer uses "mean girls" story to grab readers' attention and involve them in issue.

Two direct quotations use the authors' names in signal phrases and page numbers in parentheses. (Writer uses MLA-style documentation throughout.)

Recently Mike Males and Meda-Chesney Lind 2
wrote about how news outlets and the Internet were abuzz with reports about a group of high school girls who bullied another student who later took her own life. According to Males and Lind, these reports put many people in a panic, making them think that America was experiencing "a modern epidemic of 'mean girls'" (A23). After examining available crime statistics, Males and Lind concluded that the opposite was in fact true: "Fights, weapons possession, assaults, and violent injuries by and toward girls have been plunging for at least a decade" (A23). The story had taken on a life of its own, and the conclusions reasonable people drew from it bore little or no resemblance to reality.

Writer signals organizational plan—to present "four ways" media distorts information.

This single incident points to what seems 3
to be a significant trend: The public's expectation of "up-to-the-minute" reporting and the ease with which information can be forwarded and otherwise re-presented, often with "embellishments," means that media distortion has, according to some observers, reached an all-time high. Today, media reports are often rushed, and because they are broadcast live or otherwise disseminated shortly after a story breaks, the information that the viewer or reader receives is often distorted in one of the following four ways: It is lacking in important details or context, selectively reported, lacking more than a single perspective, or sensationalized.

Topic sentence introduces discussion of first way media distorts information.

Paraphrase of source with reference in parentheses at end.

The first way that the media can distort 4
information is by failing to provide context for a story. For example, when television news programs first aired footage of the body of a United States serviceman being dragged through the streets of the Somalian city of Mogadishu in early October 1993, the media made little attempt to explain the circumstances surrounding the incident ("Viewpoint"). Widespread outrage resulted: Many American viewers concluded that Somalians in

general couldn't be trusted and, equally important, began to wonder why Americans were there in the first place. According to ABC News, the public's reaction to the admittedly shocking image might have been different if viewers had been informed of the events surrounding the soldier's death: He had been part of a mission to bring food and other supplies in response to a growing famine— a successful policy overall that had helped save countless Somalian lives and helped restore order to an increasingly volatile part of the world. This type of misrepresentation is common in the media— witness the annual coverage of the (exceedingly rare, but panic-inducing) shark attack in Florida. Much of the anxiety surrounding stories like these could be avoided by simply providing readers and viewers with a full and accurate context for understanding them.

A second way that the media can distort nonfictional information is by selective reporting, in which stories with common elements are presented as part of a trend, despite the absence of any evidence that a trend in fact exists. One example of this can be found in a now-classic study by Mark Fishman, a professor of sociology at Brooklyn College, who analyzed the way the media reported on crimes against the elderly in New York City in 1976. Fishman noted that two newspapers and one television news channel printed and/or aired eighty-nine stories concerning crimes against the elderly during a single six-month period in 1976. During this period, the media searched through police crime dispatches for incidents of crimes against the elderly and any other news that could be related either directly to the crimes or to the senior citizen community generally. One television broadcast, for example, ran accounts about individual and unrelated crimes against the elderly coupled with pieces about crime prevention seminars for senior citizens and segments about New York City police's Senior Citizen Robbery Unit. Throughout this period of increased reporting on

5

Clear topic sentence signals discussion of second way media distorts information.

To establish Fishman's authority, in signal phrase writer gives his academic affiliation and notes that study is a "classic."

By summarizing Fishman's study, writer gives an overview of his methods and conclusions instead of quoting lengthy passages.

crimes against the elderly, police statistics actually showed a *decrease* in the murder rate for the elderly. There was a general increase in other crime during this period, but this increase affected all age groups, not just the elderly (42-58). To sell papers and advertising, the media distorted this information to make it appear that New York's elderly were being singled out and preyed upon.

> **Parenthetical page citation indicates end of summary.**

Distortions like the "crimes-against-the-elderly" story occur relatively frequently. For example, in the wake of Philip Garrido's arrest for abducting and holding Jaycee Lee Dugard captive for eighteen years, a number of media reports positioned him as a "typical" sex offender in order to make a trend out of a unique occurrence. Randall G. Shelden, a professor of criminal justice at the University of Nevada–Las Vegas, believes that similar distortions surround the reporting of youth crime. He says that if we were to believe what we see and read in the media, we'd think that "crime is being committed by people younger than ever before and, even more frightening, the crimes are getting more violent with each passing day." According to Shelden, this is quite simply not true.

> **Paraphrase and quotation of Shelden introduced with signal phrase. No page number as source is unnumbered Web page**

6

Collecting information from a select group of sources is a third way in which the media may distort information. Crime news, for example, is all too frequently reported using law enforcement officials—and only law enforcement officials—as sources. As Professor Steven Chermak of Michigan State University observes, the information is particularly liable to distortion "because it is rarely observed directly" (116) and only one point of view is presented: The offender's story is often left untold, and experts such as sociologists and criminologists are not often consulted (162-64), thus creating a one-sided, unbalanced presentation.

> **Clear topic sentence announces discussion of third way media distorts.**

7

The fourth way the media may distort information is by sensationalizing it—that is, by reporting only what makes the most exciting copy, provides the best visuals, or speaks to the public's deepest fears, whatever the reality of the case

> **Clear topic sentence announces discussion of fourth way media distorts.**

8

may be. Once again, crime reporting provides a good example of this kind of distortion. According to one study by media, crime, and justice scholar Ray Surette, murder and robbery "account for approximately 45 percent of newspaper crime news and 80 percent of television crime news" (64), although crime reports collected by the FBI show that these crimes make up less than 5% of all crimes reported to police (*Uniform Crime Reports*). Surette further notes that, as of his writing in 2007, "nonviolent crime accounted for 47 percent of known crime but only 4 percent of crime news stories" (68). This overrepresentation of the more "dramatic" types of crime leads to a general belief among the public that the crimes that are the rarest are actually the most likely to happen.

Writer cites two studies to support claim of over-representation of crime in media. Note how she weaves quotes smoothly into her text.

A similar distortion—one that seems to reflect the public's anxiety about race, rather than any reality— is seen in racial presentations of criminal offenders. According to Central Washington University criminologist Sarah Britto, "a number of studies show that minorities, particularly Black men, are disproportionately shown as criminal offenders compared to more sympathetic roles such as victims, police officers, or members of the general public." A study by Jessica M. Pollak and Charis E. Kubrin, both of George Washington University, goes so far as to suggest that "the characteristics of crime, criminals, and victims represented in the media are in most respects the polar opposite of the pattern suggested by official crime statistics" (59).

Writer quotes her instructor.

Criminal justice professor Kenneth Dowler of the California State University at Bakersfield speculates that "the majority of the public's knowledge about crime and justice is formed through media consumption" (121). If this is true of crime and justice, it stands to reason that it is also true of politics, economics, current events, and many other crucial aspects of our lives. How can we function as citizens in a democracy without reliable data on which to base our decisions, whether these decisions are about which candidate to

Writer uses outside authority to reiterate large presence of media in Americans' lives.

9

10

Writer's conclusion refers to broader importance of argument: the need for citizens of a democracy to be well-informed.

vote for or whether to venture outside at night? The public needs to be aware that the media routinely distorts information, by failing to provide context, by reporting selectively, by relying too much on single sources, and by giving in to the temptation to sensationalize. It is our responsibility—perhaps more now than ever before—to treat all media reports with a healthy degree of skepticism and to think long and hard about competing accounts before deciding what to believe.

Works Cited

Writer uses MLA style for list of Works Cited. Entries are presented in alphabetical order by authors' last names. First line of each entry begins at left margin and subsequent lines are indented.

Britto, Sarah. "Crime and Race in the News." *Crime and the Media.* Central Washington University, Ellensburg. 25 Mar. 2010. Lecture.

Chermak, Steven. "The Presentation of Drugs in the News Media: The News Sources Involved in the Construction of Social Problems." *Constructing Crime: Perspectives on Making News and Social Problems.* Ed. Gary W. Potter and Victor E. Kappeler. 2nd ed. Long Grove: Waveland P, 2006. 115-42. Print.

Dowler, Kenneth. "Media Consumption and Public Attitudes Toward Crime and Justice: The Relationship Between Fear of Crime, Punitive Attitudes, and Perceived Police Effectiveness." *Journal of Criminal Justice and Popular Culture* 10.2 (2003): 109-26. Web. 29 Mar. 2010.

Fishman, Mark. "Crime Waves as Ideology." *Constructing Crime: Perspectives on Making News and Social Problems.* Ed. Gary W. Potter and Victor E. Kappeler. 2nd ed. Long Grove: Waveland P, 2006. 42-58. Print.

Males, Mike, and Meda-Chesney Lind. "The Myth of Mean Girls." *New York Times* 2 Apr. 2010: A23. Print.

Pollak, Jessica M., and Charis E. Kubrin. "Crime in the News: How Crimes, Offenders, and Victims Are Portrayed in the Media." *Journal of Criminal Justice and Popular Culture* 14.1 (2007): 59-83. Web. 31 Mar. 2010.

Shelden, Randall G. "Media Distortions of Youth Crime." *Center on Juvenile & Criminal Justice.* CJCJ, 9 Jan. 2010. Web. 31 Mar. 2010.

Surette, Ray. *Media, Crime, and Criminal Justice: Images, Realities and Policies.* 3rd ed. Belmont: Thomson Wadsworth, 2007. Print.

United States. Dept. of Justice. Federal Bureau of Investigation. *Uniform Crime Reports: 2008 Crime in the United States.* Washington: GPO, 2010. Web. 28 Mar. 2010.

"Viewpoint: Crime, Violence and Television News." ABC News. WABC, New York, 10 Dec. 1993. Television.

Analyzing Christine Olson's Source-Based Essay

1. What is Olson's thesis? Does she support it adequately? Are there any places where you think she needs additional evidence to support her claims?

2. What kinds of sources does Olson use? Are they credible? Are they appropriately current? Do they represent a wide enough range of sources? (Is any one source or type of source overrepresented)?

3. Do you agree with Olson's conclusion? Why, or why not?

4. Generally speaking, how could Olson make her essay even stronger? What recommendations for revision would you make?

The Case of the Disappearing Rabbit

LILY HUANG

Born in Beijing, China, in 1984, Lily Huang immigrated with her parents to the United States, landing first in Columbia, Missouri, and later in South Pasadena, California, the place she now calls home. She graduated from Harvard University in 2006 and traveled in France and Switzerland on a fellowship before accepting a publishing internship at Farrar, Straus and Giroux, where she wrote jacket copy for children's books. Later she took a three-month internship at *Newsweek* in Cambridge, Massachusetts. This internship evolved into a staff writing position, which she held for nearly a year and a half. During her time at *Newsweek*, Huang wrote a series of articles focusing on environmental issues. When not writing, she worked at CYCLE Kids, a nonprofit organization that teaches children how to have active lifestyles, how to ride bikes, and how not to become overweight. Currently Huang is pursuing a doctorate in the history of science at the University of Chicago where she focuses on the study of Darwin, natural history, and ideas about consciousness.

"The Case of the Disappearing Rabbit" first appeared in the August 3, 2009, issue of *Newsweek*. For this story Huang spent ten days in and around the Crown of the Continent in Montana, interviewing local climate experts and U.S. Forest Service biologists and experiencing the wilderness area up close. She remembers riding "on the back of John Squire's snowmobile, flying across a frozen Seeley Lake toward his trapline high above the valley. Here I saw three golden eagles rise up from the carcass of an elk, and in the surrounding snow there were patches of pink and the tracks of a mountain lion. I had a sense, in that distant place, of being in the real world for the first time, and of how much of this world would always be unobserved, kept secret — would reveal itself only as tracks in the snow. I tried to capture this about the Crown in the story."

As you read this essay, notice how Huang uses her interviews to tell the story of the snowshoe rabbit and the lynx and to support and explain her central ideas about environmental change.

■ **Preparing to Read**

Where do you stand on the issue of climate change? What kinds of evidence about climate change have impressed you the most? The least? Explain why.

In the roadless, snow-muffled back-country of northwestern Montana lies   1
your best chance of ever seeing a wild Canada lynx. An improbable creature,
it is small on the spectrum of wildcats — about three times the size of a house
cat — and stands on disproportionately long legs, on which it is uncommonly
fast. Its great head seems larger and wiser for its tuft of beard and the bird-
ish plumes at the tips of its ears, but its feet spoil its air of gravitas. They are
enormous. They act like snowshoes, and they are part of what makes the lynx
supremely adapted to this part of the Rocky Mountains. Another inhabitant,
the snowshoe hare, is adapted to life here, too. A lynx, if it could, would eat
nothing but snowshoe hares its whole life, and pretty much does.

An animal so specialized that it only eats one kind of food has a tenuous   2
place in the world. But this stretch of Montana — what the 19th-century naturalist George Grinnell named the Crown of the Continent — is unlike most
places, or even most wildernesses. In an age of daily extinctions, the Crown
has not lost any of the vertebrate species present when the first Europeans ven-
tured this far west — creatures seen, heard, and feared by Lewis and Clark. If
the Crown is a window into the past, it is also a particularly privileged window:
No other intact ecosystem on the continent affords a view this grand. Only
here do you find the full suite of North America's big predators — wolves, cou-
gars, coyotes, and black and grizzly bears. Then there are the stranger beings:
cutthroat trout, bull trout, and Arctic grayling in the glacial waters; river otter,
bobcats, fishers, martens, lynxes, and wolverines. Between Glacier National
Park and the Bob Marshall Wilderness Complex, the Crown is 10 million acres
of the West as it once was and as it would have been.

Yet it is not a time capsule. Being free from development by people hasn't   3
made it a static place: The Crown rearranges itself, in a constant flux between
the living and the dying, as the planet rolls on.

> **For the first time in geological history, you can watch glacial ice move, and by the current projection, 20 years from now there will be nothing to see.**

Historically, this has happened on a time scale
largely beyond our power of perception — "glacial
pace" is not far from the mark. The problem is that
glacial pace is not what it used to be. It is speeding
up, as the glaciers melt into the Rockies, retreating up to 90 feet each year. For the first time in
geological history, you can watch glacial ice move,
and by the current projection, 20 years from now
there will be nothing to see. Altogether, climate
change is a phenomenon more keenly felt in a
place like the Crown — a mountainous landscape
with reservoirs of ice and snow — than anywhere
else. This makes it the best possible natural laboratory, a window into the large-scale ecological
change that global warming will bring. The effects of warming are magnified
two to three times in the Crown, says Dan Fagre, climate ecologist in Glacier
National Park, though the Crown's persistent biodiversity suggests that the

ecosystem is weathering the difference so far. But Fagre thinks this persistence has a limit: At some point, the pressure of the changes will be too great, and beyond this unmarked boundary the present system will come apart. An ecosystem doesn't die, but as species depart or spread, it will change the way it operates, take a different form. Potentially, the Crown has innumerable thresholds — the last of the glaciers, the first animal extinction — beyond which it could rapidly become a fundamentally altered place: different trees, different cycles, different lives. Whatever will trip that invisible wire, a look now at the Crown is a look at final moments — the last of a storied American West, of the natural wealth that once enabled this extravagant diversity of life. What awaits, in a climate-changed world, is a new era of uniformity.

What sets the Crown apart from every other ecosystem on earth is its   4 ecological schizophrenia. Straddling the Continental Divide, it is besieged by disparate climates from the fertile west, the open prairie to the east, and the cold north; even its rivers, issuing from Triple Divide Peak, flow in all four compass directions into the Pacific, the Atlantic, and the Arctic oceans. In all this, the mountains are the agents of volatility: They toss wind and snow to different sides of the Divide and wildly apportion sunlight to different slopes; historically, their dramatic nightly cooling has produced some of the coldest temperatures ever recorded below the Arctic. The convergence of these forces is what packs into the Crown the widest range of life on the continent, a diversity as distinctive as the tight profusion of Madagascar or the sweeping wealth of the Serengeti. "We have this incredible mix of microclimates," says University of Montana climate expert Steve Running, who shared the Nobel Peace Prize in 2007 with the Intergovernmental Panel on Climate Change, "which then allows an incredible mix of microhabitats for animals."

To a certain extent, this patchwork of habitats is its own refuge against   5 ecological disturbance, which is why, though records of a warming trend go back to the 19th century, no population has yet abandoned the ecosystem. "The animals can make use of those gradients," Running explains. "They can go from the Pacific side over toward the continental side, they can walk from the southern end of the Rockies farther north, and then they walk up in elevation. When their habitat goes off the top of the mountain, then it's all over." Global warming has a leveling effect on mountains: Under an atmosphere thick with carbon, mountains cool less, allowing lower-elevation plants and animals to push into the upper reaches. We get more of one kind of habitable world, but we lose the planet's extremes, along with their wholly unique strata of life — lynxes, for instance, and snow-colored hares.

On paper, the lynx population in the Crown goes back to the 1810s, in the   6 records of the old Hudson Bay Company fur trade. In 2000, when the species was pronounced "threatened" under the Endangered Species Act, trapping became illegal. This February the amount of lynx habitat singled out for protection dramatically increased, and of the nearly 43,000 square miles of new critical habitat spread across a handful of northern states, just under half is in one ecosystem: the Crown. Rarity, for a species, is a biological Catch-22: The animals are so well adapted to their particular ecological niche that they are unable to spread indiscriminately in larger numbers, but specialization is what makes their lives possible at all — by allowing them to survive in places where most others cannot. Lynxes, says Forest Service biologist John Squires, are "long, thin, and light"; with those oversized paws, they have "everything for flying through snow, trying to catch snowshoe hares." But while these animals are untouchable on their territory, they are the most vulnerable in the larger scheme of ecosystem change: As the Crown teeters toward a new balance of species and habitats, their niches will be among the first to wink out.

For the last 10 years, Squires has tracked lynxes in the Crown using radio 7
telemetry and, more recently, data-streaming GPS collars. Between one study site in the Seeley-Swan Valley, near the southern limits of the Crown, and a second in the Purcell Mountains, near Glacier National Park, he typically has about 60 cats "on air" every year. He does not know in what proportion the collared cats stand to the whole population, but from their movements he has come to understand their narrow world. "Clearly, there are places where this animal goes and places where it doesn't," he says, with GPS points plotted in clusters on a map. Unfailingly, lynx territories are boreal forests, congregations of subalpine fir, larch, and Engelmann spruce trees whose wide-reaching boughs come so low to the ground, they touch the snow. Snowshoe hares, a default prey species for nearly all predators in the Crown, cling to this protected setting, and where the hares are, so are the lynxes.

Trapping a lynx is like trapping a ghost. Even its thick coat is the color 8
of ashes. In the winter, its distinctive tracks show up in the snow. When one is caught, the invisibility cloak falls away, and it's as though the cat has been momentarily plucked from the whole mysterious whirl, a piece of the shifting wilderness held in an uncommon state of arrest. The trap Squires uses to catch and collar lynxes is his own design: a wire-mesh cage the size of a doghouse with a suspended door tautly held to an angled floor piece. The cat walks over the floor piece to reach the mounted bait and triggers the door. This year, Squires has caught fewer new cats and almost no females. In March, two weeks before the bears would emerge from their dens — at which point all bait becomes bear bait — he has collared only one female in Seeley and says, "I think something's going on." His mind goes briefly to the new surge of mountain lions in the Crown, a cat that kills lynxes on sight to eliminate competition, but reasons that lions stay out of snow-thick lynx territory in winter. But the one thing Squires can count on to affect the population of lynx is the population of hares, which has always, in this lowest fringe of the North American boreal forest, been on the brink. In fact, the fragile footing of this frontier population of hares is precisely what makes them valuable, because the moment the ecosystem falls out of balance, the hares will tell. If hare and lynx habitat ranges farther north as temperatures warm across

the map, Squires's southern outpost is the best "early-warning system" — the animals will stop showing up.

Unseasonable warmth is a problem for hares for a not-immediately-obvious reason: It isn't the heat itself but what it does to the single most important constant in the Crown — the snow. As the largest perennial food prize in the ecosystem, snowshoe hares have just one good trick — turning white in winter, brown the rest of the year—cued by the changing length of days. Now winter snow melts nearly a month earlier in the Crown than it did just a century ago, causing, says Dan Fagre, a "decoupling" between two cycles that used to be synchronized: light and temperature. This means that a snow-white hare will end up sitting on brown earth — and have no idea. Researcher Scott Mills at the University of Montana, with his own set of radio-collar signals, has found more and more compromised hares in recent years and believes that they are dying for it, in increasingly large numbers, every spring and fall. Given enough time, hares may genetically sort themselves out, along with all the other species that have evolved, over millennia, a certain exquisite timing for their migrations, for giving birth, or for coming out of the ground. But in a fast-decoupling world, expecting snowshoe hares to survive by adaptation is like trying to engineer a genetic jackpot. Statistically, it could happen, but every spring and fall, you lose a lot of chances.

Biodiversity happens when an ecosystem brings competing species to a stalemate: All have their niche, all get by, none can completely suppress another. Global warming doesn't so much tip this finely wrought balance in the Crown one way or another as knock it all down: No niche wins out; the real winners are the species that don't have a niche. These are the ones who don't have to change their genes. Grizzly bears may be the world's least choosy eaters, omnivores par excellence that can live on anything and learn what they need to survive. Wolves, mountain lions, and coyotes are also versatile generalists. Populations of these animals have become more and more robust in the Crown, and so long as they avoid getting shot by people, they will live just as well in an ecosystem restructured by climate change. So across the current range of species in the Crown "there's going to be a shakeout," says Fagre, "because some will be able to adapt better than others. The ability to change your behavior will be really important." Species that are "hard-wired" to live a certain way — hares who change color for winter, or bull trout that only spawn in clean, icy waters — will be hard pressed to do things differently in their lifetime. And the world that leaves them behind is not necessarily one we would recognize. For all life in the Crown is checked by the available water, and mountains unable to hold onto snow and glaciers trickling to nothing can no longer provide a steady supply. That leaves the species that can make do with least, and an ecosystem determined not by the resources it has but by what it lacks. In place of a lively mosaic of habitats, Fagre has a vision of Glacier National Park as a single landscape of "wall-to-wall lodgepole pine," a tree that needs little water and is always the first to leap up after a forest fire, like a weed. In this impoverished place, the lynx — built for one niche, one prey — is an impossible biological flourish, a dream.

In a last effort to find cats, John Squires sent Dustin Ranglack, a member of his Seeley Lake crew, to scout out the slopes of Fawn Peak, which had been consumed by a forest fire in 2003. It was the only place he hadn't trapped, and now he thought he might as well try. Ranglack returned to report that there was no sign of life there — no tracks of deer, or mountain lions, or hares. "When there're no hares, there's nothing," said Squires. "There's no place else to go." He loaded his truck, and with two snow machines in tow, drove north. ▪   11

▪ Thinking Critically about the Text

Why is it important that scientists find answers to the case of the disappearing rabbit? What do you see as the big-picture implications of the drama being played out at the Crown of the Continent?

▪ Questions on Subject

1. According to Huang, what makes the area called "the Crown of the Continent" unique? What sets it apart from other ecosystems?
2. According to Huang, the mountains are an important feature of the Crown. In what sense are the mountains "agents of volatility" (paragraph 4)?
3. What do you think Huang means when she says, "Rarity, for a species, is a biological Catch-22" (paragraph 6)? How does this apply to the lynx?
4. Why is unseasonable warmth a problem for snowshoe hares? How does the population of hares affect the population of lynx?
5. Who will be the winners and the losers in the Crown as a result of global warming?

▪ Questions on Strategy

1. Huang opens her essay with a description of a Canada lynx. Which specific details best help create a mental picture of this animal for you? (Glossary: *Description*) Why is it important for Huang's readers to understand what a lynx is and how it looks?
2. Identify the signal phrases that Huang uses to introduce her sources. How do these signal phrases help you as a reader? Besides giving the name of each source, what other information does Huang provide?
3. In paragraph 4, Huang quotes University of Montana climate expert Steve Running. How does Huang use this quotation in the context of the paragraph? What would have been lost had she not used the quotation?
4. Where does Huang use cause and effect analysis to explain how global warming affects mountains? Briefly describe the causal chain

of events that occurs when there is warming. (Glossary: *Cause and Effect Analysis*)

■ Questions on Diction and Vocabulary

1. In paragraph 3, Huang introduces the term "glacial pace." What did this term mean in past years? Is "glacial pace" still a useful measure of time? Why, or why not? How else could you express the same idea?
2. Huang uses a number of interesting strong verbs—*affords, apportion, toss, teeters*, and *wink out*, for example. Identify six other strong verbs. What do these verbs add to Huang's writing? (Glossary: *Verbs*)
3. Refer to your desk dictionary to determine the meanings of the following words as Huang uses them in this selection: *gravitas* (paragraph 1), *tenuous* (2), *suite* (2), *flux* (3), *convergence* (4), *decoupling* (9), *stalemate* (10), *mosaic* (10).

■ Classroom Activity for Writing with Sources

Using the examples of signal phrases and parenthetical citations on pages 640–41 as models, rewrite the following paragraphs in order to correctly and smoothly integrate the embedded quotations.

The quotation in the first example comes from Ruth Russell's "The Wounds That Can't Be Stitched Up," a firsthand account of how her family life was tragically shattered by a drunk driver. Russell's essay appeared on page 17 of the December 20, 1999, issue of *Newsweek*.

> America has a problem with drinking and driving. In 2008 drunk drivers killed almost 14,000 people and injured 500,000 others. While many are quick to condemn drinking and driving, they are also quick to defend or offer excuses for such behavior, especially when the offender is a friend. "Many local people who know the driver are surprised when they hear about the accident, and they are quick to defend him. They tell me he was a war hero. His parents aren't well. He's an alcoholic. Or my favorite: 'He's a good guy when he doesn't drink.'" When are we going to get tough on drunk drivers?

The quotation in the second example comes from page 100 of William L. Rathje's article entitled "Rubbish!" in the *Atlantic Monthly* in December 1989. Rathje teaches at the University of Arizona, where he directs the Garbage Project.

> Most Americans think that we are producing more trash per person than ever, that plastic is a huge problem, and that paper biodegrades quickly in landfills. "The biggest challenge we will face is to recognize that the conventional wisdom about garbage is often wrong."

Compare your signal phrases with those of your classmates, and discuss how smoothly each integrates the quotation into the passage.

■ Writing Suggestions

1. **Writing with Sources.** Visit the U.S. Fish and Wildlife Service Web site <http://www.fws.gov/Endangered/wildlife.html#Species> to learn about its Endangered Species Program and the Endangered Species Act. Locate the service's list of U.S. endangered species, including vertebrate and invertebrate animals and flowering and nonflowering plants. Using these lists, adopt an endangered species from your region, and write a report about it. In your report be sure to include a description of your plant or "critter," an explanation of where it is found and what it does, and an argument for why it should be protected. See Chapter 15 for documentation guidelines.

2. **Writing with Sources.** Consider the following cartoon by Joel Pett about climate change:

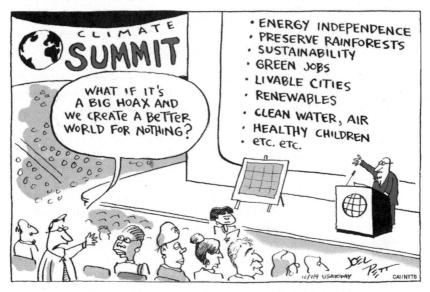

What do you think Pett is saying about the climate-change debate? Where do you stand on this issue? How did you react to the man's question in Pett's cartoon? How do you think Huang would react to this question?

Do some research online and write an essay proposing measures that could be taken on your college campus to make it more climate friendly. What energy-saving measures are already being taken? What can be done to control carbon dioxide emissions? What measures do you think would have the greatest impact? If possible, interview students and/or school officials for their reactions to your proposed solution, and integrate their perspectives into your essay. You may find it helpful to review your response to the Preparing to Read prompt for this selection before you start writing. See Chapter 15 for documentation guidelines.

▶ East Meets West: How the Brain Unites Us All

Ed Yong

 Ed Yong was fascinated by things scientific from an early age. He graduated from Cambridge University in 2002 with a degree in natural science. He pursued graduate studies in biochemistry and molecular biology at Cancer Research UK, where he discovered — after working in the lab for two years — that he "prefers to write and talk about science [rather] than do it." By day he is head of Health Evidence and Information at Cancer Research UK; by night he writes his own science blog — *Not Exactly Rocket Science* — where he tries to get readers interested in — even enthusiastic about — "the awe-inspiring, beautiful and quirky world of science." As a freelance jounalist, he's also been published in *New Scientist*, *SEED*, *Nature*, the *Times*, the *Guardian*, the *Economist*, and the *Daily Telegraph,* and a collection of his award-winning blogs was published as *Not Exactly Rocket Science* (2008). In 2007 he was awarded the Daily Telegraph Science Writers Award. He won the top three 2010 Research Blogging Awards, including Research Blog of the Year. Yong currently lives in London, England, with his wife.

In "East Meets West: How the Brain Unites Us All," published on NewScientist.com on March 6, 2009, Yong explores current research in psychology that draws into question the traditional dichotomy of Eastern thinking versus Western thinking. Yong's strength as a science writer is his ability to take the complex, sophisticated scholarly work of internationally known scientists and write about it in language that a general audience can understand. As you read, notice how he deftly uses the research work of psychologists to argue that "instead of dividing the world along cultural lines, we might be better off recognizing and cultivating our cognitive flexibility." In the original online publication, Yong provided in-text links to his sources. For this reprint, the editors have provided MLA-style in-text citations together with a Works Cited list.

■ Preparing to Read

What, for you, are the key differences between Westerners and Easterners? What are the similarities? How do you account for the fascination that Westerners and Easterners have for one another?

A s a species, we possess remarkably little genetic variation, yet we tend to overlook this homogeneity and focus instead on differences between groups and individuals. At its darkest, this tendency generates xenophobia   1 and racism, but it also has a more benign manifestation — a fascination with the exotic.

Nowhere is our love affair with otherness more romanticized than in our attitudes toward the cultures of East and West. Artists and travelers have long marveled that on opposite sides of the globe, the world's most ancient civilizations have developed distinct forms of language, writing, art, literature, music, cuisine, and fashion. As advances in communications, transport, and the Internet shrink the modern world, some of these distinctions are breaking down. But one difference is getting more attention than ever: the notion that easterners and westerners have distinct worldviews.

> Nowhere is our love affair with otherness more romanticized than in our attitudes toward the cultures of East and West.

2

Psychologists have conducted a wealth of experiments that seem to support popular notions that easterners have a holistic worldview, rooted in philosophical and religious traditions such as Taoism and Confucianism, while westerners tend to think more analytically, as befits their philosophical heritage of reductionism, utilitarianism, and so on. However, the most recent research suggests that these popular stereotypes are far too simplistic. It is becoming apparent that we are all capable of thinking both holistically and analytically — and we are starting to understand what makes individuals flip between the two modes of thought.

3

One of the pioneers of this research is Richard Nisbett from the University of Michigan, Ann Arbor. In his book *The Geography of Thought*, he recounts a study done in 2001 in which he asked American and Japanese students to describe animated videos of underwater scenes. As befits the stereotype, the Americans were more likely to start by mentioning prominent objects such as brightly colored moving fish or aquatic plants, while the vast majority of the Japanese students started by saying something about the context — the scene looked like a stream, or the water was green. They also mentioned more relationships between the objects and their environment. In another experiment, using eye-tracking equipment and a picture of a tiger in a jungle, Nisbett found that Americans tended to look at the tiger more quickly and focus on it for longer than did Chinese people, whose gaze flicked more often between the animal and the background.

4

Over the years, Nisbett and others have amassed evidence to suggest that such differences in visual attention influence the way in which people from East and West think about the world. For a start, they affect how people categorize objects, with East Asians tending to group things according to how they relate to each other and Americans tending to rely on shared features.

5

When shown pictures of a chicken, a cow, and some grass, and asked to decide which two objects belong most closely together, for example, Lian-Hwang Chiu found that most American kids choose the chicken and cow, since they are both animals, while Taiwanese children tend to group the cow and the grass together because one eats the other (235–42). Likewise, Ji, Zhang, and Nisbett found that American students usually group "monkey" with "panda," while Chinese students see "banana" as a better fit for "monkey" (57–65).

There also seem to be distinctly Eastern and Western views of causality. 6 Americans are more likely to explain murders and sports events by invoking the traits and abilities of individuals, while Chinese tend to refer to historical factors. Michael Morris and Kaiping Peng compared English-language newspaper accounts of a recent killing in the United States, in which a postal worker shot his boss along with several bystanders, with Chinese newspaper reports of a graduate student who shot his adviser and bystanders. The English-language papers speculated heavily on the killer's state of mind, while the Chinese papers emphasized his relationships with his superiors and the wider societal factors that could have led to the killings, such as the lack of religion in China or recent massacres elsewhere in the world (949–71).

Cultural differences may even extend to the way people wield logic. Chinese 7 people are happier with contradictions and try to find a middle ground between two opposing positions, while Americans are more inclined to reject one proposition for the other. For example, Peng and Nisbett found that when faced with a brief vignette of daughters rebelling against their mothers, three-quarters of Americans suggested that one party was at fault. By contrast, three-quarters of Chinese students assessed the situation from both sides and tried to reconcile the differences between mothers and daughters (741–54).

Time and again, studies like these seem to support the same basic, con- 8 trasting pattern of thought. Westerners appear to perceive the world in an analytic way, narrowing their focus onto prominent objects, lumping them into categories, and examining them through logic. Easterners take a more holistic view: They are more likely to consider an object's context and analyze it through its changing relationships with its environment.

In *The Geography of Thought*, Nisbett has suggested that historical cul- 9 tural factors are the key to understanding these differences. The intensive, large-scale agriculture of ancient China involved complex cooperation among farmers and strict hierarchies from emperor down to peasant. "You had to pay attention to what other people were doing and you had to obey orders," he explains. "These kinds of strong social constraints on behavior have been characteristic of East Asian life ever since" (49). The situation in ancient Greece, often thought of as the fount of Western culture, was very different: Agriculture on such a scale was impossible and most occupations did not require interactions with large numbers of people. The Greeks led independent lives and valued individualism. That allowed them to focus better on objects and goals in isolation, without being overly constrained by the needs of others — traits that persist to this day in Western culture. "If that story is all correct, it's not East versus West, it's interdependence versus independence" (56), says Nisbett.

False Dichotomy?

Certainly it is appealing to think that a single dimension—individualism   10
/collectivism—can account for much of the difference in people's behavior around the world. That might explain why many psychologists have been happy to go along with it. However, recently it has become apparent that the East-West dichotomy is not as clear-cut as this.

For a start, the simplistic notion of individualistic Westerners and col-   11
lectivist Easterners is undermined by studies designed to assess how people see themselves, which suggest that there is a continuum of these traits across the globe. In terms of individualism, for example, western Europeans seem to lie about midway between people in the United States and those in East Asia.

So it's not all that surprising, perhaps, that other studies find that local and   12
current social factors rather than the broad sweeps of history or geography tend to shape the way a particular society thinks. For example, Uskul, Kitayama, and Nisbett recently compared three communities living in Turkey's Black Sea region who share the same language, ethnicity, and geography but have different social lives: Farmers and fishers live in fixed communities and their trades require extensive cooperation, while herders are more mobile and independent. He found that the farmers and fishers were more holistic in their psychology than herders, being more likely to group objects based on their relationships rather than their categories: They preferred to link gloves with hands rather than with scarves, for instance ("Ecocultural Basis of Cognition" 8552–56). A similar mosaic pattern of thought can be found in the East. "Hokkaido is seen as the Wild West of Japan," says Nisbett. "The citizens are regarded as cowboys—highly independent and individualistic — and sure enough, they're more analytic in their cognitive style than mainland Japanese" (223).

Is it time we moved beyond simplistic notions of Eastern and Western psy-   13
chology? Daphna Oyserman from the University of Michigan in Ann Arbor certainly thinks so. She is not happy invoking history to explain modern human behavior. "We can't test if history mattered," she explains in an interview. "But we can test how contexts can evoke one or other mind-set."

Isolation and Conformity

Take social isolation. It has been suggested that the stereotypical Eastern worldview stems partly from a greater concern about being isolated from social groups, which makes people more likely to conform and attend to interpersonal relationships. Art Markman and his then colleague Kyungil Kim at the University of Texas in Austin wanted to see how isolation would affect the mind-set of American students, so they asked them to remember occasions either when they had been ostracized from a group or when they had excluded others. The students then studied photos of different cows against various backgrounds and later had to pick out the animals they had seen from a larger set. For students who recalled shunning others, it made little difference to their performance whether the cows appeared against new backdrops. However, students who had recalled being socially snubbed were better at spotting cows they had seen before against the same background, indicating that they paid more attention to the relationship between the cows and their environment. In fact, they behaved much as you might expect East Asians to do when given the same task (350–64). 14

This experiment suggests that while the psychology of Westerners may be superficially distinct from Easterners, when social isolation is an issue there is little difference between the two. In fact, Oyserman, Coon, and Kemmelmeier's analysis of 67 similar studies reveals just how easily social context can change the way people think. For example, psychologists have "primed" East Asian volunteers to adopt an individualistic mode of thought simply by getting them to imagine playing singles tennis, circling single-person pronouns, or unscrambling sentences containing words such as "unique," "independence," and "solitude." In many of the experiments volunteers from a single cultural background — be it Eastern or Western — show differences in behavior as large as those you normally get when comparing people from traditionally collectivist and individualist cultures. 15

The ease with which priming can alter our modes of thought makes it very unlikely that a penchant for either analytic or holistic thinking stems from deep-seated differences in the brains of westerners and easterners. Instead, it seems that the cultural context in which we grow up simply gives us more practice in thinking about the world in a particular way. "Everyone can think both ways, but on average, people tend to do more of one than the other," says Oyserman during an interview. 16

Brain imaging supports this. In an experiment that involved subjects looking at a series of squares with lines in them, Trey Hedden and his colleagues from the Massachusetts Institute of Technology found that in East Asians the areas of the brain involved in focusing attention worked harder if they had to identify lines of the same length regardless of the surrounding squares — an "absolute" task that requires you to focus on an object 17 regardless of its context. But with Americans the same brain areas were working harder to identify lines whose sizes varied proportionally with their squares — a "relative" judgment where context is key (12–17). In other words, people had to think harder to perform tasks outside their cultural comfort zone. The brain uses the same mental machinery to solve complex tasks, but cultural differences can affect how well trained these areas are.

Intriguingly, Hedden also discovered that in both groups, people who identified more strongly with American culture found the absolute task easier. Such ease of transition between different modes of thinking is even more pronounced in people with roots in more than one culture (12–17). Verónica Benet-Martínez from the University of California, Riverside, found that it takes very little to prime the perception of people who have grown up with cultural influences from both East and West. When she asked a group of Chinese students in Hong Kong to watch a video of a single fish swimming in front of a shoal, those who had previously seen American symbols such as the U.S. flag were more likely to claim that the solitary fish was leading the others. However, subjects primed with Asian symbols, including a Chinese dragon, perceived the event's context as more important and were more likely to describe the scenario as a shoal chasing after a renegade (492–516). 18

Clearly, the dichotomy between holistic Eastern and analytical Western thinking is more blurred than the stereotypes suggest. If we all flip between different modes of thought depending on social context, says Oyserman in an interview, psychologists should be trying to find out which contexts provoke the holistic and which the analytical mind-set, rather than perpetuating a false divide. 19

This approach is all the more important, she says, because the supposed dichotomy is based on limited evidence, with China and Japan representing the East in most studies and the United States and Canada flying the flag for the West. In many regions, from southern Asia to Latin America, studies are extremely scarce, and even better-studied Europe is mostly embodied by the unrepresentative duo of Germany and the Netherlands. "The kind of things that cue analytic or holistic thought may be very different in these [neglected] societies," Oyserman, Coon, and Kemmelmeier say. "Honor, for example, is a hugely important issue in areas that haven't been studied very thoroughly, like the Middle East, Africa, or Latin America" (5). 20

What is clear is that the minds of East Asians, Americans, or any other group are not wired differently. We are all capable of both analytic and holistic thought. "Different societies make one option seem to make the most sense at any given moment" (314), say Oyserman and Lee. But instead of dividing the world along cultural lines, we might be better off recognizing and cultivating our cognitive flexibility. "There are a lot of advantages 21 to both holistic and analytic perception" (87), says Nisbett. In our multicultural world it would benefit us all if we could learn to adopt the most appropriate mode of thought for the situation in which we find ourselves.

Works Cited

Benet-Martínez, Verónica, Janxin Leu, Fiona Lee, and Michael W. Morris. "Negotiating Biculturalism: Cultural Frame Switching in Biculturals with Oppositional Versus Compatible Cultural Identities." *Journal of Cross-Cultural Psychology* 33.5 (2002): 492–516. Print.

Chiu, Lian-Hwang. "A Cross-Cultural Comparison of Cognitive Styles in Chinese and American Children." *International Journal of Psychology* 7.4 (1972): 235–42. Print.

Hedden, Trey, Sarah Ketay, Arthur Aron, Hazel Rose Markus, and John D. E. Gabrieli. "Cultural Influences on Neural Substrates of Attentional Control." *Psychological Sciences* 19.1 (2008): 12–17. Print.

Ji, Li-Jun, Zhiyong Zhang, and Richard E. Nisbett. "Is It Culture, or Is It Language? Examination of Language Effects on Cross-Cultural Research on Categorization." *Journal of Personality and Social Psychology* 87.1 (2004): 57–65. Print.

Kim, Kyungil, and Arthur B. Markman. "Differences in Fear of Isolation as an Explanation of Cultural Differences: Evidence from Memory and Reasoning." *Journal of Experimental Social Psychology* 42.3 (2006): 350–64. Print.

Morris, Michael W., and Kaiping Peng. "Culture and Cause: American and Chinese Attributions for Social and Physical Events." *Journal of Personality and Social Psychology* 67.6 (1994): 949–71. Print.

Nisbett, Richard E. *The Geography of Thought: How Asians and Westerners Think Differently . . . and Why*. New York: Free Press, 2003. Print.

---. Personal interview. 16 Feb. 2009.

Oyserman, Daphna. Personal interview. 14 Feb. 2009.

Oyserman, Daphna, Heather M. Coon, and Markus Kemmelmeier. "Rethinking Individualism and Collectivism: Evaluation of Theoretical Assumptions and Meta-Analyses." *Psychological Bulletin* 128.1 (2002): 3–72. Print.

Oyserman, Daphna, and Spike W. S. Lee. "Does Culture Influence What and How We Think? Effects of Priming Individualism and Collectivism." *Psychological Bulletin* 134.2 (2008): 311–42. Print.

Peng, Kaiping, and Richard E. Nisbett. "Culture, Dialectics, and Reasoning about Contradiction." *American Psychologist* 54.9 (1999): 741–54. Print.

Uskul, Ayse K., Shinobu Kitayama, and Richard E. Nisbett. "Ecocultural Basis of Cognition: Farmers and Fishermen Are More Holistic than Herders." *Proceedings of the National Academy of Sciences* 105.25: 8552–56. Print.

■ Thinking Critically about the Text

In his conclusion Yong states that "instead of dividing the world along cultural lines, we might be better off recognizing and cultivating our cognitive flexibility" (paragraph 21). What do you see as the advantages of being able to think either holistically or analytically given the situation?

■ Questions on Subject

1. What does it mean to have a holistic worldview? An analytic worldview? Do you consider yourself a more holistic or a more analytical thinker?
2. In paragraph 4, Yong describes a 2001 study in which students were asked to describe animated videos of underwater scenes. What was the point of the study? According to Yong, how do the documented differences in visual attention influence the way people look at or think about the world?
3. During the first half of his essay, Yong cites studies that support a basic contrasting pattern of thought between Easterners and Westerners. What are the key differences? What historical cultural factors, according to Nisbett, are key to understanding these differences?
4. According to Oyserman's analysis of sixty-seven context studies, how can social context change the way people think? What other evidence does Yong provide to inform this discussion?
5. In spite of all the superficial differences between Westerners and Easterners, Yong claims that our brains are what unite us. Do you find Yong's argument convincing? Do you think that it is important for people to understand and accept this insight?

■ Questions on Strategy

1. What is Yong's thesis, and where does he present it? (Glossary: *Thesis*)
2. Identify several of the signal phrases that Yong uses to introduce borrowed material. How do these signal phrases help you as a reader, particularly in the case of paraphrase and summary? Besides giving the name of the study author or researcher for each source, what other information does Yong provide?
3. Why do you think Yong chooses to paraphrase and summarize studies — descriptions of what was investigated and the methods used — rather than to quote them directly?
4. What kinds of material does Yong quote in this essay? How is it different from the material he paraphrases and summarizes?
5. How has Yong organized his essay? (Glossary: *Organization*) You may find it helpful to outline the essay paragraph-by-paragraph so as to better identify the pattern he is using.
6. How does paragraph 10 function in the context of this essay?
7. Yong begins paragraph 13 with the question, "Is it time we moved beyond simplistic notions of Eastern and Western psychology?" How does Yong use outside sources to help answer this question?

■ Questions on Diction and Vocabulary

1. Yong has gained a reputation for being able to write about scientific topics in language that people without any training in science can understand. How well does he live up to that reputation in this essay? Do you find any of his explanations of scientific terms or descriptions of studies difficult to follow? How would you characterize Yong's diction in this essay? (Glossary: *Diction*)

2. What connotations do the words *Westerner* and *Easterner* have for you? (Glossary: *Connotation/Denotation*) Do any of these connotations shed light on what Yong calls our "fascination with the exotic" (paragraph 1)?

3. Refer to your desk dictionary to determine the meanings of the following words as Yong uses them in this selection: *xenophobia* (paragraph 1), *benign* (1), *cuisine* (2), *fount* (9), *dichotomy* (10), *cognitive* (12), *ostracized* (14), *penchant* (16), *perception* (21).

■ Classroom Activity for Writing with Sources

Using the examples on pages 638–39 and 644–45 as a model, write a *paraphrase* for each of the following paragraphs — that is, restate the original ideas in your own words, using your own sentence structure.

> The history of life on earth has been a history of interaction between living things and their surroundings. To a large extent, the physical form and the habits of the earth's vegetation and its animal life have been molded by the environment. Considering the whole span of earthly time, the opposite effect, in which life actually modifies its surroundings, has been relatively slight. Only within the moment of time represented by the present century has one species — man — acquired significant power to alter the nature of his world.
>
> — RACHEL CARSON,
> "The Obligation to Endure," *Silent Spring*

> Extroverts are energized by people, and wilt or fade when alone. They often seem bored by themselves, in both senses of the expression. Leave an extrovert alone for two minutes and he will reach for his cell phone. In contrast, after an hour or two of being socially "on," we introverts need to turn off and recharge. My own formula is roughly two hours alone for every hour of socializing. This isn't antisocial. It isn't a sign of depression. It does not call for medication. For introverts, to be alone with our thoughts is as restorative as sleeping, as nourishing as eating. Our motto: "I'm okay, you're okay — in small doses."
>
> — JONATHAN RAUCH,
> "Caring for Your Introvert"

Most of the people I've talked with say that they find social lying acceptable and necessary. They think it's the civilized way for folks to behave. Without these little white lies, they say, our relationships would be short and brutish and nasty. It's arrogant, they say, to insist on being so incorruptible and so brave that you cause other people unnecessary embarrassment or pain by compulsively assailing with your honesty. I basically agree. What about you?

— JUDITH VIORST,
"The Truth about Lying"

No, the romance and beauty were all gone from the river. All the value any feature of it had for me now was the amount of usefulness it could furnish toward compassing the safe piloting of a steamboat. Since those days, I have pitied doctors from my heart. What does the lovely flush in a beauty's cheek mean to a doctor but a "break" that ripples above some deadly disease? Are not all her visible charms sown thick with what are to him the signs and symbols of hidden decay? Does he ever see her beauty at all, or doesn't he simply view her professionally and comment upon her unwholesome condition all to himself? And doesn't he sometimes wonder whether he has gained most or lost most by learning his trade?

— MARK TWAIN,
Life on the Mississippi

■ Writing Suggestions

1. **Writing with Sources.** In his opening paragraph, Yong warns how stereotyping and prejudice come about when people focus on differences between groups and individuals instead of on similarities that unite us and bind us together. Have you or has someone you know ever been victimized by stereotyping or prejudice — as a student or as a member of a particular class, ethnic, religious, national, or racial group? After doing some research in your library or on the Internet, write an essay that examines how stereotyping has affected you, how it has perhaps changed you, and how you regard the process of stereotyping. What impact, if any, do you think what Yong calls "cognitive flexibility" (paragraph 21) would have on stereotyping and prejudice? (For documentation guidelines, see Chapter 15.)

2. **Writing with Sources.** Carefully read "Chinese in New York, American in Beijing" (page 295) by Kim Hoang and "Two Ways to Belong in America" (page 301) by Bharati Mukherjee. How do you think Yong would react to each of these essays? Write an essay in which you analyze one or both of these selections through the lens of Yong's essay. Be sure to quote, summarize, and paraphrase both authors to support

your claims, and cite them following MLA rules. (For documentation guidelines, see Chapter 15.)

3. Write an essay using the following sentence as your thesis: "Ethnic stereotypes, whether positive or negative, are harmful." Be sure to use examples from your own experience, observation, and reading to support your position.

The English-Only Movement: Can America Proscribe Language with a Clear Conscience?

Jake Jamieson

An eighth-generation Vermonter, Jake Jamieson was born in the town of Berlin and grew up in nearby Waterbury, home of Ben & Jerry's Ice Cream. He graduated from the University of Vermont with a degree in elementary education and a focus in English. After graduation Jamieson "bounced around" California and Colorado before landing in the Boston area, where he directs the Product Innovation and, Training department for iProspect, a search-engine marketing company.

Jamieson wrote the following essay while he was a college student and has updated it for inclusion in this book. As one who believes in the old axiom "If it isn't broken, don't fix it," Jamieson is intrigued by the official-English movement, which advocates fixing a system that seems to be working just fine. In this essay he tackles the issue of legislating English as the official language for the United States. As you read, notice how he uses outside sources to set out the various pieces of the English-only position and then uses his own thinking and examples, as well as experts who support his side, to undercut that position. Throughout his essay, Jamieson uses MLA-style in-text citations together with a list of works cited.

■ Preparing to Read

It is now possible to go many places in the world and get along pretty well using English, no matter what other languages are spoken in the host country. If you were to emigrate, how hard would you work to learn the predominant language of your chosen country? What advantages would there be in learning that language, even if you could get by with English? How would you feel if the country had a law that forced you to learn and use its language as quickly as possible? Write down your thoughts about these questions.

Jamieson 1

Jake Jamieson
Professor Rosa
Composition 101
May 10, 2010

The English-Only Movement:
Can America Proscribe Language with a
Clear Conscience?

Many people think of the United States as a giant cultural
"melting pot" where people from other countries come together
and bathe in the warm waters of assimilation. In this scenario
the newly arrived immigrants readily adopt American cultural
ways and learn to speak English. For others, however, this serene
picture of the melting pot does not ring true. These people see
the melting pot as a giant cauldron into which immigrants are
tossed; here their cultures, values, and backgrounds are boiled
away in the scalding waters of discrimination. At the center of
the discussion about immigrants and assimilation is language:
Should immigrants be required to learn English or should
accommodations be made so they can continue to use their
native languages?

Those who argue that the melting-pot analogy is valid
believe that immigrants who come to America do so willingly
and should be expected to become a part of its culture instead
of hanging on to their past. For them, the expectation that
immigrants will celebrate this country's holidays, dress
as Americans dress, embrace American values, and most
importantly, speak English is not unreasonable. They believe that
assimilation offers the only way for everyone in this country
to live together in harmony and the only way to dissipate the
tensions that inevitably arise when cultures clash.

A major problem with this argument, however, is that there
is no agreement on what exactly constitutes the "American way"
of doing things. Not everyone in America is of the same religious
persuasion or has the same set of values, and different people
affect vastly different styles of dress. There are so many sets of
variables that it would be hard to defend the argument that there
is only one culture in the United States.

Currently, the one common denominator in America is that
the majority of us speak English, and because of this a major
movement is being staged in favor of making English the

Jamieson 2

country's "official" language while it is still the country's national and common language. Making English America's official language would change the ground rules and expectations surrounding immigrant assimilation. According to the columnist and social commentator Charles Krauthammer, making English the official language has important implications:

> "Official" means the language of the government and its institutions. "Official" makes clear our expectations of acculturation. "Official" means that every citizen, upon entering America's most sacred political space, the voting booth, should minimally be able to identify the words president and vice president and county commissioner and judge. The immigrant, of course, has the right to speak whatever he wants. But he must understand that when he comes to the United States, swears allegiance, and accepts its bounty, he undertakes to join its civic culture. In English. (521)

Many reasons are given to support the notion that making English the official language of the land is a good idea and that it is exactly what this country needs, especially in the face of the growing diversity of languages in metropolitan areas. Indeed, the National Center for Education Statistics reports that in 2008, 21 percent of children ages 5-17 spoke a language other than English at home (Sec. 1).

Supporters of English-only contend that all government communication must be in English. Because communication is absolutely necessary for democracy to survive, they believe that the only way to ensure the existence of our nation is to make sure a common language exists. Making English official would ensure that all government business, from ballots to official forms to judicial hearings, would have to be conducted in English. According to former senator and presidential candidate Bob Dole, "Promoting English as our national language is not an act of hostility but a welcoming act of inclusion." He goes on to state that while immigrants are encouraged to continue speaking their native languages, "thousands of children [are] failing to learn the language, English, that is the ticket to the 'American Dream'" (qtd. in Donegan 51). Political and cultural commentator Greg Lewis echoes Dole's sentiments when he boldly states, "to succeed in America . . . it's important to speak, read, and

Jamieson 3

understand English as most Americans speak it. There's nothing cruel or unfair in that; it's just the way it is" (par. 5).

For those who do not subscribe to this way of thinking, however, this type of legislation is anything but the "welcoming act of inclusion" that it is described to be. Many of them, like Myriam Marquez, readily acknowledge the importance of English but fear that "talking in Spanish—or any other language, for that matter—is some sort of litmus test used to gauge American patriotism" ("Why and When" A12). Others suggest that anyone attempting to regulate language is treading dangerously close to the First Amendment and must have a hidden agenda of some type. Why, it is asked, make a language official when it is already firmly entrenched and widely used in this country without legislation to mandate it?

7

According to language diversity advocate James Crawford, the answer is plain and simple: "discrimination." He states that "it is certainly more respectable to discriminate by language than by race" or ethnicity. He points out that "most people are not sensitive to language discrimination in this nation, so it is easy to argue that you're doing someone a favor by making them speak English" (qtd. in Donegan 51). English-only legislation has been criticized as bigoted, anti-immigrant, mean-spirited, and steeped in nativism by those who oppose it, and some go so far as to say that this type of legislation will not foster better communication, as is the claim, but will instead encourage a "fear of being subsumed by a growing 'foreignness' in our midst" (Underwood 65).

8

For example, when a judge in Texas ruled that a mother was abusing her five-year-old girl by speaking to her only in Spanish, an uproar ensued. This ruling was accompanied by the statement that by talking to her daughter in a language other than English, the mother was "abusing that child and . . . relegating her to the position of housemaid." The National Association for Bilingual Education (NABE) condemned this statement for "labeling the Spanish language as abuse." The judge, Samuel C. Kiser, subsequently apologized to the housekeepers of the country, adding that he held them "in the highest esteem," but stood firm on his ruling (qtd. in Donegan 51). One might notice that he went out of his way to apologize to the housekeepers he might have offended but saw no need to apologize to the millions of Spanish speakers whose language had just been belittled in a nationally publicized case.

9

Jamieson 4

This tendency of official-English proponents to put down
other languages is one that shows up again and again, even
though they maintain that they have nothing against other
languages or the people who speak them. If there is no malice
intended toward other languages, why is the use of any language
other than English so often portrayed by them as tantamount
to lunacy? In a listing of the "New Year's Resolutions" of
various conservative organizations, a group called U.S. English,
Inc., stated that the U.S. government was not doing its job of
convincing immigrants that they "must learn English to succeed
in this country." Instead, according to Stephen Moore and his
associates, "in a bewildering display of irrationality, the U.S.
government makes it possible to vote, file a tax return, get
married, obtain a driver's license, and become a U.S. citizen in
many languages" (46).

Now, according to this mind-set, speaking any language
other than English is "abusive," "irrational," and "bewildering."
What is this world coming to when people want to speak
and make transactions in their native language? Why do
they refuse to change and become more like us? Why can't
immigrants see that speaking English is quite simply the
right way to go? These and many other questions like them
are implied by official-English proponents when they discuss
the issue.

Conservative attorney David Price argues that official-
English legislation is a good idea because most English-speaking
Americans prefer "out of pride and convenience to speak their
native language on the job" (A13). Not only does this statement
imply that the pride and convenience of non-English-speaking
Americans is unimportant but also that their native tongues are
not as important as English. The scariest prospect of all is that
this opinion is quickly gaining popularity all around the country.
It appears to be most prevalent in areas with high concentrations
of Spanish-speaking residents.

To date a number of official-English bills and one
amendment to the Constitution have been proposed in the House
and Senate. There are more than twenty-seven states—including
Missouri, North Dakota, Florida, Massachusetts, California,
Virginia, and New Hampshire—that have made English their
official language, and more are debating the issue every day. An
especially disturbing fact about this debate—and it was front and

10

11

12

13

center in 2007 during the discussions and protests about what to do with America's 12.5 million illegal immigrants—is that official-English laws always seem to be linked to anti-immigration legislation, such as proposals to limit immigration or to restrict government benefits to immigrants.

Although official-English proponents maintain that their bid for language legislation is in the best interest of immigrants, the facts tend to show otherwise. University of Texas professor Robert D. King strongly believes that "language does not threaten American unity." He recommends that "we relax and luxuriate in our linguistic richness and our traditional tolerance of language differences" (531). A decision has to be made in this country about what kind of message we will send to the rest of the world. Do we plan to allow everyone in this country the freedom of speech that we profess to cherish, or will we decide to reserve it only for those who speak English? Will we hold firm to our belief that everyone is deserving of life, liberty, and the pursuit of happiness in this country? Or will we show the world that we believe in these things only when they pertain to us and people like us? "The irony," as columnist Myriam Marquez observes, "is that English-only laws directed at government have done little to change the inevitable multicultural flavor of America" ("English-Only Laws").

14

Jamieson 6

Works Cited

Donegan, Craig. "Debate over Bilingualism: Should English Be the
　　Nation's Official Language?" *CQ Researcher* 19 Jan. 1996: 51-71.
　　Print.

King, Robert D. "Should English Be the Law?" *Subject & Strategy*.
　　Ed. Alfred Rosa and Paul Eschholz. 11th ed. Boston: Bedford,
　　2008. 522-31. Print.

Krauthammer, Charles. "In Plain English: Let's Make It Official."
　　Subject & Strategy. Ed. Alfred Rosa and Paul Eschholz. 11th ed.
　　Boston: Bedford, 2008. 519-21. Print.

Lewis, Greg. "An Open Letter to Diversity's Victims." *Washington
　　Dispatch.com*. Washington Dispatch, 12 Aug. 2003. Web.
　　11 Mar. 2010.

Marquez, Myriam. "English-Only Laws Serve to Appease Those
　　Who Fear the Inevitable." *Orlando Sentinel* 10 July 2000: A10.
　　Print.

---. "Why and When We Speak Spanish Among Ourselves in
　　Public." *Orlando Sentinel* 28 June 1998: A12. Print.

Moore, Stephen, et al. "New Year's Resolutions." *National Review*
　　29 Jan. 1996: 46-48. Print.

Price, David. "English-Only Rules: EEOC Has Gone Too Far." *USA
　　Today* 28 Mar. 1996, Final ed.: A13. Print.

Underwood, Robert L. "At Issue: Should English Be the Official
　　Language of the United States?" *CQ Researcher* 19 Jan. 1996:
　　65. Print.

United States. Dept. of Educ. Inst. of Educ. Sciences. Natl. Center
　　for Educ. Statistics. *The Condition of Education 2010*. NCES,
　　2010. Web. 13 Mar. 2010.

■ Thinking Critically about the Text

Jamieson claims that "[t]here are so many sets of variables that it would be hard to defend the argument that there is only one culture in the United States" (paragraph 3). Do you agree with him, or do you see a dominant "American culture" with many regional variations? Explain.

■ Questions on Subject

1. What question does Jamieson seek to answer in his paper? How does he answer that question?
2. How does Jamieson counter the argument that the melting-pot analogy is valid? Do you agree with his counterargument?
3. Former senator Bob Dole believes that English "is the ticket to the 'American Dream'" (paragraph 6). In what ways can it be considered a "ticket"?
4. James Crawford believes that official-English legislation is motivated by "discrimination" (paragraph 8). What exactly do you think he means? Do you think Crawford would consider Bob Dole's remarks in paragraph 6 discriminatory? Explain.
5. In his concluding paragraph, Jamieson leaves his readers with three important questions. How do you think he would answer each one? How would you answer them?

■ Questions on Strategy

1. What is Jamieson's thesis, and where does he present it? (Glossary: *Thesis*)
2. How has Jamieson organized his argument? (Glossary: *Organization*)
3. Jamieson is careful to use signal phrases to introduce each of his quotations and paraphrases. How do these signal phrases help readers follow the flow of the argument in his essay? (Glossary: *Signal Phrases*)
4. For what purpose does Jamieson quote Greg Lewis in paragraph 6? What would have been lost had he dropped the Lewis quotation? Explain.
5. In paragraph 9, Jamieson presents the example of the Texas judge who ruled that speaking to a child only in Spanish constituted abuse. What point does this example help Jamieson make?

■ Questions on Diction and Vocabulary

1. What for you constitutes the "'American way' of doing things" (paragraph 3)? Do you think the meaning of "American way" has changed in the last decade or two? Explain.
2. What are the connotations of the words *official* and *English-only*? In your opinion, do these connotations help or hinder the English-only

position? What are the connotations of the word *immigrant*? What insights into America's language debate do these connotations give you? (Glossary: *Connotation/Denotation*)

3. Consult your dictionary to determine the meanings of the following words as Jamieson uses them in this selection: *assimilation* (paragraph 1), *dissipate* (2), *implications* (4), *nativism* (8), *malice* (10).

■ Classroom Activity for Writing with Sources

For each of the following quotations, write an acceptable paraphrase and then a paraphrase including a partial quotation that avoids plagiarism (see pages 638–40 and 642–45). Pay particular attention to the word choice and the sentence structure of the original.

> The sperm whale is the largest of the toothed whales. Moby-Dick was a sperm whale. Generally, male toothed whales are larger than the females. Female sperm whales may grow 35 to 40 feet in length, while the males may reach 60 feet.
>
> — RICHARD HENDRICK,
> *The Voyage of the Mimi*

> Astronauts from over twenty nations have gone into space and they all come back, amazingly enough, saying the very same thing: The earth is a small, blue place of profound beauty that we must take care of. For each, the journey into space, whatever its original intents and purposes, became above all a spiritual one.
>
> — AL REINHERT,
> *For All Mankind*

> One of the usual things about education in mathematics in the United States is its relatively impoverished vocabulary. Whereas the student completing elementary school will already have a vocabulary for most disciplines of many hundreds, even thousands of words, the typical student will have a mathematics vocabulary of only a couple of dozen words.
>
> — MARVIN MINSKY,
> *The Society of Mind*

WRITING SUGGESTIONS

1. **Writing with Sources.** While it's no secret that English is the common language of the United States, few of us know that our country has been extremely cautious about promoting a government-mandated "official language." Why do you suppose the federal government has chosen to take a hands-off position on the language issue? If it has not been necessary to mandate it in the past, why do you think that people now feel a need to declare English the "official language" of the United States? Do you think that this need is real? Write an essay articulating your position on the English-only issue. Support your position with your own experiences and observations as well as several outside sources. (See Chapter 15 for documentation guidelines.)

2. **Writing with Sources**. In preparation for writing an essay about assimilating non-English-speaking immigrants into American society, consider the following three statements:

   a. At this time, it is highly unlikely that Congress will legislate that English is the official language of the United States.

   b. Immigrants should learn English as quickly as possible after arriving in the United States.

   c. The culture and languages of immigrants should be respected and valued so that bitterness and resentment will not be fostered, even as immigrants are assimilated into American society.

   In your opinion, what is the best way to assimilate non-English-speaking immigrants into our society? After doing some research on the issue, write an essay in which you propose how the United States, as a nation, can make the two latter statements a reality without resorting to an English-only solution. How can we effectively transition immigrants to speaking English without provoking ill will? (See Chapter 15 for documentation guidelines.)

3. **Writing with Sources.** Is the English-only debate a political issue, a social issue, an economic issue, or some combination of the three? In this context, what do you see as the relationship between language and power? After doing some research on the topic, write an essay in which you explore the relationship between language and power as it pertains to the non-English-speaking immigrants trying to live and function within the dominant English-speaking culture. (See Chapter 15 for documentation guidelines.)

A Brief Guide to Researching and Documenting Essays

In this chapter, you will learn some valuable research techniques:

- How to establish a realistic schedule for your research project

- How to conduct research online using directory and keyword searches

- How to evaluate sources

- How to analyze sources

- How to develop a working bibliography

- How to take useful notes

- How to acknowledge your sources using Modern Language Association (MLA) style in-text citations and a list of works cited

Establishing a Realistic Schedule

A research project easily spans several weeks. So as not to lose track of time and find yourself facing an impossible deadline at the last moment, establish a realistic schedule for completing key tasks. By thinking of the research paper as a multistaged process, you avoid becoming overwhelmed by the size of the whole undertaking.

Your schedule should allow at least a few days to accommodate unforeseen needs and delays. Use the following template, which lists the essential steps in writing a research paper, to plan your own research schedule:

Research Paper Schedule

Task	Completion Date
1. Choose a research topic and pose a worthwhile question.	/ /
2. Locate print and electronic sources.	/ /
3. Develop a working bibliography.	/ /
4. Evaluate your sources.	/ /
5. Read your sources, taking complete and accurate notes.	/ /
6. Develop a preliminary thesis and make a working outline.	/ /
7. Write a draft of your paper, integrating sources you have summarized, paraphrased, and quoted.	/ /
8. Visit your college writing center for help with your revision.	/ /
9. Decide on a final thesis and modify your outline.	/ /
10. Revise your paper and properly cite all borrowed materials.	/ /
11. Prepare a list of works cited.	/ /
12. Prepare the final manuscript and proofread.	/ /
13. Submit your research paper.	/ /

Finding and Using Sources

You should use materials found through a search of your school library's holdings — including books, newspapers, journals, magazines, encyclopedias, pamphlets, brochures, and government documents — as your primary tools for research. These sources, unlike many open-Internet sources,* are reviewed by experts in the field before they are published, generally overseen by a reputable publishing company or organization, and examined by editors and fact checkers for accuracy and reliability.

---

*By "open Internet," we mean the vast array of resources, ranging from Library of Congress holdings to pictures of a stranger's summer vacation, available to anyone using a search engine. Because anyone with a computer and Internet access can post information online, sources found on the open Internet should be scrutinized more carefully for relevance and reliability than those found through a search of academic databases or library holdings.

The best place to start your search, in most cases, is your college library's home page (see figure below). Here you will find links to the library's computerized catalog of hard-copy holdings, online reference works, periodical databases, electronic journals, and a list of full-text databases. Most libraries also provide links to other helpful materials, including subject study guides and guides to research.

To get started, decide on some likely search terms and try them out. You might have to try a number of different terms related to your topic in order to generate the best results. (For tips on refining your searches, see pages 685–87.) Your goal is to create a preliminary listing of books, magazine and newspaper articles, public documents and reports, and other sources that may be helpful in exploring your topic. At this early stage, it is better to err on the side of listing too many sources. Then, later on, you will not have to backtrack to find sources you discarded too hastily.

You will likely find some open-Internet sources to be informative and valuable additions to your research. The Internet is especially useful in providing recent data, stories, and reports. For example, you might find a just-published article from a university laboratory or a news story in your local newspaper's online archives. Generally, however, open-Internet sources should be used alongside other sources and not as a replacement for them. The Internet offers a vast number of useful and carefully maintained resources, but it also contains much unreliable information. It is your responsibility to determine whether a given Internet source should be trusted. (For advice on evaluating sources, see pages 687–89.)

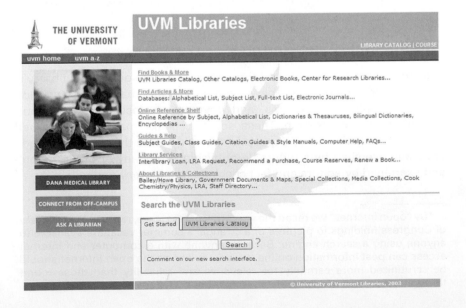

■ Conducting Keyword Searches

When searching for sources about your topic in an electronic database, in the library's computerized catalog, or on the Internet, you should start with a keyword search. To make the most efficient use of your time, you will want to know how to conduct a keyword search that is likely to yield solid sources and leads for your research project. As obvious or simple as it may sound, the key to a successful keyword search is the quality of the keywords you generate about your topic. You might find it helpful to start a list of potential keywords as you begin your research and add to it as your work proceeds. Often you will discover combinations of keywords that will lead you right to the sources you need.

Databases and library catalogs index sources by author, title, and year of publication, as well as by subject headings assigned by a cataloger who has previewed the source. In order to generate results, the keywords you use will have to match words found in one or more of these categories. Once you begin to locate sources that are on your topic, be sure to note the subject headings listed for each source. You can use these subject headings as keywords to lead you to additional book sources or, later, to articles in periodicals cataloged by full-text databases like *InfoTrac, LexisNexis, Expanded Academic ASAP*, or *JSTOR* to which your library subscribes. The figure below shows a typical book entry in a computer catalog. Notice the subject headings, all of which can be used as possible keywords.

The keyword search process is somewhat different — more wide open — when you are searching on the Web. It is always a good idea to look for search tips on the help screens or advanced search instructions for the search engine you are using before initiating a keyword

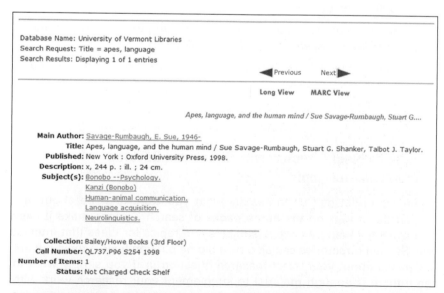

Database Name: University of Vermont Libraries
Search Request: Title = apes, language
Search Results: Displaying 1 of 1 entries

◀ Previous   Next ▶

Long View   MARC View

Apes, language, and the human mind / Sue Savage-Rumbaugh, Stuart G....

Main Author: Savage-Rumbaugh, E. Sue, 1946-
Title: Apes, language, and the human mind / Sue Savage-Rumbaugh, Stuart G. Shanker, Talbot J. Taylor.
Published: New York : Oxford University Press, 1998.
Description: x, 244 p. : ill. ; 24 cm.
Subject(s): Bonobo --Psychology.
Kanzi (Bonobo)
Human-animal communication.
Language acquisition.
Neurolinguistics.

Collection: Bailey/Howe Books (3rd Floor)
Call Number: QL737.P96 S254 1998
Number of Items: 1
Status: Not Charged Check Shelf

Computer Catalog Screen: Complete Record for a Book

search. When you type in a keyword in the "Search" box on a search engine's home page, the search engine electronically scans Web sites looking for matches to your keywords. On the Web, the quality of the keywords used determines the relevance of the hits on the first page or two that comes up. While it is not uncommon for a search on the Internet to yield between 500,000 and 1,000,000 hits, the search engine's algorithm puts the best sources up front. If after scanning the first couple of pages of results you determine that these sites seem off topic, you will need to refine your search terms to either narrow or broaden your search.

Refining Keyword Searches on the Web

While some variation in command terms and characters exists among electronic databases and popular search engines on the Internet, the following functions are almost universally accepted. If you have a particular question about refining your keyword search, seek assistance by clicking on "Help" or "Advanced Search."

▶ Use quotation marks or parentheses to indicate that you are searching for words in exact sequence — e.g., "whooping cough"; (Supreme Court).

▶ Use AND or a plus sign (+) between words to narrow your search by specifying that all words need to appear in a document — e.g., tobacco AND cancer; Shakespeare + sonnet.

▶ Use NOT or a minus sign (–) between words to narrow your search by eliminating unwanted words — e.g., monopoly NOT game, cowboys–Dallas.

▶ Use OR to broaden your search by requiring that only one of the words need appear — e.g., buffalo OR bison.

▶ Use an asterisk (*) to indicate that you will accept variations of a term — e.g., "food label*" for food labels, food labeling, and so forth.

■ Using Subject Directories to Define and Develop Your Research Topic

If you are undecided as to exactly what you want to write about, the subject directories on the home pages of search engines make it easy to browse the Web by various subjects and topics for ideas that interest you. Subject directories can also be a big help if you have a topic but are undecided about your exact research question or if you simply want to see if there is enough material to supplement your research work with print sources. Once you choose a subject area in the directory, you can select more specialized subcategories, eventually arriving at a list of sites closely related to your topic.

The most common question students have at this stage of a Web search is, "How can I tell if I'm looking in the right place?" There is no straight answer; if more than one subject area sounds plausible, you will have to dig more deeply into each of their subcategories, using logic and the process of elimination to determine which one is likely to produce the best leads for your topic. In most cases, it doesn't take long — usually just one or two clicks — to figure out whether you're searching in the right subject area. If you click on a subject area and none of the topics listed in its subcategories seems to pertain even remotely to your research topic, try a different subject area. As you browse through various subject directories, keep a running list of keywords associated with your topic that you can use in subsequent keyword searches.

Evaluating Your Sources

You do not have to spend much time in the library to realize that you do not have time to read every print and online source that appears relevant. Given the abundance of print and Internet sources, the key to successful research is identifying those books, articles, Web sites, and other online sources that will help you most. You must evaluate your potential sources to determine which materials you will read, which you will skim, and which you will simply eliminate. Here are some evaluation strategies and questions to assist you in identifying your most promising sources.

Strategies for Evaluating Print and Online Sources

Evaluating a Book

▶ Read the back or inside cover copy for insights into the book's coverage and currency as well as the author's expertise.

▶ Scan the table of contents and identify any promising chapters.

▶ Read the author's preface, looking for his or her thesis and purpose.

▶ Check the index for key words or key phrases related to your research topic.

▶ Read the opening and concluding paragraphs of any promising chapter; if you are unsure about its usefulness, skim the whole chapter.

▶ Ask yourself: Does the author have a discernible bias? If so, you must be aware that this bias will color his or her claims and evidence. (See Analyzing Your Sources, pages 689–690.)

(*continued on next page*)

(continued from previous page)

Evaluating an Article

▸ Ask yourself what you know about the journal or magazine publishing the article:

  ▸ Is the publication scholarly or popular? Scholarly journals (*American Economic Review, Journal of Marriage and the Family,* the *Wilson Quarterly*) publish articles representing original research written by authorities in the field. Such articles always cite their sources in footnotes or bibliographies, which means you can check their accuracy and delve deeper into the topic by locating these sources. Popular news and general interest magazines (*National Geographic, Smithsonian, Time, Ebony*), on the other hand, publish informative, entertaining, and easy-to-read articles written by editorial staff or freelance writers. Popular essays sometimes cite sources but often do not, making them somewhat less authoritative and less helpful in terms of extending your own research.

  ▸ What is the reputation of the journal or magazine? Determine the publisher or sponsor. Is it an academic institution or a commercial enterprise or individual? Does the publisher or publication have a reputation for accuracy and objectivity?

  ▸ Who are the readers of this journal or magazine?

▸ Try to determine the author's credentials. Is he or she an expert?

▸ Consider the title or headline of the article as well as the opening paragraph or two and the conclusion. Does the source appear to be too general or too technical for your needs and audience?

▸ For articles in journals, read the abstract (a summary of the main points) if there is one. Examine any photographs, charts, graphs, or other illustrations that accompany the article and determine how useful they might be for your research purposes.

Evaluating a Web Site or Document Found on the Open Internet

▸ Consider the original location of the document or site. Often the URL, especially the top-level domain name, can give you a clue about the kinds of information provided and the type of organization behind the site. Common suffixes include:

  .com — business/commercial/personal

  .edu — educational institution

  .gov — government sponsored

  .net — various types of networks

.org — nonprofit organization, but also some commercial or personal

(Be advised that *.org* is not regulated like *.edu* and *.gov*, for example. Most nonprofits use *.org*, but many commercial and personal sites do as well.)

▸ Examine the home page of the site:

   ▸ Does the content appear to be related to your research topic?

   ▸ Is the home page well maintained and professional in appearance?

   ▸ Is there an *About* link on the home page that takes you to background information on the site's sponsor? Is there a mission statement, history, or statement of philosophy? Can you verify whether the site is official — actually sanctioned by the organization or company?

▸ Identify the author of the document or site. What are the author's qualifications for writing on this subject?

▸ Determine whether a print equivalent is available. If so, is the Web version identical to the print version, or is it altered in some way?

▸ Determine when the site was last updated. Is the content current enough for your purposes?

You can also find sources on the Internet itself that offer useful guidelines for evaluating electronic sources. One excellent example was created by reference librarians at the Wolfgram Memorial Library of Widener University. Type *Wolfgram evaluate web pages* into a search engine to access that site. For additional guidance, go to bedfordstmartins.com/researchroom and click on "How to Evaluate Sources" and/or "Evaluating Online Sources: A Tutorial."

On the basis of your evaluation, select the most promising books, articles, and Web sites to pursue in depth for your research project.

Analyzing Your Sources

Before you begin to take notes, it is essential that you read critically and carefully analyze your sources for their theses, overall arguments, amount and credibility of evidence, bias, and reliability in helping you explore your research topic. Look for the writers' main ideas, key examples, strongest arguments, and conclusions. While it is easy to become absorbed in sources that support your own beliefs, always seek out several sources with opposing viewpoints, if only to test your own position. Look for information about the authors themselves — information that will help you determine their authority and where they position themselves in the broader conversation on the issue. You should also know the reputation and special interests of book publishers and magazines, because you are likely to get different views — conservative, liberal, international, feminist — on the same topic depending on the publication you read. Use the following checklist to assist you in analyzing your print and online sources.

Checklist for Analyzing Print and Online Sources

▸ What is the writer's thesis or claim?

▸ How does the writer support this thesis? Does the evidence seem fact-based, or is it mainly anecdotal?

▸ Does the writer consider opposing viewpoints?

▸ Does the writer have any obvious political or religious biases? Is the writer associated with any special-interest groups such as Planned Parenthood, Greenpeace, Amnesty International, or the National Rifle Association?

▸ Is the writer an expert on the subject? Do other writers mention this author in their work?

▸ Is important information documented through footnotes or links so that it can be verified or corroborated in other sources?

▸ What is the author's purpose — to inform; to argue for a particular position or action; something else?

▸ Do the writer's thesis and purpose clearly relate to your research topic?

▸ Does the source reflect current thinking and research in the field?

Developing a Working Bibliography for Your Sources

As you discover books, journal and magazine articles, newspaper stories, and Web sites that you think might be helpful, you need to start maintaining a record of important information about each source. This record, called a working bibliography, will enable you to know where sources are located as well as what they are when it comes time to consult them or acknowledge them in your list of works cited or final bibliography. In all likelihood, your working bibliography will contain more sources than you actually consult and include in your list of works cited.

Some people make separate bibliography cards, using a 3- by 5-inch index card, for each work that might be helpful to their research. By using a separate card for each book, article, or Web site, they can continually edit their working bibliography, dropping sources that did not prove helpful for one reason or another and adding new ones.

With the computerization of most library resources, you now have the option to copy and paste bibliographic information from the library computer catalog and periodical indexes or from the Internet into a document on your computer that you can edit throughout the research process. You can also track your project online with a citation manager like the Bedford Bibliographer <bedfordstmartins.com/bibliographer>. One advantage of the copy/paste option over the index card method is accuracy, especially in punctuation, spelling, and capitalization — details that are essential in accessing Internet sites.

Checklist for a Working Bibliography of Print and Online Sources

For Books

▸ Library call number

▸ Names of all authors, editors, and translators

▸ Title and subtitle

▸ Publication data:

>   Place of publication (city and state)
>   Publisher's name
>   Date of publication

▸ Edition (if not the first) and volume number (if applicable)

For Periodical Articles

▸ Names of all authors

▸ Name and subtitle of article

▸ Title of journal, magazine, or newspaper

▸ Publication data:

>   Volume number and issue number
>   Date of issue
>   Page numbers

(*continued on next page*)

(continued from previous page)

For Internet Sources

▶ Names of all authors and/or editors

▶ Title and subtitle of the document

▶ Title of the longer work to which the document belongs (if applicable)

▶ Title of the site or discussion list

▶ Name of company or organization that owns the Web site

▶ Date of release, online posting, or latest revision

▶ Format of online source (Web page, .pdf, podcast, etc.)

▶ Date you accessed the site

▶ Electronic address (URL)

For Other Sources

▶ Name of author, government agency, organization, company, recording artist, personality, etc.

▶ Title of the work

▶ Format (pamphlet, unpublished diary, interview, television broadcast, etc.)

▶ Publication or production data:

Name of publisher or producer

Date of publication, production, or release

Identifying codes or numbers (if applicable)

Taking Notes

As you read, take notes. You're looking for ideas, facts, opinions, statistics, examples, and evidence that you think will be useful in writing your paper. As you work through the articles, look for recurring themes, and mark the places where the writers are in agreement and where they differ in their views. Try to remember that the effectiveness of your paper is largely determined by the quality — not necessarily the quantity — of your notes. The purpose of a research paper is not to present a collection of quotes that show you've read all the material and can report what others have said about your topic. Your goal is to analyze, evaluate, and synthesize the information you collect — in other words, to enter into the discussion of the issues and thereby take ownership of your topic. You want to view the results of your research from your own perspective and arrive at an informed opinion of your topic. (For more on Writing with Sources, see Chapter 14.)

Now for some practical advice on taking notes: First, be systematic. If you use note cards, write one note on a card, and use cards of uniform size, preferably 4- by 6-inch cards because they are large enough to accommodate even a long note on a single card and yet small enough to be easily handled and carried. If you keep notes electronically, consider creating a separate file for each topic or source, or use an electronic research manager like Zotero <zotero.org>. If you keep your notes organized, when you get to the planning and writing stage, you will be able to sequence your notes according to the plan you have envisioned for your paper. Furthermore, should you decide to alter your organizational plan, you can easily reorder your notes to reflect those revisions.

Second, try not to take too many notes. One good way to help decide whether to take a note is to ask yourself, "How exactly does this material help prove or disprove my thesis?" You might even try envisioning where in your paper you could use the information. If it does not seem relevant to your thesis, don't bother to take a note.

Once you decide to take a note, you must decide whether to summarize, paraphrase, or quote directly. The approach that you take is largely determined by the content of the passage and the way you envision using it in your paper. For detailed advice on summary, paraphrase, and quotation, see Chapter 14, pages 637–40.

Documenting Sources

When you summarize, paraphrase, or quote a person's thoughts and ideas, and when you use facts or statistics that are not commonly known or believed, you must properly acknowledge the source of your information. You must document the source of your information when you

- Quote a source word for word

- Refer to information and ideas from another source that you present in your own words as either a paraphrase or a summary

- Cite statistics, tables, charts, or graphs

You do not need to document

- Your own observations, experiences, and ideas

- Factual information available in a number of reference works (known as "common knowledge")

- Proverbs, sayings, and familiar quotations

A reference to the source of your borrowed information is called a *citation*. There are many systems for making citations, and your citations must consistently follow one of these systems. The documentation style recommended by the Modern Language Association (MLA) is commonly used in English and the humanities and is the style used for student papers throughout this book. Another common system is American Psychological Association (APA) style, which is used in the social sciences. In general, your instructor will tell you which system to use. For more information on documentation styles, consult the appropriate manual or handbook. For MLA style, consult the *MLA Handbook for Writers of Research Papers*, 7th ed. (New York: MLA, 2009).

There are two components of documentation in a research paper: the *in-text citation*, placed in the body of your paper, and the *list of works cited*, which provides complete publication data on your sources and is placed at the end of your paper.

■ In-Text Citations

Most in-text citations, also known as parenthetical citations, consist of only the author's last name and a page reference. Usually, the author's name is given in an introductory or signal phrase (see pages 640–41) at the beginning of the borrowed material, and the page reference is given in parentheses at the end. If the author's name is not given at the beginning, it belongs in the parentheses along with the page reference. The parenthetical reference signals the end of the borrowed material and directs your readers to the list of works cited should they want to pursue a source.

Consider the following examples of in-text citations from a student paper on the debate over whether to make English America's official language.

In-Text Citations (MLA Style)

Many people are surprised to discover that English is not the official language of the United States. Today, even as English literacy becomes a necessity for people in many parts of the world, some people in the United States believe its primacy is being threatened right at home. Much of the current controversy focuses on Hispanic communities with large Spanish-speaking populations who may feel little or no pressure to learn English. Columnist and cultural critic Charles Krauthammer believes English should be America's official language. He notes that this country has been "blessed . . . with a linguistic unity that brings a critically needed

Citation with author's name in the signal phrase

> cohesion to a nation as diverse, multiracial and multiethnic as America" and that communities such as these threaten the bond created by a common language (112). There are others, however, who think that "language does not threaten American unity. Benign neglect is a good policy for any country when it comes to language, and it's a good policy for America" (King 64).

Citation with author's name in parentheses

Works Cited

King, Robert D. "Should English Be the Law?" *Atlantic Monthly* Apr. 1997: 55-64. Print.

Krauthammer, Charles. "In Plain English: Let's Make It Official." *Time* 12 June 2006: 112. Print.

In the preceding example, the student followed MLA guidelines for documentation. The following sections provide MLA guidelines for documenting periodical print publications, nonperiodical print publications, Web publications, and other common sources. For advice on documenting additional, less frequently cited sources, consult the *MLA Handbook for Writers of Research Papers*, 7th ed. (New York: MLA, 2009).

List of Works Cited

In this section, you will find general guidelines for creating a list of works cited, followed by sample entries designed to cover the citations you will use most often.

Guidelines for Constructing Your Works Cited Page

1. Begin the list on a new page following the last page of text.

2. Center the title *Works Cited* at the top of the page.

3. Double-space both within and between entries on your list.

4. Alphabetize your sources by the authors' last names. If you have two or more authors with the same last name, alphabetize by first names.

5. If you have two or more works by the same author, alphabetize by the first word of the titles, not counting *A*, *An*, or *The*. Use the

(*continued on next page*)

(continued from previous page)

author's name in the first entry and three unspaced hyphens followed by a period in subsequent entries:

Twitchell, James B. *Branded Nation: When Culture Goes Pop.* New York: Simon, 2004. Print.

---. "The Branding of Higher Ed." *Forbes* 25 Nov. 2002: 50. Print.

---. *Living It Up: America's Love Affair with Luxury.* New York: Columbia UP, 2002. Print.

6. If no author is known, alphabetize by title.

7. Begin each entry at the left margin. If the entry is longer than one line, indent the second and subsequent lines one-half inch.

8. Italicize the titles of books, journals, magazines, and newspapers. Use quotation marks for titles of periodical articles, chapters and essays within books, short stories, and poems.

9. Provide the medium of the source (i.e., Print, Web, Film, Television, Performance).

■ Periodical Print Publications: Journals, Magazines, and Newspapers

Standard Information for Periodical Print Publications

1. Name of the author of the work; for anonymous works, begin entry with the title of the work

2. Title of the work, in quotation marks

3. Name of the periodical, italicized

4. Series number or name, if relevant

5. Volume number (for scholarly journals that use volume numbers)

6. Issue number (if available, for scholarly journals)

7. Date of publication (for scholarly journals, year; for other periodicals, day, month, and year, as available)

8. Page numbers

9. Medium of publication (for print sources, use *Print*)

Scholarly Journal Article

For all scholarly journals — whether paginated continuously throughout a given year or not — provide the volume number (if one is given), the issue number, the year, the page numbers, and the medium. Separate the volume number and the issue number with a period.

Lachman, Lilach. "Time, Space, and Illusion: Between Keats and Poussin." *Comparative Literature* 55.4 (2003): 293-319. Print.

Magazine Article

When citing a weekly or biweekly magazine, give the complete date (day, month, year).

Brokaw, Tom. "Walter Cronkite: The Most Trusted Man in America." *Time* 3 Aug. 2009: 20-21. Print.

When citing a magazine published every month or every two months, provide the month or months and year. If an article in a magazine is not printed on consecutive pages — for example, an article might begin on page 45, then skip to 48 — include only the first page followed by a plus sign.

Mascarelli, Amanda Leigh. "Fall Guys." *Audubon* Nov.-Dec. 2009: 44+. Print.

Newspaper Article

Wade, Nicholas. "Museum Is Displaying Treasures of the Other Evolution Pioneer." *New York Times* 24 Nov. 2009, natl. ed.: D3. Print.

Review (Book or Film)

Ruta, Suzanne. "Midnight Minus One." Rev. of *The Point of Return*, by Siddhartha Deb. *New York Times Book Review* 23 Mar. 2003: 13. Print.
Lane, Anthony. "Under Pressure." Rev. of *K-19: The Widowmaker*, dir. Kathryn Bigelow. *New Yorker* 29 July 2002: 92-93. Print.

If the review has no title, simply begin with *Rev.* after the author's name. If there is neither a title nor an author, begin with *Rev.* and alphabetize by the title of the book or film being reviewed.

Anonymous Article

When no author's name is given, begin the entry with the title.

"Pompeii: Will the City Go from Dust to Dust?" *Newsweek* 1 Sept. 1997: 8. Print.

Editorial (Signed/Unsigned)

Jackson, Derrick Z. "The Winner: Hypocrisy." Editorial. *Boston Globe* 6 Feb. 2004: A19. Print.
"A Real Schedule for Ground Zero." Editorial. *New York Times* 18 June 2008, natl. ed.: A22. Print.

Letter to the Editor

Echevarria-Leary, Cheers. Letter. *Newsweek* 14 Sept. 2009: 4. Print.

■ Nonperiodical Print Publications: Books, Brochures, and Pamphlets

Standard Information for Nonperiodical Print Publications

1. Name of the author, editor, compiler, or translator of the work; for anonymous works, begin entry with the title

2. Title of the work, italicized

3. Edition

4. Volume number

5. City of publication, name of the publisher, and year of publication

6. Medium of publication (for print sources, use *Print*)

Book by a Single Author

Kitwana, Bakari. *Why White Kids Love Hip Hop*. New York: Basic, 2005. Print.

Use a shortened version of the publisher's name — for example, *Houghton* for "Houghton Mifflin" or *Cambridge UP* for "Cambridge University Press."

Anthology

Eschholz, Paul, and Alfred Rosa. *Subject & Strategy*. 12th ed. Boston: Bedford, 2011. Print.

Book by Two or More Authors

For a book by two or three authors, list the authors in the order in which they appear on the title page.

Douglas, Susan, and Meredith Michaels. *The Mammy Myth: The Idealization of Motherhood and How It Has Undermined Women*. New York: Free, 2004. Print.

For a book by four or more authors, list the first author in the same way as for a single-author book, followed by a comma and the abbreviation *et al.* ("and others").

Beardsley, John, et al. *Gee's Bend: The Women and Their Quilts*. Atlanta: Tinwood, 2002. Print.

Book by Corporate Author

Carnegie Foundation for the Advancement of Teaching. *Campus Life: In Search of Community*. Princeton: Princeton UP, 1990. Print.

Work in Anthology

Include the page numbers of the selection after the anthology's year of publication.

Dao, Bei. "13 Happiness Street." *Contemporary Literature of Asia*. Ed. Arthur W. Biddle, Gloria Bien, and Vinay Dharwadker. Upper Saddle River: Prentice, 1996. 281-92. Print.

Note that *Ed.* here stands for "Edited by," so no plural is necessary.

Article in Reference Book

Preuss, Harry G. "Nutrition." *The Encyclopedia Americana*. 2004 ed. Print.

If an article is unsigned, begin with the title.

"Dostoyevsky, Fyodor Mikhailovich." *Benet's Reader's Encyclopedia*. 5th ed. 2008. Print.

Note that widely used reference works such as these do not require a publisher's name.

Introduction, Preface, Foreword, or Afterword to Book

Wirzba, Norman. Introduction. *The Art of the Commonplace: The Agrarian Essays of Wendell Berry*. By Wendell Berry. Washington: Shoemaker & Hoard, 2002. vii-xx. Print.

Anonymous Book

Children of the Dragon: The Story of Tiananmen Square. New York: Collier-Macmillan, 1990. Print.

Translation

Dumas, Alexandre. *The Knight of Maison Rouge*. Trans. Julie Rose. New York: Modern Library, 2003. Print.

Illustrated Book or Graphic Novel

Clemens, Samuel L. *The Adventures of Huckleberry Finn*. Illus. Norman Rockwell. New York: Heritage, 1940. Print.

Neufield, Josh, writer and artist. *A.D.: New Orleans After the Deluge*. New York: Pantheon, 2009. Print.

Book Published in Second or Subsequent Edition

Hassan, Ihab. *The Dismemberment of Orpheus: Toward a Postmodern Literature*. 2nd ed. Madison: U of Wisconsin P, 1982. Print.

Modern Language Association of America. *MLA Handbook for Writers of Research Papers*. 7th ed. New York: MLA, 2009. Print.

Brochure or Pamphlet

Clay County Department of Parks, Recreation & Historic Sites. *Jesse James Birth Place: Clay County, Missouri*. Liberty: Clay County Parks, 2004. Print.

Government Publication

United States. Dept. of Labor. *Child Care: A Workforce Issue.* Washington: GPO, 1988.
     Print.

Give the government, the agency, and the title with a period and a space after each. For most federal publications, the publisher is the Government Printing Office (GPO).

■ Web Publications

The following guidelines and models for citing information retrieved from the World Wide Web have been adapted from the most recent advice of the MLA — as detailed in the *MLA Handbook for Writers of Research Papers*, 7th ed. (2009) — and from the "MLA Style" section on MLA's Web site <www.mla.org>. You will notice that citations of Web publications have some features in common with both print publications and reprinted works, broadcasts, and live performances.

Standard Information for Web Publications

1. Name of the author, editor, or compiler of the work
   (For works with more than one author, a corporate author, or an unnamed author, apply the guidelines for print sources; for anonymous works, begin entry with the title.)

2. Title of the work, italicized, unless it is part of a larger work, in which case put it in quotation marks

3. Title of the overall Web site, italicized (if distinct from item 2 above)

4. Version or edition of the site, if relevant

5. Publisher or sponsor of the site; if this information is not available, use *n.p.* ("no publisher")

6. Date of publication (day, month, and year); if no date is given, use *n.d.*

7. Medium of publication (for online sources use *Web*)

8. Date of access (day, month, and year)

MLA style does not require URLs in works cited entries. However, if your instructor wants you to include URLs in your citations or if you believe readers will not be able to locate the source without the URL, insert it as the last item in an entry, immediately after the date of access. Enclose the URL in angle brackets, followed by a period. The following example illustrates an entry with the URL included:

Finley, Laura L. "How Can I Teach Peace When the Book Only Covers War?" *Online Journal of Peace and Conflict Resolution* 5.1 (2003): n. pag. Web. 12 Dec. 2009. <http://www.trinstitute.org/ojpcr/5_1finley.htm>.

MLA style requires that you break URLs extending over more than one line only after a slash. Do *not* add spaces, hyphens, or any other punctuation to indicate the break.

Online Scholarly Journals. To cite an article, review, editorial, or letter to the editor in a scholarly journal existing only in electronic form on the Web, provide the author, the title of the article, the title of the journal, the volume and issue, and the date of issue, followed by the page numbers (if available), the medium, and the date of access.

Article in Online Scholarly Journal

Rist, Thomas. "Religion, Politics, Revenge: The Dead in Renaissance Drama." *Early Modern Literary Studies* 9.1 (2003): n. pag. Web. 12 Dec. 2009.

Book Review in Online Scholarly Journal

Opongo, Elias Omondi. Rev. of *Responsibility to Protect: The Global Effort to End Mass Atrocities,* by Alex J. Bellamy. *Journal of Peace, Conflict, and Development* 14.14 (2009): n. pag. Web. 27 Nov. 2009.

Editorial in Online Scholarly Journal

"Writing Across the Curriculum and Writing Centers." Editorial. *Praxis: A Writing Center Journal* 6.2 (2009): n. pag. Web. 10 Jan. 2010.

Periodical Publications in Online Databases

Journal Article from Online Database or Subscription Service

Kauver, Elaine M. "Warring Desires: The Future of Jewish American Literature." *American Literary History* 21.4 (2009): 877-90. *Project Muse.* Web. 7 Dec. 2009.

Magazine Article from Online Database or Subscription Service

Keizer, Garret. "Sound and Fury: The Politics of Noise in a Loud Society." *Harper's* Mar. 2001: 39-48. *Expanded Academic ASAP Plus.* Web. 27 July 2009.

Newspaper Article from Online Database or Subscription Service

Sanders, Joshunda. "Think Race Doesn't Matter? Listen to Eminem." *San Francisco Chronicle* 20 July 2003: n. pag. *LexisNexis.* Web. 29 Dec. 2009.
McEachern, William Ross. "Teaching and Learning in Bilingual Countries: The Examples of Belgium and Canada." *Education* 123.1 (2002): 103. *Expanded Academic ASAP Plus.* Web. 17 Sept. 2009.

Nonperiodical Web Publications. This category of Web publication includes all Web-delivered content that does not fit into one of the previous two categories (online scholarly journal publications and periodical publications from an online database).

Online Magazine Article

Lamott, Anne. "Because I'm a Mother." *Salon.com*. Salon Media Group, 4 July 2003.
Web. 4 Jan. 2010.

Huang, Lily. "The Case of the Disappearing Rabbit." *Newsweek*. Newsweek, 25 July
2009. Web. 10 Dec. 2009.

Online Newspaper Article

Hanley, Charles J., and Jan M. Olsen. "Climate Drama Climax Looks Elusive
in Copenhagen." *Seattletimes.com*. Seattle Times, 5 Dec. 2009. Web. 28 Feb.
2010.

"Beyond Copenhagen." Editorial. *New York Times*. New York Times, 6 Dec. 2009.
Web. 7 Dec. 2009.

Online Scholarly Project

Driscoll, Dana Lynn. "Irregular Verbs." Chart. *The OWL at Purdue*. Purdue U Online
Writing Lab, 13 May 2007. Web. 8 Dec. 2009.

Book or Part of Book Accessed Online

For a book available online, provide the author, the title, the editor (if any),
original publication information, the name of the database or Web site,
the medium (*Web*), and the date of access.

Hawthorne, Nathaniel. *The Blithedale Romance*. Boston: Houghton, 1894. *Google
Book Search*. Web. 28 Sept. 2009.

If you are citing only part of an online book, include the title or name
of the part directly after the author's name.

Woolf, Virginia. "Kew Gardens." *Monday or Tuesday*. New York: Harcourt, 1921.
Bartleby.com: Great Books Online. Web. 15 Nov. 2009.

Online Speech, Essay, Poem, or Short Story

Faulkner, William. "On Accepting the Nobel Prize." 10 Dec. 1950. *The History Place:
Great Speeches Collection*. Web. 12 May 2009.

Online News Service

Pressman, Gabe. "Eminent Domain: Let the Public Beware!" *NBCNewYork.com*.
NBC, 5 Dec. 2009. Web. 6 Dec. 2009.

"Iran Police Clash with Protesters." *CNN.com*. Cable News Network, 7 Dec. 2009.
Web. 7 Dec. 2009.

Online Encyclopedia or Other Reference Work

"Chili Pepper." *Encyclopaedia Britannica Online.* Encyclopaedia Britannica, 2009. Web. 20 July 2009.

"Blog." *Merriam-Webster Online Dictionary.* Merriam-Webster, 2009. Web. 30 Aug. 2009.

Online Artwork, Photographs, Maps, Charts, and Other Images

da Vinci, Leonardo. *Mona Lisa.* 1503-6. Musee du Louvre, Paris. *WebMuseum,* 19 June 2006. Web. 8 Dec. 2009.

"West Hartford, Connecticut." Map. *Google Maps.* Google, 20 June 2009. Web. 20 June 2009.

Online Government Publication

United States. Dept. of Treasury. Internal Revenue Service. *Your Rights as a Taxpayer.* GPO, May 2005. Web. 2 Nov. 2009.

Home Page for Academic Department

Dept. of English. Home page. Arizona State U, n.d. Web. 29 Aug. 2009.

Home Page for Academic Course

Magistrale, Tony. Home page. *Poe's Children.* Dept. of English. U of Vermont, 6 Nov. 2002. Web. 9 Sept. 2009.

Wiki Entry

"C. S. Lewis." *Wikipedia.* Wikimedia Foundation, 8 Dec. 2009. Web. 10 Dec. 2009.

No author is listed for a Wiki entry because the content is written collaboratively.

Blog Posting

Broadway Bob. "Defining Home." *babblebob.* Robert M. Armstrong, 24 Aug. 2009. Web. 10 Dec. 2009.

Online Video Recording

ManakinBird. "Manakin Bird." *YouTube.* YouTube, 12 Apr. 2008. Web. 12 Dec. 2009.

■ Additional Common Sources

Television or Radio Broadcast

"Everyone's Waiting." *Six Feet Under.* Dir. Alan Ball. Perf. Peter Krause, Michael C. Hall, Frances Conroy, and Lauren Ambrose. HBO. 21 Aug. 2005. Television.

Sound Recording

Beethoven, Ludwig van. *The Complete Sonatas*. Perf. Richard Goode. Warner, 1993. CD.

Film or Video Recording

Schindler's List. Dir. Steven Spielberg. Perf. Liam Neeson, Ralph Fiennes, and Ben
    Kingsley. 1993. Universal, 2004. DVD.

Work of Visual Art

Botticelli, Sandro. *Birth of Venus*. 1485-86? Tempera on panel. Uffizi Gallery,
    Florence.

If you use a reproduction of a piece of visual art, give the institution
and city as well as the complete publication information for the source,
including the medium of reproduction.

Parks, Gordon. *Muhammad Ali*. 1970. Photograph. The Capital Group
    Foundation, Atlanta. *Bare Witness: Photographs by Gordon Parks*. Milan:
    Skira, 2007. Print.

Interview

Handke, Peter. Interview. *New York Times Magazine* 2 July 2006: 13. Print.

For interviews that you conduct, provide the name of the person interviewed, the type of interview (personal, telephone, e-mail), and the date.

Dean, Howard. Telephone interview. 30 July 2009.

Cartoon or Comic Strip

Luckovich, Mike. Cartoon. *Atlanta Journal-Constitution* 24 Nov. 2009. Print.

Advertisement

Sprint. Advertisement. *Newsweek* 7 Sept. 2009: 15. Print.

Lecture, Speech, Address, or Reading

England, Paula. "Gender and Inequality: Trends and Causes." President's
    Distinguished Lecture Series. U. of Vermont. Memorial Lounge, Burlington.
    22 Mar. 2004. Lecture.

Letter, Memo, or E-Mail Message

Indicate the medium, using *MS* (handwritten manuscript), *TS* (typescript),
or *E-mail*.

Proulx, E. Annie. Letter to the author. 22 Jan. 2007. MS.
Walker, Alexis. "Re: New Visual Options." Message to the author. 10 Feb. 2010.
    E-mail.

CD-ROM or DVD-ROM Publication

Cite CD-ROMs published as a single edition as you would a book, being careful to add *CD-ROM* as the medium.

Shakespeare, William. *Macbeth*. Ed. A. R. Branmuller. New York: Voyager, 1994.
    CD-ROM.

Some CD-ROMs and DVD-ROMs are updated on a regular basis because they cover publications such as journals, magazines, and newspapers that are themselves published periodically. Start your entry with the author's name, the publication information for the print source, followed by the medium of publication, the title of the database (italicized), the name of the vendor, and the electronic publication date.

James, Caryn. "An Army Family as Strong as Its Weakest Link." *New York Times*
    16 Sept. 1994, late ed.: C8. CD-ROM. *New York Times Ondisc*. UMI-ProQuest,
    1994.

Digital File

A number of different types of work — a book, typescript, photograph, or sound recording — can be available as a digital file. It is important that you record the format of the digital file in the space reserved for publication medium (JPEG file, PDF file, *Microsoft Word* file, MP3 file).

Dengle, Isabella. *Eben Peck Cabin*. 1891. Wisconsin Historical Society, Madison.
    JPEG file.
Federman, Sarah. "An American in Paris: French Health Care." 2009. *Microsoft*
    Word file.

Editing for Grammar, Punctuation, and Sentence Style

Once you have revised your essay and you are confident that you have said what you wanted to say, you are ready to begin editing your essay. It's at the editing stage of the writing process that you identify and correct errors in grammar, punctuation, and sentence style. You don't want a series of small errors to detract from your paper: Such errors can cause confusion in some cases, and they can also cause readers to have second thoughts about your credibility as an author.

This chapter addresses twelve common writing problems that instructors from around the country told us trouble their students most. For more guidance with these or other editing concerns, be sure to refer to a writer's handbook or ask your instructor for help. To practice identifying and correcting these and other writing problems, go to bedfordstmartins .com/exercisecentral.

1 Run-ons: Fused Sentences and Comma Splices

Writers can become so absorbed in getting their ideas down on paper that they sometimes incorrectly combine two independent clauses — word groups that could stand on their own as complete sentences — incorrectly, creating a *run-on sentence*. A run-on sentence fails to show where one thought ends and another begins, and it can confuse readers. There are two types of run-on sentences: the fused sentence and the comma splice.

A *fused sentence* occurs when a writer joins two independent clauses with no punctuation and no coordinating conjunction.

fused
sentence   The delegates at the state political convention could not de-cide on a leader they were beginning to show their frustration.

A *comma splice* occurs when a writer uses only a comma to join two or more independent clauses.

comma
splice   The delegates at the state political convention could not decide on a leader, they were beginning to show their frustration.

There are five ways to fix run-on sentences.

1. Create two separate sentences with a period.

edited   The delegates at the state political convention could not decide

on a leader ~~they~~ .They were beginning to show their frustration.

2. Use a comma and a coordinating conjunction to join the two sentences.

edited   The delegates at the state political convention could not decide

on a leader ,and they were beginning to show their frustration.

3. Use a semicolon to separate the two clauses.

edited   The delegates at the state political convention could not decide

on a leader ;they were beginning to show their frustration.

4. Use a semicolon followed by a transitional word or expression and a comma to join the two clauses.

edited   The delegates at the state political convention could not decide

; consequently,
on a leader they were beginning to show their frustration.

5. Subordinate one clause to the other, using a subordinate conjunction or a relative pronoun.

When the
edited   ~~The~~ delegates at the state political convention could not decide

on a leader they were beginning to show their frustration.

, who were beginning to show their frustration,
edited   The delegates at the state political convention could not decide

on a leader ~~they were beginning to show their frustration.~~

\ 2 Sentence Fragments

A *sentence fragment* is a part of a sentence presented as if it were a complete sentence. Even if a word group begins with a capital letter and ends with a period, a question mark, or an exclamation point, it is not a sentence unless it has a subject (the person, place, or thing the sentence is about) and a verb (a word that tells what the subject does) and expresses a complete thought.

> **sentence**   My music group decided to study the early works of Mozart.
> **fragment**   *The child prodigy from Austria.*

Word groups that do not express complete thoughts are often freestanding subordinate clauses beginning with a subordinating conjunction such as *although, because, since, so, that,* or *unless.*

> **sentence**   The company president met with the management team every
> **fragment**   week. *So that problems were rarely ignored.*

You can correct sentence fragments in one of two ways.

1. **Integrate the fragment into a nearby sentence.**

    > **edited**   My music group decided to study the early works of Mozart‚ ^the^ T̶h̶e̶
    >
    > child prodigy from Austria.

    > **edited**   The company president met with the management team every
    >
    > week‚ ^so^ S̶o̶ that problems were rarely ignored.

2. **Develop the fragment into a complete sentence by adding a subject or a verb.**

    > **edited**   My music group decided to study the early works of Mozart.
    >
    > The child prodigy ^was^ from Austria.

    > **edited**   The company president met with the management team every
    >
    > week. ^Problems^ S̶o̶ t̶h̶a̶t̶ p̶r̶o̶b̶l̶e̶m̶s̶ were rarely ignored.

Sentence fragments are not always wrong. In fact, if used deliberately, a sentence fragment can add useful stylistic emphasis. In narratives, deliberate sentence fragments are most commonly used in dialogue and in descriptive passages that set a mood or tone. In the following passage taken from "Not Close Enough for Comfort" (pages 102–4), David P. Bardeen uses fragments to convey the awkwardness of the luncheon meeting he had with his brother Will:

> I asked him about his recent trip. He asked me about work. Short
> questions. One-word answers. Then an awkward pause.

3 Comma Faults

Commas help communicate meaning by eliminating possible misreadings. Consider this sentence:

> After visiting William Alan Lee went to French class.

Depending upon where you put the comma, it could be Lee, Alan Lee, or William Alan Lee who goes to French class.

> **edited**   After visiting William Alan Lee went to French class.

> **edited**   After visiting William Alan Lee went to French class.

> **edited**   After visiting William Alan Lee went to French class.

The comma, of all the marks of punctuation, has the greatest variety of uses, which can make its proper use seem difficult. It might help to think of the comma's role this way: In every case the comma functions in one of two basic ways — to *separate* or to *enclose* elements in a sentence. By learning a few basic rules based on these two functions, you will be able to identify and correct common comma errors.

1. **Use a comma to separate two independent clauses joined by a coordinating conjunction.**

   > **incorrect**   Tolstoy wrote many popular short stories but he is perhaps best known for his novels.

   > **edited**   Tolstoy wrote many popular short stories but he is perhaps
   >
   > best known for his novels.

2. **Use a comma to separate an introductory phrase or clause from the main clause of a sentence.**

   > **incorrect**   In his book *Life on the Mississippi* Mark Twain describes his days as a riverboat pilot.

   > **edited**   In his book *Life on the Mississippi* Mark Twain describes his days
   >
   > as a riverboat pilot.

   > **incorrect**   When the former Soviet Union collapsed residents of Moscow had to struggle just to survive.

   > **edited**   When the former Soviet Union collapsed residents of Moscow
   >
   > had to struggle just to survive.

3. **Use commas to enclose nonrestrictive elements.**   When an adjective phrase or clause adds information that is essential to the meaning of

a sentence, it is said to be *restrictive* and should not be set off with commas.

The woman wearing the beige linen suit works with Homeland Security.

The adjective phrase "wearing the beige linen suit" is essential and thus should not be set off with commas; without this information, we have no way of identifying which woman works with Homeland Security.

When an adjective phrase or clause does not add information that is essential to the meaning of the sentence, it is said to be *nonrestrictive* and should be enclosed with commas.

incorrect Utopian literature which was popular during the late nineteenth century seems to emerge at times of economic and political unrest.

edited Utopian literature‸which was popular during the late nineteenth century‸seems to emerge at times of economic and political unrest.

4. **Use commas to separate items in a series.**

incorrect The three staples of the diet in Thailand are rice fish and fruit.

edited The three staples of the diet in Thailand are rice‸fish‸and fruit.

＼ 4 Subject-Verb Agreement

Subjects and verbs must agree in number — that is, a singular subject (one person, place, or thing) must take a singular verb, and a plural subject (more than one person, place, or thing) must take a plural verb. While most native speakers of English use proper subject-verb agreement in their writing without thinking about it, some sentence constructions can be troublesome to native and non-native speakers alike.

▪ Intervening Prepositional Phrases

When the relationship between the subject and the verb in a sentence is not clear, the culprit is usually an intervening prepositional phrase (a phrase that begins with a preposition such as *on, of, in, at,* or *between*). To make sure the subject agrees with its verb in a sentence with an intervening prepositional phrase, mentally cross out the phrase (*of the term* in the following example) to isolate the subject and the verb and determine if they agree.

incorrect The first one hundred days of the term has passed quickly.

edited The first one hundred days of the term ~~has~~ ‸have passed quickly.

■ Compound Subjects

Writers often have difficulty with subject-verb agreement in sentences with compound subjects (two or more subjects joined together with the word *and*). As a general rule, compound subjects take plural verbs.

incorrect   My iPod, computer, and television was stolen.

edited   My iPod, computer, and television ~~was~~ ^{were} stolen.

However, in sentences with subjects joined by *either . . . or, neither . . . nor*, or *not only . . . but also*, the verb must agree with the subject closest to it.

incorrect   Neither the students nor the professor are satisfied with the lab equipment.

edited   Neither the students nor the professor ~~are~~ ^{is} satisfied with the

lab equipment.

\ 5 Unclear Pronoun References

The noun to which a pronoun refers is called its *antecedent* or *referent*. Be sure to place a pronoun as close to its antecedent as possible so that the relationship between them is clear. The more words that intervene between the antecedent and the pronoun, the more chance there is for confusion. When the relationship between a pronoun and its antecedent is unclear, the sentence becomes inaccurate or ambiguous. While editing your writing, look for and correct ambiguous, vague, or implied pronoun references.

■ Ambiguous References

Make sure all your pronouns clearly refer to specific antecedents. If a pronoun can refer to more than one antecedent, the sentence is ambiguous.

ambiguous   Adler sought to convince the reader to mark up *his* book.

In this sentence, the antecedent of the pronoun *his* could be either *Adler* or *reader*. Does Adler want his particular book marked up, or does he want the reader to mark up his or her own book? To make an ambiguous antecedent clear, either repeat the correct antecedent or rewrite the sentence.

edited   Adler sought to convince the reader to mark up ~~his~~ ^{Adler's} book.

edited   Adler sought to convince the reader to mark up ~~his~~ ^{his or her} book.

▪ Vague References

Whenever you use *it, they, you, this, that,* or *which* to refer to a general idea in a preceding clause or sentence, be sure that the connection between the pronoun and the general idea is clear. When these pronouns lack a specific antecedent, you give readers an impression of vagueness and carelessness. To correct the problem, either substitute a noun for the pronoun or provide an antecedent to which the pronoun can clearly refer.

vague   The tornadoes damaged many of the homes in the area, but it has not yet been determined.

edited   The tornadoes damaged many of the homes in the area, but

     the extent of the damage
     ~~it~~ has not yet been determined.

vague   In the book, they wrote that Samantha had an addictive personality.

edited   In the book, ~~they wrote that~~ Samantha had an addictive

     personality.

Whenever the connection between the general idea and the pronoun is simple and clear, no confusion results. Consider the following example:

The stock market rose for a third consecutive week, and *this* lifted most investors' spirits.

▪ Implied References

Make every pronoun refer to a stated, not an implied, antecedent. Every time you use a pronoun in a sentence, you should be able to identify its noun equivalent. If you cannot, use a noun instead.

implied   After all of the editing and formatting, it was finished.

                           the research report
edited   After all of the editing and formatting, ~~it~~ was finished.

Sometimes a modifier or possessive that implies a noun is mistaken for an antecedent.

implied   In G. Anthony Gorry's "Steal This MP3 File: What Is Theft?," he shows how technology might be shaping the attitudes of today's youth.

edited   In ~~G. Anthony Gorry's~~ "Steal This MP3 File: What Is Theft?,"

     G. Anthony Gorry
     ~~he~~ shows how technology might be shaping the attitudes of

     today's youth.

6 Pronoun-Antecedent Agreement

Personal pronouns must agree with their antecedents in *person*, *number*, and *gender*.

■ Agreement in Person

There are three types of personal pronouns: first person (*I* and *we*), second person (*you*), and third person (*he*, *she*, *it*, and *they*). To agree in person, first-person pronouns must refer to first-person antecedents, second-person pronouns to second-person antecedents, and third-person pronouns to third-person antecedents.

> **incorrect** A scientist should consider all the data carefully before you draw a conclusion.

> **edited** A scientist should consider all the data carefully before
> he or she draws
> ~~you draw~~ a conclusion.

■ Agreement in Number

To agree in number, a singular pronoun must refer to a singular anteced-ent, and a plural pronoun must refer to a plural antecedent. When two or more antecedents are joined by the word *and*, the pronoun must be plural.

> **incorrect** Karen, Rachel, and Sofia took her electives in history.

> **edited** Karen, Rachel, and Sofia took ~~her~~ their electives in history.

When the subject of a sentence is an indefinite pronoun such as *every-one*, *each*, *everybody*, *anyone*, *anybody*, *everything*, *either*, *one*, *neither*, *someone*, or *something*, use a singular pronoun to refer to it, or recast the sentence to eliminate the agreement problem.

> **incorrect** Each of the women submitted their résumé.

> **edited** Each of the women submitted ~~their~~ her résumé.

> **edited** Both ~~Each~~ of the women submitted their ~~résumé~~ résumés.

If a collective noun (army, community, team, herd, committee, asso-ciation) is understood as a unit, it takes a singular pronoun; if it is under-stood in terms of its individual members, it takes a plural pronoun.

> **as a unit**   The class presented its annual spring musical.

> **as individual members**   The class agreed to pay for their own art supplies.

■ Agreement in Gender

Traditionally, a masculine, singular pronoun has been used for indefinite antecedents (such as *anyone, someone,* and *everyone*) and to refer to generic antecedents (such as *employee, student, athlete, secretary, doctor,* and *computer specialist*). But *anyone* can be female or male, and women are employees (or students, athletes, secretaries, doctors, and computer specialists), too. The use of masculine pronouns to refer to both females and males is considered sexist; that is, such usage leaves out women as a segment of society or diminishes their presence. Instead, use *he or she, his or her,* or, in an extended piece of writing, alternate in a balanced way the use of *he* and *she* throughout. Sometimes the best solution is to rewrite the sentence to put it in the plural or to avoid the problem altogether.

sexist   If any student wants to attend the opening performance of *King Lear,* he will have to purchase a ticket by Wednesday.

edited   If any student wants to attend the opening performance of
           he or she
King Lear, ~~he~~ will have to purchase a ticket by Wednesday.

           students
edited   If any ~~student~~ wants to attend the opening performance of
           they   *tickets*
King Lear, ~~he~~ will have to purchase ~~a ticket~~ by Wednesday.

           All tickets for
edited   ~~If any student wants to attend~~ the opening performance of
                        must be purchased
King Lear~~, he will have to purchase a ticket~~ by Wednesday.

\ 7 Dangling and Misplaced Modifiers

A *modifier* is a word or group of words that describes or gives additional information about other words in a sentence. The words, phrases, and clauses that function as modifiers in a sentence can usually be moved around freely, so place them carefully to avoid unintentionally confusing — or amusing — your reader. As a rule, place modifiers as close as possible to the words you want to modify. Two common problems arise with modifiers: the misplaced modifier and the dangling modifier.

■ Misplaced Modifiers

A *misplaced modifier* unintentionally modifies the wrong word in a sentence because it is placed incorrectly.

misplaced   The waiter brought a steak to the man covered with onions.

                        covered with onions
edited   The waiter brought a steak to the man ~~covered with onions~~.

■ Dangling Modifiers

A *dangling modifier* usually appears at the beginning of a sentence and does not logically relate to the main clause of the sentence. The dangling modifier wants to modify a word — often an unstated subject — that does not appear in the sentence. To eliminate a dangling modifier, give the dangling phrase a subject.

dangling   Staring into the distance, large rain clouds form.

edited   Staring into the distance, _{Jon saw} large rain clouds form.

dangling   Walking on the ceiling, he noticed a beautiful luna moth.

edited   ~~Walking on the ceiling, he~~ _{He} noticed a beautiful luna moth. _{walking on the ceiling}

\8 Faulty Parallelism

Parallelism is the repetition of word order or grammatical form either within a single sentence or in several sentences that develop the same central idea. As a rhetorical device, parallel structure can aid coherence and add emphasis. Franklin Roosevelt's famous Depression-era statement "I see one-third of a nation *ill-housed*, *ill-clad*, and *ill-nourished*" illustrates effective parallelism. Use parallel grammatical structures to emphasize the similarities and differences between the items being compared. Look for opportunities to use parallel constructions with paired items or items in a series, paired items using correlative conjunctions, and comparisons using *than* or *as*.

■ Paired Items or Items in a Series

Parallel structures can be used to balance a word with a word, a phrase with a phrase, or a clause with a clause whenever you use paired items or items in a series — as in the Roosevelt example above.

1. Balance a word with a word.

faulty   Like the hunter, the photographer has to understand the animal's patterns, characteristics, and where it lives.

edited   Like the hunter, the photographer has to understand the

animal's patterns, characteristics, and ~~where it lives~~ _{habitat}.

2. Balance a phrase with a phrase.

faulty   The hunter carries a handgun and two rifles, different kinds of ammunition, and a variety of sights and telescopes to increase his chances of success.

edited   The hunter carries ~~a handgun and two rifles~~, different kinds of

several types of guns

ammunition, and a variety of sights and telescopes to increase

his chances of success.

3. Balance a clause with a clause.

faulty   Shooting is highly aggressive, photography is passive; shooting
eliminates forever, photography preserves.

edited   Shooting is ~~highly~~ aggressive, photography is passive; shooting

eliminates ~~forever~~, photography preserves.

■ Paired Items Using Correlative Conjunctions

When linking paired items with a correlative conjunction (*either/or, neither/nor, not only/but also, both/and, whether/or*) in a sentence, make sure that the elements being connected are parallel in form. Delete any unnecessary or repeated words.

incorrect   The lecture was both enjoyable and it was a form of
education.

edited   The lecture was both enjoyable and ~~it was a form of~~

educational

~~education~~.

■ Comparisons Using *Than* or *As*

Make sure that the elements of the comparison are parallel in form. Delete any unnecessary or repeated words.

incorrect   It would be better to study now than waiting until the night
before the exam.

edited   It would be better to study now than ~~waiting~~ until the night

to wait

before the exam.

\ 9   Weak Nouns and Verbs

The essence of a sentence is its subject and its verb. The subject — usually a noun or pronoun — identifies who or what the sentence is about, and the verb captures the subject's action or state of being. Sentences often lose their vitality and liveliness when the subject and the verb are lost in weak language or buried.

▪ Weak Nouns

Always opt for specific nouns when you can; they make your writing more visual. While general words like *people*, *animal*, or *dessert* name groups or classes of objects, qualities, or actions, specific words like *Samantha*, *camel*, and *pecan pie* appeal to readers more because they name individual objects, qualities, or actions within a group. Think about it — don't you prefer reading about specifics rather than generalities?

weak noun   The flowers stretched toward the bright light of the sun.

edited   The ~~flowers~~ tulips stretched toward the bright light of the sun.

▪ Strong Verbs

Strong verbs energize your writing by giving it a sense of action. Verbs like *gallop, scramble, snicker, tweak, fling, exhaust, smash, tear, smear, wrangle,* and *flog* provide readers with a vivid picture of specific actions. As you reread what you have written, be on the lookout for weak verbs like *is, are, have, deal with, make, give, do, use, get, add, become, go, appear,* and *seem.* When you encounter one of these verbs or others like them, seize the opportunity to substitute a strong action verb for a weak one.

weak verb   Local Boys and Girls Clubs in America assist in the promotion of self-esteem, individual achievement, and teamwork.

edited   Local Boys and Girls Clubs in America ~~assist in the promotion of~~ promote self-esteem, individual achievement, and teamwork.

While editing your essay, look for opportunities to replace weak nouns and verbs with strong nouns and action verbs. The more specific and strong you make your nouns and verbs, the more lively, descriptive, and concise your writing will be.

When you have difficulty thinking of strong, specific nouns and verbs, reach for a dictionary or a thesaurus — but only if you are sure you can discern the best word for your purpose. Thesauruses are available free online and in inexpensive paperback editions; most word processing programs include a thesaurus as well.

＼ 10 Shifts in Verb Tense, Mood, and Voice

▪ Shifts in Tense

A verb's tense indicates when an action takes place — sometime in the past, right now, or in the future. Using verb tense correctly helps your readers understand time changes in your writing. Shifts in tense — using different verb tenses within a sentence without a logical reason — confuse readers. Unnecessary shifts in verb tense are especially noticeable in

narration and process analysis writing, which are sequence and time oriented. Generally, you should write in the present or past tense and maintain that tense throughout your sentence.

> **incorrect** The painter studied the scene and pulls a fan brush decisively
> from her cup.
>
> **edited** The painter studied the scene and ~~pulls~~ ^{pulled} a fan brush decisively
>
> from her cup.

■ Shifts in Mood

Verbs in English have three moods: *indicative, imperative,* and *subjunctive.*
Problems with inconsistency usually occur with the imperative mood.

> **incorrect** In learning a second language, arm yourself with basic vocab-
> ulary, and it is also important to practice speaking aloud daily.
>
> **edited** In learning a second language, arm yourself with basic vocab-
>
> ulary, and ~~it is also important to~~ practice speaking aloud daily.

■ Shifts in Voice

Shifts in voice — from active voice to passive voice — usually go hand in
hand with inconsistencies in the subject of a sentence.

> **incorrect** The archeologists could see the effects of vandalism as the
> Mayan tomb was entered.
>
> **edited** The archeologists could see the effects of vandalism as the ^{they entered}
>
> Mayan tomb ~~was entered~~.

\ 11 Wordiness

Wordiness occurs in a sentence that contains words that do not contribute to the sentence's meaning. Wordiness can be eliminated by (1) using
the active voice, (2) avoiding "there is" and "it is," (3) eliminating redundancies, (4) deleting empty words and phrases, and (5) simplifying inflated
expressions.

1. **Use the active voice rather than the passive voice.** The active voice
   emphasizes the doer of an action rather than the receiver of an action.
   Not only is the active voice more concise than the passive voice, it is
   a much more vigorous form of expression.

> **passive** *The inhabitants of Londonderry were overwhelmed by the burgeon-
> ing rodent population.*
>
> **active** *The burgeoning rodent population overwhelmed the inhabitants of
> Londonderry.*

In the active sentence, *The burgeoning rodent population* is made the subject of the sentence and is moved to the beginning of the sentence — a position of importance — while the verb *overwhelmed* is made an active verb.

2. **Avoid "There is" and "It is."** "There is" and "It is" are expletives — words or phrases that do not contribute any meaning but are added only to fill out a sentence. They may be necessary with references to time and weather, but they should be avoided in other circumstances.

> **wordy**   There were many acts of heroism following the earthquake.
>
> **edited**   ~~There were many~~ ^{Many} acts of heroism ~~following~~ ^{followed} the earthquake.

Notice how the edited sentence eliminates the expletive and reveals a specific subject — *acts* — and an action verb — *followed*.

3. **Eliminate redundancies.** Unnecessary repetition often creeps into our writing and should be eliminated. For example, how often have you written expressions such as *large in size, completely filled, academic scholar,* or *I thought in my mind*? Edit such expressions by deleting the unnecessary words or using synonyms.

Sometimes our intent is to add emphasis, but the net effect is extra words that contribute little or nothing to a sentence's meaning.

> **redundant**   A big huge cloud was advancing on the crowded stadium.
>
> **edited**   A ~~big~~ huge cloud was advancing on the crowded stadium.
>
> **redundant**   After studying all night, he knew the basic and fundamental principles of geometry.
>
> **edited**   After studying all night, he knew the basic ~~and fundamental~~ principles of geometry.

4. **Delete empty words and phrases.** Look for words and phrases we use every day that carry no meaning — words that should be eliminated from your writing during the editing process.

> **empty**   One commentator believes that America is for all intents and purposes a materialistic society.
>
> **edited**   One commentator believes that America is ~~for all intents and purposes~~ a materialistic society.

Following are examples of some other words and expressions that most often can be eliminated.

basically	surely	it seems to me	extremely
essentially	truly	kind of/sort of	severely
generally	really	tend to	
very	I think/I feel/I believe	quite	

5. **Simplify inflated expressions.** Sometimes we use expressions we think sound authoritative in hopes of seeming knowledgable. We write *at this point in time* (instead of *now*) or *in the event that* (instead of *if*). However, it is best to write directly and forcefully and to use clear language. Edit inflated or pompous language to its core meaning.

inflated   The law office hired two people who have a complete knowledge of environmental policy.

edited   The law office hired two people who ~~have a complete knowledge~~ are ^
~~of~~ environmental policy. experts. ^

inflated   The president was late on account of the fact that her helicopter would not start.

edited   The president was late ~~on account of the fact that~~ because ^ her helicopter

would not start.

\ 12 Sentence Variety

While editing your essays, you can add interest and readability to your writing with more sentence variety. You should, however, seek variety in sentence structure not as an end in itself but as a more accurate means of reflecting your thoughts and giving emphasis where emphasis is needed. Look for opportunities to achieve sentence variety by combining short choppy sentences, varying sentence openings, and reducing the number of compound sentences.

■ Short Choppy Sentences

To make your writing more interesting, use one of the following five methods to combine short choppy sentences into one longer sentence.

1. **Use subordinating and coordinating conjunctions to relate and connect ideas.** The coordinating conjunctions *and, but, or, nor, for, so,* and *yet* can be used to connect two or more simple sentences. A subordinating conjunction, on the other hand, introduces a subordinate clause and connects it to a main clause. Common subordinating conjunctions include:

after	before	so	when
although	even if	than	where
as	if	that	whereas
as if	in order that	though	wherever
as though	rather than	unless	whether
because	since	until	while

short and choppy	Short words are as good as long ones. Short old words—like *sun* and *grass* and *home*—are best of all.
combined	Short words are as good as long ones ~~short~~ ^{, and short} old words—like *sun* and *grass* and *home*—are best of all.

— RICHARD LEDERER,
"The Case for Short Words," page 519

2. **Use modifiers effectively.** Instead of writing a separate descriptive sentence, combine an adjective modifier to convey a more graphic picture in a single sentence.

short and choppy	The people who breed German shepherds in Appleton, Wisconsin, are also farmers. And they are wonderful farmers.
combined	The people who breed German shepherds in Appleton, Wisconsin, are also wonderful farmers. ~~And they are wonderful farmers.~~

3. **Use a semicolon or colon to link closely related ideas.**

short and choppy	Pollution from carbon emissions remains a serious environmental problem. In some respects it is the most serious problem.
combined	Pollution from carbon emissions remains a serious environmental problem; in ~~In~~ some respects it is the most serious problem.

4. **Use parallel constructions.** Parallel constructions use repeated word order or repeated grammatical form to highlight and develop a central idea. As a rhetorical device, parallelism can aid coherence and add emphasis.

short and choppy	The school busing issue is not about comfort. It concerns fairness.
combined	The school busing issue is not about comfort, but about ~~It concerns~~ fairness.

■ Sentence Openings

More than half of all sentences in English begin with the subject of the sentence followed by the verb and any objects. The following sentences all illustrate this basic pattern:

Martha plays the saxophone.

The president vetoed the tax bill before leaving Washington for the holidays.

The upcoming lecture series will formally launch the fund-raising campaign for a new civic center.

If all the sentences in a particular passage in your essay begin this way, the effect on your readers is monotony. With a little practice, you will discover just how flexible the English language is. Consider the different ways in which one sentence can be rewritten so as to vary its beginning and add interest.

original   Candidates debated the issue of military service for women in the auditorium and did not know that a demonstration was going on outside.

varied openings   *Debating the issue of military service for women*, the candidates in the auditorium did not know that a demonstration was going on outside.

In the auditorium, the candidates debated the issue of military service for women, not knowing that a demonstration was going on outside.

As they debated the issue of military service for women, the candidates in the auditorium did not know that a demonstration was going on outside.

Another way of changing the usual subject-verb-object order of sentences is to invert — or reverse — the normal order. Do not, however, sacrifice proper emphasis to gain variety.

Usual Order	**Inverted Order**
The crowd stormed out.	Out stormed the crowd.
The enemy would never accept that.	That the enemy would never accept.
They could be friendly and civil.	Friendly and civil they could be.

■ Compound Sentences

Like a series of short, simple sentences, too many compound sentences — two or more sentences joined by coordinating conjunctions — give the impression of haste and thoughtlessness. As you edit your paper, watch for the word *and* used as a coordinating conjunction. If you discover that you have overused *and*, try one of the following four methods to remedy the situation, giving important ideas more emphasis and making it easier for your reader to follow your thought.

1. **Change a compound sentence into a simple sentence with a modifier or an appositive.**

   compound   Richard Lederer is a linguist, and he is humorous, and he has a weekly radio program about language.

   appositive   Richard Lederer ~~is a~~ , a humorous linguist, ~~and he is humorous, and he~~ has

   a weekly radio program about language.

2. **Change a compound sentence into a simple sentence with a compound predicate.**

   compound   Martin Luther King Jr. chastises America for not honoring its obligations to people of color, and he dreams of a day when racism will no longer exist.

   compound predicate   Martin Luther King Jr. chastises America for not

   honoring its obligations to people of color, and

   ~~he~~ dreams of a day when racism will no longer

   exist.

3. **Change a compound sentence into a simple sentence with a phrase or phrases.**

   compound   Women have a number of options in the military, and the responsibilities are significant.

   with a phrase   Women have a number of options in the military, with significant responsibilities ~~and the~~

   ~~responsibilities are significant.~~

4. **Change a compound sentence into a complex sentence.**

   compound   Farmers are using new technologies, and agriculture is becoming completely industrialized.

   complex   Because farmers
   ~~Farmers~~ are using new technologies, ~~and~~ agriculture is

   becoming completely industrialized.

Glossary of Rhetorical Terms

Abstract See *Concrete/Abstract*.

Allusion An allusion is a passing reference to a familiar person, place, or thing drawn from history, the Bible, mythology, or literature. An allusion is an economical way for a writer to capture the essence of an idea, atmosphere, emotion, or historical era, as in "The scandal was his Watergate," or "He saw himself as a modern Job," or "Everyone there held those truths to be self-evident." An allusion should be familiar to the reader; if it is not, it will add nothing to the meaning.

Analogy Analogy is a special form of comparison in which the writer explains something unfamiliar by comparing it to something familiar: "A transmission line is simply a pipeline for electricity. In the case of a water pipeline, more water will flow through the pipe as water pressure increases. The same is true of a transmission line for electricity." See also the discussion of analogy on page 284.

Analytical Reading Reading analytically means reading actively, paying close attention to both the content and the structure of the text. Analytical reading often involves answering several basic questions about the piece of writing under consideration:

1. What does the author want to say? What is his or her main point?

2. Why does the author want to say it? What is his or her purpose?

3. What strategy or strategies does the author use?

4. Why and how does the author's writing strategy suit both the subject and the purpose?

5. What is special about the way the author uses the strategy?

6. How effective is the essay? Why?

For a detailed example of analytical reading, see Chapter 1.

Appropriateness See *Diction*.

Argument Argument is one of the four basic types of prose. (Narration, description, and exposition are the other three.) To argue is to attempt to convince the reader to agree with a point of view, to make a given decision, or to pursue a particular course of action. Logical argument is based on reasonable explanations and appeals to the reader's intelligence. See Chapter 12 for further discussion of argumentation. See also *Logical Fallacies; Persuasion.*

Assertion   The thesis or proposition that a writer puts forward in an argument.

Assumption   A belief or principle, stated or implied, that is taken for granted.

Attitude   A writer's attitude reflects his or her opinion on a subject. For example, a writer can think very positively or very negatively about a subject. In most cases, the writer's attitude falls somewhere between these two extremes. See also *Tone.*

Audience   An audience is the intended readership for a piece of writing. For example, the readers of a national weekly newsmagazine come from all walks of life and have diverse opinions, attitudes, and educational experiences. In contrast, the readership for an organic chemistry journal is made up of people whose interests and educational backgrounds are quite similar. The essays in this book are intended for general readers — intelligent people who may lack specific information about the subject being discussed.

Beginnings/Endings   A *beginning* is the sentence, group of sentences, or section that introduces an essay. Good beginnings usually identify the thesis or controlling idea, attempt to interest the reader, and establish a tone. Some effective ways in which writers begin essays include (1) telling an anecdote that illustrates the thesis, (2) providing a controversial statement or opinion that engages the reader's interest, (3) presenting startling statistics or facts, (4) defining a term that is central to the discussion that follows, (5) asking thought-provoking questions, (6) providing a quotation that illustrates the thesis, (7) referring to a current event that helps establish the thesis, or (8) showing the significance of the subject or stressing its importance to the reader.

An *ending* is the sentence or group of sentences that brings an essay to closure. Good endings are purposeful and well planned. Endings satisfy readers when they are the natural outgrowths of the essays themselves and convey a sense of finality or completion. Good essays do not simply stop; they conclude.

Cause and Effect Analysis   Cause and effect analysis is one of the types of exposition. (Process analysis, definition, division and classification, illustration, and comparison and contrast are the others.) Cause and effect analysis answers the question *why?* It explains the reasons for an occurrence or the consequences of an action. See Chapter 11 for a detailed discussion of cause and effect analysis. See also *Exposition.*

Claim   The thesis or proposition put forth in an argument.

Classification   Classification, along with division, is one of the types of exposition. (Process analysis, definition, comparison and contrast, illustration, and cause and effect analysis are the others.) When classifying, the writer arranges and sorts people, places, or things into categories according to their differing characteristics, thus making them more manageable for the writer and more understandable for the reader. See Chapter 9 for a detailed discussion of classification. See also *Division; Exposition.*

Cliché   A cliché is an expression that has become ineffective through overuse. Expressions such as *quick as a flash, dry as dust, jump for joy,* and *slow as molasses* are all clichés. Good writers normally avoid such trite expressions and seek instead to express themselves in fresh and forceful language.

Coherence   Coherence is a quality of good writing that results when all sentences, paragraphs, and longer divisions of an essay are naturally connected. Coherent writing is achieved through (1) a logical sequence of ideas (arranged in chronological order, spatial order, order of importance, or some other appropriate order), (2) the thoughtful repetition of key words and ideas, (3) a pace suitable for your topic and reader, and (4) the use of transitional words and expressions. Coherence should not be confused with unity. See *Unity*. See also *Transitions*.

Colloquial Expressions A colloquial expression is characteristic of or appropriate to spoken language, or to writing that seeks its effect. Colloquial expressions are informal, as *chem, gym, come up with, be at loose ends, won't*, and *photo* illustrate. Thus, colloquial expressions are acceptable in formal writing only if they are used purposefully.

Comparison and Contrast Comparison and contrast is one of the types of exposition. (Process analysis, definition, division and classification, illustration, and cause and effect analysis are the others.) In comparison and contrast, the writer points out the similarities and differences between two or more subjects in the same class or category. The function of any comparison and contrast is to clarify — to reach some conclusion about the items being compared and contrasted. See Chapter 8 for a detailed discussion of comparison and contrast. See also *Exposition*.

Conclusions See *Beginnings/Endings*.

Concrete/Abstract A *concrete* word names a specific object, person, place, or action that can be directly perceived by the senses: *car, bread, building, book*, *Abraham Lincoln, Chicago*, or *hiking*. An *abstract* word, in contrast, refers to general qualities, conditions, ideas, actions, or relationships that cannot be directly perceived by the senses: *bravery, dedication, excellence, anxiety, stress, thinking*, or *hatred*.

   Although writers must use both concrete and abstract language, good writers avoid using too many abstract words. Instead, they rely on concrete words to define and illustrate abstractions. Because concrete words affect the senses, they are easily comprehended by the reader.

Connotation/Denotation Both connotation and denotation refer to the meanings of words. *Denotation* is the dictionary meaning of a word, the literal meaning. *Connotation*, on the other hand, is the implied or suggested meaning of a word. For example, the denotation of *lamb* is "a young sheep." The connotations of *lamb* are numerous: *gentle, docile, weak, peaceful, blessed, sacrificial, blood, spring, frisky, pure, innocent,* and so on. Good writers are sensitive to both the denotations and the connotations of words, and they use these meanings to their advantage in their writing. See also *Slanting*.

Controlling Idea See *Thesis*.

Deduction Deduction is the process of reasoning from a stated premise to a necessary conclusion. This form of reasoning moves from the general to the specific. See Chapter 12 for a discussion of deductive reasoning and its relation to argumentative writing. See also *Induction; Syllogism*.

Definition Definition is one of the types of exposition. (Process analysis, division and classification, comparison and contrast, illustration, and cause and effect analysis are the others.) Definition is a statement of the meaning of a word. A definition may be either brief or extended, part of an essay or an entire essay itself. See Chapter 10 for a detailed discussion of definition. See also *Exposition*.

Denotation See *Connotation/Denotation*.

Description Description is one of the four basic types of prose. (Narration, exposition, and argument are the other three.) Description tells how a person, place, or thing is perceived by the five senses. Objective description reports these sensory qualities factually, whereas subjective description gives the writer's interpretation of them. See Chapter 5 for a detailed discussion of description.

Dialogue Dialogue is conversation that is recorded in a piece of writing. Through dialogue writers reveal important aspects of characters' personalities as well as events in the narrative.

Diction   Diction refers to a writer's choice and use of words. Good diction is precise and appropriate — the words mean exactly what the writer intends, and the words are well suited to the writer's subject, intended audience, and purpose in writing. The word-conscious writer knows that there are differences among *aged*, *old*, and *elderly*; *blue*, *navy*, and *azure*; and *disturbed*, *angry*, and *irritated*. Furthermore, this writer knows in which situation to use each word. See also *Connotation/Denotation*.

Division   Like comparison and contrast, division and classification are separate yet closely related mental operations. Division involves breaking down a single large unit into smaller subunits or breaking down a large group of items into discrete categories. For example, the student body at your college or university can be divided into categories according to different criteria (by class, by home state or country, by sex, and so on).

Dominant Impression   A dominant impression is the single mood, atmosphere, or quality a writer emphasizes in a piece of descriptive writing. The dominant impression is created through the careful selection of details and is, of course, influenced by the writer's subject, audience, and purpose. See also the discussion on pages 121–32 in Chapter 5.

Draft   A draft is a version of a piece of writing at a particular stage in the writing process. The first version produced is usually called the *rough draft* or *first draft* and is a writer's beginning attempt to give overall shape to his or her ideas. Subsequent versions are called *revised drafts*. The copy presented for publication is the *final draft*.

Editing   During the editing stage of the writing process, the writer makes his or her prose conform to the conventions of the language. This includes making final improvements in sentence structure and diction, and proofreading for wordiness and errors in grammar, usage, spelling, and punctuation. After editing, the writer is ready to prepare a final copy.

Emphasis   Emphasis is the placement of important ideas and words within sentences and longer units of writing so that they have the greatest impact. In general, the end has the most impact, and the beginning nearly as much; the middle has the least. See also *Organization*.

Endings   See *Beginnings/Endings*.

Essay   An essay is a relatively short piece of nonfiction in which the writer attempts to make one or more closely related points. A good essay is purposeful, informative, and well organized.

Ethos   A type of argumentative proof having to do with the ethics of the arguer: honesty, trustworthiness, and even morals.

Evaluation   An evaluation of a piece of writing is an assessment of its effectiveness or merit. In evaluating a piece of writing, you should ask the following questions: What is the writer's purpose? Is it a worthwhile purpose? Does the writer achieve the purpose? Is the writer's information sufficient and accurate? What are the strengths of the essay? What are its weaknesses? Depending on the type of writing and the purpose, more specific questions can also be asked. For example, with an argument you could ask: Does the writer follow the principles of logical thinking? Is the writer's evidence convincing?

Evidence   Evidence is the data on which a judgment or an argument is based or by which proof or probability is established. Evidence usually takes the form of statistics, facts, names, examples or illustrations, and opinions of authorities.

Examples   Examples illustrate a larger idea or represent something of which they are a part. An example is a basic means of developing or clarifying an idea. Furthermore, examples enable writers to show and not simply tell readers what they mean. The terms *example* and *illustration* are sometimes used interchangeably. See also the discussion of illustration on pages 167–81 in Chapter 6.

Exposition Exposition is one of the four basic types of prose. (Narration, description, and argument are the other three.) The purpose of exposition is to clarify, explain, and inform. The methods of exposition presented in this text are process analysis, definition, division and classification, comparison and contrast, illustration, and cause and effect analysis. For a detailed discussion of each of these methods of exposition, see the appropriate chapter.

Fact A piece of information presented as having a verifiable certainty or reality.

Fallacy See *Logical Fallacies*.

Figures of Speech Figures of speech are brief, imaginative comparisons that highlight the similarities between things that are basically dissimilar. They make writing vivid and interesting and therefore more memorable. The most common figures of speech are these:

Simile — An implicit comparison introduced by *like* or *as*: "The fighter's hands were *like* stone."

Metaphor — An implied comparison that uses one thing as the equivalent of another: "All the world's a stage."

Personification — A special kind of simile or metaphor in which human traits are assigned to an inanimate object: "The engine coughed and then stopped."

Focus Focus is the limitation that a writer gives his or her subject. The writer's task is to select a manageable topic given the constraints of time, space, and purpose. For example, within the general subject of sports, a writer could focus on government support of amateur athletes or narrow the focus further to government support of Olympic athletes.

General See *Specific/General*.

Idiom An idiom is a word or phrase that is used habitually with a particular meaning in a language. The meaning of an idiom is not always readily apparent to nonnative speakers of that language. For example, *catch cold*, *hold a job*, *make up your mind*, and *give them a hand* are all idioms in English.

Illustration Illustration is a type of exposition. (Definition, division and classification, comparison and contrast, cause and effect analysis, and process analysis are the others.) With illustration the writer uses examples — specific facts, opinions, samples, and anecdotes or stories — to support a generalization and to make it more vivid, understandable, and persuasive. See Chapter 6 for a detailed discussion of illustration. See also *Examples*.

Induction Induction is the process of reasoning to a conclusion about all members of a class through an examination of only a few members of the class. This form of reasoning moves from the particular to the general. See Chapter 12 for a discussion of inductive reasoning and its relation to argumentative writing. Also see *Deduction*.

Introductions See *Beginnings/Endings*.

Irony Irony is the use of words to suggest something different from their literal meaning. For example, when Jonathan Swift proposes in "A Modest Proposal" that Ireland's problems could be solved if the people of Ireland fattened their babies and sold them to the English landlords for food, he meant that almost any other solution would be preferable. A writer can use irony to establish a special relationship with the reader and to add an extra dimension or twist to the meaning of a word or phrase.

Jargon See *Technical Language*.

Logical Fallacies A logical fallacy is an error in reasoning that renders an argument invalid. Some of the more common logical fallacies are these:

Oversimplification —The tendency to provide simple solutions to complex problems: "The reason we have inflation today is that OPEC has unreasonably raised the price of oil."

Non sequitur ("it does not follow") — An inference or conclusion that does not follow from established premises or evidence: "It was the best movie I saw this year, and it should get an Academy Award."

Post hoc, ergo propter hoc ("after this, therefore because of this") — Confusing chance or coincidence with causation. Because one event comes after another one, it does not necessarily mean that the first event caused the second: "I won't say I caught a cold at the hockey game, but I certainly didn't have it before I went there."

Begging the question — Assuming in a premise that which needs to be proven: "If American autoworkers built a better product, foreign auto sales would not be so high."

False analogy — Making a misleading analogy between logically unconnected ideas: "He was a brilliant basketball player; therefore, there's no question in my mind that he will be a fine coach."

Either/or thinking —The tendency to see an issue as having only two sides: "Used car salespeople are either honest or crooked."

See also Chapter 12.

Logical Reasoning   See *Deduction; Induction.*

Logos   A type of argumentative proof having to do with the logical qualities of an argument: data, evidence, and factual information.

Metaphor   See *Figures of Speech.*

Narration   Narration is one of the four basic types of prose. (Description, exposition, and argument are the other three.)To narrate is to tell a story, to tell what happened. Although narration is most often used in fiction, it is also important in nonfiction, either by itself or in conjunction with other types of prose. See Chapter 4 for a detailed discussion of narration.

Objective/Subjective   *Objective* writing is factual and impersonal, whereas subjective writing, sometimes called *impressionistic* writing, relies heavily on personal interpretation. For a discussion of objective description and subjective description, see Chapter 5.

Opinion   An opinion is a belief or conclusion not substantiated by positive knowledge or proof. An opinion reveals personal feelings or attitudes or states a position. Opinion should not be confused with argument.

Organization   In writing, organization is the thoughtful arrangement and presentation of one's points or ideas. Narration is often organized chronologically. Exposition may be organized from simplest to most complex or from most familiar to least familiar. Argument may be organized from least important to most important. There is no single correct pattern of organization for a given piece of writing, but good writers are careful to discover an order of presentation suitable for their audience and their purpose.

Paradox   A paradox is a seemingly contradictory statement that may nonetheless be true. For example, "We little know what we have until we lose it" is a paradoxical statement.

Paragraph   The paragraph, the single most important unit of thought in an essay, is a series of closely related sentences.These sentences adequately develop the central or controlling idea of the paragraph.This central or controlling idea, usually stated in a topic sentence, is necessarily related to the purpose of the whole composition.

A well-written paragraph has several distinguishing characteristics: a clearly stated or implied topic sentence, adequate development, unity, coherence, and an appropriate organizational strategy.

Parallelism   Parallel structure is the repetition of word order or form either within a single sentence or in several sentences that develop the same central idea. As a rhetorical device, parallelism can aid coherence and add emphasis. Roosevelt's statement, "I see one third of a nation ill-housed, ill-clad, ill-nourished," illustrates effective parallelism.

Pathos   A type of argumentative proof having to do with audience: emotional language, connotative diction, and appeals to certain values.

Personification   See *Figures of Speech.*

Persuasion   Persuasion, or persuasive argument, is an attempt to convince readers to agree with a point of view, to make a given decision, or to pursue a particular course of action. Persuasion appeals heavily to the emotions, whereas logical argument does not. For the distinction between logical argument and persuasive argument, see Chapter 12.

Point of View   Point of view refers to the grammatical person of the speaker in an essay. For example, a first-person point of view uses the pronoun/and is commonly found in autobiography and the personal essay; a third-person point of view uses the pronouns *he, she,* or *it* and is commonly found in objective writing. See Chapter 4 for a discussion of point of view in narration.

Prewriting   Prewriting encompasses all the activities that take place before a writer actually starts a rough draft. During the prewriting stage of the writing process, the writer selects a subject area, focuses on a particular topic, collects information and makes notes, brainstorms for ideas, discovers connections between pieces of information, determines a thesis and purpose, rehearses portions of the writing in his or her mind or on paper, and makes a scratch outline. For some suggestions about prewriting, see Chapter 2, pages 21–24.

Process Analysis   Process analysis is a type of exposition. (Definition, division and classification, comparison and contrast, illustration, and cause and effect analysis are the others.) Process analysis answers the question *how?* and explains how something works or gives step-by-step directions for doing something. See Chapter 7 for a detailed discussion of process analysis. See also *Exposition.*

Publication   The publication stage of the writing process is when the writer shares his or her writing with the intended audience. Publication can take the form of a typed or an oral presentation, a photocopy, or a commercially printed rendition. What's important is that the writer's words are read in what amounts to their final form.

Purpose   Purpose is what the writer wants to accomplish in a particular piece of writing. Purposeful writing seeks to *relate* (narration), to *describe* (description), to *explain* (process analysis, definition, division and classification, comparison and contrast, illustration, and cause and effect analysis), or to *convince* (argument).

Revision   During the revision stage of the writing process, the writer determines what in the draft needs to be developed or clarified so that the essay says what the writer intends it to say. Often the writer needs to revise several times before the essay is "right." Comments from peer evaluators can be invaluable in helping writers determine what sorts of changes need to be made. Such changes can include adding material, deleting material, changing the order of presentation, and substituting new material for old.

Rhetorical Question   A rhetorical question is a question that is asked but requires no answer from the reader. "When will nuclear proliferation end?" is such a question.

Writers use rhetorical questions to introduce topics they plan to discuss or to emphasize important points.

Rough Draft   See *Draft*.

Sequence   Sequence refers to the order in which a writer presents information. Writers commonly select chronological order, spatial order, order of importance, or order of complexity to arrange their points. See also *Organization*.

Signal Phrase   A signal phrase introduces borrowed material — a summary, paraphrase, or quotation — in a researched paper and usually consists of the author's name and a verb (*Daphna Oyserman contends*). Signal phrases let readers know who is speaking and, in the case of summaries and paraphrases, exactly where the writer's ideas end and the borrowed material begins.

Simile   See *Figures of Speech*.

Slang   Slang is the unconventional, very informal language of particular subgroups of a culture. Slang, such as *bummed, coke, split, hurt, dis, blow off*, and *cool*, is acceptable in formal writing only if it is used purposefully.

Slanting   The use of certain words or information that results in a biased viewpoint.

Specific/General   *General* words name groups or classes of objects, qualities, or actions. *Specific* words, in contrast, name individual objects, qualities, or actions within a class or group. To some extent, the terms *general* and *specific* are relative. For example, *dessert* is a class of things. *Pie*, however, is more specific than *dessert* but more general than *pecan pie* or *chocolate cream pie*.

Good writing judiciously balances the general with the specific. Writing with too many general words is likely to be dull and lifeless. General words do not create vivid responses in the reader's mind as concrete, specific words can. However, writing that relies exclusively on specific words may lack focus and direction — the control that more general statements provide.

Strategy   A strategy is a means by which a writer achieves his or her purpose. Strategy includes the many rhetorical decisions that the writer makes about organization, paragraph structure, syntax, and diction. In terms of the whole essay, strategy refers to the principal rhetorical mode that the writer uses. If, for example, a writer wishes to show how to make chocolate chip cookies, the most effective strategy would be process analysis. If it is the writer's purpose to show why sales of American cars have declined in recent years, the most effective strategy would be cause and effect analysis.

Style   Style is the individual manner in which a writer expresses ideas. Style is created by the author's particular selection of words, construction of sentences, and arrangement of ideas.

Subject   The subject of an essay is its content, what the essay is about. Depending on the author's purpose and the constraints of space, a subject may range from one that is broadly conceived to one that is narrowly defined.

Subjective   See *Objective/Subjective*.

Supporting Evidence   See *Evidence*.

Syllogism   A syllogism is an argument that utilizes deductive reasoning and consists of a major premise, a minor premise, and a conclusion. For example:

All trees that lose leaves are deciduous. (*Major premise*)

Maple trees lose their leaves. (*Minor premise*)

Therefore, maple trees are deciduous. (*Conclusion*)

See also *Deduction*.

Symbol A symbol is a person, place, or thing that represents something beyond itself. For example, the eagle is a symbol of the United States, and the bear is a symbol of Russia.

Syntax Syntax refers to the way in which words are arranged to form phrases, clauses, and sentences as well as to the grammatical relationship among the words themselves.

Technical Language Technical language, or jargon, is the special vocabulary of a trade or profession. Writers who use technical language do so with an awareness of their audience. If the audience is a group of peers, technical language may be used freely. If the audience is a more general one, technical language should be used sparingly and carefully so as not to sacrifice clarity. See also *Diction*.

Thesis A thesis is a statement of the main idea of an essay. Also known as the *controlling idea*, a thesis may sometimes be implied rather than stated directly.

Title A title is a word or phrase set off at the beginning of an essay to identify the subject, to capture the main idea of the essay, or to attract the reader's attention. A title may be explicit or suggestive. A subtitle, when used, extends or restricts the meaning of the main title.

Tone Tone is the manner in which a writer relates to an audience — the "tone of voice" used to address readers. Tone may be described as friendly, serious, distant, angry, cheerful, bitter, cynical, enthusiastic, morbid, resentful, warm, playful, and so forth. A particular tone results from a writer's diction, sentence structure, purpose, and attitude toward the subject. See also *Attitude*.

Topic Sentence The topic sentence states the central idea of a paragraph and thus limits and controls the subject of the paragraph. Although the topic sentence most often appears at the beginning of the paragraph, it may appear at any other point, particularly if the writer is trying to create a special effect. Also see *Paragraph*.

Transitions Transitions are words or phrases that link sentences, paragraphs, and larger units of a composition to achieve coherence. These devices include parallelism, pronoun references, conjunctions, and the repetition of key ideas, as well as the many conventional transitional expressions, such as *moreover, on the other hand, in addition, in contrast,* and *therefore*. Also see *Coherence*.

Unity Unity is achieved in an essay when all the words, sentences, and paragraphs contribute to its thesis. The elements of a unified essay do not distract the reader. Instead, they all harmoniously support a single idea or purpose.

Verb Verbs can be classified as either strong verbs (*scream, pierce, gush, ravage,* and *amble*) or weak verbs (*be, has, get,* and *do*). Writers prefer to use strong verbs to make their writing more specific, more descriptive, and more action filled.

Voice Verbs can be classified as being in either the active or the passive voice. In the active voice, the doer of the action is the grammatical subject. In the passive voice, the receiver of the action is the subject:

Active: Glenda questioned all the children.

Passive: All the children were questioned by Glenda.

Writing Process The writing process consists of five major stages: prewriting, writing drafts, revision, editing, and publication. The process is not inflexible, but there is no mistaking the fact that most writers follow some version of it most of the time. Although orderly in its basic components and sequence of activities, the writing process is nonetheless continuous, creative, and unique to each individual writer. See Chapter 2 for a detailed discussion of the writing process. See also *Draft; Editing; Prewriting; Publication; Revision*.

Acknowledgments

Mortimer Adler. "How to Mark a Book." Originally published in the *Saturday Review of Literature,* July 6, 1940. Copyright © 1940 by Mortimer Adler. Reprinted by permission of the author.

Mitch Albom. "If You Had One Day With Someone Who's Gone." Originally appeared in *Parade* magazine, September 17, 2006. Copyright © 2006 by Mitch Albom. Reprinted by permission.

Maya Angelou. "Sister Flowers." From *I Know Why the Caged Bird Sings* by Maya wAngelou. Copyright © 1969 and renewed 1997 by Maya Angelou. Reprinted by permission of Random House, Inc.

Stan Badgett. "Rock Dust." Originally published in *Minnetonka Review,* Winter 2008. Copyright © 2008 by Stan Badgett. Reprinted by permission of Swallow's Nest Publishing.

Russell Baker. "Discovering the Power of My Words." From *Growing Up* by Russell Baker. Copyright © 1982 by Russell Baker. Reprinted by permission of Don Congdon Associates, Inc.

David P. Bardeen. "Not Close Enough for Comfort." From the *New York Times,* February 29, 2004. Copyright © 2004 by David P. Bardeen. Reprinted by permission of the author.

Suzanne Britt. "Neat People vs. Sloppy People." Reprinted by permission of the author.

David Brooks. "The Odyssey Years." From the *New York Times,* October 9, 2008. Copyright © 2007 The New York Times. All Rights Reserved. Used by permission and protected by the Copyright Laws of the United States. The printing, copying, redistribution, or retransmission of the Material without express written permission is prohibited. www.nytimes.com

Carl M. Cannon. "The Real Computer Virus." Reprinted from *American Journalism Review,* April 2001. Copyright © 2001 by American Journalism Review. Reprinted with permission of the publisher.

Bruce Catton. "Grant and Lee: A Study in Contrasts." Originally published in *The American Story,* edited by Earl Schneck Miers. 1956.

Michael Jonas. "The Downside of Diversity." From the *New York
Times*, August 5, 2007. Copyright © 2007 The New York Times. All rights
reserved. Used by permission and protected by the Copyright Laws of
the United States. The printing, copying, redistribution, or retransmission
of the Material without express written permission is prohibited. www
.nytimes.com

Malcolm Jones. "Who Was More Important: Lincoln or Darwin?"
From *Newsweek,* July 7–14, 2008. Copyright © 2008 Newsweek, Inc. All
rights reserved. Used by permission and protected by the Copyright Laws
of the United States. The printing, copying, redistribution, or retransmission of the Material without express written permission is prohibited.
www.newsweek.com

Vernon E. Jordan. "Vernon Can Read!" From *Vernon Can Read! A Memoir* by Vernon E. Jordan, Jr. and Anne Gordon-Reed. Copyright © 2001 by
Vernon E. Jordan Jr. and Annette Gordon-Reed. Reprinted with permission.

Jon Katz. "How Boys Become Men." From *Glamour* magazine,
January 1993. Copyright © 1993 by Jon Katz. Reprinted by permission of
International Creative Management, Inc.

Andrew Keen. "Web 2.0." From the *Weekly Standard*, February 15,
2006. Copyright © 2006 by The Weekly Standard, LLC. Reprinted with
permission.

Martin Luther King Jr. Excerpt from "The Ways of Meeting
Oppression." From *Stride Toward Freedom* by Martin Luther King Jr.
Copyright @ 1958 Martin Luther King Jr. Copyright renewed 1986 by
Coretta Scott King. "I Have a Dream" speech delivered on the steps at
the Lincoln Memorial, Washington, D.C., August 28, 1963. Copyright
© 1963 Martin Luther King Jr. Copyright renewed 1991 by Coretta Scott
King. Reprinted by arrangement with The Heirs to the Estate of Martin
Luther King Jr. c/o Writers House as agent for the proprietor.

Stephen King. "Reading and Writing." From *On Writing: A Memoir of
the Craft* by Stephen King. Copyright © 2000 by Stephen King. Reprinted
by permission of Scribner, a division of Simon & Schuster, Inc. All rights
reserved.

Jim Kitchens. "The Psychology of Persuasive Messaging." Copyright
© by James Kitchens. Reprinted by permission of the author.

Anne Lamott. "Shitty First Drafts." From *Bird by Bird* by Anne Lamott.
Copyright © 1994 by Anne Lamott. Used by permission of Pantheon
Books, a division of Random House, Inc.

Richard Lederer. "The Case for Short Words." From *The Miracle of
Language* by Richard Lederer. Copyright © 1991 by Richard Lederer. Reprinted by permission of Atria Books, a division of Simon & Schuster, Inc.

Doris Lessing. "On Not Winning the Nobel Prize." From the Nobel
Lecture by Doris Lessing, December 7, 2007. Copyright © 2009 by Nobel
Web AB. Reprinted by permission. www.nobelprize.org

William Zinsser. "Simplicity." Copyright © 1976, 1980, 1985, 1988, 1990, 1994, 1998, 2001, 2006 by William K. Zinsser. Reprinted by permission of the author.

Photo/Art Credits

429, Library of Congress; **432**, © A. Inden/Corbis; **433**, Alex Wong/Getty Images; **440**, Emilia Klimiuk; **455**, James Lattanzio; **460**, Courtesy Jennie Yabroff; **466**, Peter Kramer/Getty Images; **470**, Staci Schwartz; **471**, Liz Lynch; **480**, Mary Beth Meehan; **493**, WWF-US Print Public Service Announcement; **513**, Library of Congress; **519**, Richard Lederer; **525**, © Flip Schulke/Corbis; **531**, David Levenson/Getty Images; **541**, AP Images/Andrew Shurtleff; **548**, Peter Kramer/Getty Images; **560**, Catherine Betts; **574**, Photo by Roy Rodgers; **575**, Courtesy of Claudia Goldin; **576**, © 2010 Pew Research Center, Social & Demographic Trends Project. Women, Men and the New Economics of Marriage. http://pewsocialtrends.org/pubs/750/new-economics-of-marriage; **577**, Iberia Elster; **578**, Will Kirk; **580**, Courtesy of Janet Reibstein; **581**, Courtesy of Kathleen Gerson; **582**, Courtesy of Barbara DaFoe Whitehead; **589**, Courtesy www.adbusters.org; **602**, photo source: Lars Eighner; **607**, Christopher Johnson/Stock Boston; **608**, David Levenson/Getty Images; **615**, AP Images; **624**, Beinecke Rare Book and Manuscript Library, Yale University; **653**, Thomas Gibaud; **660**, PETT, Lexington Herald-Leader/CartoonArts International/The New York Times Syndicate; **661**, Courtesy of Ed Yong; **684**, University of Vermont; **685**, University of Vermont

Index

Abstract words, 408

Academic disciplines. *See* specific types of writing

Accept/except, 407

Action-oriented argument, 495

Action verbs, 129
  in process analysis, 233

Active voice, 718–19
  in process analysis, 233

Adjective phrase or clause, comma with, 710

Adler, Mortimer, "How to Mark a Book," 236–42

Affect/effect, 407

Agreement
  pronoun-antecedent, 713–14
  subject-verb, 711

"Ain't I a Woman?" (Truth), 429–32

Albom, Mitch, "If You Had One Day with Someone Who's Gone," 186–91

Ambiguous references, 711

American Childhood, An (Dillard), 90–95

"American Dream for Sale, The" (Rashap), 373–83

Analogy
  in argumentation, 501, 511
  in comparison and contrast essay, 284

in definition essay, 406
  false, 511

Analyze, as direction word, 17

Anecdote/antidote, 407

Angelou, Maya, "Sister Flowers," 156–62

Annotation, of reading selection, 4–7

Antidote/anecdote, 407

Appeals, classical, 497–98

Appositives, in compound sentences, 723

Argue, as direction word, 17

Argumentation, 19
  in academic disciplines, 501–2
  action-oriented, 495
  analogy in, 494, 501, 511
  audience for, 498, 508–9
  blogging and, 547
  classical appeals in, 497–98
  combining strategies for, 510, 600
  comparison and contrast analysis with, 285
  conclusions in, 510–11
  defined, 493
  focused, 495
  informational/exploratory, 495
  logical, 494–95
  organizational pattern for, 509

Argumentation *(continued)*
  as organizational strategy, 2
  persuasive, 494–95
  quiet/subtle, 496
  reconciliation, 496
  refutations to, 509–10
  revising/editing of, 511–12
  as rhetorical strategy, 498
  student essay as example of,
    502–6
  thesis statement in, 508
  as writing strategy, 25, 26,
    496–501, 507–12
Argumentation (readings)
  "Benefits of the Breadwinning
    Wife, The" (Goldin), 575–76
  "Declaration of Independence,
    The" (Jefferson), 513–18
  "Housewife Anomaly, The"
    (Cherlin), 578–79
  "I Have a Dream" (King), 525–30
  "In Defense of Dangerous
    Ideas" (Pinker), 531–40
  "It's About Respect" (Reibstein),
    580–81
  "Marriage Decline, The" (Banks),
    577–78
  "No Role Reversals" (Gerson),
    581–82
  "Separate and Unequal Mating
    Markets" (Whitehead), 582–83
  "This Land Is Their Land"
    (Ehrenreich), 541–46
  "Web 2.0" (Keen), 560–64
  "Why I Blog" (Sullivan), 548–59
  "Women Finally Start to Catch
    Up" (Coontz), 574–75
Articles. *See also* Periodicals
  evaluating, 688
As, comparisons with, 716
Atmosphere, description for, 123
Audience, 19
  academic, 20
  for argumentation, 498, 508–9
  for definition essay, 404
  writer questions about, 21

Badgett, Stan, "Rock Dust," 139–43
Baker, Russell, "Discovering the
    Power of My Words," 42–46
Balance, sentence parallelism and,
    715–16
Balanced tone, words for, 453
Bambara, Toni Cade, 334–35
Banks, Ralph Richard, "Marriage
    Decline, The," 577–78
Bardeen, David P., "Not Close
    Enough for Comfort," 102–6,
    708
"Barrio, The" (Ramírez), 150–55
Begging the question, 511
Beginnings, 30, 31
Begley, Sharon, 636
"Benefits of the Breadwinning
    Wife, The" (Goldin), 575–76
"Be Specific" (Goldberg), 182–85
Bibliography, developing, 690–92
*Big Drink, The: The Story of Coca-
    Cola* (Kahn, E. J., Jr.), 73–74
Block comparison, 282–83
  in organization outline, 291–92
Blogging, argumentation and, 547
  "Blogworld and Its Gravity"
    (Welch), 565–71
"Blue-Collar Brilliance" (Rose),
    202–12
Books
  bibliography for, 691
  evaluating, 687
Borrowed material, integrating
    into text, 640–41
Both/and, paired items with, 715
Brainstorming, 21
Britt, Suzanne, "Neat People vs.
    Sloppy People," 318–22
Brooks, David, "Odyssey Years,
    The," 433–37
Brooks, John, 442

"Campus Racism 101" (Giovanni),
    270–76
Cannon, Carl M., "Real Computer
    Virus, The," 471–79

"Case for Short Words, The"
(Lederer), 519–24
"Case of the Disappearing Rabbit,
The" (Huang), 653–60
Categorize, in division and classification, 342–43
Categorize, as direction word, 17
Catton, Bruce, "Grant and Lee,"
323–28
Causal chain, 443–44
Cause and effect analysis
in academic disciplines, 445–46
combining strategies with,
510, 600
defined, 441
in definition essay, 406
errors of logic in, 451–52
focus, establishing, 450
immediate versus remote
causes, 443–44
as organizational strategy, 2
organization of, 451–53
oversimplification in, 451–52
purpose for writing, 450
revising/editing of, 453, 454
student essay as example of,
446–49
thesis statement in, 450–51
as writing strategy, 25, 26, 450–53
Chart, in division and classification
essay, 342–43
Cherlin, Andrew J., "Housewife
Anomaly, The," 578–79
"Chinese in New York, American in
Beijing" (Hoang), 295–300
Chronological organization
of illustration essay, 180
of narration essay, 81
Citations, 693–94
Classical argumentation, 497–98
Classification. *See* Division and
classification
Clauses, punctuating, 709, 710
Cliché, 250
Clustering, 22
Coarse/course, 407

Colons, sentence variety and, 721
Colored words, 252–53
Colorless words, 253
Combining strategies, 589–90
for argumentation, 510, 600
for cause and effect analysis,
510, 600
for comparison and contrast,
510, 600
for definition, 510, 600
for description, 600
for division and classification,
510, 600
dominant strategy for, 600
for illustration, 510, 600
for narration, 510, 600
in organizing essay, 600
in planning of essay, 598–99
for process analysis, 510, 600
purpose for writing, 599
revising/editing of, 601
student essay as example of,
591–98
supporting strategies and, 560
thesis statement, 599
Combining strategies (readings)
"On Dumpster Diving"
(Eighner), 602–7
"On Not Winning the Nobel
Prize" (Lessing), 608–14
"Shooting an Elephant"
(Orwell), 615–23
"Coming to an Awareness of
Language" (Malcolm X),
85–89
Commas
comma faults, 709–10
comma splices, 706, 707
uses of, 707
Commoner, Barry, 443–44
Communication, in rhetorical situ-
ations, 497–98
Compare, as direction word, 17
Comparison and contrast
in academic disciplines, 285–86
analogy as, 284

Comparison and contrast
  (continued)
  block, 282–83
  combining strategies with,
    510, 600
  conclusions from, 292–93
  defined, 281
  in definition essay, 406
  as organizational strategy, 2
  organization of, 291–93
  point-by-point, 282–83
  purpose for writing in, 290
  revising/editing of, 293–94
  student essay as example of,
    286–89
  thesis statement in, 290
  as writing strategy, 24, 25,
    284–85, 289–94
Comparison and contrast
  (readings)
  "Chinese in New York, American
    in Beijing" (Hoang), 295–300
  "Grant and Lee" (Catton),
    323–28
  "Neat People vs. Sloppy People"
    (Britt), 318–22
  "Two Ways to Belong in
    America" (Mukherjee), 301–6
  "Who Was More Important:
    Lincoln or Darwin?" (Jones),
    307–16
Comparisons, with *than/as,* 716
Compound sentences, sentence
  variety and, 722–23
Compound subjects, and subject-
  verb agreement, 711
Conclusions
  in argumentation, 510–11
  in division and classification, 343
  in logical argument, 499
Concrete words, 407–8
Connotation of words, 407
Consistency, verb tense, 233–34
Content, 4
Context (setting), in narration
  essay, 74, 80

Contrast, as direction word, 17
Contrast and compare. *See*
  Comparison and contrast
Coontz, Stephanie, 636–37
  "Women Finally Start to Catch
    Up," 574–75
Coordinating conjunctions, 707,
  709
  sentence variety and, 720
Correlative conjunctions, paired
  items with, 716
Course/coarse, 407
Critique, by peers. *See* Peer
  critiques
Critique, as direction word, 17

Dangling modifiers, 714–15
Databases, keyword searches and,
  685–86
"Declaration of Independence,
  The" (Jefferson), 513–18
Deductive reasoning, 498–501
Define, as direction word, 17
Definition
  in academic disciplines, 397–98
  audience for, 404
  combining strategies for, 510,
    600
  defined, 393
  etymological, 395
  extended, 395–96
  formal, 394
  negative, 395
  as organizational strategy, 2
  organizing and writing essay,
    405–6
  purpose of, 402–3
  revising/editing of, 406–7
  student essay as example of,
    398–402
  synonymous, 394–95
  thesis statement, 403–4
  as writing strategy, 25, 26,
    396–97, 402–9
Del Rey, Lester, 284
Denotation of words, 407

Description
in academic disciplines, 124–25
action verbs in, 129
combining strategies with,
510, 600
defined, 121
dominant impression, creating,
123, 129–30
objective, 123–24
as organizational strategy, 2
organization of, 129–31
outline for, 131
purpose for writing, 128–29
revising/editing of, 131, 132
student essay as example of,
125–28
subjective, 123, 124
visual cues for, 120, 121
as writing strategy, 24, 25,
122–24, 128–31, 132
Description (readings)
"Barrio, The" (Ramírez),
150–55
"Remembering Lobo" (Mora),
144–49
"Rock Dust" (Badgett), 139–43
"Sister Flowers" (Angelou),
156–62
"View from the Bridge, A"
(McDonald), 133–37
Details, in narration essay, 74, 81
Diagram, in division and classifica-
tion essay, 342–43
Dialogue, in narration essay, 83
Dillard, Annie, from *An American
Childhood*, 90–95
Directional process analysis, 225
Direction words
defined, 17
listing of, 17–18, 25–26
Direct quotations, 639–40
plagiarism and, 645
Disciplines, writing strategies
across, 26–27
"Discovering the Power of My
Words" (Baker), 42–46

Disinterested/uninterested, 407
Division and classification, 333
in academic disciplines, 336–37
categories of, 342–43
combining strategies with,
510, 600
conclusions in, 343
defined, 333
as organizational strategy, 2
organization of, 342–43
purpose for writing, 340–41
revising/editing of, 343–44
student essay as example of,
337–40
thesis statement for, 341–42
as writing strategy, 25, 336,
340–44
in written texts, 333–36
Division and classification
(readings)
"American Dream for Sale, The"
(Rashap), 373–83
"Psychology of Persuasive
Messaging, The" (Kitchens),
359–65
"Queen Bee and Her Court, The"
(Wiseman), 345–58
"Truth about Lying, The" (Viorst),
366–72
"Ways of Meeting Oppression,
The" (King), 384–88
Documentation, 693–94
Dominant impression, in descrip-
tion, 123, 129–30
Dove, Rita, 3, 5–7
"Downside of Diversity, The"
(Jonas), 480–88
Draft. See also Editing; Revision
first, 24–28

"East Meets West: How the Brain
Unites Us All" (Yong), 661–69
"Eating Industrial Meat" (Pollan),
256–62
Editing, 32
of argument, 511

Editing *(continued)*
of cause and effect analysis,
453, 454
combining strategies and, 601
of comparison and contrast
essay, 293–94
of definition essay, 406–7
of description essay, 131, 132
of division and classification
essay, 343–44
for grammar, punctuation, and
style, 706–23
of illustration essay, 180, 181
of narration essay, 83–84
of process analysis, 233–35
Effect/affect, 407
Ehrenreich, Barbara, "This Land Is
Their Land," 541–46
Eighner, Lars, "On Dumpster
Diving," 602–7
Either/or, paired items with, 716
Either/or thinking, 511
Electronic research. *See also*
Online sources
keyword searches, 685–86
Eminent/immanent/imminent, 407
Emphasis, narrative time for, 82
Empty words and phrases,
deleting, 719
Endings of essay, revising, 30, 31
"English-Only Movement, The"
(Jamieson), 672–80
Ethos, in classical appeals, 497
Etymological definition, 395
Euphemism, 250
Evaluate, as direction word, 17
Evaluative process analysis, 226
Evidence, for argumentation, 509
Examples
in definition essay, 406
in illustration essay, 178–79
Except/accept, 407
Explain, as direction word, 17
Exploratory argument, 495
Expressions, pat, 251
Expressive writing, 19
Extended definitions, 395–96

Facts, introducing and citing, 645
Fallows, James, 499–501
False analogy, 511
Faulty parallelism, 715–16
Faulty reasoning, in argumenta-
tion essay, 511
First draft, 24–28
Flashback, in narration essay, 81
Flower, Linda S., "Writing for an
Audience," 52–55
Focused argument, 495
Formal definition, 394
Formal writing, vs. informal
writing, 20
Fragments, sentence, 707–8
Friedman, Thomas L., 7, 8–10
Friedrich, Otto, 283–84
Fused sentences, 706–7

Gender, pronoun-antecedent
agreement in, 714
Generalizations, about words as
words, 252
Gerson, Kathleen, "No Role
Reversals," 581–82
Giovanni, Nikki, "Campus Racism
101," 270–76
Gladstone, Bernard, 223
Goldberg, Natalie, "Be Specific,"
182–85
Goldin, Claudia, "Benefits of the
Breadwinning Wife, The,"
575–76
Gorry, G. Anthony, "Steal This MP3
File," 416–21
Grammar, editing for, 706–18
"Grant and Lee" (Catton), 323–28

Harris, Sydney, 590
Hasty generalization, in argumen-
tation, 511
Heilbroner, Robert L., 644
Here Is New York (White), 333–34
"Here's Looking at You, Kids"
(Yabroff), 460–65
Hoang, Kim, "Chinese in New York,
American in Beijing," 295–300

Home page
  evaluating, 689
  of library, 684
"Housewife Anomaly, The"
  (Cherlin), 578–79
"How Boys Become Men" (Katz),
  455–59
"How to Give Orders Like a Man"
  (Tannen), 192–201
"How to Mark a Book" (Adler),
  236–42
"How to Say Nothing in 500
  Words" (Roberts), 243–55
Huang, Lily, "Case of the Disap-
  pearing Rabbit, The," 653–60

Ideas for writing, generating,
  21–23
"If You Had One Day with
  Someone Who's Gone"
  (Albom), 186–91
"I Have a Dream" (King), 21,
  525–30
Illustrate, as direction word, 17
Illustration
  in academic disciplines, 169–70
  chronological organization of,
    180
  combining strategies with,
    510, 600
  defined, 167
  examples in, 178–79
  as organizational strategy, 2
  organization of, 179–80
  revising and editing of, 180, 181
  student essay as example of,
    170–77
  thesis in, 177–78
  time sequence in, 179–80
  transitional words in, 180
  as writing strategy, 24, 25, 169
Illustration (readings)
  "Be Specific" (Goldberg), 182–85
  "Blue-Collar Brilliance" (Rose),
    202–12
  "How to Give Orders Like a
    Man" (Tannen), 192–201

"If You Had One Day with
  Someone Who's Gone"
  (Albom), 186–91
"In Full Bloom" (Walker), 213–17
Immanent/imminent/eminent, 407
Immediate cause, 444
Imperative mood, 718
Implied references, 712
"In Defense of Dangerous Ideas"
  (Pinker), 531–40
Independent clauses, commas
  with, 709
Indicative mood, 718
Inductive reasoning, 498–501
Inflated language, simplifying, 720
Informal writing vs. formal
  writing, 20
Informational argument, 495
Informational process analysis,
  225–26
Informative writing, 19
"In Full Bloom" (Walker), 213–17
Integrated quotations, 641
Internet. See also Online sources;
  Open Internet; Sources
  bibliography of sources from, 692
  resources from, 683–84
Interpret, as direction word, 17
Introductory phrase, comma with,
  709
"iPod World" (Sullivan), 466–70
It is, avoiding, 719
"It's About Respect" (Reibstein),
  580–81

Jamieson, Jake, "English-Only
  Movement, The", 672–80
Jargon, 250–51
Jefferson, Thomas, "Declaration of
  Independence, The," 513–18
Jonas, Michael, "Downside of
  Diversity, The," 480–88
Jones, Malcolm, "Who Was
  More Important: Lincoln or
  Darwin?," 307–16, 639
Jordan, Vernon E., Jr., "Vernon
  Can Read!," 108–17

Journal articles. *See* Periodicals

Journals, in Works Cited list, 696

Kahn, E. J., Jr., *Big Drink, The: The Story of Coca-Cola,* 73–74

Katz, Jon, "How Boys Become Men," 455–59

Keen, Andrew, "Web 2.0," 560–64

Keyword searches, 685–86

King, Martin Luther, Jr.
"I Have a Dream," 21, 525–30, 638
"Ways of Meeting Oppression, The," 384–88

King, Stephen, "Reading to Write," 66–70

Kitchens, Jim, "Psychology of Persuasive Messaging, The," 359–65

Lamott, Anne, "Shitty First Drafts," 47–51

Language, inflated, 720

Lederer, Richard, 637–38
"Case for Short Words, The," 519–24

Lessing, Doris, "On Not Winning the Nobel Prize," 608–14

Library, 683–84. *See also* Print sources; Sources

List, as direction word, 18

List of Works Cited. *See* Works Cited list

Loaded words, 252–53

Logic, to sequence examples, 179–80

Logical argument, 494–95

Logical errors
begging the question as, 511
in cause and effect analysis, 451–52
either/or thinking as, 511
hasty generalization as, 511
name-calling as, 511
non sequitur (it does not follow) as, 511
oversimplification as, 511

post hoc, ergo propter hoc as, 452, 511

Logos, in classical appeals, 497, 507

Main clause, punctuating, 709

Main idea. *See* Thesis statement; Topic selection

Main point (thesis), 10

"Maker's Eye, The: Revising Your Own Manuscripts" (Murray), 60–65

Malcolm X, "Coming to an Awareness of Language," 85–89

"Marriage Decline, The" (Banks), 577–78

McCullough, David, 282–83

McDonald, Cherokee Paul, "View from the Bridge, A," 133–37

Miller, Robert Keith, 393–94, 397

Miranda, Carolina A., 643

Misplaced modifiers, 714–15

MLA. *See* Modern Language Association (MLA)

Modern Language Association (MLA)
documentation style of, 693–95
in-text citations, 694–95
Works Cited list, 695–705

"Modest Proposal, A" (Swift), 624–33

Modifiers
in compound sentences, 723
dangling, 714–15
misplaced, 714–15
for sentence variety, 721

Mood
description for, 123
shifts in, 718

Mora, Pat, "Remembering Lobo," 144–49

Mukherjee, Bharati, "Two Ways to Belong in America," 301–6

Murray, Donald M., "Maker's Eye, The: Revising Your Own Manuscripts," 60–65

Name-calling, 511
Narration
  in academic disciplines, 75–76
  combining strategies with,
    510, 600
  context (setting), 80
  defined, 73
  details in, 81
  dialogue in, 83
  as organizational strategy, 2, 24
  organization of, 81–82
  outline for, 82
  point of view, 80–81
  purpose for writing, 79–80
  revising/editing of, 83–84
  student essay example of, 76–79
  time sequence, 81–82
  topic selection, 79
  transitional words in, 82–83
  as writing strategy, 24, 25,
    74–75, 79–84
  writing with sources, 118–19
  in written texts, 73–74
Narration (readings)
  American Childhood, An
    (Dillard), selection from, 90–95
  "Coming to an Awareness of
    Language" (Malcolm X), 85–89
  "Not Close Enough for Comfort"
    (Bardeen), 102–6
  "Stranger Than True" (Winston),
    96–101
  "Vernon Can Read!" (Jordan),
    108–17
"Neat People vs. Sloppy People"
  (Britt), 318–22
Negative definition, 395
Neither/nor, paired items with, 716
Newspaper articles, documenting,
  697
Nonperiodical print publications,
  documenting, 698–700
Nonrestrictive elements, commas
  with, 709–10
Non sequitur (it does not follow),
  511

"No Role Reversals" (Gerson),
  581–82
"Not Close Enough for Comfort"
  (Bardeen), 102–6, 708
Note-taking, 692–93
  bibliography cards and, 691
Not only/but also, paired items
  with, 716
Nouns, strong vs. weak, 716–17
Number, pronoun-antecedent
  agreement in, 713

Objective description, 123
"Odyssey Years, The" (Brooks),
  433–37
"On Dumpster Diving" (Eighner),
  602–7
Online sources. See also
  Documentation; Sources
  analysis of, 689–90
  bibliography for, 691–92
  common suffixes for sites,
    688–89
  documenting, 700–705
  evaluating, 687–89
  keyword searches, 685–86
"On Not Winning the Nobel Prize"
  (Lessing), 608–14
Open Internet, 683, 684
  evaluating documents from,
    688–89
Organization
  for argumentation, 509
  of cause and effect analysis,
    451–53
  of comparison and contrast
    essay, 291–93
  of definition essay, 405–6
  of description essay,
    129–31
  of division and classification
    essay, 342–43
  of illustration essay, 179–80
  of narration essay, 74, 81–82
  spatial, 180
  strategies for, 2, 24–25

Orwell, George, "Shooting an
Elephant," 615–23
Outline
block organization, 291–92
for comparison and contrast,
291–92
for description, 131
for narration essay, 82
Outline, as direction word, 18
Oversimplification
in argumentation, 511
in cause and effect analysis,
451–52

Parallel construction
faulty, 715–16
in outline, 292
sentence variety and, 721
Paraphrasing, 638–39, 645
plagiarism and, 644
Parker, Jo Goodwin, "What Is
Poverty?," 408, 410–15
Passive voice, 233, 718
Pat expressions, 251
Pathos, in classical appeals, 497–98
Peer critiques, 29
Period, uses of, 707
Periodicals
bibliography for, 691
Works Cited list, 696
Person, pronoun-antecedent
agreement in, 713
Persuasion. *See also*
Argumentation
persuasive argument, 494–95
Pew Report, on marriage trends,
572–83
Photographs. *See* Visual texts
Phrases
direction words and, 25–26
empty, 719
signal, 640–41
Pinker, Steven, "In Defense of
Dangerous Ideas," 531–40
Plagiarism
avoiding, 642–45

preventing, 645
Point-by-point comparison,
282–84
in outline, 292
Point of view, in narration essay,
74, 80–81
Points of comparison, 290–91
Pollan, Michael, "Eating Industrial
Meat," 256–62
Post hoc, ergo propter hoc (after
this, therefore because of
this), 452
in argumentation, 511
Predicates, in compound
sentences, 723
Premise, 499
Prepositional phrases, and subject-
verb agreement, 710
Principal/principle, 407
Print sources. *See also*
Documentation; Sources
analysis of, 689–90
bibliography for, 691–92
evaluating, 687–89
nonperiodical, 698–700
Works Cited, 696–97
Problem words, 407
Process analysis, 223–79
in academic disciplines,
226–27
action verbs in, 233
combining strategies with,
510, 600
in definition essay, 406
directional, 225
evaluative, 226
informational, 225–26
as organizational strategy, 2
purpose for writing, 231–32
revising/editing of, 233–35
student essay as example of,
227–31
transitional words in, 232
verb tense in, 233–34
as writing strategy, 24, 25,
224–26, 231–35

Process analysis (readings)
"Campus Racism 101"
(Giovanni), 270–76
"Eating Industrial Meat"
(Pollan), 256–62
"How to Mark a Book" (Adler),
236–42
"How to Say Nothing in 500
Words" (Roberts), 243–55
"Young Love" (Sharples),
263–69
Pronouns
pronoun-antecedent agreement,
713–14
unclear references, 711–12
Proofreading, elements of, 332
Proposition, in argumentation, 508
Prove, as direction word, 18
"Psychology of Persuasive
Messaging, The" (Kitchens),
359–65
Publication information, 4
Punctuation, 708–10
Purpose for writing, 10
of cause and effect analysis,
450
in combining strategies, 599
in comparison and contrast
essay, 290
of definition essay, 402–3
in description essay, 128–29
in division and classification
essay, 340–41
in narration essay, 79–80
process analysis, 231–32

"Queen Bee and Her Court, The"
(Wiseman), 345–58, 639–40
Quiet argument, 496
Quotation marks, for language
borrowed directly, 643
Quotations
direct, 639–40
documenting, 693
integrated, 641
unannounced, 641

Ramírez, Robert, "Barrio, The,"
150–55
Rashap, Amy, "American Dream
for Sale, The," 373–83
Reading process, 1–7
"Reading to Write" (King), 66–70
Reading-writing connection, 14–15
"Real Computer Virus, The"
(Cannon), 471–79
Reasoning. *See also* Logic; Logical
errors
faulty, 511
inductive/deductive, 498–501
Reconciliation argument, 496
Redundancies, eliminating, 719
References, pronoun, 710–11
Refutations, to argument, 509–10
Rehearsing, of ideas for writing,
22–23
Reibstein, Janet, "It's About
Respect," 580–81
Relative pronouns, 707
"Remembering Lobo" (Mora),
144–49
Remote cause, 444
Reporting. *See* Narration
Rereading, 4
Researching, for ideas, 22
Research papers. *See also*
Documentation; Online
sources; Print sources
bibliography for, 690–92
keyword searches, 685–86
note-taking for, 692–93
schedule for, 682, 683
Restrictive phrases or clauses,
709
Review, as direction word, 18
Revision, 29–31
of argument, 511–12
of cause and effect analysis,
453, 454
combining strategies, 601
of comparison and contrast
essay, 293–94
and critiques, 29

Revision *(continued)*
of definition essay, 406–7
of description essay, 131, 132
of division and classification
essay, 343–44
of first draft, 28
of illustration essay, 180, 181
of narration essay, 83–84
of process analysis, 233–35
of sentences, 30–31
Rhetorical highlights, 4
Rhetorical strategies. *See*
Organization
Roberts, Paul, "How to Say
Nothing in 500 Words," 243–55
"Rock Dust" (Badgett), 139–43
Roffman, Deborah M., "What Does
'Boys Will Be Boys' Really
Mean?," 422–28
Rose, Mike, "Blue-Collar
Brilliance," 202–13
Run-on sentences, 706–7

Schedule, for research paper, 682–83
Search engines, subject directories
of, 686–87
Semicolons
sentence variety and, 721
uses of, 707
Sentence(s)
fused, 706–7
punctuation in, 708–10
revising, 30–31, 706–8
Sentence fragments, 708
Sentence variety, 720–23
choppy sentences and, 720–21
compound sentences and, 722
sentence openings and, 721–22
"Separate and Unequal Mating
Markets" (Whitehead), 582–83
Sequence of events. *See* Time
sequence
Series, commas in, 710
Setting. *See* Context (setting)
Sharples, Tiffany, "Young Love,"
263–69

Shifts, verb tense, 233, 717–18
"Shitty First Drafts" (Lamott),
47–51
"Shooting an Elephant" (Orwell),
615–23
Signal phrases, 640–41
Similarities and differences, comparison and contrast for, 289
Simple sentences, compound sentences and, 722–23
"Simplicity" (Zinsser), 56–59
"Sister Flowers" (Angelou),
156–62
Sources. *See also* Online sources;
Print sources
analyzing, 689–90
bibliography for, 690–92
direct quotation from, 639–40
evaluating, 687–89
finding and using, 683–87
integrating borrowed material
into text, 640–41
paraphrasing, 638–39
student essay with, 646–52
summarizing, 637–38
writing with, 635–37
Sources (readings)
"Case of the Disappearing
Rabbit, The" (Huang), 653–60
"East Meets West: How the Brain
Unites Us All" (Yong), 661–69
"English-Only Movement, The"
(Jamieson), 672–80
Spatial organization, in illustration
essay, 180
Specific words, 407–8
Statistics, introducing and citing,
645
"Steal This MP3 File: What Is
Theft?" (Gorry), 416–21
"Stranger Than True" (Winston),
96–101
Strategy
organizational, 24–25
in writing, 10–11, 25–26
Subject areas, topics and, 18

Subject directories, of search engines, 686–87
Subjective description, 123
Subject-verb agreement, 710–11
Subject words, 17
Subjunctive mood, 718
Subordinate conjunctions, 707
   sentence variety and, 720
Subtle argument, 496
Suffixes, for online sites, 688–89
Sullivan, Andrew
   "iPod World: The End of Society?," 466–70
   "Why I Blog," 548–59
Summary, 645
   plagiarism and, 644
   of source material, 637–38
Swift, Jonathan, "Modest Proposal, A," 624–33
Syllogism, 499
Synonymous definition, 394–95
Synonyms, 407
Synthesize, as direction word, 18

Table, in division and classification essay, 342–43
Tannen, Deborah, "How to Give Orders Like a Man," 192–201
Teale, Edwin Way, "Wandering through Winter," 167–69
Tense, shifts in, 717–18
Than/as, comparisons with, 716
Than/then, 407
There is, avoiding, 719
Thesaurus, 129
Thesis statement, 10, 23, 24
   in argumentation, 508
   for cause and effect analysis, 450–51
   for combining strategies, 59
   in comparison and contrast essay, 289
   for definition essay, 403–4

in division and classification essay, 341–42
   formulating, 23
   in illustration essay, 177–79
   "This Land Is Their Land" (Ehrenreich), 541–46
Time sequence
   flashback in, 180
   in illustration essay, 179–80
   in narration essay, 81–82
Tone, balanced, 453
Topic selection, 10. See also Thesis statement
   choosing/narrowing topic, 18–20
   for narration essay, 79
Trace, as direction word, 18
Transitional words, 707
   in illustration essay, 180
   in narration essay, 82–83
   in process analysis, 232
Truth, Sojourner, "Ain't I a Woman?," 429–32
"Truth about Lying, The" (Viorst), 366–72
"Two Ways to Belong in America" (Mukherjee), 301–6

Unannounced quotation, 641
Uninterested/disinterested, 407

Vague references, 712
Verb(s)
   action, 129
   for integrating borrowed material, 640
   in signal phrases, 640–41
   strong vs. weak, 716–17
Verb tense
   consistency of, 233–34
   in narration essay, 82
   in process analysis, 233–34
   shifts in, 717–18
"Vernon Can Read!" (Jordan), 108–17
"View from the Bridge, A" (McDonald), 133–37

Viorst, Judith, "Truth about Lying, The," 366–72

Visual illustration, 166, 167. *See also* Illustration

Visual texts, 11–14

Voice
active and passive, 233, 718–19
shifts in, 718

Walker, Alice, "In Full Bloom," 213–17

"Wandering through Winter" (Teale), 167–69

"Ways of Meeting Oppression, The" (King), 384–88

"Web 2.0" (Keen), 560–64

Web publications, documenting, 700–705

Web sites. *See also* Online sources evaluating, 688–89

Welch, Matt, "Blogworld and Its Gravity," 565–71

"What Does 'Boys Will Be Boys' Really Mean?" (Roffman), 422–28

"What Is Poverty?" (Parker), 410–15

Whether/or, paired items with, 716

White, E. B., 333–34, 396–97

Whitehead, Barbara Dafoe, "Separate and Unequal Mating Markets," 582–83

"Who Was More Important: Lincoln or Darwin?" (Jones), 307–16, 639

"Why I Blog" (Sullivan), 548–59

Winston, Barry, "Stranger Than True," 96–101

Wiseman, Rosalind, "Queen Bee and Her Court, The," 345–58, 639–40

Women, argument roundtable on, 572–73

"Women Finally Start to Catch Up" (Coontz), 574–75

Wordiness, 718–20

Words
abstract, 408
for balanced tone, 453
empty, 719
specific and concrete, 407–8
for summarizing and paraphrasing, 644

Works Cited list, 695–705
periodicals, 696–97

"Writing for an Audience" (Flower), 52–55

Writing process, 16–40. *See also* Writing strategies
direction words, 17–18
first draft, 27–28
formal vs. informal writing, 20
student essay as example of, 32–40
subject words, 17

Writing process (readings)
"Discovering the Power of My Words" (Baker), 42–46
"Maker's Eye, The: Revising Your Own Manuscripts" (Murray), 60–65
"Reading to Write" (King), 66–70
"Shitty First Drafts" (Lamott), 47–51
"Simplicity" (Zinsser), 56–59
"Writing for an Audience" (Flower), 52–55

Writing strategies. *See also* Organization; specific strategies
listing of, 24–26

Yabroff, Jennie, "Here's Looking at You, Kids," 460–65

Yong, Ed, "East Meets West: How the Brain Unites Us All," 661–69

"Young Love" (Sharples), 263–69

Zinsser, William, "Simplicity," 56–59